Programming Data-Driven Web Applications with ASP.NET

Donny Mack

Doug Seven

SAMS

201 West 103rd St., Indianapolis, Indiana, 46290 USA

Programming Data-Driven Web Applications with ASP.NET

Copyright © 2002 by Sams Publishing

International Standard Book Number: 0-672-32106-8

Library of Congress Catalog Card Number: 00-109882

Printed in the United States of America

First Printing: August 2001

04   03   02   01   4   3   2   1

Trademarks

Warning and Disclaimer

EXECUTIVE EDITOR
Rosemarie Graham

DEVELOPMENT EDITOR
Kevin Howard

MANAGING EDITOR
Charlotte Clapp

PROJECT EDITOR
Leah Kirkpatrick

COPY EDITOR
Sean Medlock

INDEXER
Tina Trettin

PROOFREADER
Plan-It Publishing

TECHNICAL EDITORS
J. Boyd Nelson
WebF1.com

TEAM COORDINATOR
Lynne Williams

INTERIOR DESIGNER
Gary Adair

COVER DESIGNER
Alan Clements

PAGE LAYOUT
Octal Publishing, Inc.

Contents at a Glance

Table of Contents

About the Authors

Donny Mack, native of Washington State, is one of the co-founders of DotNetJunkies.com, the training company solely dedicated to ASP.NET and ADO.NET. DotNetJunkies.com is also a free online centralized resource Website used by .NET developers to feed their .NET passion. Prior to founding DotNetJunkies.com with Doug Seven, Mack worked at Microsoft Corporation as a Visual InterDev/ASP Support Professional. Mack's need for bleeding edge technology is such that he spends his waking hours, (and some of his non-waking hours), writing code and developing content for DotNetJunkies.com. Mack's real enjoyment comes from watching attendants of DotNetJunkies.com's training courses walk away as obsessed as he is with .NET.

Doug Seven, born and raised in Seattle, WA, is one of the co-founders of the .NET training company, DotNetJunkies.com. Doug comes to DotNetJunkies.com by way of technical roles at Nordstrom, Microsoft, and GiftCertificates.com; and as a Training Specialist at Seattle Coffee Company. As the son of a programmer, Doug was destined to become a developer. Growing up around computers, his career began at the tender age of 11 writing "Choose Your Own Adventure" games in BASIC on a TRS-80, (unfortunately none of his groundbreaking work from this period survived). His first professional IT job was as a lead for the long-term data storage and disaster recovery group in a dual-IBM Mainframe environment at Nordstrom. After a seven-year sojourn as a rock star (seriously!) Doug took on the role of Technical Lead in Microsoft's Developer Support group. After leaving Microsoft, Doug worked as a developer in digital certificate enablement technology for GiftCertificates.com before leaving to pursue life running his own company. DotNetJunkies.com provides hands-on training in ASP.NET and ADO.NET data access.

Dedication

This book is dedicated to:

*All the people we know who are not afraid to take a risk,
try something new, and pursue innovation.*

The memory of Leo Seven.

Milton Pavlov for all his Direct Operational Guidance.

Acknowledgments

When I was first exposed to the .NET Framework, I was blown away. I have not had this much fun programming since I was a kid and first learned how to write "Choose Your Own Adventure" programs on my older brother's TRS-80. For that, I would like to thank Scott Taylor and the development team at GiftCertificates.com for sending me to the Microsoft PDC where I was inundated with .NET. It was the beginning of the end—my life has not been the same since. I would also like to extend a great deal of thanks to Mark Anders, Scott Guthrie, Rob Howard, and Susan Warren from the Microsoft .NET development team for all the hard work they and their team have put into making .NET such a great technology, and for providing endless amounts of help and support.

Ken Scribner, co-author of *Understanding SOAP* wrote, "No book gets published without the hard work and dedication of a lot of people…" Truer words could not have been written. Prior to working on this book I had no idea the amount of work that goes into getting a technical book published. All of the people at Sams Publishing and Pearson have been tremendous. Specifically, my undying gratitude goes to Rosemarie Graham for EVERYTHING…especially the stuff we didn't deserve, like the cookies to keep us going at night, and the undying and undeserving patience. I'd like to also thank Pamalee Nelson for helping to keep us in line, Kevin Howard for reading and remarking on everything we wrote, Amy "S" Sorokas for taking very good care of us, and Leah Kirkpatrick for keeping the process going.

I have been trying to find a way to explain my level of appreciation and professional admiration for my co-author, Donny Mack, but it is too hard to explain. This book, and all things .NET I have worked on are a credit to the insane amount of time Donny and I have spent tinkering, hacking, mishandling and generally screwing around with .NET. I have yet to meet anyone other than Donny who shares my same level of passion and devotion to learning new things. It is through "The Mack" that I have managed to stay on track (I typically get bored quickly). My eternal thanks and respect go to Donny for all that we have worked on together.

I would lastly (but not leastly...can I say that?) like to thank Lance Hayes for helping Donny and me make CodeJunkies.Net and DotNetJunkies.com successful, and for being a great friend through rock stardom and code geekdom; Jon Serious...well, for being so serious; Scott Hirsch and Dan Gumm at SecureWebs.com for providing the best support from a Web host we have ever had, and doing all the things for us they didn't have to; Charlene, Lisa, and Joe for providing a wonderful and fulfilling working environment for Donny and me while we were at Microsoft; Robert Hess, Erika Weichers, and Jennie Peabody for being such great hosts and producers of MSDN's The .NET Show; Dene "425" Holdsworth and the great team of (not so serious) people at GotDotNet.com—yes, I still have my leopard skin bracelet; Scott Mitchell, Charles Carroll, Steve Smith, and Steve Schofield for helping build a tremendous ASP.NET developer community; my father, Jerry Lemmon, for helping me get my original education in Visual Basic; Antoine Victor, Michael Jimenez and Lance Baldwin at NetDesk for teaching me how to be a dev-geek; Dawniel Giebel for being there, for being you, and for being everything to me; Cathy Seven for helping to make me who I am; my mother, Ann Turner, for being extremely supportive through the really good times and the really rough times; and the rest of my family for always being there—I cannot explain how much I appreciate it. I love you all.

—Doug Seven

Shoot, I can't beat Doug's acknowledgment so I'll make mine short and sweet—essentially name drop. There are so many people that I would like to acknowledge, but I don't have the patience to go through and thank you all so if I know you, thank you! Obviously, near the top of the list is Microsoft Corporation—thank you for providing me the tools to rapidly achieve my goals (sorry you aren't at the top of the list, my mom reserves that spot). Special thanks to the Mark Anders, Rob Howard, and Scott Guthrie for their above-and-beyond help.

I'd like to thank all my close friends, family, and business partners for putting up with my ornery behavior when things weren't going "according to plan"—mom, dad, sister, grandma, aunt, uncles, Doug, Lance, V-Child, etc.—I am going to leave out the friends list because I know I'll forget someone and then I'll be in big trouble—so this goes to all my friends...Thanks!

I can't forget Sams Publishing for giving us opportunities and believing in us—RG, SS, Shelly, Leah, Jennifer, Jodie, "The Don", Paul, and so on and so forth. The great people at GotDotNet.com and ASP.net for helping us build a great Website, especially Dene "Airy Fairy" Holdsworth. Charles Carroll for having a great resource for people to learn .NET. And all the other great .NET resource sites, you know who you are...thanks.

To everyone else who put up with my often less than generous demeanor over the last year, ("I need coffee, NOW!"), I dedicate this to you, you know who you are!

—Donny Mack

Tell Us What You Think!

As the reader of this book, *you* are our most important critic and commentator. We value your opinion and want to know what we're doing right, what we could do better, what areas you'd like to see us publish in, and any other words of wisdom you're willing to pass our way.

As an Executive Editor for Sams, I welcome your comments. You can fax, email, or write me directly to let me know what you did or didn't like about this book—as well as what we can do to make our books stronger.

Please note that I cannot help you with technical problems related to the topic of this book, and that due to the high volume of mail I receive, I might not be able to reply to every message.

When you write, please be sure to include this book's title and author as well as your name and phone or fax number. I will carefully review your comments and share them with the author and editors who worked on the book.

Fax: 317-581-4770

Email: feedback@samspublishing.com

Mail: Rosemarie Graham
         Sams Publishing
         201 West 103rd Street
         Indianapolis, IN 46290 USA

Introduction

In July 2000, at the Microsoft Professional Developers Conference (PDC) in Orlando, FL, Bill Gates delivered his keynote speech. In this speech he discussed the future of application development, and how it will be so closely tied to the Internet that it would be hard to imagine an application that did not use the Internet in some fashion. Gates explained his vision for software as a service; software that can be provided on demand via the Internet using Web services. All of these things revolved around Microsoft's new strategy, something called the .NET Framework.

The .NET Framework is a completely new set of building blocks for application development, with the idea that all programming languages are created equal. In other words, all languages are created with the intent of enabling a programmer to write code efficiently to achieve the desired end result, whether that is a cataloging program, financial Web site, or a Web portal. The .NET Framework was built with the intent to allow every developer to use the programming language of his choice (eventually), and to increase the developer's efficiency.

After the keynote, the roughly 7,000 attendees of the PDC received the now infamous "pre-beta bits" of Visual Studio.NET. In a very short time, user groups and listservers began popping up all over the world. The programming community was genuinely interested in what .NET could potentially do for rapid application development. Over the next year more and more developers began taking notice and getting interested in developing applications with .NET.

As the .NET developer community grew, more and more people wanted to learn about ASP.NET and ADO.NET, two of the more significant advances bundled in the .NET Framework. ASP.NET is a completely new framework for building Web-based applications. While many of the classic ASP objects, such as Session, Application, Response and Request, exist in ASP.NET, don't be fooled. ASP.NET was written from the ground up, and was carefully planned to ensure that it would become the de facto standard for building rich Web-based applications.

In tandem with the development of ASP.NET, Microsoft began working to improve the data access strategy that could be employed with a Web-based application. The result is ADO.NET, the next evolution in Microsoft data access models. ADO.NET is a disconnected, message-based data access model. Behind the scenes ADO.NET relies heavily on XML. This allows ADO.NET to be platform independent, and interoperable with nearly any system, including legacy systems.

Who Should Read This Book

This book is intended for computer professionals who are interested in learning new and growing technologies. Although someone who's new to application development could get through this book and learn quite a bit, some areas might be a little too low-level. You don't have to be an application development expert to read this book, however. Simply understanding the concepts and principles behind application development and data access will do. ASP.NET is such a departure from traditional Web application development that you don't need to be a code expert to use it. As a matter of fact, if you *are* an expert, be prepared to do some serious unlearning and breaking of old habits.

Although many of the concepts of Web application development are applicable to ASP.NET, the means to the end have changed dramatically. You need to approach this book with an open mind to learning new and different ways of doing the tasks you've been doing for years. Ultimately, you'll thank yourself because you'll get more done in less time, your applications will be richer and more functional, and they'll perform better.

When we began writing this book, we decided to let you write code in a way that's comfortable for you. This goes hand-in-hand with one of the main ideas behind the .NET Framework—use the language with which you're most comfortable. For this reason, we've written all the code examples in both Visual Basic.NET and C#. Sorry, we left COBOL.NET out…not enough room. You need to learn how to build data-driven Web applications in the language that *you* prefer, not the language *we* prefer.

What Will You Learn from This Book?

Throughout this book, you'll learn how to build rich, data-driven Web applications using Microsoft's .NET Framework and ADO.NET. Specifically, you'll learn how to build ASP.NET Web applications that rely heavily on data access. You'll build these applications in either Visual Basic.NET or C#.

This will be followed by basic data access practices. As the book progresses, you'll build on this knowledge and begin building more advanced functionality. You'll learn how to work with ASP.NET server controls to provide data display, editing, and updating. By the end of this book, you'll be building .NET Web services that publicly expose data for others to consume.

What Software Will You Need?

The examples in this book assume that you have the .NET Framework (beta 2 or greater) and Microsoft SQL Server (7.0 or 2000) running on a Windows 2000 Server machine. Most of the examples can be completed using any platform on which the .NET Framework can run and any database application, although many of them refer to the Northwind database shipped with SQL Server and Microsoft Access.

How This Book Is Organized

This book is divided into the following parts:

- **Part I: What Is .NET?**

  This section will provide a brief overview of the .NET Framework and ADO.NET. Although it will go into some detail, this section is intended only to provide an overview of the technology.

- **Part II: Reading and Displaying Data**

  In this section, you'll begin working with ASP.NET and ADO.NET. You'll learn about the DataGrid server control first, and then you'll apply what you've learned to the DataList and Repeater server controls. As the title implies, this section is all about retrieving data from a data source and displaying it for a user. This includes using the new ADO.NET objects, reviewing SQL syntax, and building functional and attractive data display pages.

- **Part III: Updating and Inputting Data**

  In Part III, you'll build on your knowledge of ADO.NET by inserting new data and updating existing data in your data store. You'll learn about validation controls, editing functionality, and additional ADO.NET objects for inputting and updating data.

- **Part IV: Advanced Data Concepts**

  In Part IV, you'll learn about a handful of additional ASP.NET and data access functions, such as Web services, XML, and SOAP, as well as how to work with Binary Large Objects (BLOBs). You'll learn how to enable various types of authentication in your Web applications, and how to use data caching to improve the performance of your Web site by reducing the traffic to your data store.

- **Appendixes**

  Appendix A is a table of ASP.NET intrinsic server controls and their properties and methods.

  Appendix B is an ADO.NET reference that includes the charts and diagrams found throughout this book.

- **Northwind Sample Application**

  On the companion Web site for this book (http://www.samspublishing.com), you'll find a sample application that demonstrates most of the technology covered in the book. For technical reasons, it's impossible for this sample application to cover everything in this book (such as Passport authentication, which requires a paid subscription). As with all the code samples in the book, the sample application is given in both Visual Basic.NET and C#.

Conventions Used in This Book

The following typographic conventions are used in this book:

- Nearly every code sample in this book is provided in both Visual Basic.NET and C#. Some code samples are language-neutral, using only HTML and ASP.NET server controls, and are only provided once. In listings with multiple versions of the code sample, each portion will be identified by [VB] for Visual Basic.NET and [C#] for C#. Line numbers are provided for reference only and are not required in your code.

- Code lines, commands, statements, variables, and any text you type or see onscreen appears in a mono typeface. **Bold mono** typeface is used to represent the user's input.

- Placeholders in syntax descriptions appear in an *italic mono* typeface. Replace the placeholder with the actual filename, parameter, or element it represents.

- *Italics* highlight technical terms when they're being defined.

- The ➡ icon is used before a line of code that is really a continuation of the preceding line. Sometimes a line of code is too long to fit as a single line on the page. If you see ➡ before a line of code, remember that it's part of the line immediately above it.

- The book also contains Notes, Tips, and Cautions to help you spot important or useful information more quickly. Some of these are helpful shortcuts to help you work more efficiently.

What Is .NET?

PART

I

IN THIS PART

What Is ASP.NET?

IN THIS CHAPTER

At the same time that many Web developers were just starting to wrap their heads around Microsoft's Active Server Pages (ASP) 2.0, the development teams at Microsoft were hard at work preparing ASP.NET, the next generation of ASP. The development team, led by Mark Anders and Scott Guthrie, wrote ASP.NET from scratch, maintaining the good parts of ASP while radically changing its inner workings and extending its functionality to a new level. The goal was to enable Rapid Application Development (RAD) for Internet-based applications that's seamlessly integrated with the entire .NET Framework. The developer now has access to all the same APIs and components in an ASP.NET application that he would have with a Win32 application.

ASP provided a relatively easy way to create dynamic Internet applications, but the developer still had to write too much code. Unlike other Microsoft products, such as Visual Basic, ASP required code to be written for everything rather than using intrinsic controls for commonly performed functions.

For instance, let's say you want to show the results of a database query in a table on an ASP page. Unless you're using Visual Interdev or have the Script Library, there's no way to drag-and-drop a data-based table on your page, bind it to a data source, and run the page. You have to create a pretty large mix of HTML elements and server script to accomplish this. ASP.NET solves the problem of excessive coding by providing a rich set of stock server controls.

Don't panic. Learning ASP.NET will be challenging but fun. One of the great benefits of ASP.NET is that it can run side-by-side on the same installation of Internet Information Server (IIS) as ASP. You can continue to run and build your existing ASP applications while you learn how to build ASP.NET applications. As a matter of fact, most of the ASP object model was maintained in ASP.NET, with changes made only where it was absolutely necessary. The `Application`, `Session`, `Response`, `Request`, and `Server` objects from classic ASP are part of ASP.NET as well, providing a familiar development structure.

This chapter will provide a brief overview of the major features of ASP.NET and the .NET Framework.

> **NOTE**
>
> This book is intended to teach you how to program ASP.NET and ADO.NET for data-driven Web applications. It is outside the scope of this book to teach you the basics of programming ASP.NET. This chapter is meant more as a refresher or overview of ASP.NET. If you want a comprehensive book on ASP.NET read *ASP.NET: Tips, Tutorials and Code* (Sams Publishing, ISBN: 0-672-32143-2).

In this chapter you will learn about:

- The major differences between ASP and ASP.NET
- HTML server controls
- ASP.NET server controls
- Server-side event handling
- Multilanguage support
- Web services
- Session state management

The Major Differences Between ASP and ASP.NET

Although ASP.NET appears to be similar to ASP from the developer's point of view, it's actually quite different. ASP.NET is entirely object-based; every object can have its own properties, methods, and events. This structure provides an object-oriented approach to developing Web applications. ASP.NET was developed to make Web application development simpler, richer, and more available to all developers. Some of the major differences between ASP and ASP.NET that you'll learn about in this book are as follows:

- Strong-typed languages
- ADO vs. ADO.NET
- Server controls
- XML and SOAP support

Strong-Typed Languages

ASP.NET enables you to write Web applications in a variety of *strong-typed* languages, such as C#, Managed C++, Visual Basic.NET, and others. In these languages, the framework recognizes the types that are important to the user of the application.

For example, in ASP you couldn't refer to a table of customer information by name, such as Customers. But strong-typed languages treat objects, such as tables, as types that can be referred to by name. In ASP.NET, you can assign the name Customers to a table and reference it programmatically, no matter what language you're developing in.

Strong-typed languages require a shift in thinking for the developer. In traditional scripting, the things that are important to the developer are emphasized, whereas in strong-typed languages, the types are what the end user is concerned with. Take the following, for example:

```
AcctNum = Table("Customer").Cells("AccountNumber")
```

Although the table and cells are important types to the developer, the end user is more concerned with the customer and account number information. With a strong-typed language, these elements are emphasized in the programming:

```
AcctNum = Customer.AccountNumber
```

You might have grown accustomed to using VBScript to code your ASP pages. VBScript is *not* a strong-typed language, however, but rather a scripting language. ASP.NET applications cannot be written in VBScript, but you can write them in Visual Basic.NET. Much of the syntax in VBScript is similar to that in Visual Basic.NET, but there are differences you will need to learn, such as declaring variable data types. If you prefer, you can write ASP.NET applications in a number of other languages.

> **NOTE**
>
> Throughout the book, you'll see samples in both C# and Visual Basic.NET. If you don't have a language preference yet, this book should give you a good idea of which one better suits you.

Additionally, you're no longer restricted to the linear processing model of ASP, in which page script was read from top to bottom. Instead, ASP.NET pages are compiled into objects. The compiled nature of an ASP.NET page allows you to programmatically reference an object, such as a server control, that's placed further down the page.

ADO vs. ADO.NET

With the release of the .NET Framework, Microsoft introduced ADO.NET, which is the next step in the natural evolution of Microsoft's data access technologies (from DAO to RDO to ADO). ADO.NET is a new way to develop data-driven applications. ADO was great for developing connected data applications, but it was not good at providing data in a disconnected method, such as that needed by ASP. If you wanted to transmit an ADO RecordSet from the data source to a COM object, all of the data types in the RecordSet had to be converted to data types that COM understood. This type of data marshalling came at a high processing cost.

ADO.NET is a disconnected, message-based data access model. Data from a data source, such as Microsoft SQL Server, can be transmitted and persisted as an XML document and will be accessible by any application that can parse XML. The data is disconnected from the originating data source and transmitted in an application-friendly format. As a result, the data types don't need to be converted from their native types to a COM-friendly data type. This saves you in the processing cost of marshalling that ADO did not. Additionally, any COM object that can parse XML can use the data without any hard conversions, and COM objects that cannot parse XML can still save the file or pass it to another COM object as if it were plain text.

In Chapter 2, "What Is ADO.NET?", you'll learn a lot more about the ADO.NET object model.

> **NOTE**
>
> Although you'll be using ADO.NET as your data access model in this book, you can still use ADO in ASP.NET. The drawback is that you don't get the added benefits that ADO.NET provides, such as direct connections to SQL Server, disconnected XML-based data and more.

Server Controls

In classic ASP, the developer had to write code to perform almost any function. A common function, such as validating user input, had to be written every time the developer wanted to implement it. In ASP.NET, *server controls* provide an easy replacement for this model. An array of ASP.NET's intrinsic controls provides commonly used functionality. A developer can create business solutions by placing these controls and altering their properties, quickly achieving the same results that required excessive code in classic ASP.

To validate user input in ASP, you had to write code similar to Listing 1.1.

LISTING 1.1 The ASP Code for Validating User Input

```
01: <html>
02: <head>
03: <title>Programming Datadriven Web Applications with ASP.NET
➥        - Chapter 1</title>
04: </head>
05: <body>
06: <%
07: Dim strName, strPrefix
08: strName = Request.Form("txtName")
09: strPrefix = Request.Form("selPrefix")
10:
11: If Request.Form.Count > 0 Then
12:    If Not Trim(strName) = "" Then
13: %>
14:    Hello <%=strPrefix%> <%=strName%><br>
15:    <%Else%>
16:    Please enter your name.
17:    <%End If%>
18: <%End If%>
19:
20: <form method="post" action="0101.asp">
```

LISTING 1.1 Continued

```
21: Name:<br>
22: <input type="text" name="txtName" value="<%=strName%>"><br>
23:
24: Prefix:<br>
25: <select name="selPrefix">
26:   <option>--Select One--</option>
27:   <option <%If strPrefix = "Mr." Then%>selected<%End If%>>Mr.</option>
28:   <option <%If strPrefix = "Ms." Then%>selected<%End If%>>Ms.</option>
29:   <option <%If strPrefix = "Mrs." Then%>selected<%End If%>>Mrs.</option>
30: </select>
31: <p><input type="submit" value="Submit"></p>
32: </form>
33: </body>
34: </html>
```

On line 11 you have an If...Then evaluation to check if the page is being loaded as the result of a form post. On line 12 you use another If...Then to check if the txtName field has something entered into it. If the txtName field is empty you render an error message to the screen, otherwise you render a welcome message. ASP.NET's server controls provide the same functionality without requiring you to write the code, as shown in Listing 1.2.

LISTING 1.2 Required Field Validation with an ASP.NET Server Control

[VB]

```
01: <script runat="server" language="VB">
02:   Protected Sub Page_Load(Sender As Object, E As EventArgs)
03:    If Page.IsPostBack And Page.IsValid Then
04:     Welcome.Text = "Hello " & selPrefix.Value & " " &
➡       txtName.Text & "<br><br>"
05:    End If
06:   End Sub
07: </script>
```

[C#]

```
01: <script runat="server" language="C#">
02:  protected void Page_Load(object sender, EventArgs e){
03:   if(Page.IsPostBack && Page.IsValid){
04:    Welcome.Text = "Hello " + selPrefix.Value + " " +
➡      txtName.Text + "<br><br>";
05:   }
06:  }
07: </script>
```

LISTING 1.2   Continued

```
[VB & C#]

08: <html>
09: <head>
10: <title>Programming Datadriven Web Applications with ASP.NET
➥        - Chapter 1</title>
11: </head>
12: <body>
13: <form runat="server" method="post">
14:   <asp:Label runat="server" id="Welcome" />
15:   <asp:TextBox runat="server" id="txtName" />
16:   <asp:RequiredFieldValidator runat="server"
17:    ControlToValidate="txtName"
18:    ErrorMessage="Please enter your name."
19:    ForeColor="#CC3300" />
20:   <br>
21:   Prefix:<br>
22:   <select id="selPrefix" runat="server">
23:     <option>--Select One--</option>
24:     <option>Mr.</option>
25:     <option>Ms.</option>
26:     <option>Mrs.</option>
27:   </select>
28:   <asp:RequiredFieldValidator runat="server"
29:    ControlToValidate="selPrefix"
30:    InitialValue="--Select One--"
31:    ErrorMessage="Please select your prefix."
32:    ForeColor="#CC3300" />
33:   <p><input type="submit" value="Submit" runat="server"></p>
34: </form>
35: </body>
36: </html>
```

On lines 16–19, you place the RequiredFieldValidator server control. This control is set to validate the input of the TextBox named txtName. An error message is displayed if the form is posted without a value in the TextBox.

On lines 28–32 you do use the RequiredFieldValidator to validate the <select> list HtmlControl for a valid selection.

Figure 1.1 shows the output from Listing 1.2. When the form is posted without a value in the TextBox and an inappropriate selection in the <select> list, the RequiredFieldValidator controls display the error message "Please enter your name." and "Please select your prefix."

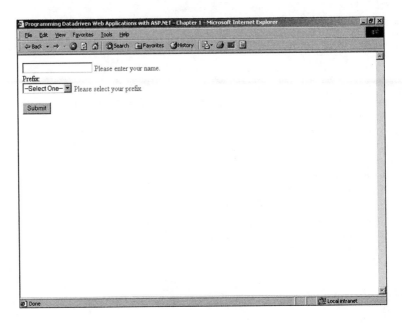

FIGURE 1.1

By using an ASP.NET server control, you can validate user input without having to write excessive code.

ASP.NET server controls let you use familiar HTML-style controls to provide functionality that previously required you to write code. This simplifies and speeds up the development process because the functionality is prebuilt and is bulletproof in most cases.

XML and SOAP Support

Extensible Markup Language (XML), a text-based, self-describing language derived from Standard Generalized Markup Language (SGML), is important in today's development environment. No matter what platform you're using, XML lets you open, read, and save data in a non-proprietary text format, making it a viable medium for transmitting that data. ASP.NET and ADO.NET use XML as the persistence and transmission format for data. As a result, ASP.NET applications can work with virtually any data source and interact with existing COM components.

Simple Object Access Protocol (SOAP) is an HTTP-based protocol used for exchanging structured and typed information on the Web, such as XML. Once received, this type of functionality requires an XML parser to convert the data to an XML file before the end user can use that data. In the past, creating these types of applications was very tedious and complicated.

ASP.NET Web services use XML as their data format and SOAP as their protocol, making this type of application much easier. You'll learn more about Web services later in this chapter.

In Chapter 12, "XML and SOAP," you'll learn more about how ASP.NET uses both XML and SOAP. You'll dive headfirst into Web services in Chapter 14, "Exposing Data Through a Web Service."

Breaking Down the Parts of ASP.NET

Now that you know a little about what ASP.NET is, it's time to go into some more detail on the parts of ASP.NET that are relevant to this book:

- Server controls
- Server-side event handling
- Multilanguage support
- Web services
- Session state management
- Caching

Server Controls

As mentioned previously, ASP.NET ships with a set of stock server controls for executing commonly used page functions, such as input validation, data-driven tables, and so on. Server controls can be broken into two major categories: HTML server controls and ASP.NET server controls.

HTML Server Controls

Any HTML element can be converted to an *HTML server control* with the addition of the `runat="server"` attribute. Once you've added this attribute, the .NET Framework will create an instance of the control for server-side page processing. Some interesting things happen once the `runat="server"` attribute is added:

- The HTML elements become visible to the server and can be accessed programmatically.
- The object model maps closely to that of the corresponding element. For example, if an input element is set to `type="text"` and is marked to be an HTML server control, you can set its background color on the server programmatically by referencing its ID attribute (`TextBoxID.BackColor= "blue"`).
- Automatic state management of page elements. That is, if you have a text box, the value will be maintained on the round trip from the client to the server and back.
- The element now supports data binding (discussed in Chapter 3, "ADO.NET Managed Providers").
- The element maintains client-side script capability.

In Listing 1.2 you added the `runat="server"` attribute to a `<select>` list HTML server control. When the page was successfully posted a welcome message was displayed to the user, and the state of the `<select>` list was maintained.

Figure 1.2 shows the output of the form after the form post. The values entered are displayed at the top of the page, and are maintained in the form fields.

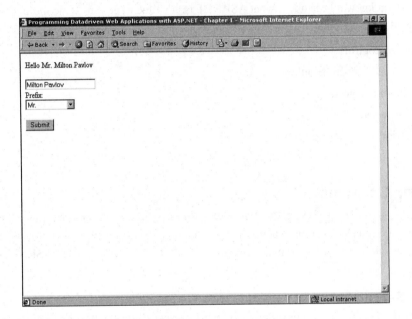

FIGURE 1.2
`HtmlControls` *maintain the values given before the form post.*

ASP.NET simplifies this programming approach through HTML server controls, which maintain their state through `ViewState`. `ViewState` uses a hidden field named `__VIEWSTATE` to maintain the server control values. The `__VIEWSTATE` field contains a reference to an in-memory copy of the values for each stateful server control, for example, every server control whose values are to be maintained.

When the ASP.NET form is posted and the results are rendered, you'll notice that the form elements, the text box and the `<select>` list, have maintained their values without any additional code. The state of these controls is maintained through `ViewState` (the `__VIEWSTATE` field). You can see this in Listing 1.3, which is part of the HTML source of the rendered page viewed in the browser.

LISTING 1.3 The Rendered Output of an ASP.NET Page

```
01: <html>
02: <head>
03: <title>Programming Datadriven Web Applications with ASP.NET
➥      - Chapter 1</title>
04: </head>
05: <body>
06: <form name="ctrl0" method="post" action="01.02.aspx" language="javascript"
➥      onsubmit="ValidatorOnSubmit();" id="ctrl0">
07: <input type="hidden" name="__VIEWSTATE"
➥value="dDwtMTc0NjQxMDYxMzt0PDtsPGk8MT47PjtsPHQ8O2w8aTwxPjs+O2w8dDxwPHA
➥8bDxUZXh0Oz47bDxIZWxsbyBNci4gTWlsdG9uIFBhdmxvdlw8YnJcPlw8YnJcPjs
➥+Pjs+Ozs+Oz4+Oz4+Oz4=" />
08:
09: <script language="javascript"
10: src="/ aspnet_client/system_web/1_0_2914_16/WebUIValidation.js"></script>
11:
12:
13:     <span id="Welcome">Hello Mr. Milton Pavlov<br><br></span>
14:     <input name="txtName" type="text" value="Milton Pavlov" id="txtName" />
15:     <span id="ctrl1" controltovalidate="txtName"
➥         errormessage="Please enter your name."
➥         evaluationfunction="RequiredFieldValidatorEvaluateIsValid"
➥         initialvalue="" style="color:#CC3300;visibility:hidden;">
➥         Please enter your name.</span>
16:     <br>
17:     Prefix:<br>
18:     <select name="selPrefix" id="selPrefix">
19:     <option value="--Select One--">--Select One--</option>
20:     <option selected="selected" value="Mr.">Mr.</option>
21:     <option value="Ms.">Ms.</option>
22:     <option value="Mrs.">Mrs.</option>
23: </select>
24:     <span id="ctrl2" controltovalidate="selPrefix"
➥         errormessage="Please select your prefix."
➥         evaluationfunction="RequiredFieldValidatorEvaluateIsValid"
➥         initialvalue="--Select One--"
➥         style="color:#CC3300;visibility:hidden;">
➥         Please select your prefix.</span>
25:     <p><input onclick="javascript:{if (typeof(Page_ClientValidate)
➥         == 'function') {Page_ClientValidate();}} " name="ctrl3"
➥         type="submit" value="Submit" /></p>
```

The ViewState is set on line 7. Although the ViewState isn't meant for people to read, it does refer to an in-memory copy of the server controls' values.

ASP.NET Server Controls

ASP.NET server controls don't map one-to-one with HTML server controls. An ASP.NET server control is essentially a black box that renders all the HTML code necessary for the control to function properly. For example, the ASP.NET Calendar control doesn't render a calendar per se; it renders a group of HTML elements, including tables, cells, rows, and hyperlinks, resulting in an object that *looks* like a calendar. The differences between HTML server controls and ASP.NET server controls are as follows:

- Template support for some controls (see Chapter 7, "Working with ASP.NET Server Controls Templates").
- A rich set of programming capabilities, including raising events, caching, and access to many other properties, methods, and events not available to HTML server controls.
- Browser compatibility. All server controls will nearly always render as browser-compatible HTML. The .NET Framework evaluates the browser on the request and renders either HTML 3.2 or HTML 4.0 and JScript. The latter is for Internet Explorer 4.0 and above, while the former is for all other browsers.

ASP.NET server controls are subdivided into four groups:

- *Intrinsic controls* render as basic HTML elements, such as <span> or <input type="text">. They're intelligent, meaning that they can maintain their state.
- *List controls* render as a variety of lists. Using a data source, they can be set to render as lists or tables of data.
- *Validation controls* are used to validate user input, such as a required field, range validation, or even custom validation.
- *Rich controls* render as complex HTML structures and can include client-side script. One example of a rich control is the Calendar control.

Server-Side Event Handling

Every ASP.NET page is compiled at runtime using Just-In-Time (JIT) compilers. The page is compiled to a tree structure of .NET objects. This enables programmatic control over all server controls on the page, exposing properties and methods available for the specified control. The ASP.NET page itself is the parent object, and it has properties, methods, and events such as the Load event. You can write your own custom event handlers or methods to execute when events are fired, or when called.

Listing 1.4 modifies the same page with which you've been working to use a server-side method to explicitly control the rendering of your page.

LISTING 1.4 Server-Side Event Handling in ASP.NET

[VB]

```
01: <script language="VB" runat="server">
02:  Protected Sub SayHello(Source As Object, E As EventArgs)
03:   divHello.InnerHtml = "Hello " & _
04:    selPrefix.Value & " " & _
05:    txtName.Value
06:   txtName.Visible = False
07:   selPrefix.Visible = False
08:   submitButton.Visible = False
09:  End Sub
10: </script>
```

[C#]

```
01: <script language="C#" runat="server">
02:  protected void SayHello(object sender, EventArgs e){
03:   divHello.InnerHtml = "Hello " +
04:    selPrefix.Value + " " +
05:    txtName.Value;
06:   txtName.Visible = false;
07:   selPrefix.Visible = false;
08:   submitButton.Visible = false;
09:  }
10: </script>
```

[VB & C#]

```
11: <html>
12: <head>
13: <title>Programming Datadriven Web Applications with ASP.NET
➥      - Chapter 1</title>
14: </head>
15: <body>
16: <div id="divHello" runat="server" />
17: <form method="post" runat="server">
18: <input type="text" id="txtName" runat="server"
19:   Value="Please Enter Name" ><br>
20: <select id="selPrefix" runat="server">
21:   <option>--Prefix--</option>
22:   <option>Mr.</option>
23:   <option>Ms.</option>
24:   <option>Mrs.</option>
25: </select>
26: <p><input type="submit" value-"Submit" id="submitButton"
27:   OnServerClick="SayHello" runat="server"></p>
28: </form>
```

LISTING 1.4 Continued

```
29: </body>
30: </html>
```

> **NOTE**
>
> Notice that the SayHello() method is placed inside <script></script> tags marked to run at the server. The .NET compliant language is specified in the <script> tag. In ASP.NET, all server-side programming is placed inside <script> tags rather than <%...%> tags.

In Figure 1.3, the page has been loaded. The HTML server controls are rendered as basic HTML elements.

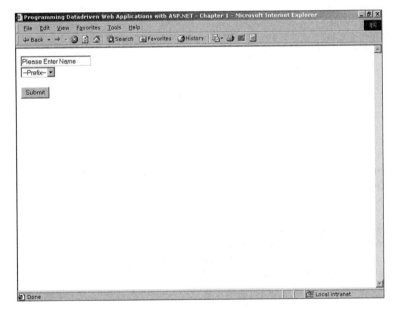

FIGURE 1.3

When the form is loaded, the HTML server controls are rendered as basic HTML elements.

In Listing 1.4, the <div> element was set to display the message "Hello" (line 3), followed by the prefix (line 4) and name (line 5) entered in the form, using the InnerHtml property.

Next, the input controls were set not to display (lines 6–8) by setting their `Visible` properties to `False`. In Figure 1.4, you see the page after the form has been posted.

FIGURE 1.4

After the form has been submitted, all the controls' `Visible` *properties are set to* `False` *on the server.*

If you're a Web developer who's never worked with strong-typed programming languages, using control properties might be new. As you'll see, it's a great way to work with and assign values. Server controls are featured prominently in upcoming chapters, so you'll have time to get familiar with them.

Multilanguage Support

You've already seen some of the benefits of strong-typed languages, such as accessing properties and methods of the page or server controls on the page. One of the ongoing debates among programmers has always been about *which* language is the best. The .NET Framework seeks to resolve this debate by equalizing the performance of the languages and letting you write ASP.NET applications in whichever language you like. When the ASP.NET page is compiled at runtime, the code you've written is emitted (translated) to Microsoft Intermediate Language (MSIL). Although the MSIL code for each language can be slightly different, the performance is nearly identical. Therefore, the language you prefer is the language you should write code in.

The final release versions of the .NET Framework and ASP.NET will support many different languages, including Visual Basic.NET, C#, Managed C++, Eiffel, COBOL, and others.

Web Services

As the Web grows and Internet data exchange becomes more important to the success of many businesses, developers are seeking new ways of providing richer Web applications. Web services provide functionality that was previously reserved for desktop applications.

A *Web service* is a class (or set of classes) that doesn't render typical browser-based HTML output, but rather outputs data. A client can consume, manipulate, and display this data in any format that's appropriate. The Web service uses XML and SOAP to expose data for consumption by a client. For example, a shipping company can expose the functionality to accept a shipping number and output the package's current location, or an online book company can expose a service to list their top ten best-selling books. Client applications can consume these services and render the output on a different site with relative ease.

The one requirement for a Web service is that both parties agree to the Web Service Description Language (WSDL) format for the exchange. The WSDL is an XML document that describes the service transports or protocols, the invocation semantics, and the call order.

Figure 1.5 shows how a Web service provider and consumer interact.

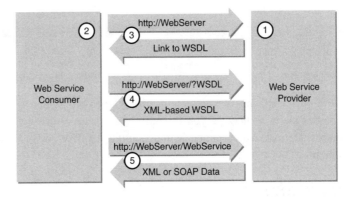

FIGURE 1.5

A provider exposes a Web service that a consumer uses.

A Web service provider (1) makes a Web service publicly available on the Internet. The consumer (2) goes through the discovery process (3) to find out what Web services are available from the provider. The discovery process returns a link to the WSDL document. When the consumer knows where to find the WSDL, she can request it by appending the URL with ?WSDL (4). The WSDL can be used to build classes for consuming the Web service. The consumer can then call the Web service with an Http-Get, Http-Post, or a SOAP message (5). The data is returned to the client as either an XML document, or XML-formatted data in a SOAP message.

In Chapter 14 you'll build your own Web service to expose data to other sites.

Session State Management

In classic ASP, managing state always meant writing a lot of extra code. This process became even more difficult when the ASP application was hosted on multiple servers in a Web farm. State values needed to be either written to hidden fields and passed from page to page or written to a database and accessed on each page view.

Recall how ASP.NET manages state for you in the form of ViewState. The state values are passed from page to page in the hidden ViewState field. All controls that use the runat="server" attribute have their state managed by ASP.NET.

There *is* a solution for managing session state in the present ASP model, using the ASP Session object, but it can't handle some of today's common server setups, such as Web farms. Most of those problems have been solved in ASP.NET with a Web farm compatible, memory-based ASP.NET State Store, or a Microsoft SQL Server database. The latter is done through the SQL State Store. The state values are stored in a SQL Server database and are accessed with each page view. It takes a minimal amount of code to use either method, making either state management option viable and easy to use.

Caching

Caching is a highly anticipated feature of ASP.NET and will help immensely in your creation of high-performance Web applications. Basically, caching in ASP.NET means taking a figurative snapshot of a page after it's been compiled and rendered once, and then holding it in memory until specific conditions you've set are met. Then the page is recompiled and rendered and the process starts all over.

For example, let's say you have a page that makes a call to a database and returns a rather large result set back to the client. That page might take 10 seconds to render. With ASP.NET, you can add the page directive shown in Listing 1.5 to your page, and the results of that query will be cached for 30 seconds. When a user refreshes the page or the next user visits it, the page will be served from the cache and no query to the database will take place. This can increase performance dramatically.

LISTING 1.5   Page Directive to Set Caching to 30 Seconds

```
<%@ OutputCache Duration="30" %>
```

This example assumes that the page makes the same query to the database every time. But let's say that this is a search engine of some sort that serves up different results every time, based on the user's search criteria. You can't serve up a cached page for every user based on the first query, or the next user would get incorrect data. However, it's conceivable that two users might search using the same criteria. In that case, the second user would indeed get the cached results of the first user's query.

ASP.NET has two types of caching:

- Output caching—The caching of a dynamic response generated by a request.
- Data caching—Programmatic caching of arbitrary objects across HTTP requests.

Beyond page-level caching, you can cache individual parts of your page. *Fragment caching* enables you to cache the results of a database query without caching your rotating banner advertisement on the same page. Put all these ingredients together and you have the recipe for a high-performance, highly optimized Web solution. Chapter 16, "Data Caching," will go into some advanced caching techniques.

Summary

In this chapter, you learned what ASP.NET is. You got a high-level overview of some of the major advantages of ASP.NET over traditional ASP and other Web development platforms in general. You also learned about some of the new features of ASP.NET:

- Encapsulating common functionality into server controls that can be placed on the page without any additional code.
- Server-side event handling, which enables you to react to events from the page or from any server control on the page.
- Multilanguage support, which enables you to write rich Web applications in the language with which you're most comfortable.
- Web services, which let you share data with other Web sites in an agreed-upon format.
- Session state management, which means you no longer need to deal with the complexity of state management.
- Caching, which enables reduced processing on the server by storing output on the server for quick access.

In the following chapters, you'll learn more about the benefits of ASP.NET over other Web development platforms. This will include ADO.NET, working with data-bound server controls, Web services, and some advanced features such as data caching.

What Is ADO.NET?

IN THIS CHAPTER

In the beginning, there was Microsoft ActiveX Data Objects (ADO). Okay, that was a long way from the beginning, but ADO has been around a few years—a lifetime in Internet terms. As with all things, ADO came to us through a normal evolutionary process, based on Data Access Objects (DAO) and Remote Data Objects (RDO). Following in this evolutionary model, Microsoft created ADO.NET.

This chapter provides a high-level look at the ADO.NET object model. You'll learn about the following:

- What ADO.NET is
- The Benefits of ADO.NET
- ADO.NET Document Object Model (DOM)

ADO.NET Explained

ADO.NET is a standards-based programming model for creating distributed, data-sharing applications.

If you have experience with ADO, you know that the RecordSet was the centerpiece of the model. . .where the rubber met the road, so to speak. In ADO.NET, the DataSet is the centerpiece. It's an in-memory copy of the data from a data store. Unlike an ADO RecordSet, a DataSet can contain any number of DataTables, each of which could represent the data from a database table or view. The DataSet resides in memory, disconnected from the original data store. In other words, the DataSet can exist without an active connection to the data store.

The underlying technology at work is XML, which is the persistence and transmission format for the DataSet. At runtime, components (such as a business logic object or an ASP.NET Web Form) need to exchange the data in the DataSet. The data is transmitted from one component to the other in the form of an XML file, and the receiving component materializes the file in the form of a DataSet. The DataSet is built with methods consistent with the relational data model. As mentioned earlier, the DataSet has a collection of DataTables. Each DataTable has a collection of DataRows and DataColumns, as well as relationships to other DataTables.

Figure 2.1 shows you the major components in an ADO.NET-based solution.

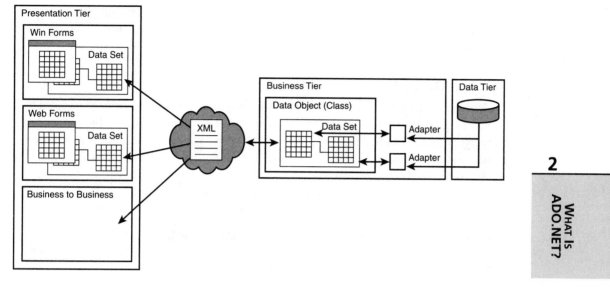

FIGURE 2.1

The major components of an ADO.NET solution.

The Benefits of ADO.NET

With evolution comes new, and often great things. Such is the case with the evolution of ADO into ADO.NET. The prime benefits can be broken down into five categories: Interoperability, Maintainability, Programmability, Performance, and Scalability.

Interoperability

As XML becomes more widely accepted, the benefits of the XML-based persistence and transmission of ADO.NET become more obvious. ADO.NET is designed to take advantage of the acceptance of XML. Because the work being done out-of-sight, out-of-mind is in XML, any component that can parse XML can use ADO.NET. Programming languages and lack of compatibility no longer stand in the way. With ADO.NET, a PERL component can pass an ADO.NET `DataSet` to a C# component, which can manipulate it and pass it to an ASP.NET Web Form written in Visual Basic.NET. Throughout the whole process, the data is transmitted as an XML file and materialized as a `DataSet` without need for concern.

Even if the component being used cannot parse XML, that component can still play a part. Since the DataSet is being transmitted as an XML file, it can be saved to the file system or retransmitted to another component without doing any damage to the file.

Maintainability

The Web and Internet exchange have come a long way since they became widely accepted by the non-programmer community. Every day more and more people get on the Internet, and every day businesses around the world need to find ways to maintain their Web site infrastructure to handle the increased traffic. Commonly, they do this by dividing the Web site structure into layers to even out the processing demand across multiple servers. Perhaps the presentation processing, business logic, and data services are all moved to separate servers, as in typical three-tier architecture. Maybe the business logic layer is subdivided to multiple servers.

Using ADO.NET makes this type of division a little easier. The layers of the solution must be able to communicate. With ADO.NET, they can communicate through XML-based DataSets, making the communication a little less painful.

Programmability

ADO.NET enables developers to write code against data using strong-typed programming, in which things of interest to the user become more evident. In traditional weak-typed programming, the things most important to the developer become more evident, such as the table and cells in the following example:

```
AcctNum = Table("Customer").Cells("AccountNumber")
```

ADO.NET enables programmers to manipulate data through strong-typed programming. Under this style, the AccountNumber becomes a property of the Customer object. From a programmer's point of view, Customer might refer to a DataTable and AccountNumber might refer to a DataColumn of that table.

```
AcctNum = Customer.AccountNumber
```

This type of programming makes the vocabulary more evident, making the code easier to read. A non-programmer could look at this code and infer it's meaning easily.

As well as being easier to read, strong-typed code is easier to write. Among the benefits are the possibilities of automatic statement completion in a code editor. When the programmer types the following, a drop-down list appears, and AccountNumber is one of the options to be selected, as seen in Figure 2.2:

```
AcctNum = Customer.
```

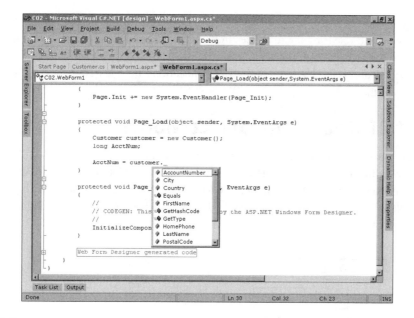

FIGURE 2.2
Strong-types programming has automatic statement completion as one of its benefits, as long as you are using a code editor that provides that feature, such as Visual Studio.NET.

Performance

Web applications are inherently disconnected; the client does not maintain an active connection to the server, and the server does not maintain an active connection to the data source. ADO.NET `DataSets` offer performance advantages over traditional ADO disconnected `RecordSets`. In the past, when data was passed from one component to another, the application's performance took a heavy hit due to the cost of COM marshalling. The values in the `RecordSet` had to be converted to data types recognized by COM. As a result, there was a significant processing cost. In ADO.NET, this data type conversion isn't required because you're simply passing an XML file.

Scalability

In any Web solution, scalability is a huge concern. Everyone wants Web traffic to increase, and as it does the solution needs to accommodate the higher levels of throughput. Often, applications will perform well for a small number of users, instilling a false sense of confidence. As the user base grows, application performance can suffer because the users are fighting over a limited number of resources, such as database connections, records locked by other users, etc.

ADO.NET inherently encourages you to work in a disconnected manner, retrieving the data that is required and releasing the resources immediately. Because you can pull your data into a disconnected `DataSet` in the form of an XML file, scalability is increased without the need for additional hardware. Database locks and active connections are released, giving additional users access to the resources.

ADO.NET Document Object Model

ADO.NET is made up of two basic parts, the `DataSet` and the Managed Providers. You'll learn about the latter in Chapter 3, "Managed Providers in ADO.NET." For now, let's take a high-level look at the Document Object Model (DOM) for the ADO.NET `DataSet` (each piece of the ADO.NET DOM will be more thoroughly dissected throughout this book). Figure 2.3 shows you the ADO.NET Document Object Model.

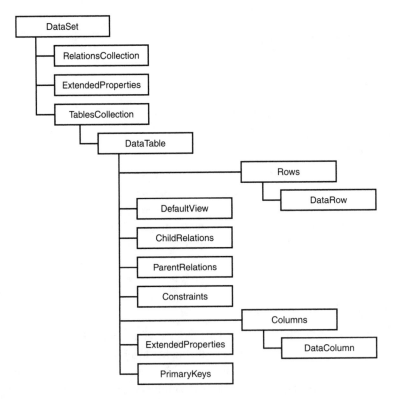

FIGURE 2.3

The ADO.NET Document Object Model.

As previously mentioned, the DataSet is an in-memory copy of data that provides a consistent programming model regardless of the original data store.

The DataSet is made up of a RelationsCollection and a TablesCollection. Each DataTable in the TablesCollection has Columns and Rows collections. The following sections will take a quick look at the objects in these collections.

> **NOTE**
>
> To use ADO.NET in ASP.NET, you must import the System.Data namespace. The following code samples are provided as a demonstration. You're not expected to fully understand everything at this point, but this will give you a glimpse of what the code looks like.

DataTables

A *DataTable* represents one table of in-memory data in the DataSet. It contains a collection of DataColumns that represent the table schema and a collection of DataRows that represent the data in the table. The DataTable maintains the original state of the data along with its current state, and it tracks the changes that have occurred.

The following code adds a new DataTable to a DataSet:

[VB]

```
Dim myDataSet As New DataSet
myDataSet.Tables.Add(New DataTable("Products"))
```

[C#]

```
DataSet myDataSet = new DataSet();
myDataSet.Tables.Add(new DataTable("Products"));
```

DataColumns

The *DataColumns* represent the database table's schema. The DataTable allows you to create a variety of DataColumns within the table's columns collection, including the following:

- Standard column
- Expression column (used for filtering, computing, and aggregating column information)
- AutoIncrement column

Listing 2.1 demonstrates how to add three columns—ID, Name and Cost—to an existing DataTable in a DataSet. Then the ID column is set as the primary key.

LISTING 2.1   Adding a `DataColumn` to a `DataTable`

[VB]

```
01: Imports System
02: Imports System.Data
03:
04: Namespace Chapter02
05:
06:   Public Class C0202
07:
08:    Public Function CreateCustomDataSet() As DataSet
09:     Dim myDataSet As New DataSet
10:     Dim keys(1) As DataColumn
11:
12:     myDataSet.Tables.Add(new DataTable("Products"))
13:     myDataSet.Tables("Products").Columns.Add("ID",
➥         System.Type.GetType("System.Int32"))
14:     myDataSet.Tables("Products").Columns.Add("Name",
➥         System.Type.GetType("System.String"))
15:     myDataSet.Tables("Products").Columns.Add("Cost",
➥         System.Type.GetType("System.Double"))
16:
17:     keys(0) = myDataSet.Tables("Products").Columns("ID")
18:     myDataSet.Tables("Products").PrimaryKey = keys
19:
20:     Return myDataSet
21:    End Function
22:   End Class
23: End Namespace
```

[C#]

```
01: using System;
02: using System.Data;
03:
04: namespace Chapter02{
05:
06:   public class C0202{
07:
08:    public DataSet CreateCustomDataSet(){
09:     DataSet myDataSet = new DataSet();
10:     DataColumn[] keys = new DataColumn[1];
11:
12:     myDataSet.Tables.Add(new DataTable("Products"));
13:     myDataSet.Tables["Products"].Columns.Add("ID",
➥         System.Type.GetType("System.Int32"));
```

LISTING 2.1 Continued

```
14:    myDataSet.Tables["Products"].Columns.Add("Name",
➡        System.Type.GetType("System.String"));
15:    myDataSet.Tables["Products"].Columns.Add("Cost",
➡        System.Type.GetType("System.Double"));
16:
17:    keys[0] = myDataSet.Tables["Products"].Columns["ID"];
18:    myDataSet.Tables["Products"].PrimaryKey = keys;
19:
20:    return myDataSet;
21:    }
22:    }
23: }
```

In Listing 2.1 you dynamically create a new `DataTable` in a `DataSet` (line 12). On lines 13–15 you add three `DataColumns` to the `DataTable` using the `Add()` method of the `DataColumnCollection` class. The `Add()` method takes two arguments, the name of the `DataColumn` (`string`) and the data type for the `DataColumn` (`Type`).

On line 10 you create a 1-dimensional array of `DataColumns`, and on line 17 you assign the `ID` column to the only object in the array. You use an array because the `DataTable`'s `PrimaryKey` property accepts an array of `DataColumns`. On line 18 you assign the `keys` array (which only has the `ID` column in it) as the `PrimaryKey` property of the `Products` `DataTable`.

DataRows

A *DataRow* is a child element of the `DataTable`. Each `DataRow` represents a row of data from the original data store and has a `RowState` property. The possible `RowStates` are shown in Table 2.1.

TABLE 2.1 ADO.NET DataRow RowStates

RowState	Description
Unchanged	No changes have been made since the last call to `AcceptChanges()`.
New	The row has been added to the table, but `AcceptChanges()` has not been called.
Modified	Some element of the row has been changed.
Deleted	The row has been deleted from the table using the `Delete()` method.
Detached	Either the row has been deleted but `AcceptChanges()` has not been called, or the row has been created but not added to the table.

Listing 2.2 adds a new DataRow to an existing DataTable.

LISTING 2.2 Adding a DataRow to a DataTable

```
[VB]
01: Imports System
02: Imports System.Data
03:
04: Namespace Chapter02
05:
06:  Public Class C0202
07:
08:   Public Function CreateCustomDataSet() As DataSet
09:    Dim myDataSet As New DataSet
10:    Dim keys(1) As DataColumn
11:
12:    myDataSet.Tables.Add(new DataTable("Products"))
13:    myDataSet.Tables("Products").Columns.Add("ID",
➥        System.Type.GetType("System.Int32"))
14:    myDataSet.Tables("Products").Columns.Add("Name",
➥        System.Type.GetType("System.String"))
15:    myDataSet.Tables("Products").Columns.Add("Cost",
➥        System.Type.GetType("System.Double"))
16:
17:    keys(0) = myDataSet.Tables("Products").Columns("ID")
18:    myDataSet.Tables("Products").PrimaryKey = keys
19:
20:    Dim myRow As DataRow
21:    myRow = myDataSet.Tables("Products").NewRow()
22:    myRow("ID") = 1
23:    myRow("Name") = "Doug's Doomsday Device"
24:    myRow("Cost") = 19.95
25:    myDataSet.Tables("Products").Rows.Add(myRow)
26:
27:    Return myDataSet
28:   End Function
29:  End Class
30: End Namespace

[C#]
01: using System;
02: using System.Data;
03:
04: namespace Chapter02{
05:
```

LISTING 2.2   Continued

```
06:  public class C0202{
07:
08:   public DataSet CreateCustomDataSet(){
09:    DataSet myDataSet = new DataSet();
10:    DataColumn[] keys = new DataColumn[1];
11:
12:    myDataSet.Tables.Add(new DataTable("Products"));
13:    myDataSet.Tables["Products"].Columns.Add("ID",
➥        System.Type.GetType("System.Int32"));
14:    myDataSet.Tables["Products"].Columns.Add("Name",
➥        System.Type.GetType("System.String"));
15:    myDataSet.Tables["Products"].Columns.Add("Cost",
➥        System.Type.GetType("System.Double"));
16:
17:    keys[0] = myDataSet.Tables["Products"].Columns["ID"];
18:    myDataSet.Tables["Products"].PrimaryKey = keys;
19:
20:    DataRow myRow = null;
21:    myRow = myDataSet.Tables["Products"].NewRow();
22:    myRow["ID"] = 1;
23:    myRow["Name"] = "Doug's Doomsday Device";
24:    myRow["Cost"] = 19.95;
25:    myDataSet.Tables["Products"].Rows.Add(myRow);
26:
27:    return myDataSet;
28:   }
29:  }
30: }
```

In Listing 2.2 you extend the code from Listing 2.1 by adding lines 20–25. In these lines of code you create and add a new DataRow to the Products table. On line 20 you create an instance of the DataRow class, and on line 21 you set it to the result of the NewRow() method of the Products table. This creates a new DataRow using the DataColumn values from the Products table. On lines 22–24 you set the values of each column in the row, and on line 25 you add the new DataRow to the Rows collection of the Products table.

DataRelation

A *DataRelation* relates two tables in a DataSet to each other. The arguments of a DataRelation are the two columns that serve as the primary key and the foreign key columns in the relationship, as well as the name of the DataRelation. A DataRelation isn't restricted to only two columns, and it can use DataColumn arrays as its primary and foreign keys.

The following example shows how to create a DataRelation between two DataTables in a DataSet, representing the relationship between Products and OrderDetail.

Listing 2.3 creates a DataRelation between two DataTables in the DataSet.

LISTING 2.3 Adding a DataRelation

```
[VB]

01: Imports System
02: Imports System.Data
03:
04: Namespace Chapter02
05:
06:   Public Class C0203
07:
08:   Public Function CreateCustomDataSet() As DataSet
09:     Dim myDataSet As New DataSet
10:     Dim keys(1) As DataColumn
11:
12:     myDataSet.Tables.Add(new DataTable("Products"))
13:     myDataSet.Tables("Products").Columns.Add("ID",
➥        System.Type.GetType("System.Int32"))
14:     myDataSet.Tables("Products").Columns.Add("Name",
➥        System.Type.GetType("System.String"))
15:     myDataSet.Tables("Products").Columns.Add("Cost",
➥        System.Type.GetType("System.Double"))
16:
17:     keys(0) = myDataSet.Tables("Products").Columns("ID")
18:     myDataSet.Tables("Products").PrimaryKey = keys
19:
20:     Dim myRow As DataRow
21:     myRow = myDataSet.Tables("Products").NewRow()
22:     myRow("ID") = 1
23:     myRow("Name") = "Doug's Doomsday Device"
24:     myRow("Cost") = 19.95
25:     myDataSet.Tables("Products").Rows.Add(myRow)
26:
27:     ' Add OrderDetail Table
28:     myDataSet.Tables.Add(new DataTable("OrderDetail"))
29:     myDataSet.Tables("OrderDetail").Columns.Add("ProductID",
➥        System.Type.GetType("System.Int32"))
30:     myDataSet.Tables("OrderDetail").Columns.Add("Quantity",
➥        System.Type.GetType("System.Int32"))
31:
32:     keys(0) = myDataSet.Tables("OrderDetail").Columns("ProductID")
33:     myDataSet.Tables("OrderDetail").PrimaryKey = keys
34:
```

LISTING 2.3 Continued

```
35:    myRow = myDataSet.Tables("OrderDetail").NewRow()
36:    myRow("ProductID") = 1
37:    myRow("Quantity") = 7
38:    myDataSet.Tables("OrderDetail").Rows.Add(myRow)
39:
40:    ' Add DataRelations
41:    myDataSet.Relations.Add("ProductToOrderDetails",
➥         myDataSet.Tables("Products").Columns("ID"),
➥         myDataSet.Tables("OrderDetail").Columns("ProductID"))
42:
43:    Return myDataSet
44:   End Function
45:  End Class
46: End Namespace

[C#]

01: using System;
02: using System.Data;
03:
04: namespace Chapter02{
05:
06:   public class C0203{
07:
08:    public DataSet CreateCustomDataSet(){
09:     DataSet myDataSet = new DataSet();
10:     DataColumn[] keys = new DataColumn[1];
11:
12:     myDataSet.Tables.Add(new DataTable("Products"));
13:     myDataSet.Tables["Products"].Columns.Add("ID",
➥         System.Type.GetType("System.Int32"));
14:     myDataSet.Tables["Products"].Columns.Add("Name",
➥         System.Type.GetType("System.String"));
15:     myDataSet.Tables["Products"].Columns.Add("Cost",
➥         System.Type.GetType("System.Double"));
16:
17:     keys[0] = myDataSet.Tables["Products"].Columns["ID"];
18:     myDataSet.Tables["Products"].PrimaryKey = keys;
19:
20:     DataRow myRow = null;
21:     myRow = myDataSet.Tables["Products"].NewRow();
22:     myRow["ID"] = 1;
23:     myRow["Name"] = "Doug's Doomsday Device";
24:     myRow["Cost"] = 19.95;
25:     myDataSet.Tables["Products"].Rows.Add(myRow);
26:
```

LISTING 2.3 Continued

```
27:    // Add OrderDetail Table
28:    myDataSet.Tables.Add(new DataTable("OrderDetail"));
29:    myDataSet.Tables["OrderDetail"].Columns.Add("ProductID",
➥        System.Type.GetType("System.Int32"));
30:    myDataSet.Tables["OrderDetail"].Columns.Add("Quantity",
➥        System.Type.GetType("System.Int32"));
31:
32:    keys[0] = myDataSet.Tables["OrderDetail"].Columns["ProductID"];
33:    myDataSet.Tables["OrderDetail"].PrimaryKey = keys;
34:
35:    myRow = myDataSet.Tables["OrderDetail"].NewRow();
36:    myRow["ProductID"] = 1;
37:    myRow["Quantity"] = 7;
38:    myDataSet.Tables["OrderDetail"].Rows.Add(myRow);
39:
40:    // Add DataRelations
41:    myDataSet.Relations.Add("ProductToOrderDetails",
➥        myDataSet.Tables["Products"].Columns["ID"],
➥        myDataSet.Tables["OrderDetail"].Columns["ProductID"]);
42:
43:    return myDataSet;
44:    }
45:  }
46: }
```

In Listing 2.3 you continue to extend the code from the previous examples. On lines 27–38 you add a new DataTable, OrderDetail, to the DataSet, and a new DataRow to the OrderDetail table. On line 41 you create a DataRelation between the Products table and the OrderDetail table. The DataRelation is called ProductToOrderDetail, and it links the Products.ID (primary key) column to the OrderDetail.ProductID (foreign key) column.

Constraints

As with any data structure, maintaining data integrity is imperative. ADO.NET enables *constraints* as one means of maintaining data integrity. There are two kinds of constraints:

- ForeignKeyConstraints
- UniqueConstraints

ForeignKeyConstraint

When a row is deleted or updated, and the value that has changed is used also as a foreign key in one or more related tables, the *ForeignKeyConstraint* is used to determine how to react to the change. The possible ForeignKeyConstraint actions are shown in Table 2.2.

TABLE 2.2 ForeignKeyConstraint Actions

Action	Description
Cascade	Deletes or updates the related rows.
SetNull	Sets the values in the related rows to Null.
SetDefault	Sets the values in the related rows to their default values.
None	No action. The values in the related rows are unaffected.
Default	The default action is to cascade.

Listing 2.4 creates a ForeignKeyConstraint for a DataTable in your DataSet.

LISTING 2.4 Adding a ForeignKeyConstraint

```
[VB]

01: Imports System
02: Imports System.Data
03:
04: Namespace Chapter02
05:
06:   Public Class C0204
07:
08:     Public Function CreateCustomDataSet() As DataSet
09:       Dim myDataSet As New DataSet
10:       Dim keys(1) As DataColumn
11:
12:       myDataSet.Tables.Add(new DataTable("Products"))
13:       myDataSet.Tables("Products").Columns.Add("ID",
➡           System.Type.GetType("System.Int32"))
14:       myDataSet.Tables("Products").Columns.Add("Name",
➡           System.Type.GetType("System.String"))
15:       myDataSet.Tables("Products").Columns.Add("Cost",
➡           System.Type.GetType("System.Double"))
16:
17:       keys(0) = myDataSet.Tables("Products").Columns("ID")
18:       myDataSet.Tables("Products").PrimaryKey = keys
19:
20:       Dim myRow As DataRow
21:       myRow = myDataSet.Tables("Products").NewRow()
22:       myRow("ID") = 1
23:       myRow("Name") = "Doug's Doomsday Device"
24:       myRow("Cost") = 19.95
25:       myDataSet.Tables("Products").Rows.Add(myRow)
26:
```

2

**WHAT IS
ADO.NET?**

LISTING 2.4   Continued

```
27:    ' Add OrderDetail Table
28:    myDataSet.Tables.Add(new DataTable("OrderDetail"))
29:    myDataSet.Tables("OrderDetail").Columns.Add("ProductID",
➡        System.Type.GetType("System.Int32"))
30:    myDataSet.Tables("OrderDetail").Columns.Add("Quantity",
➡        System.Type.GetType("System.Int32"))
31:
32:    keys(0) = myDataSet.Tables("OrderDetail").Columns("ProductID")
33:    myDataSet.Tables("OrderDetail").PrimaryKey = keys
34:
35:    myRow = myDataSet.Tables("OrderDetail").NewRow()
36:    myRow("ProductID") = 1
37:    myRow("Quantity") = 7
38:    myDataSet.Tables("OrderDetail").Rows.Add(myRow)
39:
40:    ' Add DataRelations
41:    myDataSet.Relations.Add("ProductToOrderDetails",
➡        myDataSet.Tables("Products").Columns("ID"), 42:
➡        myDataSet.Tables("OrderDetail").Columns("ProductID"))
42:
43:    Dim fk As ForeignKeyConstraint
44:    fk = New ForeignKeyConstraint(
➡        myDataSet.Tables("Products").Columns("ID"),
➡        myDataSet.Tables("OrderDetail").Columns("ProductID"))
45:    fk.DeleteRule = Rule.Cascade
46:    fk.UpdateRule = Rule.SetDefault
47:    myDataSet.Tables("Products").Constraints.Add(fk)
48:
49:    Return myDataSet
50:   End Function
51:  End Class
52: End Namespace

[C#]

01: using System;
02: using System.Data;
03:
04: namespace Chapter02{
05:
06:   public class C0204{
07:
08:    public DataSet CreateCustomDataSet(){
09:     DataSet myDataSet = new DataSet();
10:     DataColumn[] keys = new DataColumn[1];
11:
```

LISTING 2.4 Continued

```
12:     myDataSet.Tables.Add(new DataTable("Products"));
13:     myDataSet.Tables["Products"].Columns.Add("ID",
➡          System.Type.GetType("System.Int32"));
14:     myDataSet.Tables["Products"].Columns.Add("Name",
➡          System.Type.GetType("System.String"));
15:     myDataSet.Tables["Products"].Columns.Add("Cost",
➡          System.Type.GetType("System.Double"));
16:
17:     keys[0] = myDataSet.Tables["Products"].Columns["ID"];
18:     myDataSet.Tables["Products"].PrimaryKey = keys;
19:
20:     DataRow myRow = null;
21:     myRow = myDataSet.Tables["Products"].NewRow();
22:     myRow["ID"] = 1;
23:     myRow["Name"] = "Doug's Doomsday Device";
24:     myRow["Cost"] = 19.95;
25:     myDataSet.Tables["Products"].Rows.Add(myRow);
26:
27:     // Add OrderDetail Table
28:     myDataSet.Tables.Add(new DataTable("OrderDetail"));
29:     myDataSet.Tables["OrderDetail"].Columns.Add("ProductID",
➡          System.Type.GetType("System.Int32"));
30:     myDataSet.Tables["OrderDetail"].Columns.Add("Quantity",
➡          System.Type.GetType("System.Int32"));
31:
32:     keys[0] = myDataSet.Tables["OrderDetail"].Columns["ProductID"];
33:     myDataSet.Tables["OrderDetail"].PrimaryKey = keys;
34:
35:     myRow = myDataSet.Tables["OrderDetail"].NewRow();
36:     myRow["ProductID"] = 1;
37:     myRow["Quantity"] = 7;
38:     myDataSet.Tables["OrderDetail"].Rows.Add(myRow);
39:
40:     // Add DataRelations
41:     myDataSet.Relations.Add("ProductToOrderDetails",
➡          myDataSet.Tables["Products"].Columns["ID"],
➡          myDataSet.Tables["OrderDetail"].Columns["ProductID"]);
42:
43:     ForeignKeyConstraint fk = null;
44:     fk = new ForeignKeyConstraint(
➡          myDataSet.Tables["Products"].Columns["ID"],
➡          myDataSet.Tables["OrderDetail"].Columns["ProductID"]);
45:     fk.DeleteRule = Rule.Cascade;
46:     fk.UpdateRule = Rule.SetDefault;
```

LISTING 2.4 Continued

```
47:      myDataSet.Tables["Products"].Constraints.Add(fk);
48:
49:      return myDataSet;
50:    }
51:  }
52: }
```

In Listing 2.4 you continue extending the code from the previous examples. On lines 43–47 you add a ForeignKeyConstraint between the Products and OrderDetail tables. On line 44 you set the constraint between Products.ID and OrderDetail.ProductID (Products.ID is the parent column and primary key; OrderDetail.ProductID is the foreign key). On line 45 you set the DeleteRule to Cascade; the appropriate rows in OrderDetail will be deleted when a product is deleted from the Products table. On line 46 you set the UpdateRule to SetDefault, which will set the values in related rows to their default values. On line 47 you add the constraint to the Products table.

UniqueConstraint

A *UniqueConstraint* is used to ensure that all values in a DataColumn are unique. It can be assigned to either an individual column or an array of columns in a single DataTable. Listing 2.5 shows how to add a UniqueConstraint.

LISTING 2.5 Adding a UniqueConstraint

```
[VB]
01: Imports System
02: Imports System.Data
03:
04: Namespace Chapter02
05:
06:   Public Class C0204
07:
08:    Public Function CreateCustomDataSet() As DataSet
09:     Dim myDataSet As New DataSet
10:     Dim keys(1) As DataColumn
11:
12:     myDataSet.Tables.Add(new DataTable("Products"))
13:     myDataSet.Tables("Products").Columns.Add("ID",
➡         System.Type.GetType("System.Int32"))
14:     myDataSet.Tables("Products").Columns.Add("Name",
➡         System.Type.GetType("System.String"))
15:     myDataSet.Tables("Products").Columns.Add("Cost",
➡         System.Type.GetType("System.Double"))
16:
```

LISTING 2.5 Continued

```
17:    keys(0) = myDataSet.Tables("Products").Columns("ID")
18:    myDataSet.Tables("Products").PrimaryKey = keys
19:
20:    Dim myRow As DataRow
21:    myRow = myDataSet.Tables("Products").NewRow()
22:    myRow("ID") = 1
23:    myRow("Name") = "Doug's Doomsday Device"
24:    myRow("Cost") = 19.95
25:    myDataSet.Tables("Products").Rows.Add(myRow)
26:
27:    ' Add OrderDetail Table
28:    myDataSet.Tables.Add(new DataTable("OrderDetail"))
29:    myDataSet.Tables("OrderDetail").Columns.Add("ProductID",
➥         System.Type.GetType("System.Int32"))
30:    myDataSet.Tables("OrderDetail").Columns.Add("Quantity",
➥         System.Type.GetType("System.Int32"))
31:
32:    keys(0) = myDataSet.Tables("OrderDetail").Columns("ProductID")
33:    myDataSet.Tables("OrderDetail").PrimaryKey = keys
34:
35:    myRow = myDataSet.Tables("OrderDetail").NewRow()
36:    myRow("ProductID") = 1
37:    myRow("Quantity") = 7
38:    myDataSet.Tables("OrderDetail").Rows.Add(myRow)
39:
40:    ' Add DataRelations
41:    myDataSet.Relations.Add("ProductToOrderDetails",
➥         myDataSet.Tables("Products").Columns("ID"), 42:
➥         myDataSet.Tables("OrderDetail").Columns("ProductID"))
42:
43:    Dim fk As ForeignKeyConstraint
44:    fk = New ForeignKeyConstraint(
➥         myDataSet.Tables("Products").Columns("ID"),
➥         myDataSet.Tables("OrderDetail").Columns("ProductID"))
45:    fk.DeleteRule = Rule.Cascade
46:    fk.UpdateRule = Rule.SetDefault
47:    myDataSet.Tables("Products").Constraints.Add(fk)
48:
49:    Dim uc As UniqueConstraint
50:    uc = New UniqueConstraint(myDataSet.Tables("Products").Columns("ID"))
51:    myDataSet.Tables("Products").Constraints.Add(uc)
52:
53:    Return myDataSet
54:   End Function
55:  End Class
56: End Namespace
```

LISTING 2.5 Continued

[C#]

```
01: using System;
02: using System.Data;
03:
04: namespace Chapter02{
05:
06:   public class C0204{
07:
08:    public DataSet CreateCustomDataSet(){
09:     DataSet myDataSet = new DataSet();
10:     DataColumn[] keys = new DataColumn[1];
11:
12:     myDataSet.Tables.Add(new DataTable("Products"));
13:     myDataSet.Tables["Products"].Columns.Add("ID",
➡         System.Type.GetType("System.Int32"));
14:     myDataSet.Tables["Products"].Columns.Add("Name",
➡         System.Type.GetType("System.String"));
15:     myDataSet.Tables["Products"].Columns.Add("Cost",
➡         System.Type.GetType("System.Double"));
16:
17:     keys[0] = myDataSet.Tables["Products"].Columns["ID"];
18:     myDataSet.Tables["Products"].PrimaryKey = keys;
19:
20:     DataRow myRow = null;
21:     myRow = myDataSet.Tables["Products"].NewRow();
22:     myRow["ID"] = 1;
23:     myRow["Name"] = "Doug's Doomsday Device";
24:     myRow["Cost"] = 19.95;
25:     myDataSet.Tables["Products"].Rows.Add(myRow);
26:
27:     // Add OrderDetail Table
28:     myDataSet.Tables.Add(new DataTable("OrderDetail"));
29:     myDataSet.Tables["OrderDetail"].Columns.Add("ProductID",
➡         System.Type.GetType("System.Int32"));
30:     myDataSet.Tables["OrderDetail"].Columns.Add("Quantity",
➡         System.Type.GetType("System.Int32"));
31:
32:     keys[0] = myDataSet.Tables["OrderDetail"].Columns["ProductID"];
33:     myDataSet.Tables["OrderDetail"].PrimaryKey = keys;
34:
35:     myRow = myDataSet.Tables["OrderDetail"].NewRow();
36:     myRow["ProductID"] = 1;
37:     myRow["Quantity"] = 7;
38:     myDataSet.Tables["OrderDetail"].Rows.Add(myRow);
39:
40:     // Add DataRelations
```

LISTING 2.5 Continued

```
41:    myDataSet.Relations.Add("ProductToOrderDetails",
➥        myDataSet.Tables["Products"].Columns["ID"],
➥        myDataSet.Tables["OrderDetail"].Columns["ProductID"]);
42:
43:    ForeignKeyConstraint fk = null;
44:    fk = new ForeignKeyConstraint(
➥        myDataSet.Tables["Products"].Columns["ID"],
➥        myDataSet.Tables["OrderDetail"].Columns["ProductID"]);
45:    fk.DeleteRule = Rule.Cascade;
46:    fk.UpdateRule = Rule.SetDefault;
47:    myDataSet.Tables["Products"].Constraints.Add(fk);
48:
49:    UniqueConstraint uc = null;
50:    uc = new UniqueConstraint(myDataSet.Tables["Products"].Columns["ID"]);
51:    myDataSet.Tables["Products"].Constraints.Add(uc);
52:
53:    return myDataSet;
54:    }
55:  }
56: }
```

In Listing 2.5 you continue extending the code from the previous examples. On lines 49–51 you add a UniqueConstraint to the Products table. The UniqueConstraint ensures that all values added to the Products.ID column must be unique.

Summary

In this chapter you learned about ADO.NET, the most recent evolution of ActiveX Data Objects. You saw that there are great benefits to using ADO.NET, including the following:

- Interoperability
- Maintainability
- Programmability
- Performance
- Scalability

You also received a high-level overview of the ADO.NET object model, and you learned that the DataSet is the centerpiece of an ADO.NET solution. In each DataSet, there's a RelationsCollection and a TablesCollection. In each DataTable of the TablesCollection, there's a columns collection and a rows collection. You also saw some code samples for dynamically building an ADO.NET DataSet.

As you progress through this book, you'll look deeper into the object model and write code against the ADO.NET objects.

Reading and Displaying Data

PART
II

IN THIS PART

ADO.NET Managed Providers

IN THIS CHAPTER

In the last chapter, you began looking at how an ASP.NET data-driven solution works. You looked at the ADO.NET object model, and how to build a `DataSet` dynamically. In this chapter, you'll dig into the two data access Managed Providers offered in ADO.NET: the SQL Managed Provider and the OleDB Managed Provider.

In this chapter, you'll learn the following:

- How the .NET Managed Providers are a bridge from the application, such as an ASP.NET Web Form, to a data store, such as Microsoft SQL Server.
- How to create Managed Connections to connect to a data store.
- How to use Managed Commands to execute SQL statements on a database.
- How to use `DataAdapters` to retrieve data and populate a `DataSet`.
- How to create custom table and column mappings.

Managed Providers, as shown in Figure 3.1, are ADO.NET's bridge from an application, such as an ASP.NET Web Form to the data source. Data sources include Microsoft's SQL Server, Access, Oracle, or any other such data storage device.

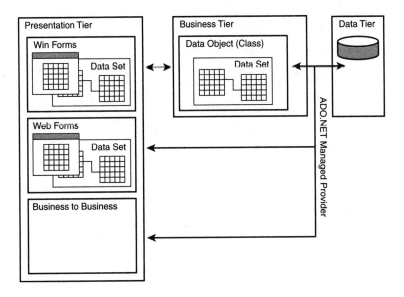

FIGURE 3.1
Managed Providers are the bridge from a data store to a .NET application.

The Managed Providers have four core components:

- **Connection**

  The Connection represents a unique session to a data store. This might be manifested as a network connection in a client/server database application.

- **Command**

  The Command represents a SQL statement to be executed on a data store.

- **DataReader**

  The DataReader is a forward-only, read-only stream of data records from a data store to a client.

- **DataAdapter**

  The DataAdapter represents a set of Commands and a Connection which are used to retrieve data from a data store and fill a DataSet.

The Two Managed Providers

ADO.NET, the successor to Microsoft's highly successful ActiveX Data Objects (ADO), offers two Managed Providers. These providers are similar in their object model, but are chosen at design-time based on the data provider being used. The SQL Managed Provider offers a direct link into Microsoft's SQL Server database application (version 7.0 or higher), while the OleDb Managed Provider is used for all other data providers. Following is a brief description of each of the Managed Providers. Throughout this chapter we will show you how the Managed Providers work, and specify when a particular object, property, method or event is unique to only one of the Managed Providers.

OleDb Managed Provider

The *OleDb Managed Provider* uses native OLEDB and COM Interop to establish a connection to a data store and negotiate commands. The OleDb Managed Provider is the data access provider to use when you are working with data from any data source that is not Microsoft's SQL Server 7.0 or higher. To use the OleDb Managed Provider, you must import the System.Data.OleDb namespace.

SQL Managed Provider

The *SQL Managed Provider* is designed to work directly with Microsoft SQL Server 7.0 or greater. It connects and negotiates directly with SQL Server without using OLEDB. This provides a better performance model than the OleDb Managed Provider, but it's restricted to use with Microsoft SQL Server 7.0 or higher. To use the SQL Managed Provider, you must import the System.Data.SqlClient namespace.

Managed Connections

Much like classic ADO, the OleDb and SQL Managed Connection objects (OleDbConnection and SqlConnection) provide a set of properties that might be familiar to you. These are listed in Table 3.1. Properties that apply to only one of the Managed Providers are indicated.

Table 3.1 Managed Connection Properties

Property	Description
ConnectionString	Gets or sets the string used to open a data store.
ConnectionTimeout	Gets or sets the time to wait while establishing a connection before terminating the attempt and generating an error.
Container	Returns the IContainer that contains the object.
Database	Gets or sets the name of the current database or the database to be used once a connection is open.
DataSource	Gets or sets the name of the database to connect to.
PacketSize (SqlConnection only)	Gets the size of the packets the data is transferred in.
Provider (OleDbConnection only)	Gets or sets the name of the OLEDB provider.
ServerVersion (SqlConnection only)	Gets a string containing the version of the connected SQL Server.
Site	Gets or sets the site of the component.
State	Gets the current state of the connection.

OleDbConnection

The OleDb Managed Provider uses a ConnectionString property format identical to that of a classic ADO connection object. Listing 3.1 shows how to connect to an Access 2000 database using the OleDbConnection object.

> **Warning**
>
> In the following code listing, the OleDb Managed Connection object is pointing to an Access 2000 database file using the path, C:\Program Files\Microsoft Office\Office\Samples\Northwind.mdb. This is the default path to the Northwind sample database that is installed when Access 2000 is installed. The path on your machine might vary. Alter the code as necessary.

Listing 3.1 Connecting to an Access 2000 Database with the OleDbConnection

[VB]

```
01: <%@ Page Language="VB" %>
02: <%@ Import Namespace="System.Data.OleDb" %>
03: <script runat="server">
```

LISTING 3.1 Continued

```
04: Sub Page_Load(Sender As Object, E As EventArgs)
05:   Dim myConnection As OleDbConnection
06:   myConnection = New OleDbConnection("Provider=Microsoft.Jet.OLEDB.4.0;
➡     Data Source=C:\Program Files\Microsoft
➡     Office\Office\Samples\Northwind.mdb;")
07:   myConnection.Open()
08:   ConnectionState.Text = myConnection.State.ToString()
09:   myConnection.Close()
10:   End Sub
11: </script>

[C#]

01: <%@ Page Language="C#" %>
02: <%@ Import Namespace="System.Data.OleDb" %>
03: <script runat="server">
04:   void Page_Load(Object sender, EventArgs e){
05:   OleDbConnection myConnection;
06:   myConnection = new OleDbConnection("Provider=Microsoft.Jet.OLEDB.4.0;
➡     Data Source=C:\\Program Files\\Microsoft
➡     Office\\Office\\Samples\\Northwind.mdb;");
07:   myConnection.Open();
08:   ConnectionState.Text = myConnection.State.ToString();
09:   myConnection.Close();
10:   }
11: </script>

[VB & C#]

12: <html>
13: <body>
14: <form runat="server" method="post">
15:   Connection State: <asp:Label runat="server" id="ConnectionState" />
16: </form>
17: </body>
18: </html>
```

3

ADO.NET MANAGED PROVIDERS

In Listing 3.1, you import the System.Data.OleDb namespace on line 2. On line 5, you declare a variable for the OleDbConnection class and on line 6, you instantiate the OleDbConnection class, passing in the ConnectionString as the connection's only parameter. The ConnectionString property specifies that the OLEDB Provider is Microsoft.Jet.OLEDB.4.0, the provider necessary to connect to an Access 2000 database.

On line 7 you open the connection with the Open() method of the OleDbConnection class. On line 8 you set the Text property of an ASP.NET Label to the string representation of the State property of the OleDbConnection class.

> **WARNING**
>
> In the C# example in Listing 3.1 you will notice that the `ConnectionString` property of the Managed Connection object uses a double slash (\\) between the tree hierarchy of the path to the Northwind sample database file. This is because C# treats the slash (\) as an escape character in a string. Using a double slash (\\) lets the compiler know that you really want to use a slash character in that spot.

> **NOTE**
>
> If you are using Access 2000 with user name and password security, you might see an error indicating that Access can not find the installable ISAM. This error is related to your Access 2000 installation, and not the .NET Framework. For more information, see `http://support.microsoft.com/support/kb/articles/Q209/8/05.ASP`.

SqlConnection

The SQL Managed Provider uses a `ConnectionString` property format that's similar to that of a classic ADO connection object. Since you know what the database application is from using the SQL Managed Provider, the Provider property isn't required (it isn't even allowed, for that matter). Listing 3.2 shows sample code for connecting to a Microsoft SQL Server database using the `SqlConnection` object.

LISTING 3.2 Connecting to a SQL Server Database with the SqlConnection

```
[VB]
01: <%@ Page Language="VB" %>
02: <%@ Import Namespace="System.Data.SqlClient" %>
03: <script runat="server">
04:   Sub Page_Load(Sender As Object, E As EventArgs)
05:    Dim myConnection As SqlConnection
06:    myConnection = New SqlConnection("server=localhost;
➥      database=Northwind; uid=sa; pwd=;")
07:    myConnection.Open()
08:    ConnectionState.Text = myConnection.State.ToString()
09:    myConnection.Close()
10:   End Sub
11: </script>
```

LISTING 3.2   Continued

```
[C#]

01: <%@ Page Language="C#" %>
02: <%@ Import Namespace="System.Data.SqlClient" %>
03: <script runat="server">
04:   void Page_Load(Object sender, EventArgs e){
05:     SqlConnection myConnection;
06:     myConnection = new SqlConnection("server=localhost;
➥        database=Northwind; uid=sa; pwd=;");
07:     myConnection.Open();
08:     ConnectionState.Text = myConnection.State.ToString();
09:     myConnection.Close();
10:   }
11: </script>

[VB & C#]


12: <html>
13: <body>
14: <form runat="server" method="post">
15:   Connection State: <asp:Label runat="server" id="ConnectionState" />
16: </form>
17: </body>
18: </html>
```

In Listing 3.2 you create a connection to a SQL Server database. The code in Listing 3.2 is nearly identical to that of Listing 3.1. The only two differences are on lines 2 and 6. On line 2 you import the System.Data.SqlClient namespace rather than the System.Data.OleDb namespace. This allows you access to the SQL Managed Provider classes, like the SqlConnection class. On line 6 you create an instance of the SqlConnection class and pass in the ConnectionString property as the only parameter. In the ConnectionString property you *do not* specify a provider since the SqlConnection is designed to connect only to a Microsoft SQL Server database.

Managed Commands

Managed Commands represent SQL syntax to be executed on the data store. Managed Commands can be simple SELECT statements or complex, parameterized commands.

Once a connection to a data store is established, you can retrieve, update, or insert data. One way of accomplishing this is to use a Managed Command. This is the most direct way to execute a SQL statement on a data store.

As with the Managed Connection object, there are both OleDb and SQL versions of the Managed Command—OleDbCommand and SqlCommand.

The Managed Command is similar to the classic ADO command object. In its simplest form, you create a Managed Command with the SQL statement and the connection (as either a ConnectionString or a Managed Connection object) as its parameters. In Listing 3.3 you create a SqlCommand to execute a simple SELECT statement against the Northwind database. This example will not render any output, but you will build on it in the following examples.

> **NOTE**
>
> For the bulk of this chapter I will be showing samples using the SQL Managed Provider. You can use the OleDb Managed Provider by changing the Managed Provider classes from SqlWidget to OleDbWidget. For example, in Listing 3.3 you could use the OleDbCommand class in replacement of the SqlCommand class. Remember that the OleDb Managed Provider uses the System.Data.OleDb namespace instead of the System.Data.SqlClient namespace.

LISTING 3.3 Creating a SqlCommand Object

[VB]

```
01: <%@ Page Language="VB" %>
02: <%@ Import Namespace="System.Data.SqlClient" %>
03: <script runat="server">
04:  Sub Page_Load(Sender As Object, E As EventArgs)
05:   Dim myConnection As SqlConnection
06:   Dim myCommand As SqlCommand
07:   myConnection = New SqlConnection("server=localhost;
➡      database=Northwind; uid=sa; pwd=;")
08:   myCommand = New SqlCommand("SELECT * FROM Customers", myConnection)
09:  End Sub
10: </script>
```

[C#]

```
01: <%@ Page Language="C#" %>
02: <%@ Import Namespace="System.Data.SqlClient" %>
03: <script runat="server">
04:  void Page_Load(Object sender, EventArgs e){
05:   SqlConnection myConnection;
06:   SqlCommand myCommand;
07:   myConnection = new SqlConnection("server=localhost;
➡      database=Northwind; uid=sa; pwd=;");
08:   myCommand = new SqlCommand("SELECT * FROM Customers", myConnection);
09:  }
10: </script>
```

LISTING 3.3   Continued

```
[VB & C#]
11: <html>
12: <body>
13: <form runat="server" method="post">
14:   <asp:DataGrid runat="server" id="myDataGrid" />
15: </form>
16: </body>
17: </html>
```

In Listing 3.3 you create a Web Form that uses the SQL Managed Provider to create a SqlConnection and a SqlCommand. To execute the SqlCommand on the database you call one of the provided execute methods.

- ExecuteNonQuery: Executes a SQL statement that does not return any records.
- ExecuteReader: Returns a DataReader object.
- ExecuteScalar: Executes the SQL statement and returns the first column of the first row.
- ExecuteXmlReader (SQL Managed Provider only): Executes a SQL statement and returns the results as an XML stream.

The only thing you're missing before calling one of the execute methods is an object to hold the results that are returned. For this example you will use the ExecuteReader() method and return the results as a DataReader object (SqlDataReader or OleDbDataReader). Once you have a DataReader object you can work with the data. For now you will bind the DataReader to a DataGrid server control. In Listing 3.4 you will use the ExecuteReader() method to return the results of the command execution into a DataReader object.

LISTING 3.4   Executing a SqlCommand Object and Returning the Results in a DataReader

```
[VB]
01: <%@ Page Language="VB" %>
02: <%@ Import Namespace="System.Data.SqlClient" %>
03: <script runat="server">
04:   Sub Page_Load(Sender As Object, E As EventArgs)
05:   Dim myConnection As SqlConnection
06:   Dim myCommand As SqlCommand
07:   myConnection = New SqlConnection("server=localhost;
➥     database=Northwind; uid=sa; pwd=;")
08:   myCommand = New SqlCommand("SELECT * FROM Customers", myConnection)
09:   myConnection.Open()
10:   Dim myDataReader As SqlDataReader = myCommand.ExecuteReader()
11:   myDataGrid.DataSource = myDataReader
```

3

ADO.NET MANAGED PROVIDERS

LISTING 3.4   Continued

```
12:    myDataGrid.DataBind()
13:    myConnection.Close()
14:    End Sub
15: </script>
```

[C#]

```
01: <%@ Page Language="C#" %>
02: <%@ Import Namespace="System.Data.SqlClient" %>
03: <script runat="server">
04:   void Page_Load(Object sender, EventArgs e){
05:     SqlConnection myConnection;
06:     SqlCommand myCommand;
07:     myConnection = new SqlConnection("server=localhost;
➥        database=Northwind; uid=sa; pwd=;");
08:     myCommand = new SqlCommand("SELECT * FROM Customers", myConnection);
09:     myConnection.Open();
10:     SqlDataReader myDataReader = myCommand.ExecuteReader();
11:     myDataGrid.DataSource = myDataReader;
12:     myDataGrid.DataBind();
13:     myConnection.Close();
14:   }
15: </script>
```

[VB & C#]

```
16: <html>
17: <body>
18: <form runat="server" method="post">
19:   <asp:DataGrid runat="server" id="myDataGrid" />
20: </form>
21: </body>
22: </html>
```

In Listing 3.4 you extend the code in Listing 3.3 to execute the SqlCommand object using the
ExecuteReader() method. Since this method returns the results in a DataReader object, you
first create an instance of the SqlDataReader class on line 10, and set it to the returned result
of the SqlCommand.ExecuteReader() method. You will notice that I create an instance of the
DataReader and assign it to the results of the ExecuteReader() on the same line. This is just
another way of constructing an object in .NET, rather than doing the same thing across two
lines of code.

Once the command has executed and the DataReader has been created, you bind the
DataReader to a DataGrid server control (line 11) by setting the DataSource property of the
DataGrid as the DataReader. Once the DataSource property is set you call the DataBind()
method of the DataGrid to bind the command results to the output of the DataGrid.

Figure 3.2 shows the ASP.NET Web Form with the results from the Managed Command execution in a DataGrid.

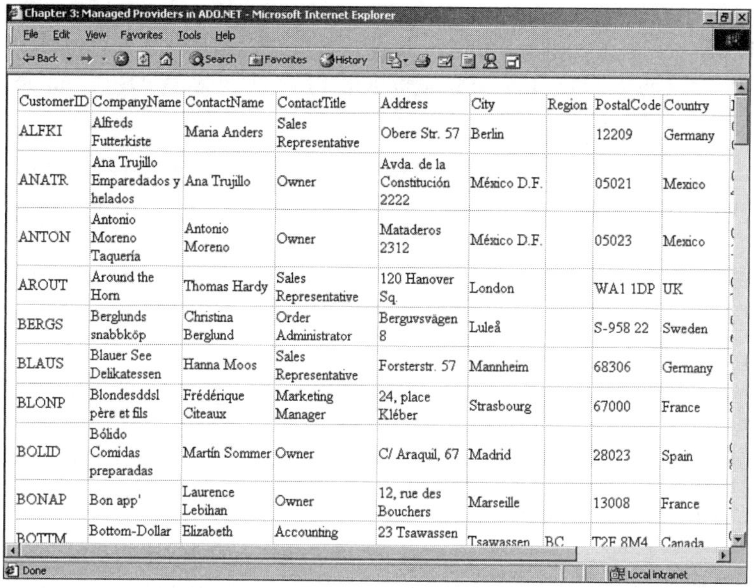

CustomerID	CompanyName	ContactName	ContactTitle	Address	City	Region	PostalCode	Country
ALFKI	Alfreds Futterkiste	Maria Anders	Sales Representative	Obere Str. 57	Berlin		12209	Germany
ANATR	Ana Trujillo Emparedados y helados	Ana Trujillo	Owner	Avda. de la Constitución 2222	México D.F.		05021	Mexico
ANTON	Antonio Moreno Taquería	Antonio Moreno	Owner	Mataderos 2312	México D.F.		05023	Mexico
AROUT	Around the Horn	Thomas Hardy	Sales Representative	120 Hanover Sq.	London		WA1 1DP	UK
BERGS	Berglunds snabbköp	Christina Berglund	Order Administrator	Berguvsvägen 8	Luleå		S-958 22	Sweden
BLAUS	Blauer See Delikatessen	Hanna Moos	Sales Representative	Forsterstr. 57	Mannheim		68306	Germany
BLONP	Blondesddsl père et fils	Frédérique Citeaux	Marketing Manager	24, place Kléber	Strasbourg		67000	France
BOLID	Bólido Comidas preparadas	Martín Sommer	Owner	C/ Araquil, 67	Madrid		28023	Spain
BONAP	Bon app'	Laurence Lebihan	Owner	12, rue des Bouchers	Marseille		13008	France
BOTTM	Bottom-Dollar	Elizabeth	Accounting	23 Tsawassen	Tsawassen	BC	T2F 8M4	Canada

FIGURE 3.2

Using the Managed Providers you can create a connection to a database, execute a command, and display the results on an ASP.NET Web Form.

The DataReader

The `DataReader` provides a forward-only, read-only stream of data from the data store. The `DataReader` is best used when either there are many records in the result set and pulling them all in at once would use too much memory, or when you want to iterate through the records to work with the data returned. As a stream of records, the `DataReader` helps manage memory allocation. Rather than all of the records in the result set being returned at once and using up a chunk of memory on the server, the `DataReader` streams in one record at a time.

You've seen how to execute a command against a data store, and in the previous listings, the results weren't too big. But imagine if your Managed Command returned a result set with over 100,000 records in it. Now imagine 1,000 users doing that all at the same time. It would use up the memory space for 100,000,000 records of data, and that could spell disaster for your Web application.

What would be ideal is a way to connect to the data store, bring the results back in a stream, and evaluate those results one record at a time. Ideally, this would only use up the memory for one record at a time.

This type of functionality is exactly what the DataReader provides. The DataReader is the classic "fire hose" of data access—a forward-only, read-only stream returned from the data store. In Listing 3.4, you bound a DataGrid server control to the DataReader. The DataGrid is covered in depth in Chapter 5, "Using a Basic DataGrid," and Chapter 6, "Altering DataGrid Output." This will set up the DataGrid to display the entire contents of the stream. However, with a data stream, you can step through the data that's returned very easily and decide how to react to it.

The DataReader exposes a Read() method which advances to the next record in the stream. Using the Read() method you can iterate through the result set evaluating or working with the data.

[VB]

```
While myDataReader.Read
  'Do something with the current row
End While
```

[C#]

```
while (myDataReader.Read()){
  //Do something with the current row
}
```

You should be able to come up with a good reason to step through the results of a command execution and evaluate the results. This is something you've done relentlessly as a classic ASP developer (does Do While Not RecordSet.EOF sound familiar?). How often have you looped through ADO RecordSets, checking the values of a particular column and using Response.Write on the RecordSet row if the criterion is met? Or granted access to a page if the user name and password columns match the submitted values?

In Listing 3.5 you will use the DataReader class to iterate through the result set and add any record with the value "USA" to a new DataTable. The DataTable and DataRow classes you learned about in Chapter 2, "What Is ADO.NET?" are used in Listing 3.5.

LISTING 3.5 Evaluating Data with the DataReader

[VB]

```
01: <%@ Page Language="VB" %>
02: <%@ Import Namespace="System.Data" %>
03: <%@ Import Namespace="System.Data.SqlClient" %>
04: <script runat="server">
05:   Sub Page_Load(Sender As Object, E As EventArgs)
06:    Dim myConnection As SqlConnection
07:    Dim myCommand As SqlCommand
08:    Dim myDataTable As New DataTable
09:    Dim myRow As DataRow
```

LISTING 3.5 Continued

```
10:
11:    myConnection = New SqlConnection("server=localhost;
➡       database=Northwind; uid=sa; pwd=;")
12:    myCommand = New SqlCommand("SELECT * FROM Customers", myConnection)
13:    myConnection.Open()
14:    Dim myDataReader As SqlDataReader = myCommand.ExecuteReader()
15:
16:    myDataTable.Columns.Add("CustomerID",
➡       System.Type.GetType("System.String"))
17:    myDataTable.Columns.Add("CompanyName",
➡       System.Type.GetType("System.String"))
18:    myDataTable.Columns.Add("Address",
➡       System.Type.GetType("System.String"))
19:    myDataTable.Columns.Add("City",
➡       System.Type.GetType("System.String"))
20:    myDataTable.Columns.Add("Region",
➡       System.Type.GetType("System.String"))
21:    myDataTable.Columns.Add("Country",
➡       System.Type.GetType("System.String"))
22:
23:    While myDataReader.Read
24:      If myDataReader("Country") = "USA" Then
25:        myRow = myDataTable.NewRow()
26:        myRow("CustomerID") = myDataReader("CustomerID")
27:        myRow("CompanyName") = myDataReader("CompanyName")
28:        myRow("Address") = myDataReader("Address")
29:        myRow("City") = myDataReader("City")
30:        myRow("Region") = myDataReader("Region")
31:        myRow("Country") = myDataReader("Country")
32:        myDataTable.Rows.Add(myRow)
33:      End If
34:    End While
35:
36:    myDataGrid.DataSource = myDataTable
37:    myDataGrid.DataBind()
38:
39:    myConnection.Close()
40:  End Sub
41: </script>


[C#]

01: <%@ Page Language="C#" %>
02: <%@ Import Namespace="System.Data" %>
03: <%@ Import Namespace="System.Data.SqlClient" %>
04: <script runat="server">
```

LISTING 3.5   Continued

```
05:  void Page_Load(Object sender, EventArgs e){
06:    SqlConnection myConnection;
07:    SqlCommand myCommand;
08:    DataTable myDataTable = new DataTable();
09:    DataRow myRow;
10:
11:    myConnection = new SqlConnection("server=localhost;
➥      database=Northwind; uid=sa; pwd=;");
12:    myCommand = new SqlCommand("SELECT * FROM Customers", myConnection);
13:    myConnection.Open();
14:    SqlDataReader myDataReader = myCommand.ExecuteReader();
15:
16:    myDataTable.Columns.Add("CustomerID",
➥      System.Type.GetType("System.String"));
17:    myDataTable.Columns.Add("CompanyName",
➥      System.Type.GetType("System.String"));
18:    myDataTable.Columns.Add("Address",
➥      System.Type.GetType("System.String"));
19:    myDataTable.Columns.Add("City",
➥      System.Type.GetType("System.String"));
20:    myDataTable.Columns.Add("Region",
➥      System.Type.GetType("System.String"));
21:    myDataTable.Columns.Add("Country",
➥      System.Type.GetType("System.String"));
22:
23:    while(myDataReader.Read()){
24:      if(myDataReader["Country"].ToString() == "USA"){
25:        myRow = myDataTable.NewRow();
26:        myRow["CustomerID"] = myDataReader["CustomerID"].ToString();
27:        myRow["CompanyName"] = myDataReader["CompanyName"].ToString();
28:        myRow["Address"] = myDataReader["Address"].ToString();
29:        myRow["City"] = myDataReader["City"].ToString();
30:        myRow["Region"] = myDataReader["Region"].ToString();
31:        myRow["Country"] = myDataReader["Country"].ToString();
32:        myDataTable.Rows.Add(myRow);
33:      }
34:    }
35:
36:    myDataGrid.DataSource = myDataTable;
37:    myDataGrid.DataBind();
38:
39:    myConnection.Close();
40:  }
41: </script>
```

LISTING 3.5 Continued

```
[VB & C#]

42: <html>
43: <body>
44: <form runat="server" method="post">
45:  <asp:DataGrid runat="server" id="myDataGrid" />
46: </form>
47: </body>
48: </html>
```

In Chapter 2, you read an overview of the ADO.NET Document Object Model and saw samples of creating `DataTables` dynamically. Listing 3.5 makes use of that knowledge. On line 08, you create a `DataTable` dynamically. On lines 16–21, you add columns to the `DataTable`'s `Columns` collection. On lines 23–34, you step through the results of the SqlCommand execution with the `DataReader.Read()` method. If the "Country" field is "USA", you create a new `DataRow` (line 25) and add the values of the current record in the `DataReader` stream to the row (lines 26–31). On line 32, you add the new `DataRow` object to the `DataTable`'s `Rows` collection. Finally, you bind the dynamically created `DataTable` to the `DataGrid` server control. You end up with a table limited to customers in the USA, as shown in Figure 3.3.

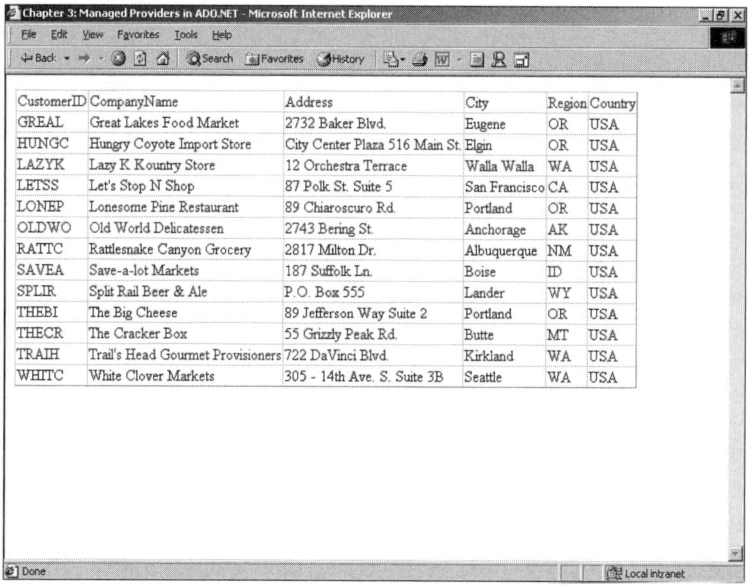

CustomerID	CompanyName	Address	City	Region	Country
GREAL	Great Lakes Food Market	2732 Baker Blvd.	Eugene	OR	USA
HUNGC	Hungry Coyote Import Store	City Center Plaza 516 Main St.	Elgin	OR	USA
LAZYK	Lazy K Kountry Store	12 Orchestra Terrace	Walla Walla	WA	USA
LETSS	Let's Stop N Shop	87 Polk St. Suite 5	San Francisco	CA	USA
LONEP	Lonesome Pine Restaurant	89 Chiaroscuro Rd.	Portland	OR	USA
OLDWO	Old World Delicatessen	2743 Bering St.	Anchorage	AK	USA
RATTC	Rattlesnake Canyon Grocery	2817 Milton Dr.	Albuquerque	NM	USA
SAVEA	Save-a-lot Markets	187 Suffolk Ln.	Boise	ID	USA
SPLIR	Split Rail Beer & Ale	P.O. Box 555	Lander	WY	USA
THEBI	The Big Cheese	89 Jefferson Way Suite 2	Portland	OR	USA
THECR	The Cracker Box	55 Grizzly Peak Rd.	Butte	MT	USA
TRAIH	Trail's Head Gourmet Provisioners	722 DaVinci Blvd.	Kirkland	WA	USA
WHITC	White Clover Markets	305 - 14th Ave. S. Suite 3B	Seattle	WA	USA

FIGURE 3.3
You can use the `DataReader.Read()` *method to iterate through the result set and react to the data.*

Managed Commands with Stored Procedures

Although the example in Listing 3.5 allows you to evaluate data and output only what is desired, a more economical way to get a restricted result set is to use a SQL statement with a WHERE clause. Rather than querying the data store and bringing back all of the records in the table, you can write a SQL statement or stored procedure to bring back only the data you want. Stored procedures typically give better performance to your application than a SQL statement passed via a command.

You can use the Managed Command to call a stored procedure. In many cases, the stored procedure will have the parameters you pass it to determine the result set, such as the country abbreviation in the previous examples.

Listing 3.6 is the syntax for a SQL stored procedure. In the SQL Server Enterprise Manager, create a new stored procedure in the Northwind database named GetCustomersByCountry.

> **WARNING**
>
> Listing 3.6 shows a stored procedure called GetCustomersByCountry. This must be added to the Northwind database before the following samples will work.

LISTING 3.6 GetCustomersByCountry Stored Procedure for SQL Server Northwind Database

```
CREATE PROCEDURE [GetCustomersByCountry]
@country varchar (50)
AS
SELECT * FROM Customers WHERE Country = @country
```

When using a Managed Command to execute a stored procedure you must set the CommandType property. The default value of the CommandType property is Text. To execute a stored procedure you set the CommandType property to CommandType.StoredProcedure and pass in the name of the stored procedure.

Just as classic ADO command objects have a Parameters collection for passing parameters to the stored procedure, ADO.NET Managed Command classes (SqlCommand and OleDbCommand) also have a Parameters collection. You can call to a stored procedure, passing the required parameters in the collection using the following steps:

1. Create a Managed Command object (SqlCommand or OleDbCommand).

2. Set the Managed Command's CommandType property to CommandType.StoredProcedure.

3. Declare a parameter variable (SqlParameter or OleDbParameter).

4. Add a new instance of the parameter class to the Managed Command's `Parameters` collection, passing in its name and data type (`SqlDbType` for `SqlParameter` and `OleDbType` for `OleDbParameter`—see Appendix B for a list of valid `SqlDbTypes` and `OleDbTypes`).

5. Set the parameter's `Direction` property. (Optional—"Input" is the default.)

6. Set the Parameter's `Value` property.

7. Repeat steps 4-6 for additional parameters.

8. Execute the Managed Command.

Listing 3.7 demonstrates these steps.

> **WARNING**
>
> When you're using the SqlCommand object, the names of the parameters added to the Parameters collection must match the names of the markers in the stored procedure. The SQL Managed Provider will treat the parameters as named parameters, and it will look for markers in the stored procedure of the same name.

LISTING 3.7   Calling a Parameterized Stored Procedure with a SqlCommand

[VB]

```
01: <%@ Page Language="VB" %>
02: <%@ Import Namespace="System.Data" %>
03: <%@ Import Namespace="System.Data.SqlClient" %>
04: <script runat="server">
05:  Sub Page_Load(Sender As Object, E As EventArgs)
06:   Dim myConnection As SqlConnection
07:   Dim myCommand As SqlCommand
08:   Dim myParameter As SqlParameter
09:
10:   myConnection = New SqlConnection("server=localhost;
➥     database=Northwind; uid=sa; pwd=;")
11:   myCommand = New SqlCommand("GetCustomersByCountry", myConnection)
12:   myCommand.CommandType = CommandType.StoredProcedure
13:   myParameter = myCommand.Parameters.Add(New SqlParameter("@country",
➥     SqlDbType.VarChar, 50))
14:   myParameter.Direction = ParameterDirection.Input
15:   myParameter.Value = "USA"
16:   myConnection.Open()
17:   Dim myDataReader As SqlDataReader = myCommand.ExecuteReader()
18:
19:   myDataGrid.DataSource = myDataReader
20:   myDataGrid.DataBind()
21:
```

3

ADO.NET MANAGED PROVIDERS

LISTING 3.7 Continued

```
22:   myConnection.Close()
23:  End Sub
24: </script>
```

[C#]

```csharp
01: <%@ Page Language="C#" %>
02: <%@ Import Namespace="System.Data" %>
03: <%@ Import Namespace="System.Data.SqlClient" %>
04: <script runat="server">
05:  void Page_Load(Object sender, EventArgs e){
06:    SqlConnection myConnection;
07:    SqlCommand myCommand;
08:    SqlParameter myParameter;
09:
10:    myConnection = new SqlConnection("server=localhost;
➥      database=Northwind; uid=sa; pwd=;");
11:    myCommand = new SqlCommand("GetCustomersByCountry", myConnection);
12:    myCommand.CommandType = CommandType.StoredProcedure;
13:    myParameter = myCommand.Parameters.Add(new SqlParameter("@country",
➥      SqlDbType.VarChar, 50));
14:    myParameter.Direction = ParameterDirection.Input;
15:    myParameter.Value = "USA";
16:    myConnection.Open();
17:    SqlDataReader myDataReader = myCommand.ExecuteReader();
18:
19:    myDataGrid.DataSource = myDataReader;
20:    myDataGrid.DataBind();
21:
22:    myConnection.Close();
23:  }
24: </script>
```

[VB & C#]

```html
25: <html>
26:  <head>
27:   <title>Chapter 3: Managed Providers in ADO.NET</title>
28:  </head>
29: <body>
30: <form runat="server" method="post">
31:   <asp:DataGrid runat="server" id="myDataGrid" />
32: </form>
33: </body>
34: </html>
```

In Listing 3.7, you create a SqlConnection, SqlCommand, and SqlDataReader, the same as in previous listings. On line 8, you declare a SqlParameter object that will be used to create and add parameters to the SqlCommand. On line 13, you instantiate the SqlParameter object and set its name to @country, which is the same name given to the input parameter in the stored procedure in Listing 3.6. Additionally, you set the data type to SqlDbType.VarChar, 50, as required by the database table. On line 14, you set the SqlParameter's direction to ParameterDirection.Input, and you set the SqlParameter's Value to "USA" on line 15. Lastly, you open the connection and execute the command.

> **NOTE**
>
> In Listing 3.5 you created a series of new DataRow objects, and assigned their values after all the DataRows were created. The same approach can be used for SqlParameters.
>
> ```
> myCommand.Parameters["@country"].Value = "USA";
> ```

> **NOTE**
>
> Input is the default direction for a Managed Command's parameter. There's no need to set a parameter's direction to Input explicitly. Listing 3.7 demonstrated how to set the parameter's Direction property. The possible values are ParameterDirection.Input and ParameterDirection.Output.

The DataAdapter

In Chapter 2, you looked at the DataSet as a collection of DataTable objects. You used the DataTables in the DataSet to populate one or more server controls on an ASP.NET Web Form. The *DataAdapter* is the bridge between the DataSet and the data store.

Unlike the past model of connection-based data processing, the DataAdapter works on a disconnected message-based model, revolving around and delivering chunks of information in a disconnected fashion. The DataAdapter is made up of four command methods, a TableMappings collection, a Command collection, and an Exception collection (for OleDbErrors). Like the other objects in the Managed Providers, the DataAdapter comes in two stock flavors, the SqlDataAdapter and the OleDbDataAdapter. Figure 3.4 illustrates the DataAdapter Object Model.

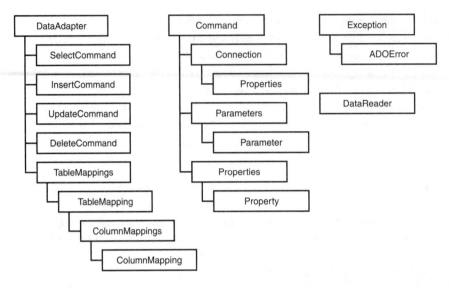

FIGURE 3.4

The DataAdapter *Object Model.*

The primary function of a DataAdapter is to retrieve data from a data store and push it into a DataTable in the DataSet. To complete this task, the DataAdapter requires two pieces of information, or parameters:

- A Managed Connection
- A Select Command

The DataAdapter constructor can accept either the command and connection values as text, or a Managed Command object as a single parameter. Listing 3.7 demonstrated constructing a DataAdapter with text values, while Listing 3.8 demonstrates constructing the DataAdapter with a single Managed Command.

LISTING 3.8 Creating a SqlDataAdapter with Connection and Command Text Values

```
[VB]
01: <%@ Page Language="VB" %>
02: <%@ Import Namespace="System.Data" %>
03: <%@ Import Namespace="System.Data.SqlClient" %>
04: <script runat="server">
05:  Sub Page_Load(Sender As Object, E As EventArgs)
06:   Dim myDataAdapter As SqlDataAdapter
07:   Dim myDataSet As New DataSet
08:   myDataAdapter = New SqlDataAdapter("SELECT * FROM Customers",
➥      "server=localhost; database=Northwind; uid=sa; pwd=;")
09:   myDataAdapter.Fill(myDataSet, "Customers")
```

LISTING 3.8 Continued

```
10:    myDataGrid.DataSource = myDataSet.Tables("Customers").DefaultView
11:    myDataGrid.DataBind()
12:  End Sub
13: </script>
```

```
[C#]
```

```
01: <%@ Page Language="C#" %>
02: <%@ Import Namespace="System.Data" %>
03: <%@ Import Namespace="System.Data.SqlClient" %>
04: <script runat="server">
05:  void Page_Load(Object sender, EventArgs e){
06:   SqlDataAdapter myDataAdapter;
07:   DataSet myDataSet = new DataSet();
08:   myDataAdapter = new SqlDataAdapter("SELECT * FROM Customers",
➥    "server=localhost; database=Northwind; uid=sa; pwd=;");
09:   myDataAdapter.Fill(myDataSet, "Customers");
10:   myDataGrid.DataSource = myDataSet.Tables["Customers"].DefaultView;
11:   myDataGrid.DataBind();
12:  }
13: </script>
```

```
[VB & C#]
```

```
14: <html>
15: <body>
16: <form runat="server" method="post">
17:  <asp:DataGrid runat="server" id="myDataGrid" />
18: </form>
19: </body>
20: </html>
```

In Listing 3.8 you create an instance of the SqlDataAdapter class. When instantiating the class, on line 8 you pass in the command and connection values as text. The DataAdapter uses these values to create SqlCommand and SqlConnection objects behind the scenes. These objects are used to connect to the database and retrieve the appropriate data.

In Listing 3.9 you achieve the same result as in Listing 3.8, using explicit SqlCommand and SqlConnection objects.

LISTING 3.9 Creating an SqlDataAdapter with Connection and Command Objects

```
[VB]
```

```
01: <%@ Page Language="VB" %>
02: <%@ Import Namespace="System.Data" %>
03: <%@ Import Namespace="System.Data.SqlClient" %>
```

3

ADO.NET
MANAGED
PROVIDERS

LISTING 3.9 Continued

```
04: <script runat="server">
05:  Sub Page_Load(Sender As Object, E As EventArgs)
06:   Dim myConnection As SqlConnection
07:   Dim myCommand As SqlCommand
08:   Dim myDataAdapter As SqlDataAdapter
09:   Dim myDataSet As New DataSet
10:   myConnection = New SqlConnection("server=localhost;
➡     database=Northwind; uid=sa; pwd=;")
11:   myCommand = New SqlCommand("SELECT * FROM Customers", myConnection)
12:   myDataAdapter = New SqlDataAdapter(myCommand)
13:   myDataAdapter.Fill(myDataSet, "Customers")
14:   myDataGrid.DataSource = myDataSet.Tables("Customers")
15:   myDataGrid.DataBind()
16:  End Sub
17: </script>
```

[C#]

```
01: <%@ Page Language="C#" %>
02: <%@ Import Namespace="System.Data" %>
03: <%@ Import Namespace="System.Data.SqlClient" %>
04: <script runat="server">
05:  void Page_Load(Object sender, EventArgs e){
06:   SqlConnection myConnection;
07:   SqlCommand myCommand;
08:   SqlDataAdapter myDataAdapter;
09:   DataSet myDataSet = new DataSet();
10:   myConnection = new SqlConnection("server=localhost;
➡     database=Northwind; uid=sa; pwd=;");
11:   myCommand = new SqlCommand("SELECT * FROM Customers", myConnection);
12:   myDataAdapter = new SqlDataAdapter(myCommand);
13:   myDataAdapter.Fill(myDataSet, "Customers");
14:   myDataGrid.DataSource = myDataSet.Tables["Customers"];
15:   myDataGrid.DataBind();
16:  }
17: </script>
```

[VB & C#]

```
18: <html>
19: <body>
20: <form runat="server" method="post">
21:  <asp:DataGrid runat="server" id="myDataGrid" />
22: </form>
23: </body>
24: </html>
```

In Listing 3.9 you explicitly create `SqlCommand` and `SqlConnection` objects. The `SqlConnection` object is used when constructing the `SqlCommand` object, and the `SqlCommand` object is passed into the `SqlDataAdapter` when it is instantiated.

While this might seem logical, it is more efficient to create the `DataAdapter` using the text values. The `DataAdapter` will manage the creation and destruction of the connection and command objects it requires. The explicit creation of these objects is only useful if you will be using either or both of them again, separate of the `DataAdapter`.

DataAdapter.Fill() Method

In Listings 3.8 and 3.9, you used various techniques and languages to create an instance of the Managed Provider `DataAdapter`. In one fashion or another, you created the `DataAdapter` and passed it values for the `SelectCommand` and `Connection` properties (either as inline values or as objects). Once the `DataAdapter` was created, the `Fill()` method of the `DataAdapter` was called.

The `DataAdapter.Fill()` method is like the switch that makes it go. Up until the `Fill()` method is called, the `DataAdapter` is idle. When the `Fill()` method is called, the connection to the database is made, and the SQL statement is executed. The results from the execution are filled into a `DataSet`, specified as a parameter of the `Fill()` method.

Specifying only a `DataSet` to fill the result set will cause a new `DataTable` object to be created in the `DataSet`. The `DataTable` is then accessible by its index value.

```
DataAdapter.Fill([DataSet])
DataGrid.DataSource = DataSet.Tables(0)
```

Optionally, you can also pass in a string value representing the name you would like assigned to the `DataTable` that is created. This makes your code easier to follow and more readable, as you can then access the `DataTable` by name rather than by its index value.

```
DataAdapter.Fill([DataSet], "[Table Name]")
DataGrid.DataSource = DataSet.Tables("[Table Name]")
```

On line 13 of Listing 3.9 you invoke the `Fill()` method of the `DataAdapter` and fill the results of the executed SQL statement into an empty `DataSet`, creating a new `DataTable` named "Customers".

When the `Fill()` method is invoked, the bridge to the data store is extended. Then the data is retrieved and brought back to the calling application in the form of an XML file. This XML file is materialized as a `DataTable` in the `DataSet` you specified. The `DataTable` schema (table/column/primary key definitions) will be created automatically based on the schema of the database. Figure 3.5 illustrates the process when you're invoking the `DataAdapter.Fill()` method.

3

ADO.NET MANAGED PROVIDERS

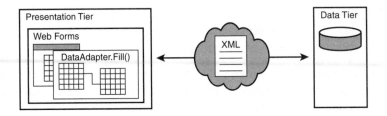

FIGURE 3.5

Invoking the Fill() *method of the* DataAdapter *class causes a bridge to be extended to the data store and the results to be returned to the calling application in the form of an XML file. The XML file is materialized as a* DataTable *in a* DataSet.*

While the Fill() method will create the DataTable dynamically, it can also fill an existing DataTable that you create explicitly, as shown in Listing 3.10.

LISTING 3.10   Using the DataAdapter with an Existing DataTable

[VB]

```
01: <%@ Page Language="VB" %>
02: <%@ Import Namespace="System.Data" %>
03: <%@ Import Namespace="System.Data.SqlClient" %>
04: <script runat="server">
05:  Sub Page_Load(Sender As Object, E As EventArgs)
06:   Dim myDataAdapter As SqlDataAdapter
07:   Dim myDataSet As New DataSet
08:
09:   myDataSet.Tables.Add(New DataTable("Customers"))
10:   myDataSet.Tables("Customers").Columns.Add("CompanyName",
➥     System.Type.GetType("System.String"))
11:   myDataSet.Tables("Customers").Columns.Add("ContactName",
➥     System.Type.GetType("System.String"))
12:   myDataSet.Tables("Customers").Columns.Add("Region",
➥     System.Type.GetType("System.String"))
13:
14:   myDataAdapter = New SqlDataAdapter("SELECT
➥     CompanyName, ContactName, Region FROM Customers",
➥     "server=localhost; database=Northwind; uid=sa; pwd=;")
15:   myDataAdapter.Fill(myDataSet, "Customers")
16:   myDataGrid.DataSource = myDataSet.Tables("Customers")
17:   myDataGrid.DataBind()
18:  End Sub
19: </script>
```

LISTING 3.10 Continued

```
[C#]

01: <%@ Page Language="C#" %>
02: <%@ Import Namespace="System.Data" %>
03: <%@ Import Namespace="System.Data.SqlClient" %>
04: <script runat="server">
05:  void Page_Load(Object sender, EventArgs e){
06:   SqlDataAdapter myDataAdapter;
07:   DataSet myDataSet = new DataSet();
08:
09:   myDataSet.Tables.Add(new DataTable("Customers"));
10:   myDataSet.Tables["Customers"].Columns.Add("CompanyName",
       System.Type.GetType("System.String"));
11:   myDataSet.Tables["Customers"].Columns.Add("ContactName",
       System.Type.GetType("System.String"));
12:   myDataSet.Tables["Customers"].Columns.Add("Region",
       System.Type.GetType("System.String"));
13:
14:   myDataAdapter = new SqlDataAdapter("SELECT
       CompanyName, ContactName, Region FROM Customers",
       "server=localhost; database=Northwind; uid=sa; pwd=;");
15:   myDataAdapter.Fill(myDataSet, "Customers");
16:   myDataGrid.DataSource = myDataSet.Tables["Customers"];
17:   myDataGrid.DataBind();
18:  }
19: </script>

[VB & C#]

20: <html>
21: <body>
22: <form runat="server" method="post">
23:  <asp:DataGrid runat="server" id="myDataGrid" />
24: </form>
25: </body>
26: </html>
```

3

ADO.NET
MANAGED
PROVIDERS

In Listing 3.10 you create a DataTable explicitly on lines 9–12. Using the Fill() method of the DataAdapter you fill this newly created DataTable with the results from the SQL statement execution. This is done by calling the Fill() method and passing in the DataSet and DataTable name for the DataTable you just created. If data already exists in the DataTable, then the Fill() method will update, or add rows to the DataTable. You can use the same DataAdapter, change its SelectCommand.CommandText property, and invoke the Fill() method again. In Listing 3.11 you use the DataAdapter to return two different result sets from similar SQL statements. You use the Fill() method to add the records to the same DataTable in the DataSet.

LISTING 3.11   Using the `Fill()` Method to Add Records to a `DataTable`

[VB]

```
01: <%@ Page Language="VB" %>
02: <%@ Import Namespace="System.Data" %>
03: <%@ Import Namespace="System.Data.SqlClient" %>
04: <script runat="server">
05:  Sub Page_Load(Sender As Object, E As EventArgs)
06:   Dim myDataAdapter As SqlDataAdapter
07:   Dim myDataSet As New DataSet
08:
09:   myDataSet.Tables.Add(New DataTable("Customers"))
10:   myDataSet.Tables("Customers").Columns.Add("CompanyName",
➡       System.Type.GetType("System.String"))
11:   myDataSet.Tables("Customers").Columns.Add("ContactName",
➡       System.Type.GetType("System.String"))
12:   myDataSet.Tables("Customers").Columns.Add("Region",
➡       System.Type.GetType("System.String"))
13:
14:   myDataAdapter = new SqlDataAdapter("GetCustomersByCountry",
➡       "server=localhost; database=Northwind; uid=sa; pwd=;")
15:   myDataAdapter.SelectCommand.CommandType = CommandType.StoredProcedure
16:   myDataAdapter.SelectCommand.Parameters.Add(new
➡       SqlParameter("@country", SqlDbType.VarChar, 50))
17:   myDataAdapter.SelectCommand.Parameters("@country").Value = "Canada"
18:   myDataAdapter.Fill(myDataSet, "Customers")
19:
20:   myDataAdapter.SelectCommand.Parameters("@country").Value = "Spain"
21:   myDataAdapter.Fill(myDataSet, "Customers")
22:
23:   myDataGrid.DataSource = myDataSet.Tables("Customers")
24:   myDataGrid.DataBind()
25:  End Sub
26: </script>
```

[C#]

```
01: <%@ Page Language="C#" %>
02: <%@ Import Namespace="System.Data" %>
03: <%@ Import Namespace="System.Data.SqlClient" %>
04: <script runat="server">
05:  void Page_Load(Object sender, EventArgs e){
06:   SqlDataAdapter myDataAdapter;
07:   DataSet myDataSet = new DataSet();
08:
09:   myDataSet.Tables.Add(new DataTable("Customers"));
```

LISTING 3.11 Continued

```
10:    myDataSet.Tables["Customers"].Columns.Add("CompanyName",
➥        System.Type.GetType("System.String"));
11:    myDataSet.Tables["Customers"].Columns.Add("ContactName",
➥        System.Type.GetType("System.String"));
12:    myDataSet.Tables["Customers"].Columns.Add("Region",
➥        System.Type.GetType("System.String"));
13:
14:    myDataAdapter = new SqlDataAdapter("GetCustomersByCountry",
➥        "server=localhost; database=Northwind; uid=sa; pwd=;");
15:    myDataAdapter.SelectCommand.CommandType = CommandType.StoredProcedure;
16:    myDataAdapter.SelectCommand.Parameters.Add(new
➥        SqlParameter("@country", SqlDbType.VarChar, 50));
17:    myDataAdapter.SelectCommand.Parameters["@country"].Value = "Canada";
18:    myDataAdapter.Fill(myDataSet, "Customers");
19:
20:    myDataAdapter.SelectCommand.Parameters["@country"].Value = "Spain";
21:    myDataAdapter.Fill(myDataSet, "Customers");
22:
23:    myDataGrid.DataSource = myDataSet.Tables["Customers"];
24:    myDataGrid.DataBind();
25:    }
26: </script>

[VB & C#]

27: <html>
28: <body>
29: <form runat="server" method="post">
30:   <asp:DataGrid runat="server" id="myDataGrid" />
31: </form>
32: </body>
33: </html>
```

3

In Listing 3.11 you use the `DataAdapter` to select a small set of records from the database (line 14) with the stored procedure from Listing 3.6. On line 15 you specify that the `SelectCommand` property of the `DataAdapter` is a stored procedure. On line 16 you add a parameter for the expected "@country" parameter in the stored procedure. On line 17 you set the value of the parameter to "Canada." Using the `Fill()` method you add those records to the Customers `DataTable` on line 18. On line 20 you change the parameter's value to "Spain." Since you are using the same `DataAdapter` to execute the second `Fill()` method, you do not need to set the `ConnectionString` property, or recreate the parameter you are using. Using the `Fill()` method, on line 18, you add the new result set to the existing records in the Customers table. Figure 3.6 shows the result of executing the code in Listing 3.11.

As you've learned, the DataAdapter works on a disconnected message-based model. You can reuse the DataAdapter to fill additional DataTables in the same DataSet, or in other DataSets, because there's no physical link between the DataAdapter and the DataSet or DataTable. You only need to change the SelectCommand property of the DataSet (if you want to use a new SQL statement), or change a parameter value (if you want to use the same SQL statement), and call the Fill() method, passing it the new DataSet and DataTable name (see Listing 3.12).

CompanyName	ContactName	Region	CustomerID	ContactTitle	Address	City	PostalCode	Country	Phone	Fax
Bottom-Dollar Markets	Elizabeth Lincoln	BC	BOTTM	Accounting Manager	23 Tsawassen Blvd.	Tsawassen	T2F 8M4	Canada	(604) 555-4729	(604) 555-3745
Laughing Bacchus Wine Cellars	Yoshi Tannamuri	BC	LAUGB	Marketing Assistant	1900 Oak St.	Vancouver	V3F 2K1	Canada	(604) 555-3392	(604) 555-7293
Mère Paillarde	Jean Fresnière	Québec	MEREP	Marketing Assistant	43 rue St. Laurent	Montréal	H1J 1C3	Canada	(514) 555-8054	(514) 555-8055
Bólido Comidas preparadas	Martín Sommer		BOLID	Owner	C/ Araquil, 67	Madrid	28023	Spain	(91) 555 22 82	(91) 555 91 99
FISSA Fabrica Inter. Salchichas S.A.	Diego Roel		FISSA	Accounting Manager	C/ Moralzarzal, 86	Madrid	28034	Spain	(91) 555 94 44	(91) 555 55 93
Galería del gastrónomo	Eduardo Saavedra		GALED	Marketing Manager	Rambla de Cataluña, 23	Barcelona	08022	Spain	(93) 203 4560	(93) 203 4561
Godos Cocina Típica	José Pedro Freyre		GODOS	Sales Manager	C/ Romero, 33	Sevilla	41101	Spain	(95) 555 82 82	
Romero y tomillo	Alejandra Camino		ROMEY	Accounting Manager	Gran Vía, 1	Madrid	28001	Spain	(91) 745	(91) 745

FIGURE 3.6

The DataAdapter.Fill() method can be used to add records to a DataTable, or update existing records.

LISTING 3.12   Adding a Second DataTable to a DataSet

[VB]

```
01: <%@ Page Language="VB" %>
02: <%@ Import Namespace="System.Data" %>
03: <%@ Import Namespace="System.Data.SqlClient" %>
04: <script runat="server">
05:  Sub Page_Load(Sender As Object, E As EventArgs)
06:   Dim myDataAdapter As SqlDataAdapter
07:   Dim myDataSet As New DataSet
08:
09:   myDataAdapter = new SqlDataAdapter("GetCustomersByCountry",
➡       "server=localhost; database=Northwind; uid=sa; pwd=;")
```

LISTING 3.12 Continued

```
10:   myDataAdapter.SelectCommand.CommandType = CommandType.StoredProcedure
11:   myDataAdapter.SelectCommand.Parameters.Add(new
➥     SqlParameter("@country", SqlDbType.VarChar, 50))
12:   myDataAdapter.SelectCommand.Parameters("@country").Value = "Canada"
13:   myDataAdapter.Fill(myDataSet, "Canada_Customers")
14:
15:   myDataAdapter.SelectCommand.Parameters("@country").Value = "Spain"
16:   myDataAdapter.Fill(myDataSet, "Spain_Customers")
17:
18:   myDataGrid.DataSource = myDataSet.Tables("Canada_Customers")
19:   myDataGrid.DataBind()
20:
21:   myOtherDataGrid.DataSource = myDataSet.Tables("Spain_Customers")
22:   myOtherDataGrid.DataBind()
23:  End Sub
24: </script>

[C#]
01: <%@ Page Language="C#" %>
02: <%@ Import Namespace="System.Data" %>
03: <%@ Import Namespace="System.Data.SqlClient" %>
04: <script runat="server">
05:  void Page_Load(Object sender, EventArgs e){
06:   SqlDataAdapter myDataAdapter;
07:   DataSet myDataSet = new DataSet();
08:
09:   myDataAdapter = new SqlDataAdapter("GetCustomersByCountry",
➥     "server=localhost; database=Northwind; uid=sa; pwd=;");
10:   myDataAdapter.SelectCommand.CommandType = CommandType.StoredProcedure;
11:   myDataAdapter.SelectCommand.Parameters.Add(new
➥     SqlParameter("@country", SqlDbType.VarChar, 50));
12:   myDataAdapter.SelectCommand.Parameters["@country"].Value = "Canada";
13:   myDataAdapter.Fill(myDataSet, "Canada_Customers");
14:
15:   myDataAdapter.SelectCommand.Parameters["@country"].Value = "Spain";
16:   myDataAdapter.Fill(myDataSet, "Spain_Customers");
17:
18:   myDataGrid.DataSource = myDataSet.Tables["Canada_Customers"];
19:   myDataGrid.DataBind();
20:
21:   myOtherDataGrid.DataSource = myDataSet.Tables["Spain_Customers"];
22:   myOtherDataGrid.DataBind();
23:  }
24: </script>
```

3

ADO.NET
MANAGED
PROVIDERS

LISTING 3.12 Continued

```
[VB & C#]
25: <html>
26: <form runat="server" method="post">
27: <body>
28:  <asp:DataGrid runat="server" id="myDataGrid" />
29:  <asp:DataGrid runat="server" id="myOtherDataGrid" />
30: </form>
31: </body>
32: </html>
```

In Listing 3.12 you use the same data access code from Listing 3.11. You use the Fill() method to create a new DataTable named Canada_Customers. Then, by resetting the parameter value you retrieve another set of data from the database. Using the Fill() method you create a second DataTable named Spain_Customers. Finally you bind each of these DataTables to a separate DataGrid. The resulting page is shown in Figure 3.7.

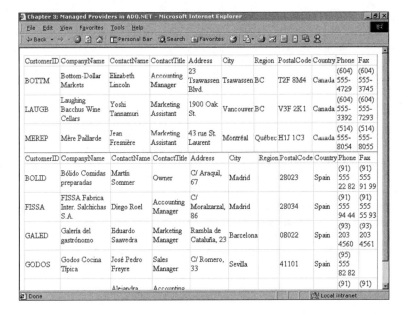

FIGURE 3.7

The DataAdapter *can be used to create multiple* DataTables *in one or more* DataSets. *This is allowed because the* DataAdapter *is not explicitly tied to a single* DataSet *or* DataTable.

Table and Column Mappings

Table and column mappings enable you to alter the schema of the `DataTable` that's dynamically created in the `DataSet`. In the previous listings you filled the `DataSet`, taking in the schema provided to you by the data store. There are certainly instances when you'll want to change this. Often, database column names can be a bit cryptic, and changing them can make writing your code easier. Table and column mappings allow you to create a master mapping between the data returned from the data store and the `DataTable` in the `DataSet`. The `DataSet` maintains the table and column mappings and can translate them back to their original names when reconciling the data with the data store.

> **NOTE**
>
> In the previous listings, you've been filling a `DataSet` with the Customers table from the Northwind database. In the following listings, you'll create a new `TableMapping` for the Authors table in the Pubs database. Pubs is a sample database installed with Microsoft SQL Server. I chose to switch to it because of its notoriously cryptic naming conventions.

In the following example, you'll create table and column mappings for the Authors table in the Pubs database. When you add a new `TableMapping`, you must pass in the `TableMapping` source name and the `DataTable` name. If you specify "Table" (the default) as the source name, when you fill the `DataSet` you do not need to pass in the `DataTable` name. The data retrieved will use the `TableMappings` for "Table" by default, and a `DataTable` with the name you specified when you created the `TableMappings` will be created. This is demonstrated in Listing 3.13.

LISTING 3.13 Creating Table and Column Mappings for the Default Table

```
[VB]
01: <%@ Page Language="VB" %>
02: <%@ Import Namespace="System.Data" %>
03: <%@ Import Namespace="System.Data.SqlClient" %>
04: <script runat="server">
05:  Sub Page_Load(Sender As Object, E As EventArgs)
06:   Dim myDataAdapter As SqlDataAdapter
07:   Dim myDataSet As New DataSet
08:
09:   myDataAdapter = new SqlDataAdapter("SELECT * FROM Authors",
➥      "server=localhost; database=Pubs; uid=sa; pwd=;")
10:
```

LISTING 3.13 Continued

```
11:    myDataAdapter.TableMappings.Add("Table", "Authors")
12:    With myDataAdapter.TableMappings("Table").ColumnMappings
13:        .Add("au_id", "ID")
14:        .Add("au_lname", "Last Name")
15:        .Add("au_fname", "First Name")
16:        .Add("phone", "Phone")
17:        .Add("address", "Address")
18:        .Add("city", "City")
19:        .Add("state", "State")
20:        .Add("zip", "Zipcode")
21:        .Add("contract", "Contract")
22:    End With
23:
24:    myDataAdapter.Fill(myDataSet)
25:
26:    myDataGrid.DataSource = myDataSet.Tables("Authors")
27:    myDataGrid.DataBind()
28:  End Sub
29: </script>

[C#]

01: <%@ Page Language="C#" %>
02: <%@ Import Namespace="System.Data" %>
03: <%@ Import Namespace="System.Data.SqlClient" %>
04: <script runat="server">
05:  void Page_Load(Object sender, EventArgs e){
06:    SqlDataAdapter myDataAdapter;
07:    DataSet myDataSet = new DataSet();
08:
09:    myDataAdapter = new SqlDataAdapter("SELECT * FROM Authors",
➡        "server=localhost; database=Pubs; uid=sa; pwd=;");
10:
11:    myDataAdapter.TableMappings.Add("Table", "Authors");
12:
13:    myDataAdapter.TableMappings["Table"].
➡        ColumnMappings.Add("au_id", "ID");
14:    myDataAdapter.TableMappings["Table"].
➡        ColumnMappings.Add("au_lname", "Last Name");
15:    myDataAdapter.TableMappings["Table"].
➡        ColumnMappings.Add("au_fname", "First Name");
16:    myDataAdapter.TableMappings["Table"].
➡        ColumnMappings.Add("phone", "Phone");
17:    myDataAdapter.TableMappings["Table"].
➡        ColumnMappings.Add("address", "Address");
18:    myDataAdapter.TableMappings["Table"].
➡        ColumnMappings.Add("city", "City");
```

LISTING 3.13 Continued

```
19:    myDataAdapter.TableMappings["Table"].
➡      ColumnMappings.Add("state", "State");
20:    myDataAdapter.TableMappings["Table"].
➡      ColumnMappings.Add("zip", "Zipcode");
21:    myDataAdapter.TableMappings["Table"].
➡      ColumnMappings.Add("contract", "Contract");
22:
23:
24:    myDataAdapter.Fill(myDataSet);
25:
26:    myDataGrid.DataSource = myDataSet.Tables["Authors"];
27:    myDataGrid.DataBind();
28:    }
29: </script>

[VB & C#]

30: <html>
31: <body>
32: <form runat="server" method="post">
33:   <asp:DataGrid runat="server" id="myDataGrid" />
34:   <asp:DataGrid runat="server" id="myOtherDataGrid" />
35: </form>
36: </body>
37: </html>
```

On line 9, you create a new `SqlDataAdapter`, selecting all of the fields in the Authors table of the Pubs database. On line 11, you add a new default table mapping by passing in the name "Table" as the first parameter. Any table created in the `DataSet` that doesn't have a name specified in the `Fill()` method will use this table mapping and will be given the name "Authors", as indicated on line 11. On lines 13–21 you create the column mappings for all of the fields in the Authors table. The first parameter passed into the `ColumnMappings` collection's `Add()` method is the name of the field in the database. The second parameter is the name you're giving the field in the `DataTable`.

In case you'd rather not alter the `DataSet`'s default table and column mappings, the `DataAdapter` allows you to add named table and column mappings. Rather than specifying "Table" as the source name, you can provide a new source name. When you call the `Fill()` method, you pass in the new source name as the table parameter. The `DataSet` checks for a table mapping for the source name passed in. If no table mapping exists, the schema is built on the fly based on the data store's schema, the same as in earlier examples. If there's a table mapping for the name passed in, it's used.

```
11:    myDataAdapter.TableMappings.Add("BookAuthors", "BookAuthors");

24:    myDataAdapter.Fill(myDataSet, "BookAuthors");
```

Line 11 shows a table mapping named "BookAuthors", specifying the name "BookAuthors" to be used when the `DataTable` is created. (Lines 12–23 did not change from Listing 3.13.) On line 24, you call the `Fill()` method, passing in the name of your table mapping ("BookAuthors"). The `DataSet` finds this table mapping and creates a `DataTable` named "BookAuthors", using the schema you created.

Summary

Chapter 1 looked at what ASP.NET is, and Chapter 2 looked at what ADO.NET is. This chapter pulled the two pieces together.

In this chapter you learned that the ADO.NET Managed Providers are the bridge from a data store to your data-driven application. The Managed Providers come in two stock flavors: the SQL Managed Provider and the OleDb Managed Provider. The SQL Managed Provider is used to connect directly to a Microsoft SQL Server database (version 7.0 or higher), and bypasses OLEDB to provider better performance. The OleDb Managed Provider is used to connect to non-Microsoft SQL Server databases, such as Access, Oracle, and a host of others.

In this chapter you created connections to a database, built command objects to execute SQL statements on the database, and used the `DataReader` to iterate through data before binding it to a server control. You also learned about the `DataAdapter` class; a specific class for bridging between the Web application and the database to return the result set as a `DataTable` in a `DataSet`.

Throughout this chapter you built sample Web forms that connected to the database and returned records as either a data stream (`DataReader`), or a `DataTable` (`DataAdapter`).

By now you should be comfortable with the two Managed Providers and should be ready to start building data-driven Web applications. For the rest of this book you'll be working with both the Managed Providers. You'll be pulling data into an application with the Managed Command or the `DataAdapter`, and you'll use the `DataSet` to persist the data, or the `DataReader` to iterate through the data.

If it felt as though you covered a lot in this chapter, you did. You'll be using it repetitively throughout this book, so don't worry. . . you'll get lots of practice.

Basic ANSI-SQL

IN THIS CHAPTER

This chapter will go over Structured Query Language, or SQL, which can be pronounced either "ess-cue-ell" or "sequel." Some people insist that it must be called one or the other. I prefer "sequel" because it's one less syllable to say.

SQL was invented by IBM in 1970 and became an ANSI standard in 1986. It's an English-like, nonprocedural language that aids in the definition, manipulation, and administration of data in a relational database management system (RDMS). I'll be going over today's most commonly used statements and clauses when working with SQL in a sub language environment, such as the writing of Web applications. The statements and clauses introduced in this chapter will be used throughout the rest of the book in code examples. This chapter will not make you an expert in SQL, but if you have not used SQL that much it will give you the foundation you need to start building data driven web applications.

All the example code used in this chapter assumes that you have the Northwind database, which is commonly distributed with either Microsoft's SQL Server or Microsoft Access. If you don't have either one on your computer, you can download the Access 2000 Northwind database at http://officeupdate.microsoft.com/2000/downloadDetails/Nwind2K.htm.

In this chapter, you'll learn about the following:

- Using the SELECT statement to retrieve data
- Using the FROM clause to specify which table to retrieve data
- Using the WHERE clause to filter and return specific rows
- Using a SubQuery to retrieve a value from a table nested in a different SQL statement
- Using SQL Joins to join two tables together into one result set
- Sorting data in descending or ascending order
- Using the ORDER BY clause to sort rows
- Using the GROUP BY clause to group rows together
- Using the UPDATE clause to update rows
- Using the INSERT statement to insert rows
- Using the DELETE statement to delete rows

Setting Up Your Workspace

In this chapter, your workspace is going to be an ASP.NET Web Form. If you prefer working in an application that's similar to Microsoft's SQL Server Query Analyzer, you also can run all the queries in that.

The first step is to create a new web form. In the example in Listing 4.1, I created one called myqueries.aspx. Listing 4.1 contains the code you're going to be using to walk through the different SQL statements. Since this code is for demonstration purposes only, we won't be spending a lot of time looking at it; by now you should be familiar with most of the ADO.NET code after going through Chapter 2, "What Is ADO.NET?" and Chapter 3, "ADO.NET Managed Providers." In Chapter 5, "Using a Basic DataGrid," the DataGrid will be explained in greater detail.

Myqueries.aspx uses the DataGrid to display the result from our SQL Statements, although not all of the SQL statements that we'll be going through have a result. It uses the SQLConnection object and the SQLDataSetCommand for the database connectivity and the DataSet object for the in memory cache of data. You can test all the example code by typing it directly into the text area of the page in your browser and clicking the Submit Query button, or you can choose to hand-code it in the source code and execute the page. Listing 4.1 contains the source code for myqueries.aspx. You can also find myqueries.aspx in the Chapter 4 folder on the disk located in the back of the book.

LISTING 4.1   This ASP.NET Web Form Can Be Used for Your Workspace

```
01: <%@ Import Namespace="System.Data" %>
02: <%@ Import Namespace="System.Data.SqlClient" %>
03: <html>
04:   <head>
05: <script language="C#" runat="server">
06:   void Page_Load(Object src, EventArgs e)
07:   {
08:   try{
09:   if (Page.IsPostBack) {
10:
11:    string strSQL;
12:    strSQL = SQL.Text;
13:
14:    SqlConnection sCon = new SqlConnection("SERVER=LOCALHOST;" +
15:    "UID=sa;DataBase=Northwind");
16:    SqlDataAdapter sda;
17:    sda = new SqlDataAdapter(strSQL,sCon);
18:    DataSet ds = new DataSet();
19:    sda.Fill(ds,"Products");
20:    datagrid1.DataSource = ds.Tables[0].DefaultView;
21:    Page.DataBind();
22:   }
23:   } catch (SqlException Sex)
24:   {
25:    Message.Text = "<b>Error Processing Query - [" + Sex.Message.ToString() +
26:    " ] Check Syntax and Try Again...</b>"; }
27:   }
28:   </script>
29:   <title>Go To DotNetJunkies.com for .NET news and
30:   tutorials!!</title>
31:   </head>
```

LISTING 4.1   Continued

```
32: <body>
33: <form method="post" runat="server">
34:   <asp:Label
35:   Runat="Server"
36:   ForeColor="Red"
37:   Id="Message"
38:   MaintainState="False" />
39:   <br>
40:   <asp:TextBox id="SQL"
41:   Runat="server"
42:   Width="400"
43:   Height="200"
44:   TextMode="MultiLine"
45:   MaintainState="True" />
46:   <asp:Button id="button1"
47:   Runat="server"
48:   Text="Submit Query" />
49:   <asp:DataGrid id="datagrid1"
50:   Runat="server"
51:   MaintainState="False" font-size="10"/>
52: </form>
53: </body>
54: </html>
```

If you choose to hand-code your SQL queries, you can simply change line 12 from this:

```
12: strSQL  = SQL.Text;
```

to this:

```
12: strSQL = "SQL statement to be executed"
```

"SQL statement to be executed" is where the SQL code you want to execute should be placed. Also, take out lines 40–45, which create the large text field where you type in your SQL statements.

If you're using an Access database as your data source, or any other data source besides Microsoft's SQL Server, you must use the OleDbConnection and OleDbDataAdapter objects and change the code accordingly.

Now that you have your workspace finished, let's begin!

Getting Data from a Database

The SELECT statement is the most commonly used statement when you're using SQL. This is what enables you to retrieve data from a relational database. Listing 4.2 illustrates the basic structure of the SELECT statement.

LISTING 4.2   The Basic Structure of a SELECT Statement

```
SELECT select_list
[ INTO new_table ]
FROM table_source
[ WHERE search_condition ]
[ GROUP BY group_by_expression ]
[ HAVING search_condition ]
[ ORDER BY order_expression [ ASC | DESC ] ]
```

In its simplest form, a SELECT statement begins with the word SELECT. SELECT is followed by one or more fields from the database table, each field separated by a comma. Then there's the FROM clause, which specifies the source of the data being queried. It ends with a table name, your source. After the WHERE clause you'll notice a couple of other expressions: GROUP BY, HAVING, and ORDER BY. These are covered later in the chapter and deal with sorting and filtering your result set (the rows returned from the query).

The following is a simple real-world example using a SELECT statement against the Northwind database:

```
1: SELECT ProductName
2: FROM Products
```

Figure 4.1 illustrates the results of the query.

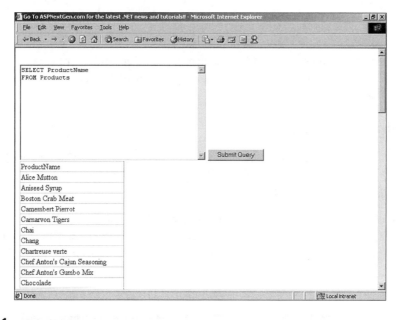

FIGURE 4.1

A Web page displaying the results of the query.

4

BASIC ANSI-SQL

When the SQL Statement in the proceeding example is executed, all rows in the `ProductName` field found in the `Products` table will be returned in the result set. In this query, the data will be returned exactly as it appears in the database, meaning that it's basically a snapshot of that column in the database.

If retrieving all the records from a table is what you need to do, you can bypass the need to comma delimitate all the field names by using an asterisk (*) after the `SELECT` statement and before the `FROM` clause, as shown in the following code:

```
1: SELECT *
2: FROM Products
```

> **NOTE**
>
> Be careful, though, because running this query will return all the data in the table. This could be a hefty load on your server, depending on how big your database is.

It's said to be good form to use the table name before any fields in the table when you're doing queries as the following code demonstrates. You want to do this in case you're returning data from more than one table and for ease of readability:

```
1: Select Products.*
2: FROM Products
```

The `SELECT` statement can be simple, as in this example, or it can be very complicated, spanning many lines. You can use the `SELECT` statement to return one million rows out of a database, or narrow it down to one record out of a million by giving the statement a set of criteria on which to search.

The WHERE Clause

Filters allow you to limit the number of rows returned by your queries. You set criteria to filter out rows that don't match a certain conditional statement. The SQL `WHERE` clause is always going to be in front of any conditions you specify.

You can filter which rows will be returned when running SQL queries by using the SQL `WHERE` clause. This clause enables you specify a search condition in the query to restrict the number of rows returned in the result set. Listing 4.3 illustrates the basic structure of the SQL `WHERE` clause.

LISTING 4.3   The Basic Structure of the WHERE Clause

```
[ WHERE < search_condition >
```

Using the preceding SELECT statement example, you can filter out all products except those supplied by the supplier with the SupplierID of 2:

```
1: SELECT *
2: FROM Products
3: WHERE SupplierID = 2
```

When the preceding query is executed, rows in the Products table will be returned only if they have a SupplierID that equals 2. You can limit the returned data even further by using an additional condition statement. If you do use more than one condition statement you separate the criteria by using the AND operator, as shown in the following example:

```
1: SELECT *
2: FROM Products
3: WHERE SupplierID = 2 AND UnitPrice = 22
```

In the preceding situation, the only rows that will be returned are those that contain a SupplierID equal to 2 and a UnitPrice equal to 22. When this query is executed, only one row is returned in the result set.

I would suggest researching all the different search condition arguments available to you using SQL (see Table 4.1). Using search conditions can significantly reduce your application's overhead. I have seen some applications that return twice as many rows as needed for their function. This is all fine and good for a single-user application, but it could be devastating to the performance of a Web site that gets 1,000+ concurrent users and could potentially crash your server.

TABLE 4.1   Some Useful Arguments for Search Criteria

Argument	Condition It Tests
=	Equality between two expressions
<>	Two expressions not equal to each other
!=	Two expressions not equal to each other
>	One expression greater than the other
>=	One expression greater than or equal to the other
!>	One expression not greater than the other
<	One expression less than the other
<=	One expression less than or equal to the other
!<	One expression not less than the other

4

The SubQuery

A SubQuery is a SELECT query that's nested inside a top-level SELECT, DELETE, UPDATE or INSERT statement, a HAVING or WHERE clause, or inside another SubQuery. A SubQuery must be constructed so it only will return a single value. Otherwise you will get an error because it is executed for each row returned in the result set and one row cannot have multiple values for one field. The following example contains a SubQuery that will be used to select all the rows from the Products table that are supplied by Exotic Liquids:

```
1: SELECT *
2: FROM Products
3: WHERE SupplierID =
4: (SELECT SupplierID FROM Suppliers
5: WHERE CompanyName = 'Exotic Liquids')
```

Essentially, you're doing a SELECT statement that will retrieve all fields from the Products table. Then you are stating that you only want to see Exotic Liquids products. This is achieved by stating that the SupplierID must be equal to the results of a SubQuery against the Suppliers table, which returns Exotic Liquids SupplierID value. Now try the following code example with a SubQuery that returns more than one row in its result set.

```
SELECT *
FROM Products
WHERE SupplierID =
(SELECT SupplierID FROM Suppliers)
```

When the preceding code is executed you will get the following error: *Subquery returned more than 1 value. This is not permitted when the subquery follows =, !=, <, <= , >, >= or when the subquery is used as an expression.*

Not only can a SubQuery be used in the FROM clause, it can also be used in the SELECT clause. The following example returns all the rows in the Suppliers table for Exotic Liquids. Additionally, it will return how many products they currently supply by using the SubQuery:

```
1: SELECT *,(SELECT Count(*) FROM Products WHERE SupplierID = '1') AS [Number Of
2: Products]
3: FROM Suppliers
4: Where SupplierID = '1'
```

The result of your SubQuery doesn't have a field name assigned to it by default, but you can assign it your own name by using the AS clause. In this example I used "Number Of Products" as the field name. This clause can be used to change the name of a result set column regardless of whether column was created by a SubQuery. The new name is put into brackets because there are spaces in the name and an error would occur. Without the brackets, you'll receive an error.

SQL Joins

There are many types of `Join` statements that allow you to retrieve data from two or more tables based on logical relationships between those tables. For instance, let's say you have a `Students` and `Classes` table in a database used by a local college, and each of the tables has a field named StudentID. By using a join statement, you can converge the two tables in a SQL query into one result set. For the most part, a `Join` condition needs two things:

- To specify a column from each table to be joined; typically it's a primary key/foreign key relationship

- A logical operator to be used when comparing values from the specified columns (such as Column A = Column B)

Take a look at the following example illustrating how to use a `Join`. This example joins the `Products` and `Suppliers` table based on the `SupplierID column value`:

```
1: SELECT *
2: FROM Suppliers AS S
3: INNER JOIN Products AS P
4: ON
5: S.SupplierID = P.SupplierID
6: WHERE
7: S.SupplierID = '1'
```

When the previous code example executes, 4 rows will be returned in the result set, one for each product in the `Products` table. Each row in the result set will contain every column from both the `Suppliers` and `Products` table. There are three types of joins; the following list contains the name and description of each:

- `INNER JOIN` The most commonly used `JOIN` statement. It uses a comparison operator, such as the equals sign (=), to match rows on tables based on the specified columns of each table.

- `OUTER JOIN` There are multiple types of `OUTER JOINS`; included is the `LEFT OUTER JOIN`, `RIGHT OUTER JOIN`, and `FULL JOIN`. An `OUTER JOIN` returns all the rows in the joined table, either the `LEFT` or `RIGHT`. In the case of the FULL JOIN, all the rows from both tables are returned.

- `CROSS JOIN` Returns all rows from the left table. Each row from the left table is combined with all rows from the right table.

Sorting Data

Now that you know how to get and limit the amount of rows returned in a result set to only the rows you need, let's talk a little about how to organize the data.

4

BASIC ANSI-SQL

The ORDER BY Clause

The ORDER BY clause specifies the sort of a result set using one or more column names separated by commas. The sort is how the rows are organized; for instance, you can sort the result set in a query to the Products table so the ProductName column is listed in alphabetical order.

> **NOTE**
>
> Sort order cannot be used with SubQueries or to sort data of the type nText, Text, or image.

The sort can be both alphabetical and/or chronological. The following example returns all the rows in the Products table and orders them by the ProductName column in alphabetical order:

```
1: SELECT *
2: FROM Products
3: ORDER BY ProductName
```

You can alter the order further by specifying that you want the data in ascending or descending order. The default order is ascending. Adding the DESC argument changes the result set to display data in descending order. In the following example it's reverse alphabetical order:

```
1: SELECT *
2: FROM Products
3: ORDER BY ProductName DESC
```

If you want to hard-code ascending order, you can use the argument ASC. You also can specify more than one column in the sort order, as the following code example demonstrates:

```
1: SELECT *
2: FROM Products
3: ORDER BY ProductName DESC, SupplierID
```

In a situation like this, all rows and columns are returned in the result set. First, the result set is sorted in descending order determined by the ProductName column, and then its additionally sorted by SupplierID column in ascending order within each product. This means that if you have two products with the same name, such as "peanuts," they will be returned with each other in the result set. But you also specified that the results should be ordered by SupplierID, so if Company A has a SupplierID of 1 and Company B has a SupplierID of 5, Company A will be listed in the result set prior to Company B.

The GROUP BY Clause

The GROUP BY clause can be used to summarize data based on particular columns. The following example contains a SQL statement that will return a list of all company names and a total of how many products they currently have available. Additionally, it will sort the results by company name in ascending order:

```
1: SELECT Suppliers.CompanyName AS [Company Name], COUNT(Products.ProductName) AS
2: [Number Of Products]
3: FROM
4: Products
5: INNER JOIN
6: Suppliers
7: ON
8: Suppliers.SupplierID = Products.SupplierID
9: GROUP BY Suppliers.CompanyName
10: ORDER BY Suppliers.CompanyName ASC
```

The preceding example uses an aggregate function named COUNT, which returns the number of items in a group. In this example, it counts the number of different products for a particular company.

Notice also that all of the columns are given human-readable names. The CompanyName column is given the name "Company Name," and the total number of products returned by your Count function is given the name "Number of Products". This is a personal choice and isn't necessary. In my personal experience, though, it has saved time on the front end. If the result set is going to be shown on a Web page or any other type of presentation layer, you don't want the column headers to look like they do in the database, so you can either hard-code new ones on the front end or take care of it on the back-end in your SQL statement, or do nothing. If you rename them in the query, you don't have to worry about doing it later, and if your result set is used in many places you can change the query once in your stored procedure and the changes will be reflected on every page.

If you would like to see an example of what I am talking about, run the preceding query without the AS clause and check out what the column names are. Then do the same with the AS clause.

Okay, on with the statement. Because you're retrieving data from two tables, you're performing an INNER JOIN and the two columns you're comparing for the join are the SupplierID columns. Once those are returned, you tell the result set that you want it to be grouped by the CompanyName column. Hence, it will add up all the products for that company name and sort the whole result set in alphabetical order by the company name.

Updating Existing Data

The UPDATE statement is used to update existing data in a database. For example, if you want to change the company name in the Suppliers table you can run an UPDATE statement to edit it. Listing 4.4 shows the basic structure of an UPDATE statement.

4

BASIC ANSI-SQL

LISTING 4.4   The Basic Structure of an UPDATE Statement

```
UPDATE
        {
         table_name WITH ( < table_hint_limited > [ ...n ] )
         | view_name
         | rowset_function_limited
        }
        SET
        { column_name = { expression | DEFAULT | NULL }
        | @variable = expression
        | @variable = column = expression } [ ,...n ]

    { { [ FROM { < table_source > } [ ,...n ] ]
        [ WHERE
            < search_condition > ] }
        |
        [ WHERE CURRENT OF
        { { [ GLOBAL ] cursor_name } | cursor_variable_name }
        ] }
        [ OPTION ( < query_hint > [ ,...n ] ) ]
```

The UPDATE statement is very powerful, and I recommend that you look over your statement a couple of times before executing it so you don't change data that you don't mean to. Take the following UPDATE statement, for example:

```
1: UPDATE Products SET UnitsInStock = 50
```

When this statement is executed, it will change every row in the UnitsInStock column of the Products table to be equal to 50. I don't know of anyone who hasn't accidentally done this and changed all the data in a table.

The following statement states that you're going to update the Products table and set the UnitsInStock column to 50. You use conditions to narrow the amount of data changed during the UPDATE; you can use the same things you used in a SELECT statement: WHERE, SubQueries, LIKE, etc. The best way to minimize mistakes is to use the WHERE clause against the primary key column of the table; for example, if you are updating a table in which the primary key is a product number you would call the UPDATE TABLE SET ? = ? WHERE ProductNumber = ?. Go ahead and UPDATE the UnitsInStock table using the following code. When executed it will add 50 new units to the product named Alice Mutton:

```
1: UPDATE Products
2: SET UnitsInStock = 50
3: WHERE ProductName = Alice Mutton
```

You've narrowed down the number of rows you're changing to those that have a value of Alice Mutton in the ProductName column. If you are hand coding these examples or using the Query

Analyzer you'll receive errors if you attempt to set a string value without single quotes surrounding the value as in the following example. Please keep this in mind during the following sections:

```
1: UPDATE Products
2: SET UnitsInStock = '50'
3: WHERE ProductName = 'Alice Mutton'
```

Inserting New Data

The INSERT statement is used to create new rows of data in a database. It appends a new row to a table in the database. Listing 4.5 shows the basic structure of the INSERT statement.

LISTING 4.5   The Basic Structure of the INSERT Statement

```
INSERT [ INTO]
    { table_name WITH ( < table_hint_limited > [ ...n ] )
        | view_name
        | rowset_function_limited
    }

    {    [ ( column_list ) ]
        { VALUES
            ( { DEFAULT | NULL | expression } [ ,...n] )
            | derived_table
            | execute_statement
        }
    }
```

The following code example demonstrates how to add a new product to the Products table for *Exotic Liquids* using the SQL INSERT statement:

```
1: INSERT INTO Products
2: (
3: ProductName,
4: SupplierID,
5: CategoryID,
6: QuantityPerUnit,
7: UnitPrice,
8: UnitsInStock,
9: UnitsOnOrder,
10: ReorderLevel
11: )
12: VALUES
13: (
14: 'Fast Acting Pheromone Liquid',
15: 1,
16: 1,
```

4

```
17: '1000 Per Case',
18: 100,
19: 100,
20: 100,
21: 10
22: )
```

The reason the `ProductID` value wasn't set is that it's a Primary Key and is Auto Incremented by SQL Server. This is done so we are guaranteed not to have duplicates. You didn't set the value for `Discontinued` because it has a default value of False. To make sure the new row was added to the `Products` table, you can run the following `SELECT` statement:

```
1: SELECT Products.*
2: FROM Products
3: WHERE SupplierID = 1
```

The results from the proceeding SQL SELECT query can be seen in Figure 4.2

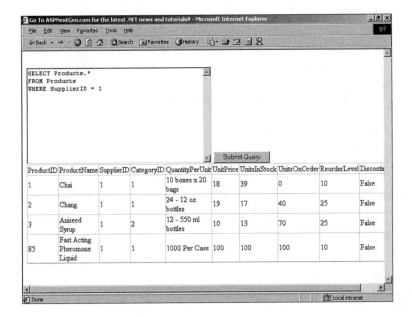

FIGURE 4.2

Results of the query to see if new products have been added.

Sure enough, Exotic Liquids' new Fast Acting Pheromone Liquid is now added to the table and ready for distribution. Looks like they're expecting it to be a top-seller!

Deleting Existing Data

The DELETE statement is used to delete existing rows of data from a database. Listing 4.6 shows the basic structure of the DELETE statement.

LISTING 4.6 The Basic Structure of the DELETE Statement

```
DELETE
    [ FROM ]
        { table_name WITH ( < table_hint_limited > [ ...n ] )
        | view_name
        | rowset_function_limited
        }

        [ FROM { < table_source > } [ ,...n ] ]
    [ WHERE
        { < search_condition >
        | { [ CURRENT OF
                { { [ GLOBAL ] cursor_name }
                    | cursor_variable_name
                }
            ] }
        }
    ]
    [ OPTION ( < query_hint > [ ,...n ] ) ]
```

The DELETE statement will completely wipe out a row, so be careful! If you accidentally ran the statement DELETE Products, every row in the Products table would be deleted. Use the following DELETE statement to delete the row you just added to the Products Table. Your ProductID number might be different than 85; double check the accuracy of the number before running the following DELETE statement:

```
1: DELETE Products
2: WHERE ProductID = 85
```

You use the ProductID column as your condition because it's a Primary Key and won't be repeated anywhere. That way you won't delete anything by accident. If you run the SELECT statement from the previous section you will find that the product we added no longer shows up in the result set.

Summary

This chapter was only meant to give you a high-level overview of Structured Query Language to help you understand future chapters. You learned how to use SQL statements to do the following:

- Retrieve data from a database
- Organize the data before it's returned
- Use SubQuerys in your SQL statements
- Update data in a database
- Insert new data into a database
- Delete existing data from a database

I can guarantee that if you're participating in third-generation Web site development, you *will* be using Structured Query Language. This chapter demonstrated the use of page-level SQL statements, which isn't recommended when you're building your solution. We're using inline SQL primarily for simplicity.

Well, enough primers—let's get down to the nitty-gritty!

Using a Basic DataGrid

IN THIS CHAPTER

In Chapter 3, "ADO.NET Managed Providers," you learned how the Managed Providers are the bridge from a .NET application, such as an ASP.NET Web Form, to a data store, such as Microsoft SQL Server. You used the DataGrid server control to display the output. This chapter will drill down into the DataGrid server control to show you what it can do. You'll begin using the Managed Providers to retrieve data from a database, and you'll be displaying the data with the ASP.NET DataGrid control.

In this chapter, you'll learn the following:

- The basics of the DataGrid control
- What data binding is in ASP.NET
- Binding server controls to a `DataTable` in a `DataSet`
- Binding server controls to Arrays
- Binding server controls to Collections
- Binding server controls to Properties
- Binding server controls to XML files

The ASP.NET DataGrid

The `DataGrid` server control is a multicolumn data-bound grid control...now say that five times fast! In English, the `DataGrid` renders a basic HTML `<table>` element. In its most basic form, the `DataGrid` renders a `<table>` element with `<tr>` elements for each row in its data source and `<td>` elements for each column in the row. The `DataGrid` also supports selecting, editing, sorting, and paging the data, as well as customizing the layout of the data. This chapter is going to show you a basic `DataGrid` and introduce you to the concept of data binding. In Chapter 6, "Altering DataGrid Output," you'll see how to use properties of the `DataGrid` to customize its output. In Chapter 10, "Inputting and Editing Data with the `DataGrid` and `DataList`," you'll delve into the editing functionality of the `DataGrid`.

The DataGrid is a control from the `System.Web.UI.WebControls` namespace. It's the first of three data server controls. The others are the `DataList` and the `Repeater`, which you'll learn about in Chapter 7, "Working With ASP.NET Server Controls Templates."

NOTE

Unlike the namespaces you saw in Chapter 3, `System.Data`, `System.Data.SqlClient` and `System.Data.OleDb`, you don't have to import the `System.Web.UI.WebControls` namespace to use the DataGrid on a Web Form. It's imported by default for all ASP.NET pages.

As with all ASP.NET intrinsic controls, you use the prefix asp when placing the DataGrid on an ASP.NET page and include the runat="server" property/value pair to identify it as a server control. This notifies the .NET Framework that this server control is to be processed on the server and rendered as HTML output appropriate for the browser making the request:

```
<asp:DataGrid runat="server" />
```

You can have any number of DataGrid controls on one Web Form. Listing 5.1 demonstrates how to add a DataGrid to an ASP.NET Web Form.

LISTING 5.1   Adding the DataGrid to an ASP.NET Web Form

```
01:  <%@ Page Language="[VB | C#]"%>
02:  <html>
03:  <head>
04:   <script runat="server">
05:   </script>
06:  </head>
07:  <body>
08:   <asp:DataGrid id="myDataGrid" runat="server" />
09:  </body>
10:  </html>
```

On line 8 of Listing 5.1 you place the DataGrid control, indicating that it's a server control with the runat="server" property/value pair. You add the ID property so you can have declarative control over the DataGrid. Using the ID property enables you to reference the DataGrid object by name. You can then declaratively set its properties, such as its DataSource property, and call its methods, such as DataBind().

Data Binding

Data binding in .NET is different than it was in previous Microsoft products. In .NET, *data binding* means binding any property of any .NET control to any publicly available information. It accesses data in the form of classes that expose raw data as properties and, in many cases, defines methods for updating the data. "Data" is a rather broad term in .NET. It might be values from a data store, names of controls from a collection, or attribute values from an object property. As you can see, this requires a slight shift in thinking from previous data access methods.

Complex controls that include embedded controls, such as the DataGrid, can bind to any class that supports the ICollection interface, such as a DataTable, DataReader, array, collection, or an object's properties. The ICollection interface defines size, enumerators, and synchronization methods for all collections, and it guarantees that the data class provides at least a basic means of data access and data navigation.

One example of an object that supports the ICollection interface is the DataSet object. One of its collections is the Tables collection, which supports the ICollection interface. This means that you could use the DataSet.Tables collection as a data source for a server control to render a list of all DataTables in the current DataSet.

Binding a data source to a DataGrid requires three steps:

1. Define a data source.
2. Set the DataGrid's DataSource property to the data source class you defined.
3. Call the DataBind() method.

Define a Data Source

In Chapter 3, you learned how to use the Managed Providers to retrieve data from a data source such as Microsoft's SQL Server. While this is the most typical type of data you'll be binding to, you could also bind a DataGrid to any other publicly available data. We'll get into other data sources later in this chapter. For now, let's look at how to bind to data from a database. Listing 5.2 shows how to create two DataTable classes in a DataSet.

LISTING 5.2   Creating a Data Source with the SQL Managed Provider

[VB]

```
01: <%@ Page Language="VB" %>
02: <%@ Import Namespace="System.Data" %>
03: <%@ Import Namespace="System.Data.SqlClient" %>
04:
05: <script runat="server">
06:    Sub Page_Load(Sender As Object, E As EventArgs)
07:       Dim myDataSet As New DataSet
08:       Dim myDataAdapter As SqlDataAdapter
09:
10:       myDataAdapter = New SqlDataAdapter("SELECT * FROM Customers",
➥        "server=localhost;database=Northwind;uid=sa;pwd=;")
11:       myDataAdapter.Fill(myDataSet, "Customers")
12:
13:       myDataAdapter.SelectCommand.CommandText = "SELECT * FROM Products"
14:       myDataAdapter.Fill(myDataSet, "Products")
15:    End Sub
16: </script>
```

[C#]

```
01: <%@ Page Language="C#" %>
02: <%@ Import Namespace="System.Data" %>
03: <%@ Import Namespace="System.Data.SqlClient" %>
04:
05: <script runat="server">
```

LISTING 5.2   Continued

```
06:    void Page_Load(Object sender, EventArgs e){
07:       DataSet myDataSet = new DataSet();
08:       SqlDataAdapter myDataAdapter;
09:
10:       myDataAdapter = new SqlDataAdapter("SELECT * FROM Customers",
➡          "server=localhost;database=Northwind;uid=sa;pwd=;");
11:       myDataAdapter.Fill(myDataSet, "Customers");
12:
13:       myDataAdapter.SelectCommand.CommandText = "SELECT * FROM Products";
14:       myDataAdapter.Fill(myDataSet, "Products");
15:    }
16: </script>

[VB & C#]

17: <html>
18: <head>
19: <title>Programming Datadriven Web Applications with ASP.NET
➡          - Chapter 5</title>
20: </head>
21: <body>
22:   <asp:DataGrid id="myDataGrid" runat="server" />
23: </body>
24: </html>
```

On lines 2 and 3 of Listing 5.2, you import the namespaces necessary for using the basic data functionality and the SQL Managed Provider. On line 7, you create a new instance of the DataSet class, inside the Page_Load() event handler. You follow that on line 8 by declaring a new instance of the SqlDataAdapter class. On line 10 you create the instance of the SqlDataAdapter, passing in a SQL SELECT statement and a connection string. On line 11, you execute the SQL statement by calling the Fill() method of the SqlDataAdapter. The result of the Fill() method is a new DataTable object in the DataSet. On line 13 you reset the SelectCommand.CommandText property of the SqlDataAdapter to a new SQL SELECT statement. Since the connection string is not changing for this new SQL statement, you only need to reset the CommandText property of the SelectCommand in the SqlDataAdapter. On line 14 you use the Fill() method again to execute the SQL statement, and create a new (second) DataTable in the DataSet.

Set the DataSource of the DataGrid

In the preceding example, you created two DataTable objects in the DataSet. Both of these DataTables are suitable candidates as a data source for the DataGrid. On the other hand, the DataSet.Tables collection is also a suitable candidate as the data source. Before you use an obvious data source for the DataGrid, such as a DataTable, you should know how to bind to a collection. This will teach you more about how the collection is built.

In Listing 5.2, insert the following code after line 14 and before line 15:

[VB]

```
14a:        myDataGrid.DataSource = myDataSet.Tables
```

[C#]

```
14a:        myDataGrid.DataSource = myDataSet.Tables;
```

Line 14a programmatically sets the DataSource property of the DataGrid to the Tables collection of the DataSet object. Now, there's one last step before you can see the fruits of your labor.

Call the `DataBind()` Method

The *DataBind()* method executes the binding of the control to the data source. When this method is called, a row is generated for each record in the data source and a cell is generated in each row for each column in the data source. The DataBind() method can be called by the individual data server control (myDataGrid.DataBind()) or by the Page object (Page.DataBind()), which will bind any child control(s) that has a data source defined.

> **NOTE**
>
> The DataBind() method is read-only. In Chapter 10 you'll learn how to create your own logic to update the data store with new values.

The following line of code, inserted between line 14a and line 15 in Listing 5.2, will call the DataBind() method on the DataGrid object:

[VB]

```
14b:        myDataGrid.DataBind()
```

[C#]

```
14b:        myDataGrid.DataBind();
```

The DataBind() method call executes the built-in data binding logic. When the page is viewed in a browser, a basic HTML table is rendered displaying all of the information about the two DataTable objects in the DataSet.Tables collection. Figure 5.1 shows this page in Internet Explorer 6.0.

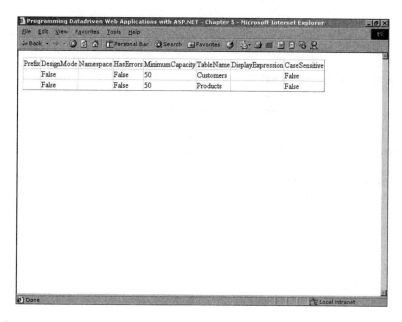

The DataGrid *is bound to the* DataSet.Tables *collection. It contains all the information about the collection.*

Binding to a `DataTable` in a `DataSet`

In the preceding example, you bound the DataGrid output to the DataSet.Tables collection, causing a table with a row for each DataTable to be rendered. This is cool and all, but it's not terribly useful. What you really want to do is display the data from one of the DataTables in the DataGrid, or display multiple DataGrids, each one with the data from a different DataTable.

Listing 5.3 shows the ASP.NET Web Form from Listing 5.2 with the Customers DataTable bound to the DataGrid.

LISTING 5.3   Binding a DataGrid to a DataTable

```
[VB]

01: <%@ Page Language="VB" %>
02: <%@ Import Namespace="System.Data" %>
03: <%@ Import Namespace="System.Data.SqlClient" %>
04:
05: <script runat="server">
06:   Sub Page_Load(Sender As Object, E As EventArgs)
07:     Dim myDataSet As New DataSet
```

LISTING 5.3 Continued

```
08:     Dim myDataAdapter As SqlDataAdapter
09:
10:     myDataAdapter = New SqlDataAdapter("SELECT * FROM Customers",
➥        "server=localhost;database=Northwind;uid=sa;pwd=;")
11:     myDataAdapter.Fill(myDataSet, "Customers")
12:
13:     myDataAdapter.SelectCommand.CommandText = "SELECT * FROM Products"
14:     myDataAdapter.Fill(myDataSet, "Products")
15:
16:     myDataGrid.DataSource = myDataSet.Tables("Customers")
17:     myDataGrid.DataBind()
18:   End Sub
19: </script>
```

[C#]

```
01: <%@ Page Language="C#" %>
02: <%@ Import Namespace="System.Data" %>
03: <%@ Import Namespace="System.Data.SqlClient" %>
04:
05: <script runat="server">
06:   void Page_Load(Object sender, EventArgs e){
07:     DataSet myDataSet = new DataSet();
08:     SqlDataAdapter myDataAdapter;
09:
10:     myDataAdapter = new SqlDataAdapter("SELECT * FROM Customers",
➥        "server=localhost;database=Northwind;uid=sa;pwd=;");
11:     myDataAdapter.Fill(myDataSet, "Customers");
12:
13:     myDataAdapter.SelectCommand.CommandText = "SELECT * FROM Products";
14:     myDataAdapter.Fill(myDataSet, "Products");
15:
16:     myDataGrid.DataSource = myDataSet.Tables["Customers"];
17:     myDataGrid.DataBind();
18:   }
19: </script>
```

[VB & C#]

```
20: <html>
21: <head>
22: <title>Programming Datadriven Web Applications with ASP.NET
➥       - Chapter 5</title>
23: </head>
24: <body>
25:  <asp:DataGrid id="myDataGrid" runat="server" />
26: </body>
27: </html>
```

For the most part, Listing 5.3 works the same as Listing 5.2. The only real change is on line 16, where you set the DataSource property of the DataGrid to the Customers DataTable in the DataSet. The resulting Web page renders a row for each DataRow in the DataTable and a cell in each row for each DataColumn (see Figure 5.2).

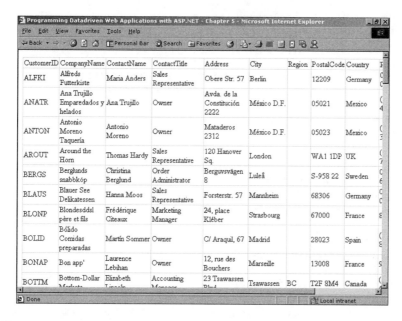

FIGURE 5.2

A basic DataGrid *renders a row for each* DataRow *in the* DataTable *and a cell in each row for each* DataColumn.

To display multiple DataGrids, each one bound to a different DataTable in the DataSet, you only need to define the DataSource for each DataGrid, and use the Page.DataBind() method to bind all data server controls on the page to their data source. Listing 5.4 changes the SQL statement to return only five rows for each DataTable.

LISTING 5.4   Displaying Multiple DataGrids on One Web Form

```
[VB]

01: <%@ Page Language="VB" %>
02: <%@ Import Namespace="System.Data" %>
03: <%@ Import Namespace="System.Data.SqlClient" %>
04:
05: <script runat="server">
06:    Sub Page_Load(Sender As Object, E As EventArgs)
07:       Dim myDataSet As New DataSet
08:       Dim myDataAdapter As SqlDataAdapter
09:
```

LISTING 5.4 Continued

```
10:    myDataAdapter = New SqlDataAdapter("SELECT TOP 5 * FROM Customers",
➡      "server=localhost;database=Northwind;uid=sa;pwd=;")
11:    myDataAdapter.Fill(myDataSet, "Customers")
12:
13:    myDataAdapter.SelectCommand.CommandText =
➡      "SELECT TOP 5 * FROM Products"
14:    myDataAdapter.Fill(myDataSet, "Products")
15:
16:    myDataGrid.DataSource = myDataSet.Tables("Customers")
17:    myOtherDataGrid.DataSource = myDataSet.Tables("Products")
18:    Page.DataBind()
19:  End Sub
20: </script>

[C#]

01: <%@ Page Language="C#" %>
02: <%@ Import Namespace="System.Data" %>
03: <%@ Import Namespace="System.Data.SqlClient" %>
04:
05: <script runat="server">
06:   void Page_Load(Object sender, EventArgs e){
07:     DataSet myDataSet = new DataSet();
08:     SqlDataAdapter myDataAdapter;
09:
10:     myDataAdapter = new SqlDataAdapter("SELECT TOP 5 * FROM Customers",
➡       "server=localhost;database=Northwind;uid=sa;pwd=;");
11:     myDataAdapter.Fill(myDataSet, "Customers");
12:
13:     myDataAdapter.SelectCommand.CommandText =
➡       "SELECT TOP 5 * FROM Products";
14:     myDataAdapter.Fill(myDataSet, "Products");
15:
16:     myDataGrid.DataSource = myDataSet.Tables["Customers"];
17:     myOtherDataGrid.DataSource = myDataSet.Tables["Products"];
18:     Page.DataBind();
19:   }
20: </script>

[VB & C#]

21: <html>
22: <head>
23: <title>Programming Datadriven Web Applications with ASP.NET
➡       - Chapter 5</title>
24: </head>
25: <body>
26:   <p><asp:DataGrid id="myDataGrid" runat="server" /></p>
```

LISTING 5.4 Continued

```
27:    <p><asp:DataGrid id="myOtherDataGrid" runat="server" /></p>
28: </body>
29: </html>
```

On lines 10 and 13, you add a TOP 5 argument to the SQL statement so it returns only five records in each DataTable. On line 27, you add another DataGrid named myOtherDataGrid to display the data from the Products DataTable. On line 17, you set the DataSource property of myOtherDataGrid to the Products table, the same way that you set the DataSource property of myDataGrid in Listing 5.3.

One change in Listing 5.4 is on line 18. Rather than calling the DataBind() method for each DataGrid, you call it just for the Page object, which binds any child control of the Page object that has its DataSource set. Figure 5.3 shows the rendered Web page with two DataGrid controls.

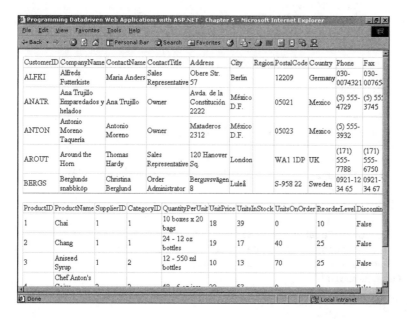

FIGURE 5.3

Multiple DataGrids can be used to display the data from multiple DataTables. The Page.DataBind() method can be used to bind all child controls on the Web Form.

Binding to Arrays

Just as you can bind a server control to a DataTable, you can also bind a server control to an array. The concept is the same. The DataBind() method works for any data source. Listing 5.5 shows an ASP.NET Web Form that creates an ArrayList object and binds it to a DataGrid, a DropDownList, and a RadioButtonList.

LISTING 5.5   Binding Server Controls to an `ArrayList`

[VB]

```
01: <%@ Page Language="VB" %>
02:
03: <script runat="server">
04:    Sub Page_Load(Source As Object, E As EventArgs)
05:      Dim al As New ArrayList
06:      al.Add("Item 1")
07:      al.Add("Item 2")
08:      al.Add("Item 3")
09:      al.Add("Item 4")
10:      al.Add("Item 5")
11:      myDataGrid.DataSource = al
12:      myDropDownList.DataSource = al
13:      myRadioButtonList.DataSource = al
14:      Page.DataBind()
15:    End Sub
16: </script>
```

[C#]

```
01: <%@ Page Language="C#" %>
02:
03: <script runat="server">
04:    void Page_Load(Object sender, EventArgs e){
05:      ArrayList al = new ArrayList();
06:      al.Add("Item 1");
07:      al.Add("Item 2");
08:      al.Add("Item 3");
09:      al.Add("Item 4");
10:      al.Add("Item 5");
11:      myDataGrid.DataSource = al;
12:      myDropDownList.DataSource = al;
13:      myRadioButtonList.DataSource = al;
14:      Page.DataBind();
15:    }
16: </script>
```

[VB & C#]

```
17: <html>
18: <head>
19: <title>Programming Datadriven Web Applications with ASP.NET
➥      - Chapter 5</title>
20: </head>
21: <body>
22:    <p>
```

LISTING 5.5   Continued

```
23:    <b>Binding to a DataGrid</b><br>
24:    <asp:DataGrid id="myDataGrid" runat="server" />
25: </p>
26: <p>
27:    <b>Binding to a DropDownList</b><br>
28:    <asp:DropDownList id="myDropDownList" runat="server" />
29: </p>
30: <p>
31:    <b>Binding to a RadioButtonList</b><br>
32:    <asp:RadioButtonList id="myRadioButtonList" runat="server" />
33: </p>
34: </body>
35: </html>
```

In Listing 5.5, you create an ArrayList on line 5. On Lines 6–10, you add some items to the ArrayList using the Add() method of the ArrayList class. Just as in previous examples, on lines 11–13, you set the DataSource property of each of the server controls. You use the ArrayList as the data source. Lastly, on line 14, you use the Page.DataBind() method to bind all of the controls in the Web Form to their data source. Figure 5.4 shows the rendered Web page created in Listing 5.5.

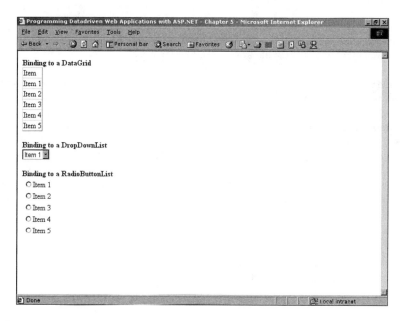

FIGURE 5.4

An ArrayList can be bound to any server control that has a DataSource property.

Binding to Collections

As explained in the "Data Binding" section earlier in the chapter, a class that supports the ICollection interface can be treated as a data source. A server control that has a DataSource property can be bound to a collection. If you bind a DataGrid server control to the DataSet.Tables collection, as you did in Listing 5.2, you'll get a table detailing all of the properties of the DataTables in the DataSet.

Listing 5.6 shows an ASP.NET Web Form that creates a DataSet object, fills it with two DataTables, and binds it to a DataGrid, a ListBox, and a RadioButtonList.

LISTING 5.6   Binding Server Controls to a Collection

```
[VB]
01: <%@ Page Language="VB" %>
02: <%@ Import Namespace="System.Data" %>
03: <%@ Import Namespace="System.Data.SqlClient" %>
04:
05: <script runat="server">
06:   Sub Page_Load(Sender As Object, E As EventArgs)
07:     Dim myDataSet As New DataSet
08:     Dim myDataAdapter As SqlDataAdapter
09:
10:     myDataAdapter = New SqlDataAdapter("SELECT * FROM Customers",
➡       "server=localhost;database=Northwind;uid=sa;pwd=;")
11:     myDataAdapter.Fill(myDataSet, "Customers")
12:
13:     myDataAdapter.SelectCommand.CommandText = "SELECT * FROM Products"
14:     myDataAdapter.Fill(myDataSet, "Products")
15:
16:     myDataGrid.DataSource = myDataSet.Tables
17:     myListBox.DataSource = myDataSet.Tables
18:     myCheckboxList.DataSource = myDataSet.Tables
19:     Page.DataBind()
20:   End Sub
21: </script>

[C#]
01: <%@ Page Language="C#" %>
02: <%@ Import Namespace="System.Data" %>
03: <%@ Import Namespace="System.Data.SqlClient" %>
04:
05: <script runat="server">
06:   void Page_Load(Object sender, EventArgs e){
07:     DataSet myDataSet = new DataSet();
```

LISTING 5.6   Continued

```
08:     SqlDataAdapter myDataAdapter;
09:
10:     myDataAdapter = new SqlDataAdapter("SELECT * FROM Customers",
➥       "server=localhost;database=Northwind;uid=sa;pwd=;");
11:     myDataAdapter.Fill(myDataSet, "Customers");
12:
13:     myDataAdapter.SelectCommand.CommandText = "SELECT * FROM Products";
14:     myDataAdapter.Fill(myDataSet, "Products");
15:
16:     myDataGrid.DataSource = myDataSet.Tables;
17:     myListBox.DataSource = myDataSet.Tables;
18:     myCheckboxList.DataSource = myDataSet.Tables;
19:     Page.DataBind();
20:   }
21: </script>

[VB & C#]

22: <html>
23: <head>
24: <title>Programming Datadriven Web Applications with ASP.NET
➥        - Chapter 5</title>
25: </head>
26: <body>
27:   <p>
28:     <b>Binding to a DataGrid</b><br>
29:     <asp:DataGrid id="myDataGrid" runat="server" />
30:   </p>
31:   <p>
32:     <b>Binding to a ListBox</b><br>
33:     <asp:ListBox id="myListBox" runat="server" />
34:   </p>
35:   <p>
36:     <b>Binding to a CheckboxList</b><br>
37:     <asp:CheckboxList id="myCheckboxList" runat="server" />
38:   </p>
39: </body>
40: </html>
```

In Listing 5.6, you create a DataSet and fill it with two DataTables, the same as you did in Listing 5.2. On lines 16–18, you set the DataSource property of three different server controls, a DataGrid, a ListBox, and a CheckboxList, to the Tables collection of the DataSet. On line 19, you call the page-level DataBind() method. Figure 5.5 shows the resulting Web page.

5

USING A BASIC DATAGRID

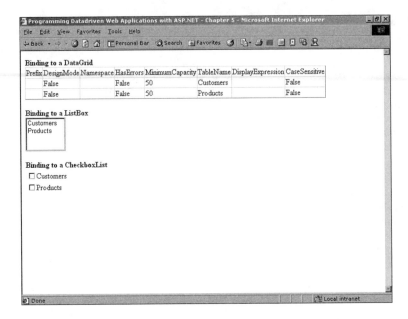

FIGURE 5.5

Collections of classes supporting the ICollection *interface can be used as data sources for server controls.*

Binding to Properties

Data binding to properties is slightly different than binding to traditional data sources. In the previous examples, you've been binding a DataGrid or similar server control to a data source that exposes data values in grid-like structures. Properties are different because they typically consist of a single value. You can't bind a DataGrid to a property because the property doesn't contain a traditional row/column structure. However, you *can* bind a server control, such as a Label control, to a property. The single value of the property can be rendered as the Label.Text property.

This type of data binding requires a slightly different syntax. You don't have to set a DataSource property. Rather, you bind a property of the server control to the property value you wish to render. This type of data binding uses the <%# and %> tags to delimit the binding expression. Alternatively, you can set the server control's property declaratively. Listing 5.7 shows an ASP.NET Web Form that binds two Label server controls to the Page.IsPostBack property (a Boolean value).

LISTING 5.7   Data Binding Server Controls to Properties

```
[VB]

01: <%@ Page Language="VB" %>
02:
```

LISTING 5.7 Continued

```
03: <script runat="server">
04:    Sub Page_Load(Source As Object, E As EventArgs)
05:       Label1.Text = Page.IsPostBack
06:       Page.DataBind()
07:    End Sub
08: </script>
```

[C#]

```
01: <%@ Page Language="C#" %>
02:
03: <script runat="server">
04:    void Page_Load(Object sender, EventArgs e){
05:       Label1.Text = Page.IsPostBack.ToString();
06:       Page.DataBind();
07:    }
08: </script>
```

[VB & C#]

```
09: <html>
10: <head>
11: <title>Programming Datadriven Web Applications with ASP.NET
➥       - Chapter 5</title>
12: </head>
13: <body>
14: </head>
15: <body>
16:    <p>Label 1: <asp:Label id="Label1" runat="server" /></p>
17:    <p>Label 2: <asp:Label id="Label2" Text='<%# Page.IsPostBack %>'
➥       runat="server" /></p>
18: </body>
19: </html>
```

In Listing 5.7, you create an ASP.NET Web Form with two Label server controls. Each control displays the same Page.IsPostBack property value. This is done with two different approaches. On line 5, you set the Text property of the first Label control to the Page.IsPostBack property value. The Text value is being set declaratively, and will render correctly without calling DataBind(). For the other control, you use the <%#...%> data binding expression. This is done on line 17 with the expression <%# Page.IsPostBack %>. Figure 5.6 shows the rendered Web page.

NOTE

In Listing 5.7, you used the ToString() method only in the C# example. Visual Basic.Net can implicitly convert a Boolean value to a String data type, whereas in C# this must be done explicitly.

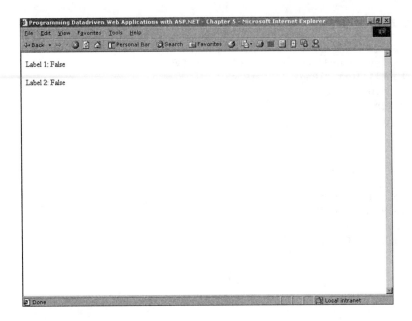

FIGURE 5.6
Server controls can be bound to properties of .NET objects, such as the `Page.IsPostBack` *property.*

Binding to XML Files

Although an in-depth analysis of XML and its place in the .NET Framework is beyond the
scope of this chapter, you do need to know how to use an XML file as a data source for server
controls, and the `DataGrid` in particular. Chapter 12, "XML and SOAP," will explore what
XML is and its role in the .NET Framework. This section will only show you how to open and
read an existing XML file and bind the data to a `DataGrid`.

An XML file is nothing more than a text file that's been marked up according to the XML standard, much like an HTML file is simply marked-up text. Since you cannot connect to a text file
the way you connect to a database, you don't use the ADO.NET Managed Providers to access the
XML file. Instead, you must open and read the XML file using functionality from the `System.IO`
namespace. The class libraries in `System.IO` include the `FileStream` and `StreamReader` classes.
You'll use these classes to open and read an XML file. As with any namespace that isn't included
by default, you must import `System.IO` using the `@ Import` directive.

The `FileStream` class is used to read from or write to files in the Web server's file system.
`FileStream` can open a file either synchronously (by default) or asynchronously.

Asynchronously opening a file (`BeginRead`, `BeginWrite`) will begin accessing the file and
move on to the next operation without waiting for the function to complete. This method of
opening files can cause uncertain completion order when multiple files are opened at once.

When files are opened *synchronously* (Read, Write), each function starts, and completes before the next function begins.

To read an XML file, you use the FileMode.Open and FileAccess.Read parameters of the FileStream class.

```
myFileStream = new FileStream([fileName], [fileMode], [fileAccess])
```

The StreamReader class implements a TextReader and reads bytes from a stream. In this case, the FileStream class creates the stream. StreamReader takes FileStream as a parameter and defaults to UTF-8 encoding, which handles Unicode characters correctly and makes the StreamReader appropriate for localized versions of the operating system:

```
myStreamReader = new StreamReader([fileStream])
```

The DataSet class exposes a ReadXml() method, which is used to read XML data from the StreamReader and fill a DataTable with it. The DataTable is created dynamically when ReadXml() is called. Listing 5.8 shows an ASP.NET Web Form that uses FileStream, StreamReader, and DataSet.ReadXml() to open an XML file and stream it into a DataTable in the DataSet. Once it's in the DataSet, you can bind the DataTable of XML data to a DataGrid.

LISTING 5.8   Data Binding to XML Data

[VB]

```
01: <%@ Page Language="VB" %>
02: <%@ Import Namespace="System.Data" %>
03: <%@ Import Namespace="System.IO" %>
04:
05: <script runat="server">
06:    Sub Page_Load(Source As Object, E As EventArgs)
07:       Dim myDataSet As New DataSet
08:
09:       Dim myFileStream As FileStream = New
➡          FileStream(Server.MapPath("states.xml"),
➡          FileMode.Open, FileAccess.Read)
10:       Dim myXmlStream As StreamReader = New StreamReader(myFileStream)
11:       myDataSet.ReadXml(myXmlStream)
12:       myFileStream.Close
13:
14:       myDataGrid.DataSource = myDataSet.Tables("State")
15:       myDataGrid.DataBind()
16:    End Sub
17: </script>

[C#]

01: <%@ Page Language="C#" %>
02: <%@ Import Namespace="System.Data" %>
```

LISTING 5.8   Continued

```
03: <%@ Import Namespace="System.IO" %>
04:
05: <script runat="server">
06:    void Page_Load(Object sender, EventArgs e){
07:      DataSet myDataSet = new DataSet();
08:
09:      FileStream myFileStream = new
➥      FileStream(Server.MapPath("states.xml"),
➥      FileMode.Open, FileAccess.Read);
10:      StreamReader myXmlStream = new StreamReader(myFileStream);
11:      myDataSet.ReadXml(myXmlStream);
12:      myFileStream.Close();
13:
14:      myDataGrid.DataSource = myDataSet.Tables["State"];
15:      myDataGrid.DataBind();
16:    }
17: </script>

[VB & C#]

18: <html>
19: <head>
20: <title>Programming Datadriven Web Applications with ASP.NET
➥        - Chapter 5</title>
21: </head>
22: <body>
23:    <asp:DataGrid id="myDataGrid" runat="server" />
24: </body>
25: </html>
```

> **NOTE**
>
> The states.xml file can be downloaded from the companion Web site for this book at
> <http://www.samspublishing.com>. Copy the states.xml file to the same directory as
> the ASP.NET Web Form in Listing 5.8.

In Listing 5.8, you stream in data from an XML file named states.xml. On line 3, you import
the System.IO namespace, which enables the Input/Output functionality that's required to read
from a file in the file system. On line 9, you create a new FileStream to open and read the
states.xml file. The path to the file was created dynamically using the Server.MapPath()
method that has been retained from previous versions of ASP. On line 10, you create a new
StreamReader named myXmlStream and pass in FileStream as its path. On line 11, you use the
DataSet.ReadXml() method to read the XML data from StreamReader.

At this point, you've created a `DataTable` in the `DataSet` and filled it with the XML file's data. The `DataSet.DataSetName` property is set to the XML file's schema ID (`States`), and the `DataTable.TableName` property is set to the element name (`State`). The XML schema for the states.xml file is shown in Listing 5.9.

LISTING 5.9   The states.xml Schema

```
01: <?xml version="1.0"?>
02: <root>
03: <xsd:schema id="States" targetNamespace=""
04:   xmlns="" xmlns:xsd=http://www.w3.org/2001/XMLSchema
05:   xmlns:msdata="urn:schemas-microsoft-com:xml-msdata">
06:   <xsd:element name="State">
07:     <xsd:complexType>
08:       <xsd:all>
09:         <xsd:element name="Name" minOccurs="0" type="xsd:string" />
10:         <xsd:element name="Abbreviation" minOccurs="0" type="xsd:string" />
11:       </xsd:all>
12:     </xsd:complexType>
13:   </xsd:element>
14: </xsd:schema>
```

On line 14 of Listing 5.8, you set the `DataSource` property of the `DataGrid` to the `State` `DataTable` in the `DataSet`. When the page is requested, the XML data is bound to the `DataGrid`. The resulting Web page is shown in Figure 5.7.

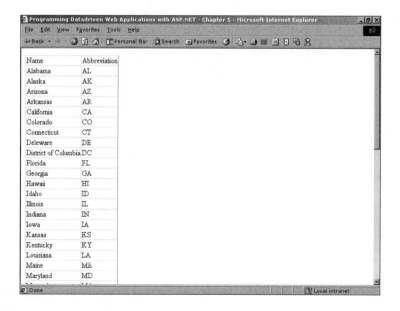

FIGURE 5.7

XML data can be streamed into a `DataSet`. *Then a server control, such as the* `DataGrid`, *can bind to the* `DataTable`.

Summary

In this chapter, you put to use the knowledge you gained from Chapters 1 through 4. You used the ASP.NET Managed Providers to retrieve data from a data store, and you learned the following:

- The basics of the DataGrid control
- Data binding
- Binding to a DataTable in your DataSet
- Binding to arrays
- Binding to collections
- Binding to properties
- Binding to XML files

In this chapter, you learned the basics of the `DataGrid` server control. The next chapter will show you some of the extended functionality of the `DataGrid`, including how to alter the output appearance, sort data, and create a paging `DataGrid`.

Altering DataGrid Output

IN THIS CHAPTER

In Chapter 5, "Using a Basic DataGrid," you learned how to work with the basic ASP.NET DataGrid server control. You also learned how to get data and bind it to a DataGrid so it can be rendered as HTML on a client browser. In this chapter, you're going to learn how to alter the DataGrid cosmetically. You'll also learn how to build DataGrids that use paging to show only a select amount of data at a time, and that use sorting to allow the user to click on a column heading. Finally you'll learn to re-sort the data in the DataGrid.

This chapter will cover the following:

- Properties for altering a DataGrid's appearance
- Paging DataGrids—Using the built-in paging and custom paging
- Sorting the DataGrid by columns
- Using BoundColumns

Understanding DataGrid Properties

Like all ASP.NET server controls, the DataGrid exposes a rich set of properties and methods. In the previous chapter, you worked with a few of these properties and methods, including the DataSource property and the DataBind() method. You built DataGrids that were rendered as basic HTML <table> elements. Although this is where the core functionality of the DataGrid is found, the table that was rendered wasn't the most attractive table ever. Altering the DataGrid's appearance is as simple as setting a few property values. You can be as creative as you like because the property set accounts for nearly everything you'll want.

Listing 6.1 builds a DataGrid that renders a plain old table. The following examples will expand on this code to alter the output.

> **WARNING**
>
> In this chapter I am using ASP.NET's code behind functionality in the example code. The reason for this is that several code listings use the same logic to render data. All the changes are made in the Web Form. By using code behind, several of the Web Form listings can share the same code behind file. Each listing will show a code behind sample in Visual Basic.NET and in C#. Save the code behind file to the same directory as the Web Form. In the Web Form I use the @ Page SRC attribute, which enables Just-In-Time compilers for the code behind class. You do not need to precompile the code behind class into a DLL.

LISTING 6.1 A Basic DataGrid

[Code Behind VB - 0601.vb]

```
01: Imports System
02: Imports System.Web
03: Imports System.Web.UI
04: Imports System.Web.UI.WebControls
05: Imports System.Data
06: Imports System.Data.SqlClient
07:
08: Public Class Listing0601 : Inherits Page
09:
10:    Protected myDataGrid As DataGrid
11:
12:    Protected Sub Page_Load(Source As Object, E As EventArgs)
13:      Dim myConnection As New SqlConnection(
➥        "server=localhost;database=Northwind;uid=sa;pwd=;")
14:      Dim myCommand As New SqlCommand("SELECT CompanyName,
➥        ContactName, ContactTitle, Phone, Fax FROM Customers",
➥        myConnection)
15:      Dim myReader As SqlDataReader = Nothing
16:
17:      Try
18:       myConnection.Open()
19:       myReader = myCommand.ExecuteReader()
20:       myDataGrid.DataSource = myReader
21:       myDataGrid.DataBind()
22:
23:      Finally
24:       myConnection.Close()
25:      End Try
26:
27:    End Sub
28:
29: End Class
```

[Code Behind C# - 06.01.cs]

```
01: using System;
02: using System.Web;
03: using System.Web.UI;
04: using System.Web.UI.WebControls;
05: using System.Data;
```

LISTING 6.1   Continued

```
06: using System.Data.SqlClient;
07:
08: public class Listing0601 : Page{
09:
10:    protected DataGrid myDataGrid;
11:
12:    protected void Page_Load(Object sender, EventArgs e){
13:     SqlConnection myConnection = new SqlConnection(
➥        "server=localhost;database=Northwind;uid=sa;pwd=;");
14:     SqlCommand myCommand = new SqlCommand("SELECT CompanyName,
➥        ContactName, ContactTitle, Phone, Fax FROM Customers",
➥        myConnection);
15:     SqlDataReader myReader = null;
16:
17:     try{
18:      myConnection.Open();
19:      myReader = myCommand.ExecuteReader();
20:      myDataGrid.DataSource = myReader;
21:      myDataGrid.DataBind();
22:     }
23:     finally{
24:      myConnection.Close();
25:     }
26:
27:    }
28:
29: }
```

[Web Form VB]

```
01: <%@ Page Inherits="Listing0601" Src="06.01.vb" %>
```

[Web Form C#]

```
01: <%@ Page Inherits="Listing0601" Src="06.01.cs" %>
```

[Web Form VB & C#]

```
02: <html>
03: <head></head>
04: <body>
05: <form runat="server" method="post">
06:   <asp:DataGrid runat="server" id="myDataGrid" />
07: </form>
08: </body>
09: </html>
```

Altering DataGrid Output

CHAPTER 6

125

6

ALTERING
DATAGRID
OUTPUT

Listing 6.1 is very similar to the code you worked with in Chapter 5. In the Page_Load() event handler in the code behind class, you create a SqlDataReader to retrieve the data from the Customers table in the database. On line 20, you set the SqlDataReader as the DataSource for the DataGrid. On line 21, you bind the SqlDataReader to the DataGrid. Figure 6.1 shows the rendered output from Listing 6.1.

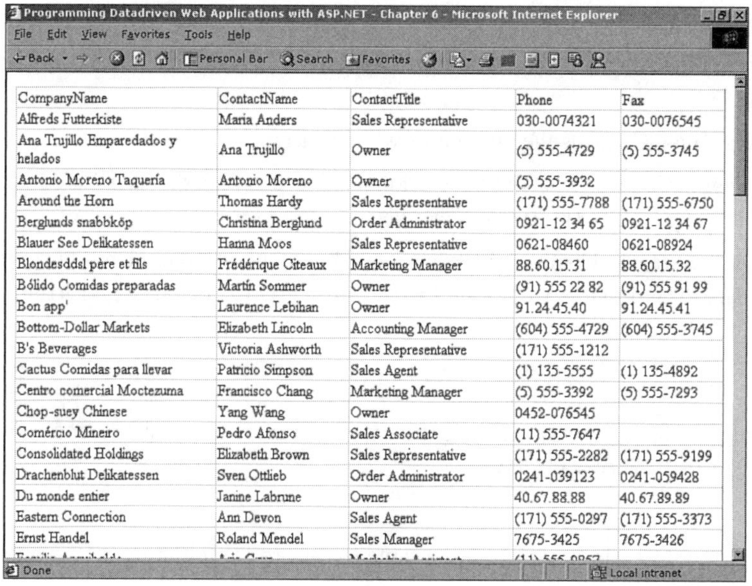

FIGURE 6.1
A basic DataGrid.

Using Basic DataGrid Properties to Alter the Rendered Table

The DataGrid exposes the basic table attributes as properties, such as Width, Cellspacing, Cellpadding, and so on. These properties are used to alter the rendered output of the DataGrid in a very basic way. You can control the border style, width, and spacing as if you were hard-coding those values into a table element in HTML.

The HTML for a table is replicated easily using DataGrid properties. The following HTML is a table element with some basic attributes:

```
<table border="0" cellpadding="4" cellspacing="0" width="100%">
```

This HTML can be replicated with a `DataGrid` using the basic properties:

```
<asp:DataGrid runat="server" id="myDataGrid" BorderWidth="0" Width="100%"
  Cellpadding="4" Cellspacing="0" />
```

In Listing 6.2, you add five properties to the `DataGrid`:

- `Width`—Controls the width of the rendered table. This can be an absolute pixel value or a percentage value.
- `CellPadding`—Controls the amount of white space between the cell border and the cell content.
- `CellSpacing`—Controls the amount of white space between cells.
- `Gridlines`—Controls how the table gridlines (borders between cells) are rendered. The possible values are `Both`, `Horizontal`, `None`, or `Vertical`.
- `HorizontalAlign`—Controls the horizontal alignment of the rendered table in the available space. The possible values are `Center`, `Justify`, `Left`, `NotSet`, or `Right`.

NOTE

For a complete list of the `DataGrid` properties and methods, see Appendix A, "ASP.NET Intrinsic Server Controls."

Listing 6.2 shows the code for creating the same `DataGrid` from Listing 6.1 with the added properties.

LISTING 6.2   Using `DataGrid` Properties

```
[Web Form VB & C#]
06: <asp:DataGrid runat="server" id="myDataGrid"
06a:    Width="740"
06b:    CellPadding="4"
06c:    CellSpacing="0"
06d:    Gridlines="Horizontal"
06e:    HorizontalAlign="Center"
06f:    />
```

Listing 6.2 extends the code from Listing 6.1. On line 6a, you add a `Width` property to set the rendered table to an absolute pixel width of 740 pixels. On line 6b, you add a `Cellpadding` property of 4 pixels. On line 6c, you add a `Cellspacing` property of 0 pixels. On line 6d,

Altering DataGrid Output

CHAPTER 6

127

6

ALTERING
DATAGRID
OUTPUT

you use the `GridLines` property to specify that only the horizontal gridlines should be visible. On line 6, you use the `HorizontalAlign` property to center the DataGrid on the page. Figure 6.2 shows the rendered output from Listing 6.1 with the extended code from Listing 6.2.

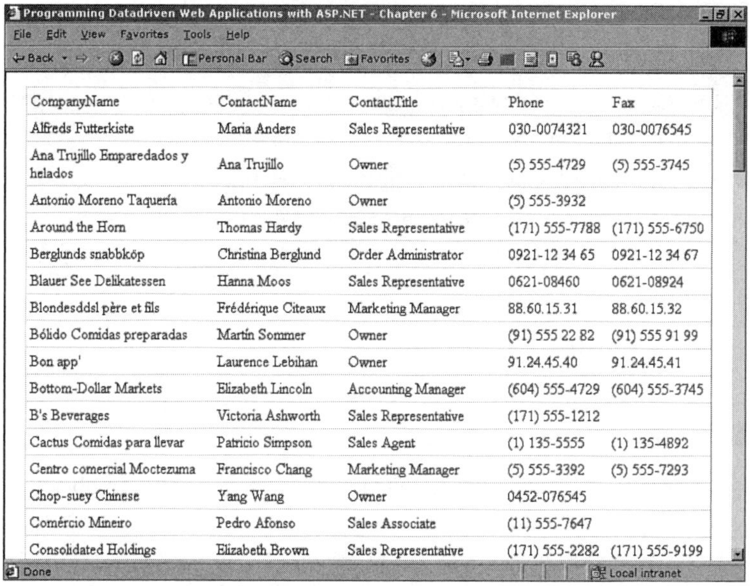

FIGURE 6.2
`DataGrid` *properties can be used to render an HTML table with typical attribute values.*

`DataGrid` Style Objects

The `DataGrid` is a *complex control*, meaning that it's the parent to many child controls. Complex controls are simply controls that contain other controls in a parent/child relationship. The control in question, such as a `DataGrid`, is the parent control, and it contains one or more dependent controls, called child controls.

Each row in the `DataGrid` is a child, and each cell in each row is a child of that row. Complex controls such as the `DataGrid`, `DataList`, `Repeater`, and `Calendar` expose *style objects* that allow you to control the appearance of certain child controls. You can use these style objects to alter the rendered output of a complex control. In classic ASP, you had to write a lot of code to do simple things such as changing the `background-color` attribute of every other row in a table. Style objects enable the same functionality through properties.

The `DataGrid` exposes *seven* style objects, each derived from the `TableItemStyle` class:

- `AlternatingItemStyle`—Controls the appearance of every other row.
- `EditItemStyle`—Controls the appearance of a row while being edited.
- `FooterStyle`—Controls the appearance of the footer row in the table.
- `HeaderStyle`—Controls the appearance of the header row of the table.
- `ItemStyle`—Controls the appearance of each row in the table. `AlternatingItemStyle` will override property settings on every other row.
- `PagerStyle`—Controls the appearance of the page-navigation links.
- `SelectedItemStyle`—Controls the appearance of the row that's currently selected.

Each style object exposes a rich set of properties, including `BackColor`, `ForeColor`, `Font-Name`, and so on. The style object property can be set inline or declaratively. To set a style object property, you specify the style object and the property name:

```
style object-property = value
```

```
ItemStyle-BackColor = "Red"
```

The `AlternatingItemStyle`, `FooterStyle`, `HeaderStyle`, and `ItemStyle` objects can be used on any `DataGrid`. The `PagerStyle` only applies to `DataGrids` that use the paging functionality that you'll learn about in this chapter. The `EditItemStyle` and `SelectedItemStyle` are used in very specific instances, which you'll learn about in Chapter 10, "Inputting and Editing Data with the DataGrid."

NOTE

For a complete list of style object properties, see Appendix A.

Listing 6.3 continues with the Web Form from Listings 6.1 and 6.2. It sets the properties for three of the style objects.

LISTING 6.3   Using Style Objects with the `DataGrid`

```
[Web Form VB & C#]
06: <asp:DataGrid runat="server" id="myDataGrid"
06a:    Width="740"
06b:    CellPadding="4"
06c:    CellSpacing="0"
06d:    Gridlines="Horizontal"
06e:    HorizontalAlign="Center"
```

Altering DataGrid Output

CHAPTER 6

129

6

ALTERING
DATAGRID
OUTPUT

LISTING 6.3   Continued

```
06g:    HeaderStyle-Font-Bold="True"
06h:    HeaderStyle-Font-Name="Arial"
06i:    HeaderStyle-Font-Size="small"
06j:    HeaderStyle-ForeColor="#663300"
06k:    HeaderStyle-BackColor="#CCCC66"
06l:
06m:    ItemStyle-Font-Names="Verdana, Arial, sans-serif"
06n:    ItemStyle-Font-Size="x-small"
06o:    AlternatingItemStyle-BackColor="#FFFFCC"
06p:    />
```

Listing 6.3 extends the previous examples by specifying the properties for three style objects. On lines 6g–6k, you specify values for the HeaderStyle object, which alters the appearance of the header row in the table (the row with the column titles). On lines 6m–6n, you set properties of the ItemStyle object, which affects the appearance of every row. On line 6o, you set the AlternatingItemStyle-BackColor property, which sets the background color for every other row. If an ItemStyle-BackColor property were set, the AlternatingItemStyle-BackColor property would override it on every other row. Figure 6.3 shows the rendered output from Listing 6.3.

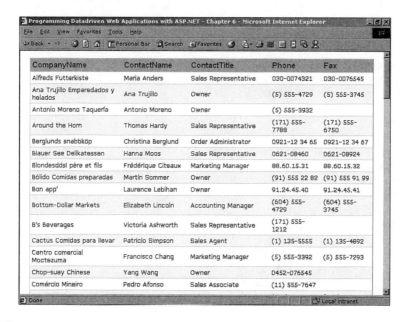

FIGURE 6.3

You use style objects to alter the appearance of child controls of the DataGrid.

Just as all of the properties for a user control can be set individually, you also can define the output with a cascading style sheet. Each of the style objects includes a CssClass property, which identifies the custom class of a style sheet. This, in turn, defines the appearance of the output from the style object:

style object-CssClas=*value*

In Listing 6.4, you re-create the same Web Form from the previous examples, but you use a cascading style sheet rather than setting the individual properties. The Web Form in Listing 6.4 uses the same code behind class from Listing 6.1.

LISTING 6.4   Using the CssClass of the Style Objects with the DataGrid

```
[Web Form VB]

01: <%@ Page Inherits="Listing0601" Src="06.01.vb" %>

[Web Form C#]

01: <%@ Page Inherits="Listing0601" Src="06.01.cs" %>

[Web Form VB & C#]

01: <html>
02: <head>
03:   <style ref="stylesheet" type="text/css">
04:     .tableItem {font: x-small Verdana, Arial, sans-serif;}
05:     .tableHeader {font: bold small Arial; color:#663300;
➥       background-color:#CCCC66;}
06:     .alternatingItem {font: x-small Verdana, Arial, sans-serif;
➥       background-color:#FFFFCC;}
07:   </style>
08: </head>
09: <body>
10: <form runat="server" method="post">
11:   <asp:DataGrid runat="server" id="myDataGrid"
12:     Width="740"
13:     Cellpadding="4"
14:     Cellspacing="0"
15:     Gridlines="Horizontal"
16:     HorizontalAlign="Center"
17:     HeaderStyle-CssClass="tableHeader"
18:     ItemStyle-CssClass="tableItem"
19:     AlternatingItemStyle-CssClass="alternatingItem"
20:   />
21: </form>
22: </body>
23: </html>
```

Altering DataGrid Output

CHAPTER 6

131

6

ALTERING
DATAGRID
OUTPUT

On lines 3–7, you create a cascading style sheet and define three (3) classes: `tableItem` (for the `ItemStyle` object), `tableHeader` (for the `HeaderStyle` object) and `alternatingItem` (for the `AlternatingItemStyle` object). These style sheet definitions are referred to using the `CssClass` property of the style objects on lines 17–19. Figure 6.4 shows the rendered output of Listing 6.4.

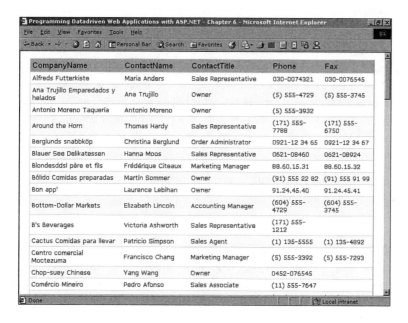

FIGURE 6.4
You can use the CssClass *property to reference cascading style sheet classes that control the output.*

ASP.NET complex server controls, such as the `DataGrid`, `Calendar`, `DataList`, and `Repeater`, provide a rich set of properties that give you full control over their rendered output. Refer to Appendix A for a complete list of all of the properties available. You'd be bored to death if we went through each of them here, but now you understand how complex controls use properties and the style objects.

Paging with the DataGrid

Letting the user page through data from a data store has become an important part of Web site development. An online retailer with 500 products doesn't want to provide one big list of all those products. It's much better to display a short list of products and provide links so the user can scroll through pages of the remaining products. The `DataGrid` lets you add paging functionality with either the built-in paging functions or a custom function.

The paging functionality works with the DataGrid's CurrentPageIndex property, which defines the page of data that's to be displayed, based on the number of records in the data source and the PageSize property of the DataGrid. The PageSize default value is 10 records per page. This property can be overridden with any integer value. The CurrentPageIndex value is set each time a user navigates to another page of data, and the DataGrid is bound to the data source again.

Built-In Paging

The built-in paging functionality is designed to work best with smaller data sources. Each time CurrentPageIndex is set, the data source is retrieved. For instance, a DataTable in a DataSet is retrieved from the database, and the DataGrid is bound to the data source. Before the DataBind() method is called, the CurrentPageIndex property must be set. When the DataBind() method is called, the appropriate range of records from the data source is bound to the DataGrid.

The built-in paging functionality requires an event handler to manage the paging. For the paging to work, the data binding of the DataGrid has to be moved out of the Page_Load() event handler. This is because you need to ensure that the CurrentPageIndex property is set prior to calling the DataBind() method. Every time a page-navigation link is clicked, such as a "Next Page" link or a page number link, a post-back to the page occurs. You want the DataGrid to be bound to the data source on the first page request. On a post-back from a page-navigation link, you want to make sure the CurrentPageIndex property is set prior to any data binding. In Listing 6.5, you create the same Web Form from the previous examples, but you set the DataGrid to use the built-in paging functionality.

LISTING 6.5 Using Built-In Paging with the DataGrid

```
[Code Behind VB - 06.05.vb]

01: Imports System
02: Imports System.Web
03: Imports System.Web.UI
04: Imports System.Web.UI.WebControls
05: Imports System.Data
06: Imports System.Data.SqlClient
07:
08: Public Class Listing0605 : Inherits Page
09:
10:   Protected myDataGrid As DataGrid
11:
12:   Protected Sub Page_Load(Source As Object, E As EventArgs)
13:     If Not Page.IsPostBack Then
```

LISTING 6.5   Continued

```
14:     BindData()
15:    End If
16:   End Sub
17:
18:   Protected Sub BindData()
19:    Dim myDataSet As New DataSet
20:    Dim myDataAdapter As SqlDataAdapter = New SqlDataAdapter("SELECT
➥     CompanyName, ContactName, ContactTitle, Phone, Fax
➥     FROM Customers",
➥     "server=localhost;database=Northwind;uid=sa;pwd=;")
21:    myDataAdapter.Fill(myDataSet, "Customers")
22:
23:    myDataGrid.DataSource = myDataSet.Tables("Customers")
24:    myDataGrid.DataBind()
25:   End Sub
26:
27:   Protected Sub PageIndexChanged_OnClick(Sender As Object,
➥     E As DataGridPageChangedEventArgs)
28:    myDataGrid.CurrentPageIndex = e.NewPageIndex
29:    BindData()
30:   End Sub
31:
32: End Class
```

[Code Behind C# - 06.05.cs]

```
01: using System;
02: using System.Web;
03: using System.Web.UI;
04: using System.Web.UI.WebControls;
05: using System.Data;
06: using System.Data.SqlClient;
07:
08: public class Listing0605 : Page{
09:
10:   protected DataGrid myDataGrid;
11:
12:   protected void Page_Load(Object sender, EventArgs e){
13:    if(!Page.IsPostBack){
14:      BindData();
15:    }
16:   }
17:
18:   protected void BindData(){
19:    DataSet myDataSet = new DataSet();
```

LISTING 6.5   Continued

```
20:    SqlDataAdapter myDataAdapter = new SqlDataAdapter("SELECT CompanyName,
➡      ContactName, ContactTitle, Phone, Fax FROM Customers",
➡      "server=localhost;database=Northwind;uid=sa;pwd=;");
21:    myDataAdapter.Fill(myDataSet, "Customers");
22:
23:    myDataGrid.DataSource = myDataSet.Tables["Customers"];
24:    myDataGrid.DataBind();
25:    }
26:
27:    protected void PageIndexChanged_OnClick(Object sender,
➡      DataGridPageChangedEventArgs e){
28:    myDataGrid.CurrentPageIndex = e.NewPageIndex;
29:    BindData();
30:    }
31:
32: }
```

[Web Form VB]

```
01: <%@ Page Inherits="Listing0605" Src="06.05.vb" %>
```

[Web Form C#]

```
01: <%@ Page Inherits="Listing0605" Src="06.05.cs" %>
```

[Web Form VB & C#]

```
02: <html>
03: <head>
04:   <style ref="stylesheet" type="text/css">
05:     .tableItem {font: x-small Verdana, Arial, sans-serif;}
06:     .tableHeader {font: bold small Arial; color:#663300;
➡      background-color:#CCCC66;}
07:     .alternatingItem {font: x-small Verdana, Arial, sans-serif;
➡      background-color:#FFFFCC;}
08:     A {color:#663300}
09:     A:hover {color:red}
10:   </style>
11: </head>
12: <body>
13: <form runat="server" method="post">
14:   <asp:DataGrid runat="server" id="myDataGrid"
15:   Width="740"
16:   Cellpadding="4"
17:   Cellspacing="0"
18:   Gridlines="Horizontal"
19:   HorizontalAlign="Center"
```

Altering DataGrid Output

CHAPTER 6

135

6

ALTERING
DATAGRID
OUTPUT

LISTING 6.5   Continued

```
20:    HeaderStyle-CssClass="tableHeader"
21:    ItemStyle-CssClass="tableItem"
22:    AlternatingItemStyle-CssClass="alternatingItem"
23:    AllowPaging="True"
24:    OnPageIndexChanged="PageIndexChanged_OnClick"
25:    PageSize="10"
26:    />
27: </form>
28: </body>
29: </html>
```

In Listing 6.5, you use the data access code from Listing 6.1. However, this time it's moved into a method named BindData(). This allows you to call BindData() anytime you need to bind the DataGrid to the data source. On lines 12–16 in the code behind class, you change the Page_Load() event handler to call BindData(), only when the request for the page is not a post-back event. This is done using the Page object's Boolean property, IsPostBack. If IsPostBack is true, the request is a result of a post-back from one of the page-navigation links. Rather than simply binding the data source to the DataGrid, you need to ensure that the CurrentPageIndex property is set.

On lines 27–30 of the code behind class, you create an event handler for the DataGrid's PageIndexChanged event. In this event handler you set the myDataGrid.CurrentPageIndex to the NewPageIndex value passed in the DataGridPageChangedEventArgs. Next you make a call to the BindData() method, and the DataGrid is bound. The NewPageIndex is the page index for the page to be rendered, depending on the link that was clicked and the PageSize property of the DataGrid. When BindData() is called, the data is retrieved from the database again, and the DataGrid is bound to the appropriate records based on the values of the aforementioned properties.

The properties for handling the DataGrid's paging values are set on lines 23–25 of the Web Form. When the AllowPaging property is set to true, it turns on the built-in paging functionality. The default value is false. The OnPageIndexChanged property specifies the event handler to refer to when a page-navigation link is clicked. Lastly, the PageSize property can be set to any integer, and the default value is 10. This defines how many records to display per page. Figure 6.5 shows the rendered page from Listing 6.5.

In Figure 6.5, you can see the page-navigation links in the lower-left corner of the table. Less-than and greater-than symbols are used to navigate to the previous and next pages in the data source. The DataGrid exposes a number of properties for altering the display of the page-navigation links.

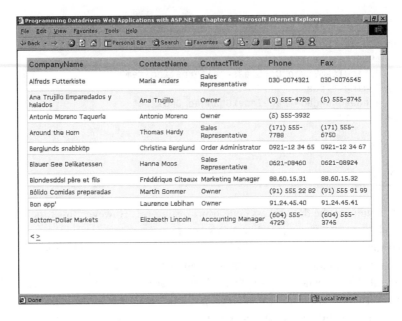

FIGURE 6.5

The built-in paging functionality of the DataGrid *renders pages of data in blocks according to the* PageSize *property.*

As you learned earlier, there's a PagerStyle style object for controlling the appearance of the page-navigation links. All of the same properties you used with the other style objects are available with the PagerStyle object. Additionally, there are a few extra properties that only apply to the PagerStyle object:

- Mode—Determines the page-navigation link type. Possible values are NextPrev and NumericPages.

- NextPageText—The text to display for the link to navigate to the next page. Only available when the Mode property is NextPrev.

- PageButtonCount—The number of page links to display when the Mode property is NumericPages. If more pages exist beyond the number displayed, an ellipsis will be rendered after the last link. The default value is 10.

- Position—Determines the position of the page-navigation links. Possible values are Top, Bottom, TopAndBottom.

- PrevPageText—The text to display for the link to navigate to the previous page. Only available when the Mode property is NextPrev.

- Visible—Boolean property to show or hide the page-navigation links. The default is true.

In Listing 6.6, you use the same Web Form from the preceding example. By adding a couple of property values, you easily can alter the output of the page-navigation links.

LISTING 6.6   Changing the Appearance of the Page-Navigation Links

```
[Web Form VB]

01: <%@ Page Inherits="Listing0605" Src="06.05.vb" %>

[Web Form C#]

01: <%@ Page Inherits="Listing0605" Src="06.05.cs" %>

[Web Form VB & C#]

02: <html>
03: <head>
04:   <style ref="stylesheet" type="text/css">
05:     .tableItem {font: x-small Verdana, Arial, sans-serif;}
06:     .tableHeader {font: bold small Arial; color:#663300;
➡    background-color:#CCCC66;}
07:     .alternatingItem {font: x-small Verdana, Arial, sans-serif;
➡    background-color:#FFFFCC;}
08:     A {color:#663300}
09:     A:hover {color:red}
10:     .pageLinks {font: bold x-small Verdana, Arial, sans-serif;}
11:   </style>
12: </head>
13: <body>
14: <form runat="server" method="post">
15:   <asp:DataGrid runat="server" id="myDataGrid"
16:     Width="740"
17:     Cellpadding="4"
18:     Cellspacing="0"
19:     Gridlines="Horizontal"
20:     HorizontalAlign="Center"
21:     HeaderStyle-CssClass="tableHeader"
22:     ItemStyle-CssClass="tableItem"
23:     AlternatingItemStyle-CssClass="alternatingItem"
24:     AllowPaging="True"
25:     OnPageIndexChanged="PageIndexChanged_OnClick"
26:     PageSize="10"
27:     PagerStyle-CssClass="pageLinks"
28:     PagerStyle-Mode="NextPrev"
29:     PagerStyle-NextPageText="Next"
30:     PagerStyle-PrevPageText="Previous"
31:     PagerStyle-HorizontalAlign="Center"
32:     PagerStyle-Position="TopAndBottom"
33:   />
34: </form>
35: </body>
36: </html>
```

In Listing 6.6, you add six PagerStyle properties to the data grid. On line 27, you specify the cascading style sheet class to use for the page-navigation links. (The style sheet class was added on line 10.) On line 28, you specify that the page-navigation links should be the next and previous links (this is also the default value). On lines 29 and 30, you specify the text to be displayed for the next and previous links. On line 31, you specify that the page-navigation links should be centered. Lastly, on line 32, you specify that the page-navigation links should be rendered at both the top and bottom of the DataGrid output. Figure 6.6 shows the rendered output from Listing 6.6.

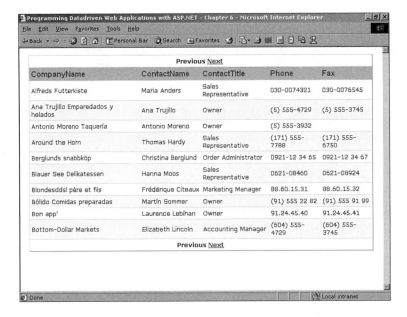

FIGURE 6.6
Next and previous links can be created by specifying the NextPageText *and* PrevPageText *properties of the DataGrid.*

In Listing 6.7, you use the same Web Form, but set the DataGrid to use the NumericPages mode of page navigation.

LISTING 6.7   Using the NumericPages Mode with the DataGrid

```
[VB & C#]

15:   <asp:DataGrid runat="server" id="myDataGrid"
16:     Width="740"
17:     Cellpadding="4"
18:     Cellspacing="0"
19:     Gridlines="Horizontal"
```

6

LISTING 6.7 Continued

```
20:    HorizontalAlign="Center"
21:    HeaderStyle-CssClass="tableHeader"
22:    ItemStyle-CssClass="tableItem"
23:    AlternatingItemStyle-CssClass="alternatingItem"
24:    AllowPaging="True"
25:    OnPageIndexChanged="PageIndexChanged_OnClick"
26:    PageSize="10"
27:    PagerStyle-CssClass="pageLinks"
28:    PagerStyle-Mode="NumericPages"
29:    PagerStyle-HorizontalAlign="Right"
30:    PagerStyle-Position="TopAndBottom"
31:    />
```

In Listing 6.7 you do not have to set as many `PagerStyle` properties, since there are no next and previous links. On line 28 you simply specify that the `DataGrid` will use the `NumericPages` style of page-navigation links. Additionally, you could specify the `PageButtonCount` but the default value of ten (10) is reasonable. Figure 6.7 shows the rendered output of Listing 6.7.

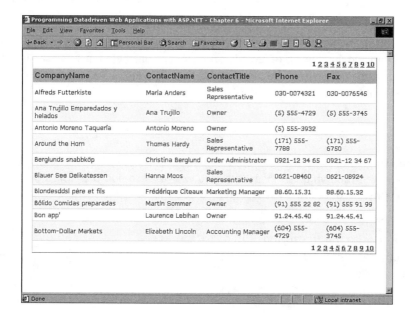

FIGURE 6.7

You easily can use page numbers as the page-navigation links by specifying the `PagerStyle-Mode="NumericPages"`.

Custom Paging

The best part of the built-in paging is that it's easy to use and there's very little code you have to write to implement it. The downside is that on each page request, you retrieve all the data from the data store, even if it is not being rendered on the current DataGrid page. Imagine you're querying a table with thousands of rows of data, and thousands of users are requesting the page at the same time. This type of load on a Web server and a database server could cause sub-optimal performance, to say the least. In this kind of scenario, the best alternative is to query only the records of data needed for the page being viewed, and to handle the paging yourself.

The DataGrid provides a custom-paging alternative if the built-in paging doesn't suit your needs. With custom paging, the CurrentPageIndex isn't used. Rather, the DataGrid binds to rows 0-*n*, *n* being the number of the PageSize property of the DataGrid. This allows you to query only the records required for the current page request and handle the paging manually.

To make the custom paging work, you must set the AllowCustomPaging property of the DataGrid to true. This tells the DataGrid to enable the PageSize property, but not to handle the paging itself. Basically the DataGrid is displaying records as if paging were not enabled, except that a few properties, such as PageSize, *are* enabled. You then must return data from the data source according to your paging scheme.

Listing 6.8 shows a SQL Server stored procedure that takes two input parameters (the page number to return and the number of records per page) and one output parameter (the total number of records in the table). Like the previous examples, this stored procedure works against the Customers table in the Northwind database.

WARNING

The following code sample is restricted to a SQL Server 7.0+ database. In order for the code in the following listings to run, you will need to add the stored procedure to the Northwind database in SQL Server. To add the stored procedure:

1. Open the SQL Server Enterprise Manager.
2. Navigate to the Northwind Stored Procedures node.
3. Right click on the Northwind Stored Procedures node, and choose New Stored Procedure.
4. Enter the code in Listing 6.8 and click OK.

Altering DataGrid Output

CHAPTER 6

141

6

ALTERING
DATAGRID
OUTPUT

LISTING 6.8 SQL Server Stored Procedure to Retrieve One Page of Data

```
01: CREATE PROCEDURE [spGet_Customers_By_Page]
02:  @CurrentPage int,
03:  @PageSize int,
04:  @TotalRecs int output
05: AS
06:   --Create a temp table
07:   --Add and ID column to count the records
08:   CREATE TABLE #TempTable
09:   (
10:    ID int IDENTITY PRIMARY KEY,
11:    CompanyName nvarchar(40),
12:    ContactName nvarchar (30),
13:    ContactTitle nvarchar (30),
14:    Phone nvarchar (24),
15:    Fax nvarchar (24)
16:   )
17:   --Fill the temp table with the Customers data
18:   INSERT INTO #TempTable
19:     (CompanyName, ContactName, ContactTitle, Phone, Fax)
20:   SELECT CompanyName, ContactName, ContactTitle, Phone, Fax
21:   FROM Customers
22:   --Create variable to identify the first and
23:   --last record that should be selected
24:   DECLARE @FirstRec int, @LastRec int
25:   SELECT @FirstRec = (@CurrentPage - 1) * @PageSize
26:   SELECT @LastRec = (@CurrentPage * @PageSize + 1)
27:   --Select one page of data based on the record numbers above
28:   SELECT CompanyName, ContactName, ContactTitle, Phone, Fax
29:   FROM #TempTable
30:   WHERE ID > @FirstRec AND ID < @LastRec
31:   --Return the total number of records available as an output parameter
32:   SELECT @TotalRecs = COUNT(*) FROM Customers
```

In Listing 6.8, you create a SQL stored procedure that returns records for one page of data based on the current page requested and the number of records in the page. On lines 2 and 3, you specify the input parameters, @CurrentPage and @PageSize. @CurrentPage specifies the page number being requested, and @PageSize is the PageSize property of the DataGrid. On line 4, you create an output parameter to return the number of records in the table.

On lines 8–16, you create a temporary table to hold the Customers table data that you're querying. Since the Customers table doesn't have sequential numbering in an Identity column, you add an Identity column in the temporary table. On lines 18–21, you select all of the rows from the Customers table (only the columns you need) and insert them into the temporary table.

Using the @CurrentPage and @PageSize variables, you identify the first and last record to select. On lines 28–30, you select one page of data to return to the Web Form. Finally, on line 32, you get the total number of records in the Customers table and return that value as the @TotalRecs parameter.

In Listing 6.9, you build a code behind class and a Web Form that use the custom paging functionality of the DataGrid. You make a call to the stored procedure in Listing 6.8, passing in the page number being requested and the PageSize property of the DataGrid.

LISTING 6.9   Using Custom Paging with the DataGrid

```
[Code Behind VB - 06.09.vb]
01: Imports System
02: Imports System.Web
03: Imports System.Web.UI
04: Imports System.Web.UI.WebControls
05: Imports System.Data
06: Imports System.Data.SqlClient
07:
08: Public Class Listing0609 : Inherits Page
09:
10:    Protected myDataGrid As DataGrid
11:    Protected CurrentPage As Label
12:    Protected TotalPages As Label
13:    Protected NextPage As LinkButton
14:    Protected PreviousPage As LinkButton
15:    Protected FirstPage As LinkButton
16:    Protected LastPage As LinkButton
17:    Protected CurrentPageNumber As Integer
18:
19:    Sub Page_Load(Sender As Object, E As EventArgs)
20:     If Not Page.IsPostBack Then
21:       CurrentPageNumber = 1
22:       BindData()
23:     End If
24:    End Sub
25:
26:    Sub BindData()
27:     Dim myConnection As SqlConnection = new SqlConnection(
➥       "server=localhost;database=Northwind;uid=sa;pwd=;")
28:     Dim myCommand As SqlCommand = new
➥       SqlCommand("spGet_Customers_By_Page", myConnection)
29:     Dim myReader As SqlDataReader = Nothing
30:
31:     With myCommand
```

Altering DataGrid Output

CHAPTER 6

143

6

**ALTERING
DATAGRID
OUTPUT**

LISTING 6.9   Continued

```
32:      .CommandType = CommandType.StoredProcedure
33:      .Parameters.Add(new SqlParameter("@CurrentPage", SqlDbType.Int))
34:      .Parameters("@CurrentPage").Value = CurrentPageNumber
35:      .Parameters.Add(new SqlParameter("@PageSize", SqlDbType.Int))
36:      .Parameters("@PageSize").Value = myDataGrid.PageSize
37:      .Parameters.Add(new SqlParameter("@TotalRecs", SqlDbType.Int))
38:      .Parameters("@TotalRecs").Direction = ParameterDirection.Output
39:    End With
40:
41:    Try
42:     myConnection.Open()
43:     myReader = myCommand.ExecuteReader()
44:     myDataGrid.DataSource = myReader
45:     myDataGrid.DataBind()
46:
47:    Finally
48:     myConnection.Close()
49:    End Try
50:
51:    CurrentPage.Text = CurrentPageNumber.ToString()
52:
53:    If Not Page.IsPostBack Then
54:     Dim Total_Records As Integer =
➡      CInt(myCommand.Parameters("@TotalRecs").Value)
55:     Dim Total_Pages As Decimal =
➡      Decimal.Parse(Total_Records.ToString())/myDataGrid.PageSize
56:     TotalPages.Text = (System.Math.Ceiling(
➡      Double.Parse(Total_Pages.ToString())))).ToString()
57:    End If
58:
59:    Select Case CurrentPageNumber
60:     Case 1
61:      PreviousPage.Enabled = False
62:      NextPage.Enabled = True
63:     Case Int32.Parse(TotalPages.Text)
64:      NextPage.Enabled = False
65:      PreviousPage.Enabled = True
66:     Case Else
67:      PreviousPage.Enabled = True
68:      NextPage.Enabled = True
69:    End Select
70:
71:    End Sub
72:
```

LISTING 6.9   Continued

```
73:  Sub NavigationLink_OnClick(Sender As Object, E As CommandEventArgs)
74:    Select Case e.CommandName
75:     Case "First"
76:      CurrentPageNumber = 1
77:
78:     Case "Last"
79:      CurrentPageNumber = Int32.Parse(TotalPages.Text)
80:
81:     Case "Next"
82:      CurrentPageNumber = Int32.Parse(CurrentPage.Text) +1
83:
84:     Case "Prev"
85:      CurrentPageNumber = Int32.Parse(CurrentPage.Text) -1
86:
87:     End Select
88:
89:     BindData()
90:
91:   End Sub
92:
93: End Class
```

[Code Behind C# - 06.09.cs]

```
01: using System;
02: using System.Web;
03: using System.Web.UI;
04: using System.Web.UI.WebControls;
05: using System.Data;
06: using System.Data.SqlClient;
07:
08: public class Listing0609 : Page{
09:
10:    protected DataGrid myDataGrid;
11:    protected Label CurrentPage;
12:    protected Label TotalPages;
13:    protected LinkButton NextPage;
14:    protected LinkButton PreviousPage;
15:    protected LinkButton FirstPage;
16:    protected LinkButton LastPage;
17:    protected int CurrentPageNumber;
18:
19:    protected void Page_Load(Object sender, EventArgs e){
20:     if (!Page.IsPostBack){
21:      CurrentPageNumber = 1;
```

Altering DataGrid Output

CHAPTER 6

145

6

ALTERING
DATAGRID
OUTPUT

LISTING 6.9   Continued

```
x22:      BindData();
23:    }
24:  }
25:
26:  protected void BindData(){
27:   SqlConnection myConnection = new SqlConnection(
➡      "server=localhost;database=Northwind;uid=sa;pwd=;");
28:   SqlCommand myCommand = new
➡     SqlCommand("spGet_Customers_By_Page", myConnection);
29:   SqlDataReader myReader = null;
30:
31:
32:    myCommand.CommandType = CommandType.StoredProcedure;
33:    myCommand.Parameters.Add(new SqlParameter("@CurrentPage",
➡     SqlDbType.Int));
34:    myCommand.Parameters["@CurrentPage"].Value = CurrentPageNumber;
35:    myCommand.Parameters.Add(new SqlParameter("@PageSize",
➡     SqlDbType.Int));
36:    myCommand.Parameters["@PageSize"].Value = myDataGrid.PageSize;
37:    myCommand.Parameters.Add(new SqlParameter("@TotalRecs",
➡     SqlDbType.Int));
38:    myCommand.Parameters["@TotalRecs"].Direction =
➡     ParameterDirection.Output;
39:
40:
41:    try{
42:     myConnection.Open();
43:     myReader = myCommand.ExecuteReader();
44:     myDataGrid.DataSource = myReader;
45:     myDataGrid.DataBind();
46:    }
47:    finally{
48:     myConnection.Close();
49:    }
50:
51:    CurrentPage.Text = CurrentPageNumber.ToString();
52:
53:    if (!Page.IsPostBack){
54:     int Total_Records = ((int) myCommand.Parameters["@TotalRecs"].Value);
55:     decimal Total_Pages = Decimal.Parse(
➡     Total_Records.ToString())/myDataGrid.PageSize;
56:     TotalPages.Text = (System.Math.Ceiling(Double.Parse(
➡     Total_Pages.ToString())))).ToString();
57:    }
58:
```

LISTING 6.9 Continued

```
59:    if(CurrentPageNumber == 1){
60:     PreviousPage.Enabled = false;
61:     NextPage.Enabled=true;
62:    }else{
63:     if(CurrentPageNumber == Int32.Parse(TotalPages.Text)){
64:      NextPage.Enabled=false;
65:      PreviousPage.Enabled=true;
66:     }else{
67:      PreviousPage.Enabled=true;
68:      NextPage.Enabled=true;
69:     }
70:    }
71:   }
72:
73:   protected void NavigationLink_OnClick(Object sender, CommandEventArgs e){
74:    switch (e.CommandName){
75:     case "First":
76:      CurrentPageNumber = 1;
77:      break;
78:     case "Last":
79:      CurrentPageNumber = Int32.Parse(TotalPages.Text);
80:      break;
81:     case "Next":
82:      CurrentPageNumber = Int32.Parse(CurrentPage.Text) +1;
83:      break;
84:     case "Prev":
85:      CurrentPageNumber = Int32.Parse(CurrentPage.Text) -1;
86:      break;
87:     }
88:
89:     BindData();
90:
91:   }
92:
93: }
```

[Web Form VB]

```
<%@ Page Inherits="Listing0609" Src="06.09.vb" %>
```

[Web Form VB]

```
<%@ Page Inherits="Listing0609" Src="06.09.cs" %>
```

[Web Form VB & C#]

```
01: <html>
02: <head>
```

Altering DataGrid Output

CHAPTER 6

147

6

ALTERING
DATAGRID
OUTPUT

LISTING 6.9   Continued

```
03:   <style ref="stylesheet" type="text/css">
04:     .tableItem {font: x-small Verdana, Arial, sans-serif;}
05:     .tableHeader {font: bold small Arial; color:#663300;
➥       background-color:#CCCC66;}
06:     .alternatingItem {font: x-small Verdana, Arial, sans-serif;
➥       background-color:#FFFFCC;}
07:     A {color:#663300}
08:     A:hover {color:red}
09:     .pageLinks {font: bold x-small Verdana, Arial, sans-serif;}
10:   </style>
11:   </head>
12:   <body>
13:   <form runat="server" method="post">
14:     <asp:DataGrid runat="server" id="myDataGrid"
15:       Width="740"
16:       Cellpadding="4"
17:       Cellspacing="0"
18:       Gridlines="Horizontal"
19:       HorizontalAlign="Center"
20:       HeaderStyle-CssClass="tableHeader"
21:       ItemStyle-CssClass="tableItem"
22:       AlternatingItemStyle-CssClass="alternatingItem"
23:       AllowPaging="True"
24:       AllowCustomPaging="True"
25:       PageSize="10"
26:       PagerStyle-Visible="False"
27:     />
28:     <center>
29:     <p class="pageLinks">
30:     <b>Page
31:     <asp:Label id="CurrentPage" CssClass="pageLinks" runat="server" />
32:     of
33:     <asp:Label id="TotalPages" CssClass="pageLinks" runat="server" />
34:     </p>
35:     <asp:LinkButton runat="server" CssClass="pageLinks"
36:       id="FirstPage" Text="[First Page]"
37:       OnCommand="NavigationLink_OnClick" CommandName="First" />
38:     <asp:LinkButton runat="server" CssClass="pageLinks"
39:       id="PreviousPage" Text="[Previous Page]"
40:       OnCommand="NavigationLink_OnClick" CommandName="Prev" />
41:     <asp:LinkButton runat="server" CssClass="pageLinks"
42:       id="NextPage" Text="[Next Page]"
43:       OnCommand="NavigationLink_OnClick" CommandName="Next" />
44:     <asp:LinkButton runat="server" CssClass="pageLinks"
45:       id="LastPage" Text="[Last Page]"
46:       OnCommand="NavigationLink_OnClick" CommandName="Last" />
```

LISTING 6.9   Continued

```
47:  </center>
48:  </form>
49:  </body>
50:  </html>
```

In Listing 6.9, you create a Web Form that calls to the stored procedure in Listing 6.8. The stored procedure returns one page of records based on the PageSize property of the DataGrid and the page number being requested.

On line 11 of the code behind class, you create a page-level variable named CurrentPage. This variable holds the page number of the page of data being requested. In the Page_Load() event handler, you specify the CurrentPage value as 1 only when the request is *not* a post-back; that is, when the request is the first visit to the page. Any clicks on the page-navigation links will trigger a post-back, and the CurrentPage value will be set in the BindData() method.

Lines 26–71 are the BindData() method. Here you create a SqlCommand and a SqlDataReader to retrieve the data from the database. The SqlCommand executes the stored procedure, which requires setting the SqlCommand.CommandType property to CommandType.StoredProcedure. You create and set the input parameters on lines 32–36. On lines 41–46, in a Try/Finally block, you open the SqlConnection and use the SqlCommand.ExecuteReader() method to execute the stored procedure and create a SqlDataReader stream of data. You set the DataGrid.DataSource property to the SqlDataReader, and call the DataGrid.DataBind() method to bind the data in the SqlDataReader to the DataGrid. You now have one page of data displayed in the DataGrid.

Next, you add values for page navigation. Just below the DataGrid but above the page-navigation links, you'll display a page counter indicating the page number the user is viewing and the total number of pages. On line 51, you set the Text property of an ASP.NET Label control to the value of CurrentPage. Next, you set the TotalPages.Text property (also a Label control), but only on the first page request. For this example, you're safe in assuming that the total number of records won't change as you navigate through the pages, so it only needs to be set on the first request. ViewState will maintain the TotalPages.Text value on subsequent page requests.

In the stored procedure, you return the total number of records (@TotalRecs), not the total number of pages. Although you could add the math into the stored procedure and return the total number of pages, you might want the versatility of having the total number of records available. The code in Listing 6.9 doesn't take advantage of the @TotalRecs value, in terms of displaying it to the user, but it does use the value to calculate the total number of pages, which is displayed to the user.

Altering DataGrid Output

CHAPTER 6

149

6

ALTERING
DATAGRID
OUTPUT

Using the `System.Math` class, you make a call to the `Ceiling()` method. This method takes a `Double` data type as its input parameter and returns the same value rounded up to the nearest whole number equal to or greater than the value passed in. For example, calling `Ceiling(1.2)` would return the value 2. The value returned is also a `Double` data type. Since it's likely that the total number of records won't be divisible evenly by the `DataGrid.PageSize` property, you can use the `Ceiling()` method to round it up to the nearest whole number. For example, say there are 91 records in the `Customers` table and the `PageSize` property is 10. The result of dividing the number of records by the `PageSize` value is 9.1. There are nine full pages and one extra record. Really, what you want is 10 pages with only one record on the last page. Using `Ceiling()`, 9.1 gets rounded to 10, which is the result you want.

Before exiting the `BindData()` method, you check the `CurrentPage` number and enable or disable the navigation links as appropriate. You're using ASP.NET `LinkButtons` for the navigation control, which allows you to set the `Enabled` property. A value of `True` (the default) will make the link perform as expected and trigger a post-back event. A value of `False` will render the text of the link, but it won't provide the HTML to trigger a post-back.

Before you add all of the server controls to the Web Form, you need to create an event handler for the `LinkButton` click event. On line 73, you create the `NavigationLink_OnClick()` event handler, which will work for all four `LinkButtons`. With each `LinkButton`, you'll add a `CommandName` property (First, Last, Next, Prev). The event handler evaluates the `CommandName` (`e.CommandName`) and sets the `CurrentPage` value accordingly before calling the `BindData()` method.

Once the event handler for the navigation controls is in place, you finish the Web Form by adding the server controls. With the `DataGrid`, you set `AllowPaging` to `True` to enable the `PageSize` property, and you set `AllowCustomPaging` to `True` to disable the built-in paging functionality. On line 26 of the Web Form, you specify the `PageSize` property (10 in this example), and on line 27, you set the `PagerStyle-Visible` property to `False` to hide the standard `DataGrid` navigation.

On lines 32 and 34, you add two `Label` controls for the `CurrentPage` value and the `TotalPages` value set previously. Next you add four `LinkButtons`: one for the first page, one for the previous page, one for the next page, and one for the last page. Each `LinkButton` control specifies the `NavigationLink_OnClick()` event handler in the `OnCommand` property, specifying that the `NavigationLink_OnClick()` event handler should be called when the page posts back. The `CommandName` properties are set according to the `Select Case` evaluator (`switch` in C#) in the event handler.

The Web Form built in Listing 6.9 will render a page with a table of 10 records and four navigation links. Figure 6.8 shows the rendered page from Listing 6.9.

FIGURE 6.8

The custom paging options available with the DataGrid *allow you to build any type of paging that's appropriate for your application.*

Sorting Columns

The DataGrid offers both built-in and custom paging solutions. It also offers simple solutions for enabling column sorting in a rendered table. Using the built-in sorting features of the DataGrid, you easily can allow your Web site visitors to click on column headings to re-sort the DataGrid.

The sorting functionality requires you to handle the sorting of the data, but it handles the tracking of which column to sort by. Much like paging, sorting is enabled by setting the DataGrid.AllowSorting property to True. This tells the DataGrid that you want the column headings to be links that the user can click on to re-sort the DataGrid.

Once AllowSorting is set to True, you need to specify the OnSortCommand event handler. In the event handler, you'll capture the name of the column to sort by and re-create the data source sorted as necessary. Since you must re-create the data source on each post-back to the page, you can simply alter the parameters of the SQL statement that retrieves the data. Listing 6.10 shows an ASP.NET code behind and Web Form with sorting implemented.

LISTING 6.10   Column Sorting with the `DataGrid`

6

[VB]

```vb
01: Imports System
02: Imports System.Web
03: Imports System.Web.UI
04: Imports System.Web.UI.WebControls
05: Imports System.Data
06: Imports System.Data.SqlClient
07:
08: Public Class Listing0610 : Inherits Page
09:
10:   Protected myDataGrid As DataGrid
11:
12:   Protected SqlStmt As String = "SELECT CompanyName, ContactName,
➥     ContactTitle, Phone, Fax FROM Customers"
13:
14:   Sub Page_Load(Source As Object, E As EventArgs)
15:    If Not Page.IsPostBack Then
16:     BindData()
17:    End If
18:   End Sub
19:
20:   Sub BindData()
21:    Dim myConnection As SqlConnection = New SqlConnection(
➥     "server=localhost;database=Northwind;uid=sa;pwd=;")
22:    Dim myCommand As SqlCommand = New SqlCommand(SqlStmt, myConnection)
23:    Dim myReader As SqlDataReader = Nothing
24:
25:    Try
26:     myConnection.Open()
27:     myReader = myCommand.ExecuteReader()
28:     myDataGrid.DataSource = myReader
29:     myDataGrid.DataBind()
30:
31:    Finally
32:     myConnection.Close()
33:    End Try
34:
35:   End Sub
36:
37:   Sub SortCommand_OnClick(Source As Object,
➥     E As DataGridSortCommandEventArgs)
38:    SqlStmt = SqlStmt & " ORDER BY " & E.SortExpression
39:    BindData()
40:   End Sub
```

LISTING 6.10   Continued

```
41:
42: End Class
```

[Code Behind C# - 06.10.cs]

```
01: using System;
02: using System.Web;
03: using System.Web.UI;
04: using System.Web.UI.WebControls;
05: using System.Data;
06: using System.Data.SqlClient;
07:
08: public class Listing0610 : Page{
09:
10:    protected DataGrid myDataGrid;
11:
12:    protected string SqlStmt = "SELECT CompanyName, ContactName,
➥      ContactTitle, Phone, Fax FROM Customers";
13:
14:    protected void Page_Load(Object sender, EventArgs e){
15:    if (!Page.IsPostBack){
16:       BindData();
17:    }
18:  }
19:
20:    protected void BindData(){
21:     SqlConnection myConnection = new SqlConnection(
➥      "server=localhost;database=Northwind;uid=sa;pwd=;");
22:     SqlCommand myCommand = new SqlCommand(SqlStmt, myConnection);
23:     SqlDataReader myReader = null;
24:
25:     try{
26:      myConnection.Open();
27:      myReader = myCommand.ExecuteReader();
28:      myDataGrid.DataSource = myReader;
29:      myDataGrid.DataBind();
30:     }
31:     finally{
32:      myConnection.Close();
33:     }
34:
35:  }
36:
```

LISTING 6.10   Continued

```
37:    protected void SortCommand_OnClick(Object sender,
➡        DataGridSortCommandEventArgs e){
38:    SqlStmt = SqlStmt + " ORDER BY " + e.SortExpression;
39:    BindData();
40:    }
41:
42: }
```

[Web Form VB]

```
01: <%@ Page Inherits="Listing0610" Src="06.10.vb" %>
```

[Web Form C#]

```
01: <%@ Page Inherits="Listing0610" Src="06.10.cs" %>
```

[Web Form VB & C#]

```
02: <html>
03: <head>
04:  <style ref="stylesheet" type="text/css">
05:    .tableItem {font: x-small Verdana, Arial, sans-serif;}
06:    .tableHeader {font: bold small Arial; color:#663300;
➡        background-color:#CCCC66;}
07:    .alternatingItem {font: x-small Verdana, Arial, sans-serif;
➡        background-color:#FFFFCC;}
08:    A {color:#663300}
09:    A:hover {color:red}
10:    .pageLinks {font: bold x-small Verdana, Arial, sans-serif;}
11:  </style>
12: </head>
13: <body>
14: <form runat="server" method="post">
15:  <asp:DataGrid runat="server" id="myDataGrid"
16:    Width="740"
17:    Cellpadding="4"
18:    Cellspacing="0"
19:    Gridlines="Horizontal"
20:    HorizontalAlign="Center"
21:    HeaderStyle-CssClass="tableHeader"
22:    ItemStyle-CssClass="tableItem"
23:    AlternatingItemStyle-CssClass="alternatingItem"
24:    AllowSorting="True"
25:    OnSortCommand="SortCommand_OnClick"
26:  />
```

LISTING 6.10 Continued

```
27: </form>
28: </body>
29: </html>
```

In Listing 6.10, you implement column sorting with the DataGrid. This requires a few code modifications from the previous examples. On line 12 of the code behind class, you create a page-level variable for the SQL statement (SqlStmt). This allows you to set the variable value in any method in the Web Form code behind. That way you can set an initial SQL statement on the first request of the page and modify it to sort by a column when its column heading is clicked.

On lines 37–40, you create the SortCommand_OnClick() event handler. In this event handler, you add an ORDER BY clause to the SQL statement. The parameter to order the data by is set using the SortExpression property of the DataGridSortCommandEvenArgs (e.SortExpression). Each column in a DataGrid can specify a SortExpression, which is used to identify how to sort the results when a sort link is clicked. Since none of the columns have a specified SortExpression property, it defaults to the column name. Once you've modified the SQL statement with an ORDER BY clause, you call to the BindData() method to retrieve the data from the database and bind it to the DataGrid. The new page is rendered as a table sorted by the column that was clicked on. Figure 6.9 shows the rendered page from Listing 6.10.

One of the truly great things about the DataGrid's advanced functionality is that none of the features, such as paging and sorting, are mutually exclusive. The advance features of the DataGrid can be used together. To implement both paging and sorting on a DataGrid, you need to make sure that the event handlers for both features are in place and the correct properties of the DataGrid are set. The only difference from what you've done so far is that the SQL statement needs to be maintained from one page request to the next. If you sort a DataGrid by a column and then navigate to the next page of data, you want to ensure that the sorting remains consistent.

To implement both paging and sorting, you'll write code similar to the examples in this section and the "Paging with the DataGrid" section earlier in this chapter. You'll need to add a hidden field for the SQL statement ORDER BY clause. A Label control with the Visible property set to False is ideal for this. Using a Label control ensures the value of the control (its state) is maintained by ViewState from one page request to the next. Additionally, when a Label control's Visible property is set to False, no HTML for that control is rendered to the client. This means your SQL statement ORDER BY clause is completely hidden from the client. Listing 6.11 shows a Web Form that implements both paging and sorting.

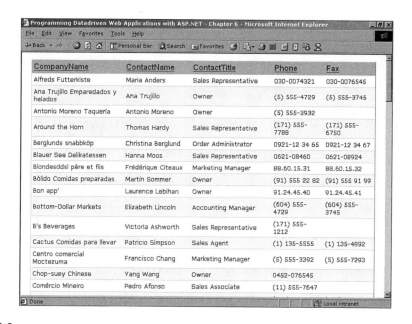

FIGURE 6.9

The DataGrid *implements column sorting by capturing the* SortExpression *and binding to the data source again.*

LISTING 6.11   Using Paging and Sorting on a DataGrid

[VB]

```
01: Imports System
02: Imports System.Web
03: Imports System.Web.UI
04: Imports System.Web.UI.WebControls
05: Imports System.Data
06: Imports System.Data.SqlClient
07:
08: Public Class Listing0611 : Inherits Page
09:
10:   Protected myDataGrid As DataGrid
11:   Protected SqlStatement As Label
12:
13:   Protected SqlStmt As String = "SELECT CompanyName, ContactName,
➥     ContactTitle, Phone, Fax FROM Customers"
14:
15:   Sub Page_Load(Source As Object, E As EventArgs)
16:     If Not Page.IsPostBack Then
17:       BindData()
18:     End If
```

LISTING 6.11   Continued

```
19:   End Sub
20:
21:   Sub BindData()
22:    SqlStmt = SqlStmt + SqlStatement.Text
23:    Dim myDataSet As DataSet = new DataSet()
24:    Dim myDataAdapter As SqlDataAdapter = new SqlDataAdapter(SqlStmt,
➡       "server=localhost;database=Northwind;uid=sa;pwd=;")
25:    myDataAdapter.Fill(myDataSet, "Customers")
26:
27:    myDataGrid.DataSource = myDataSet.Tables("Customers")
28:    myDataGrid.DataBind()
29:   End Sub
30:
31:   Sub SortCommand_OnClick(Source As Object,
➡       E As DataGridSortCommandEventArgs)
32:    SqlStatement.Text = " ORDER BY " + e.SortExpression
33:    BindData()
34:   End Sub
35:
36:   Sub PageIndexChanged_OnClick(Source As Object,
➡       E As DataGridPageChangedEventArgs)
37:    myDataGrid.CurrentPageIndex = e.NewPageIndex
38:    BindData()
39:   End Sub
40:
41: End Class

[Code Behind C# - 06.11.cs]

01: using System;
02: using System.Web;
03: using System.Web.UI;
04: using System.Web.UI.WebControls;
05: using System.Data;
06: using System.Data.SqlClient;
07:
08: public class Listing0611 : Page{
09:
10:   protected DataGrid myDataGrid;
11:   protected Label SqlStatement;
12:
13:   protected string SqlStmt = "SELECT CompanyName, ContactName,
➡       ContactTitle, Phone, Fax FROM Customers";
14:
15:   protected void Page_Load(Object sender, EventArgs e){
```

Altering DataGrid Output

CHAPTER 6

157

6

**ALTERING
DATAGRID
OUTPUT**

LISTING 6.11   Continued

```
16:    if (!Page.IsPostBack){
17:      BindData();
18:    }
19:  }
20:
21:  protected void BindData(){
22:    SqlStmt = SqlStmt + SqlStatement.Text;
23:    DataSet myDataSet = new DataSet();
24:    SqlDataAdapter myDataAdapter = new SqlDataAdapter(SqlStmt,
       "server=localhost;database=Northwind;uid=sa;pwd=;");
25:    myDataAdapter.Fill(myDataSet, "Customers");
26:
27:    myDataGrid.DataSource = myDataSet.Tables["Customers"];
28:    myDataGrid.DataBind();
29:  }
30:
31:  protected void SortCommand_OnClick(Object sender,
       DataGridSortCommandEventArgs e){
32:    SqlStatement.Text = " ORDER BY " + e.SortExpression;
33:    BindData();
34:  }
35:
36:  protected void PageIndexChanged_OnClick(Object sender,
       DataGridPageChangedEventArgs e){
37:    myDataGrid.CurrentPageIndex = e.NewPageIndex;
38:    BindData();
39:  }
40:
41: }
```

```
[Web Form VB]

01: <%@ Page Inherits="Listing0611" Src="06.11.vb" %>

[Web Form VB]

01: <%@ Page Inherits="Listing0611" Src="06.11.cs" %>

[Web Form VB & C#]

02: <html>
03: <head>
04:   <style ref="stylesheet" type="text/css">
05:     .tableItem {font: x-small Verdana, Arial, sans-serif;}
06:     .tableHeader {font: bold small Arial; color:#663300;
       background-color:#CCCC66;}
```

LISTING 6.11   Continued

```
07:    .alternatingItem {font: x-small Verdana, Arial, sans-serif;
➥      background-color:#FFFFCC;}
08:    A {color:#663300}
09:    A:hover {color:red}
10:    .pageLinks {font: bold x-small Verdana, Arial, sans-serif;}
11:    </style>
12:  </head>
13:  <body>
14:  <form runat="server" method="post">
15:    <asp:Label id="SqlStatement" runat="server" Visible="False" />
16:    <asp:DataGrid runat="server" id="myDataGrid"
17:      Width="740"
18:      Cellpadding="4"
19:      Cellspacing="0"
20:      Gridlines="Horizontal"
21:      HorizontalAlign="Center"
22:      HeaderStyle-CssClass="tableHeader"
23:      ItemStyle-CssClass="tableItem"
24:      AlternatingItemStyle-CssClass="alternatingItem"
25:      AllowPaging="True"
26:      OnPageIndexChanged="PageIndexChanged_OnClick"
27:      PageSize="10"
28:      PagerStyle-Mode="NumericPages"
29:      PagerStyle-HorizontalAlign="Right"
30:      PagerStyle-CssClass="pageLinks"
31:      AllowSorting="True"
32:      OnSortCommand="SortCommand_OnClick"
33:    />
34:  </form>
35:  </body>
36:  </html>
```

In Listing 6.11, you create a Web Form that implements both paging and sorting. This is done by adding event handlers for both the OnPageIndexChanged and OnSortCommand events and then setting the paging and sorting properties of the DataGrid. The code in Listing 6.11 is similar to the code in previous examples, using the event handler for paging from Listing 6.5 and the event handler for sorting from Listing 6.10. The only real difference is that the ORDER BY clause of the SQL statement is maintained across page requests by setting it as the Text property of an invisible Label control (line 32 of the code behind and line 15 of the Web Form). On each call to BindData(), the ORDER BY clause from the Label control is appended to the SqlStmt variable, which is used to retrieve the data. If the user sorts the table by a column and then clicks on a page-navigation link, the ORDER BY clause is maintained by ViewState.

Altering DataGrid Output

CHAPTER 6

159

6

**ALTERING
DATAGRID
OUTPUT**

The result is that when the user clicks on another column to sort by, the page number is retained and the DataGrid is re-sorted. Figure 6.10 shows the rendered output of Listing 6.11 after navigating to page 3 and sorting on the ContactTitle column.

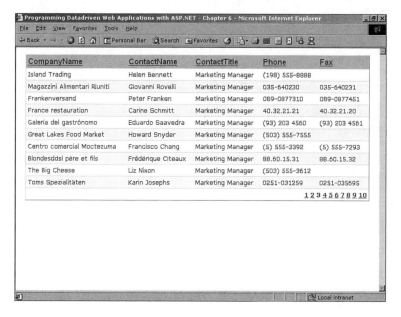

FIGURE 6.10
Both paging and sorting can be used on a DataGrid *simultaneously.*

BoundColumns

In the previous examples, the DataGrid has been bound to a data source and the columns have been created dynamically based on the columns in the DataTable. *BoundColumns* can be used to create a custom column layout for the DataGrid. Each BoundColumn can define the column heading text and the field in the table to sort on. Like all controls in ASP.NET, BoundColumns includes basic properties such as Visible, among others. In Chapter 7, "Working with ASP.NET Server Controls Templates," you'll learn about other properties of BoundColumns. This chapter covers only the basic properties.

BoundColumns are encapsulated inside a property declaration. The DataGrid property is named Columns. Each BoundColumn renders a table column populated with the data from the data source specified by a DataField property. Listing 6.12 shows the DataGrid code to use BoundColumns with the programmatic code from Listing 6.11.

Listing 6.12   Using BoundColumns with the DataGrid

[Web Form VB & C#]

```
16: <asp:DataGrid runat="server" id="myDataGrid"
17:    Width="740"
18:    Cellpadding="4"
19:    Cellspacing="0"
20:    Gridlines="Horizontal"
21:    HorizontalAlign="Center"
22:    HeaderStyle-CssClass="tableHeader"
23:    ItemStyle-CssClass="tableItem"
24:    AlternatingItemStyle-CssClass="alternatingItem"
25:    AllowPaging="True"
26:    OnPageIndexChanged="PageIndexChanged_OnClick"
27:    PageSize="10"
28:    PagerStyle-Mode="NumericPages"
29:    PagerStyle-HorizontalAlign="Right"
30:    PagerStyle-CssClass="pageLinks"
31:    AllowSorting="True"
32:    OnSortCommand="SortCommand_OnClick"
33:    AutoGenerateColumns="False"
34:    >
35:    <Columns>
36:     <asp:BoundColumn DataField="CompanyName"
37      HeaderText="Company Name" SortExpression="CompanyName" />
38:     <asp:BoundColumn DataField="ContactName"
39      HeaderText="Contact Name" SortExpression="ContactName" />
40:     <asp:BoundColumn DataField="ContactTitle"
41      HeaderText="Contact Title" SortExpression="ContactTitle" />
42:     <asp:BoundColumn DataField="Phone" HeaderText="Phone" />
43:     <asp:BoundColumn DataField="Fax" HeaderText="Fax" />
44:    </Columns>
45: </asp:DataGrid>
```

In Listing 6.12, you modify the DataGrid properties to use BoundColumns. The benefit of using BoundColumns is that you can specify the column heading text (HeaderText) and the name of the field to sort on (SortExpression). In Listing 6.12, you add spaces to column names that are two words (such as Company Name, Contact Name, and Contact Title), and disable sorting on the Phone and Fax columns by not adding a SortExpression value to those columns.

On line 33, you add the AutoGenerateColumns property to the DataGrid and set it to False. This tells the .NET Framework that you'll specify how the columns are generated. If AutoGenerateColumns is set to True, the BoundColumns you specify will be rendered, followed by all the columns in the data source. True is the default value.

Each `BoundColumn` specifies a `DataField` property (lines 37, 39, 41, 42, and 43). This is the name of the field in the data source that the `BoundColumn` will display when data-bound. Additionally, you specify the `HeaderText` property and a `SortExpression` property. For the `Phone` (line 42) and `Fax` (line 43) columns, no `SortExpression` is specified. The .NET Framework will disable sorting on a column when `BoundColumns` are used and no `SortExpression` is specified. Figure 6.11 shows the rendered page from Listing 6.12.

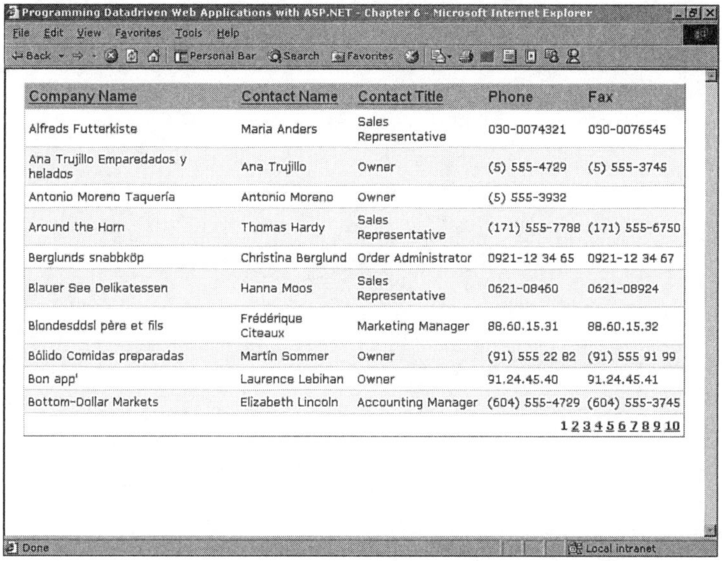

Company Name	Contact Name	Contact Title	Phone	Fax
Alfreds Futterkiste	Maria Anders	Sales Representative	030-0074321	030-0076545
Ana Trujillo Emparedados y helados	Ana Trujillo	Owner	(5) 555-4729	(5) 555-3745
Antonio Moreno Taquería	Antonio Moreno	Owner	(5) 555-3932	
Around the Horn	Thomas Hardy	Sales Representative	(171) 555-7788	(171) 555-6750
Berglunds snabbköp	Christina Berglund	Order Administrator	0921-12 34 65	0921-12 34 67
Blauer See Delikatessen	Hanna Moos	Sales Representative	0621-08460	0621-08924
Blondesddsl père et fils	Frédérique Citeaux	Marketing Manager	88.60.15.31	88.60.15.32
Bólido Comidas preparadas	Martín Sommer	Owner	(91) 555 22 82	(91) 555 91 99
Bon app'	Laurence Lebihan	Owner	91.24.45.40	91.24.45.41
Bottom-Dollar Markets	Elizabeth Lincoln	Accounting Manager	(604) 555-4729	(604) 555-3745
				1 2 3 4 5 6 7 8 9 10

FIGURE 6.11

Using `BoundColumns` in a `DataGrid`, you can specify the column order, the column heading text, and the field to sort on.

Summary

The `DataGrid` is one of the most powerful and versatile server controls shipped with ASP.NET. It includes properties and methods for altering the display of data, paging through data, and sorting data. Additionally, it has properties and methods for updating data and refreshing the data source. Those properties and methods will be covered in the next chapter.

In this chapter, you learned:

- How to work with `DataGrid` properties to alter the appearance of the rendered table.
- How to use the `DataGrid` paging properties and events with both built-in and custom paging.
- How to enable column sorting in the `DataGrid`.
- How to use `DataGrid` `BoundColumns`.

Working with ASP.NET Server Controls Templates

IN THIS CHAPTER

Up to this point you've seen how to retrieve data from multiple data stores and how to bind different server controls to that data. Though useful and efficient, the pages you've created thus far have been quite plain and your control on how the page is rendered has been limited to the default rendering of that particular control. In this chapter you will learn how to make your pages look exquisite using templates. Not all server controls support the use of templates. We will be demonstrating the three intrinsic server controls that do inherently support templates—the `DataGrid`, `DataList`, and `Repeater` controls.

In this chapter we will cover the following:

- What a template is
- `DataGrid` column controls
- How to use templates with the `DataGrid`
- How to use templates with the `DataList`
- How to use templates with the `Repeater`

What Is a Template?

Essentially, a template is a repeating or non-repeating set of HTML elements or .NET controls mixed with data that make up part of the layout of a web form or user control. Whereas styles affect the appearance of elements, templates create a pattern of elements that makes up a layout. Of course, you can use styles with templates (as we will demonstrate) to affect the look of the elements that are rendered when you're using templates.

As stated, there are currently three intrinsic .NET server controls support templates: `DataGrid`, `DataList`, and `Repeater`.

Beyond using the intrinsic .NET server controls, you can develop your own server controls to support templates. In our next book, *Developing Server Controls for ASP.NET,* we will go into greater detail on how to create custom .NET server and user controls and we will discuss how to develop controls that support templates. In this chapter, however, we will only be going over intrinsic server controls and their inherent support of templates.

Each of the server controls supports a similar set of templates—although as you'll see a template might behave differently from control to control. The following sections will examine each of the three server controls and the templates they support. Each section will contain one or more code examples illustrating how to implement templates using that particular control.

DataGrid .NET Server Control

The `DataGrid` control is a multicolumn, data-bound (bound to a data source—an object that supports an `ICollection` interface—`ArrayList`, `DataView`) grid that displays data in a tabular fashion (rows and columns). In order for the `DataGrid` to render any HTML elements to the page, the `DataGrid` must be bound to a data source that supports this interface—`ICollection`. When the `DataGrid` is rendered to a web form, an HTML table is created (`<table>`). As you probably are aware an HTML table has four parts:

- `Table Header`—The top row in the table.
- `Table Row`—Spans the width of the table, containing one or more columns.
- `Table Column`—Spans the height of the table, containing one or more rows.
- `Table Footer`—The last row in the table.

The `DataGrid` has a set of intrinsic features that gives you access to which columns are rendered from its data source and in what order. By default the `DataGrid` is rendered automatically based on the structure of its data source. For instance, if the `DataGrid.DataSource` is a `DataTable` that has four fields and 20 rows, the `DataGrid` will render a table that has a header with the value of each field name from the data source, four columns (one for each field in the data source), and 20 rows (one for each row in the data source). Each cell will contain the value of the row and field for that record in the data source.

You can override this default behavior by using column objects. Using column objects enables you to manipulate both the style and content of your `DataGrid` column-by-column. The following list contains all the different column objects available when using the `DataGrid`:

- `BoundColumn`—Enables you to specify a particular field from your data source to bind to. A `BoundColumn` also enables you to specify the style and format of the data displayed.
- `HyperLinkColumn`—Enables you to specify a particular field from your data source to bind to and displays the data in the column as a hyperlink (`<a href="">DataItem</a>`).
- `ButtonColumn`—Renders a Button control for each item (row) in your data source. You can either manually set its Text attribute or bind it to a field from your data source.
- `EditCommandColumn`—Enables you to create editing features for your DataGrid. Buttons for putting the DataGrid into different modes (edit) are rendered for each item (row) in your data source. (Editing is covered in Chapter 10.)
- `TemplateColumn`—Gives you precise control over what is rendered by the `DataGrid`. You can create combinations of HTML and server controls and design a custom layout for a column.

The most powerful entry in this list is the `TemplateColumn`. The `TemplateColumn` supports the following templates within it:

- `HeaderTemplate`—Defines how the columns header is rendered.
- `FooterTemplate`—Defines how the columns footer is rendered.
- `ItemTemplate`—Defines how items are rendered within the column.
- `EditItemTemplate`—Defines how items in Edit Mode are rendered within the columns.

In the following sections, first I'll go over using the basic `DataGrid`. Second, I'll go over how to use the column objects in the `DataGrid` (ex: `BoundColumn`). Finally, I'll go over how to use template columns with the `DataGrid`.

The Basic DataGrid

As you'll remember from previous chapters, the basic `DataGrid` is very easy to implement and can be done in as little as one line of code. Listing 7.1 demonstrates how to use some of `DataGrid`'s inherent attributes to improve the way the `DataGrid` looks when it's rendered to the page.

LISTING 7.1   Code to Render a Simple `DataGrid` to a Web Form

```
[VisualBasic.NET]

01: <%@ Import Namespace="System.Data" %>
02: <%@ Import Namespace="System.Data.SqlClient" %>
03:
04: <script language="VB" runat="server">
05:
06:   sub Page_Load(sender as Object, e as EventArgs)
07:
08:     dim SqlCmd as new StringBuilder()
09:     SqlCmd.Append("SELECT S.CompanyName [Company Name],")
10:     SqlCmd.Append("P.ProductName [Product Name],")
11:     SqlCmd.Append("P.QuantityPerUnit [Quantity Per Unit],")
12:     SqlCmd.Append("P.UnitPrice [Unit Price],")
13:     SqlCmd.Append("P.UnitsInStock [Units In Stock],")
14:     SqlCmd.Append("P.UnitsOnOrder [Units On Order] ")
15:     SqlCmd.Append("FROM Products P ")
16:     SqlCmd.Append("INNER JOIN Suppliers S ")
17:     SqlCmd.Append("ON ")
18:     SqlCmd.Append("S.SupplierID = P.SupplierID")
19:
20:     dim SqlCon as new SqlConnection("server=localhost;
➥   uid=sa;pwd=;database=northwind")
```

LISTING 7.1 Continued

```
21:   dim sqlcommand as new SqlCommand(SqlCmd.ToString(), SqlCon)
22:
23:   SqlCon.Open()
24:    MyDataGrid.DataSource = sqlcommand.ExecuteReader()
25:    MyDataGrid.DataBind()
26:   SqlCon.Close()
27:
28: End Sub
29:
30: </script>

[C#.NET]

01: <%@ Import Namespace="System.Data" %>
02: <%@ Import Namespace="System.Data.SqlClient" %>
03:
04: <script language="c#" runat="server">
05:
06:   public void Page_Load(Object sender, EventArgs e) {
07:
08:     StringBuilder SqlCmd = new StringBuilder();
09:     SqlCmd.Append("SELECT S.CompanyName [Company Name],");
10:     SqlCmd.Append("P.ProductName [Product Name],");
11:     SqlCmd.Append("P.QuantityPerUnit [Quantity Per Unit],");
12:     SqlCmd.Append("P.UnitPrice [Unit Price],");
13:     SqlCmd.Append("P.UnitsInStock [Units In Stock],");
14:     SqlCmd.Append("P.UnitsOnOrder [Units On Order] ");
15:     SqlCmd.Append("FROM Products P ");
16:     SqlCmd.Append("INNER JOIN Suppliers S ");
17:     SqlCmd.Append("ON ");
18:     SqlCmd.Append("S.SupplierID = P.SupplierID");
19:
20:     SqlConnection SqlCon = new SqlConnection("server=localhost;
➥ uid=sa;pwd=;database=northwind");
21:     SqlCommand sqlcommand = new SqlCommand(SqlCmd.ToString(), SqlCon);
22:
23:     SqlCon.Open();
24:      MyDataGrid.DataSource = sqlcommand.ExecuteReader();
25:      MyDataGrid.DataBind();
26:     SqlCon.Close();
27:
28: }
29:
30: </script>
```

7

ASP.NET SERVER CONTROLS TEMPLATES

Listing 7.1 Continued

```
[VisualBasic.NET & C#.NET]
31: <html>
32: <head><title>DotNetJunkies.com</title></head>
33: <body>
34:         <asp:DataGrid
35:          id="MyDataGrid"
36:          runat="server"
37:          AutoGenerateColumns="True"
38:          GridLines="Vertical"
39:          Width="100%"
40:          CellPadding="4"
41:          CellSpacing="0"
42:
43:          HeaderStyle-BackColor="maroon"
44:          HeaderStyle-ForeColor="#FFFFFF"
45:          HeaderStyle-Font-Size="10"
46:          HeaderStyle-Font-Bold="true"
47:          HeaderStyle-Font-Name="Verdana"
48:
49:          ItemStyle-BackColor="Green"
50:          ItemStyle-ForeColor="White"
51:          ItemStyle-Font-Size="8"
52:          ItemStyle-Font-Bold="true"
53:          ItemStyle-Font-Name="Verdana"
54:
55:          AlternatingItemStyle-BackColor="White"
56:          AlternatingItemStyle-ForeColor="Black"
57:          AlternatingItemStyle-Font-Size="8"
58:          AlternatingItemStyle-Font-Bold="true"
59:          AlternatingItemStyle-Font-Name="Verdana"
60:
61:          />
62: </body>
63: </html>
```

In Listing 7.1, fields from both the Supplier and the Products table are returned from the SQL query. Within the SQL statement I gave the field names human-readable names because in this type of DataGrid the header text will be populated from the field names in its DataGrid.DataSource. For example, if I didn't change the names in the SQL statement, the first column of the DataGrid would be called CompanyName instead of Company Name (line 9).

As previously mentioned this `DataGrid` is in one of its most basic forms. However, I did use some of its attributes to improve on its looks (lines 43-59). On line 37 the `AutoGenerateColumns` attribute is set to `True`. This means that each column will be automatically generated for the `DataGrid` based on its data source, one column for each field. In this example, if this value were `false` nothing would render to the client. Figure 7.1 contains an illustration of this page when rendered. Notice the header text and its enhanced appearance.

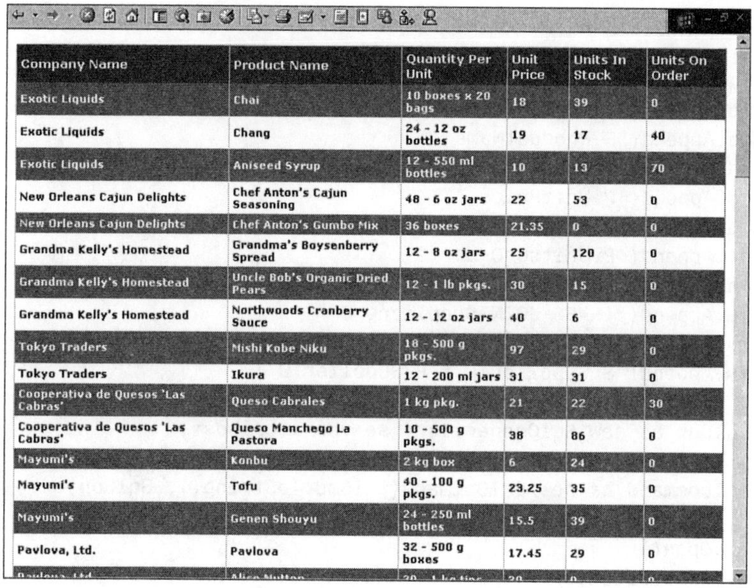

Company Name	Product Name	Quantity Per Unit	Unit Price	Units In Stock	Units On Order
Exotic Liquids	Chai	10 boxes x 20 bags	18	39	0
Exotic Liquids	Chang	24 - 12 oz bottles	19	17	40
Exotic Liquids	Aniseed Syrup	12 - 550 ml bottles	10	13	70
New Orleans Cajun Delights	Chef Anton's Cajun Seasoning	48 - 6 oz jars	22	53	0
New Orleans Cajun Delights	Chef Anton's Gumbo Mix	36 boxes	21.35	0	0
Grandma Kelly's Homestead	Grandma's Boysenberry Spread	12 - 8 oz jars	25	120	0
Grandma Kelly's Homestead	Uncle Bob's Organic Dried Pears	12 - 1 lb pkgs.	30	15	0
Grandma Kelly's Homestead	Northwoods Cranberry Sauce	12 - 12 oz jars	40	6	0
Tokyo Traders	Mishi Kobe Niku	18 - 500 g pkgs.	97	29	0
Tokyo Traders	Ikura	12 - 200 ml jars	31	31	0
Cooperativa de Quesos 'Las Cabras'	Queso Cabrales	1 kg pkg.	21	22	30
Cooperativa de Quesos 'Las Cabras'	Queso Manchego La Pastora	10 - 500 g pkgs.	38	86	0
Mayumi's	Konbu	2 kg box	6	24	0
Mayumi's	Tofu	40 - 100 g pkgs.	23.25	35	0
Mayumi's	Genen Shouyu	24 - 250 ml bottles	15.5	39	0
Pavlova, Ltd.	Pavlova	32 - 500 g boxes	17.45	29	0

FIGURE 7.1
The basic `DataGrid`.

Getting More Control Using Column Objects

As previously mentioned, the `DataGrid` enables you to control which fields from your data source to display, and how to display them, by using column objects. There are a total of five different column objects, as listed in the "`DataGrid` .NET Server Control" section earlier in the chapter. This section covers `BoundColumn` and `HyperlinkColumn`. The `ButtonColumn` will be discussed in Chapter 10, "Inputting and Editing Data with the DataGrid."

Listing 7.2 contains the code example illustrating how to use these two types of column objects. The server code used in this example is very similar to that of Listing 7.1, but you'll notice that we don't rename the fields from our database from within the SQL statement. Instead, we use the column objects `HeaderText` attribute.

LISTING 7.2   Code for DataGrid Using Column Objects

[VisualBasic.NET]

```
01: <%@ Import Namespace="System.Data" %>
02: <%@ Import Namespace="System.Data.SqlClient" %>
03:
04: <script language="VB" runat="server">
05:
06:  sub Page_Load(sender as Object, e as EventArgs)
07:
08:    dim SqlCmd as new StringBuilder()
09:    SqlCmd.Append("SELECT S.CompanyName,")
10:    SqlCmd.Append("P.ProductName,")
11:    SqlCmd.Append("P.QuantityPerUnit,")
12:    SqlCmd.Append("P.UnitPrice,")
13:    SqlCmd.Append("P.UnitsInStock,")
14:    SqlCmd.Append("P.UnitsOnOrder ")
15:    SqlCmd.Append("FROM Products P ")
16:    SqlCmd.Append("INNER JOIN Suppliers S ")
17:    SqlCmd.Append("ON ")
18:    SqlCmd.Append("S.SupplierID = P.SupplierID")
19:
20:    dim SqlCon as new SqlConnection("server=localhost;
➥ uid=sa;pwd=;database=northwind")
21:    dim sqlcommand as new SqlCommand(SqlCmd.ToString(), SqlCon)
22:
23:    SqlCon.Open()
24:    MyDataGrid.DataSource = sqlcommand.ExecuteReader()
25:    MyDataGrid.DataBind()
26:    SqlCon.Close()
27:
28: End Sub
29:
30: </script>
```

[C#.NET]

```
01: <%@ Import Namespace="System.Data" %>
02: <%@ Import Namespace="System.Data.SqlClient" %>
03:
04: <script language="c#" runat="server">
05:
06:  public void Page_Load(Object sender, EventArgs e) {
07:
08:    StringBuilder SqlCmd = new StringBuilder();
09:    SqlCmd.Append("SELECT S.CompanyName,");
10:    SqlCmd.Append("P.ProductName,");
```

LISTING 7.2 Continued

```
11:    SqlCmd.Append("P.QuantityPerUnit,");
12:    SqlCmd.Append("P.UnitPrice,");
13:    SqlCmd.Append("P.UnitsInStock,");
14:    SqlCmd.Append("P.UnitsOnOrder ");
15:    SqlCmd.Append("FROM Products P ");
16:    SqlCmd.Append("INNER JOIN Suppliers S ");
17:    SqlCmd.Append("ON ");
18:    SqlCmd.Append("S.SupplierID = P.SupplierID");
19:
20:    SqlConnection SqlCon = new SqlConnection("server=localhost;
➥ uid=sa;pwd=;database=northwind");
21:    SqlCommand sqlcommand = new SqlCommand(SqlCmd.ToString(), SqlCon);
22:
23:    SqlCon.Open();
24:     MyDataGrid.DataSource = sqlcommand.ExecuteReader();
25:     MyDataGrid.DataBind();
26:    SqlCon.Close();
27:
28: }
29:
30: </script>

[VisualBasic.NET & C#.NET]

31: <html>
32: <head><title>DotNetJunkies.com</title>
33: <style rel="stylesheet">
34:
35:  A {text-decoration:none;color:black}
36:  A:Hover {color:maroon;text-decoration:underline}
37:  A:Visited {color:red}
38:
39: </style>
40: </head>
41: <body>
42:         <asp:DataGrid
43:         id="MyDataGrid"
44:         runat="server"
45:         AutoGenerateColumns="False"
46:         GridLines="Both"
47:         Width="100%"
48:         CellPadding="4"
49:         CellSpacing="0"
50:         >
51:
```

7

ASP.NET SERVER
CONTROLS
TEMPLATES

LISTING 7.2   Continued

```
52:        <columns>
53:
54:          <asp:BoundColumn
55:            DataField="CompanyName"
56:            HeaderText="Company Name"
57:            HeaderStyle-BackColor="maroon"
58:            HeaderStyle-ForeColor="#FFFFFF"
59:            HeaderStyle-Font-Size="10"
60:            HeaderStyle-Font-Bold="true"
61:            HeaderStyle-Font-Name="Verdana"
62:
63:            ItemStyle-BackColor="#FFFFFF"
64:            ItemStyle-ForeColor="#000000"
65:            ItemStyle-Font-Size="8"
66:            ItemStyle-Font-Bold="true"
67:            ItemStyle-Font-Name="Verdana"
68:
69:            />
70:
71:          <asp:BoundColumn
72:            DataField="ProductName"
73:            HeaderText="Product Name"
74:
75:            HeaderStyle-BackColor="maroon"
76:            HeaderStyle-ForeColor="#FFFFFF"
77:            HeaderStyle-Font-Size="10"
78:            HeaderStyle-Font-Bold="true"
79:            HeaderStyle-Font-Name="Verdana"
80:
81:            ItemStyle-BackColor="#FFFFFF"
82:            ItemStyle-ForeColor="#000000"
83:            ItemStyle-Font-Size="8"
84:            ItemStyle-Font-Bold="true"
85:            ItemStyle-Font-Name="Verdana"
86:
87:            />
88:
89:          <asp:BoundColumn
90:            DataField="UnitPrice"
91:            HeaderText="Price Per Unit"
92:            DataFormatString="{0:C}"
93:
```

LISTING 7.2 Continued

```
94:             HeaderStyle-BackColor="maroon"
96:             HeaderStyle-ForeColor="#FFFFFF"
97:             HeaderStyle-Font-Size="10"
98:             HeaderStyle-Font-Bold="true"
99:             HeaderStyle-Font-Name="Verdana"
100:
101:            ItemStyle-BackColor="#FFFFFF"
102:            ItemStyle-ForeColor="#000000"
103:            ItemStyle-Font-Size="8"
104:            ItemStyle-Font-Bold="true"
105:            ItemStyle-Font-Name="Verdana"
106:
107:            />
108:
109:         <asp:HyperLinkColumn
110:            Text="Click Here"
111:            HeaderText="More Info"
112:            DataNavigateUrlField="ProductName"
113:            DataNavigateUrlFormatString=
➥   "ProductDetails.aspx?ProductName={0}"
114:            Target="_blank"
115:
116:            HeaderStyle-BackColor="maroon"
117:            HeaderStyle-ForeColor="#FFFFFF"
118:            HeaderStyle-Font-Size="10"
119:            HeaderStyle-Font-Bold="true"
120:            HeaderStyle-Font-Name="Verdana"
121:
122:            ItemStyle-BackColor="#FFFFFF"
123:            ItemStyle-ForeColor="White"
124:            ItemStyle-Font-Size="8"
125:            ItemStyle-Font-Bold="true"
126:            ItemStyle-Font-Name="Verdana"
127:
128:            />
129:
130:         </columns>
131:
132:         </asp:DataGrid>
133: </body>
134: </html>
```

7

ASP.NET SERVER
CONTROLS
TEMPLATES

Beginning with the starting `DataGrid` tag (line 42) let's walk through the `DataGrid` code from Listing 7.2. The first thing you might have noticed is I changed the value of the `AutoGenerateColumns` attribute from `true` to `false`. The reason I did this is because when it is set to `true` the `DataGrid` will render a column for each field in the `DataGrid.DataSource` even when using column objects. Hence, if the value were `true` for this example, there would be 10 columns rendered—the 6 default fields from the data source and the 4 from the bound columns.

There are a total of 4 column objects used in this example. There are three `BoundColumns` and one `HyperLinkColumn`. The three `BoundColumns` are located in lines 54–107. You'll notice that I set their style attributes within their individual tags. This gives you greater control on how the columns appear when rendered because one column `BackColor` can be different than another.

You also have complete control on which fields from the data source are displayed when using column objects and where within the `DataGridColumnCollection` they'll be shown. In this example only 3 out of the 6 fields are displayed from the `DataGrid.DataSource`. Additionally, you can also use one field more than once as I did in this example by using the `ProductName` field value for both a `BoundColumn` and the `HyperLinkColumn`.

Displaying data within a `BoundColumn` is quite simple. You use the `DataField` attribute to set the field from the data source you wish to display in that column and the `HeaderText` attribute to set the Header for the column. For instance, in the first `BoundColumn` starting on line 54 the `DataField` is set to be the `CompanyName` field value (line 55) from the `DataGrid.DataSource` and the `HeaderText` is set to "Company Name"—a hard coded, static value.

Displaying data within the `HyperLinkColumn` is quite different than the `BoundColumn`. The reason is that it doesn't necessarily have to bind to any field from the data source; but even if not bound to a field, the `HyperLinkColumn` will still be rendered once for each row in the data source. In this example it is bound to a field, the `ProductName` field. I use the `HyperLinkColumn.DataNavigateUrlField` attribute to bind the `HyperLinkColumn` to the `ProductName` field (line 112) and the `HyperLinkColumn.DataNavigateUrlFormatString` (line 113) to access the value and append it to a `URL` as a parameter value. On line 110 I use its `Text` attribute to set the text rendered for each row to a static value `Click Here`. Alternatively, you can use the `DataTextField` attribute to bind the text displayed to a field in its data source. Some additional attributes can be found in the following list:

- `HyperLinkColumn.NavigateUrl`   The value is a static URL that should be navigated to when clicked on. You cannot have both this and `DataNavigateUrlField` attributes set at the same time.

- `HyperLinkColumn.Target`   Used to get or set the "target" window or frame to display the page being navigated to (ex: `Target="_blank"`).

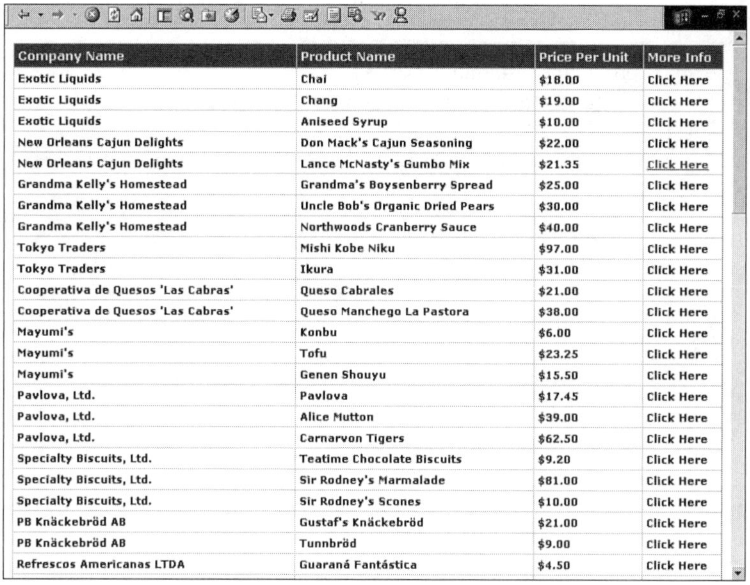

FIGURE 7.2
The DataGrid using column objects.

The Ultimate Control: Template Columns

For the ultimate control over what is rendered in each column you can use the TemplateColumn. This enables you to add any type of HTML elements or server controls to the DataGrid and control which fields are shown and where. Using the same server code from Listing 7.2 replace the code between the starting <html> and ending </html> tags with the code example found in Listing 7.3.

LISTING 7.3 Using a Template Column in the DataGrid

```
[VisualBasic.NET and C#.NET]

31: <html>
32: <head><title>DotNetJunkies.com</title>
33: <style rel="stylesheet">
34:
35:   A {text-decoration:none;color:black}
36:   A:Hover {color:maroon;text-decoration:underline}
37:   A:Visited {color:red}
38:   .body { font: 9pt Verdana, Arial, sans-serif; }
```

Listing 7.3   Continued

```
39:   .head { font: bold 9pt Verdana, Arial,
➥  sans-serif; background-color:Maroon; color:white; }
40:   .tablehead { font: bold 9pt Verdana, Arial,
➥  sans-serif; background-color:green; color:white; }
41: </style>
42: </head>
43: <body>
44:  <center>
45:   <asp:DataGrid
46:   id="MyDataGrid"
47:   runat="server"
48:   AutoGenerateColumns="False"
49:   GridLines="Both"
50:   Width="500"
51:   CellPadding="4"
52:   CellSpacing="0"
53:   >
54:
55:    <columns>
56:
57:     <asp:TemplateColumn
58:     HeaderStyle-CssClass="head"
59:     ItemStyle-CssClass="body"
60:     >
61:
62:      <HeaderTemplate>
63:      <center>Northwind Products</center>
64:      </HeaderTemplate>
65:
66:      <ItemTemplate>
67:       <table width="100%">
68:        <tr>
69:         <td align="center" class="tablehead" ColSpan="2">
70:          <%# DataBinder.Eval(Container.DataItem, "ProductName" )%>
71:         </td>
72:        </tr>
73:        <tr>
74:         <td class="body" align="left" valign="top">
75:          <b>Price</b>
76:         </td>
77:         <td class="body" align="right" valign="top">
78:          <b><%# DataBinder.Eval(
➥  Container.DataItem, "UnitPrice",  "{0:C}")%></b>
79:         </td>
80:        </tr>
```

LISTING 7.3 Continued

```
81:        <tr>
82:         <td class="body" align="left" valign="top">
83:          <b>Quantity Per Unit</b>
84:         </td>
85:         <td class="body" align="right" valign="top">
86:          <b><%# DataBinder.Eval(
➥  Container.DataItem, "QuantityPerUnit")%></b>
87:         </td>
88:        </tr>
89:        <tr>
90:         <td align="center" class="head" ColSpan="2"></td>
91:        </tr>
92:        <tr>
93:         <td class="body" ColSpan="2" align="center">
94:          <a Target="_blank"
95:           href="ProductDetails.aspx?ProductName=<%# DataBinder.Eval(
➥  Container.DataItem, "ProductName")%>">
96:           [ More Information Click Here ]
97:          </a>
98:         </td>
99:        </tr>
100:        </table>
101:       </ItemTemplate>
102:
103:      </asp:TemplateColumn>
104:
105:     </columns>
106:
107:    </asp:DataGrid>
108:   </center>
109: </body>
110: </html>
```

As previously mentioned there are four parts to the `TemplateColumn`:

- `HeaderTemplate`—The HTML or text that should be rendered for the Header
- `FooterTemplate`—The HTML or text that should be rendered for the Footer
- `ItemTemplate`—The HTML or text that should be rendered for each item
- `EditItemTemplate`—The HTML or text that should be rendered when the DataGrid is in "edit mode"

In this example I used only the `HeaderTemplate` (lines 62–64) and the `ItemTemplate` (lines 66–101) and I kept the example simple by only using the `TemplateColumn` to contain all the data. However, you can use any number of different column objects within the `DataGrid`.

For instance, you can have a TemplateColumn and a BoundColumn within the same DataGrid or two different TemplateColumns or two different TemplateColumns.

You'll also notice that I set the style for the column differently than I did in previous examples. I use the CssClass attribute to set the HeaderStyle and ItemStyle in this DataGrid (lines 58–59); this enables you to use an external style sheet to set the style for DataGrid items.

The ItemTemplate (lines 66–101) in Listing 7.3 uses a table to organize the data. One thing to be aware of when using HTML elements within the TemplateColumn is that all the elements will be repeated for every row in the data source. So if you have server controls or HTML elements (ex: images) that are large in size (Bytes) then the page might render very slowly. Figure 7.3 contains an illustration of this page when rendered.

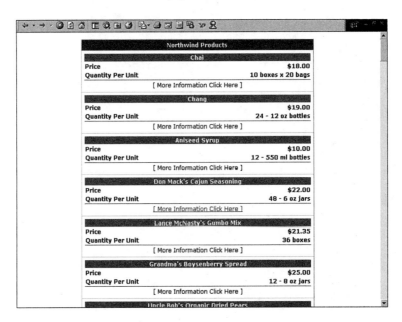

FIGURE 7.3
The DataGrid using a TemplateColumn.

DataList .NET Server Control

The DataList is next on the list of server controls that support templates we'll be discussing. The DataList differs from the DataGrid because you must use templates to display data; you cannot simply set its DataList.DataSource attribute and call the DataList.DataBind method as you can with the DataGrid. Although, it is similar to the DataGrid, in that it must be bound to a data source that supports the ICollection interface to render HTML.

The `DataList` contains 7 templates. The following list contains each:

- `HeaderTemplate`—Defines how the header is rendered.
- `ItemTemplate`—Defines how items are rendered.
- `AlternatingItemTemplate`—Defines how alternating items are rendered (every other item).
- `EditItemTemplate`—Defines how items in edit mode should be rendered (not discussed in this chapter).
- `SelectedItemTemplate`—Defines how selected items should be rendered (not discussed in this chapter).
- `SeparatorTemplate`—Defines a separator for each item to be rendered (ex: <hr>).
- `FooterTemplate`—Defines how the footer is rendered.

7

ASP.NET SERVER
CONTROLS
TEMPLATES

NOTE

At a minimum, you need to define the `ItemTemplate` to render output to a page using the `DataList`.

By default, the `DataList` renders items in a single vertical column. However, by setting the `RepeatColumns` property, you can specify that more than one column is rendered. You set the `RepeatColumns` property in the opening `DataList` tag:

```
<asp:DataList RepeatColumns="2" />
```

If `RepeatColumns` is set to more than one column, a couple of new properties can be taken advantage of. The first is the `RepeatLayout` property. `RepeatLayout` enables you to control how items in the `DataList` are positioned with respect to one another. `RepeatLayout` has two options:

- `Flow`—List items are rendered inline, much like a word document (left to right). Flow Layout uses the `<SPAN>` HTML element for placement; hence attributes such as `GridLines` disappear when `RepeatLayout` is `Flow`.
- `Table`—List items are rendered in a `<TABLE>` HTML element. `Table` Layout gives you more flexibility than `Flow` Layout in manipulating the look of the data contained in each cell. You can set any property you would normally set for a table cell or table such as setting the `GridLines` attribute. (Table Layout is the default value for `RepeatLayout`.)

You can set the `RepeatLayout` property using code similar to the following:

```
<asp:DataList RepeatColumns="2" RepeatLayout="Table" />
```

The third layout property I want to discuss is the RepeatDirection property, which indicates whether the control is rendered horizontally or vertically:

- Vertical—Items are ordered vertically, like a newspaper or magazine column. (This is the default value for RepeatDirection.) What this means is items are rendered from index 0 to *n* from your data source top to bottom in the DataList.

- Horizontal—Items are ordered like the content of a calendar. What this means is items are rendered from index 0 to *n* from your data source left to right.

You set the RepeatDirection using code similar to the following:

```
<asp:DataList RepeatColumns="2" RepeatLayout="Table"
RepeatDirection="Vertical" />
```

Listing 7.4 illustrates how all these properties affect the way things are rendered to the page. There's only so much room in this book, so I'm keeping these examples very concise. For more detailed examples, please visit our web site at http://www.DotNetJunkies.com. When you are through with this example, I recommend playing around with the RepeatColumns, RepeatDirection, and RepeatLayout properties further to get a better idea of how they affect the rendering of the page.

LISTING 7.4   Using the DataList

```
[VisualBasic.NET]
01: <%@ Import Namespace="System.Data" %>
02: <%@ Import Namespace="System.Data.SqlClient" %>
03:
04: <script language="VB" runat="server">
05:
06:   sub Page_Load(sender as Object, e as EventArgs)
07:
08:     dim SqlCmd as new StringBuilder()
09:     SqlCmd.Append("SELECT S.CompanyName,")
10:     SqlCmd.Append("P.ProductName,")
11:     SqlCmd.Append("P.QuantityPerUnit,")
12:     SqlCmd.Append("P.UnitPrice,")
13:     SqlCmd.Append("P.UnitsInStock,")
14:     SqlCmd.Append("P.UnitsOnOrder ")
15:     SqlCmd.Append("FROM Products P ")
16:     SqlCmd.Append("INNER JOIN Suppliers S ")
17:     SqlCmd.Append("ON ")
18:     SqlCmd.Append("S.SupplierID = P.SupplierID")
19:
20:     dim SqlCon as new SqlConnection("server=localhost;
➥  uid=sa;pwd=;database=northwind")
```

LISTING 7.4 Continued

```
21:    dim sqlcommand as new SqlCommand(SqlCmd.ToString(), SqlCon)
22:
23:    SqlCon.Open()
24:      DLProducts.DataSource =
sqlcommand.ExecuteReader(CommandBehavior.CloseConnection)
25:      DLProducts.DataBind()
26:
27:
28: End Sub
29:
30: </script>
```

```
[C#.NET]
```

```
01: <%@ Import Namespace="System.Data" %>
02: <%@ Import Namespace="System.Data.SqlClient" %>
03:
04: <script language="c#" runat="server">
05:
06:   public void Page_Load(Object sender, EventArgs e) {
07:
08:     StringBuilder SqlCmd = new StringBuilder();
09:     SqlCmd.Append("SELECT S.CompanyName,");
10:     SqlCmd.Append("P.ProductName,");
11:     SqlCmd.Append("P.QuantityPerUnit,");
12:     SqlCmd.Append("P.UnitPrice,");
13:     SqlCmd.Append("P.UnitsInStock,");
14:     SqlCmd.Append("P.UnitsOnOrder ");
15:     SqlCmd.Append("FROM Products P ");
16:     SqlCmd.Append("INNER JOIN Suppliers S ");
17:     SqlCmd.Append("ON ");
18:     SqlCmd.Append("S.SupplierID = P.SupplierID");
19:
20:     SqlConnection SqlCon = new SqlConnection("server=localhost;
➡ uid=sa;pwd=;database=northwind");
21:     SqlCommand sqlcommand = new SqlCommand(SqlCmd.ToString(), SqlCon);
22:
23:     SqlCon.Open();
24:       DLProducts.DataSource =
sqlcommand.ExecuteReader(CommandBehavior.CloseConnection);
25:       DLProducts.DataBind();
26:
27:
28: }
29:
30: </script>
```

7

ASP.NET SERVER CONTROLS TEMPLATES

Listing 7.4   Continued

```
[VisualBasic.NET & C#.NET]
31: <html>
32: <head><title>DotNetJunkies.com</title>
33: <style rel="stylesheet">
34:
35:  A {text-decoration:none;color:black}
36:  A:Hover {color:maroon;text-decoration:underline}
37:  A:Visited {color:red}
38:  .body { font: 9pt Verdana, Arial, sans-serif; }
39:  .head { font: bold 9pt Verdana, Arial,
➥ sans-serif; background-color:Maroon; color:white; }
40:  .tablehead { font: bold 9pt Verdana, Arial,
➥ sans-serif; background-color:green; color:white; }
41: </style>
42: </head>
43: <body>
44:  <center>
45:  <asp:DataList
46:    id="DLProducts"
47:    Runat="server"
48:    Width="100%"
49:    GridLines="Both"
50:    CellPadding="4"
51:    CellSpacing="0"
52:    RepeatColumns="3"
53:    RepeatLayout="Table"
54:    RepeatDirection="Horizontal"
55:
56:    HeaderStyle-CssClass="head"
57:    ItemStyle-CssClass="body"
58:
59:  >
60:
61:    <HeaderTemplate>
62:     <center>Northwind Products</center>
63:    </HeaderTemplate>
64:
65:    <ItemTemplate>
66:     <table width="100%">
67:      <tr>
68:       <td align="center" class="tablehead" ColSpan="2">
69:        <%# DataBinder.Eval(Container.DataItem, "ProductName" )%>
```

LISTING 7.4 Continued

```
70:          </td>
71:          </tr>
72:          <tr>
73:          <td class="body" align="left" valign="top">
74:           <b>Price</b>
75:          </td>
76:          <td class="body" align="right" valign="top">
77:           <b><%# DataBinder.Eval(
➥ Container.DataItem, "UnitPrice",  "{0:C}")%></b>
78:          </td>
79:          </tr>
80:          <tr>
81:          <td class="body" align="left" valign="top">
82:           <b>Quantity Per Unit</b>
83:          </td>
84:          <td class="body" align="right" valign="top">
85:           <b><%# DataBinder.Eval(
➥ Container.DataItem, "QuantityPerUnit")%></b>
86:          </td>
87:          </tr>
88:          <tr>
89:          <td align="center" class="head" ColSpan="2"></td>
90:          </tr>
91:          <tr>
92:          <td class="body" ColSpan="2" align="center">
93:           <a Target="_blank"
94:           href="ProductDetails.aspx?ProductName=<%# DataBinder.Eval(
➥ Container.DataItem, "ProductName")%>">
95:              [ More Information Click Here ]
96:           </a>
97:          </td>
98:          </tr>
99:          </table>
100:         </ItemTemplate>
101:
102:     </asp:DataList>
103:     </center>
104: </body>
105: </html>
```

First let's look at the rendered page from Listing 7.4 found in Figure 7.4 and then go through what attributes made it render in this fashion.

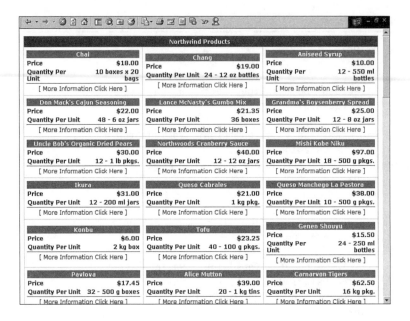

FIGURE 7.4
DataList using the HeaderTemplate *and* ItemTemplate.

The first thing you'll notice is that there are three columns within the DataList and only one Header. This was achieved by using the RepeatColumns attribute (line 52) in conjunction with the RepeatLayout (line 53). The value of RepeatColumns is 3, which indicates that the items should render 3 columns wide, but if the RepeatLayout is set to Flow rather than Table there are no columns rendered; hence, setting this attribute would be ineffective.

Something that may not jump out at you is the effect of setting the RepeatDirection attribute. As previously mentioned the RepeatDirection attribute determines whether items from the DataList.DataSource are rendered from left to right or from top to bottom. I recommend changing the value from Horizontal to Vertical in order to see the difference in the way the items are rendered.

In this example I only took advantage of two templates. The first template is the HeaderTemplate (lines 61–63). Whatever is located between the HeaderTemplate elements will only be rendered once. In this example there are a mix of HTML elements and raw text "Northwind Products". The second template used is the ItemTemplate. Recall that the ItemTemplate contents will be rendered once for each item in the DataList.DataSource. In this example a table HTML element is used to structure the item and the DataBinder.Eval method is used to populate data from the DataList.DataSource.

Now let's add a little more pizzazz to the DataList by adding the AlternatingItemTemplate, which lets you change the display of every other item that's rendered. Using the DataList the AlternatingItemTemplate can differ from the ItemTemplate merely by style attributes such as the background color of the header or you can change the entire structure of the item. Listing 7.5 contains example code illustrating how to use the AlternatingItemTemplate. Insert the code from Listing 7.5 between lines 100 & 102 in Listing 7.4.

LISTING 7.5   Adding an AlternatingItemTemplate to Listing 7.4

```
101:       <AlternatingItemTemplate>
102:        <table width="100%">
103:         <tr>
104:          <td align="center" class="Head" ColSpan="2">
105:           <%# DataBinder.Eval(Container.DataItem, "ProductName" )%>
106:          </td>
107:         </tr>
108:         <tr>
109:          <td class="body" ColSpan="2" align="center">
110:           <a Target="_blank"
111:           href="ProductDetails.aspx?ProductName=<%# DataBinder.Eval(
➥ Container.DataItem, "ProductName")%>">
112:             [ More Information Click Here ]
113:           </a>
114:          </td>
115:         </tr>
116:         <tr>
117:          <td align="center" class="head" ColSpan="2"></td>
118:         </tr>
119:         <tr>
120:          <td class="body" align="left" valign="top">
121:           <b>Price</b>
122:          </td>
123:          <td class="body" align="right" valign="top">
124:            <b><%# DataBinder.Eval(
➥ Container.DataItem, "UnitPrice",  "{0:C}")%></b>
125:          </td>
126:         </tr>
127:         <tr>
128:          <td class="body" align="left" valign="top">
129:           <b>Quantity Per Unit</b>
130:          </td>
131:          <td class="body" align="right" valign="top">
132:           <b><%# DataBinder.Eval(
➥ Container.DataItem, "QuantityPerUnit")%></b>
133:          </td>
134:         </tr>
135:        </table>
136:       </AlternatingItemTemplate>
```

Again, let's look at the rendered page for Listing 7.5 before discussion (see Figure 7.5).

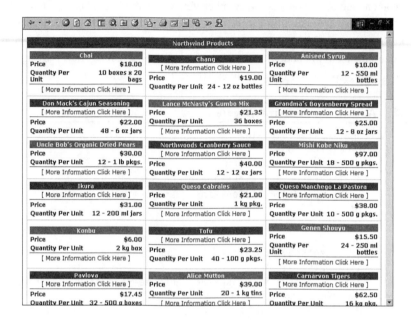

FIGURE 7.5
DataList using the HeaderTemplate, ItemTemplate, *and the* AlternatingItemTemplate.

Ok, this isn't the prettiest page possible, but it demonstrates my point for this section. Every other item is different within the DataList both in style and structure. The first item in the top-left corner has a green header with a hyperlink at the bottom of the item. The item found directly to the right of that has a maroon header and the link is located at the top of the item.

As you can imagine you easily can make some very complicated user interfaces using the DataList since you have absolute control over how items are rendered. Also, you only have to create your user interface for an item once and it is repeated for you for all other items. For instance, a DataList would be great for a master detail list.

Repeater .NET Server Control

The Repeater .NET server control is different from the previous controls because it doesn't have an inherent look to it. However, similar to the previous server controls, the Repeater must be bound to a data source to render. The Repeater does exactly what the name states: It repeats. Anything contained within the ItemTemplate is rendered once for each item in the Repeater. DataSource from the top to bottom. Because the Repeater doesn't have a default structure, it's great for creating lists quickly and has less overhead than the DataGrid or DataList.

> **TIP**
>
> The Repeater control is optimized for speed; hence, it has better performance than the DataGrid and DataList. Because you will typically use the Repeater for read only data, use either the SqlDataReader or OleDbDataReader as the data source for performance gains over using the DataSet.

The following list contains all the templates supported by the Repeater control:

The Repeater supports the following five templates:

- ItemTemplate—This template contains the HTML elements or server controls that are rendered for each row in the Repeater.DataSource.

- AlternatingItemTemplate—Similar to the ItemTemplate but rendered for every other row in the Repeater control. You can have a different look for the data contained in AlternatingItemTemplate.

- HeaderTemplate and FooterTemplate—Elements to render once before all data-bound rows have been rendered and once afterward. You'll probably use these templates to open and close an element (for example, a <TABLE> element in the HeaderTemplate and a </TABLE> element in the FooterTemplate).

- SeparatorTemplate—Elements to render between each row, such as line breaks (
 tags), lines (<HR> tags), or a comma.

Listing 7.6 contains an example of implementing the Repeater control. In this example we will make use of the HeaderTemplate, ItemTemplate, AlternatingItemTemplate, and FooterTemplate.

LISTING 7.6   Using the Repeater Control

```
[VisualBasic.NET]
01: <%@ Import Namespace="System.Data" %>
02: <%@ Import Namespace="System.Data.SqlClient" %>
03:
04: <script language="VB" runat="server">
05:
06:  sub Page_Load(sender as Object, e as EventArgs)
07:
08:    dim SqlCmd as new StringBuilder()
09:    SqlCmd.Append("SELECT S.CompanyName,")
10:    SqlCmd.Append("P.ProductName,")
11:    SqlCmd.Append("P.QuantityPerUnit,")
```

LISTING 7.6   Continued

```
12:    SqlCmd.Append("P.UnitPrice,")
13:    SqlCmd.Append("P.UnitsInStock,")
14:    SqlCmd.Append("P.UnitsOnOrder ")
15:    SqlCmd.Append("FROM Products P ")
16:    SqlCmd.Append("INNER JOIN Suppliers S ")
17:    SqlCmd.Append("ON ")
18:    SqlCmd.Append("S.SupplierID = P.SupplierID")
19:
20:    dim SqlCon as new SqlConnection("server=localhost;
➥  uid=sa;pwd=;database=northwind")
21:    dim sqlcommand as new SqlCommand(SqlCmd.ToString(), SqlCon)
22:
23:    SqlCon.Open()
24:     RProducts.DataSource = sqlcommand.ExecuteReader()
25:     RProducts.DataBind()
26:    SqlCon.Close()
27:
38: End Sub
29:
30: </script>
```

[C#.NET]

```
01: <%@ Import Namespace="System.Data" %>
02: <%@ Import Namespace="System.Data.SqlClient" %>
03:
04: <script language="c#" runat="server">
05:
06:  public void Page_Load(Object sender, EventArgs e) {
07:
08:    StringBuilder SqlCmd = new StringBuilder();
09:    SqlCmd.Append("SELECT S.CompanyName,");
10:    SqlCmd.Append("P.ProductName,");
11:    SqlCmd.Append("P.QuantityPerUnit,");
12:    SqlCmd.Append("P.UnitPrice,");
13:    SqlCmd.Append("P.UnitsInStock,");
14:    SqlCmd.Append("P.UnitsOnOrder ");
15:    SqlCmd.Append("FROM Products P ");
16:    SqlCmd.Append("INNER JOIN Suppliers S ");
17:    SqlCmd.Append("ON ");
18:    SqlCmd.Append("S.SupplierID = P.SupplierID");
19:
20:    SqlConnection SqlCon = new SqlConnection("server=localhost;
➥  uid=sa;pwd=;database=northwind");
21:    SqlCommand sqlcommand = new SqlCommand(SqlCmd.ToString(), SqlCon);
22:
23:    SqlCon.Open();
```

LISTING 7.6   Continued

```
24:     RProducts.DataSource = sqlcommand.ExecuteReader();
25:     RProducts.DataBind();
26:    SqlCon.Close();
27:
28: }
29:
30: </script>


[VisualBasic.NET and C#.NET]

31: <html>
32: <head><title>DotNetJunkies.com</title>
33: <style rel="stylesheet">
34:
35:  A {text-decoration:none;color:black}
36:  A:Hover {color:maroon;text-decoration:underline}
37:  A:Visited {color:red}
38:  .body { font: 9pt Verdana, Arial, sans-serif; }
39:  .head { font: bold 9pt Verdana, Arial,
➥ sans-serif; background-color:Maroon; color:white; }
40:  .tablehead { font: bold 9pt Verdana, Arial,
➥ sans-serif; background-color:green; color:white; }
41:
42: </style>
43:
44: </head>
45: <body>
46: <center>
47:
48:  <asp:Repeater
49:   id="RProducts"
50:   Runat="Server"
51:  >
52:
53:      <HeaderTemplate>
54:
55:       <table CellPadding="4" CellSpacing="0"
➥ rules="all" border="1" style="width:500;border-collapse:collapse;">
56:          <tr>
57:           <td class="Head">
58:            <center>
59:             Northwind Products
60:            </center>
61:           </td>
62:          </tr>
63:
64:      </HeaderTemplate>
```

LISTING 7.6   Continued

```
65:
66:          <ItemTemplate>
67:
68:          <tr>
69:           <td>
70:            <table width="100%" Class="body">
71:             <tr>
72:              <td align="center" class="tablehead" ColSpan="2">
73:                <%# DataBinder.Eval(Container.DataItem, "ProductName" )%>
74:              </td>
75:             </tr>
76:             <tr>
77:              <td class="body" align="left" valign="top">
78:                <b>Price</b>
79:              </td>
80:              <td class="body" align="right" valign="top">
81:                <b><%# DataBinder.Eval(
➥ Container.DataItem, "UnitPrice",   "{0:C}")%></b>
82:              </td>
83:             </tr>
84:             <tr>
85:              <td class="body" align="left" valign="top">
86:                <b>Quantity Per Unit</b>
87:              </td>
88:              <td class="body" align="right" valign="top">
89:                <b><%# DataBinder.Eval(
➥ Container.DataItem, "QuantityPerUnit")%></b>
90:              </td>
91:             </tr>
92:             <tr>
93:              <td align="center" class="head" ColSpan="2"></td>
94:             </tr>
95:             <tr>
96:              <td class="body" ColSpan="2" align="center">
97:               <a Target="_blank"
98:                  href="ProductDetails.aspx?ProductName=<%# DataBinder.Eval(
➥ Container.DataItem, "ProductName")%>">
99:                 [ More Information Click Here ]
100:               </a>
101:              </td>
102:             </tr>
103:            </table>
104:           </td>
105:          </tr>
106:
```

LISTING 7.6   Continued

```
107:      </ItemTemplate>
108:
109:      <AlternatingItemTemplate>
110:
111:       <tr>
112:        <td>
113:         <table width="100%">
114:          <tr>
115:           <td align="center" class="Head" ColSpan="2">
116:            <%# DataBinder.Eval(Container.DataItem, "ProductName" )%>
117:           </td>
118:          </tr>
119:          <tr>
120:           <td class="body" ColSpan="2" align="center">
121:            <a Target="_blank"
122:             href="ProductDetails.aspx?ProductName=<%# DataBinder.Eval(
➥ Container.DataItem, "ProductName")%>">
123:             [ More Information Click Here ]
124:            </a>
125:           </td>
126:          </tr>
127:          <tr>
128:           <td align="center" class="head" ColSpan="2"></td>
129:          </tr>
130:          <tr>
131:           <td class="body" align="left" valign="top">
132:            <b>Price</b>
133:           </td>
134:           <td class="body" align="right" valign="top">
135:            <b><%# DataBinder.Eval(
➥ Container.DataItem, "UnitPrice",  "{0:C}")%></b>
136:           </td>
137:          </tr>
138:          <tr>
140:           <td class="body" align="left" valign="top">
141:            <b>Quantity Per Unit</b>
142:           </td>
143:           <td class="body" align="right" valign="top">
144:            <b><%# DataBinder.Eval(
➥ Container.DataItem, "QuantityPerUnit")%></b>
145:           </td>
146:          </tr>
147:         </table>
148:        </td>
149:       </tr>
150:
```

LISTING 7.6   Continued

```
151:        </AlternatingItemTemplate>
152:
153:        <FooterTemplate>
154:
155:         </table>
156:
157:        </FooterTemplate>
158:
159:   </asp:Repeater>
160: </center>
161: </body>
162: </html>
```

The Repeater is different from the previous two template controls in a few different ways. First, notice that the Repeater has no default structure—it simply repeats. This is why there are no attributes such as ItemTemplate-Style as with the DataGrid or DataList controls. Instead, when using the Repeater you must define all of its output structure and style.

Let's walk through each of the different sections of the Repeater. First, the HeaderTemplate (lines 53–64)—this section of the Repeater will only be rendered once. This section is where you would most likely put the Header for the output. In this example I first start a <table> HTML element to provide structure to the output data and for the header I text I used, "Northwind Products."

The next section is the ItemTemplate (lines 66–107)—the ItemTemplate, like the DataList and DataGrid is rendered once for each item in the Repeater.DataSource unless the AlternatingItemTemplate is being used. Within the ItemTemplate I nest an additional table to achieve even more control over the way each item is rendered. The ItemTemplate behaves exactly like the DataList and DataGrid's ItemTemplate—note: The more complicated the structure is in the ItemTemplate, the slower the rendering.

The AlternatingItemTemplate is the next item in the Repeater. It too behaves like the DataList's AlternatingItemTemplate. In this example we create another nested table. The next template is something you haven't used yet—the FooterTemplate. In this example I use the FooterTemplate to close our <TABLE> HTML tag. Figure 7.6 contains an illustration of this page when rendered.

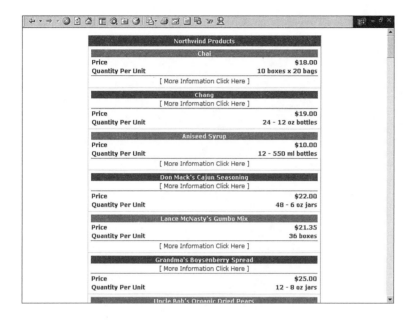

FIGURE 7.6
Repeater server control using the HeaderTemplate, ItemTemplate, AlternatingItemTemplate, *and* FooterTemplate.

Summary

Using templates in ASP.NET will save you an incredible amount of time in the development of very complicated user interfaces by cutting out the need to do complicated loop structures intermixed with HTML elements and data rendering. This chapter introduced you to the following concepts:

- What templates are
- How to use templates with the DataGrid
- How to use templates with the DataList
- How to use templates with the Repeater

The DataList and DataGrid server controls can support updating, editing, item selection, and the deletion of items rendered by the controls, but that won't be covered in this chapter. Stay tuned for Chapter 10, "Inputting and Editing Data Using the DataGrid and DataList" where we will go into these features in depth. It is noteworthy to mention that the Repeater also can be tweaked to support the above features (editing, selecting, etc.). However, this will not be covered simply because it isn't efficient to reinvent the wheel.

Updating and Inputting Data

PART

III

IN THIS PART

Gathering Data with ASP.NET Web Forms

Up to this point in the book we have discussed a number of ways to retrieve and show data using ASP.NET, but haven't touched on how to collect data from users and return it back to the server. We use a combination of a FORM (<form runat="server">) and controls to collect data from the user. A FORM is essentially a container that provides a way to exchange data between the client and server. ASP.NET comes with a rich collection of useful controls you can use within a FORM that makes data collection a very speedy and reliable process.

This chapter will discuss some of the more commonly used server controls—be careful not to confuse these with HTML server controls, which also can collect data from users. Specifically, in this chapter we will cover the following ASP.NET server controls:

- Button
- TextBox
- DropDownList
- ListBox
- CheckBox
- CheckBoxList
- RadioButton
- RadioButtonList

We will be going over each of the proceeding server controls in some detail. We'll explain how to raise and handle some of the controls events, how to retrieve attributes from the control programmatically on the server, and, finally, we'll demonstrate how to bind the control to a data source, if applicable.

As you may or may not know, an ASP.NET server control that has a user interface doesn't render any special objects to the client (browser). If you were to view the source code sent to the client's browser you would see only a collection of HTML elements. For instance, there is a Calendar server control available to you right out of the box when you install .NET. When you drop this control into your web form and a client requests the page, a calendar is not rendered in the client's browser; instead, a mix of HTML elements is rendered that looks like a calendar. My point is, every server control has an HTML counterpart. In some of the sections of this chapter I'll demonstrate this fact by showing you both the server control code and the code that is actually sent to the client. I recommend viewing source on all new controls you use so you become famililar with what HTML is actually sent to the client.

Typically when gathering information or data from users you must validate the data they give you. For instance, if you have a field in your form where the user must enter their date of birth, you probably want to make sure that they enter a valid date. In this chapter we will not be validating the data collected. In Chapter 9, "Evaluating Data with ASP.NET Validation Controls," we'll discuss using the ASP.NET validation controls to validate data. Validation controls are server controls that can be wired or bound to other controls and automatically validate their values.

Button ASP.NET Server Control

A button is used by nearly all user interface applications, and its function is the same across every application. A button lets a user choose an option, tell the application she is done with a task, or exit an application. The ASP.NET `Button` server control is no different. The `Button` control comes in three flavors:

- `Button`—Renders as a typical HTML Button
  `<Input Type"="Button"">`
- `LinkButton`—Renders as a hyperlink
- `ImageButton`—Renders as an image for your `Button`

All three of the buttons do the same thing; they cause an HTML form to be submitted back to the server when it is clicked. However, ASP.NET adds an additional feature that enables you to call methods on the server on the post back. Later in this section, I'll demonstrate this functionality in detail. In the following sections we will go through each of the three button types, illustrating how to use each and how to use some of their attributes to effect the way they are rendered.

Button

The first of the three different types of buttons looks like a typical HTML button that you can render by inserting `<input type="button">` into your code. Listing 8.1 shows how to use the Button control.

LISTING 8.1   Using the Button Control

```
01: <html>
02:   <body>
03:    <form runat="server">
04:     <h3>Button Server Control - Button</h3>
05:     <asp:button id="Button1"
06:      runat="server"
07:      BackColor="maroon"
08:      ForeColor="white"
09:      BorderWidth="2"
10:      BorderStyle="Solid"
11:      BorderColor="Black"
12:      Font-Bold="true"
13:      Text="Click Me"
14:      Width="200"
15:     />
16:    </form>
17:   </body>
18: </html>
```

The server-side code and the HTML code rendered to the page are quite different. The following bit of code is the ASP.NET server control when the page is requested and rendered:

```
01: <input type="submit" name="Button1" value="Click Me"
02: id="Button1" style="color:White;background-color:Maroon;
03: border-color:Black;border-width:2px;border-style:Solid;
04: font-weight:bold;width:200px;" />
```

Code is converted into legitimate HTML and style code behind the scenes. Slick? I think so!

LinkButton

The second type of button is the LinkButton and it has all the same members of the button type, but instead of a typical button showing up, a hyperlink is rendered. You can test it using the same code from Listing 8.1, but replacing lines 5–15 with the code from Listing 8.2.

LISTING 8.2   LinkButton Control

```
01:      <asp:LinkButton id="Button1"
02:       runat="server"
03:       ForeColor="Maroon"
04:       Font-Bold="true"
05:       Text="Click Here"
06:       />
```

If you were to view the source on the rendered page when using the LinkButton, you would see the following code:

```
01:   <html>
02:    <body>
03:     <form name="ctrl0" method="post" action="Listing8.2.aspx" id="ctrl0">
04: <input type="hidden" name="__VIEWSTATE" value="dDwtMTAwOTA0ODU1NTs7Pg==" />
05:
06:      <h3>Button Server Control - LinkButton</h3>
07:      <a id="Button1" href="javascript:__doPostBack('Button1','')"
➥  style="color:Maroon;font-weight:bold;">Click Here</a>
08:
09: <input type="hidden" name="__EVENTTARGET" value="" />
10: <input type="hidden" name="__EVENTARGUMENT" value="" />
11: <script language="javascript">
12: <!--
13:         function __doPostBack(eventTarget, eventArgument) {
14:                 var theform = document.ctrl0
15:                 theform.__EVENTTARGET.value = eventTarget
16:                 theform.__EVENTARGUMENT.value = eventArgument
17:                 theform.submit()
18:         }
19: // -->
```

```
20: </script>
21: </form>
22:  </body>
23: </html>
```

Not only is the LinkButton translated into HTML and text, but it adds JavaScript to the page to post the form back to the server when the link is clicked. Can it get any easier?

> **NOTE**
>
> The HTML that is rendered by your browser might be different from mine depending on what type and version of browser you have.

ImageButton

The last of the three types of button controls is the ImageButton. It too has the same members as the previous two buttons, but also has some of its own unique attributes associated with it:

- AlternateText   Used to get or set the alternate text in the event the image that should be displayed cannot be—for example: AlternateText="Putting The Dot in .NET"

- ImageAlign   Used to get or set the alignment of the image when rendered—for example: Left, Right, BaseLine, Top, or NotSet (default)—ImageAlign="Left"

- ImageUrl   Used to get or set the location of the image to display—for example: ImageUrl="myimages/dotnetjunkieslogo.gif"

Again you can just replace lines 5–15 of Listing 8.1 with the following code.

LISTING 8.3   An example Using the ImageButton

```
01:     <asp:imagebutton id="Button1"
02:       runat="server"
03:       BorderWidth="0"
04:       AlternateText="Putting the Dot In .NET"
05:       ImageUrl="http://www.dotnetjunkies.com/images/dnj_logo2.gif"
06:       />
```

If you were to view the source on the rendered page when using the ImageButton, you would see the code for the ImageButton rendered as the following:

```
01: <input type="image" name="Button1" id="Button1"
02: src="http://www.DotNetJunkies.com/images/dnj_logo2.gif"
03: alt="Putting the Dot In .NET" style="border-width:0px;" />
```

The ImageButton is converted into an INPUT element of the type image.

Handling Button Events

You will most likely be using one of the Button controls for users to submit a form to the server, whether it is to submit data or make some kind of selection. When a Button control is clicked and the form is posted back to the server there are certain events that can be raised and handled. Although there are other events raised when a button control is clicked (Command), in this section we will go over the Click event—the Command event will be discussed later in the book.

When you want to handle the Click event you set the Buttons OnClick attribute equal to the method you want to use as the event handler. Listing 8.4 demonstrates how to handle the Button Controls Click event. Additionally, the code example will illustrate how to programmatically manipulate some properties of the Buttons on the server.

LISTING 8.4 Handling the Button Controls Click Event

```
[VisualBasic.NET]
01: <script runat="server" language="vb">
02:
03:  public sub Button1_Click(sender as Object, e as EventArgs)
04:
05:   message.Text = "Button Has Been Clicked"
06:   Button1.Text = "Been Clicked"
07:
08:  end sub
09:
10:  public sub LinkButton1_Click(sender as Object, e as EventArgs)
11:
12:   message.Text = "Link Button Has Been Clicked"
13:   LinkButton1.Text = "Been Clicked"
14:
15:  end sub
16:
17:  public sub ImageButton1_Click(sender as Object, e as ImageClickEventArgs)
18:
19:   message.Text = "Image Button Has Been " & _
20:    "Clicked at X = " + e.X.ToString() + " Y = " + e.Y.ToString()
21:
22:   ImageButton1.ImageUrl = "http://msdn.microsoft.com/msdn-online/
➥  shared/graphics/banners/net-banner.gif"
23:   ImageButton1.AlternateText="Microsoft .NET"
24:  end sub
25:
26: </script>

[C#.NET]
```

LISTING 8.4 Continued

```
01: <script runat="server" language="C#">
02:
03:  void Button1_Click(Object sender, EventArgs e) {
04:
05:   message.Text = "Button Has Been Clicked";
06:   Button1.Text = "Been Clicked";
07:
08:  }
09:
10:  void LinkButton1_Click(Object sender, EventArgs e) {
11:
12:   message.Text = "Link Button Has Been Clicked";
13:   LinkButton1.Text = "Been Clicked";
14:
15:  }
16:
17:  void ImageButton1_Click(Object sender, ImageClickEventArgs e) {
18:
19:   message.Text = "Image Button Has Been " +
20:    "Clicked at X = " + e.X.ToString() + " Y = " + e.Y.ToString();
21:
22:   ImageButton1.ImageUrl = "http://msdn.microsoft.com/msdn-online/
➥ shared/graphics/banners/net-banner.gif";
23:   ImageButton1.AlternateText="Microsoft .NET";
24:  }
25:
26: </script>

[VisualBasic.NET & C#.NET]

27: <html>
28:  <body>
29:   <form runat="server">
30:    <asp:label id="message"
31:     runat="server"
32:     Font-Size="10"
33:    />
34:
35:    <p>
36:     <asp:button id="Button1"
37:      runat="server"
38:      BackColor="maroon"
39:      ForeColor="white"
40:      BorderWidth="2"
41:      BorderStyle="Solid"
42:      BorderColor="Black"
```

LISTING 8.4 Continued

```
43:        Font-Bold="true"
44:        Text="Click Me"
45:        Width="200"
46:        OnClick="Button1_Click"
47:      />
48:
49:    </p><p>
50:
51:     <asp:LinkButton id="LinkButton1"
52:      runat="server"
53:      ForeColor="Maroon"
54:      Font-Bold="true"
55:      Text="Click Here"
56:      OnClick="LinkButton1_Click"
57:      />
58:
59:    </p><p>
60:
61:     <asp:imagebutton id="ImageButton1"
62:      runat="server"
63:      BorderWidth="0"
64:      AlternateText="Putting the Dot In .NET"
65:      ImageUrl="http://www.DotNetJunkies.com/images/dnj_logo2.gif"
66:      OnClick="ImageButton1_Click"
67:      />
68:
69:     </p>
70:
71:    </form>
72:   </body>
73: </html>
```

When the code example in Listing 8.4 initially renders, you will receive a page similar to that in Figure 8.1.

On the top of the page is the Button that reads "Click Me". Below that is the LinkButton that reads "Click Here", and finally is the ImageButton with an image of our logo, DotNetJunkies.com.

Click each one. As you click you'll notice that the text in the Label control changes—the Label control is located at the top of the page above the first Button. Also, the text of the LinkButton and Button is changed to "Been Clicked" and the ImageButton's image is changed from our DotNetJunkies.com logo to MSDN's .NET logo. Now that you have seen how things are working cosmetically, let's see how they are working on the server.

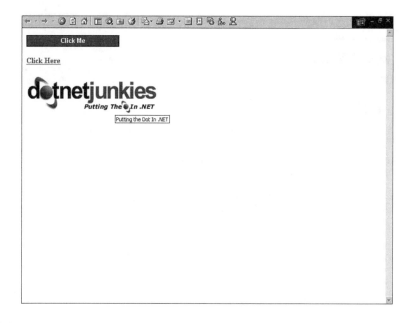

FIGURE 8.1

The three types of Button *controls*—Button, LinkButton, *and* ImageButton.

The Button control can be found in lines 36–47. Its Click event is handled by Button1_Click (lines 3–8); the Button is wired together with the event handler by setting the OnClick attribute equal to Button1_Click (line 46). When the Click event is handled, two things happen. First, the message Label control's Text attribute is changed to "Button Has Been Clicked" and the Text attribute of the Button is changed to "Been Clicked". The LinkButton behaves exactly the same as the Button as far as how the Click event is handled (setting the OnClick attribute) and the actions taken once the event is handled.

You will notice a difference in the ImageButton's event handler (lines 17–24). In the Button and LinkButton Click, the two parameters passed in are Object and the EventArgs. The ImageButton's parameters are Object and ImageClickEventArgs. This is because additional information is passed in that is not applicable to the other two Buttons. This information is specific to the image that is clicked—the XY coordinates of where the image was clicked by the client. These coordinates would come in handy for image mapping—the method of breaking an image into sectors. In this example, when the ImageButton is clicked, I print out its X and Y coordinates of where the image was clicked in the Label and change the ImageUrl attribute. Figure 8.2 contains the page after all three buttons are clicked. The Label control contains the data from the ImageButton.

FIGURE 8.2

All three buttons have been clicked. Notice that the ImageButton's *XY coordinates are printed out as well.*

Binding a Button to a Data Source

The Button controls don't have a DataSource property, but you can certainly bind the attributes of the Button to fields from your data source. For instance, you can bind the name of a product from your data source to the Text attribute of the Button as seen in Listing 8.5.

LISTING 8.5   Binding a Button's Text Attribute

```
[VisualBasic.NET]
01: <script runat="server" language="vb">
02:
03:  public sub Page_Load(sender as Object, e as EventArgs)
04:
05:   DataBind()
06:
07:  end sub
08:
09:  public function ButtonText() as string
10:
11:   return "Click Here"
12:
13:  end function
14:
```

LISTING 8.5   Continued

```
15:
16: </script>

[C#.NET]

01: <script runat="server" language="C#">
02:
03:  void Page_Load(Object sender, EventArgs e){
04:
05:    DataBind();
06:
07:  }
08:
09:  public string ButtonText() {
10:
11:    return "Click Here";
12:
13:  }
14:
15:
16: </script>

[VisualBasic.NET & C#.NET]

17: <html>
18:  <body>
19:   <form runat="server">
20:    <asp:label id="message"
21:     runat="server"
22:     Font-Size="10"
23:    />
24:
25:    <p>
26:     <asp:button id="Button1"
27:      runat="server"
28:      BackColor="maroon"
29:      ForeColor="white"
30:      BorderWidth="2"
31:      BorderStyle="Solid"
32:      BorderColor="Black"
33:      Font-Bold="true"
34:      Text='<%# ButtonText() %>'
35:      Width="200"
36:     />
37:
38:   </form>
39:  </body>
40: </html>
```

Although a very simple example, Listing 8.5 illustrates how to make attributes of controls data bound. In this example I bind the `Text` attribute (line 34) to a function which returns a string—"Click Here" (lines 9–13). Always remember to invoke the `Page.DataBind` method (line 5)—if this isn't called then data binding will not take place and the text for the `Button` will be blank. When invoked, the `Page.DataBind` method causes all databinding syntax to be evaluated. Databinding expressions are contained between the `<%#` and `%>` characters.

TextBox ASP.NET Server Control

The `TextBox` server control provides a way for users to enter information such as numbers, text, dates, and passwords. There are three types of `TextBox` controls: Single-Line, Multi-Line, and Password—the type of TextBox is determined by the value of the `TextMode` attribute. In the following sections, I will demonstrate how to use each type of `TextBox` control and I'll also go over some of their individual attributes you can use to control the data that is entered.

Single-Line `TextBox`

The single-line `TextBox` can be used for a variety of purposes. For example, obtaining a username, or the first and last name of a user. You could use a multi-line, but it wouldn't be prudent in these examples because our examples will consist of very small string values. You should use the multi-line for longer strings—a sentence or paragraph worth of text. I think a good rule of thumb is if the user might not be able to fit all the text they have to enter in a single-line `TextBox` then use a multi-line, but it all falls back to your design patterns. Listing 8.6 is a code example that uses the single-line `TextBox` control.

LISTING 8.6   Single-line `TextBox`

```
01: <html>
02:  <body Style="Font-Size:12">
03:   <form runat="server">
04:   <h3>TextBox - TextMode="SingleLine"</h3>
05:    Enter Your Name:
06:    <asp:TextBox
07:      id="txtSingle"
08:      runat="server"
09:      TextMode="SingleLine"
10:      BackColor="lightGray"
11:      ForeColor="Black"
12:      Font-Bold="true"
13:      BorderWidth="2"
14:      BorderColor="Black"
15:    />
16:   </form>
17:  </body>
18: </html>
```

The `TextBox` members contain every style attribute available to an `HTML` INPUT box, such as `ForeColor`, `BackColor`, and `Font` as seen in Listing 8.6. On line 9 I set the type of `Textbox` I want by setting the `TextMode` attribute to `SingleLine`.

Another attribute I want to talk about is the `MaxLength` attribute. The `MaxLength` attribute gets or sets the maximum number of characters allowed in the `TextBox`. For example, you can set `MaxLength` to 9 to restrict the length of usernames to 9 characters. If you want to play around with the `MaxLength` attribute add `MaxLength="9"` to Listing 8.6 between lines 14 and 15 and try typing more than 9 characters in the `TextBox`. This attribute works for all three types of `TextBox` controls. `Columns` Attribute is another attribute worth discussing. `Columns` sets the width of the control in characters. Don't confuse the `Columns` attribute with `MaxLength`. `MaxLength` is the total amount of characters that can be entered in the control while `Columns` is the display width in characters for the control. When using a single-line `TextBox`, characters can still be entered once the `Columns` value has been exceeded. However, as you'll see in the next section the multi-line `TextBox` behaves differently when the `Columns` attribute is set.

If you were to view the source on the rendered page when using the single-line `TextBox`, you would see the following:

```
01: <input name="txtSingle" type="text" maxlength="9" id="txtSingle"
02: style="color:Black;background-color:LightGrey;border-color:Black;
03: border-width:2px;border-style:solid;font-weight:bold;" />
```

The `TextBox` is conveted into an `INPUT` HTML element of the type `text`.

Multi-line `TextBox`

The multi-line `TextBox` is exactly what the name entails. It is a `TextBox` with multiple rows so a user can enter multiple lines of text. The `TextMode` value for a multi-line `TextBox` is `MultiLine`. The multi-line `TextBox` has additional attributes that the single-line or password `TextBox`'s don't have. The first is `Rows`, which specifies the number of rows within a `TextBox`. The second is `Wrap`, and can have a value of either `true` (default) or `false`. When set to `true` text will wrap to the next row (line) within the `TextBox` when the text has reached the end of the line—much like Microsoft Word. When set to `false`, a scroll bar will be rendered at the bottom of the control and text will continue indefinitely until the user presses Enter to go to the next line.

Keep in mind that attributes for one type of `TextBox` do not work with another. For instance, you can set the `Rows` attribute for a single-line `TextBox` and not get an error, but the `TextBox` can't use it because it doesn't exist for that type of `TextBox`. On the flip side, the `MaxLength` attribute won't work with a multi-line `TextBox`. If the situation arises where you have to limit the amount of characters allowed in a multi-line `TextBox` you will have to use another type of validation to make sure that the correct values are entered—for instance a custom validator. Listing 8.7 is a code example of how to use the multi-line `TextBox`.

LISTING 8.7   The Multi-line TextBox

```
01:  <html>
02:  <body Style="Font-Size:12">
03:   <form runat="server">
04:   <h3>TextBox - TextMode="MultiLine"</h3>
05:    Enter Your Address:
06:    <asp:TextBox
07:     id="txtMulti"
08:     runat="server"
09:     TextMode="MultiLine"
10:     BackColor="lightGray"
11:     ForeColor="Black"
12:     Font-Bold="true"
13:     BorderWidth="2"
14:     BorderColor="Black"
15:     Columns="25"
16:     Rows="5"
17:    />
18:   </form>
19:   </body>
20:  </html>
```

On lines 15 and 16 I set the Columns and Rows attributes. Columns is set to 25, which means that up to 25 characters can be entered on each line of the TextBox. Rows is set to 5, which means that only 5 lines are viewable at any one time.

If you were to view the source on the rendered page when using the multi-line TextBox, you would see the following:

```
<textarea name="txtMulti" rows="5" cols="25" id="txtMulti"
style="color:Black;background-color:LightGrey;border-color:Black;
border-width:2px;border-style:solid;font-weight:bold;"></textarea>
```

The TextBox is converted into a TEXTAREA HTML element.

Password TextBox

The Password TextBox masks all the characters entered by the user with an *—the asterisk, rather than the actual characters being typed, appears on the user's screen. The Password TextBox is, in fact, a single-line TextBox and supports the exact same attributes as the regular single-line; the only difference is that the characters entered are masked. Listing 8.8 shows how to use the Password type TextBox.

LISTING 8.8   The Password TextBox

```
01:  <html>
02:   <body Style="Font-Size:12">
```

LISTING 8.8   Continued

```
03:     <form runat="server">
04:     <h3>TextBox - TextMode="Password"</h3>
05:      Enter Your Password:
06:      <asp:TextBox
07:       id="txtPassword"
08:       runat="server"
09:       TextMode="Password"
10:       BackColor="lightGray"
11:       ForeColor="Black"
12:       Font-Bold="true"
13:       BorderWidth="2"
14:       BorderColor="Black"
15:       MaxLength="9"
16:      />
17:     </form>
18:     </body>
19:     </html>
```

Notice that the code in Listings 8.8 and 8.6 are nearly identical. The only differences are the ID attribute in Listing 8.8 is txtPassword, the TextMode is set to Password, and a MaxLength value is given. If you were to view the source on the rendered page using the Password TextBox, you would see the following:

```
<input name="txtPassword" type="password" maxlength="9" id="txtPassword"
style="color:Black;background-color:LightGrey;border-color:Black;
border-width:2px;border-style:solid;font-weight:bold;" />
```

The TextBox is converted into an INPUT HTML element of the type password.

Raising and Handling Events With the TextBox

In this section I'll demonstrate some of the built-in functionality of the Textbox server control. You'll learn how to wire up the TextBox so that when the Text of the TextBox changes, automatic page postback will occur. For example, you can automatically postback the page as soon as a user changes the contents of a TextBox and then leaves TextBox. Additionally, you will learn how to raise and handle the TextChanged event. The TextChanged event is fired when the value of the TextBox is changed from its rendered state and posted back to the server. This feature is handy if you need to validate how many characters are entered in a multi-line TextBox.

You can enable automatic page postback by setting the TextBox's AutoPostBack attribute to true, the default is false. You use the OnTextChanged attribute of the TextBox to wire up a method to handle the TextChanged event—the value of OnTextChanged should be equal to the name of the method. Listing 8.9 contains a code example demonstrating how to raise and handle events using the TextBox.

LISTING 8.9   Raising and Handling Events Using the `TextBox`

[VisualBasic.NET]

```
01: <script language="vb" runat="server">
02:
03:  public sub txtSingle_TextChanged(sender as Object, e as EventArgs)
04:
05:   lblSingle.Text = txtSingle.Text
06:
07:  end sub
08:
09:  public sub txtMulti_TextChanged(sender as Object, e as EventArgs)
10:
11:   lblMulti.Text = txtMulti.Text
12:
13:  end sub
14:
15:  public sub txtPassword_TextChanged(sender as Object, e as EventArgs)
16:
17:   lblPassword.Text = txtPassword.Text
18:
19:  end sub
20:
21: </script>
```

[C#.NET]

```
01: <script language="c#" runat="server">
02:
03:  void txtSingle_TextChanged(Object sender, EventArgs e){
04:
05:   lblSingle.Text = txtSingle.Text;
06:
07:  }
08:
09:  void txtMulti_TextChanged(Object sender, EventArgs e){
10:
11:   lblMulti.Text = txtMulti.Text;
12:
13:  }
14:
15:  void txtPassword_TextChanged(Object sender, EventArgs e){
16:
17:   lblPassword.Text = txtPassword.Text;
18:
19:  }
```

LISTING 8.9   Continued

```
20:
21: </script>

[VisualBasic.NET & C#.NET]

22: <html>
23:   <body Style="Font-Size:12">
24:    <form runat="server">
25:    <h3>Raising and Handling Events</h3>
26:
27:     Enter Your Name:
28:
29:     <br>
30:     <asp:TextBox
31:      id="txtSingle"
32:      runat="server"
33:      TextMode="SingleLine"
34:      BackColor="lightGray"
35:      ForeColor="Black"
36:      Font-Bold="true"
37:      BorderWidth="2"
38:      BorderColor="Black"
39:      MaxLength="10"
40:      AutoPostBack="false"
41:      OnTextChanged="txtSingle_TextChanged"
42:      />
43:     <asp:Label id="lblSingle" runat="server" />
44:
45:     <p>
46:     Enter Your Address:
47:
48:     <br>
49:     <asp:TextBox
50:      id="txtMulti"
51:      runat="server"
52:      TextMode="MultiLine"
53:      BackColor="lightGray"
54:      ForeColor="Black"
55:      Font-Bold="true"
56:      BorderWidth="2"
57:      BorderColor="Black"
58:      Columns="15"
59:      Rows="5"
60:      AutoPostBack="true"
61:      OnTextChanged="txtMulti_TextChanged"
```

LISTING 8.9   Continued

```
62:    />
63:    <asp:Label id="lblMulti" runat="server" />
64:
65:    <p>
66:    Enter A Password:
67:
68:    <br>
69:    <asp:TextBox
70:      id="txtPassword"
71:      runat="server"
72:      TextMode="Password"
73:      BackColor="lightGray"
74:      ForeColor="Black"
75:      Font-Bold="true"
76:      BorderWidth="2"
77:      BorderColor="Black"
78:      MaxLength="10"
79:      AutoPostBack="true"
80:      OnTextChanged="txtPassword_TextChanged"
81:
82:    />
83:    <asp:Label id="lblPassword" runat="server" />
84:
85:    </form>
86:    </body>
87:  </html>
```

Let's walk through each of the three TextBox controls from Listing 8.9. The single-line TextBox (lines 30–42) has AutoPostBack set to false and OnTextChanged set to txtSingle_TextChanged. What this means is when the value within the TextBox changes, the page will not be posted back to the server, but in the event the page is posted back the txtSingle_TextChanged method (lines 3–7) will handle the TextChanged event. The multi-line TextBox (lines 49–62) has AutoPostBack set to true and the OnTextChanged set to txtMulti_TextChanged. What this means is the page will be posted back to the server when the value within the TextBox changes and the txtMulti_TextChanged method will handle its TextChanged event. The Password TextBox (lines 69–82) also has AutoPostBack set to true and the OnTextChanged set to txtPassword_TextChanged.

To see the effects, do the following:

1. Enter your name in the single-line TextBox.

2. Navigate to the multi-line TextBox and enter your address. (The page will not post back to the server because AutoPostBack is set to false.)

3. Navigate to the Password TextBox. (The page will post back to the server because AutoPostBack is set to true and the TextChanged event will be raised for the single-line and multi-line TextBox.)

Figure 8.3 contains the page from Listing 8.9 after step 3 in the previous list is executed.

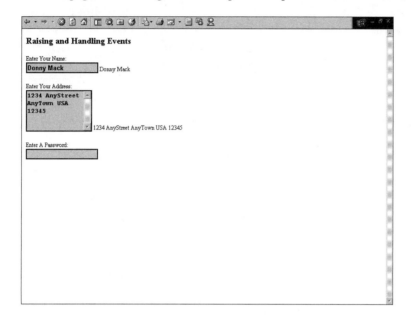

FIGURE 8.3

Page after post back.

Notice that the Label control to the right of the single-line and multi-line TextBox controls have the text entered in the TextBox displayed.

Binding a TextBox to a Data Source

The TextBox control also doesn't have a DataSource property, but you can certainly bind the attributes of the TextBox to fields from your data source. For example, if your site has membership and you allow the user to edit this information you can use a TextBox to load the initial value and then save the edited value back to your database. Rest assured this is covered in detail later in the book.

DropDownList ASP.NET Server Control

The DropDownList control enables item selection from a drop-down ListBox. For example, if your site requires a user to enter their year of birth you can have a DropDownList populated with years ranging from 1900 to present from which the user can select.

Another example would be if your site wanted users to enter their address and, instead of the full state name, only the states' abbreviations—(Washington–WA). You can force them to enter it correctly by making them choose it from the DropDownList.

The DropDownList is the first of the list controls that we will go over. Even though each of the list controls are different in their functionality they are made up of the same guts—the ListItem. The ListItem represents one item in the list control. When you want to add an item to the list control you add a ListItem object. There are three ways to add a ListItem to the DropDownList—Listing 8.10 demonstrates all of them. The DropDownList can also be dynamically populated by setting its DropDownList.DataSource, which I'll discuss later in the chapter.

LISTING 8.10   Adding Items to the DropDownList

```
[VisualBasic.NET]

01: <script runat="server" language="vb" >
02:
03:  public sub Page_Load(sender as Object, e as EventArgs)
04:
05:   ddl.Items.Add(new ListItem("This is Method Three", 3.ToString()))
06:
07:  end sub
08:
09: </script>
```

```
[C#.NET]

01: <script runat="server" language="C#" >
02:
03:  void Page_Load(Object sender, EventArgs e) {
04:
05:   ddl.Items.Add(new ListItem("This is Method Three", 3.ToString()));
06:
07:  }
08:
09: </script>
```

```
[VisualBasic.NET & C#.NET]

10: <html>
11:  <body>
12:   <form runat="server">
13:
```

LISTING 8.10 Continued

```
14:     <asp:DropDownList runat="server" id="ddl" >
15:      <asp:ListItem Value="1" Text="This is Method One" />
16:      <asp:ListItem Value="2">This is Method Two</asp:ListItem>
17:     </asp:DropDownList>
18:
19:    </form>
20:   </body>
21: </html>
```

The `DropDownList` control can be found on lines 14–17. The first method I use to add a `ListItem` can be found on line 15 where all values are contained within one `ListItem` element. The second method is on line 16 where the `Value` attribute is within the opening `ListItem` element and the text is between the opening and closing `ListItem` element. The third method is done dynamically through code (lines 3–7) in the `Page.Load` event. I use the `ListItemsCollection.Add` method passing in a new `ListItem` object (line 5). You might be wondering where the `ListItemsCollection` object came from—it was accessed through the `DropDownList.Items` property. The `ListItemCollection` is a zero-based collection of `ListItem` objects. Like nearly everything in .NET you can write code to add a new `ListItem` many different ways. I wrote it this way for the simple fact that it requires the least amount of code.

In Listing 8.10, I created a new `ListItem` by passing in the `Text` and `Value` of the `ListItem` directly into the object constructor. There are actually three overloads for the `ListItem` constructor. We will not being going into detail for each one, but the following list contains them:

- `ListItem myListItem = new ListItem();`
- `ListItem myListItem = new ListItem(string-for-text);`
- `ListItem myListItem = new ListItem(string-for-text, string-for-value);`

If you were to view the source on the rendered page when using the single-line `TextBox`, you would see the following:

```
01:    <select name="ddl" id="ddl">
02:         <option value="1">This is Method One</option>
03:         <option value="2">This is Method Two</option>
04:         <option value="3">This is Method Three</option>
05:    </select>
```

Look familiar? The `DropDownList` generates a `SELECT` HTML element. Figure 8.4 is an illustration of the page once rendered with the `ListBox` open showing all three items added.

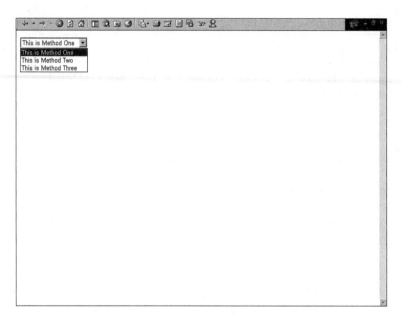

FIGURE 8.4
All three ListItems *have been added to the same* DropDownList.

Raising and Handling Events and Determining Item Selection

I have often seen drop-down lists used for Web site navigation where a user will select an item from the list and the page will immediately navigate to the desired section of the site. This is nothing new and exciting, but is a bit different to implement when using the DropDownList.

The DropDownList.AutoPostBack property behaves similar to that of the TextBox.AutoPostBack in that when a user makes a change to the DropDownList the page is automatically posted back to the server. The difference is that the text isn't changing in the DropDownList as in the TextBox. Instead, when a user changes the DropDownList.SelectedItem the page is posted back to the server. The DropDownList.SelectedIndex is the index of the ListItem within the ListItemCollection that is selected—as a reminder the ListItemCollection is zero based.

The DropDownList.OnSelectedIndexChanged attribute behaves similar to that of the TextBox.OnTextChanged attribute. When a user makes a change to the DropDownList and the page is posted back to the server an event is raised— (DropDownList.SelectedIndexChanged)—and you can handle this event by setting the DropDownList.OnSelectedIndexChanged equal to the name of the method you want to handle it. The difference between the two the change that takes place—a change to the DropDownList.SelectedIndex.

In Listing 8.11, I demonstrate how to use these two attributes. Additionally, I show how to retrieve and set the `DropDownList.SelectedItem`.

LISTING 8.11   Raising and Handling Events and Determining Item Selection

```
[VisualBasic.NET]
01: <script runat="server" language="vb" >
02:
03:   public sub Page_Load(sender as Object, e as EventArgs)
04:
05:    if (Not IsPostBack) then
06:     ddl_AddItems()
07:    end if
08:
09:   end sub
10:
11:   public sub ddl_AddItems()
12:
13:    dim i as integer
14:    for i = 0 to 4
15:     ddl.Items.Add(new ListItem("This is Index - " & i))
16:    next
17:
18:   end sub
19:
20:   public sub ddl_SelectedIndexChanged(sender as Object, e as EventArgs)
21:
22:    dim sb as new StringBuilder()
23:    sb.Append("DropDownList.SelectedIndex = ")
24:    sb.Append(ddl.SelectedIndex)
25:    sb.Append("<br>")
26:    sb.Append("DropDownList.SelectedItem = ")
27:    sb.Append(ddl.SelectedItem.Text)
28:
29:    lblSelectedItem.Text = sb.ToString()
30:
31:   end sub
32:
33: </script>

[C#.NET]
01: <script runat="server" language="C#" >
02:
03:   void Page_Load(Object sender, EventArgs e) {
04:
```

LISTING 8.11   Continued

```
05:   if (! IsPostBack) {
06:     ddl_AddItems();
07:   }
08:
09:  }
10:
11:  void ddl_AddItems(){
12:
13:    int i;
14:    for (i = 0; i < 5; i++){
15:     ddl.Items.Add(new ListItem("This is Index - " + i));
16:    }
17:
18:  }
19:
20:  void ddl_SelectedIndexChanged(Object sender, EventArgs e){
21:
22:    StringBuilder sb = new StringBuilder();
23:    sb.Append("DropDownList.SelectedIndex = ");
24:    sb.Append(ddl.SelectedIndex);
25   sb.Append("<br>");
26:    sb.Append("DropDownList.SelectedItem = ");
27:    sb.Append(ddl.SelectedItem.Text);
28:
29:    lblSelectedItem.Text = sb.ToString();
30:
31:  }
32:
33: </script>

[VisualBasic.NET & C#.NET]

34: <html>
35:  <body Style="font-Size:10">
36:   <form runat="server">
37:    <h3>DropDownList</h3>
38:
39:    <asp:Label id="lblSelectedItem" runat="server" />
40:
41:    <p>
42:
43:    <asp:DropDownList
44:     runat="server"
45:     id="ddl"
46:     AutoPostBack="true"
```

LISTING 8.11   Continued

```
47:     OnSelectedIndexChanged="ddl_SelectedIndexChanged"
48:     />
49:
50:   </form>
51:   </body>
52: </html>
```

Let's start with the `DropDownList` control (lines 43–48) in Listing 8.11. On line 46 I have the `AutoPostBack` property set to `true`. This means that as soon as the `DropDownList.SelectedIndex` changes the page will post back to the server. On line 47 is `OnSelectedIndexChanged` and it is set to `ddl_SelectedIndexChanged`. This means that when the `DropDownList.SelectedIndex` changes and the page is posted back to the server, `ddl_SelectedIndexChanged` (lines 20–31) will handle the `SelectedIndexChaned` event.

You might be wondering why the `DropDownList` is only populated on the first page request and not on a post back (lines 3-9). This is because the `Page.Load` event is fired before the `DropDownList.SelectedIndexChanged` event is. If you were to re-bind the `DropDownList` on every request, then the `DropDownList` would be refreshed to its original state and the `DropDownList.SelectedIndex` value would always be 0.

Within the `ddl_SelectedIndexChanged` I retrieve two values. The first is the `DropDownList.SelectedIndex` and the second is the `DropDownList.SelectedItem.Text`—this is the selected items text that is displayed to the user—"This is Index–2". The `DropDownList.SelectedItem` exposes a `ListItem` object for the item that selected. What this means is you have access to all the `ListItem` attributes—for example, `Text`, `Value`, `Selected`. In this example I access the `Text` attribute.

Binding a `DropDownList` to a Data Source

One of the greatest things about all the list controls is that they can be bound to a data source with more than one record and the `ListItemCollection` automatically will be made. For example, you can populate a `DropDownList` from a `DataTable` and a `ListItem` automatically will be generated for each row in the `DataTable`.

If you want to bind the `DropDownList` to a data source then you must set the `DropDownList.DataSource` equal to the object you want to bind to—this can be any data source that supports the `ICollection` interface—`DataTable`, `DataView`, or `ArrayList`.

You can control which fields from the `DropDownList.DataSource` are used when the `DropDownList`'s `ListItemCollection` is created by using two properties:

- `DataTextField` The name of the field you want to populate `ListItem.Text` (this is what's shown to the user)

- `DataValueField` The name of the field you want to populate `ListItem.Value` (this is the value for the item)

Listing 8.12 demonstrates how to dynamically populate the `DropDownList` from a database.

LISTING 8.12 Data Binding the `DropDownList`

```
[VisualBasic.NET]
01: <%@ Import Namespace="System.Data" %>
02: <%@ Import Namespace="System.Data.SqlClient" %>
03: <script runat="server" language="vb" >
04:
05:  public sub Page_Load(sender as Object, e as EventArgs)
06:
07:   if (not IsPostBack) then
08:    ddl_DataBind()
09:   end if
10:
11:  end sub
12:
13:  public sub ddl_DataBind()
14:
15:   dim SqlCon as new SqlConnection("server=localhost;
➥ uid=sa;pwd=;database=northwind")
16:   dim SqlCmd as new SqlCommand("SELECT ProductName,
➥ ProductID FROM Products", SqlCon)
17:
18:   SqlCon.Open()
19:   ddl.DataSource = SqlCmd.ExecuteReader(CommandBehavior.CloseConnection)
20:   ddl.DataTextField = "ProductName"
21:   ddl.DataValueField = "ProductID"
22:   ddl.DataBind()
23:
24:
25:  end sub
26:
27:  public sub ddl_SelectedIndexChanged(sender as Object, e as EventArgs)
28:
29:   dim sb as new StringBuilder()
30:   sb.Append("DropDownList.SelectedItem Value = ")
31:   sb.Append(ddl.SelectedItem.Value)
32:   sb.Append("<br>")
```

LISTING 8.12   Continued

```
33:    sb.Append("DropDownList.SelectedItem = ")
34:    sb.Append(ddl.SelectedItem.Text)
35:
36:    lblSelectedItem.Text = sb.ToString()
37:
38:  end sub
39:
40: </script>
```

```
[C#.NET]
01: <%@ Import Namespace="System.Data" %>
02: <%@ Import Namespace="System.Data.SqlClient" %>
03: <script runat="server" language="C#" >
04:
05:  void Page_Load(Object sender, EventArgs e) {
06:
07:    if (! IsPostBack) {
08:     ddl_DataBind();
09:    }
10:
11:  }
12:
13:  void ddl_DataBind(){
14:
15:    SqlConnection SqlCon = new SqlConnection("server=localhost;
➡ uid=sa;pwd=;database=northwind");
16:    SqlCommand SqlCmd = new SqlCommand("SELECT ProductName,
➡ ProductID FROM Products", SqlCon);
17:
18:    SqlCon.Open();
19:    ddl.DataSource = SqlCmd.ExecuteReader(CommandBehavior.CloseConnection);
20:    ddl.DataTextField = "ProductName";
21:    ddl.DataValueField = "ProductID";
22:    ddl.DataBind();
23:
24:
25:  }
26:
27:  void ddl_SelectedIndexChanged(Object sender, EventArgs e){
28:
29:    StringBuilder sb = new StringBuilder();
30:    sb.Append("DropDownList.SelectedItem Value = ");
31:    sb.Append(ddl.SelectedItem.Value);
32:    sb.Append("<br>");
```

8

LISTING 8.12   Continued

```
33:    sb.Append("DropDownList.SelectedItem = ");
34:    sb.Append(ddl.SelectedItem.Text);
35:
36:    lblSelectedItem.Text = sb.ToString();
37:
38:  }
39:
40: </script>

[VisualBasic.NET & C#.NET]

41: <html>
42:   <body Style="font-Size:10">
43:    <form runat="server">
44:     <h3>DropDownList</h3>
45:
46:     <asp:Label id="lblSelectedItem" runat="server" />
47:
48:     <p>
49:
50:     <asp:DropDownList
51:      runat="server"
52:      id="ddl"
53:      AutoPostBack="true"
54:      OnSelectedIndexChanged="ddl_SelectedIndexChanged"
55:      />
56:
57:    </form>
58:   </body>
59: </html>
```

Binding to the DropDownList is very simple as Listing 8.12 demonstrates. First, you'll need an object to bind to—in this example I use a SqlDataReader (lines 15–19). After setting the DropDownList.DataSource I use the DropDownList.DataTextField attribute to set which field from the data source should be shown to the user in the list—DropDownList.DataValueField. I use the DropDownList.DataValueField to set which field should be used as the DropDownList.Value.

In this example I also have set AutoPostBack to true and when the page is posted back to the server after a selected index change in the DropDownList, the Text and Value attributes are printed out to the page as seen in Figure 8.5.

FIGURE 8.5
After the page is posted back to the server the selected item details are printed out to the page.

ListBox ASP.NET Server Control

The ListBox server control is very similar to the DropDownList, but differs in its display. You can have more than one item at a time shown to the user. The ListBox also enables users to select more than one item at time. For example, if you have a site that delivers news to its users you can allow users to select the type of news they want (for example: sports, world) using the ListBox.

Multiple item selection is a behavior over which you have control. By default the ListBox allows users to select only a single item in the list, but by setting the ListBox.SelectionMode attribute to Multiple multiple item selection is enabled. The following lists the two values you can use for the SelectionMode attribute:

- Single   Single item selection (default)
- Multiple   Multiple item selection

Because the ListBox enables you to display more than one item at a time there is one other attribute you can use to affect how the control is rendered to the client. The Rows attribute controls how many items are displayed to the user in the ListBox. If the amount of items in the Listbox exceeds this value, then scroll bars are rendered for ListBox navigation.

Listing 8.13 demonstrates how to use a ListBox control. There are four different types of ListBoxes in this example because I wanted to illustrate how setting the SelectionMode and Rows attributes to different values affect the way the control is rendered.

LISTING 8.13   Using the Different Styles of the ListBox Control

```
[VisualBasic.NET]
01: <script runat="server" language="vb" >
02:
03:  public sub Page_Load(sender as Object, e as EventArgs)
04:
05:   if (Not IsPostBack) then
06:    lb_AddItems()
07:   end if
08:
09:  end sub
10:
11:  public sub lb_AddItems()
12:
13:   dim i as integer
14:   for i = 0 to 4
15:    lb.Items.Add(new ListItem("This is Index - " & i))
16:    lb2.Items.Add(new ListItem("This is Index - " & i))
17:    lb3.Items.Add(new ListItem("This is Index - " & i))
18:    lb4.Items.Add(new ListItem("This is Index - " & i))
19:   next
20:
21:  end sub
22:
23: </script>

[C#.NET]
01: <script runat="server" language="C#" >
02:
03:  void Page_Load(Object source, EventArgs e ) {
04:
05:   if (! Page.IsPostBack) {
06:    lb_AddItems();
07:   }
08:
09:  }
10:
11:  void lb_AddItems(){
12:
13:   int i;
14:   for (i = 0; i < 5; i++){
```

LISTING 8.13   Continued

```
15:     lb.Items.Add(new ListItem("This is Index - " + i));
16:     lb2.Items.Add(new ListItem("This is Index - " + i));
17:     lb3.Items.Add(new ListItem("This is Index - " + i));
18:     lb4.Items.Add(new ListItem("This is Index - " + i));
19:     }
20:
21:   }
22:
23: </script>

[VisualBasic.NET & C#.NET]

24: <html>
25:   <body>
26:    <form method="post" runat="server">
27:
28:     5 Rows Multiple Item Selection
29:     <br>
30:     <asp:ListBox runat="server" rows="5" id="lb" SelectionMode="Multiple" />
31:
32:     <p>
33:
34:     5 Rows Single Item Selection
35:     <br>
36:     <asp:ListBox runat="server" rows="5" id="lb2" SelectionMode="Single" />
37:
38:     <p>
39:
40:     1 Row Single Line Selection
41:     <br>
42:     <asp:ListBox runat="server" rows="1" id="lb3" SelectionMode="Single" />
43:
44:     <p>
45:
46:     1 Row Multiple Line Selection
47:     <br>
48:     <asp:ListBox runat="server" rows="1" id="lb4"
➥  SelectionMode="Multiple" />
49:
50:    </form>
51:   </body>
52: </html>
```

As previously mentioned there are four types of ListBox controls in Listing 8.13. Each has five items (ListItems). In the following paragraphs we'll go through each one and look at which attributes are used and the effect they have on the rendered element.

The first ListBox (line 30) has the Rows attribute set to five and SelectionMode set to Multiple. Because there are only five items a scroll bar is not rendered, and because SelectionMode is Multiple the user can select more than one item from the list. The following HTML is rendered to the client for this ListBox—a SELECT element just like the DropDownList, but with two new attributes—size and multiple:

```
01: <select name="lb" id="lb" size="5" multiple="multiple">
02:     <option value="This is Index - 0">This is Index - 0</option>
03:     <option value="This is Index - 1">This is Index - 1</option>
04:     <option value="This is Index - 2">This is Index - 2</option>
05:     <option value="This is Index - 3">This is Index - 3</option>
06:     <option value="This is Index - 4">This is Index - 4</option>
07: </select>
```

The next ListBox (line 36) also has Rows set to five, but the SelectionMode attribute is set to Single so the user can select only one item from the list. The following HTML is rendered to the client for this ListBox—because SelectionMode is Single, only the size attribute is rendered:

```
01: <select name="lb2" id="lb2" size="5">
02:     <option value="This is Index - 0">This is Index - 0</option>
03:     <option value="This is Index - 1">This is Index - 1</option>
04:     <option value="This is Index - 2">This is Index - 2</option>
05:     <option value="This is Index - 3">This is Index - 3</option>
06:     <option value="This is Index - 4">This is Index - 4</option>
07: </select>
```

On line 42 is the next ListBox and it has Rows set to one and SelectionMode set to Single. When this ListBox is rendered you will notice that it's essentially a DropDownList control as seen in Figure 8.6. The following HTML is rendered to the client for this ListBox—compare this HTML to that of the DropDownList—they are identical:

```
01: <select name="lb3" id="lb3" size="1">
02:     <option value="This is Index - 0">This is Index - 0</option>
03:     <option value="This is Index - 1">This is Index - 1</option>
04:     <option value="This is Index - 2">This is Index - 2</option>
05:     <option value="This is Index - 3">This is Index - 3</option>
06:     <option value="This is Index - 4">This is Index - 4</option>
07: </select>
```

The final ListBox, located on line 48, also has Rows set to 1, but has SelectionMode set to Multiple. This means the user can see only one item at a time, but can choose multiple items from the list. The following HTML is rendered to the client for this ListBox:

```
01: <select name="lb4" id="lb4" size="1" multiple="multiple">
02:     <option value="This is Index - 0">This is Index - 0</option>
03:     <option value="This is Index - 1">This is Index - 1</option>
04:     <option value="This is Index - 2">This is Index - 2</option>
```

```
05:    <option value="This is Index - 3">This is Index - 3</option>
06:    <option value="This is Index - 4">This is Index - 4</option>
07: </select>
```

Size is set to 1 and multiple is set to multiple. Let's take a look at what this page looks like! Figure 8.6 contains the page created in Listing 8.14—the ListBox controls discussed in the previous paragraphs are shown in order.

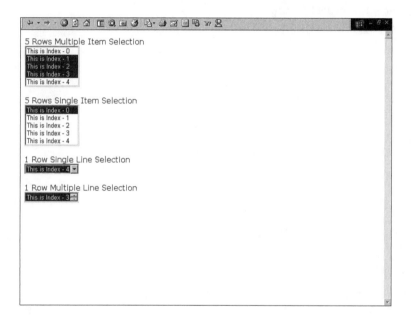

FIGURE 8.6
All four types of Listbox.

Raising and Handling Events and Determining Item Selection

The ListBox supports the same events and attributes of the DropDownList—AutoPostBack, SelectedIndex, OnSelectedIndexChanged, and SelectedItem. But, because the ListBox supports multiple item selection, you have to do things a little differently to get the selected values.

As previously mentioned, the List controls are made up of ListItem objects—ListItemCollection. Again, the ListItem object contains the Value, and Text of the item in the control; additionally, it contains a Selected attribute which is either going to be true or false. It will be true if the ListItem is selected and false if not. We use this ListItemCollection to determine which item or items are selected within List controls. Listing 8.14 demonstrates how to loop through a ListBox with multiple item selection enabled.

LISTING 8.14   Retrieving All the Selected Items in a `ListBox`

[VisualBasic.NET]

```
01: <script runat="server" language="vb">
02:
03:  public sub Page_Load(sender as Object, e as EventArgs)
04:
05:   if (Not IsPostBack) then
06:    lb_AddItems()
07:   end if
08:
09:  end sub
10:
11:  public sub lb_AddItems()
12:
13:   dim i as integer
14:   for i = 0 to 4
15:    lb.Items.Add(new ListItem("This is Index - " & i))
16:   next
17:
18:  end sub
19:
20:  public sub lblMulti_OnSelectedIndexChanged(
➥ sender as Object, e as EventArgs)
21:
22:   dim sb as new StringBuilder()
23:   dim i as integer
24:
25:   for i = 0 to lb.Items.Count - 1
26:    if lb.Items(i).Selected = true then
27:       sb.Append(i)
28:       sb.Append(". ")
29:       sb.Append(lb.Items(i).Text)
30:       sb.Append("<br>")
31:    end if
32:   next
33:
34:   lblMulti.Text = sb.ToString()
35:
36:  end sub
37:
38: </script>
```

LISTING 8.14   Continued

[C#.NET]

```
01: <script runat="server" language="C#">
02:
03:  void Page_Load(Object source, EventArgs e ) {
04:
05:   if (! Page.IsPostBack) {
06:    lb_AddItems();
07:   }
08:
09:  }
10:
11:  void lb_AddItems(){
12:
13:   int i;
14:   for (i = 0; i < 5; i++){
15:    lb.Items.Add(new ListItem("This is Index - " + i));
16:   }
17:
18:  }
19:
20:  void lblMulti_OnSelectedIndexChanged(Object sender, EventArgs e){
21:
22:   StringBuilder sb = new StringBuilder();
23:   int i;
24:
25:   for (i = 0; i < lb.Items.Count; i ++){
26:    if (lb.Items[i].Selected == true) {
27:      sb.Append(i);
28:      sb.Append(". ");
29:      sb.Append(lb.Items[i].Text);
30:      sb.Append("<br>");
31:    }
32:   }
33:
34:   lblMulti.Text = sb.ToString();
35:
36:  }
37:
38: </script>
```

8

LISTING 8.14 Continued

```
[VisualBasic.NET & C#.NET]
39: <html>
40:  <body>
41:   <form runat="server">
42:
43:    5 Rows Multiple Item Selection
44:
45:    <br>
46:
47:    <asp:ListBox runat="server"
48:     rows="5" id="lb"
49:     SelectionMode="Multiple"
50:     AutoPostBack="True"
51:     OnSelectedIndexChanged="lblMulti_OnSelectedIndexChanged"
52:    />
53:
54:    <br>
55:
56:    <asp:Label id="lblMulti" runat="server" />
57:
58:   </form>
59:  </body>
60: </html>
```

The ListBox control in Listing 8.14 is located on lines 47–52. I have Rows set to 5, AutoPostBack to true, SelectionMode to Multiple, and I have OnSelectedIndexChanged set to lblMulti_OnSelectedIndexChanged—the SelectedIndexChanged event handler. When this page first renders you'll receive a ListBox with five items in it and no scroll bars. You can select an item(s) by clicking on it. You can also click on an item and, while holding down the right mouse button, dragging the cursor up or down. Finally, you can click on an item while holding the Ctrl button down and then clicking another.

After a selection is made, the page is posted back to the server and the SelectedIndexChanged event is handled by lblMulti_OnSelectedIndexChanged. Within the event handler a for loop is used to loop through the ListItemCollection looking for ListItems with the Selected property of true, concatenated together using a StringBuilder, and finally written to the page using a Label control. Figure 8.7 contains an illustration of this page after the first and last items are selected from the ListBox.

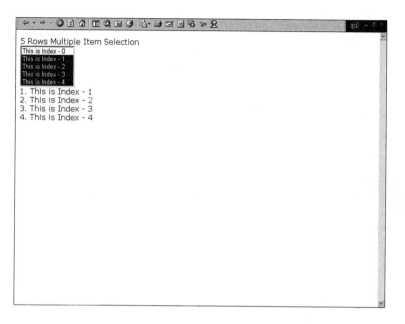

FIGURE 8.7
The Label *control contains a list of selected items.*

Binding a `ListBox` to a Data Source

The `ListBox` control supports binding just as the `DropDownList` control does. You set the `ListBox.DataSource`, `DataTextField`, and `DataValueField` and call the `DataBind` method. Listing 8.15 demonstrates how to bind a `ListBox` control to a data source that was derived from a database query.

LISTING 8.15   Binding the `ListBox` Control to a Data Source

```
[VisualBasic.NET]

01: <%@ Import Namespace="System.Data" %>
02: <%@ Import Namespace="System.Data.SqlClient" %>
03: <script runat="server" language="vb" >
04:
05:  public sub Page_Load(sender as Object, e as EventArgs)
06:
07:   if (not IsPostBack) then
08:    lb_DataBind()
09:   end if
10:
```

LISTING 8.15   Continued

```
11:   end sub
12:
13:   public sub lb_DataBind()
14:
15:    dim SqlCon as new SqlConnection("server=localhost;
➥ uid=sa;pwd=;database=northwind")
16:    dim SqlCmd as new SqlCommand("SELECT ProductName,
➥ ProductID FROM Products", SqlCon)
17:
18:    SqlCon.Open()
19:    lb.DataSource = SqlCmd.ExecuteReader(CommandBehavior.CloseConnection)
20:    lb.DataTextField = "ProductName"
21:    lb.DataValueField = "ProductID"
22:    lb.DataBind()
23:
24:   end sub
25:
26: </script>

[C#.NET]

01: <%@ Import Namespace="System.Data" %>
02: <%@ Import Namespace="System.Data.SqlClient" %>
03: <script runat="server" language="C#" >
04:
05:   void Page_Load(Object sender, EventArgs e) {
06:
07:    if (! IsPostBack) {
08:     lb_DataBind();
09:    }
10:
11:   }
12:
13:   void lb_DataBind(){
14:
15:    SqlConnection SqlCon = new SqlConnection("server=localhost;
➥ uid=sa;pwd=;database=northwind");
16:    SqlCommand SqlCmd = new SqlCommand("SELECT ProductName,
➥ ProductID FROM Products", SqlCon);
17:
18:    SqlCon.Open();
19:    lb.DataSource = SqlCmd.ExecuteReader(CommandBehavior.CloseConnection);
20:    lb.DataTextField = "ProductName";
21:    lb.DataValueField = "ProductID";
22:    lb.DataBind();
23:
```

LISTING 8.15   Continued

```
24:  }
25:
26: </script>
```

[VisualBasic.NET & C#.NET]

```
27: : <html>
28:  <body>
29:   <form runat="server">
30:
31:    <asp:ListBox
32:     runat="server"
33:     Rows="15"
34:     SelectionMode="Multiple"
35:     id="lb" />
36:
37:   </form>
38:  </body>
39: </html>
```

If you compared the data binding code in Listing 8.16 to the data binding code from Listing 8.13 the only difference you would see is the name of the control which is being bound—ddl (DropDownList) versus lb (ListBox). First you construct a valid data source and use it as the ListBox.DataSource. Then set the DataTextField and DataValueField, invoke the DataBind method and you're done.

CheckBox ASP.NET Server Control

There are two types of CheckBox server controls: CheckBox and CheckBoxList. The Checkbox control provides a way for users to input Boolean data, either a true or false value. For example, you could provide a CheckBox on your site so users could indicate whether they would like to receive a weekly newsletter. If they would not like to receive it, they wouldn't check the box.

One attribute with which you should be familiar when using the CheckBox control is the Checked attribute. The Checked attribute expects a Boolean value (true or false) and if true the CheckBox will be selected; if false then it is not. Listing 8.16 demonstrates the use of the CheckBox control—the top CheckBox has Checked set to true and the bottom is false.

LISTING 8.16   The CheckBox Control

```
01: <html>
02:  <body>
03:   <form runat="server">
```

LISTING 8.16   Continued

```
04:
05:    <asp:Checkbox runat="server"
06:     id="cb"
07:     Checked="true"
08:     Text="Check Me Out"
09:     />
10:
11:    <br>
12:
13:    <asp:Checkbox runat="server"
14:     id="cb2"
15:     Checked="false"
16:     Text="Check Me Out"
17:     />
18:
19:    </form>
20:   </body>
21: </html>
```

When the page from Listing 8.16 is rendered you'll get a page with two CheckBox controls, both with the text "Check Me Out" to the right. The top CheckBox is checked when it first loads because I set the Checked attribute to true— the bottom is set to false so it will not be checked. The following HTML is what is actually rendered to the client:

```
01: <input id="cb" type="checkbox" name="cb" checked="checked" /><label
for="cb">Check Me Out</label>
02:
03: <br>
04:
05: <input id="cb2" type="checkbox" name="cb2" /><label for="cb2">Check Me
Out</label>
```

Two HTML INPUT elements of the type checkbox are rendered along with LABEL elements that contain text.

Raising and Handling Events and Determining Item Selection

As with all the other controls, you can raise an event when the CheckBox control changes from checked to unchecked, and vice versa. This event is the CheckedChanged event. You use OnCheckedChanged to indicate which method will handle this event. Note that, as with all the rest of the controls, the form will only post back on the change if AutoPostBack is set to true for the control unless a Button is used to submit the form.

LISTING 8.17   Responding to Changes to the CheckBox Control

```
[VisualBasic.NET]

01: <script runat="server" language="vb">
02:
03:   public sub cb_CheckedChanged(sender as Object, e as EventArgs)
04:
05:   if(cb.Checked)then
06:
07:    cb.Text = "Item Is Checked"
08:
09:   else
10:
11:    cb.Text = "Item Is Not Checked"
12:
13:   end if
14:
15:   end sub
16:
17: </script>
```

```
[C#.NET]

01: <script runat="server" language="C#">
02:
03:   void cb_CheckedChanged(Object sender, EventArgs e) {
04:
05:   if(cb.Checked){
06:
07:    cb.Text = "Item Is Checked";
08:
09:   }else{
10:
11:    cb.Text = "Item Is Not Checked";
12:
13:   }
14:
15:   }
16:
17: </script>
```

```
[VisualBasic.NET & C#.NET]

18 :<html>
19:   <body style="font-size:10">
20:    <form runat="server">
21:
```

LISTING 8.17 Continued

```
22:    <asp:Checkbox runat="server"
23:     id="cb"
24:     Checked="true"
25:     Text="Item Is Checked"
26:     AutoPostBack="true"
27:     OnCheckedChanged="cb_CheckedChanged"
28:     />
29:
30:    </form>
31:   </body>
32: </html>
```

You'll notice similarities in the way all these controls work. The only differences are in the names of events and methods. The CheckBox control is located on lines 22–28 and you'll notice that Checked is true, AutoPostBack is true, and OnCheckedChanged is cb_CheckedChanged—which means cb_CheckedChanged will handle the CheckedChanged event.

Within cb_CheckedChanged (lines 3–15) there is an if...then statement and depending on whether or not the cb CheckBox Checked attribute is true or false, the Text attribute of the CheckBox is changed. Figure 8.8 contains an illustration of the page on a post back after the CheckBox is unchecked.

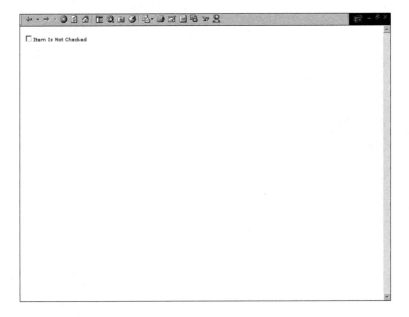

FIGURE 8.8

The CheckBox is unchecked.

Binding a `CheckBox` to a Data Source

The `CheckBox` server control does not have a `DataSource` property, but you can bind individual attributes of the `CheckBox` to a data source as you have seen in the previous sections. For instance, you could set the `Checked` property to checked or unchecked, depending on whether or not a product is in stock.

CheckBoxList ASP.NET Server Control

The `CheckBoxList` server control differs from the previous `CheckBox` control in that, when the `CheckBox` control is used, a single `Checkbox` control is rendered. On the other hand a single `CheckBoxList` control can render multiple check boxes. The `CheckBoxList` is another one of the controls that is part of the List controls suite.

The `CheckBox` control does give you greater flexibility in positioning than a `CheckBoxList` does because it renders as a list. However, the `CheckBox`'s data binding support is limited when compared to the `CheckBoxList` because it fully supports data binding using its `DataSource`, `DataTextField`, and `DataValueField` properties.

The `CheckBoxList` does give you some control over how its list is created by exposing some style attributes. You'll notice that these style attributes are also found in the `DataList` control. The following list contains a description of each:

- `RepeatColumns`   The number of columns to display—if set to three, `CheckBoxes` will render three across

- `RepeatDirection`   Controls which direction items from the data source are rendered—values can be `Horizontal` or `Vertical`

- `RepeatLayout`   Determines whether the list is rendered within a `TABLE` or `SPAN`—values can be `Table` or `Flow`

If `RepeatLayout` is set to `Table`, then two other attributes become available:

- `CellPadding`   The CellPadding for the container `Table`
- `CellSpacing`   The CellSpacing for the container `Table`

Listing 8.18 demonstrates how to bind the `CheckBoxList` to a data source and what attributes you can use to affect the way the control is rendered.

LISTING 8.18   Using the `CheckBoxList` Control

```
[VisualBasic.NET]

01: <%@ Import Namespace="System.Data" %>
02: <%@ Import Namespace="System.Data.SqlClient" %>
```

8

GATHERING DATA
WITH ASP.NET
WEB FORMS

LISTING 8.18 Continued

```
03: <script runat="server" language="vb" >
04:
05:  public sub Page_Load(sender as Object, e as EventArgs)
06:
07:   if (not IsPostBack) then
08:    cbl_DataBind()
09:   end if
10:
11:  end sub
12:
13:  public sub cbl_DataBind()
14:
15:   dim SqlCon as new SqlConnection("server=localhost;
➡ uid=sa;pwd=;database=northwind")
16:   dim SqlCmd as new SqlCommand("SELECT TOP 21 ProductName,
➡ ProductID FROM Products", SqlCon)
17:
18:   SqlCon.Open()
19:   cbl.DataSource = SqlCmd.ExecuteReader(CommandBehavior.CloseConnection)
20:   cbl.DataTextField = "ProductName"
21:   cbl.DataValueField = "ProductID"
22:   cbl.DataBind()
23:
24:  end sub
25:
26:  </script>

[C#.NET]
01: <%@ Import Namespace="System.Data" %>
02: <%@ Import Namespace="System.Data.SqlClient" %>
03: <script runat="server" language="C#" >
04:
05:  void Page_Load(Object sender, EventArgs e) {
06:
07:   if (! IsPostBack) {
08:    cbl_DataBind();
09:   }
10:
11:  }
12:
13:  void cbl_DataBind(){
14:
15:   SqlConnection SqlCon = new SqlConnection("server=localhost;
➡ uid=sa;pwd=;database=northwind");
```

LISTING 8.18   Continued

```
16:    SqlCommand SqlCmd = new SqlCommand("SELECT TOP 21 ProductName,
➡  ProductID FROM Products", SqlCon);
17:
18:    SqlCon.Open();
19:    cbl.DataSource = SqlCmd.ExecuteReader(CommandBehavior.CloseConnection);
20:    cbl.DataTextField = "ProductName";
21:    cbl.DataValueField = "ProductID";
22:    cbl.DataBind();
23:
24:  }
25:
26:  </script>

[VisualBasic.NET & C#.NET]

27:  <html>
28:    <body>
29:     <form runat="server">
30:
31:      <asp:Label
32:       width="100%"
33:       runat="server"
34:       text="<center>Pick Products</center>"
35:       BackColor="white"
36:       ForeColor="Navy"
37:       Font-Bold="true"
38:       Font-Size="13"
39:      />
40:
41:      <asp:CheckBoxList
42:       runat="server"
43:       id="cbl"
44:
45:       CellPadding="4"
46:       CellSpacing="0"
47:
48:       RepeatLayout="table"
49:       RepeatColumns="3"
50:       RepeatDirection="Vertical"
51:
52:       font-size="10"
53:       BackColor="white"
54:       ForeColor="Navy"
55:       Font-Bold="true"
56:       width="100%"
```

Listing 8.18   Continued

```
57:        BorderWidth="1"
58:        BorderColor="Navy"
59:     />
60:
61:     </form>
62:   </body>
63: </html>
```

Listing 8.18 renders the page illustrated in Figure 8.9.

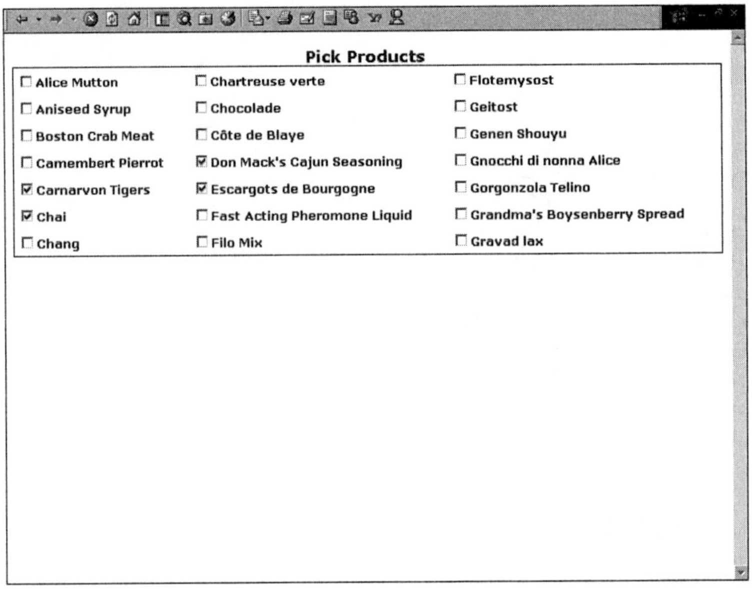

Figure 8.9

The rendered CheckBoxList *control.*

In this example I have RepeatLayout set to Table (line 48) so each CheckBox is in its own TableCell. RepeatColumns is set to 3 (line 49) so the control is rendered three columns wide. RepeatDirection is set to Vertical, so items are ordered from the top to the bottom from the data source. I suggest playing around with the different values you can use for these three attributes so you can see the effects of each value. For instance, change RepeatLayout to Flow and leave all the other attributes the same.

Raising and Handling Events and Determining Item Selection

In this section, we'll demonstrate how to respond and handle events with the CheckBoxList control. Because the way you raise and handle events with the CheckBoxList is identical to that of the other List controls, we won't go into great detail explaining it. Listing 8.19 contains example code illustrating how to determine item selection on a post back.

LISTING 8.19   Handling Events and Determining Item Selection

```
[VisualBasic.NET]
01: <%@ Import Namespace="System.Data" %>
02: <%@ Import Namespace="System.Data.SqlClient" %>
03: <script runat="server" language="vb" >
04:
05:  public sub Page_Load(sender as Object, e as EventArgs)
06:
07:   if (not IsPostBack) then
08:    cbl_DataBind()
09:   end if
10:
11:  end sub
12:
13:  public sub cbl_DataBind()
14:
15:   dim SqlCon as new SqlConnection("server=localhost;
➥  uid=sa;pwd=;database=northwind")
16:   dim SqlCmd as new SqlCommand("SELECT TOP 21 ProductName,
➥  ProductID FROM Products", SqlCon)
17:
18:   SqlCon.Open()
19:   cbl.DataSource = SqlCmd.ExecuteReader(CommandBehavior.CloseConnection)
20:   cbl.DataTextField = "ProductName"
21:   cbl.DataValueField = "ProductID"
22:   cbl.DataBind()
23:
24:  end sub
25:
26:  public sub CheckBoxList_SelectedIndexChanged(
➥  sender as Object, e as EventArgs)
27:
28:   dim sb as new StringBuilder("<b><u>Items Selected</u></b><p>")
29:
```

8

LISTING 8.19 Continued

```
30:    dim i as integer
31:    for i = 0 to cbl.Items.Count - 1
32:
33:     if(cbl.Items(i).Selected) then
34:
35:      sb.Append(i)
36:      sb.Append(" - ")
37:      sb.Append(cbl.Items(i).Text)
38:      sb.Append("<br>")
39:
40:     end if
41:
42:    next
43:
44:   lCheckBoxList.Text = sb.ToString()
45:
46:  end sub
47:
48: </script>
```

[C#.NET]

```
01: <%@ Import Namespace="System.Data" %>
02: <%@ Import Namespace="System.Data.SqlClient" %>
03: <script runat="server" language="C#" >
04:
05:  void Page_Load(Object sender, EventArgs e) {
06:
07:   if (! IsPostBack) {
08:    cbl_DataBind();
09:   }
10:
11:  }
12:
13:  void cbl_DataBind(){
14:
15:    SqlConnection SqlCon = new SqlConnection("server=localhost;
➥  uid=sa;pwd=;database=northwind");
16:    SqlCommand SqlCmd = new SqlCommand("SELECT TOP 21 ProductName,
➥  ProductID FROM Products", SqlCon);
17:
18:    SqlCon.Open();
19:    cbl.DataSource = SqlCmd.ExecuteReader(CommandBehavior.CloseConnection);
20:    cbl.DataTextField = "ProductName";
21:    cbl.DataValueField = "ProductID";
```

LISTING 8.19   Continued

```
22:    cbl.DataBind();
23:
24:    }
25:
26:    void CheckBoxList_SelectedIndexChanged(Object sender, EventArgs e) {
27:
28:      StringBuilder sb = new StringBuilder("<b><u>Items Selected</u></b><p>");
29:
30:      int i;
31:      for(i = 0; i<cbl.Items.Count; i++){
32:
33:       if(cbl.Items[i].Selected) {
34:
35:        sb.Append(i);
36:        sb.Append(" - ");
37:        sb.Append(cbl.Items[i].Text);
38:        sb.Append("<br>");
39:
40:       }
41:
42:      }
43:
44:      lCheckBoxList.Text = sb.ToString();
45:
46:    }
47:
48: </script>

[VisualBasic.NET & C#.NET]

49: <html>
50:   <body>
51:     <form runat="server">
52:
53:       <asp:Label
54:        width="100%"
55:        runat="server"
56:        text="<center>Pick Products</center>"
57:        BackColor="white"
58:        ForeColor="Navy"
59:        Font-Bold="true"
60:        Font-Size="13"
61:       />
62:
63:       <asp:CheckBoxList
```

LISTING 8.19 Continued

```
64:          runat="server"
65:          id="cbl"
66:
67:          CellPadding="4"
68:          CellSpacing="0"
69:
70:          RepeatLayout="table"
71:          RepeatColumns="3"
72:          RepeatDirection="Vertical"
73:
74:          AutoPostBack="true"
75:          OnSelectedIndexChanged="CheckBoxList_SelectedIndexChanged"
76:
77:          font-size="10"
78:          BackColor="white"
79:          ForeColor="Navy"
80:          Font-Bold="true"
81:          width="100%"
82:          BorderWidth="1"
83:          BorderColor="Navy"
84:       />
85:
86:       <p>
87:
88:       <asp:label
89:         runat="server"
90:         id="lCheckBoxList"
91:         Font-Bold="false"
92:         Font-Size="8"
93:         ForeColor="Navy"
94:       />
95:
96:  </form>
97:  </body>
98:  </html>
```

When Listing 8.19 is executed and a check box is selected, the resulting page is posted back, and the Label control under the CheckBoxList control is populated with the names of the products next to all selected check boxes. Figure 8.10 shows a page with a few check boxes selected.

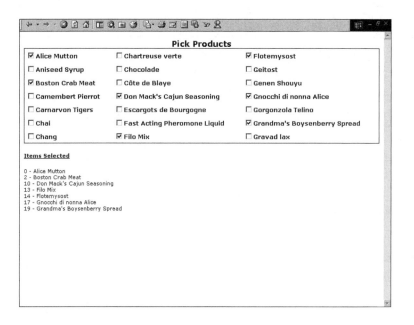

FIGURE 8.10

The Label *control under the* CheckBoxList *control lists all currently selected items.*

RadioButton ASP.NET Server Control

The RadioButton and RadioButtonList are implemented in exactly the same way as the CheckBox and CheckBoxList, but their functionality is quite different. The RadioButton and RadioButtonList controls enable users to select one option from a group of options. For instance, you might give a user on your Web site the option of paying for purchases or services with VISA, Master Card, or American Express. However, they cannot pay with more than one during any one purchase, so you would want to make them choose one or the other. The RadioButton, demonstrated in Listing 8.20, would be the perfect control to use for this purpose.

LISTING 8.20 Using the RadioButton Control

```
01: <html>
02:   <body Style="Font-Size:10">
03:     <form runat="server">
04:
05:       <h5>Method of Paymant</h5>
06:
```

LISTING 8.20   Continued

```
07:     <asp:RadioButton
08:      runat="server"
09:      id="cb"
10:      Text="Visa"
11:      GroupName="GroupOne"
12:      Checked="true"
13:      />
14:
15:     <br>
16:
17:     <asp:RadioButton
18:      runat="server"
19:      id="cb2"
20:      Text="Master Card"
21:      GroupName="GroupOne"
22:      />
23:
24:     <br>
25:
26:     <asp:RadioButton
27:      runat="server"
28:      id="cb3"
29:      Text="American Express"
30:      GroupName="GroupOne"
31:      />
32:
33:    </form>
34:   </body>
35:  </html>
```

Because radio buttons are put together as a group, there must be a way to bind them together. Setting the GroupName attribute does this. In Listing 8.20, I set the three different RadioButton controls' GroupName attributes to Charge. When the page renders, a user can only select one of the three radio buttons—Visa, Master Card, or American Express. You'll notice the Checked attribute in the top RadioButton (line 12) is set to true. This RadioButton will be selected when the page loads automatically.

Raising and Handling Events and Determining Item Selection

Like the CheckBox, the RadioButton has an OnCheckedChanged event that fires when the RadioButton control becomes checked or unchecked. Again, because these controls are so similar discussion will be minimal. Listing 8.21 contains a code example illustrating how to determine item selection on a post back.

LISTING 8.21   Determining Item Selection Using the `RadioButton`

[VisualBasic.NET]

```
01: <script runat="server" language="vb" >
02:
03:  public sub Charge_CheckedChanged(source as Object, e as EventArgs)
04:
05:   if(cb.Checked)then
06:
07:    lblCharge.Text = cb.Text & " Was Charged"
08:
09:   elseif(cb2.Checked) then
10:
11:    lblCharge.Text = cb2.Text & " Was Charged"
12:
13:   elseif(cb3.Checked) then
14:
15:    lblCharge.Text = cb3.Text & " Was Charged"
16:
17:   end if
18:
19:  end sub
20:
21: </script>
```

[C#.NET]

```
01: <script runat="server" language="C#" >
02:
03:  void Charge_CheckedChanged(Object source, EventArgs e) {
04:
05:   if(cb.Checked){
06:
07:    lblCharge.Text = cb.Text + " Was Charged";
08:
09:   } else if(cb2.Checked){
10:
11:    lblCharge.Text = cb2.Text + " Was Charged";
12:
13:   } else if(cb3.Checked){
14:
15:    lblCharge.Text = cb3.Text + " Was Charged";
16:
17:   }
18:
19:  }
20
21: </script>
```

8

GATHERING DATA
WITH ASP.NET
WEB FORMS

LISTING 8.21 Continued

```
[VisualBasic.NET & C#.NET]
22: <html>
23:  <body Style="Font-Size:10">
24:   <form runat="server">
25:
26:    <h5>Method of Paymant</h5>
27:
28:    <asp:RadioButton
29:     runat="server"
30:     id="cb"
31:     Text="Visa"
32:     GroupName="Charge"
33:     Checked="true"
34:     AutoPostBack="true"
35:     OnCheckedChanged="Charge_CheckedChanged"
36:    />
37:
38:    <br>
39:
40:    <asp:RadioButton
41:     runat="server"
42:     id="cb2"
43:     Text="Master Card"
44:     GroupName="Charge"
45:     AutoPostBack="true"
46:     OnCheckedChanged="Charge_CheckedChanged"
47:    />
48:
49:    <br>
50:
51:    <asp:RadioButton
52:     runat="server"
53:     id="cb3"
54:     Text="American Express"
55:     GroupName="Charge"
56:     AutoPostBack="true"
57:     OnCheckedChanged="Charge_CheckedChanged"
58:    />
59:
60:    <p>
61:
62:    <asp:label
63:     runat="server"
64:     id="lblCharge"
65:     Font-Bold="false"
66:     Font-Size="8"
```

LISTING 8.21   Continued

```
67:    ForeColor="Navy"
68:    />
69:
70:    </form>
71:  </body>
72: </html>
```

The rendered page from Listing 8.21 can be seen in Figure 8.11. When you select one of the option buttons, text appears on the page and tells you which of the three credit cards you selected. I use a simple If...Then statement to figure out which of the RadioButton controls is selected.

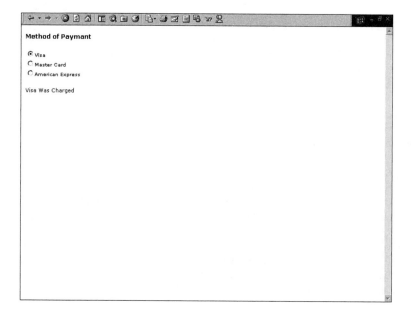

FIGURE 8.11
The Visa RadioButton *is selected.*

RadioButtonList ASP.NET Server Control

The RadioButtonList control's programmatic functionality is nearly identical to the CheckBoxList, but its functionality is different. When rendered, each item from the RadioButtonList.DataSource will be part of a group of RadioButton controls and only one RadioButton out of the group can ever be selected at one time.

The RadioButtonList is part of the List controls suite, so its behavior is the same as the proceeding List controls as far as how you enable automatic post back (AutoPostBack), how you tell if an item is checked (ListItem.Selected), and how to handle the SelectedIndexChanged on the post back. So, not to sound redundant, I will be jumping right into the code example. Listing 8.22 illustrates how to use all the proceeding attributes and events to determine item selection.

LISTING 8.22   Using the RadioButtonList Control

```
[VisualBasic.NET]

01: <%@ Import Namespace="System.Data" %>
02: <%@ Import Namespace="System.Data.SqlClient" %>
03: <script runat="server" language="vb" >
04:
05:   public sub Page_Load(sender as Object, e as EventArgs)
06:
07:    if (not IsPostBack) then
08:     rbl_DataBind()
09:    end if
10:
11:   end sub
12:
13:   public sub rbl_DataBind()
14:
15:    dim SqlCon as new SqlConnection("server=localhost;
➥ uid=sa;pwd=;database=northwind")
16:    dim SqlCmd as new SqlCommand("SELECT TOP 21 ProductName,
➥ ProductID FROM Products", SqlCon)
17:
18:    SqlCon.Open()
19:    rbl.DataSource = SqlCmd.ExecuteReader(CommandBehavior.CloseConnection)
20:    rbl.DataTextField = "ProductName"
21:    rbl.DataValueField = "ProductID"
22:    rbl.DataBind()
23:
24:   end sub
25:
26:   public sub RadioButtonList_SelectedIndexChanged(
➥ sender as Object, e as EventArgs)
27:
28:    dim sb as new StringBuilder("<b><u>Items Selected</u></b><p>")
29:
30:    dim i as integer
31:    for i = 0 to rbl.Items.Count - 1
32:
```

LISTING 8.22   Continued

```
33:    if(rbl.Items(i).Selected) then
34:
35:     sb.Append(i)
36:     sb.Append(" - ")
37:     sb.Append(rbl.Items(i).Text)
38:     sb.Append("<br>")
39:
40:    end if
41:
42:   next
43:
44:   lCheckBoxList.Text = sb.ToString()
45:
46:  end sub
47:
48: </script>
```

[C#.NET]

```
01: <%@ Import Namespace="System.Data" %>
02: <%@ Import Namespace="System.Data.SqlClient" %>
03: <script runat="server" language="C#" >
04:
05:  void Page_Load(Object sender, EventArgs e) {
06:
07:   if (! IsPostBack) {
08:    rbl_DataBind();
09:   }
10:
11:  }
12:
13:  void rbl_DataBind(){
14:
15:    SqlConnection SqlCon = new SqlConnection("server=localhost;
➥ uid=sa;pwd=;database=northwind");
16:    SqlCommand SqlCmd = new SqlCommand("SELECT TOP 21 ProductName,
➥ ProductID FROM Products", SqlCon);
17:
18:    SqlCon.Open();
19:    rbl.DataSource = SqlCmd.ExecuteReader(CommandBehavior.CloseConnection);
20:    rbl.DataTextField = "ProductName";
21:    rbl.DataValueField = "ProductID";
22:    rbl.DataBind();
23:
24:  }
25:
```

8

LISTING 8.22   Continued

```
26:   void RadioButtonList_SelectedIndexChanged(Object sender, EventArgs e) {
27:
28:     StringBuilder sb = new StringBuilder("<b><u>Item Selected</u></b><p>");
29:
30:     int i;
31:     for(i = 0; i < rbl.Items.Count; i++){
32:
33:      if(rbl.Items[i].Selected) {
34:
35:       sb.Append(i);
36:       sb.Append(" - ");
37:       sb.Append(rbl.Items[i].Text);
38:       sb.Append("<br>");
39:
40:      }
41:
42:     }
43:
44:     lCheckBoxList.Text = sb.ToString();
45:
46:   }
47:
48: </script>

[VisualBasic.NET & C#.NET]

49: <html>
50:   <body>
51:    <form runat="server">
52:
53:      <asp:Label
54:       width="100%"
55:       runat="server"
56:       text="<center>Pick Products</center>"
57:       BackColor="white"
58:       ForeColor="Navy"
59:       Font-Bold="true"
60:       Font-Size="13"
61:      />
62:
63:      <asp:RadioButtonList
64:       runat="server"
65:       id="rbl"
66:
67:        CellPadding="4"
```

LISTING 8.22   Continued

```
68:      CellSpacing="0"
69:
70:      RepeatLayout="table"
71:      RepeatColumns="3"
72:      RepeatDirection="Vertical"
73:
74:      AutoPostBack="true"
75:      OnSelectedIndexChanged="RadioButtonList_SelectedIndexChanged"
76:
77:      font-size="10"
78:      BackColor="white"
79:      ForeColor="Navy"
80:      Font-Bold="true"
81:      width="100%"
82:      BorderWidth="1"
83:      BorderColor="Navy"
84:      />
85:
86:      <p>
87:
88:      <asp:label
89:       runat="server"
90:       id="lCheckBoxList"
91:       Font-Bold="false"
92:       Font-Size="8"
93:       ForeColor="Navy"
94:       />
95:
96: </form>
97: </body>
98: </html>
```

When Listing 8.22 is executed, you'll get a page with three columns of RadioButton controls and a product name next to each. When you select one, the page is posted back to the server and the name of the product you selected is printed out to the screen. Unlike the CheckBoxList you can only check one product at a time when using the RadioButtonList control. Figure 8.12 contains an illustration of the page after an item is selected and the page is posted back to the server.

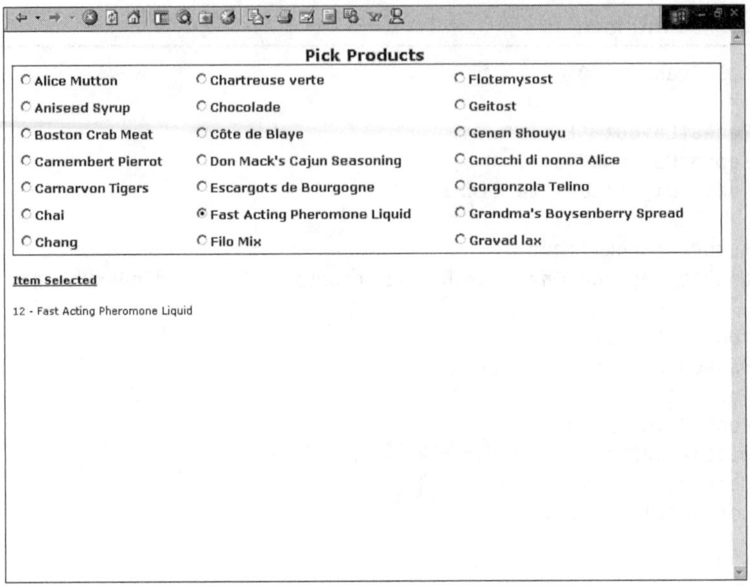

FIGURE 8.12
The RadioButtonList *control.*

Summary

The quicker you realize that nearly all the different server controls act and react in similar ways, the quicker you'll master developing in ASP.NET. Of course, when you start getting under the covers of some of the controls, you'll see some major differences, but that's a topic for a different book!

This chapter described some of ASP.NET's new server controls, how to implement each one, how to capture events, and how to bind the controls to a data source. Specifically, I discussed the following ASP.NET server controls:

- Button
- TextBox
- DropDownList
- ListBox

- CheckBox
- CheckBoxList
- RadioButton
- RadioButtonList

Chapter 9 will cover using ASP.NET's validation controls to make sure that data collected in a Web form is accurate before you insert it into the database.

Evaluating Data with ASP.NET Validation Controls

IN THIS CHAPTER

In Chapter 8, "Gathering Data with ASP.NET Web Forms," I discussed how to use many of the new ASP.NET server controls to gather data from users. In this chapter, I'll demonstrate how to use ASP.NET's collection of validation controls to validate data on both the client side and the server-side before a database edit is made. Specifically, we will explore the following topics:

- What validation controls are and how they work
- Using the `RequiredFieldValidator` control
- Using the `CompareValidator` control
- Using the `RangeValidator` control
- Using the `RegularExpressionValidator` control
- Using the `CustomValidator` control
- Displaying error information using the `ValidationSummary` control
- Multiple validator controls on one input control

Validation Controls and How They Work

Validation controls are used between `<FORM>` tags in a Web Form, and they validate that the user enters or selects the proper data from `INPUT` controls, such as the `TextBox`, `TextArea`, or `ListBox`. For example, you might validate that the user entered data into a required `TextBox` field or that an e-mail address was entered into a `TextBox` in the correct format (donny.mack@dotnetjunkies.com)—the correct format being:

1. donny.mack—One or more characters
2. @—sign
3. DotNetJunkies—One or more characters
4. .—a Period
5. com—a URL Extension

When using a .NET validation control, you have the option to validate data on the server-side, the client side, or both. For security reasons, server-side validation occurs regardless of whether or not you have client-side validation enabled unless you explicitly disable server validation. The reason for this is mischievous users with a little programming experience can bypass your client-side validation with relatively little effort. On the other hand bypassing server-side code would be extremely difficult if not impossible. By no means does this imply you shouldn't use client-side validation. Ninety-nine percent of your users will be legitimate non-hacking individuals, and validating data on the client will save a round-trip to the server if the user mistakenly forgot to fill out a field or filled out a field with an incorrect type of data.

For example, if you have a `RequiredFieldValidator` wired up to a required `TextBox` on your page and a user tries to submit the page without filling it out, they will get a warning message that the `TextBox` must be filled out before you will allow the page to be submitted thus saving a round-trip to the server.

Shared Validator Attributes

All of the validation controls share a base set of properties and methods. As you go though this chapter, you will see us use them in nearly every example, so we thought it prudent to go over these first. The following quick reference lists and discusses the eight we will be using most often (for a list of all, see the `BaseValidator` class):

- `ControlToValidate` The `ID` property of the control you wish to have validated by the validation control.

- `IsValid` A Boolean value (true or false) indicating whether or not the control which is being validated is valid. True if valid and false if not.

- `ErrorMessage` The error message you want displayed to the user if the control is found to be invalid.

- `Text` The inner contents of the control.

- `EnableClientScript` A Boolean value (`true` or `false`) indicating whether client-side validation is enabled.

- `Enabled` A Boolean value indicating whether the validation control is enabled—client and server-side validation.

- `Validate` Method used to perform validation on the associated `INPUT` control.

- `Display` The display of the validation control when it gives the user an error message. The following three values are acceptable for this attribute:

  - `None` The validation control isn't displayed inline. If there is not a ValidationSummary control, no error message will be given to the user.

  - `Static` The validation control is displayed inline and is part of the page layout even when not visible. For instance, if your error message contains a paragraph worth of text, it will take up a paragraph worth of space on the page.

  - `Dyanamic` The validation control is displayed inline, but doesn't make up part of the page layout until the control is found to be invalid.

Of course many of the validation controls have their own set of properties that are used as well, but we will be going over those in each of the different controls sections.

What Controls Can Be Validated

Not all server controls support the use of validation controls. The following list contains each control that supports the use of validation contols and what property can be validated:

- `RadioButtonList` server control `SelectedItem.Value`
- `DropDownList` server control `SelectedItem.Value`
- `ListBox` server control `SelectedItem.Value`
- `TextBox` server control `TextBox.Text`
- `HtmlInputFile` HTML server control `HtmlInputFile.Value`
- `HtmlSelect` HTML server control `HtmlSelect.Value`
- `HtmlTextArea` HTML server control `HtmlTextArea.Value`
- `HtmlInputText` HTML server control `HtmlInputText.Value`

Server-Side Validation

As previously mentioned, validation occurs on both the client-side (client-side JavaScript) and server-side. So you may be wondering what happens on the server-side. In this section, we'll give you a high-level overview of just that. All the topics discussed in this section will apply to all validation controls. We'll also be giving you a few code examples of some commonly asked questions regarding validation controls, for instance, programmatically affecting validation.

The first thing we want to discuss is when validation occurs on the server. When I say "when validation occurs" I am talking about within the page processing model. The following list is a simplified model of the page processing model after a post back has occured. There is much more to this model, but for our discussion this is what you need to know, because quite frankly, I can talk about the page processing model for hours:

- The Page and its controls are created.
- The Page and its controls properties are populated.
- The Page and its controls are updated to new values based on data the user enters, for example, if the user changes their phone number in a `TextBox`.
- The `Page.Load` is fired.
- Validation takes place on controls.
- Event Handling occurs—This is where events like `SelectedIndexChanged`, which we saw in the previous chapter, are handled. At this point, you can access the `Page.IsValid` property (discussed later in chapter).

As you can see, if you try to check the `Page.IsValid` property in the `Page.Load` event, it will always return `true` since validation hasn't occurred yet. You can override this default functionality by invoking the `Page.Validate` method before checking the `Page.IsValid` property.

A question that comes up often is how to disable server-side validation? Well, there are a couple ways; first, by using the Validation controls `Enabled` attribute (`false = disabled, true = enabled`), but the side effect is that client-side validation also is disabled. The second way is overriding the `Page.Validate` method. The differences between the two methods are you can disable all validation by overriding the `Page.Validate` method and you can only disable an individual control by using its `Enabled` property.

Listing 9.1 contains an example of disabling validation by overriding the `Page.Validate` method. In this example, there is a `CheckBox` and when its `Checked` attribute is `true`, validation occurs; otherwise, validation doesn't occur. This example uses the `RequiredFieldValidator`.

LISTING 9.1 Disabling Validation Controls

```
[VisualBasic.NET]

01: <script language="vb" runat="server">
02:
03:   public overrides sub Validate()
04:
05:     if (validater.Checked) then
06:
07:       mybase.Validate()
08:
09:     end if
10:
11:   end sub
12:
13: </script>

[C#.NET]

01: <script language="C#" runat="server">
02:
03:   public override void Validate(){
04:
05:     if(validater.Checked) {
06:
07:       base.Validate();
08:
09:     }
10:
11:   }
12:
13: </script>

[VisualBasic.NET & C#.NET]

14: <html>
```

LISTING 9.1 Continued

```
15:    <body Style="font-size:10">
16:     <form runat="server">
17:      <center>
18:
19:      <asp:RequiredFieldValidator
20:       runat="server"
21:       ControlToValidate="Required"
22:       id="rfv"
23:       EnableClientScript="False"
24:      >
25:      * Not Valid
26:      </asp:RequiredFieldValidator>
27:
28:      <asp:TextBox
29:       runat="server"
30:       id="Required"
31:      />
32:
33:      <asp:Button
34:       runat="server"
35:       Text="Validate"
36:      />
37:
38:      <br>
39:
40:      <asp:CheckBox
41:       runat="server"
42:       id="validater"
43:       text="Validate Page?"
44:      />
45:      </center>
46:
47:     </form>
48:    </body>
49:  </html>
```

Because this section is not intended to teach you about validation controls, but rather the validation process, we'll not be discussing the RequiredFieldValidator in this section. Lines 3–9 contain the Page.Validate method. Within it, I have an if…end if statement that checks if the CheckBox is checked or not. If it is checked, then I invoke the base.Validate method, and if it isn't checked then validation doesn't occur.

> **TIP**
>
> The base (C#) and mybase (VB) keywords are used to call a method on a base class that has been overridden by another method—in this case, the Validate method. If I were just to call the Page.Validate method again, an exception would occur because my method would invoke itself.

After the base.Validate method is called, the pages default validation process occurs. Using this functionality enables you to modify each of the validation controls and then revalidate them. For example, you can change all the validation controls IsValid attribute to false and then call base.Validate and each control will be invalid or you can manipulate the values of the controls somehow before they are validated. Beyond disabling page validation, you can override the Page.Validate method to do custom validation.

The Page object has a property you can use to check if the page as a whole is valid. The Page.IsValid property returns a Boolean value indicating if the page is valid. A page is considered valid if every enabled validation controls IsValid property is true. If one controls IsValid property is false, then the whole page is considered invalid.

Another property of the Page I want to go over is the Page.Validators property. This property exposes a ValidatorCollection object, which is an array of all validation controls for the page. For an example on how to use this property, replace the server code from Listing 9.1 with that contained in Listing 9.2. This code loops through the ValidatorCollection and outputs whether or not the individual validation controls IsValid property value.

LISTING 9.2 Looping through the ValidatorCollection

```
[VisualBasic.NET]
01: <script language="vb" runat="server">
02:
03:  public overrides sub Validate()
04:
05:   if (validater.Checked) then
06:
07:    mybase.Validate()
08:
09:   end if
10:
11:   CheckValidators()
12:
13:  end sub
14:
```

9

ASP.NET VALIDATION CONTROLS

LISTING 9.2 Continued

```
15:   sub CheckValidators()
16:
17:    dim ValCol as ValidatorCollection = Page.Validators
18:    dim IVal as IValidator
19:
20:    for each IVal in ValCol
21:
22:     dim sb as new StringBuilder("<center>")
23:     sb.Append("Control is Valid: ")
24:     sb.Append((CType(IVal,RequiredFieldValidator).IsValid))
25:     sb.Append("</center>")
26:     Response.Write(sb.ToString())
27:
28:    next IVal
29:
30:   end sub
31:
32: </script>
```

[C#.NET]

```
01: <script language="C#" runat="server">
02:
03:  public override void Validate(){
04:
05:   if(validater.Checked) {
06:
07:    base.Validate();
08:
09:   }
10:
11:   CheckValidators();
12:
13:  }
14:
15:  void CheckValidators(){
16:
17:   ValidatorCollection ValCol = Page.Validators;
18:
19:
20:   foreach(IValidator IVal in ValCol) {
21:
22:    StringBuilder sb = new StringBuilder("<center>");
23:    sb.Append("Control is Valid: ");
24:    sb.Append(((RequiredFieldValidator) IVal).IsValid);
```

LISTING 9.2 Continued

```
25:    sb.Append("</center>");
26:    Response.Write(sb.ToString());
27:
28:    }
29:
30:  }
31:
32: </script>
```

In Listing 9.2, I created a `CheckValidator` (lines 15–30) method which is invoked from the `Validate` (lines 3–13) method. Within the `CheckValidator` method, I have a `for each` statement which loops through the `ValidatorCollection` object (lines 20–28). Notice the `IValidator` object on line 20—the `ValidatorCollection` is made up of references to these objects—each one being a validation control located in the page. *The `IValidator` class defines all the properties and methods that all validation controls must implement.*

Client-Side Validation

Client side validation comes in the form of automatically generated JavaScript and most of the functionality is kept in the `WebUIValidation.js` that is distributed with ASP.NET. Because of this fact, support for client side validation is browser independent and this is yet another reason why server-side validation takes place even if client script is disabled. Client-side validation can be disabled by setting a single property available for all validation controls:

- `EnableClientScript`   A `Boolean` value (`true` or `false`) indicating whether client-side validation is enabled.

When client-validation is enabled, it's important to know what is going on behind the scenes. Initial validation occurs as the user moves from field to field (`INPUT` control to `INPUT` control). If all the validation controls are valid and the user submits the page (clicking a submit button), the page then will be posted back to the server and server-side validation takes place. If one or more of the controls are not valid when the user tries to submit the page, the submit is cancelled and all the invalid validators become visible. If there is a `ValidationSummary` control, which we will examine in a later section, it will become visible as well with a list of errors messages. If the `ValidationSummary` has message box output, then a client-side message box with a list of errors will be generated.

You might run into a situation where you need multiple buttons on a page. You might not want to submit the form for one of those buttons, but if you don't take preventative measures, a user could get stuck on that form because it is not validated. An example would be if you not only have information collection forms on a page, but you also have fields for search functionality.

Listing 9.3 contains code example illustrating how to cancel validation if a user clicks on one button, but how to make it work if he clicks on another. In this example, I am using a RequiredFieldValidator, a TextBox, and three Buttons. The reason for the three buttons is I want to show you two ways to disable client script. The first is through a client-side function call and the second is by setting the Buttons CausesValidation attribute to false. By settting the CausesValidation attribute to false, a post back to the server still occurs.

LISTING 9.3   Disabling Client-side Validation

```
01: <html>
02:  <head>
03:   <script language="c#" runat="server">
04:
05:    void ButtonTwo_Click(Object sender, EventArgs e){
06:     lblMessage.Text = "Validation Was Cancelled - PostBack Occured";
07:    }
08:
09:   </script>
10:
11:   <script language="JavaScript">
12:
13:    function ButtonOne_Click(){
14:
15:     document.all["lblMessage"].innerText =
➥ "Validation Was Cancelled - No PostBack";
16:
17:
18:    }
19:
20:   </script>
21:  </head>
22: <body Style="font-size:10">
23:  <form runat="server">
24:   <center>
25:
26:   <h3>RequiredFieldValidator</h3>
27:
28:   First Name:  
29:
30:   <asp:TextBox
31:    id="txtFirstName"
32:    runat="server"
33:    />
34:
35:   <asp:RequiredFieldValidator
```

LISTING 9.3 Continued

```
36:    id="rfv"
37:    Runat="Server"
38:    ControlToValidate="txtFirstName"
39:    Display="Dynamic"
40:    >
41:    * Required Field
42:    </asp:RequiredFieldValidator>
43:
44:    <p>
45:
46:    <asp:Button
47:     id="ButtonTwo"
48:     runat="server"
49:     Text="Submit"
50:    />
51:
52:    <input type="button"
53:     id="ButtonOne"
54:     value="Cancel One"
55:     runat="server"
56:     OnClick="ButtonOne_Click()"
57:    />
58:
59:    <asp:Button
60:     runat="server"
61:     CausesValidation="false"
62:     Text="Cancel Two"
63:     OnClick="ButtonTwo_Click"
64:    />
65:
66:    <p>
67:
68:    <asp:Label
69:     runat="server"
70:     id="lblMessage"
71:     name="lblMessage"
72:     ForeColor="Red"
73:     Font-Bold="true"
74:    />
75:
76:    </center>
77:    </form>
78:   </body>
79: </html>
```

As previously mentioned, there is a `TextBox` control (lines 30–33) in Listing 9.3, which is wired to a `RequiredFieldValidator` (lines 35–42) effect: The `TextBox` must be filled out to be valid. There are three possible buttons to click on in the page. The first, lines 46–50, submits the page and validation occurs—both client and server-side validation. The `HtmlButton`, lines 52–57, has an `OnClick` value of `ButtonOne_Click`—a client side JavaScript function found on lines 13–18. Within the `ButtonOne_Click` function, you can do what you wish. In this example, I simply write out to the page. The important point is that the form isn't automatically submitted (you can use the OnServer). The third button (lines 59–64) uses one of its own attributes to prevent validation—on both the server and client—`CausesValidation` attribute. `CausesValidation` expects a `Boolean` value which indicates whether or not validation should occur when that particular button is clicked—default is `true`.

Now that you have a high-level view on how validation works, and some of their shared attributes, let's go over each of the individual controls from the validation controls suite.

The `RequiredFieldValidator` Control

The `RequiredFieldValidator` is by far the simplest validator control to use. The `Required FieldValidator` will find a control invalid if the value the user entered is equal to the `InitialValue` attribute. The `InitialValue` attribute is the value contained in the control that is to be validated (ex:TextBox) when the page is first rendered to the client. If an `InitialValue` is not specified, then the value defaults to `String.Empty` (an empty string). For example, if you have a `TextBox` control with a `RequiredFieldValidator` and you don't set the `InitialValue` attribute, then the `Page` will not be valid until the user adds at least one character. A code example using the `RequiredFieldValidator` can be found in Listing 9.4.

LISTING 9.4 Using the `RequiredFieldValidator` Control

```
[VisualBasic.NET]
01: <script language="vb" runat="server">
02:
03:   sub Validate_Page(sender as Object, e as EventArgs)
04:
05:    if (Page.IsValid) then
06:
07:      lblmessage.Text = "* Page Is Valid"
08:
09:    else
10:
```

LISTING 9.4 Continued

```
11:     lblmessage.Text = "* Page Is Invalid"
12:
13:   end if
14:
15:  end sub
16:
17: </script>
```

```
[C#.NET]
01: <script language="c#" runat="server">
02:
03:   void Validate_Page(Object sender, EventArgs e) {
04:
05:    if (Page.IsValid) {
06:
07:      lblmessage.Text = "* Page Is Valid";
08:
09:    } else {
10:
11:      lblmessage.Text = "* Page Is Invalid";
12:
13:    }
14:
15:  }
16:
17: </script>
```

```
[VisualBasic.NET & C#.NET]
18: <html>
19:   <body Style="font-size:10">
20:    <form runat="server">
21:     <center>
22:
23:     <h3>RequiredFieldValidator</h3>
24:     <asp:Label runat="server" id="lblmessage" />
25:
26:     <p>
27:
28:     <asp:TextBox
29:      id="txtFirstName"
30:      runat="server"
```

LISTING 9.4   Continued

```
31:        Text="First Name"
32:        />
33:
34:        <asp:RequiredFieldValidator
35:         id="rfv"
36:         runat="server"
37:         ControlToValidate="txtFirstName"
38:         Display="Dynamic"
39:         InitialValue="First Name"
40:        >
41:         * This is a Required Field
42:        </asp:RequiredFieldValidator>
43:
44:        <br>
45:
46:        <asp:Button id="SubmitButton"
47:         runat="server"
48:         Text="Validate"
49:         OnClick="Validate_Page"
50:        />
51:
52:      </center>
53:     </form>
54:    </body>
55: </html>
```

The RequiredFieldValidator in Listing 9.4 is on lines 34–42 and is wired to the TextBox on lines 28–32. The Button on lines 46–50 is used to submit the page for server-side validation. You'll notice that the TextBox has an initial value of "First Name" (line 31) and because the TextBox control will only be valid once the initial value has changed, this value must somehow change. I used the InitialValue attribute (line 39) of the RequiredFieldValidator to wire gain this functionality. If I were not to use the InitialValue attribute, the page could be posted back to the server with "First Name" as the TextBox value. Figure 9.1 contains an image of the page on the first request. Notice the TextBox has "First Name" for a value.

Try to submit the page without changing the value of the TextBox. The result will be that the page will not be submitted. Now change the value of the TextBox and try resubmitting the page. You'll receive a page similar to Figure 9.2.

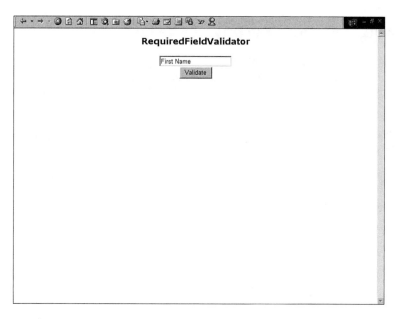

FIGURE 9.1
The page on first request.

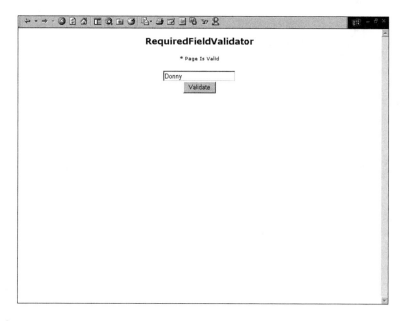

FIGURE 9.2
The page is valid and submitted to the server.

The RegularExpressionValidator Control

Through the use of regular expressions, the RegularExpressionValidator gives you tremendous control over how data is entered in to input controls and in what format. *Regular expressions* are used to match text character patterns to actual character strings. They also can be used to edit, extract, replace, or delete substrings (strings within strings). In this section, I am going to concentrate on the pattern-matching aspects of regular expressions with regard to the RegularExpressionValidator.

The RegularExpressionValidator has one unique attribute, ValidationExpression. The value for this attribute is the regular expression to be used for validation. Listing 9.5 contains a code example illustrating how to use the RegularExpressionValidator. In this example, we created a Regular Expression used to verify e-mail address syntax as described in the beginning of this chapter.

LISTING 9.5   Using the RegularExpressionValidator to Validate a Phone Number

```
01: <html>
02:  <body style="font-size:10">
03:   <form runat="server">
04:
05:    <h3>RegularExpressionValidator</h3>
06:
07:    Email Address:
08:    <asp:TextBox id="txtEmail" runat="server" width="200"/>
09:
10:    <p>
11:
12:    <asp:RegularExpressionValidator
13:     runat="server"
14:     ControlToValidate="txtEmail"
15:     Display="Dynamic"
16:     ValidationExpression=
➥ "[\w\x2E\x2D]{2,}\x40{1}[\w\x2E\x2D]{2,}\x2E{1}[\w\x2E\x2D]{2,}"
17:     >
18:      * Email Address is formatted incorrectly
➥ Ex: donny.mack@dotnetjunkies.com
19:    </asp:RegularExpressionValidator>
20:
21:    <p>
22:
23:    <asp:Button id="SubmitButton"
24:     runat="server"
25:     Text="Submit"
```

LISTING 9.5   Continued

```
26:    />
27:
28:    </form>
29:  </body>
30: </html>
```

The RegularExpressionValidator is located on lines 12-19 and is wired to the txtEmail TextBox located on line 8. We won't be going through the Regular Expression used as the ValidationExpression value, but essentially it assures that a valid e-mail address is entered. Figure 9.3 contains an illustration of the page after the URL extension is left off of an e-mail address.

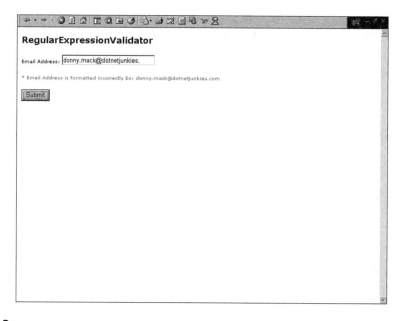

FIGURE 9.3

E-mail is not valid because there isn't a URL extension.

The ability to match and validate character patterns is only inhibited by your imagination and knowledge of regular expression syntax. Each of the regular expressions I used in Listings 9.3 through 9.5 can be written in different ways. This book isn't about regular expressions, so I am not going into great detail about the syntax, but for more information on regular expressions, please see http://msdn.microsoft.com/library/dotnet/cpguide/cpconintroduction toregularexpressions.htm.

The `CompareValidator` Control

The next validator control we'll be talking about is the `CompareValidator` control. The `CompareValidator` differs from the previous validator controls because it enables you to compare the value entered by the user with another value. The other value can be that of either another control or a constant value. For instance, if you have a site that has membership that is password controlled during user registration, it is customary to have the user enter their password twice to lessen the chance of entering it incorrectly. You could use the `CompareValidator` and quickly wire the two Password `TextBox` controls together to ensure the same value was entered into both.

You can use a couple different attributes to wire up controls to the `CompareValidator`. The following list contains a description of each:

- `ControlToCompare` The `ID` attribute of the INPUT control you want to compare against. Do not confuse this with the `ControlToValidate`. `ControlToValidate` will be the control you want to compare to the `ControlToCompare` control.

- `ValueToCompare` A constant value you want to compare against.

The `CompareValidator` doesn't just support comparing string against string. By using the `Type` attribute, you can specify what data type you want validated. The following list contains each supported data type:

- `Currency`
- `Date`
- `Double`
- `Integer`
- `String`

Not only can you ensure that two values are equal, you can choose from the following seven compare operators, which would be applied to the `Operator` attribute of the control:

- `Equal`—The values should equal to one another.
- `GreaterThan`—The `ControlToValidate` value must be greater than the `ControlToCompare` or `ValueToCompare` value.
- `GreaterThanEqual`—The `ControlToValidate` value must be equal to or greater than the `ControlToCompare` value or `ValueToCompare`.
- `LessThan`—The `ControlToValidate` value must be less than the `ControlToCompare` or `ValueToCompare` value.
- `LessThanEqual`—The `ControlToValidate` value must be less than or equal to the `ControlToCompare` or `ValueToCompare` value.

- NotEqual—The ControlToValidate value cannot equal the ControlToCompare or ValueToCompare value.

- DataTypeCheck—The data type of the ControlToValidate must be the same as the ControlToCompare or ValueToCompare data type.

Listing 9.6 demonstrates how to implement the CompareValidator. This example compares the values of two different dates.

LISTING 9.6   Comparing two dates

```
01: <html>
02:  <body style="font-size:10">
03:   <form runat="server">
04:
05:    Beginning Date:
06:    <asp:textbox
07:     runat="server"
08:     id="BeginningDate"
09:    />
10:
11:
12:    Ending Date:
13:    <asp:textbox
14:     runat="server"
15:    id="EndDate"
16:     Text="01/11/2001"
17:    />
18:
19:    <p>
20:
21:    <asp:CompareValidator
22:     runat="server"
23:     ControlToValidate="BeginningDate"
24:     ControlToCompare="EndDate"
25:     Operator="LessThan"
26:     Type="Date"
27:     ErrorMessage="You MUST Enter A Valid Date And The
➥ Beginning Date Must Not Be Greater Than Ending Date"
28:    />
29:
30:    <p>
31:
32:    <asp:Button
33:     runat="server"
34:     Text="Submit"
```

9

**ASP.NET
VALIDATION
CONTROLS**

LISTING 9.6 Continued

```
35:      />
36:
37:   </form>
38:   </body>
39: </html>
```

The `CompareValidator` from Listing 9.6 is located on lines 21–28, and has the `ControlToValidate` set to the `TextBox` located on lines 6–9, and the `ControlToCompare` set to the `TextBox` on lines 12–17. The `Operator` is set to `LessThan` with a `Type` equal to `Date`. When the page initially loads, a date is already populated in the `ControlToCompare` `TextBox` and the `ControlToValidate` is blank. Now that you have the page up, do the following:

1. Enter a date greater than the `ControlToValidate` and try to submit the page. An error message will be displayed.

2. Enter a date less than the `ControlToValidate` and try to submit the page. The page will submit.

3. Now enter nothing into the `ControlToValidate` and try to submit the page. The page will submit.

4. Now enter a date larger than the `ControlToValidate` and then delete the `ControlToValidate`'s date or enter in something other than a date and try to submit the page. The page will submit.

Well, now you might be confused as to why the page is submitting for 3 and 4. If you think about it, it's logical. When we do number 3, the `InitialValue` of the property is never changed so validation doesn't occur. We can solve this problem by wiring up a `RequiredField Validator` on it. As for number 4, by deleting the value for the `ControlToValidate` to compare against, it will always return `true`. You also can solve this situation by wiring up a `RequiredFieldValidator` to it. You will find more often than not you will have to wire up more than one validator control to any one control to achieve proper validation. Later in this chapter, we will discuss how to wire up multiple validator controls to one `INPUT` control.

The `RangeValidator` Control

The `RangeValidator` control enables you to specify a range for the values entered into the input control. Such a range would be applicable if you have a B2B e-commerce site, and you wanted to set minimum and maximum order rates on some products. There are two ways to specify the minimum and maximum values. The first is to set the `MinimumValue` and `Maximum Value` to specified values. The second is to set the `MinimumControl` and `MaximumControl` values with the `ID` value of other `HTML` controls. As with the `CompareValidator` control, you can assign the range's data type with the `Type` attribute of the `RangeValidator` control.

Listing 9.7 contains an example using the `RangeValidator`. This is a very simple example that checks an integer value entered into a `TextBox`. If the value entered is at least one and not more than 100, it is considered valid.

LISTING 9.7   Using the `RangeValidator` Control

```
01: <html>
02:  <body style="font-size:10">
03:  <form runat="server">
04:
05:  <h3>RangeValidator</h3>
06:
07:  Pick a number between 1 and 100
08:
09:  <asp:TextBox
10:   runat="server"
11:   id="txtNumber"
12:  />
13:
14:  <p>
15:
16:  <asp:RangeValidator
17:   runat="server"
18:   Type="Integer"
19:   ControlToValidate="txtNumber"
20:   MinimumValue="1"
21:   MaximumValue="100"
22:   ErrorMessage="You must enter a number between 1 and 100"
23:   Display="Dynamic"
24:  />
25:
26:  <p>
27:
28:  <asp:Button id="SubmitButton"
29:      runat="server"
30:      Text="Submit"
31:  />
32:
33:  </form>
34:  </body>
35: </html>
```

Listing 9.7 uses the `MinimumValue` and `MaximumValue` attribute to determine what to compare to validate the `TextBox` value. The `Type` attribute is set to `Integer`, so only integers are accepted. In this example, the value of the `TextBox` must be at least 1 but not more than 100.

9

**ASP.NET
VALIDATION
CONTROLS**

Try entering a number less than 1 or greater than 100 and the page will not submit. Also try entering something other than an integer; again the page will not submit. Although, if nothing is entered, the page will submit because we are lacking a `RequiredFieldValidator`. Figure 9.4 contains the page after something other than an integer is entered as the value.

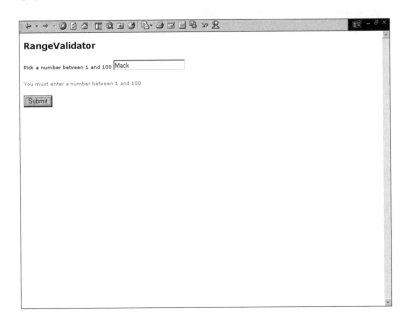

FIGURE 9.4

The page is invalid because my name was entered.

The `CustomValidator` Control

The `CustomValidator` control enables you to create your own validation function in both client and server code. The server code you write can be developed in your default language (for example: C#.NET), but, for your client script, you must write in a scripting language that your target browser supports. Today's most widely used client-scripting languages are JavaScript and its competing Microsoft version, JScript. If you're developing strictly for Internet Explorer, you can write in VBScript.

We'll focus primarily on two things. The first is the `ServerValidate` event. You need to handle this event to perform server-side validation using the `CustomValidator` control. This event expects two parameters: `Object`, and `ServerValidateEventArgs`. `ServerValidateEventArgs` contains a string of the value that needs to be validated accessed through the `ServerValidate EventArgs.Value` property. You use the Boolean `ServerValidateEventArgs.IsValid` attribute to store the result of your validation routine. You use `OnServerValidate` to wire the event handler to the `CustomValidator` control.

The second thing I want to discuss is the `ClientValidationFunction` property, which is what you'll use to either GET or SET the name of a client-side script that will be used to validate the control. This method should have two parameters, source and value, with value being the characters you want to validate. This function should return a Boolean value.

Listing 9.8 demonstrates how to use the `CustomValidator` and how to implement both server- and client-side validation. The validation in this example merely checks that the amount of characters entered into a `TextBox` doesn't exceed 100 characters.

LISTING 9.8 Using the `CustomValidation` Control

```
[VisualBasic.NET]
01: <script language="vb" runat="server">
02:
03:  public sub txtDescription_Validate(sender as Object,
➥   args as ServerValidateEventArgs)
04:
05:   if (args.Value.Length > 100) then
06:
07:    args.IsValid = false
08:
09:   else
10:
11:    args.IsValid = true
12:
13:   end if
14:
15:  end sub
16:
17: </script>

[C#.NET]
01: <script language="C#" runat="server">
02:
03:  void txtDescription_Validate(Object sender,
➥   ServerValidateEventArgs args){
04:
05:   if (args.Value.Length > 100) {
06:
07:    args.IsValid = false;
08:
09:   } else {
10:
11:    args.IsValid = true;
```

LISTING 9.8 Continued

```
12:
13:   }
14:
15:  }
16:
17: </script>
```

[VisualBasic.NET & C#.NET]

```
18: <html>
19:  <head>
20:   <script language="JavaScript">
21:
22:    function txtDescription_ClientValidate(source, value){
23:
24:     if(value.Value.length > 100) {
25:
26:      value.IsValid = false;
27:
28:     } else {
29:
30:      value.IsValid = true;
31:
32:     }
33:
34:    }
35:
36:   </script>
37:  </head>
38: <body Style="font-size:10">
39:  <form runat="server">
40:
41:     <h3>CustomValidator</h3>
42:
43:     <asp:TextBox
44:      id="txtDescription"
45:      runat="server"
46:      TextMode="MultiLine"
47:      Rows="10"
48:     />
49:
50:     <p>
51:
52:     <asp:CustomValidator
53:      runat="server"
```

LISTING 9.8 Continued

```
54:        ControlToValidate="txtDescription"
55:        OnServerValidate="txtDescription_Validate"
56:        ClientValidationFunction="txtDescription_ClientValidate"
57:        ErrorMessage="Text must be 100 characters or less"
58:        Display="Dynamic"
59:     />
60:
61:     <p>
62:
63:     <asp:Button
64:      runat="server"
65:      Text="Submit"
66:     />
67:
68:   </form>
69:   </body>
70: </html>
```

Listing 9.8 contains a multi-line TextBox which is wired up with the CustomValidator control
(lines 52–59). Within the CustomValidator control, I have OnServerValidate set to
txtDescription_Validate—the ServerValidate event handler. ClientValidationFunction
is set to the client-side function txtDescription_ClientValidate. Within both the server-side
event handler and the client-side function, I have the same code, which checks the Length
property of the string passed in. If the string is greater than 100, then the control is found to be
invalid. Figure 9.5 contains an illustration of the page after more than 100 characters were
entered into the TextBox.

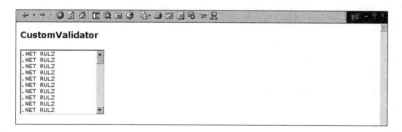

FIGURE 9.5

The control is invalid because more than 100 characters were entered into the TextBox.

Now enter less than 100 characters and try submitting the page again—the page is valid. As
you can see, there are many posiblilities available when using the CustomValidator control.

The `ValidationSummary` Control

The `ValidationSummary` control does not do actual evaluation like the previously mentioned controls. Instead it summarizes all the invalid controls after validation takes place. The `ValidationSummary` control loops through the validation controls array, gathers all the `ErrorMessage` properties of each invalid control, and displays the results in a specified manner.

The `ValidationSummary` control enables you to display the summary in a few different ways. This is accomplished by setting its `DisplayMode` property. There are three different "Modes" or Values to choose from for this property:

- `BulletList` (default)
- `List`
- `SingleParagraph`

The `ValidationSummary` also has a `ShowMessageBox` property which is a `Boolean`. The `ShowMessageBox` property enables you to have the validation summary displayed in a pop-up message box. The default value for this attribute is `false`. Alternatively, the `ShowSummary` attribute, also Boolean, enables you to show the validation summary inline. The default value for this attribute is true.

If none of the above displays are adequate for your Web site, you can alternatively loop through the validation controls collection through code and create a custom summary.

In Listing 9.9, there is an example using the `ValidationSummary` control. In this example, there are two `TextBox` controls—one for your first name and one for your second name. Both controls have `RequiredFieldValidators` wired to them.

LISTING 9.9   The `ValidationSummary` Control

```
01: <html>
02:   <body style="font-size:10">
03:    <form runat="server">
04:
05:     <h3>ValidationSummary</h3>
06:
07:     <asp:ValidationSummary
08:      runat="server"
09:      DisplayMode="BulletList"
10:      ShowMessageBox="true"
11:      ShowSummary="True"
12:      HeaderText="The following fields are missing:"
13:      />
14:
15:     <p>
```

LISTING 9.9   Continued

```
16:
17:      First Name:
18:
19:      <asp:TextBox
20:        runat="Server"
21:        id="txtFName"
22:      />
23:
24:      <asp:RequiredFieldValidator
25:        runat="server"
26:        ControlToValidate="txtFName"
27:        ErrorMessage="* First Name is Required"
28:      />
29:
30:      <br>
31:
32:      Last Name:
33:
34:      <asp:TextBox
35:        runat="server"
36:        id="txtLName"
37:      />
38:
39:      <asp:RequiredFieldValidator
40:        runat="server"
41:        ControlToValidate="txtLName"
42:        ErrorMessage="* Last Name is Required"
43:      />
44:
45:      <p>
46:
47:      <asp:Button
48:        runat="server"
49:        Text="Submit"
50:      />
51:
52:    </form>
53:  </body>
54: </html>
```

In Listing 9.9, we have two TextBox controls being validated. The first, (lines 19–22), is wired to the RequiredFieldValidator on lines 24–28. The second, (lines 34–37), is wired to the RequiredFieldValidator on lines 39–43. Finally, the ValidationSummary control is located on lines 7–13. You'll notice right away that the ValidationSummary isn't wired to anything.

This is because everything is done for you "behind the scenes." This is nice because you don't have to worry about writing any code—hence, productivity is increased.

Let's try it out: Submit the page without filling out any fields. You will get a screen similar to Figure 9.6.

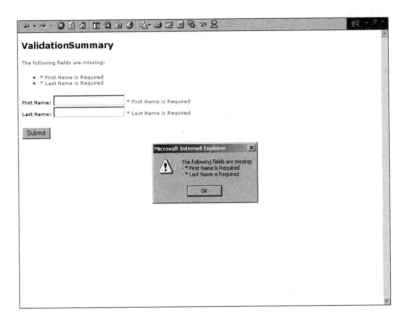

FIGURE 9.6
No fields have been filled out.

Because I have ShowMessageBox and ShowSummary both set to true you get an inline summary of all invalid controls, a message box, and individual control summaries. Do you think the user will get the point? Now fill in just the first name field and try to submit the page to see the effects. Finally, fill in all the fields and submit the page—the page submits fine without any errors.

One Control, Multiple Validators

As previously mentioned, you most likely will need to wire up more than one valiator to one control; for example, the registration page that requires the user to enter a password twice. You most likely would want to make sure they have the fields filled out and the same password is in both TextBox controls. There are a couple benefits to using multiple validators.

One benefit is that you can ensure proper data is entered by the user, and the other is that you can give the user different error messages. For instance, if you are using a RequiredFieldValidator and a CompareValidator you can set the RequiredFieldValidators error message to read "Required Field" and the the CompareValidator's to read, "Passwords must match". Listing 9.10 contains code illustrating how to use multiple validators. This example uses code similar to the CompareValidator section of this chapter. There are two TextBox's and one is used to enter a beginning date and the second, an ending date.

LISTING 9.10 Muliple Validation Controls

```
01:    <html>
02:    <body style="font-size:10">
03:     <form runat="server">
04:     <center>
05:     <H3>Multiple Validation Controls Example</h3>
06:
07:      <asp:ValidationSummary
08:       runat="server"
09:       DisplayMode="BulletList"
10:       ShowMessageBox="false"
11:       ShowSummary="True"
12:       HeaderText="The following fields are missing:"
13:      />
14:
15:      <p>
16:
17:      Beginning Date:
18:      <asp:textbox
19:       runat="server"
20:       id="BeginningDate"
21:      />
22:
23:      <asp:RequiredFieldValidator
24:       runat="server"
25:       ControlToValidate="BeginningDate"
26:       ErrorMessage="Beginning Date"
27:       Display="Dynamic"
28:      >
29:      <b>*</b>
30:      </asp:RequiredFieldValidator>
31:
32:      <asp:CompareValidator
```

LISTING 9.10   Continued

```
33:        runat="server"
34:        ControlToValidate="BeginningDate"
35:        ControlToCompare="EndDate"
36:        Operator="LessThan"
37:        Type="Date"
38:        ErrorMessage="You must enter a valid date and the beginning
➥   date must be earlier than the ending date."
39:        Display="Dynamic"
40:        >
41:        *
42:      </asp:CompareValidator>
43:
44:      Ending Date:
45:      <asp:textbox
46:       runat="server"
47:       id="EndDate"
48:       />
49:
50:      <asp:RequiredFieldValidator
51:       runat="server"
52:       ControlToValidate="EndDate"
53:       ErrorMessage="Ending Date"
54:       Display="Dynamic"
55:       >
56:       <b>*</b>
57:      </asp:RequiredFieldValidator>
58:
59:      <asp:CompareValidator
60:       runat="server"
61:       ControlToValidate="EndDate"
62:       ControlToCompare="BeginningDate"
63:       Operator="GreaterThan"
64:       Type="Date"
65:       ErrorMessage="You must enter a valid date and the beginning
➥   date must be earlier than the ending date."
66:       Display="Dynamic"
67:       >
68:       *
69:      </asp:CompareValidator>
70:
71:      <p>
72:
73:      <asp:Button
74:       runat="server"
```

LISTING 9.10   Continued

```
75:      Text="Submit"
76:      />
77:
78:    </center>
79:    </form>
80:  </body>
81: </html>
```

In Listing 9.10, each `TextBox` control has a `RequiredFieldValidator` and a
`CompareValidator` wired to it. Because of the way the `TextBox` controls are being validated,
the page will not be valid until both `TextBox` controls are filled out with a valid date. The
`TextBox` on lines 18–21 has a date that is before that of the `TextBox` on lines 45–48. You can
try whatever you like to bypass this, but it will be impossible using standard means. Try running through the four steps from the `CompareValidator` section again and see if it will bypass
the validation process again.

Summary

Using validation controls is a very quick, easy, and dependable way to validate data. ASP.NET
offers you some very good stock validation controls you can use, and also enables you to create your own custom validation controls. Using these controls not only saves you development
time, but also is a very clean way to implement data validation. In this chapter, you learned
how to use the following validation controls:

- What are validation controls and how do they work?
- Using the `RequiredFieldValidator` control
- Using the `CompareValidator` control
- Using the `RangeValidator` control
- Using the `RegularExpressionValidator` control
- Using the `CustomValidator` control
- Displaying error information using the `ValidationSummary` control
- Multiple validator controls on one input control

I have one final suggestion for you. To really learn the power of these validation controls, play
around with all of them—change attributes, apply the different styles, and try implementing
multiple validation controls on single input controls. Try to hack them before you go live with
them, because, if you can find a loophole in your validation process, I can guarantee that
someone else will also!

Inputting and Editing Data Using the DataGrid and DataList

IN THIS CHAPTER

When you're building Web applications, sometimes you want to enable your users to change stored information. For instance, you might want to allow a user to change their user profile. Another case might be an online inventory management system in which you want to allow your sales force to update inventory numbers from remote locations via the web. This chapter will show you how to enable editing in both the `DataGrid` and `DataList` server controls in your Web applications. The first thing you'll learn is how editing works using these controls. Then you'll learn the steps you have to take to enable editing and how to save the edited items back to your database. You'll also look at how to change an item's appearance in the `DataGrid` and `DataList` based on certain criteria by using the `ItemCreated` event. Finally, you're going to look at how to enable item selection using the `DataList` and `DataGrid`. Specifically, we'll be going over the following:

- Enabling editing using the `DataGrid` and `DataList`
- Changing certain items using the `ItemCreated` event
- Enabling item selection using the `DataGrid` and `DataList`

An Overview of Editing Functions

The way you enable editing for the `DataGrid` is similar to the method for the `DataList`, which is why we are combining them in this chapter. In this section, I want to give you a high-level picture of how editing works. I'll be mentioning certain attributes and events that might not make sense to you right now, but they'll become clear to you later in the chapter when we start building and dissecting the example code.

When editing is enabled for a `DataGrid`, you must have an `EditCommandColumn`. This is nothing more than a container column for an object that the users click to go into edit mode. The DataList also has a way for users to put it into edit mode, but you have to create the buttons manually using either a Button or LinkButton control because the `DataList` is built entirely from templates. Once the page is rendered and a user clicks the *Edit* button, then the form is posted back to the server and the `EditCommand` event is raised. This is where you'll code to put the `DataGrid` or `DataList` into edit mode.

After it's in edit mode, the row selected by the user to be edited will contain editable controls such as a text box. Two new buttons can be used while in edit mode: `Update` and `Cancel` button. `Update` is used to raise the `UpdateCommmand` event, which is where you save any changes back to your data source. `Cancel` is used to raise the `CancelCommand` event, which switches the `DataGrid` or `DataList` out of edit mode without making changes to the underlying data source.

There are four different events used for enabling editing data using the `DataGrid` and `DataList`. You must handle these events appropriately to make editing work:

- `EditCommand`—Raised by the `OnEditCommand` method when the Edit button is clicked.
- `UpdateCommand`—Raised by the `OnUpdateCommand` method when the Update button is clicked.

- DeleteCommand—Raised by the OnDeleteCommand method when the Delete button is clicked
- CancelCommand—Raised by the OnCancelCommand method when the Cancel button is clicked.

In order for these events to be fired, you must tell the DataGrid or DataList by setting the following attributes:

- OnEditCommand—The value is the method name you're using to handle the EditCommand event.
- OnUpdateCommand—The value is the method name you're using to handle the UpdateCommand event.
- OnDeleteCommand—The value is the method name you're using to handle the DeleteCommand event.
- OnCancelCommand—The value is the method name you're using to handle the CancelCommand event.

Enabling Editing Using the DataGrid

Chapter 7, "Working with ASP.NET Server Controls Templates," discussed working with templates and columns, and you learned what bound columns are. The EditCommandColumn is one of these columns; it's a single row within a DataGrid and by default doesn't contain any data from your data source. Listing 10.1 shows how to insert the EditCommandColumn in your DataGrid.

LISTING 10.1   Inserting the EditCommandColumn

```
01: <asp:DataGrid
02:   id="DGProducts"
03:   runat="server"
04:   AutoGenerateColumns="true"
05:   OnEditCommand="DGProducts_Edit"
06:   OnCancelCommand="DGProducts_Cancel"
07:   OnUpdateCommand="DGProducts_Update"
08:   OnDeleteCommand="DGProducts_Delete"
09:   >
10:   <Columns>
11:   <asp:EditCommandColumn
12:     ButtonType="LinkButton"
13:     CancelText="Cancel"
14:     EditText="Edit"
15:     UpdateText="Update"
16:     Visible="true"
17:     />
18:   </columns>
19: </asp:DataGrid>
```

Notice that the `EditCommandColumn` isn't bound to any field from the data source (lines 11–17), but instead is bound to the row as a whole from the data source. This means you can use the `DataGrid` in any way you want even when you enable editing. For example, you can set `AutoGenerateColumns` to false and create a custom layout for the `DataGrid`. You also can enable paging and/or sorting without having to change any code within the `EditCommandColumn`.

The `EditCommandColumn` contains all the styling information for edit mode, but it doesn't contain information about server events. (The use of event handlers will be discussed later in this chapter.)

One attribute from the `EditCommandColumn` I would like to discuss is the `ButtonType` attribute, which is used to determine what type of button should be used for the column for the user to click on. You have the choice of two types of buttons:

- `LinkButton`—The button comes in the form of a hyperlink.
- `PushButton`—The button comes in the form of an HTML input button.

TIP

When you use the `LinkButton` as the `ButtonType`, you can use an image for the button with the following code:

```
ButtonType="LinkButton"
EditText="<img src='/images/edit.gif' border='0'>"
```
The image will be placed between the `<a href=""></a>` tags.

You set the text for the three buttons by using the following attributes:

- `EditText`—Attribute used to set the text for the Edit button.
- `UpdateText`—Attribute used to set the text of the Update button.
- `CancelText`—Attribute used to set the text of the Cancel button.

Listing 10.2 shows how to use the `DataGrid` with editing enabled. After this example, we will dissect the code.

LISTING 10.2   Enabling Editing in the `DataGrid`

```
[Visual Basic]

01: <%@ import namespace="System.Data" %>
02: <%@ import namespace="System.Data.SqlClient" %>
```

LISTING 10.2   Continued

```vb
03: <script language="vb" runat="server">
04:   private sSqlCon as string   =
➥"server=localhost;uid=sa;pwd=;database=northwind"
05:
06:   public sub Page_Load(sender as Object, e as EventArgs)
07:
08:     if not IsPostBack then
09:      Bind()
10:     end if
11:
12:   end sub
13:
14:  private sub Bind()
15:
16:     dim SqlCon as new SqlConnection(sSqlCon)
17:     dim SqlCmd as new StringBuilder()
18:     SqlCmd.Append("SELECT ProductName,UnitPrice,")
19:     SqlCmd.Append("UnitsInStock,UnitsOnOrder,")
20:     SqlCmd.Append("ProductID FROM Products")
21:     dim sda as new SqlDataAdapter(SqlCmd.ToString(),SqlCon)
22:     dim ds as new DataSet()
23:     sda.Fill(ds,"products")
24:     DGProducts.DataSource = ds.Tables("Products").DefaultView
25:     DGProducts.DataBind()
26:
27:  end sub
28:
29:  public sub DGProducts_Edit(sender as Object, e as DataGridCommandEventArgs)
30:
31:   DGProducts.EditItemIndex = e.Item.ItemIndex
32:   Bind()
33:
34:  end sub
35:
36:  public sub DGProducts_Cancel(sender as Object, e as
➥DataGridCommandEventArgs)
37:
38:   DGProducts.EditItemIndex = -1
39:   Bind()
40:
41:  end sub
42:
43:  public sub DGProducts_Update(sender as Object, e as
➥DataGridCommandEventArgs)
```

EDITING DATA
USING DATAGRID
AND DATALIST

LISTING 10.2   Continued

```
44:
45:  dim sProductName,sUnitsInStock,sUnitsOnOrder,sProductID as string
46:    sProductName = CType(e.Item.Cells(1).Controls(0), TextBox).Text
47:    sUnitsInStock = CType(e.Item.Cells(2).Controls(0), TextBox).Text
48:    sUnitsOnOrder = CType(e.Item.Cells(3).Controls(0), TextBox).Text
49:    sProductID = e.Item.Cells(5). Text
50:
51:  dim sSqlCmd as new StringBuilder()
52:    sSqlCmd.Append("UPDATE Products ")
53:    sSqlCmd.Append("SET ProductName = @ProductName,")
54:    sSqlCmd.Append("UnitsInStock = @UnitsInStock,")
55:    sSqlCmd.Append("UnitsOnOrder = @UnitsOnOrder ")
56:    sSqlCmd.Append("WHERE ProductID = @ProductID")
57:
58:  dim SqlCon as new SqlConnection(sSqlCon)
59:  Dim SqlCmd as new SqlCommand(sSqlCmd.ToString(),SqlCon)
60:    SqlCmd.Parameters.Add(new SqlParameter("@ProductName",
➥SqlDbType.NVarChar, 40))
61:    SqlCmd.Parameters("@ProductName").Value = sProductName
62:    SqlCmd.Parameters.Add(new SqlParameter("@UnitsInStock",
➥SqlDbType.SmallInt))
63:    SqlCmd.Parameters("@UnitsInStock").Value = sUnitsInStock
64:    SqlCmd.Parameters.Add(new SqlParameter("@UnitsOnOrder",
➥SqlDbType.SmallInt))
65:    SqlCmd.Parameters("@UnitsOnOrder").Value = sUnitsOnOrder
66:    SqlCmd.Parameters.Add(new SqlParameter("@ProductID", SqlDbType.SmallInt))
67:    SqlCmd.Parameters("@ProductID").Value = sProductID
68:
69:  SqlCon.Open()
70:  SqlCmd.ExecuteNonQuery()
71:  SqlCon.Close()
72:
73:  DGProducts.EditItemIndex = -1
74:  Bind()
75:
76: end sub
77:
78: </script>
79: <html>
80:   <body>
81:     <head>
82:
83:       <style rel="stylesheet">
84:         H3 { font: bold 11pt Verdana, Arial, sans-serif; }
```

LISTING 10.2   Continued

```
85:        .products { font: 9pt Verdana, Arial, sans-serif; }
86:        .productsHead { font: bold 9pt Verdana, Arial, sans-serif;
87:         background-color:Maroon; color:white; }
88:        a { text-decoration:none; }
89:        a:hover { text-decoration:underline; color:maroon; }
90:      </style>
91:
92:    </head>
93:        <form runat="server">
94: <H3>Northwind Inventory Management - VisualBasic.NET</H3>
95:
96: <asp:DataGrid
97:   id="DGProducts"
98:   runat="server"
99:   Cellpadding="4" Cellspacing="0" Width="750"
100:  BorderWidth="1" Gridlines="None"
101:  AlternatingItemStyle-BackColor="Tan"
102:  HeaderStyle-CssClass="productsHead"
103:  Font-Size="12"
104:  AutoGenerateColumns="false"
105:  OnEditCommand="DGProducts_Edit"
106:  OnCancelCommand="DGProducts_Cancel"
107:  OnUpdateCommand="DGProducts_Update"
108:  >
109:  <Columns>
110: <asp:EditCommandColumn
111:   ButtonType="LinkButton"
112:   CancelText="Cancel"
113:   EditText="Edit"
114:   UpdateText="Update"
115:   />
116:  <asp:BoundColumn DataField="ProductName" HeaderText="Product Name" />
117:  <asp:BoundColumn DataField="UnitsInStock" HeaderText="Units in Stock" />
118:  <asp:BoundColumn DataField="UnitsOnOrder" HeaderText="Units on Order" />
119:  <asp:BoundColumn DataField="UnitPrice" HeaderText="Price Per Unit"
120:   DataFormatString="{0:C}" ReadOnly="true" />
121:  <asp:BoundColumn DataField="ProductID"
122:   HeaderText="Product ID" ReadOnly="true" />
123:  </columns>
124: </asp:DataGrid>
125:   </form>
126:  </body>
127: </html>
```

10

EDITING DATA
USING DATAGRID
AND DATALIST

LISTING 10.2   Continued

[C#—Replace server code]

```
01: <%@ import namespace="System.Data" %>
02: <%@ import namespace="System.Data.SqlClient" %>
03: <script language="c#" runat="server">
04:   private string sSqlCon = ➥"server=localhost;uid=sa;pwd=;database=north-
wind";
05:
06:   public void Page_Load(Object sender, EventArgs e){
07:
08:     if (! IsPostBack){
09:       Bind();
10:     }
11:
12:   }
13:
14: private void Bind() {
15:
16:     SqlConnection SqlCon = new SqlConnection(sSqlCon);
17:     StringBuilder SqlCmd = new StringBuilder();
18:      SqlCmd.Append("SELECT ProductName,UnitPrice,");
19:      SqlCmd.Append("UnitsInStock,UnitsOnOrder,");
20:      SqlCmd.Append("ProductID FROM Products");
21:     SqlDataAdapter sda = new SqlDataAdapter(SqlCmd.ToString(),SqlCon);
22:     DataSet ds = new DataSet();
23:     sda.Fill(ds,"products");
24:     DGProducts.DataSource = ds.Tables["Products"].DefaultView;
25:     DGProducts.DataBind();
26:
27: }
28:
29: public void DGProducts_Edit(Object sender, DataGridCommandEventArgs e) {
30:
31:  DGProducts.EditItemIndex = e.Item.ItemIndex;
32:  Bind();
33:
34: }
35:
36: public void DGProducts_Cancel(Object sender, DataGridCommandEventArgs e) {
37:
38:  DGProducts.EditItemIndex = -1;
39:  Bind();
40:
```

LISTING 10.2   Continued

```
41: }
42:
43: public void DGProducts_Update(Object sender, DataGridCommandEventArgs e) {
44:
45:   string sProductName,sUnitsInStock,sUnitsOnOrder,sProductID;
46:    sProductName = ((TextBox)e.Item.Cells[1].Controls[0]).Text;
47:    sUnitsInStock = ((TextBox)e.Item.Cells[2].Controls[0]).Text;
48:    sUnitsOnOrder = ((TextBox)e.Item.Cells[3].Controls[0]).Text;
49:    sProductID = e.Item.Cells[5]. Text;
50:
51:   StringBuilder sSqlCmd = new StringBuilder();
52:    sSqlCmd.Append("UPDATE Products ");
53:    sSqlCmd.Append("SET ProductName = @ProductName,");
54:    sSqlCmd.Append("UnitsInStock = @UnitsInStock,");
55:    sSqlCmd.Append("UnitsOnOrder = @UnitsOnOrder ");
56:    sSqlCmd.Append("WHERE ProductID = @ProductID");
57:
58:   SqlConnection SqlCon = new SqlConnection(sSqlCon);
59:   SqlCommand SqlCmd = new SqlCommand(sSqlCmd.ToString(),SqlCon);
60:    SqlCmd.Parameters.Add(new SqlParameter("@ProductName",
➥SqlDbType.NVarChar, 40));
61:    SqlCmd.Parameters["@ProductName"].Value = sProductName;
62:    SqlCmd.Parameters.Add(new SqlParameter("@UnitsInStock",
➥SqlDbType.SmallInt));
63:    SqlCmd.Parameters["@UnitsInStock"].Value = sUnitsInStock;
64:    SqlCmd.Parameters.Add(new SqlParameter("@UnitsOnOrder",
➥SqlDbType.SmallInt));
65:    SqlCmd.Parameters["@UnitsOnOrder"].Value = sUnitsOnOrder;
66:    SqlCmd.Parameters.Add(new SqlParameter("@ProductID",
➥SqlDbType.SmallInt));
67:    SqlCmd.Parameters["@ProductID"].Value = sProductID;
68:
69:   SqlCon.Open();
70:   SqlCmd.ExecuteNonQuery();
71:   SqlCon.Close();
72:
73:   DGProducts.EditItemIndex = -1;
74:   Bind();
75:
76: }
77:
78: </script>
```

10

EDITING DATA
USING DATAGRID
AND DATALIST

We will go over Listing 10.2 in detail in the following three sections. The first section, "Putting the `DataGrid` into Edit Mode" explains how to configure the `DataGrid` to support editing. The next section, "Updating Data with the `DataGrid`," explains how to update your database with the edited data. Finally, "Cancelling out of Edit Mode," explains how to cancel out of edit mode without saving the edited data back to the database.

Putting the `DataGrid` into Edit Mode

Going through Listing 10.2 you'll notice that putting the `DataGrid` into edit mode isn't as simple as setting one attribute to true or false. You must tell the `DataGrid` that you want it to go into edit mode and handle certain events appropriately. First, you need to set the `OnEditCommand` attribute of the `DataGrid` (line 105). As previously mentioned the `OnEditCommand` method raises the `EditCommand` event which will be handled by the event named as the value of the `OnEditCommand` attribute. This brings us to the second step: handling the `EditCommand` event. This code is found on lines 29–34; the method name is `DGProducts_Edit`. The event handler expects two parameters; `Object` and `DataGridCommandEventArgs`.

The `DataGridCommandEventArgs` object contains all the information you need to retrieve information about what raised the event. The following list contains all the properties contained in the `DataGridCommandEventArgs`:

- `Item`—Gets the selected item (the row within the `DataGrid` that the event was raised by) (see `DataGridItem` class for more detail).
- `CommandArgument`—Gets the argument for the command.
- `CommandName`—Gets the name of the command.
- `CommandSource`—Gets the source of the command.

Once you have handled the `EditCommand` event, you will need to use an attribute of the Item property to figure out which row of the `DataGrid` you want to put into edit mode. You do this by setting the `DataGrid`'s `EditItemIndex` attribute to be equal to the index of the item that raised the event. This code can be found on line 31 and you use the `Item` objects `ItemIndex` property to retrieve it. Once in edit mode, you need to re-bind the `DataGrid` to its data source (line 32). Any columns within the `DataGrid` that are visible and are not read-only will contain TextBox's with the original values in them—very similar to Figure 10.1.

You can use the `ReadOnly` Attribute to disable editing of certain fields in the `DataGrid` as I did for the `ProductID` column on line 121. This attribute is set to false by default, and a text box will appear for every field from the data source. To disable a certain field, set this attribute to true.

Now that some of the `DataGrid`'s columns can be changed we need to save these changes back to our database. In the next section we will be illustrating how to handle these updates using the `UpdateCommand`.

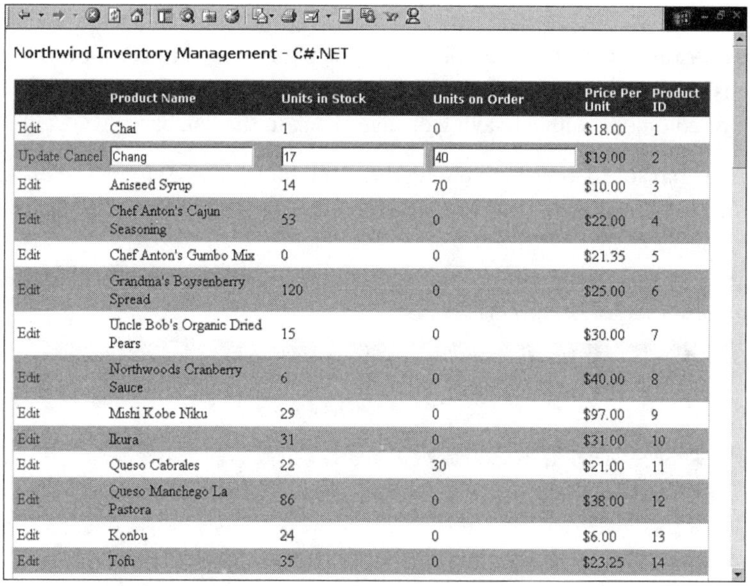

FIGURE 10.1
The DataGrid *in edit mode—TextBox controls are used to edit data.*

Updating Data with the DataGrid

Updating data with the DataGrid requires a little more work than putting the DataGrid into edit mode. The first thing we have to do is set up the DataGrid to allow updating. You can accomplish this by setting the OnUpdateCommand attribute to the name of the method that will handle the event (line 107). The method you use to handle the event expects the same two arguments as the DataGrid_Edit from the previous section. In this example, the name for this method is DGProducts_Update (lines 43–76). This is the method you want to use to gain access to the edited items within the DataGrid, validate it, and save it back to the database.

Retrieving the edited data is a bit tricky because the entire row from the DataGrid is contained within the Item object. Because the edited data is located in controls (ex: TextBox) that are in turn located within table cells we have to drill down through the Item object to each individual control; first through the cells collection and then through the controls collection within each cell. This is done in lines 45–49. First, on line 45 I create 4 variables that I'll use to hold the values of the edited item(s). In lines 46–49 I assign values to each variable by accessing the Text property of the first control within the cells that are allowed to be edited. On line 49 I need to only access the Cell's Text attribute since the ProductID is not contained within a control but rather within the Cell itself.

Next I construct my SQL UPDATE statement and update the backend database (lines 51–71). On line 73 the DataGrid is taken out of edit mode by setting its EditItemIndex to -1 and finally the DataGrid is re-bound (line 74). In the next section we will demonstrate how to take the DataGrid out of edit mode without saving changes back to the database.

Figure 10.2 is the DataGrid after I edited the row containing *Chef Anton's Cajun Seasoning* to *Don Mack's Cajun Seasoning*.

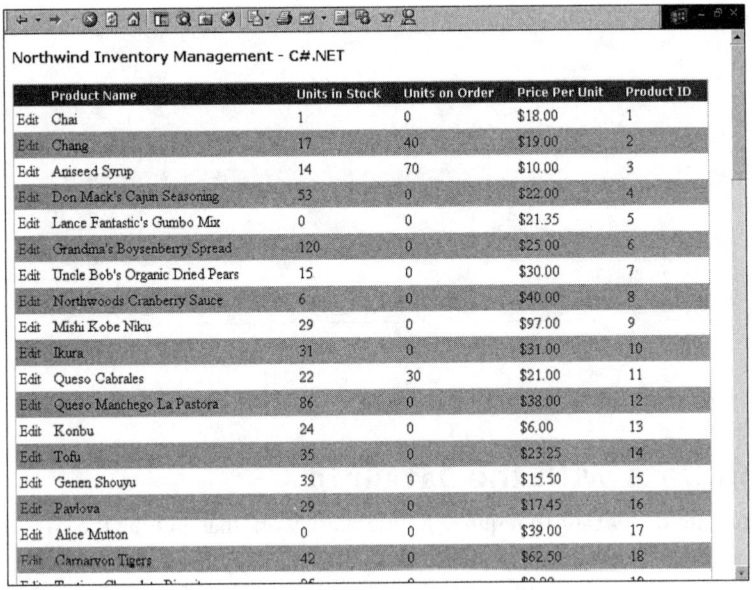

FIGURE 10.2

Edited DataGrid—*Chef Anton's Cajun Seasoning has been changed to Don Mack's Cajun Seasoning.*

Cancelling Out of Edit Mode

Cancelling out of edit mode is a very simple task. You enable this feature by setting the OnCancelCommand attribute equal to what you're going to use to handle the event (line 106). Next you need to create the event handler (lines 36–41). When you're cancelling out of edit mode, you need only set its EditItemIndex attribute to -1.

Enabling Editing Using the DataList

Using the DataList control rather than the DataGrid gives you significantly more control over the layout of the rendered page. For example, since the DataList doesn't have a default look, you can have one look for items while in edit mode and another for those that are not. Listing 10.3 uses the DataList with editing enabled. After this listing, we'll dissect the code used for editing to show you exactly what's going on.

LISTING 10.3 Enabling Editing in the `DataList`

```
[Visual Basic]

01: <%@ import namespace="System.Data" %>
02: <%@ import namespace="System.Data.SqlClient" %>
03: <script language="vb" runat="server">
04:   private sSqlCon as string   =
➥"server=localhost;uid=sa;pwd=;database=northwind"
05:
06:   public sub Page_Load(sender as Object, e as EventArgs)
07:
08:     if not IsPostBack then
09:      Bind()
10:     end if
11:
12:   end sub
13:
14: private sub Bind()
15:
16:    dim SqlCon as new SqlConnection(sSqlCon)
17:    dim SqlCmd as new StringBuilder()
18:     SqlCmd.Append("SELECT ProductName,UnitPrice,")
19:     SqlCmd.Append("UnitsInStock,UnitsOnOrder,")
20:     SqlCmd.Append("ProductID FROM Products")
21:    dim sda as new SqlDataAdapter(SqlCmd.ToString(),SqlCon)
22:    dim ds as new DataSet()
23:    sda.Fill(ds,"products")
24:    DLProducts.DataSource = ds.Tables("Products").DefaultView
25:    DLProducts.DataBind()
26:
27: end sub
28:
29: public sub DLProducts_Edit(sender as Object, e as DataListCommandEventArgs)
30:
31:  DLProducts.EditItemIndex = e.Item.ItemIndex
32:  Bind()
33:
34: end sub
35:
36: public sub DLProducts_Cancel(sender as Object, e as
➥DataListCommandEventArgs)
37:
38:  DLProducts.EditItemIndex = -1
39:  Bind()
40:
41: end sub
42:
```

10

EDITING DATA
USING DATAGRID
AND DATALIST

LISTING 10.3 Continued

```
43: public sub DLProducts_Update(sender as Object, e as
➥DataListCommandEventArgs)
44:
45:  dim sProductName,sUnitsInStock,sUnitsOnOrder,sProductID as string
46:   sProductName = CType(e.Item.FindControl("tProductName"), TextBox).Text
47:   sUnitsInStock = CType(e.Item.FindControl("tUnitsInStock"), TextBox).Text
48:   sUnitsOnOrder = CType(e.Item.FindControl("tUnitsOnOrder"), TextBox).Text
49:   sProductID = CType(e.Item.FindControl("lProductID"), Label).Text
50:
51:  dim sSqlCmd as new StringBuilder()
52:   sSqlCmd.Append("UPDATE Products ")
53:   sSqlCmd.Append("SET ProductName = @ProductName,")
54:   sSqlCmd.Append("UnitsInStock = @UnitsInStock,")
55:   sSqlCmd.Append("UnitsOnOrder = @UnitsOnOrder ")
56:   sSqlCmd.Append("WHERE ProductID = @ProductID")
57:
58:  dim SqlCon as new SqlConnection(sSqlCon)
59:  Dim SqlCmd as new SqlCommand(sSqlCmd.ToString(),SqlCon)
60:   SqlCmd.Parameters.Add(new SqlParameter("@ProductName",
➥SqlDbType.NVarChar, 40))
61:   SqlCmd.Parameters("@ProductName").Value = sProductName
62:   SqlCmd.Parameters.Add(new SqlParameter("@UnitsInStock",
➥SqlDbType.SmallInt))
63:   SqlCmd.Parameters("@UnitsInStock").Value = sUnitsInStock
64:   SqlCmd.Parameters.Add(new SqlParameter("@UnitsOnOrder",
➥SqlDbType.SmallInt))
65:   SqlCmd.Parameters("@UnitsOnOrder").Value = sUnitsOnOrder
66:   SqlCmd.Parameters.Add(new SqlParameter("@ProductID", SqlDbType.SmallInt))
67:   SqlCmd.Parameters("@ProductID").Value = sProductID
68:
69:  SqlCon.Open()
70:  SqlCmd.ExecuteNonQuery()
71:  SqlCon.Close()
72:
73:  DLProducts.EditItemIndex = -1
74:  Bind()
75:
76: end sub
77:
78: </script>
79: <html>
80:   <body>
81:    <head>
82:
83:     <style rel="stylesheet">
84:      H3 { font: bold 11pt Verdana, Arial, sans-serif; }
```

LISTING 10.3 Continued

```
85:        .products { font: 9pt Verdana, Arial, sans-serif; }
86:        .productsHead { font: bold 9pt Verdana, Arial, sans-serif;
87:         background-color:Maroon; color:white; }
88:        a { text-decoration:none; }
89:        a:hover { text-decoration:underline; color:maroon; }
90:      </style>
91:
92:    </head>
93:       <form runat="server">
94: <center>
95: <H3>Northwind Inventory Management - VisualBasic.NET</H3>
96: </center>
97: <asp:DataList
98:   id="DLProducts"
99:   runat="server"
100:  Cellpadding="0" Cellspacing="0" Width="750"
101:  BorderWidth="1" Gridlines="Both"
102:  AlternatingItemStyle-BackColor="Tan"
103:  HeaderStyle-CssClass="productsHead"
104:  Font-Size="12"
105:  RepeatColumns="1"
106:  Align="Center"
107:  OnCancelCommand="DLProducts_Cancel"
108:  OnEditCommand="DLProducts_Edit"
109:  OnUpdateCommand="DLProducts_Update"
110:
111:  >
112:   <ItemTemplate>
113:
114:     <Table cellpadding="4" cellspacing="0" width="100%">
115:      <TR>
116:       <TD ColSpan="2" class="ProductsHead">
117:        <h3><%# DataBinder.Eval(Container.DataItem, "ProductName") %></b>
118:       </TD>
119:      </TR>
120:      <TR>
121:       <TD Width="50%" Align="Left">
122:        <b>Units In Stock</b>
123:       </TD>
124:       <TD Width="50%" Align="Right">
125:        <%# DataBinder.Eval(Container.DataItem, "UnitsInStock") %>
126:       </TD>
127:      </TR>
128:      <TR>
129:       <TD Width="50%" Align="Left">
```

10

EDITING DATA
USING DATAGRID
AND DATALIST

LISTING 10.3 Continued

```
130:          <b>Units On Order</b>
131:        </TD>
132:        <TD Width="50%" Align="Right">
133:         <%# DataBinder.Eval(Container.DataItem, "UnitsOnOrder") %>
134:        </TD>
135:       </TR>
136:       <TR>
137:        <TD Width="50%" Align="Left">
138:          <b>Price Per Unit</b>
139:        </TD>
140:        <TD Width="50%" Align="Right">
141:         <%# DataBinder.Eval(Container.DataItem, "UnitPrice", "{0:C}") %>
142:        </TD>
143:       </TR>
144:       <TR>
145:        <TD Width="50%" Align="Left">
146:          <b>Edit This Item</b>
147:        </TD>
148:        <TD Width="50%" Align="Right">
149:         <asp:LinkButton Runat="server" CommandName="edit" Text="Edit" />
150:        </TD>
151:       </TR>
152:      </Table>
153:
154:   </ItemTemplate>
155:
156:   <EditItemTemplate>
157:
158:    <Table cellpadding="4" cellspacing="0" width="100%">
159:     <TR>
160:      <TD ColSpan="2" class="ProductsHead">
161:       <h3><%# DataBinder.Eval(Container.DataItem, "ProductName") %></b>
162:      </TD>
163:     </TR>
164:     <TR>
165:      <TD Width="50%" Align="Left">
166:        <b>Product Name</b>
167:      </TD>
168:      <TD Width="50%" Align="Right">
169:       <asp:TextBox id="tProductName" runat="server"
170:        Text='<%# DataBinder.Eval(Container.DataItem, "ProductName") %>'
171:        />
172:      </TD>
173:     </TR>
174:      <TR>
```

LISTING 10.3 Continued

```
175:          <TD Width="50%" Align="Left">
176:           <b>Units In Stock</b>
177:          </TD>
178:          <TD Width="50%" Align="Right">
179:           <asp:TextBox id="tUnitsInStock" Runat="server"
180:            Text='<%# DataBinder.Eval(Container.DataItem, "UnitsInStock") %>'
181:            />
182:          </TD>
183:         </TR>
184:         <TR>
185:          <TD Width="50%" Align="Left">
186:           <b>Units On Order</b>
187:          </TD>
188:          <TD Width="50%" Align="Right">
189:           <asp:TextBox id="tUnitsOnOrder" Runat="server"
190:            Text='<%# DataBinder.Eval(Container.DataItem, "UnitsOnOrder") %>'
191:            />
192:          </TD>
193:         </TR>
194:         <TR>
195:          <TD ColSpan="2">
196:           <asp:Label id="lProductID" runat="server"
197:            Text='<%# DataBinder.Eval(Container.DataItem, "ProductID") %>'
198:            Visible="false"
199:            />
200:          </TD>
201:         </TR>
201:         <TR>
202:          <TD Width="50%" Align="Left">
203:           <b>Edit This Item</b>
204:          </TD>
205:          <TD Width="50%" Align="Right">
206:           <asp:LinkButton Runat="server" CommandName="update" Text="Update"
/>
207:           <asp:LinkButton Runat="server" CommandName="cancel" Text="Cancel"
/>
208:          </TD>
209:         </TR>
210:        </Table>
211:
212:     </EditItemTemplate>
213:
214: </asp:DataList>
215:    </form>
216:   </body>
217: </html>
```

LISTING 10.3   Continued

```csharp
[C#—Replace server code]
01: <%@ import namespace="System.Data" %>
02: <%@ import namespace="System.Data.SqlClient" %>
03: <script language="c#" runat="server">
04:   private string sSqlCon = ➡"server=localhost;uid=sa;pwd=;database=north-
wind";
05:
06:   public void Page_Load(Object sender, EventArgs e){
07:
08:     if (! IsPostBack){
09:       Bind();
10:     }
11:
12:   }
13:
14: private void Bind() {
15:
16:     SqlConnection SqlCon = new SqlConnection(sSqlCon);
17:     StringBuilder SqlCmd = new StringBuilder();
18:      SqlCmd.Append("SELECT ProductName,UnitPrice,");
19:      SqlCmd.Append("UnitsInStock,UnitsOnOrder,");
20:      SqlCmd.Append("ProductID FROM Products");
21:     SqlDataAdapter sda = new SqlDataAdapter(SqlCmd.ToString(),SqlCon);
22:     DataSet ds = new DataSet();
23:     sda.Fill(ds,"products");
24:     DLProducts.DataSource = ds.Tables["Products"].DefaultView;
25:     DLProducts.DataBind();
26:
27: }
28:
29: public void DLProducts_Edit(Object sender, DataListCommandEventArgs e) {
30:
31:   DLProducts.EditItemIndex = e.Item.ItemIndex;
32:   Bind();
33:
34: }
35:
36: public void DLProducts_Cancel(Object sender, DataListCommandEventArgs e) {
37:
38:   DLProducts.EditItemIndex = -1;
39:   Bind();
40:
41: }
42:
43: public void DLProducts_Update(Object sender, DataListCommandEventArgs e) {
44:
```

LISTING 10.3 Continued

```
45:  string sProductName,sUnitsInStock,sUnitsOnOrder,sProductID;
46:    sProductName = ((TextBox)e.Item.FindControl("tProductName")).Text;
47:    sUnitsInStock = ((TextBox)e.Item.FindControl("tUnitsInStock")).Text;
48:    sUnitsOnOrder = ((TextBox)e.Item.FindControl("tUnitsOnOrder")).Text;
49:    sProductID = ((Label)e.Item.FindControl("lProductID")).Text;
50:
51:  StringBuilder sSqlCmd = new StringBuilder();
52:    sSqlCmd.Append("UPDATE Products ");
53:    sSqlCmd.Append("SET ProductName = @ProductName,");
54:    sSqlCmd.Append("UnitsInStock = @UnitsInStock,");
55:    sSqlCmd.Append("UnitsOnOrder = @UnitsOnOrder ");
56:    sSqlCmd.Append("WHERE ProductID = @ProductID");
57:
58:  SqlConnection SqlCon = new SqlConnection(sSqlCon);
59:  SqlCommand SqlCmd = new SqlCommand(sSqlCmd.ToString(),SqlCon);
60:    SqlCmd.Parameters.Add(new SqlParameter("@ProductName",
➥SqlDbType.NVarChar, 40));
61:    SqlCmd.Parameters["@ProductName"].Value = sProductName;
62:    SqlCmd.Parameters.Add(new SqlParameter("@UnitsInStock",
➥SqlDbType.SmallInt));
63:    SqlCmd.Parameters["@UnitsInStock"].Value = sUnitsInStock;
64:    SqlCmd.Parameters.Add(new SqlParameter("@UnitsOnOrder",
➥SqlDbType.SmallInt));
65:    SqlCmd.Parameters["@UnitsOnOrder"].Value = sUnitsOnOrder;
66:    SqlCmd.Parameters.Add(new SqlParameter("@ProductID",
➥SqlDbType.SmallInt));
67:    SqlCmd.Parameters["@ProductID"].Value = sProductID;
68:
69:  SqlCon.Open();
70:  SqlCmd.ExecuteNonQuery();
71:  SqlCon.Close();
72:
73:  DLProducts.EditItemIndex = -1;
74:  Bind();
75:
76: }
77:
78: </script>
```

We will go over Listing 10.3 in detail in the following three sections. The first section, "Putting the DataList into Edit Mode," explains how to configure the DataList to support editing. The next section, "Updating Data with the DataList," explains how to update your database with the edited data. Finally, "Cancelling out of Edit Mode," explains how to cancel out of edit mode without saving the edited data back to the database.

Putting the `DataList` into Edit Mode

Looking at Listing 10.3 you'll notice that editing using `DataList` is a little different than with the `DataGrid`. The first thing you probably noticed is that there isn't an `EditCommandColumn`. Instead you have to use button controls to raise the `CancelCommand`, `UpdateCommand`, and `EditCommand` events. You might also have noticed that you have to manually create the user interface for both normal and edit mode by use of templates.

First, let's take a look at the structure of the `DataList` itself. There are two templates used in Listing 10.3: the `ItemTemplate` (lines 112–154), which as you remember is rendered once for each row in the data source, and the `EditItemTemplate` (lines 156–213), which is rendered only when the `DataList` is in edit mode. It will only be used for the item that has been chosen by the user to edit. You can use similar HTML code as you do in the `ItemTemplate` or you can use completely different HTML code. Whether or not you decide to use a similar html structure within the `EditItemTemplate` you have to decide what controls you are going to use to allow the user to edit data such as a TextBox control or a `DropDownList` control. In Listing 10.3 we use TextBox controls.

As previously mentioned, you need to use Button controls to raise the `EditCommand` event. On line 149 you will find the `LinkButton` we use to enter into edit mode in Listing 10.3. The `CommandName` attribute of the Button control is how you control which event is raised when using the `DataList` control. As with the `DataGrid`, the `DataList` has 4 different events that you will use when dealing with editing data. Each event is raised by using a key word as the `CommandName` attribute value of the button control and by setting its correlating method's value (`OnEditCommand`) equal to event which will handle the command (`EditCommand`). Table 10.1 contains each.

TABLE 10.1   The button `ColumnName` attribute signals the `DataList` method to raise the correlating `DataList` event.

`DataList` *Method*	*Event Button or LinkButton*	`DataList` *CommandName*
`EditCommand`	`OnEditCommand`	`edit`
`DeleteCommand`	`OnDeleteCommand`	`delete`
`CancelCommand`	`OnCancelCommand`	`cancel`
`DeleteCommand`	`OnDeleteCommand`	`delete`

Once the `LinkButton` is clicked and the `EditCommand` event is handled by `DLProducts_Edit` (lines 29–34) that item is put into edit mode exactly as you would using the `DataGrid`. First, you set the `DataList`'s `EditItemIndex` attribute equal to the selected item's `ItemIndex`. You retrieve the `ItemIndex` through the `Item` property of the `DataListCommandEventArgs` parameter. The `DataListCommandEventArgs` contains and behaves similar to the `DataGrid`'s `DataGridCommandEventArgs`. After setting the `EditItemIndex` you want to rebind the `DataList` to its data source (i.e. `Bind` method). Figure 10.3 shows this `DataList` in edit mode.

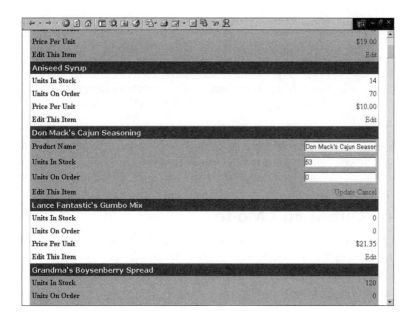

FIGURE 10.3

This DataList *in edit mode.*

Updating Data with the `DataList`

Now that you have the basics of how to handle editing events with the `DataList` the rest is easy. You will see the `UpdateCommand` behaves nearly the same way as the `DataGrid` with two differences. The first difference is how you raise the `EditCommand` event. The event is handled by the `DLProducts_Update` method found on lines 43–76 and is raised by the `LinkButton` control on line 207—notice the `CommandName` for the button is `update`. The second difference is the way you retrieve the edited values from their perspective controls. This is because the `DataList` has no default structure so you cannot depend on the Cells and Controls collection to retrieve the values. Instead you use the `Control` classes `FindControl` method.

The `FindControl` method expects the `ID` attribute as a parameter and will search the naming container for that attribute and will return a `Control` object. Because the return is a `Control` you must cast or convert this `Control` object to the original control. In Listing 10.3, you need the values from four different controls: three TextBox controls and one Label control. This is shown in the following code and on lines 45–49 from Listing 10.3:

```visualbasic
[Visual Basic]

dim sProductName,sUnitsInStock,sUnitsOnOrder,sProductID as string
  sProductName = CType(e.Item.FindControl("tProductName"), TextBox).Text
  sUnitsInStock = CType(e.Item.FindControl("tUnitsInStock"), TextBox).Text
  sUnitsOnOrder = CType(e.Item.FindControl("tUnitsOnOrder"), TextBox).Text
  sProductID = CType(e.Item.FindControl("lProductID"), Label).Text
```

10

**EDITING DATA
USING DATAGRID
AND DATALIST**

```
[C#]
string sProductName,sUnitsInStock,sUnitsOnOrder,sProductID;
  sProductName = ((TextBox)e.Item.FindControl("tProductName")).Text;
  sUnitsInStock = ((TextBox)e.Item.FindControl("tUnitsInStock")).Text;
  sUnitsOnOrder = ((TextBox)e.Item.FindControl("tUnitsOnOrder")).Text;
  sProductID = ((Label)e.Item.FindControl("lProductID")).Text;
```

First I create four `string` variables and then I retrieve each of the four controls `Text` attribute values. The rest of the code is exactly the same as the code in the `DataGrid`'s update method. You construct your SQL statement, insert the data, take the `DataList` out of edit mode, and rebind the `DataList` to its data source.

Cancelling Out of Edit Mode

Cancelling out of edit mode is done in the `CancelCommand` event. In our example this is handled by the `DLProducts_Cancel` method (lines 36–41) which is raised by the `LinkButton` control on line 208 (the `CommandName` for this `LinkButton` is cancel). It's just a matter of setting the DataList's `EditItemIndex` attribute to -1.

Changing Output with the `ItemCreated` Event Using the `DataGrid` and `DataList`

You might want to alter the way an item is rendered based on certain criteria, using either the `DataGrid` or `DataList` controls. For example, you might have a `DataGrid` which displays accounting information and you want negative numbers to be red instead of black. You can use the `ItemCreated` event to accomplish this. This event is fired every time an item is created for either control. Listing 10.4 illustrates how to use this feature in the `DataGrid`.

LISTING 10.4   Using the `ItemCreated` Event with the `DataGrid`

```
[Visual Basic]
01: <%@ import namespace="System.Data" %>
02: <%@ import namespace="System.Data.SqlClient" %>
03: <script language="c#" runat="server">
04:   private string sSqlCon = ➥"server=localhost;uid=sa;pwd=;database=north-
wind";
05:
06:   public void Page_Load(Object sender, EventArgs e){
07:
08:     if (! IsPostBack){
09:       Bind();
10:     }
11:
12:   }
```

LISTING 10.4   Continued

```
13:
14: private void Bind() {
15:
16:    SqlConnection SqlCon = new SqlConnection(sSqlCon);
17:    StringBuilder SqlCmd = new StringBuilder();
18:     SqlCmd.Append("SELECT ProductName,UnitPrice,");
19:     SqlCmd.Append("UnitsInStock,UnitsOnOrder,");
20:     SqlCmd.Append("ProductID FROM Products");
21:    SqlDataAdapter sda = new SqlDataAdapter(SqlCmd.ToString(),SqlCon);
22:    DataSet ds = new DataSet();
23:    sda.Fill(ds,"products");
24:    DGProducts.DataSource = ds.Tables["Products"].DefaultView;
25:    DGProducts.DataBind();
26:
27: }
28:
29: public void DGProducts_ItemCreated(Object sender, DataGridItemEventArgs e)
{
30:
31:   if (e.Item.ItemType == ListItemType.Item || e.Item.ItemType ==
➡ListItemType.AlternatingItem) {
32:     int iUnitsInStock = int.Parse(DataBinder.Eval(e.Item.DataItem,
➡"UnitsInStock").ToString());
33:     if (iUnitsInStock <= 10) {
34:      e.Item.Cells[1].ForeColor = System.Drawing.Color.Red;
35:    }
36:   }
37:
38:  }
39:
40: </script>
41: <html>
42:   <body>
43:     <head>
44:
45:      <style rel="stylesheet">
46:       H3 { font: bold 11pt Verdana, Arial, sans-serif; }
47:        .products { font: 9pt Verdana, Arial, sans-serif; }
48:        .productsHead { font: bold 9pt Verdana, Arial, sans-serif;
49:         background-color:Maroon; color:white; }
50:        a { text-decoration:none; }
51:        a:hover { text-decoration:underline; color:maroon; }
52:      </style>
53:
54:     </head>
```

LISTING 10.4   Continued

```
55:      <form runat="server">
56: <H3>ItemCreated Example - Visual Basic.NET</H3>
57:
58: <asp:DataGrid
59:   id="DGProducts"
60:   runat="server"
61:   Cellpadding="4" Cellspacing="0" Width="750"
62:   BorderWidth="1" Gridlines="None"
63:   AlternatingItemStyle-BackColor="Tan"
64:   HeaderStyle-CssClass="productsHead"
65:   Font-Size="12"
66:   AutoGenerateColumns="false"
67:   OnItemCreated="DGProducts_ItemCreated"
68:   >
69:   <Columns>
70:   <asp:BoundColumn DataField="ProductName" HeaderText="Product Name" />
71:   <asp:BoundColumn DataField="UnitsInStock" HeaderText="Units in Stock" />
72:   <asp:BoundColumn DataField="UnitsOnOrder" HeaderText="Units on Order" />
73:   <asp:BoundColumn DataField="UnitPrice" HeaderText="Price Per Unit"
74:    DataFormatString="{0:C}" ReadOnly="true" />
75:   <asp:BoundColumn DataField="ProductID"
76:    HeaderText="ProductID" visible="false"/>
77:   </columns>
78: </asp:DataGrid>
79:   </form>
80:   </body>
81: </html>

[C#—Replace server code]

01: <%@ import namespace="System.Data" %>
02: <%@ import namespace="System.Data.SqlClient" %>
03: <script language="vb" runat="server">
04:   private sSqlCon as string   =
➥"server=localhost;uid=sa;pwd=;database=northwind"
05:
06:   public sub Page_Load(sender as Object, e as EventArgs)
07:
08:     if not IsPostBack then
09:      Bind()
10:     end if
11:
12:   end sub
13:
```

LISTING 10.4 Continued

```
14: private sub Bind()
15:
16:    dim SqlCon as new SqlConnection(sSqlCon)
17:    dim SqlCmd as new StringBuilder()
18:     SqlCmd.Append("SELECT ProductName,UnitPrice,")
19:     SqlCmd.Append("UnitsInStock,UnitsOnOrder,")
20:     SqlCmd.Append("ProductID FROM Products")
21:    dim sda as new SqlDataAdapter(SqlCmd.ToString(),SqlCon)
22:    dim ds as new DataSet()
23:    sda.Fill(ds,"products")
24:    DGProducts.DataSource = ds.Tables("Products").DefaultView
25:    DGProducts.DataBind()
26:
27: end sub
28:
29: public sub DGProducts_ItemCreated(sender as Object,e as
➥DataGridItemEventArgs)
30:
31:  if (e.Item.ItemType = ListItemType.Item or e.Item.ItemType =
ListItemType.AlternatingItem) then
32:    dim iUnitsInStock as integer =
➥integer.Parse(DataBinder.Eval(e.Item.DataItem, "UnitsInStock").ToString())
33:    if (iUnitsInStock <= 10) then
34:      e.Item.Cells(1).ForeColor = System.Drawing.Color.Red
35:    end if
36:   end if
37:
38: end sub
39:
40: </script>
```

One of the things to do when you want to use the ItemCreated event is set the OnItemCreated attribute equal to the name of the method that will handle the ItemCreated event (line 67). In this example, it's DGProducts_ItemCreated (lines 29–38) and it expects Object and DataGridItemEventArgs as parameters. DataGridItemEventArgs contains the Item that's going to be added to the container, and you have programmatic access to all its attributes. In our example we are going to check the value of the UnitsInStock field from our data source. If it is equal to 10 or less than that cells ForeColor will be red.

Because the ItemCreated event is fired for each item including the DataGrid's Header and Footer we need to evaluate the item to make sure it is either of the Item or AlternatingItem type (line 31); otherwise you would receive an exception. Figure 10.4 is an illustration of this page.

10

EDITING DATA USING DATAGRID AND DATALIST

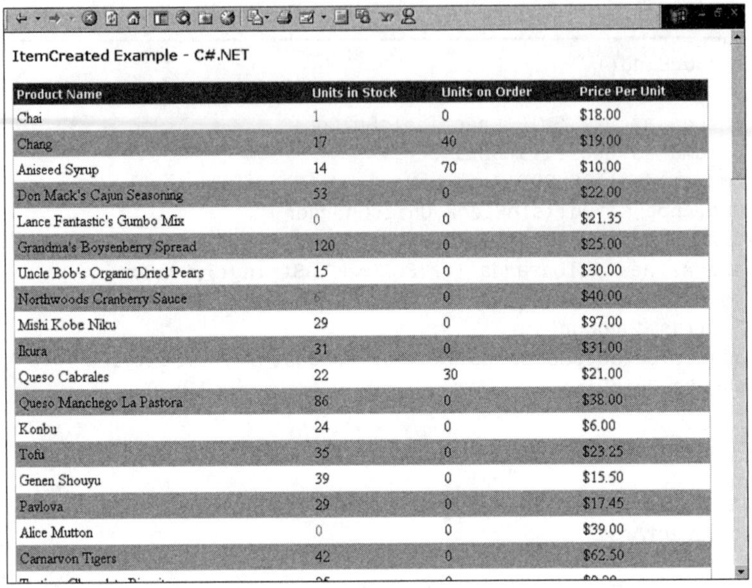

FIGURE 10.4

Using the ItemCreated *event to change the* ForeColor *attribute of the item to red if the value of the* UnitsInStock *field is less than 10.*

Listing 10.5 illustrates how to handle the ItemCreated event using the DataList control.

LISTING 10.5 Using the ItemCreated Event with the DataList

```
[Visual Basic]
01: <%@ import namespace="System.Data" %>
02: <%@ import namespace="System.Data.SqlClient" %>
03: <script language="vb" runat="server">
04:   private sSqlCon as string  =
➥"server=localhost;uid=sa;pwd=;database=northwind"
05:
06:   public sub Page_Load(sender as Object, e as EventArgs)
07:
08:     if not IsPostBack then
09:       Bind()
10:     end if
11:
12:   end sub
13:
14: private sub Bind()
15:
```

LISTING 10.5 Continued

```
16:    dim SqlCon as new SqlConnection(sSqlCon)
17:    dim SqlCmd as new StringBuilder()
18:     SqlCmd.Append("SELECT ProductName,UnitPrice,")
19:     SqlCmd.Append("UnitsInStock,UnitsOnOrder,")
20:     SqlCmd.Append("ProductID FROM Products")
21:    dim sda as new SqlDataAdapter(SqlCmd.ToString(),SqlCon)
22:    dim ds as new DataSet()
23:    sda.Fill(ds,"products")
24:    DLProducts.DataSource = ds.Tables("Products").DefaultView
25:    DLProducts.DataBind()
26:
27: end sub
28:
29: public sub DLProducts_ItemCreated(sender as Object,e as
➥DataListItemEventArgs)
30:
31:   if (e.Item.ItemType = ListItemType.Item or e.Item.ItemType =
➥ListItemType.AlternatingItem) then
32:     dim iUnitsInStock as integer =
➥integer.Parse(DataBinder.Eval(e.Item.DataItem, "UnitsInStock").ToString())
33:     if (iUnitsInStock <= 10) then
34:       CType(e.Item.FindControl("lUnitsOnOrder"), Label).ForeColor =
➥System.Drawing.Color.Red
35:     end if
36:   end if
37:
38: end sub
39:
40: </script>
41: <html>
42:   <body>
43:     <head>
44:
45:      <style rel="stylesheet">
46:        H3 { font: bold 11pt Verdana, Arial, sans-serif; }
47:        .products { font: 9pt Verdana, Arial, sans-serif; }
48:        .productsHead { font: bold 9pt Verdana, Arial, sans-serif;
49:         background-color:Maroon; color:white; }
50:        a { text-decoration:none; }
51:        a:hover { text-decoration:underline; color:maroon; }
52:      </style>
53:
54:    </head>
55:      <form runat="server">
```

10

EDITING DATA
USING DATAGRID
AND DATALIST

LISTING **10.5**   Continued

```
56: <center>
57:  <H3>Northwind Inventory Management - VisualBasic.NET</H3>
58: </center>
59: <asp:DataList
60:  id="DLProducts"
61:  runat="server"
62:  Cellpadding="0" Cellspacing="0" Width="750"
63:  BorderWidth="1" Gridlines="Both"
64:  AlternatingItemStyle-BackColor="Tan"
65:  HeaderStyle-CssClass="productsHead"
66:  Font-Size="12"
67:  RepeatColumns="1"
68:  Align="Center"
69:  OnItemCreated="DLProducts_ItemCreated"
70:  >
71:   <ItemTemplate>
72:
73:    <Table cellpadding="4" cellspacing="0" width="100%">
74:     <TR>
75:      <TD ColSpan="2" class="ProductsHead">
76:       <h3><%# DataBinder.Eval(Container.DataItem, "ProductName") %></b>
77:      </TD>
78:     </TR>
79:     <TR>
80:      <TD Width="50%" Align="Left">
81:       <b>Units In Stock</b>
82:      </TD>
83:      <TD Width="50%" Align="Right">
84:       <asp:Label id="lUnitsOnOrder" runat="server"
85:        Text='<%# DataBinder.Eval(Container.DataItem, "UnitsInStock") %>'
86:        />
87:      </TD>
88:     </TR>
89:     <TR>
90:      <TD Width="50%" Align="Left">
91:       <b>Units On Order</b>
92:      </TD>
93:      <TD Width="50%" Align="Right">
94:       <%# DataBinder.Eval(Container.DataItem, "UnitsOnOrder") %>      </TD>
95:     </TR>
96:     <TR>
97:      <TD Width="50%" Align="Left">
98:       <b>Price Per Unit</b>
99:      </TD>
```

LISTING 10.5 Continued

```
100:        <TD Width="50%" Align="Right">
101:          <%# DataBinder.Eval(Container.DataItem, "UnitPrice", "{0:C}") %>
102:        </TD>
103:      </TR>
104:    </Table>
105:
106:    </ItemTemplate>
107: </asp:DataList>
108:    </form>
109:  </body>
110: </html>

[C#—Replace server code]

01: <%@ import namespace="System.Data" %>
02: <%@ import namespace="System.Data.SqlClient" %>
03: <script language="c#" runat="server">
04:   private string sSqlCon = "server=localhost;uid=sa;pwd=;database=north-
wind";
05:
06:   public void Page_Load(Object sender, EventArgs e){
07:
08:     if (! IsPostBack){
09:       Bind();
10:     }
11:
12:   }
13:
14: private void Bind() {
15:
16:     SqlConnection SqlCon = new SqlConnection(sSqlCon);
17:     StringBuilder SqlCmd = new StringBuilder();
18:      SqlCmd.Append("SELECT ProductName,UnitPrice,");
19:      SqlCmd.Append("UnitsInStock,UnitsOnOrder,");
20:      SqlCmd.Append("ProductID FROM Products");
21:     SqlDataAdapter sda = new SqlDataAdapter(SqlCmd.ToString(),SqlCon);
22:     DataSet ds = new DataSet();
23:     sda.Fill(ds,"products");
24:     DLProducts.DataSource = ds.Tables["Products"].DefaultView;
25:     DLProducts.DataBind();
26:
27: }
28:
29: public void DLProducts_ItemCreated(Object sender, DataListItemEventArgs e)
{
```

10

EDITING DATA
USING DATAGRID
AND DATALIST

LISTING 10.5 Continued

```
30:
31:  if (e.Item.ItemType == ListItemType.Item || e.Item.ItemType ==
➥ListItemType.AlternatingItem) {
32:    int iUnitsInStock = int.Parse(DataBinder.Eval(e.Item.DataItem,
➥"UnitsInStock").ToString());
33:    if (iUnitsInStock <= 10) {
34:      ((Label)e.Item.FindControl("lUnitsOnOrder")).ForeColor =
➥System.Drawing.Color.Red;
35:    }
36:  }
37:
38: }
39:
40: </script>
```

To handle the ItemCreated event using the DataList, first you set the OnItemCreated attribute to be equal to the method that will handle the event. In this case, it's DataList_ItemCreated. The only difference between handling the ItemCreated event in the DataGrid and doing so in the DataList is how you tell the control. Figure 10.5 is an illustration of this page.

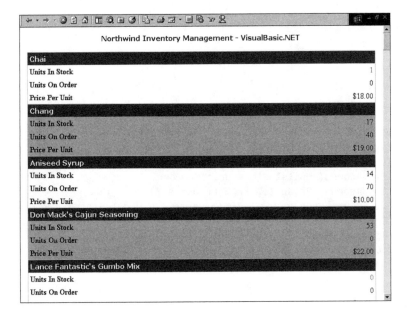

FIGURE 10.5

Using the ItemCreated event to change the ForeColor attribute of the item to red if the value of the UnitsInStock field is less than 10.

Enabling Item Selection Using the `DataGrid` and `DataList`

The final feature I want to discuss is how to enable item selection. When you enable item selection, users can click on a button or LinkButton to select a row out of the `DataGrid` or `DataList`. For example, the user could highlight a particular row in the control for easy reading. Listing 10.6 illustrates how to implement Item Selection using the `DataGrid`.

LISTING 10.6 Enabling Item Selection Using the `DataGrid`

[Visual Basic]

```
01: <%@ import namespace="System.Data" %>
02: <%@ import namespace="System.Data.SqlClient" %>
03: <script language="vb" runat="server">
04:   private sSqlCon as string   =
➥"server=localhost;uid=sa;pwd=;database=northwind"
05:
06:   public sub Page_Load(sender as Object, e as EventArgs)
07:
08:     if not IsPostBack then
09:       Bind()
10:       end if
11:
12:   end sub
13:
14: private sub Bind()
15:
16:    dim SqlCon as new SqlConnection(sSqlCon)
17:    dim SqlCmd as new StringBuilder()
18:     SqlCmd.Append("SELECT ProductName,UnitPrice,")
19:     SqlCmd.Append("UnitsInStock,UnitsOnOrder,")
20:     SqlCmd.Append("ProductID FROM Products")
21:    dim sda as new SqlDataAdapter(SqlCmd.ToString(),SqlCon)
22:    dim ds as new DataSet()
23:    sda.Fill(ds,"products")
24:    DGProducts.DataSource = ds.Tables("Products").DefaultView
25:    DGProducts.DataBind()
26:
27: end sub
28:
29: public sub DGProducts_ItemCommand(sender as Object, e as
➥DataGridCommandEventArgs)
30:
31:   if e.CommandName = "select" then
32:     DGProducts.SelectedIndex = e.Item.ItemIndex
33:     Bind()
```

LISTING 10.6   Continued

```
34:  end if
35:
36: end sub
37:
38: </script>
39: <html>
40:   <body>
41:    <head>
42:
43:     <style rel="stylesheet">
44:       H3 { font: bold 11pt Verdana, Arial, sans-serif; }
45:       .products { font: 9pt Verdana, Arial, sans-serif; }
46:       .productsHead { font: bold 9pt Verdana, Arial, sans-serif;
47:        background-color:Maroon; color:white; }
48:       a { text-decoration:none; }
49:       a:hover { text-decoration:underline; color:maroon; }
50:    </style>
51:
52:    </head>
53:     <form runat="server">
54: <H3>Allowing Item Selection - VB.NET</H3>
55:
56: <asp:DataGrid
57:  id="DGProducts"
58:  runat="server"
59:  Cellpadding="4" Cellspacing="0" Width="750"
60:  BorderWidth="1" Gridlines="None"
61:  AlternatingItemStyle-BackColor="Tan"
62:  HeaderStyle-CssClass="productsHead"
63:  Font-Size="12"
64:  AutoGenerateColumns="false"
65:  SelectedItemStyle-BackColor = "Blue"
66:  SelectedItemStyle-ForeColor = "white"
67:
68:  OnItemCommand = "DGProducts_ItemCommand"
69:  >
70:  <Columns>
71:  <asp:ButtonColumn CommandName="select" Text="Select Row"
➥ButtonType="LinkButton" />
72:  <asp:BoundColumn DataField="ProductName" HeaderText="Product Name" />
73:  <asp:BoundColumn DataField="UnitsInStock" HeaderText="Units in Stock" />
74:  <asp:BoundColumn DataField="UnitsOnOrder" HeaderText="Units on Order" />
75:  <asp:BoundColumn DataField="UnitPrice" HeaderText="Price Per Unit"
76:   DataFormatString="{0:C}" ReadOnly="true" />
77:  <asp:BoundColumn DataField="ProductID" HeaderText="ProductID"
➥visible="false"/>
```

LISTING 10.6   Continued

```
78:   </columns>
79: </asp:DataGrid>
80:    </form>
81:   </body>
82: </html>

[C#—Replace server code]

01: <%@ import namespace="System.Data" %>
02: <%@ import namespace="System.Data.SqlClient" %>
03: <script language="c#" runat="server">
04:  private string sSqlCon = "server=localhost;uid=sa;pwd=;database=northwind";
05:
06:  public void Page_Load(Object sender, EventArgs e){
07:
08:    if (! IsPostBack){
09:     Bind();
10:    }
11:
12:  }
13:
14: private void Bind() {
15:
16:   SqlConnection SqlCon = new SqlConnection(sSqlCon);
17:   StringBuilder SqlCmd = new StringBuilder();
18:    SqlCmd.Append("SELECT ProductName,UnitPrice,");
19:    SqlCmd.Append("UnitsInStock,UnitsOnOrder,");
20:    SqlCmd.Append("ProductID FROM Products");
21:   SqlDataAdapter sda = new SqlDataAdapter(SqlCmd.ToString(),SqlCon);
22:   DataSet ds = new DataSet();
23:   sda.Fill(ds,"products");
24:   DGProducts.DataSource = ds.Tables["Products"].DefaultView;
25:   DGProducts.DataBind();
26:
27: }
28:
29: public void DGProducts_ItemCommand(Object sender, DataGridCommandEventArgs
e) {
30:
31:  if(e.CommandName == "select") {
32:   DGProducts.SelectedIndex = e.Item.ItemIndex;
33:   Bind();
34:  }
35:
36: }
37:
38: </script>
```

When you enable item selection using the DataGrid, the first thing you want to do is create a way for the user to select an item. This example uses a Button control. Then you must set the OnItemCommand attribute to the name of the method that will handle the event. In this case, it's DGProducts_ItemCommand (lines 29–36). In order to select a particular item out of the DataGrid, you set the DataGrid's SelectedIndex attribute to be equal to the ItemIndex of the Item passed into the ItemCommand event in the DataGridCommandEventArgs parameter. Figure 10.6 shows the results of Listing 10.6, with an item selected.

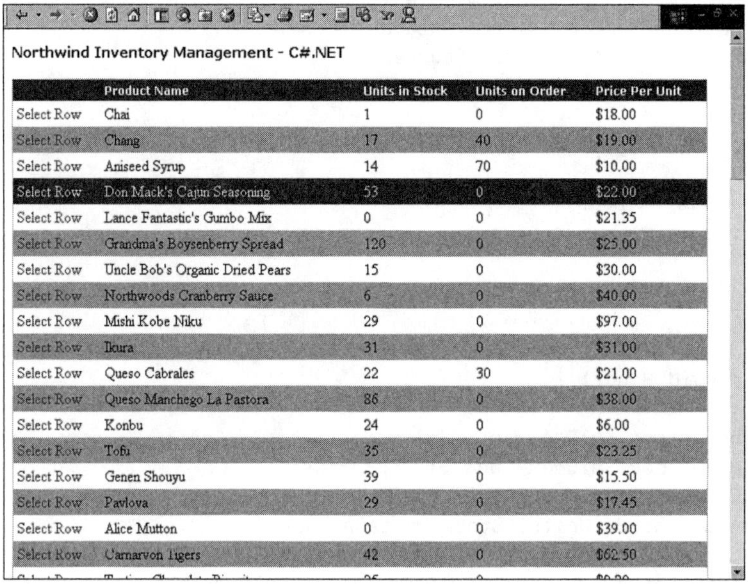

FIGURE 10.6
DataGrid with an item selected.

Like all the other samples, enabling item selecting using the DataList is a little different than the DataGrid. The following, Listing 10.7, contains an example on how to enable item selection using the DataList.

LISTING 10.7 Enabling Item Selection Using the DataList Control

```
[Visual basic]

01: <%@ import namespace="System.Data" %>
02: <%@ import namespace="System.Data.SqlClient" %>
03: <script language="vb" runat="server">
04:   private sSqlCon as string   =
➥"server=localhost;uid=sa;pwd=;database=northwind"
```

LISTING 10.7 Continued

```
05:
06:  public sub Page_Load(sender as Object, e as EventArgs)
07:
08:    if not IsPostBack then
09:     Bind()
10:    end if
11:
12:  end sub
13:
14: private sub Bind()
15:
16:    dim SqlCon as new SqlConnection(sSqlCon)
17:    dim SqlCmd as new StringBuilder()
18:    SqlCmd.Append("SELECT ProductName,UnitPrice,")
19:    SqlCmd.Append("UnitsInStock,UnitsOnOrder,")
20:    SqlCmd.Append("ProductID FROM Products")
21:    dim sda as new SqlDataAdapter(SqlCmd.ToString(),SqlCon)
22:    dim ds as new DataSet()
23:    sda.Fill(ds,"products")
24:    DLProducts.DataSource = ds.Tables("Products").DefaultView
25:    DLProducts.DataBind()
26:
27: end sub
28:
29: public sub DLProducts_ItemCommand(sender as Object,e as
➥DataListCommandEventArgs)
30:
31:  if e.CommandName = "select" then
32:   DLProducts.SelectedIndex = e.Item.ItemIndex
33:   Bind()
34:  end if
35:
36: end sub
37:
38: </script>
39: <html>
40:   <body>
41:    <head>
42:
43:     <style rel="stylesheet">
44:      H3 { font: bold 11pt Verdana, Arial, sans-serif; }
45:      .products { font: 9pt Verdana, Arial, sans-serif; }
46:      .productsHead { font: bold 9pt Verdana, Arial, sans-serif;
47:       background-color:Maroon; color:white; }
```

10

LISTING 10.7 Continued

```
48:        a { text-decoration:none; }
49:        a:hover { text-decoration:underline; color:maroon; }
50:      </style>
51:
52:    </head>
53:       <form runat="server">
54: <center>
55: <H3>Northwind Inventory Management - VisualBasic.NET</H3>
56: </center>
57: <asp:DataList
58:   id="DLProducts"
59:   runat="server"
60:   Cellpadding="0" Cellspacing="0" Width="750"
61:   BorderWidth="1" Gridlines="Both"
62:   AlternatingItemStyle-BackColor="Tan"
63:   HeaderStyle-CssClass="productsHead"
64:   Font-Size="12"
65:   RepeatColumns="1"
66:   Align="Center"
67:   OnItemCommand="DLProducts_ItemCommand"
68:   >
69:    <ItemTemplate>
70:
71:     <Table cellpadding="4" cellspacing="0" width="100%">
72:      <TR>
73:       <TD ColSpan="2" class="ProductsHead">
74:        <h3><%# DataBinder.Eval(Container.DataItem, "ProductName") %></b>
75:       </TD>
76:      </TR>
77:      <TR>
78:       <TD Width="50%" Align="Left">
79:        <b>Units In Stock</b>
80:       </TD>
81:       <TD Width="50%" Align="Right">
82:        <asp:Label id="lUnitsOnOrder" runat="server"
83:        Text='<%# DataBinder.Eval(Container.DataItem, "UnitsInStock") %>'
84:        />
85:       </TD>
86:      </TR>
87:      <TR>
88:       <TD Width="50%" Align="Left">
89:        <b>Units On Order</b>
90:       </TD>
91:       <TD Width="50%" Align="Right">
```

LISTING 10.7 Continued

```
92:              <%# DataBinder.Eval(Container.DataItem, "UnitsOnOrder") %>        </TD>
93:        </TR>
94:        <TR>
95:         <TD Width="50%" Align="Left">
96:          <b>Price Per Unit</b>
97:         </TD>
98:         <TD Width="50%" Align="Right">
99:          <%# DataBinder.Eval(Container.DataItem, "UnitPrice", "{0:C}") %>
100:        </TD>
101:       </TR>
102:       <TR>
103:        <TD ColSpan="2" Width="100%" Align="Left">
104:           <asp:LinkButton CommandName="select" Text="Select Item"
➥runat="server" />
105:        </TD>
106:       </TR>
107:      </Table>
108:
109:    </ItemTemplate>
110:
111:    <SelectedItemTemplate>
112:       <Table cellpadding="4" cellspacing="0" width="100%">
113:        <TR>
114:         <TD ColSpan="2" Style="color:white;background-color:blue">
115:          <h3><%# DataBinder.Eval(Container.DataItem, "ProductName") %></b>
116:         </TD>
117:        </TR>
118:        <TR>
119:         <TD Width="50%" Align="Left">
120:          <b>Units In Stock</b>
121:         </TD>
122:         <TD Width="50%" Align="Right">
123:          <asp:Label id="lUnitsOnOrder" runat="server"
124:          Text='<%# DataBinder.Eval(Container.DataItem, "UnitsInStock") %>'
125:          />
126:         </TD>
127:        </TR>
128:        <TR>
129:         <TD Width="50%" Align="Left">
130:          <b>Units On Order</b>
131:         </TD>
132:         <TD Width="50%" Align="Right">
133:            <%# DataBinder.Eval(Container.DataItem, "UnitsOnOrder") %>
</TD>
```

10

EDITING DATA
USING DATAGRID
AND DATALIST

LISTING 10.7 Continued

```
134:         </TR>
135:         <TR>
136:          <TD Width="50%" Align="Left">
137:           <b>Price Per Unit</b>
138:          </TD>
139:          <TD Width="50%" Align="Right">
140:           <%# DataBinder.Eval(Container.DataItem, "UnitPrice", "{0:C}") %>
141:          </TD>
142:         </TR>
143:       </Table>
144:
145:     </SelectedItemTemplate>
146:
147: </asp:DataList>
148:    </form>
149:   </body>
150: </html>

[C#—Replace server code]

01: <%@ import namespace="System.Data" %>
02: <%@ import namespace="System.Data.SqlClient" %>
03: <script language="c#" runat="server">
04:   private string sSqlCon = ➥"server=localhost;uid=sa;pwd=;database=north-
wind";
05:
06:   public void Page_Load(Object sender, EventArgs e){
07:
08:     if (! IsPostBack){
09:       Bind();
10:     }
11:
12:   }
13:
14: private void Bind() {
15:
16:     SqlConnection SqlCon = new SqlConnection(sSqlCon);
17:     StringBuilder SqlCmd = new StringBuilder();
18:      SqlCmd.Append("SELECT ProductName,UnitPrice,");
19:      SqlCmd.Append("UnitsInStock,UnitsOnOrder,");
20:      SqlCmd.Append("ProductID FROM Products");
21:     SqlDataAdapter sda = new SqlDataAdapter(SqlCmd.ToString(),SqlCon);
22:     DataSet ds = new DataSet();
23:     sda.Fill(ds,"products");
24:     DLProducts.DataSource = ds.Tables["Products"].DefaultView;
```

LISTING 10.7   Continued

```
25:    DLProducts.DataBind();
26:
27: }
28:
29: public void DLProducts_ItemCommand(Object sender, DataListCommandEventArgs e)
{
30:
31:   if(e.CommandName == "select") {
32:   DLProducts.SelectedIndex = e.Item.ItemIndex;
33:   Bind();
34:   }
35:
36: }
37:
38: </script>
```

The only real difference between the DataGrid and DataList is that with the DataList, you must use templates to enable item selection. You need to define an ItemTemplate and a SelectedItemTemplate. This means that a regular item can look entirely different than a selected item, which would be good for a master/detail page. An illustration of the rendered page from Listing 10.7 can be seen in Figure 10.7.

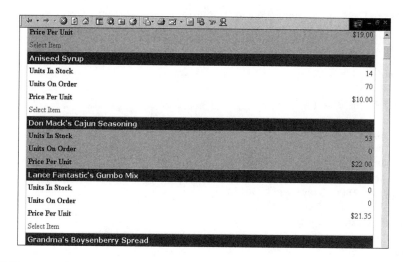

FIGURE 10.7

The DataList with an item selected.

Tip—Using a `DropDownList` in a `DataGrid`

This section was really just an afterthought, but we think you'll enjoy it. Many people have asked us how to put some kind of `List` control (ex: `DropDownList`) in a `DataGrid` or `DataList`. At first thought you might think it would be difficult because each row in the `DataGrid` or `DataList` is generated once for each row in the data source. In actuality it is really quite simple to do. In this example (Listing 10.8) we will demonstrate how to use a `DropDownList` in a `DataGrid`. We are going to keep the example very simple, but the technique used is going to work for all other situations and controls. The `DataGrid` in Listing 10.8 has two columns, one is the `Company Name` and the other is `Products`. The `Products` column will contain a `DropDownList` control with a list of all the suppliers products.

LISTING 10.8   Using a `DropDownList` in a `DataGrid`

```
[VisualBasic.NET]
01: <%@ import namespace="System.Data" %>
02: <%@ import namespace="System.Data.SqlClient" %>
03:
04: <script language="vb" runat="server">
05:
06:   private DTProducts as DataView
07:
08:   protected sub Page_Load(sender as Object, e as EventArgs)
09:
10:    Bind()
11:
12:   end sub
13:
14:   private sub Bind()
15:
16:    dim SqlCon as new SqlConnection("server=localhost;
➥  uid=sa;pwd=;database=northwind")
17:    dim SqlCmd as new StringBuilder()
18:    dim sda as new SqlDataAdapter("SELECT CompanyName,
➥  SupplierID FROM Suppliers",SqlCon)
19:    dim ds as new DataSet()
20:    sda.Fill(ds,"suppliers")
21:    sda.SelectCommand = new SqlCommand("SELECT ProductName,
➥  ProductID, SupplierID FROM Products", SqlCon)
22:    sda.Fill(ds, "products")
23:    DTProducts = ds.Tables("Products").DefaultView
24:    DGProducts.DataSource = ds.Tables("suppliers")
```

LISTING 10.8 Continued

```
25:    DGProducts.DataBind()
26:
27:   end sub
28:
29:   private function GetProducts(SupplierID as integer) as DataView
30:
31:    DTProducts.RowFilter = "SupplierID = " & SupplierID
32:    return DTProducts
33:
34:   end function
35:
36: </script>
```

[C#.NET]

```
01: <%@ import namespace="System.Data" %>
02: <%@ import namespace="System.Data.SqlClient" %>
03:
04: <script language="c#" runat="server">
05:
06:   private DataView DTProducts;
07:
08:   protected void Page_Load(Object sender, EventArgs e){
09:
10:    Bind();
11:
12:   }
13:
14:   private void Bind() {
15:
16:    SqlConnection SqlCon = new SqlConnection("server=localhost;
➥ uid=sa;pwd=;database=northwind");
17:    StringBuilder SqlCmd = new StringBuilder();
18:    SqlDataAdapter sda = new SqlDataAdapter("SELECT CompanyName,
➥ SupplierID FROM Suppliers",SqlCon);
19:    DataSet ds = new DataSet();
20:    sda.Fill(ds,"suppliers");
21:    sda.SelectCommand = new SqlCommand("SELECT ProductName,
➥ ProductID, SupplierID FROM Products", SqlCon);
22:    sda.Fill(ds, "products");
23:    DTProducts = ds.Tables["Products"].DefaultView;
24:    DGProducts.DataSource = ds.Tables["suppliers"];
25:    DGProducts.DataBind();
26:
```

Listing 10.8   Continued

```
27:  }
28:
29:  private DataView GetProducts(int SupplierID){
30:
31:   DTProducts.RowFilter = "SupplierID = " + SupplierID;
32:   return DTProducts;
33:
34:  }
35:
36: </script>

[VisualBasic.NET & C#.NET]

37: <html>
38:   <body>
39:    <head>
40:
41:     <style rel="stylesheet">
42:      H3 { font: bold 11pt Verdana, Arial, sans-serif; }
43:      .products { font: 9pt Verdana, Arial, sans-serif; }
44:      .productsHead { font: bold 9pt Verdana, Arial, sans-serif;
45:       background-color:Maroon; color:white; }
46:      a { text-decoration:none; }
47:      a:hover { text-decoration:underline; color:maroon; }
48:     </style>
49:
50:    </head>
51:    <center>
52:      <form runat="server">
53:      <H3>Products on File</H3>
54:
55:      <asp:DataGrid
56:       id="DGProducts"
57:        runat="server"
58:        Cellpadding="4" Cellspacing="0"
59:        BorderWidth="1" Gridlines="None"
60:        AlternatingItemStyle-BackColor="Tan"
61:        HeaderStyle-CssClass="productsHead"
62:        Font-Size="12"
63:        AutoGenerateColumns="false"
64:        >
65:        <Columns>
66:
67:        <asp:BoundColumn DataField="CompanyName" HeaderText="Company" />
68:
```

LISTING 10.8 Continued

```
69:              <asp:TemplateColumn>
70:              <HeaderTemplate>
71:               Products
72:              </HeaderTemplate>
73:              <ItemTemplate>
74:               <asp:DropDownList
75:               id="DDL"
76:               runat="server"
77:               Width="200"
78:               Border="0"
79:               DataSource='<%# GetProducts(CType(DataBinder.Eval(
➥    Container.DataItem, "SupplierID"), integer)) %>'
80:               DataTextField="ProductName"
81:               DataValueField="ProductID" />
82:              </ItemTemplate>
83:              </asp:TemplateColumn>
84:
85:            </columns>
86:          </asp:DataGrid>
87:        </form>
88:      <center>
89:    </body>
90:  </html>
```

In Listing 10.8 you'll find the *Company Name* column on line 67. The *Products* column, a
TemplateColumn, is on lines 69–83 and has a DropDownList control on lines 74–81 within the
ItemTemplate. The DataList is bound to a data source in the Bind method, but you'll notice
that the DropDownList.DataSource (line 79) is set to the following databinding expression:

[VisualBasic.NET]

```
<%# GetProducts(CType(DataBinder.Eval(Container.DataItem, "SupplierID"),
integer)) %>
```

[C#.NET]

```
<%# GetProducts((int)DataBinder.Eval(Container.DataItem, "SupplierID")) %>
```

The GetProducts method, lines 29–34, returns a filtered DataView object and has one parameter, SupplierID. Within the GetProducts method the DataView.RowFilter property is used to
filter out all the products for a particular supplier based on the SupplierID parameter and uses
the DataView created in the Bind method, line 23, as the DataView. Figure 10.8 contains an
illustration of this page.

10

EDITING DATA
USING DATAGRID
AND DATALIST

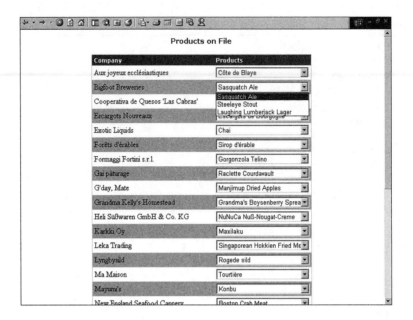

Figure 10.8

`DataGrid` *with a* `DropDownList` *server control in one of its columns.*

Summary

In this chapter you learned how to enable editing using the `DataGrid` and `DataList` controls. These built-in features allow users to edit, select, or delete data in a `DataGrid` in a very simple and logical manner, without a lot of complicated code. Specifically in this chapter you learned:

- Enabling editing using the `DataGrid` and `DataList`
- Changing certain items using the `ItemCreated` event
- Enabling item selection using the `DataGrid` and `DataList`

We illustrated how you enter these two controls into different modes (edit vs normal), and how you handle certain events to gain programmatic access to both data and child controls found within said control. The hard part is over now; you know the basics of both these controls. Now you can take this basic knowledge, and start adding even more functionality such as rendering populated `DropDownList` controls within cells in edit mode for the user to select from as seen in the *Tip* section. The possibilities are nearly endless.

Editing and Filtering Data

IN THIS CHAPTER

In this chapter, we will be discussing some of the ways you can work with data once it has been retrieved from your data store and put into a `DataSet`. Specifically, we will be going over the objects that make up a `DataSet` and how you can use these objects to filter, edit, delete, and add new items (rows). After going through each of the `DataTable` and `DataViews` individual properties and methods you can use to manipulate their prospective `DataRowCollection`—*rows that make up a `DataTable`*, we'll discuss ways to save these changes back to your database. Finally, in the "Bringing It All Together" section, we'll provide a rather lengthy example that brings everything in the chapter together. Specifically, we will be covering the following topics in this chapter.

- An introduction to the `DataTable` and `DataView`
- Working with the `DataTable`
- Working with the `DataView`
- Using the `SqlCommandBuilder` to save changes back to your database
- Bringing it all together

In the first part of the chapter we briefly discuss the `DataTable` and `DataView` objects and what they are. The second section covers manipulating data in the `DataTable`, and the third section looks at the `DataView` and how to use it to create customized views of the data in `DataTables`. We are going to end the chapter by illustrating an easy way to save changes made to a `DataTable` back to your database.

The `DataTable` Versus `DataView`

On the outside, a `DataTable` and `DataView` are identical in structure. They are both made up of columns and rows. The difference between the two objects is how they are derived. A `DataView` is derived from a `DataTable` and is a customized view of that `DataTable`. At a high-level, a `DataTable` can be compared to a table from a database and a `DataView` can be compared to a SQL View.

One or more `DataViews` can be created from a single `DataTable` and each one of the `DataViews` can have rows edited, updated, deleted, filtered, and searched. As previously mentioned, both the `DataView` and `DataTable` are constructed of columns and rows and in this chapter those are the two pieces we will be concentrating on. Both the `DataTable` and the `DataView` are constructed with a `DataRowCollection` and `DataColumnCollection`. The diff-ence is when working with a `DataView` you are working with a "view" of this data and in order to manipulate its data (rows) you will use a `DataRowView` rather than the `DataRow` as you do with the `DataTable`. In the following sections, I'll be giving you a high-level view of the `DataRow`, `DataRowView`, and `DataColumn` objects.

DataRow and DataRowView

A DataTable contains a collection of rows called the DataRowCollection; this collection holds all the actual data (rows) in the table. You can think of the DataRowCollection as rows in a database table.

Just as a DataView is a customized view of a DataTable, a DataRowView is a customized view of a DataRow, and as you will see in this chapter, changes to the data to either one of these objects can have a direct effect on the other. For instance, if you have two DataView objects derived from one DataTable and a row is deleted from one of them; the second DataView and the DataTable also will reflect this row deletion unless specific measures are taken—which we will cover later in the chapter. Even though the the DataView and DataRowView are derived, and to a degree, dependent on the DataTable and DataRows from which they were derived, they have many of their own properties and methods available to manipulate their data (as you will see in this chapter)

The DataColumn Object

The DataColumn object is identical in both the DataTable and DataView. The DataColumn is the foundation of a table; it, among other things, describes the schema for the table including the columns data type, whether it allows null values, whether it's read only, or whether the column should be auto-incremented.

You can construct the DataColumn to mimic a schema from your database so that you can merge its data directly into a database without having to format or change data types. In the next section on DataTables, you'll see code demonstrating how you can construct a DataTable from scratch rather than populating it from data derived from a database. Beyond that, you will see some of the properties of the DataColumn that describe data contained in each column's rows.

The DataTable: Filtering, Adding, Editing, Sorting, and Deleting DataRows

Because we believe it is important to develop a good fundamental understanding of new technology, we thought we should start this chapter with code illustrating how to create a DataTable and DataSet from "scratch." We are going to dynamically build the DataSet, DataTable, DataColumn, and DataRow objects and then bind to a DataGrid (Listing 11.1).

LISTING 11.1   Constructing a DataTable

```
[VisualBasic.NET]

01: <%@ import namespace="System.Data" %>
02:
03: <script language="vb" runat="server">
```

LISTING 11.1   Continued

```
04:
05:   sub Page_Load(sender as Object, e as EventArgs)
06:
07:    dim DS as new DataSet()
08:    dim DC as DataColumn
09:    dim DR as DataRow
10:
11:    dim DT as new DataTable("Counters")
12:
13:    dim i as integer
14:    for i = 0 to 4
15:
16:     dc = new DataColumn("Column " & i, System.Type.GetType("System.String"))
17:     DT.Columns.Add(DC)
18:
19:    next
20:
21:    DS.Tables.Add(DT)
22:
23:    for i = 0 to  9
24:
25:     DR = DT.NewRow()
26:     DR(0) = "Row " & i
27:     DR(1) = "Row " & i
28:     DR(2) = "Row " & i
29:     DR(3) = "Row " & i
30:     DR(4) = "Row " & i
31:
32:     DT.Rows.Add(DR)
33:   next
34:
35:   DG.DataSource = DS.Tables("Counters")
36:   DG.DataBind()
37:
38:   end sub
39:
40: </script>

[C#.NET]

01: <%@ import namespace="System.Data" %>
02:
03: <script language="c#" runat="server">
04:
05:   void Page_Load(Object sender, EventArgs e){
06:
07:    DataSet DS = new DataSet();
```

LISTING 11.1 Continued

```
08:    DataColumn DC;
09:    DataRow DR;
10:
11:    DataTable DT = new DataTable("Counters");
12:
13:    int i;
14:    for (i = 0; i < 5; i++) {
15:
16:      DC = new DataColumn("Column " + i, System.Type.GetType(
➥ "System.String"));
17:      DT.Columns.Add(DC);
18:
19:    }
20:
21:    DS.Tables.Add(DT);
22:
23:    for (i = 0; i < 10; i ++) {
24:
25:      DR = DT.NewRow();
26:      DR[0] = "Row " + i;
27:      DR[1] = "Row " + i;
28:      DR[2] = "Row " + i;
29:      DR[3] = "Row " + i;
30:      DR[4] = "Row " + i;
31:
32:      DT.Rows.Add(DR);
33:    }
34:
35:    DG.DataSource = DS.Tables["Counters"];
36:    DG.DataBind();
37:
38:    }
39:
40: </script>

[VisualBasic.NET & C#.NET]

41: <html>
42:   <body>
43:    <asp:DataGrid
44:     font-size="10"
45:     runat="server"
46:     id="DG"
47:    />
48:   </body>
49: </html>
```

The steps for constructing the `DataTable` in this example (Listing 11.1) are as follows:

1. Created a `DataTable` object—line 11, a `DataTable` named "Counters" is created.

2. Created and added 5 `DataColumns` to the `DataTable`. On lines 13–19, a loop is performed creating a new `DataColumn` object (line 16) and then adding that `DataColumn` to the `DataTable` (line 17) by calling the `DataColumnsCollection.Add` method. In this example, I only specify two attributes for the `DataColumn` using the `DataColumn` constructor—`ColumnName` and `DataType`.

3. Add the `DataTable` to the `DataSet`—This is done by calling the `DataTableCollection.Add` method—(line 21).

4. Add 10 `DataRows` to the `DataTable`—lines 23–33, this is accomplished by first calling the `DataTable.NewRow` method. The `NewRow` method returns a `DataRow` object with the schema of the `DataTable`. After you have a `DataRow` to work with, give each field in the row values and call the `DataRowCollection.Add` method, which adds the row to the `DataTable`.

You can see an illustration of the page from Listing 11.1 in Figure 11.1.

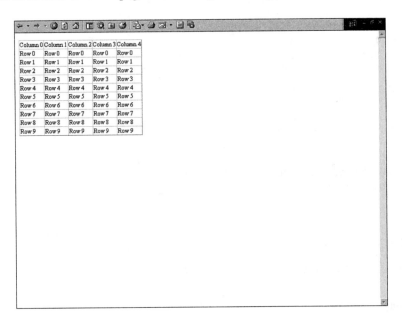

FIGURE 11.1

A DataGrid *control bound to a constructed* DataTable *with five columns and 10 rows.*

As you can see, constructing a `DataTable` isn't too difficult after you understand what it is and what it's made of. All you do is construct each piece and put them together somewhat like a puzzle. When you retrieve data from your database and put it into a `DataSet`, the creation of the `DataTable` is done automatically behind the scenes, but you might run into a situation where you must make your own.

Filtering Rows in a `DataTable`

The `DataTable.Select` method enables you to filter out specific rows from a `DataTable` into an array of `DataRow` objects. For example, say you're using a `DropDownList` to show a list of animals in a zoo and you want to let the user see all animals whose names start with the letter A, but the `DataTable` you're working with has all the animals in the zoo in it. You can use the `DataTable.Select` method and filter out all the rows where the animal's name starts with A and show only those to the user instead of creating an additional call to the database to get those specific records.

There are four overloads to the `DataTable.Select` method and three different parameters. The following list describes each.

- `DataTable.Select()`   This is the only parameterless overload. This will return all the `DataRow` objects from the `DataTable` ordered by the *Primary Key*. If a *Primary Key* doesn't exsist, then the array is created by the order in which the `DataRow` objects are in the `DataRowCollection`.

- `DataTable.Select(FilterExpression)`   The *FilterExpression* is a string value in which you'll supply a valid Expression which is used to filter by *Primary Key*. (Ex: `DataTable.Select("AnimalNameColumn LIKE 'A%'")`)

- `DataTable.Select(FilterExpression, Sort)`   A new parameter is added here, the `Sort` parameter. The Sort parameter is also a string value indicating the sort for the `DataRow` objects. For instance, after you have filtered out all the animals whose names start with A, you can order them by what type of animal they are, Mammal or Reptile. (Ex: `DataTable.Select("AnimalNameColumn LIKE 'A%'"`, `"TypeOfAnimalColumn DESC")`

- `DataTable.Select(FilterExpression, Sort, DataViewRowState)`   The third parameter deals with the `DataRows` state. We will be going over this later in this section, but essentially this is the state of the `DataRow` at the time of the filter. Some of the values can be Added, Deleted, or Modified. (Ex: `DataTable.Select("AnimalNameColumn LIKE 'A%'"`, `"TypeOfAnimalColumn DESC"`, `DataViewRowState.Added`)

In Listing 11.2, the `DataTable.Select` method is used to filter out all rows from a `DataTable`, populated with the `Products` table from `Northwind`, where the `ProductName` columns value begins with the letter C.

LISTING 11.2   Using the `Select` Method

```
[VisualBasic.NET]

01: <%@ import namespace="System.Data" %>
02: <%@ import namespace="System.Data.SqlClient" %>
03:
```

Listing 11.2 Continued

```vb
04: <script language="vb" runat="server">
05:
06:   protected sub Page_Load(sender as Object, e as EventArgs)
07:
08:     dim SqlCon as new SqlConnection("server=localhost;
➥ uid=sa;pwd=;database=northwind")
09:     dim SqlDA as new SqlDataAdapter("SELECT * FROM Products", SqlCon)
10:     dim ds as new DataSet()
11:
12:     SqlDA.Fill(ds, "Products")
13:
14:     dim DR() as DataRow = ds.Tables("Products").Select(
➥ "ProductName LIKE 'C%'")
15:
16:     dim i as integer
17:     for i = 0 to DR.Length - 1
18:
19:       me.DDL.Items.Add(new ListItem(DR(i)("ProductName").ToString()))
20:
21:     next
22:
23:   end sub
24:
25: </script>
```

```csharp
[C#.NET]

01: <%@ import namespace="System.Data" %>
02: <%@ import namespace="System.Data.SqlClient" %>
03:
04: <script language="C#" runat="server">
05:
06:   protected void Page_Load(Object sender, EventArgs e){
07:
08:     SqlConnection SqlCon = new SqlConnection("server=localhost;
➥ uid=sa;pwd=;database=northwind");
09:     SqlDataAdapter SqlDA = new SqlDataAdapter(
➥ "SELECT * FROM Products", SqlCon);
10:     DataSet ds = new DataSet();
11:
12:     SqlDA.Fill(ds, "Products");
13:
14:     DataRow[] DR = ds.Tables["Products"].Select("ProductName LIKE 'C%'");
15:
16:     int i;
17:     for (i = 0; i < DR.Length; i ++){
18:
```

LISTING 11.2   Continued

```
19:    this.DDL.Items.Add(new ListItem(DR[i]["ProductName"].ToString()));
20:
21:    }
22:
23:  }
24:
25: </script>

[VisualBasic.NET & C#.NET]

26: <html>
27:  <body>
28:
29:   <asp:DropDownList id="DDL" runat="Server" font-size="10" />
30:
31:  </body>
32: </html>
```

The DataTable.Select method in Listing 11.2 can be found on line 14. After calling the DataTable.Select method, we loop through the returned array of DataRow objects on lines 17–21, dynamically building a ListItems and adding them to the DropDownList control. You can see this page in Figure 11.2.

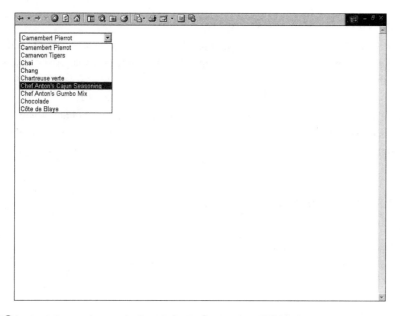

FIGURE 11.2
A DropDownList control containing all product names that start with the letter "C".

> **NOTE**
>
> You don't have to set all the parameters when using the `DataTable.Select` method. For example, if you want to change the sort order for the `DataTable` you can specify nothing (VB) or `null` (C#) for the *FilterExpression* parameter (ex: `DataTable.Select(null, "ProductName DESC")`.

As previously mentioned, the fourth overload for the `DataTable.Select` method expects a `DataViewRowState` enumeration value. The following list contains a description of each:

- `CurrentRows`—The current rows
- `Deleted`—All deleted rows
- `ModifiedCurrent`—The current version of modified data
- `ModifiedOriginal`—The original version of modified data
- `Added`—A new row
- `None`—None
- `OriginalRows`—The original rows
- `Unchanged`—Unchanged rows

Adding New Rows to a `DataTable`

Just like you can add new rows to a table in a database, you can add new rows to a `DataTable`. When adding a new row to a `DataTable`, you must do three things. First, create a new `DataRow` object with the same schema as the `DataTable` you want to add it to. Second, apply values to each field in the `DataRow`. Third, add the new `DataRow` to the `DataTable`'s `DataRowCollection`. The `DataTable.NewRow` method must be used to create a new `DataRow` object and as previously mentioned, the `DataTable.NewRow` method returns a `DataRow` object with the exact schema of the `DataTable`. Listing 11.3 is an example illustrating how to add a new row to a `DataTable`.

LISTING 11.3   Demonstrating the `DataTable`'s `NewRow` Method

```
[VisualBasic.NET]

01: <%@ import namespace="System.Data" %>
02: <%@ import namespace="System.Data.SqlClient" %>
03:
04: <script language="vb" runat="server">
05:
```

LISTING 11.3   Continued

```
06:  protected sub Page_Load(sender as Object, e as EventArgs)
07:
08:    dim SqlCon as new SqlConnection("server=localhost;
➡ uid=sa;pwd=;database=northwind")
09:    dim SqlDA as new SqlDataAdapter("SELECT TOP 10 ProductName,
➡ ProductID FROM Products", SqlCon)
10:    dim ds as new DataSet()
11:
12:    SqlDA.Fill(ds, "Products")
13:
14:    dim dt as DataTable = ds.Tables(0)
15:
16:    dim NewDataRow as DataRow = dt.NewRow()
17:
18:    NewDataRow("ProductName") = "DotNetJunkies .NET Power Bar"
19:    NewDataRow("ProductID") = "4999"
20:
21:    dt.Rows.Add(NewDataRow)
22:    'dt.Rows.InsertAt(NewDataRow, 0)
23:
24:    DG.DataSource = dt
25:    DG.DataBind()
26:
27:  end sub
28:
29: </script>
```

[C#.NET]

```
01: <%@ import namespace="System.Data" %>
02: <%@ import namespace="System.Data.SqlClient" %>
03:
04: <script language="C#" runat="server">
05:
06:  protected void Page_Load(Object sender, EventArgs e){
07:
08:    SqlConnection SqlCon = new SqlConnection("server=localhost;
➡ uid=sa;pwd=;database=northwind");
09:    SqlDataAdapter SqlDA = new SqlDataAdapter("SELECT TOP 10 ProductName,
➡ ProductID FROM Products", SqlCon);
10:    DataSet ds = new DataSet();
11:
12:    SqlDA.Fill(ds, "Products");
13:
14:    DataTable dt = ds.Tables[0];
```

LISTING 11.3   Continued

```
15:
16:    DataRow NewDataRow = dt.NewRow();
17:
18:    NewDataRow["ProductName"] = "DotNetJunkies .NET Power Bar";
19:    NewDataRow["ProductID"] = "4999";
20:
21:    dt.Rows.Add(NewDataRow);
22:    //dt.Rows.InsertAt(NewDataRow, 0);
23:
24:    DG.DataSource = dt;
25:    DG.DataBind();
26:
27:  }
28:
29: </script>

[VisualBasic.NET & C#.NET]

30: <html>
31:   <body>32:
33:     <asp:DataGrid id="DG" runat="Server" font-size="10" />
34:
35:   </body>
36: </html>
```

The DataTable.NewRow method is invoked on line 16 of Listing 11.3. Values are given to each field of the new DataRow (NewDataRow) on lines 18–19. Finally, the new DataRow object is added to the DataTables DataRowCollection on line 21 by calling the DataRowCollection.Add method. You will notice that there is a commented out piece of code on line 22, dt.Rows.InsertAt(NewDataRow, 0); this is the DataRowCollection.InsertAt method and it can be used to insert a new DataRow to a DataRowCollection at a specified location within the DataRowCollection index. This code will add the DataRow object to the 0 index of the DataRowCollection. After running the code that utilizes the Add method comment out line 21 and run the code that uses the InsertAt method (line 22) to see the effect.

Figure 11.3 is this page after using the DataRowCollection.InsertAt method to add a new DataRow to the DataTable.

Notice in Figure 11.3 that the new DataRow is located at the very top of the DataGrid. This is because by using the InsertAt method, I was able to insert the DataRow at 0 index of the DataRowCollection.

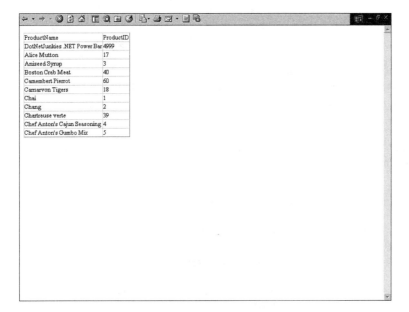

FIGURE 11.3
DataGrid *bound to* DataTable *with a new* DataRow *added to its* DataRowCollection.

Editing Rows in a `DataTable`

You are going to run into situations where you will enable users to edit one or more rows in your web applications. For instance, you might have a web application that allows users to make changes to data, but you don't want to save the changes back to the database until the user is completely finished with the edits; hence the edited data will be persisted in the DataTable.

There are a few steps you must do to edit a DataRow:

1. Determine which DataRow you want to edit with the DataRowCollection.
2. Put the DataRow into edit mode by invoking the DataRow.BeginEdit method.
3. Edit the DataRow column values.
4. Invoke the DataRow.EndEdit method.

The following list contains a description of the preceding methods:

- DataRow.BeginEdit—This method puts a DataRow into edit mode.
- DataRow.EndEdit—This method takes the DataRow out of edit mode. (Note: when you invoke the DataTable.AcceptChanges, the EndEdit method is called implicitly.)

Another important method:

- `DataRow.CancelEdit`—This method cancels the current edit. This method cannot be called after the `EndEdit` method to cancel changes.

Listing 11.4 contains an example on how to edit a DataRow. In this example, I determine which `DataRow` I want to edit by using the `DataTable.Select` method to return a `DataRow`.

LISTING 11.4   Editing a `DataRow`

```
[VisualBasic.NET]

01: <%@ import namespace="System.Data" %>
02: <%@ import namespace="System.Data.SqlClient" %>
03:
04: <script language="vb" runat="server">
05:
06:   protected sub Page_Load(sender as Object, e as EventArgs)
07:
08:     dim SqlCon as new SqlConnection("server=localhost;
➥   uid=sa;pwd=;database=northwind")
09:     dim SqlDA as new SqlDataAdapter("SELECT TOP 10 ProductName,
➥   ProductID FROM Products", SqlCon)
10:     dim ds as new DataSet()
11:
12:     SqlDA.Fill(ds, "Products")
13:
14:     dim dt as DataTable = ds.Tables(0)
15:
16:     dim dr() as DataRow = dt.Select("ProductID = '17'")
17:
18:     dr(0).BeginEdit()
19:     dr(0)("ProductName") = "New and Improved Alice Mutton"
20:     dr(0).EndEdit()
21:
22:     DG.DataSource = dt
23:     DG.DataBind()
24:
25:   end sub
26:
27: </script>

[C#.NET]

01: <%@ import namespace="System.Data" %>
02: <%@ import namespace="System.Data.SqlClient" %>
03:
04: <script language="C#" runat="server">
```

LISTING 11.4   Continued

```
05:
06:   protected void Page_Load(Object sender, EventArgs e){
07:
08:     SqlConnection SqlCon = new SqlConnection("server=localhost;
➥  uid=sa;pwd=;database=northwind");
09:     SqlDataAdapter SqlDA = new SqlDataAdapter("SELECT TOP 10 ProductName,
➥  ProductID FROM Products", SqlCon);
10:     DataSet ds = new DataSet();
11:
12:     SqlDA.Fill(ds, "Products");
13:
14:     DataTable dt = ds.Tables[0];
15:
16:     DataRow[] dr = dt.Select("ProductID = '17'");
17:
18:     dr[0].BeginEdit();
19:     dr[0]["ProductName"] = "New and Improved Alice Mutton";
20:     dr[0].EndEdit();
21:
22:     DG.DataSource = dt;
23:     DG.DataBind();
24:
25:   }
26:
27: </script>

[VisualBasic.NET & C#.NET]

28: <html>
29:   <body>
30:
31:     <asp:DataGrid id="DG" runat="Server" font-size="10" />
32:
33:   </body>
34: </html>
```

I found the DataRow I wanted to edit on line 16 using the DataTable.Select method to search the DataRowCollection for a DataRow with a ProductID value of 17. In this example, I knew only one row would be returned, so I immediately put the DataRow into edit mode. (If multiple rows could have been returned, I would have had to loop through the returned DataRow array.)

To begin editing, I invoked the DataRow.BeginEdit method (line 18). After calling the BeginEdit method, you can change some or all the columns values by simply supplying new values (line 19) to the columns. After editing is finished, the DataRow.EndEdit method is invoked and the DataGrid is bound to the DataTable (lines 20–23).

The rendered page from Listing 11.4 can be seen in Figure 11.4. The first product is now named "New and Improved Alice Mutton" instead of "Alice Mutton."

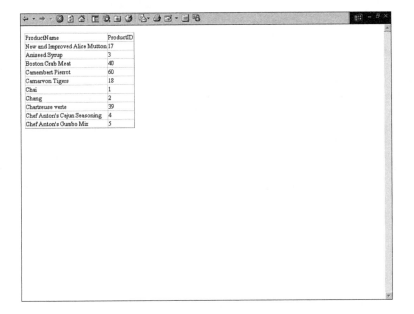

FIGURE 11.4
The first row of the DataGrid is "New and Improved Alice Mutton" instead of "Alice Mutton," as it is in the database.

Sorting Rows in a DataTable

Sorting can be achieved in two ways when using a DataTable. You can sort data with your SQL statement before it is put into a DataTable. Or you can sort by the DataTable.Select method's second parameter like this:

```
dr = dt.Select(Nothing, "ProductName DESC")
```

Deleting Rows in a DataTable

Deleting a row from a DataTable is a very simple task. Just determine which row you would like to delete and call the DataRow.Delete method, as shown in Listing 11.5.

LISTING 11.5   Deleting a `DataRow` Using the `DataRow.Delete` Method

[VisualBasic.NET]

```
01: <%@ import namespace="System.Data" %>
02: <%@ import namespace="System.Data.SqlClient" %>
03:
04: <script language="vb" runat="server">
05:
06:  protected sub Page_Load(sender as Object, e as EventArgs)
07:
08:   dim SqlCon as new SqlConnection("server=localhost;
➥ uid=sa;pwd=;database=northwind")
09:   dim SqlDA as new SqlDataAdapter("SELECT TOP 10 ProductName,
➥ ProductID FROM Products", SqlCon)
10:   dim ds as new DataSet()
11:
12:   SqlDA.Fill(ds, "Products")
13:
14:   dim dt as DataTable = ds.Tables(0)
15:
16:   dim dr() as DataRow = dt.Select("ProductID = '17'")
17:
18:   dr(0).Delete()
19:   dt.AcceptChanges()
20:
21:   DG.DataSource = dt
22:   DG.DataBind()
23:
24:  end sub
25:
26: </script>
```

[C#.NET]

```
01: <%@ import namespace="System.Data" %>
02: <%@ import namespace="System.Data.SqlClient" %>
03:
04: <script language="C#" runat="server">
05:
06:  protected void Page_Load(Object sender, EventArgs e){
07:
08:   SqlConnection SqlCon = new SqlConnection("server=localhost;
➥ uid=sa;pwd=;database=northwind");
09:   SqlDataAdapter SqlDA = new SqlDataAdapter("SELECT TOP 10 ProductName,
➥ ProductID FROM Products", SqlCon);
10:   DataSet ds = new DataSet();
11:
12:   SqlDA.Fill(ds, "Products");
```

LISTING 11.5   Continued

```
13:
14:    DataTable dt = ds.Tables[0];
15:
16:    DataRow[] dr = dt.Select("ProductID = '17'");
17:
18:    dr[0].Delete();
19:    dt.AcceptChanges();
20:
21:    DG.DataSource = dt;
22:    DG.DataBind();
23:
24:  }
25:
26: </script>

[VisualBasic.NET & C#.NET]

27: <html>
28:   <body>
29:
30:     <asp:DataGrid id="DG" runat="Server" font-size="10" />
31:
32:   </body>
33: </html>
```

The DataRow.Delete method is invoked on line 18. This particular DataRow was retrieved via the DataTable.Select method. On line 19, I invoke the DataTable.AcceptChanges method to commit the DataRow deletion and finally bind the DataGrid to the DataTable. Figure 11.5 is an illustration of this page after the deletion.

NOTE

You could delete all DataRows in a DataTable by invoking the DataTable.Clear method as seen in the following code: MyDataTable.Clear().

CAUTION

If the DataTable has a relationship to one or more other DataTables, an exception will occur if you call the DataTable.Clear method.

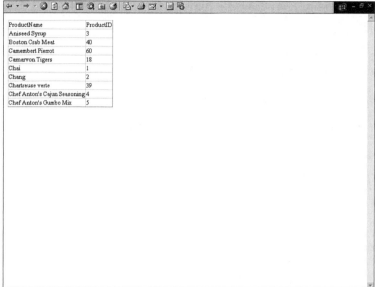

FIGURE 11.5
The first DataRow *of the* DataTable *has been deleted (Alice Mutton).*

The DataView: Filtering, Adding, Editing, Sorting, and Deleting DataRowViews

As previously mentioned, a DataView is a customized view of a DataTable. Essentially, when you create a DataView you are taking a snapshot of the DataTable and then manipulating the data some how—whether it be sorting, filtering, adding, etc. For instance, you can create two DataView objects from one DataTable and filter out all rows where the primary key value starts with "A" in one of them and in the second you can filter out all rows where the primary key value starts with "B". Each of the two DataView objects is a separate entity to a degree, but they are still dependent and bound to the DataTable from which they were both derived.

A DataView can be created using an existing DataTable. The following code creates a new DataView:

```
[VisualBasic.NET] - dim dv as new DataView(MyDataTable)

[C#.NET] -  DataView dv = new DataView(MyDataTable);
```

We have included Listing 11.6 so you can get a good feel for how a DataView works before we jump into some of its more rich features such as editing, sorting, and filtering. Listing 11.6 illustrates how to create multiple DataView objects from one DataTable object and binds each to a separate DataGrid.

LISTING 11.6 Creating Two `DataViews` from the Same `DataTable`

[VisualBasic.NET]

```
01: <%@ import namespace="System.Data" %>
02: <%@ import namespace="System.Data.SqlClient" %>
03:
04: <script language="vb" runat="server">
05:
06:  protected sub Page_Load(sender as Object, e as EventArgs)
07:
08:    dim SqlCon as new SqlConnection("server=localhost;
➥  uid=sa;pwd=;database=northwind")
09:    dim SqlDA as new SqlDataAdapter("SELECT TOP 10 ProductName,
➥  ProductID FROM Products", SqlCon)
10:    dim ds as new DataSet()
11:
12:    SqlDA.Fill(ds, "Products")
13:
14:    dim dt as DataTable = ds.Tables(0)
15:
16:    dim MyDataView1 as new DataView(dt)
17:    MyDataView1.Sort = "ProductName ASC" 'Default
18:
19:    dim MyDataView2 as new DataView(dt)
20:    MyDataView2.Sort = "ProductName DESC"
21:
22:    DG.DataSource = MyDataView1
23:    DG.DataBind()
24:
25:    DG2.DataSource = MyDataView2
26:    DG2.DataBind()
27:
28:  end sub
29:
30: </script>
```

[C#.NET]

```
01: <%@ import namespace="System.Data" %>
02: <%@ import namespace="System.Data.SqlClient" %>
03:
04: <script language="C#" runat="server">
05:
06:  protected void Page_Load(Object sender, EventArgs e){
07:
08:    SqlConnection SqlCon = new SqlConnection("server=localhost;
➥  uid=sa;pwd=;database=northwind");
09:    SqlDataAdapter SqlDA = new SqlDataAdapter("SELECT TOP 10 ProductName,
➥  ProductID FROM Products", SqlCon);
```

LISTING 11.6 Continued

```
10:    DataSet ds = new DataSet();
11:
12:    SqlDA.Fill(ds, "Products");
13:
14:    DataTable dt = ds.Tables[0];
15:
16:    DataView MyDataView1 = new DataView(dt);
17:    MyDataView1.Sort = "ProductName ASC"; //Default
18:
19:    DataView MyDataView2 = new DataView(dt);
20:    MyDataView2.Sort = "ProductName DESC";
21:
22:    DG.DataSource = MyDataView1;
23:    DG.DataBind();
24:
25:    DG2.DataSource = MyDataView2;
26:    DG2.DataBind();
27:
28:  }
29:
30: </script>

[VisualBasic.NET & C#.NET]

31: <html>
32:   <body>
33:
34:     <h3>DataGrid - Ordered ASC by ProductName</h3>
35:     <asp:DataGrid id="DG" runat="Server" font-size="10" />
36:
37:     <br>
38:
39:     <h3>DataGrid - Ordered DESC by ProductName</h3>
40:     <asp:DataGrid id="DG2" runat="Server" font-size="10" />
41:
42:   </body>
43: </html>
```

In Listing 11.6, two DataView objects are created from the same DataTable. The first DataView created is on line 16 and named MyDataView1. The rows in MyDataView1 are sorted in ascending order by the ProductName value (line 17), and is the DataGrid named DG DataSource. The second DataView is created on line 19 and is named MyDataView2. MyDataView2 is sorted in descending order by the ProductName column value (line 20), and is the DataGrid named DG2 DataSource. We will be going over the DataView.Sort attribute later in this section. When this page loads, there will be two different DataGrids displayed. The top DataGrids contents are sorted in alphabetical order, and the bottom is in reverse alphabetical order, as seen in Figure 11.6.

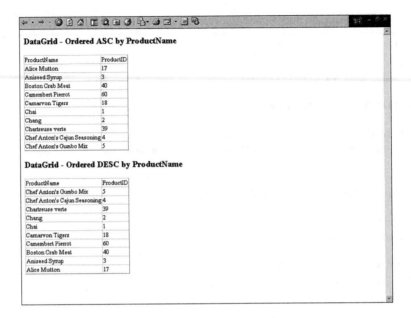

FIGURE 11.6

The top DataGrid *contents are in alphabetical order and the bottom in reverse alphabetical order.*

Now that you have a basic understanding of how to create and use a DataView, let's move on to some of its attributes you can use to manipulate its DataRowCollection.

Filtering Rows in a DataView

You can filter rows in a DataView by using the DataView.RowFilter property. The syntax for the value of this property is a column name followed by an operator (for example: <, >, =) and ending in a value to filter on—for more information on filter expressions see the DataColumn.Expression property. The DataView.RowFilter is similar to the DataTable.Select(FilterExpression) method and if given access to the same DataRowCollection both will contain the same rows if the same filterexpression is used. The difference is how the rows are returned: In the DataTable.Select method an array of DataRows is returned while the DataView.RowFilter merely affects what rows are in the DataView.

Listing 11.7 contains an example using the DataView.RowFilter attribute. In this example, I again use two different DataView objects: The first DataView will be filtered to just contain rows where the ProductName column value starts with "A" and the second DataView will only contain rows where the ProductName column value starts with "B".

LISTING 11.7   Using the `DataView.RowFilter` Attribute

[VisualBasic.NET]

```vb
01: <%@ import namespace="System.Data" %>
02: <%@ import namespace="System.Data.SqlClient" %>
03:
04: <script language="vb" runat="server">
05:
06:   protected sub Page_Load(sender as Object, e as EventArgs)
07:
08:     dim SqlCon as new SqlConnection("server=localhost;
➥ uid=sa;pwd=;database=northwind")
09:     dim SqlDA as new SqlDataAdapter("SELECT TOP 10 ProductName,
➥ ProductID FROM Products", SqlCon)
10:     dim ds as new DataSet()
11:
12:     SqlDA.Fill(ds, "Products")
13:
14:     dim dt as DataTable = ds.Tables(0)
15:
16:     dim  MyDataView1 as new DataView(dt)
17:     MyDataView1.RowFilter = "ProductName LIKE 'A%'"
18:
19:     dim MyDataView2 as new DataView(dt)
20:     MyDataView2.RowFilter = "ProductName LIKE 'B%'"
21:
22:     DG.DataSource = MyDataView1
23:     DG.DataBind()
24:
25:     DG2.DataSource = MyDataView2
26:     DG2.DataBind()
27:
28:   end sub
29:
30: </script>
```

[C#.NET]

```csharp
01: <%@ import namespace="System.Data" %>
02: <%@ import namespace="System.Data.SqlClient" %>
03:
04: <script language="C#" runat="server">
05:
06:   protected void Page_Load(Object sender, EventArgs e){
07:
08:     SqlConnection SqlCon = new SqlConnection("server=localhost;
➥ uid=sa;pwd=;database=northwind");
```

LISTING 11.7   Continued

```
09:    SqlDataAdapter SqlDA = new SqlDataAdapter("SELECT TOP 10 ProductName,
➥    ProductID FROM Products", SqlCon);
10:    DataSet ds = new DataSet();
11:
12:    SqlDA.Fill(ds, "Products");
13:
14:    DataTable dt = ds.Tables[0];
15:
16:    DataView MyDataView1 = new DataView(dt);
17:    MyDataView1.RowFilter = "ProductName LIKE 'A%'";
18:
19:    DataView MyDataView2 = new DataView(dt);
20:    MyDataView2.RowFilter = "ProductName LIKE 'B%'";
21:
22:    DG.DataSource = MyDataView1;
23:    DG.DataBind();
24:
25:    DG2.DataSource = MyDataView2;
26:    DG2.DataBind();
27:
28:  }
29:
30: </script>

[VisualBasic.NET & C#.NET]

01: <html>
02:   <body>
03:
04:    <h3>ProductName Starts With A</h3>
05:    <asp:DataGrid id="DG" runat="Server" font-size="10" />
06:
07:    <br>
08:
09:    <h3>ProductName Starts With B</h3>
10:    <asp:DataGrid id="DG2" runat="Server" font-size="10" />
11:
12:   </body>
13: </html>
```

In Listing 11.7, I use the DataView.DataRowFilter to filter all rows that start with the letter "A" (line 17) for the DataView named MyDataView1 and on line 20, I use the DataView.DataRowFilter to filter rows that start with the letter "B". Figure 11.7 contains an illustration of this page.

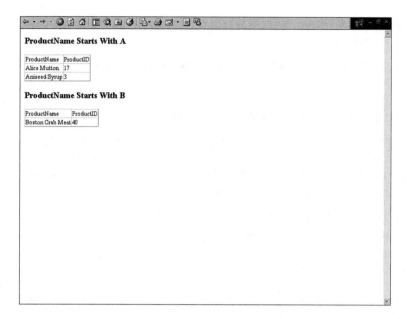

FIGURE 11.7

The top DataGrid *contains all rows where the* ProductName *value starts with "A", and the bottom* DataGrid *contains just rows that start with "B".*

Recall that you can use the `DataTable.Select` method's third parameter to filter rows based on their state—you also can do this using the `DataView` by setting the `DataView.RowStateFilter` property. This functionality is exactly the same as the `DataTables`. The following list contains all the possible values. These values can be found in the `DataViewRowState` enumeration.

- `CurrentRows`—The current rows
- `Deleted`—All deleted rows
- `ModifiedCurrent`—The current version of modified data
- `ModifiedOriginal`—The original version of modified data
- `Added`—A new row
- `None`—None
- `OriginalRows`—The original rows
- `Unchanged`—Unchanged rows

In the following code, you'll find an example of implementing this type of filtering:

```
[Visual Basic] - DataView.RowStateFilter = DataViewRowState.Added
```

```
[C#] - DataView.RowStateFilter = DataViewRowState.Added;
```

You can optionally filter with more than one `DataViewRowState` enumerator by using the `OR` Boolean operator (`C# = |`)(`VB = OR`) as seen in the following.

```
[Visual Basic] - DataView.RowStateFilter = DataViewRowState.New OR
DataViewRowState.Deleted
```

```
[C#] - DataView.RowStateFilter = DataViewRowState.New |
DataViewRowState.Deleted;
```

Adding a New Row to a `DataView`

Adding a new row to a `DataView` is much like adding a new row to the `DataTable` except that you use a `DataRowView` object instead of a `DataRow` object, and the `DataView` method you invoke to return the `DataRowView` is slightly different. There is one method and one property I want to introduce to you before we get to the code example:

- `DataView.AllowNew`—This property expects a boolean value indicating whether or not this `DataView` can have new rows added.

- `DataView.AddNew`—This method adds a new row to the `DataView` and returns it so you can give the different fields values.

Listing 11.8 shows how to add a new row to a `DataView`. In this example, you are going to add one new row to a `DataView` and then bind it to a `DataGrid`.

LISTING 11.8   Adding a New `DataRowView`

```
[VisualBasic.NET]
01: <%@ import namespace="System.Data" %>
02: <%@ import namespace="System.Data.SqlClient" %>
03: <script language="vb" runat="server">
04:
05:   protected sub Page_Load(sender as Object, e as EventArgs)
06:
07:     dim SqlCon as new SqlConnection("server=localhost;
➥  uid=sa;pwd=;database=northwind")
08:     dim SqlDA as new SqlDataAdapter("SELECT TOP 10 ProductName,
➥  ProductID FROM Products", SqlCon)
09:     dim ds as new DataSet()
10:
11:     SqlDA.Fill(ds, "Products")
12:
13:     dim dt as DataTable = ds.Tables(0)
14:
15:     dim MyDataView1 as new DataView(dt)
16:     MyDataView1.AllowNew = true
17:     dim MyDataRowView as DataRowView = MyDataView1.AddNew()
18:     MyDataRowView("ProductName") = "An Dim Sum"
19:     MyDataRowView("ProductID") = "12"
20:
```

LISTING 11.8   Continued

```
21:    DG.DataSource = MyDataView1
22:    DG.DataBind()
23:
24:   end sub
25:
26: </script>
```

[C#.NET]

```
01: <%@ import namespace="System.Data" %>
02: <%@ import namespace="System.Data.SqlClient" %>
03: <script language="C#" runat="server">
04:
05:   protected void Page_Load(Object sender, EventArgs e){
06:
07:     SqlConnection SqlCon = new SqlConnection("server=localhost;
➥ uid=sa;pwd=;database=northwind");
08:     SqlDataAdapter SqlDA = new SqlDataAdapter("SELECT TOP 10 ProductName,
➥ ProductID FROM Products", SqlCon);
09:     DataSet ds = new DataSet();
10:
11:     SqlDA.Fill(ds, "Products");
12:
13:     DataTable dt = ds.Tables[0];
14:
15:     DataView MyDataView1 = new DataView(dt);
16:     MyDataView1.AllowNew = true;
17:     DataRowView MyDataRowView = MyDataView1.AddNew();
18:     MyDataRowView["ProductName"] = "An Dim Sum";
19:     MyDataRowView["ProductID"] = "12";
20:
21:     DG.DataSource = MyDataView1;
22:     DG.DataBind();
23:
24:   }

</script>
```

[VisualBasic.NET & C#.NET]

```
25: <html>
26:   <body>
27:    <h3>
28:     Adding a new DataRowView
29:    </h3>
30:     <asp:DataGrid id="DG" runat="Server" font-size="10" />
31:   </body>
32: </html>
```

Listing 11.8 might look famililar to you. It is very similar to adding a new `DataRow` to the `DataTable` except when using the `DataTable` you use the `DataTable.NewRow` method. In a `DataView`, you use the `DataView.AddNew` method to add the new row—line 17. On the line before the `DataView.AddNew` method is invoked, I set the `DataView.AllowNew` property to `true`. This indicates that new rows can be added to the `DataView`. Finally, on lines 18 and 19, I apply values to both fields from the `DataView`—`ProductName` and `ProductID` and then I bind the `DataGrid` to the `DataView`. If I wanted to add more than one row to the `DataView`, I would have to invoke the `DataView.AddNew` method again after applying the values to the first `DataRowView` added.

> **CAUTION**
>
> When you call the `DataView.AddNew` method, a new `DataRowView` is added regardless of whether you apply values to the new row. So if you call the `DataView.AddNew` method and don't apply values, an empty row will be in the `DataView`.

You can see this page in Figure 11.8. You will see the newly added product at the very bottom of the `DataGrid`.

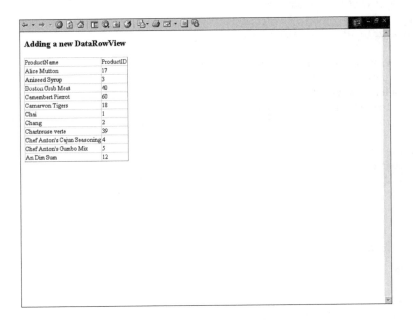

FIGURE 11.8

A Dim Sum can be seen at the very bottom of the `DataGrid`*.*

NOTE

Adding a new row to a `DataView` doesn't affect either the `DataTable` from which it was derived or any other `DataView` objects that were derived from the `DataTable`.

Editing Rows in a `DataView`

Editing using the `DataView` object is very similar to editing in the `DataTable` object. You must determine which row or rows you want to edit within the `DataRowCollection`, make sure the `DataView` is indeed editable, and finally edit the `DataRowView`.

There are a couple of properties and methods with which to be concerned when editing a row in a `DataView`. The following list goes over each. Note that some are `DataView` properties or methods and some are `DataRowView`s.

- `DataView.AllowEdit`—This boolean property enables you to get or set whether or not edits are allowed.
- `DataRowView.BeginEdit`—The method that puts the `DataRowView` into edit mode.
- `DataRowView.EndEdit`—The method that takes the `DataRowView` out of edit mode.
- `DataRowView.CancelEdit`—Cancels and rolls back any edits made on the `DataRowView`.

Now let's look at a code example—Listing 11.9 contains an example editing a `DataRowView`.

LISTING 11.9   Editing a `DataRowView`

```
[VisualBasic.NET]
01: <%@ import namespace="System.Data" %>
02: <%@ import namespace="System.Data.SqlClient" %>
03: <script language="vb" runat="server">
04:
05:   protected sub Page_Load(sender as Object, e as EventArgs)
06:
07:     dim SqlCon as new SqlConnection("server=localhost;
➥   uid=sa;pwd=;database=northwind")
08:     dim SqlDA as new SqlDataAdapter("SELECT TOP 10 ProductName,
➥   ProductID FROM Products", SqlCon)
09:     dim ds as new DataSet()
10:
11:     SqlDA.Fill(ds, "Products")
12:
13:     dim dt as DataTable = ds.Tables(0)
14:
```

LISTING 11.9   Continued

```
15:    dim MyDataView1 as new DataView(dt)
16:    dim DRV as DataRowView = MyDataView1(0)
17:    MyDataView1.AllowEdit = true
18:    DRV.BeginEdit()
19:    DRV("ProductName") = "New and Improved " + DRV("ProductName")
20:    DRV.EndEdit()
21:
22:    DG.DataSource = MyDataView1
23:    DG.DataBind()
24:
25:   end sub
26:
27: </script>
```

```
[C#.NET]
01: <%@ import namespace="System.Data" %>
02: <%@ import namespace="System.Data.SqlClient" %>
03: <script language="C#" runat="server">
04:
05:   protected void Page_Load(Object sender, EventArgs e){
06:
07:    SqlConnection SqlCon = new SqlConnection("server=localhost;
➥ uid=sa;pwd=;database=northwind");
08:    SqlDataAdapter SqlDA = new SqlDataAdapter("SELECT TOP 10 ProductName,
➥ ProductID FROM Products", SqlCon);
09:    DataSet ds = new DataSet();
10:
11:    SqlDA.Fill(ds, "Products");
12:
13:    DataTable dt = ds.Tables[0];
14:
15:    DataView MyDataView1 = new DataView(dt);
16:    DataRowView DRV = MyDataView1[0];
17:    MyDataView1.AllowEdit = true;
18:    DRV.BeginEdit();
19:    DRV["ProductName"] = "New and Improved " + DRV["ProductName"];
20:    DRV.EndEdit();
21:
22:    DG.DataSource = MyDataView1;
23:    DG.DataBind();
24:
25:   }
26:
27: </script>
```

LISTING 11.9   Continued

```
[VisualBasic.NET & C#.NET]
28: <html>
29:  <body>
30:    <h3>
31:     Adding a new DataRowView
32:    </h3>
33:     <asp:DataGrid id="DG" runat="Server" font-size="10" />
34:  </body>
35: </html>
```

In Listing 11.9, I enable editing within the DataView on line 17 by setting the
DataView.AllowEdit property. On line 18, I put the first DataRowView in the DataView into
edit mode by invoking DataRowView.BeginEdit. I change the value of the ProductName column on line 19, and invoke the DataRowView.EndEdit method on line 20 to save the changes
and bind the DataGrid on lines 22 and 23. You can see this page in Figure 11.9.

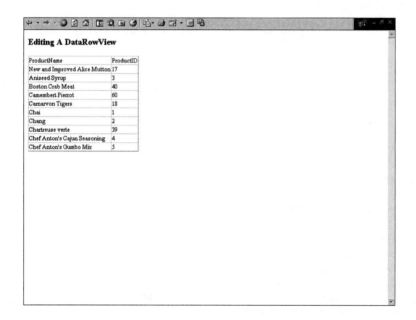

FIGURE 11.9
The "Alice Mutton" field is now "New and Improved Alice Mutton."

In Listing 11.9, I took the easy way out and just edited the first row in the DataRowCollection,
but you might want to edit the third or three-hundreth row. In the following sections I'll illustrate how you can search a DataView for specific DataRowView's based on their columns values by using the DataView.Find method.

Finding `DataRowViews`

The `DataView.Find` method finds a row based on a primary key value and returns an integer value indicating the index of the row where the value was found in the `DataRowCollection`.

There is an additional property you need to set before using the `DataView.Find` method, `DataView.Sort`. The `DataView.Sort` method gets or sets how the `DataView` is sorted. The value can be one or more column names followed by an optional `ASC` or `DESC` (sort in ascending or descending order). Listing 11.10 illustrates how to use the `DataView.Find` and `DataView.Sort` method. In this example, we will use the `Find` and `Sort` method to find a specific row, and then we'll edit it and bind to a `DataGrid`.

LISTING 11.10   Using the `Find` Method

```
[VisualBasic.NET]

01: <%@ import namespace="System.Data" %>
02: <%@ import namespace="System.Data.SqlClient" %>
03: <script language="vb" runat="server">
04:
05:  protected sub Page_Load(sender as Object, e as EventArgs)
06:
07:    dim SqlCon as new SqlConnection("server=localhost;
  ➥ uid=sa;pwd=;database=northwind")
08:    dim SqlDA as new SqlDataAdapter("SELECT TOP 10 ProductName,
  ➥ ProductID FROM Products", SqlCon)
09:    dim ds as new DataSet()
10:
11:    SqlDA.Fill(ds, "Products")
12:
13:    dim dt as DataTable = ds.Tables(0)
14:
15:    dim MyDataView1 as new DataView(dt)
16:
17:    MyDataView1.Sort = "ProductID DESC"
18:    dim row as integer = MyDataView1.Find("17")
19:    MyDataView1.AllowEdit = true
20:    MyDataView1(row).BeginEdit()
21:    MyDataView1(row)("ProductName") = "New and Improved "
  ➥  + MyDataView1(row)("ProductName")
22:    MyDataView1(row).EndEdit()
23:
24:    DG.DataSource = MyDataView1
25:    DG.DataBind()
26:
27:  end sub
28:
29: </script>
```

LISTING 11.10   Continued

[C#.NET]

```
01: <%@ import namespace="System.Data" %>
02: <%@ import namespace="System.Data.SqlClient" %>
03: <script language="C#" runat="server">
04:
05:   protected void Page_Load(Object sender, EventArgs e){
06:
07:     SqlConnection SqlCon = new SqlConnection("server=localhost;
➥ uid=sa;pwd=;database=northwind");
08:     SqlDataAdapter SqlDA = new SqlDataAdapter("SELECT TOP 10 ProductName,
➥ ProductID FROM Products", SqlCon);
09:     DataSet ds = new DataSet();
10:
11:     SqlDA.Fill(ds, "Products");
12:
13:     DataTable dt = ds.Tables[0];
14:
15:     DataView MyDataView1 = new DataView(dt);
16:
17:     MyDataView1.Sort = "ProductID DESC";
18:     int row = MyDataView1.Find("17");
19:     MyDataView1.AllowEdit = true;
20:     MyDataView1[row].BeginEdit();
21:     MyDataView1[row]["ProductName"] = "New and Improved "
➥   + MyDataView1[row]["ProductName"];
22:     MyDataView1[row].EndEdit();
23:
24:     DG.DataSource = MyDataView1;
25:     DG.DataBind();
26:
27:   }
28:
29: </script>
```

[VisualBasic.NET & C#.NET]

```
28: <html>
29:   <body>
30:     <h3>
31:       Adding a new DataRowView
32:     </h3>
33:       <asp:DataGrid id="DG" runat="Server" font-size="10" />
34:   </body>
35: </html>
```

In Listing 11.10, the first thing I do is sort the `DataView`, line 17. I sort by the `ProductID` column in descending order which not only sets the `DataViews` sort order, but also sets the `ProductID` column as the column to search when using the `DataView.Find` method. On line 18, I call the `DataView.Find` method passing a value of 17, which is "Alice Muttton's" `ProductID` (Note: Your Alice Mutton `ProductID` may be different). This method returns an integer value of where this row is located within the `DataRowCollection`. I put the returned integer in the variable row. I use this integer (row) to edit this row in lines 20–22 and finally bind the `DataGrid`. Figure 11.10 contains this page. Notice that "Alice Mutton" has been edited to read "New and Improved Alice Mutton".

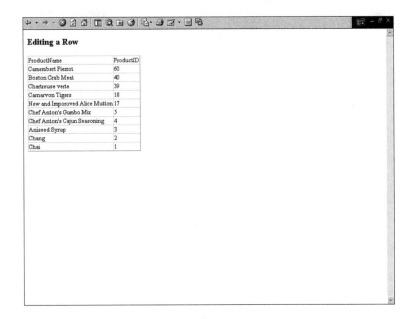

FIGURE 11.10
The "Alice Mutton" field is now New and Improved Alice Mutton.

Deleting `DataRowViews`

There are two ways you can delete a `DataRowView` from a `DataView`. The first is by using the `DataView.Delete` method and the second is by using the `DataRowView.Delete` method. The following describes each:

- `DataView.Delete`—This method deletes a row at a specified index. `DataView.Delete` expects one parameter, the index you want to delete.

- `DataRowView.Delete`—Deletes the row that invoked the method.

Listing 11.11 contains an example using both methods. In this example, there are two different `DataViews` created and the `DataRowView` with the value "*Alice Mutton*" will be deleted from both.

11

LISTING 11.11   Deleting a Row in a DataView

[VisualBasic.NET]

```
01: <%@ import namespace="System.Data" %>
02: <%@ import namespace="System.Data.SqlClient" %>
03: <script language="vb" runat="server">
04:
05:   protected sub Page_Load(sender as Object, e as EventArgs)
06:
07:     dim SqlCon as new SqlConnection("server=localhost;
➡  uid=sa;pwd=;database=northwind")
08:     dim SqlDA as new SqlDataAdapter("SELECT TOP 10 ProductName,
➡  ProductID FROM Products", SqlCon)
09:     dim ds as new DataSet()
10:
11:     SqlDA.Fill(ds, "Products")
12:
13:     dim dt as DataTable = ds.Tables(0)
14:
15:     dim MyDataView1 as new DataView(dt)
16:     dim MyDataView2 as new DataView(dt)
17:
18:     MyDataView1.Sort = "ProductID DESC"
19:     dim row as integer = MyDataView1.Find("17")
20:     MyDataView1.AllowDelete = true
21:     MyDataView1(row).Delete()
22:     DG.DataSource = MyDataView1
23:     DG.DataBind()
24:
25:     dt.RejectChanges() 'Rollback First Delete
26:
27:     MyDataView2.Sort = "ProductID DESC"
28:     row = MyDataView2.Find("17")
29:     MyDataView2.AllowDelete = true
30:     MyDataView2.Delete(row)
31:     DG2.DataSource = MyDataView2
32:     DG2.DataBind()
33:
34:   end sub
35:
36: </script>
```

[C#.NET]

```
01: <%@ import namespace="System.Data" %>
02: <%@ import namespace="System.Data.SqlClient" %>
03: <script language="C#" runat="server">
04:
05:   protected void Page_Load(Object sender, EventArgs e){
06:
```

LISTING 11.11   Continued

```
07:    SqlConnection SqlCon = new SqlConnection("server=localhost;
➥    uid=sa;pwd=;database=northwind");
08:    SqlDataAdapter SqlDA = new SqlDataAdapter("SELECT TOP 10 ProductName,
➥    ProductID FROM Products", SqlCon);
09:    DataSet ds = new DataSet();
10:
11:    SqlDA.Fill(ds, "Products");
12:
13:    DataTable dt = ds.Tables[0];
14:
15:    DataView MyDataView1 = new DataView(dt);
16:    DataView MyDataView2 = new DataView(dt);
17:
18:    MyDataView1.Sort = "ProductID DESC";
19:    int row = MyDataView1.Find("17");
20:    MyDataView1.AllowDelete = true;
21:    MyDataView1[row].Delete();
22:    DG.DataSource = MyDataView1;
23:    DG.DataBind();
24:
25:    dt.RejectChanges(); //Rollback First Delete
26:
27:    MyDataView2.Sort = "ProductID DESC";
28:    row = MyDataView2.Find("17");
29:    MyDataView2.AllowDelete = true;
30:    MyDataView2.Delete(row);
31:    DG2.DataSource = MyDataView2;
32:    DG2.DataBind();
33:
34:  }
35:
36: </script>

[VisualBasic.NET & C#.NET]

37: <html>
38:  <body>
39:   <h3>
40:   DataRowView.Delete()
41:   </h3>
42:   <asp:DataGrid id="DG" runat="Server" font-size="10" />
43:   <br>
44:   <h3>
45:   DataView.Delete()
46:   </h3>
47:   <asp:DataGrid id="DG2" runat="Server" font-size="10" />
48:  </body>
49: </html>
```

First let's go through the DataRowView.Delete section of Listing 11.11. On line 18, I sort the DataView, then on line 19, I use the DataView.Find method to get the index within the DataRowCollection of "Alice Mutton". On line 20, I set DataView.AllowDelete to true and invoke the DataRowView.Delete method passing in the proper row index on line 21. Lastly, I bind the DataGrid to the MyDataView1.

You might be wondering why I invoke the DataTable.RejectChanges method on line 25. I do this to roll back the first deletion because when a row is deleted from the DataRowCollection, it affects all objects associated with it—the parent DataTable and associated DataViews. For instance, if I did not invoke the DataTable.RejectChanges, I would have gotten an exception on line 30 (the DataView.Delete method) because the DataView.Find method would not return an index and I would be passing in an invalid index as a parameter for the DataView.Delete method. Try commenting out line 25 to see the effects.

Let's move on to the DataView.Delete method section of the code. Lines 27–29 are identical to the first method. First, I sort the rows (line 27), then I find the specific row I want to delete (line 28), and enable deleting for the DataView (line 29). The DataView.Delete method is invoked on line 30 and I use the row variable as a parameter. Finally, I bind the second DataGrid to this DataView. Figure 11.11 contains this page.

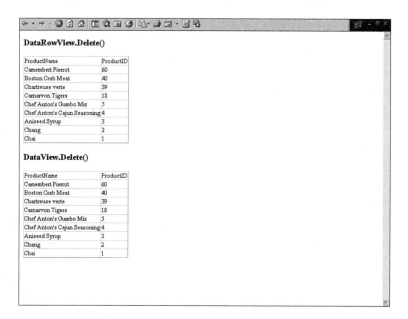

FIGURE 11.11

Alice Mutton is deleted in both DataGrids.

I also would like to suggest trying the following to show the relationship between the DataTable and the DataViews derived from it:

1. Change the parameter passed into the `DataView.Find` method on line 28 to a different `ProductID` value, comment out line 25 and re-execute the page. You will see that the bottom `DataGrid` will have two different rows deleted.

2. Leaving the code from number 1 intact, add another `DataGrid`, but bind this one to the `DataTable` from which the two `DataViews` were derived. Put the data binding code after all other code. You will see that both rows are deleted from the `DataTable`.

Using the `SqlCommandBuilder` to Save Changes Back to Your Database

Now that you have seen how easy it is to manipulate data in both a `DataView` and `DataTable` you're probably wondering how hard is it to save these changes back to your database. Well, the answer is very easy. In this section I'll demonstrate how to use some of ADO.NET's built-in functionality to easily save data edited within a `DataTable` back to your database. I'll also be demonstrating how to use the `SqlCommandBuilder` to automatically generate your UPDATE, DELETE, and INSERT SQL statements. In the next section, "Bringing It All Together," I'll demonstrate another turnkey method to save your changes back to your database.

Using the `SqlCommandBuilder` (or one of its counterparts, `OleDbCommandBuilder` or `OdbcCommandBuilder`) to generate your SQL statements is very quick and easy for single table changes. What that means is if all your data in a particular `DataTable` is from a single database table, this works great. If not, you can't use it and you'll have to manually supply the command text for each command by using the `DataAdapter DeleteCommand`, `InsertCommand`, and `UpdateCommand` as we'll demonstrate in the following section.

At a minimum, you must set the `SqlDataAdpater.SelectCommand` property to use the `SqlCommandBuilder`. The `SqlCommandBuilder` uses the `SelectCommand` to retrieve information about the table in which the edits will be made and uses this information to automatically generate Transact-SQL statements for the other commands. Note: If you set one of the additional commands, for example, `UpdateCommand`, the `SqlCommandBuilder` will not automatically generate an `UpdateCommand` and will use the one you created.

After being created and associated with a `SqlDataAdpater`, the `SqlCommandBuilder` becomes a listener for the `SqlDataAdapter.RowUpdating` event. This event occurs right before a command gets executed against a datasource. The `SqlCommandBuilder` then tells the `SqlDataAdapter` what command object to use. You associate a `SqlCommandBuilder` with a `SqlDataAdapter` in the `SqlCommandBuilder` constructer; you pass the `SqlDataAdapter` object in as a parameter.

After all row edits, inserts, or deletions are done to the `DataTable`, all you need to do is call the `SqlDataAdapter.Update` method and the rest is done for you under the covers. Essentially, the `SqlDataAdapter` examines all the `DataRow.RowState` values and executes the correlating SQL command. For instance, if `DataRow.RowState` is `DataRowState.Added`, then the INSERT command is executed and if its `DataRowState.Deleted`, the DELETE command is executed and so on.

Easy enough? Let's look at an example. In Listing 11.12, I demonstrate how to use the SqlCommandBuilder to insert a new row into the Products table of the Northwind database. Because the SqlCommandBuilder does all the work for us, I am keeping this example as simple as possible and just inserting a new record. Editing and deleting is done the exact same way as inserting. First, you manipulate the DataTable and then call the DataAdapter.Update method.

LISTING 11.12   Using the SqlCommandBuilder

[VisualBasic.NET]

```
01: <%@ import namespace="System.Data" %>
02: <%@ import namespace="System.Data.SqlClient" %>
03: <script language="vb" runat="server">
04:
05:  protected sub Page_Load(sender as Object, e as EventArgs)
06:
07:   if (not IsPostBack) then
08:    Bind()
09:   end if
10:
11:  end sub
12:
13:  sub Bind()
14:
15:   dim SqlCon as new SqlConnection("server=localhost;
➥ uid=sa;pwd=;database=northwind")
16:   dim SqlDA as new SqlDataAdapter("SELECT ProductName,
➥ ProductID FROM Products", SqlCon)
17:   dim ds as new DataSet()
18:   SqlDA.Fill(ds, "Products")
19:   DG.DataSource = ds.Tables(0)
20:   DG.DataBind()
21:
22:  end sub
23:
24:  sub InsertRecord(sender as Object, e as EventArgs)
25:
26:   dim SqlCon as new SqlConnection("server=localhost;
➥ uid=sa;pwd=;database=northwind")
27:   dim SqlDA as new SqlDataAdapter("SELECT ProductName,
➥ ProductID FROM Products", SqlCon)
28:   dim SCB as new SqlCommandBuilder(SqlDA)
29:   dim ds as new DataSet()
30:   SqlDA.Fill(ds, "Products")
31:   dim dt as DataTable = ds.Tables(0)
32:   dim dr as DataRow = dt.NewRow()
33:   dr(0) = ChangeTo.Text
34:   dt.Rows.Add(dr)
```

LISTING 11.12   Using the `SqlCommandBuilder`

```
35:    SqlDA.Update(ds, "Products")
36:    Bind()
37:
38: end sub
39:
40: </script>
```

[C#.NET]

```
01: <%@ import namespace="System.Data" %>
02: <%@ import namespace="System.Data.SqlClient" %>
03: <script language="C#" runat="server">
04:
05:   protected void Page_Load(Object sender, EventArgs e){
06:
07:    if (! IsPostBack) { Bind(); }
08:
09:   }
10:
11:   void Bind(){
12:
13:    SqlConnection SqlCon = new SqlConnection("server=localhost;
➥   uid=sa;pwd=;database=northwind");
14:    SqlDataAdapter SqlDA = new SqlDataAdapter("SELECT ProductName,
➥   ProductID FROM Products", SqlCon);
15:    DataSet ds = new DataSet();
16:    SqlDA.Fill(ds, "Products");
17:    DG.DataSource = ds.Tables[0];
18:    DG.DataBind();
19:
20:   }
21:
22:   void InsertRecord(Object sender, EventArgs e){
23:
24:    SqlConnection SqlCon = new SqlConnection("server=localhost
➥   ;uid=sa;pwd=;database=northwind");
25:    SqlDataAdapter SqlDA = new SqlDataAdapter("SELECT ProductName,
➥   ProductID FROM Products", SqlCon);
26:    SqlCommandBuilder SCB = new SqlCommandBuilder(SqlDA);
27:    DataSet ds = new DataSet();
28:    SqlDA.Fill(ds, "Products");
29:    DataTable dt = ds.Tables[0];
30:    DataRow dr = dt.NewRow();
```

LISTING 11.12 Continued

```
31:    dr[0] = ChangeTo.Text;
32:    dt.Rows.Add(dr);
33:    SqlDA.Update(ds, "Products");
34:    Bind();
35:
36: }
37:
38: </script>

[VisualBasic.NET & C#.NET]

39: <html>
40:   <body style="font:10">
41:     <form runat="server">
42:       <h3>
43:       SqlCommandBuilder
44:       </h3>
45:       Enter Product Name:
46:       <asp:TextBox ID="ChangeTo" Runat="server" />
47:       <asp:Button Text="Submit" Runat="server" OnClick="InsertRecord" />
48:       <p>
49:       <asp:DataGrid id="DG" runat="Server" font-size="10" />
50:       </p>
51:     </form>
52:   </body>
53: </html>
```

In Listing 11.12, there are three methods—Page_Load (lines 5–9), Bind (lines 11–20), InsertRecord (lines 22–36). Within the Page_Load event, I check if Page.IsPostBack is true. If it is not, then I invoke the Bind method. All the Bind method does is populates the DataGrid with the contents of the Products table. The InsertRecord method is used to handle the Button controls Click event and within it is where I make use of the SqlCommandBuilder. Notice I create my SqlConnection and SqlDataAdapter in the usual way (lines 24 and 25). On line 26 is where I create the SqlCommandBuilder object. Notice that I pass in the SqlDataAdapter as a parameter. In lines 29–32, I add the new row to the DataTable ("*Products*") and then on line 33 I invoke the DataAdapter.Update method, ending by invoking the Bind method so the DataGrid gets fresh data. You can see this page after a new row is added in Figure 11.12. You will notice that there is a ProductID associated with the new row even though we didn't specify one. This is because the ProductID field is autogenerated by SQL Server.

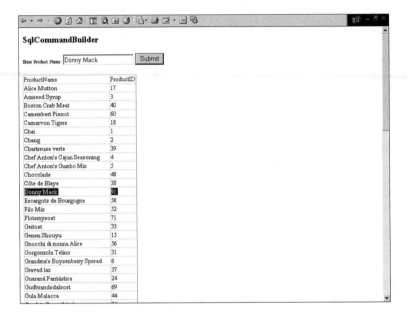

FIGURE 11.12

My name is shown as a product.

Bringing It Together

So we have seen how to manipulate the data in a `DataTable` and `DataView`, and how to use the `SqlCommandBuilder` to save changes back to the datasource. Now let's see how they all work together. In this rather lengthy example we are going to create a product edit page for `Northwind`. This two-page example will contain a list of all the suppliers available in the `Suppliers` table and a means to edit, insert, and delete each one of their products. Once all edits have been done to their products, there is a confirmation page that lists all inserts, edits, and deletions. From this page, you will be able to decide to save or reject the changes. If you choose to save the changes, then the `Products` table will be updated. If you choose not to save the changes, then all the changes made will be rolled back and you can start again with the original data.

An interesting thing about this example is that there are only two connections ever made to the database. The first is when you first enter the page, and the second is if you save the changes back to the database. What this means is that all edits, inserts, and deletions are held in memory until the user has completed. Then a batch update is performed. So let's look at the code. Because of the length of this example, we will only be showing the C# version; you can find the VB.NET version in this chapter's code folder.

LISTING 11.13   Northwind Product Edit Page

```
01: <%@ import namespace="System.Data" %>
02: <%@ import namespace="System.Data.SqlClient" %>
03:
04: <script language="C#" runat="Server">
05:
06:   protected void Page_Load(Object sender, EventArgs e){
07:
08:     if (! Page.IsPostBack) {
09:
10:       Bind();
11:
12:     }
13:
14:   }
15:
16:   void SaveToSession(DataSet ds){
17:
18:     Session["WorkingDataSet"] = ds;
19:
20:   }
21:
22:   DataSet GetFromSession() {
23:
24:     return (DataSet)Session["WorkingDataSet"];
25:
26:   }
27:
28:   void Bind(){
29:
30:     if (Session["WorkingDataSet"] == null) {
31:
32:       DDLSuppliers.DataSource = GetFromDatabase().Tables["Suppliers"];
33:
34:     } else {
35:
36:       DDLSuppliers.DataSource = GetFromSession().Tables["Suppliers"];
37:
38:     }
39:
40:     Page.DataBind();
41:     GetProducts();
42:
43:   }
44:
45:   DataSet GetFromDatabase(){
46:
```

LISTING **11.13**   Continued

```
47:   SqlConnection SqlCon = new SqlConnection("server=localhost;
➡ uid=sa;pwd=;database=northwind");
48:   SqlDataAdapter SqlDA = new SqlDataAdapter("SELECT ProductName,
➡ ProductID, SupplierID FROM Products ORDER By ProductName", SqlCon);
49:
50:   SqlDA.UpdateCommand = new SqlCommand("UPDATE Products SET
➡ ProductName = @ProductName WHERE ProductID = @ProductID");
51:   SqlDA.UpdateCommand.Parameters.Add(new SqlParameter(
➡ "@ProductName", SqlDbType.NVarChar, 20, "ProductName"));
52:   SqlDA.UpdateCommand.Parameters.Add(new SqlParameter(
➡ "@ProductID", SqlDbType.Int, 4, "ProductID"));
53:
54:   SqlDA.InsertCommand = new SqlCommand("INSERT INTO Products
➡ (ProductName, SupplierID) VALUES (@ProductName,@SupplierID)");
55:   SqlDA.InsertCommand.Parameters.Add(new SqlParameter(
➡ "@ProductName", SqlDbType.NVarChar, 20, "ProductName"));
56:   SqlDA.InsertCommand.Parameters.Add(new SqlParameter(
➡ "@SupplierID", SqlDbType.Int, 4, "SupplierID"));
57:
58:   SqlDA.DeleteCommand = new SqlCommand("DELETE Products
➡ WHERE ProductID = @ProductID");
59:   SqlDA.DeleteCommand.Parameters.Add(new SqlParameter(
➡ "@ProductID", SqlDbType.Int, 4, "ProductID"));
60:
61:   DataSet ds = new DataSet();
62:   SqlDA.Fill(ds, "Products");
63:
64:   SqlDA.SelectCommand = new SqlCommand("SELECT CompanyName,
➡ SupplierID FROM Suppliers ORDER BY CompanyName", SqlCon);
65:   SqlDA.Fill(ds, "Suppliers");
66:
67:   SaveToSession(ds);
68:   Session["WorkingDataAdpater"] = SqlDA;
69:   SqlCon.Close();
70:
71:   return ds;
72:
73:   }
74:
75:   protected void GetProducts_Click(Object sender, EventArgs e)
➡ { GetProducts(); }
76:
77:   protected void GetProducts(){
78:
79:   lbProducts.Items.Clear();
80:
```

LISTING 11.13 Continued

```
81:    DataView dv = new DataView(GetFromSession().Tables["Products"]);
82:    dv.Sort = DDLColumn.SelectedItem.Value + " " +
➥ DDLSortOrder.SelectedItem.Value;
83:    dv.RowFilter = "SupplierID =" + DDLSuppliers.SelectedItem.Value;
84:    lbProducts.SelectedIndex = 0;
85:    lbProducts.DataSource = dv;
86:    lbProducts.DataBind();
87:    txtEdit.Text = null;
88:  }
89:
90:
91:   protected void Delete_Click(Object sender, EventArgs e){
92:
93:    DataSet ds = GetFromSession();
94:    DataTable dt = ds.Tables["Products"];
95:    DataRow[] dr = dt.Select("ProductID = " + lbProducts.SelectedItem.Value);
96:    dr[0].Delete();
97:    SaveToSession(ds);
98:    GetProducts();
99:
100:  }
101:
102:   protected void Insert_Click(Object sender, EventArgs e){
103:
104:    DataSet ds = GetFromSession();
105:    DataTable dt = ds.Tables["Products"];
106:    DataRow dr = dt.NewRow();
107:    dr["ProductName"]  =txtEdit.Text;
108:    dr["SupplierID"] = DDLSuppliers.SelectedItem.Value;
109:    Random RA = new Random();
110:    string sProductID = "1234" + RA.Next(1000).ToString();
111:    dr["ProductID"] = int.Parse(sProductID);
112:    dt.Rows.Add(dr);
113:    SaveToSession(ds);
114:    GetProducts();
115:
116:  }
117:
118:   protected void Edit_Click(Object sender, EventArgs e){
119:
120:    DataSet ds = GetFromSession();
121:    DataTable dt = ds.Tables["Products"];
122:    DataRow[] dr = dt.Select("ProductID = " +
➥  lbProducts.SelectedItem.Value);
123:    dr[0].BeginEdit();
124:    dr[0]["ProductName"] = txtEdit.Text;
```

LISTING 11.13   Continued

```
125:    dr[0].EndEdit();
126:    SaveToSession(ds);
127:    GetProducts();
128:
129:  }
130:
131: </script>
132: <html>
133:  <body>
134:   <form runat="server">
135:    <TABLE CellPadding="4" CellSpacing="4" Border="0">
136:
137:       <TR>
138:        <TD Style="font-size:18;background-color:green;
➥ color:white;text-align:center">
139:
140:        Select A Supplier To Edit
141:
142:       </TD>
143:      </TR>
144:
145:       <TR>
146:
147:       <TD Style="text-align:center">
148:
149:        <b>Get All Products For</b>
150:
151:        <asp:DropDownList
152:         id="DDLSuppliers"
153:         runat="server"
154:         DataTextField="CompanyName"
155:         DataValueField="SupplierID" />
156:
157:        <b>Sort Results by </b>
158:
159:        <asp:DropDownList id="DDLColumn" runat="Server" >
160:         <asp:ListItem Value="ProductID" Text="Product ID" />
161:         <asp:ListItem Value="ProductName" Text="Product Name" />
162:        </asp:DropDownList>
163:
164:        <b> in </b>
165:
166:        <asp:DropDownList id="DDLSortOrder" runat="Server" >
167:         <asp:ListItem Value="DESC" Text="DESC" />
168:         <asp:ListItem Value="ASC" Text="ASC" />
```

LISTING 11.13   Continued

```
169:        </asp:DropDownList>
170:
171:        <b>Order</b>
172:
173:       </TD>
174:     </TR>
175:
176:     <TR>
177:
178:       <TD Style="text-align:left">
179:
180:        <asp:Button
181:         Text="Get Products" Width="200"
182:         BackColor="green" ForeColor="White"
183:         OnClick="GetProducts_Click" Runat="server"
184:         Font-Bold="true" Border="none" />
185:
186:       </TD>
187:     </TR>
188:
189:     <TR>
190:       <TD Style="font-size:18;background-color:green;
➥ color:white;text-align:left">
191:
192:          Edit Products
193:
194:       </TD>
195:     </TR>
196:
197:     <TR>
198:       <TD Style="text-align:left">
199:
200:        <b>Choose Product From List to Edit or Delete</b>
201:        <br>
202:        <asp:ListBox
203:         Id="lbProducts" Runat="server"
204:         Rows="5" Width="100%"
205:         DataTextField="ProductName" DataValueField="ProductID" />
206:        <BR>
207:        <b>Edit or Insert Product </b><font size="1">{insert item by
➥ filling out textbox and clicking on the insert button}</font>
208:        <BR>
209:        <asp:TextBox
210:         Id="txtEdit" Runat="server"
211:         Width="100%"/>
212:
```

LISTING 11.13 Continued

```
213:          </TD>
214:          </TR>
215:
216:
217:          <TR>
218:           <TD Style="text-align:left">
219:
220:            <asp:Button
221:             Id="Delete"
222:             Runat="Server" Text="Delete"
223:             OnClick="Delete_Click" Width="200"
224:             BackColor="green" ForeColor="White"
225:             Runat="server"  Font-Bold="true"
226:             Border="none" />
227:            <asp:button
228:             Id="Edit" Runat="server"
229:             Text="Edit" OnClick="Edit_Click"
230:             Width="200" BackColor="green"
231:             ForeColor="White" Runat="server"
232:             Font-Bold="true" Border="none" />
233:            <asp:button
234:             Id="Insert" Runat="server"
235:             Text="Insert" OnClick="Insert_Click"
236:             Width="200" BackColor="green"
237:             ForeColor="White" Runat="server"
238:             Font-Bold="true" Border="none" />
239:            <p>
240:            <a href="listing11.15.aspx">Save Changes</a>
241:
242:          </TD>
243:          </TR>
244:
245:         </TABLE>
246:        </form>
247:       </body>
248:      </html>
```

Okay, let's walk through the event chain. On the first request of this page, the Bind method is invoked (line 10) in the Page_Load event (lines 6–14). The Bind method (lines 28–43) has an if...then statement that checks if there is a session object with the name of WorkingDataSet—WorkingDataSet is a DataSet which holds all of our data. Since this is the first request there isn't a session object with that name, so the code in the if statement is executed. Within the if statement, the DropDownList named DDLSuppliers is bound to the result of the method GetFromDatabase (line 32). The GetFromDatabase method (lines 45–73) returns a DataSet object that is constructed from a database query.

Let's take a moment and look at the code in the GetFromDatabase method because this is where all our primary objects are created. The SqlDataAdapter is constructed on line 48. You'll notice that I create a SelectCommand, UpdateCommand, InsertCommand, and DeleteCommand for it (lines 48–59). You'll recall in the previous section that this is done for us by using the SqlCommandBuilder object. Next, in lines 61–65, I fill a DataSet with two queries—the contents of the Products and Suppliers table. You'll understand why I create two DataTables later in this section. On line 67, I invoke the SaveToSession method passing in the DataSet. The SaveToSession method saves the DataSet to the users session. On line 68, I save the SqlDataAdapter to the session. We'll be using the SqlDataAdapter again on the next page of our sample. We finish up by returning the DataSet.

After the if...then statement, the Page.DataBind method is invoked, followed by the GetProducts method. To understand why the Page.DataBind method was invoked before the GetProducts method, we must look at the GetProducts method. The GetProducts method is used to populate a ListBox named lbProducts that contains a list of all products that a particular supplier carries. Because there is always going to be a supplier selected in the DDLSuppliers we need to wait until it is populated, and invoking the Page.DataBind method does this.

Within the GetProducts method, we first clear the present contents of lbProducts—line 79. Then, on line 81, a new DataView is created with the Product DataTable named dv. We use this DataView to enable the user to sort the products shown in lbProducts—line 82. We also use dv to filter out all the products for a particular supplier—line 83. On line 84, the ListBox.SelectedIndex is set to 0, the first item in the list, and on lines 85 and 86, lbProducts is bound to dv. Finally, any contents of the TextBox named txtEdit are cleared—txtEdit is used to insert or edit a product in lbProducts.

At this point, the page load process is complete and you should have a page similar to Figure 11.13.

The top of the page has a DropDownList with a list of suppliers. To the right of that is a DropDownList with fields you can sort by, and on the far right is a DropDownList you can use to determine if the sort order should be in ascending or descending order. Beneath that is a button you use to retrieve all the products for a particular supplier. When this button is clicked, the GetProducts_Click handles the click event. The GetProducts_Click, in turn, invokes the GetProducts method.

Once the products for a supplier have been retrieved, you can edit the product's name by selecting the product from lbProducts and typing the new product name in the TextBox with the heading "Edit or Insert Product" and clicking the edit button. You can delete a product by selecting an item from lbProducts and clicking the delete button. Finally, you can insert a new product by typing in a product name in a new product name and clicking the insert button.

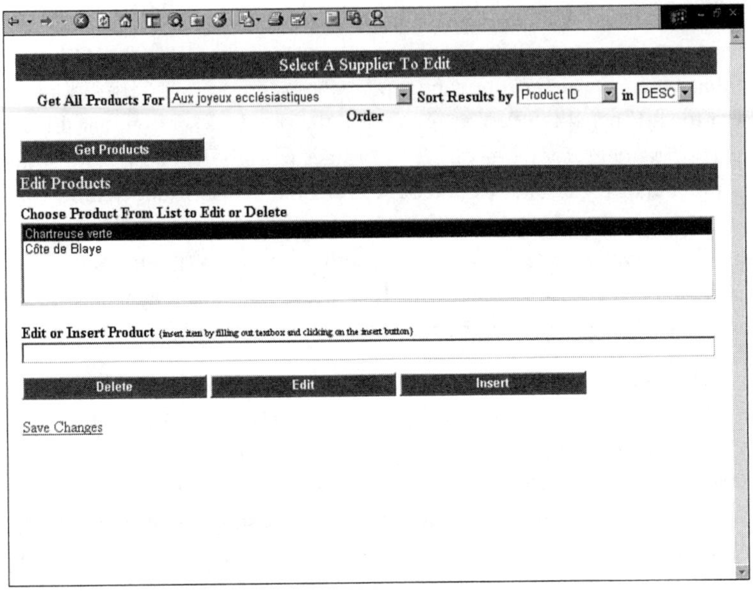

FIGURE **11.13**

Page on first request.

Once an item is selected and the delete button is clicked Delete_Click handles the event (lines 91–100). Within Delete_Click the GetFromSession method (line 93) is invoked to get our working DataSet. Then the DataTable.Select method is used to return the DataRow of the product you want to delete in the Products DataTable—line 95. The ProductID value is used to find the proper row. On line 96, we invoke the returned DataRow's Delete method to delete it from the DataTable. Then we put the edited DataSet back into the session and invoke the GetProducts method again to rebind the ListBox with the updated data.

When the edit button is clicked, Edit_Click handles the event (lines 118–129). The only difference between the Edit_Click and Delete_Click method is what is done with the DataRow. Instead of invoking the DataRow.Delete method, the DataRow is put into edit mode—line 123. The ProductName column is changed to the value found in txtEdit—line 124. Finally, the DataRow.EndEdit method is invoked to take it out of edit mode—line 125.

When the insert button is clicked, Insert_Click handles the event (lines 102–116). In this method, the DataTable.NewRow method is invoked to return a new DataRow—line 106. Only three column values are set in this example, the ProductName column value is set on line 107 by using the value of txtEdit, the SupplierID column is set on line 108 by using DDLSuppliers.SelectedItem.Value, and the ProductID value is set on line 111.

I set the ProductID with a random number that will never see the light of the database because when a new row is inserted into the Products table, the ProductID is autogenerated. Although, in this example it is needed; if you choose to delete or edit the ProductName after it has been added, this value finds the DataRow in the DataTable.

Figure 11.14 contains a screenshot of this page after a new item was added, and one was edited. Following Figure 11.14, in Listing 11.14, is the code for our page that will save this data back to the database.

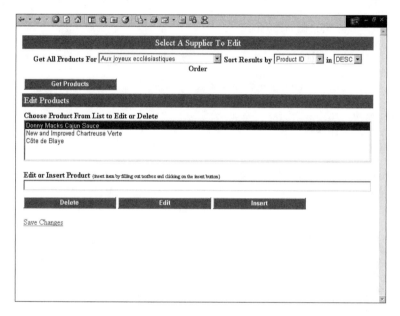

Figure 11.14

The edited page.

Listing 11.14 Accept Changes Page

```
01: <%@ Page EnableViewState ="false" %>
02: <%@ import namespace="System.Data" %>
03: <%@ import namespace="System.Data.SqlClient" %>
04:
05: <script language="C#" runat="server">
06:
07:   protected void RejectChanges(Object sender, EventArgs e){
08:
09:     ((DataSet)Session["WorkingDataSet"]).Tables["Products"].RejectChanges();
10:     Response.Redirect("listing11.14.aspx");
11:
```

LISTING 11.14   Accept Changes Page

```
12:  }
13:
14:  protected void Update_Click(Object sender, EventArgs e){
15:
16:   try {
17:     SqlDataAdapter SqlDa = (SqlDataAdapter)Session["WorkingDataAdpater"];
18:     SqlConnection SqlCon = new SqlConnection("server=localhost;
➥ uid=sa;pwd=;database=northwind");
19:     SqlDa.UpdateCommand.Connection = SqlCon;
20:     SqlDa.InsertCommand.Connection = SqlCon;
21:     SqlDa.DeleteCommand.Connection = SqlCon;
22:     SqlDa.Update(((DataSet)Session["WorkingDataSet"]).Tables["Products"]);
23:     Session.Remove("WorkingDataSet");
24:     Message.Text = "Changes Successfully Saved <a href='listing11.14.aspx'>
➥ Click Here</a> to start again";
25:     Update.Visible = false;
26:     Reject.Visible = false;
27:   } catch (SqlException SqlEx) {
28:
29:     Message.Text = "The Following Error Occured:<br>" +
➥ SqlEx.Message.ToString() + "<p>You may be trying to delete a restricted
item!";
30:
31:   }
32:
33:  }
34:
35:  protected void Page_Load(Object sender, EventArgs e){
36:
37:   DataTable dt = ((DataSet)Session["WorkingDataSet"]).Tables["Products"];
38:
39:   foreach (DataRow row in dt.Rows) {
40:
41:    if (row.RowState == DataRowState.Added){
42:
43:     Added.Items.Add(new ListItem(row["ProductName"].ToString()));
44:
45:    } else if (row.RowState == DataRowState.Deleted) {
46:
47:     row.RejectChanges();
48:     Deleted.Items.Add(new ListItem(row["ProductName"].ToString()));
49:     row.Delete();
50:
51:    } else if (row.RowState == DataRowState.Modified) {
52:
```

LISTING 11.14   Continued

```
53:      Modified.Items.Add(new ListItem(row["ProductName"].ToString()));
54:
55:    } else if (row.RowState == DataRowState.Unchanged) {
56:
57:    Unchanged.Items.Add(new ListItem(row["ProductName"].ToString()));
58:
59:    }
60:
61:   }
62:
63:  }
64:
65: </script>
66:
67: <html>
68:  <body>
69:   <form runat="server">
70:     <center>
71:
72:     <table CellPadding="4" CellSpacing="0" Border="0" Width="500">
73:      <tr>
74:       <td Style="font-size:18;background-color:green;
➥  color:white;text-align:center">
75:
76:         Confirm Changes
77:
78:       </td>
79:      </tr>
80:      <tr>
81:       <td align="center">
82:
83:        <b>Rows Added</b>
84:        <br>
85:        <asp:ListBox runat="server" font-size="10" id="Added" Width="410" />
86:
87:       </td>
88:      </tr>
89:      <tr>
90:       <td align="center">
91:
92:        <b>Rows Deleted</b>
93:        <br>
94:        <asp:ListBox runat="server" font-size="10"
➥  id="Deleted" Width="410" />
05:
```

Listing 11.14   Continued

```
96:        </td>
97:        </tr>
98:        <tr>
99:         <td align="center">
100:
101:          <b>Rows Modified</b>
102:          <br>
103:          <asp:ListBox runat="server" font-size="10"
➥   id="Modified" Width="410"        />
104:
105:         </td>
106:        </tr>
107:        <tr>
108:         <td align="center">
109:
110:          <b>Rows Unchanged</b>
111:          <br>
112:          <asp:ListBox runat="server" font-size="10"
➥   id="Unchanged" Width="410" />
113:
114:         </td>
115:        </tr>
116:        <tr>
117:         <td align="center">
118:
119:          <asp:Button
120:           Text="Update Database"
121:           runat="server" OnClick="Update_Click"
122:           Width="200" BackColor="green"
123:           ForeColor="White" Runat="server"
124:           Font-Bold="true" Border="none" />
125:
126:          <asp:Button
127:           Text="Reject Changes and Go Back"
128:           runat="server" OnClick="RejectChanges"
129:           Width="200" BackColor="green"
130:           ForeColor="White" Runat="server"
131:           Font-Bold="true" Border="none" />
132:
133:
134:         </td>
135:        </tr>
136:        <tr>
137:         <td align="Left">
138:
```

LISTING 11.14 Continued

```
139:          <asp:Label runat="server" Font-Color="Red"
➡ Font-Bold="true" id="Message" />
140:
141:        </td>
142:      </tr>
143:    </table>
144:    </center>
145:  </form>
146: </body>
147: </html>
```

By clicking on "Save Changes," as shown in Figure 11.14, you can navigate to Listing 11.14. When Listing 11.14 first renders, you'll receive a page with four multiple-lined TextBox controls. The top will contain all products that were added during the session. The second will contain all products that were deleted. The third contains all items that were edited. And the last TextBox contains all items that were unchanged.

These TextBoxes are populated in the Page_Load event handler (lines 35–61). First, I retrieve the Products DataTable on line 37. Then I loop through its DataRowCollection and check each DataRow.RowState property for its value, and depending on the value I insert the row into its correlating TextBox. You will notice in lines 47–49, I have to invoke the DataRow.RejectChanges method before I can get the value of the ProductName field for deleted DataRows. If I didn't rollback the changes before trying to access the columns, I would get a DeletedRowInaccessibleException because the DataRow has indeed been deleted from this version of the DataTable. Then after I get the value to display, I delete the DataRow again.

At the bottom of this page are two buttons. The first "Update Database" will execute code that will attempt to save the changes to the rows DataTable back to the database. The second, "Reject Changes and Go Back" will reject all the changes made to the DataTable and send the user back to the original page.

When the "Update Database" button is clicked, Update_Click handles the event. In this method is where I retrieve the SqlDataAdapter we created in the first code example from sessionstate. The SqlDataAdapter is pretty much ready to use right when we get it. We set it up before we threw it into sessionstate. The only thing we have to do is wire it to a valid SqlConnection object. This is done on lines 18–21, where the Connection property of each of the commands (UpdateCommand, InsertCommand, and DeleteCommand) is set to the SqlConnection object created on line 18—SqlCon. On line 22, I use the SqlDataAdapter.Update method to save the changes back to the database.

After updating the database, I remove the DataSet from sessionstate and provide a means for the user to start a new session. Figure 11.15 contains the page after edits have been made and saved back to the database. Notice the different values in the different TextBox controls.

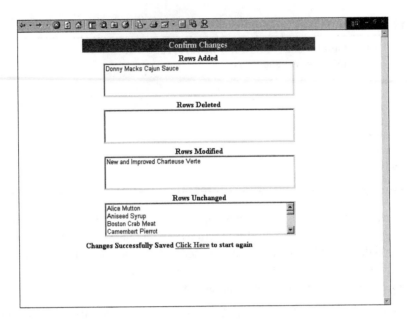

FIGURE 11.15
Edited page after data has been saved back to the database.

If you're trying this on your own computer, be aware: If you try to delete one of the products already contained in the Products table, you will receive an exception because of a foreign key constraint with the "Order Details" table. Edits and inserts will update fine, and you can delete any products that you add yourself. In this code example, there is no exception handling so it will break if you try to use it outside the bounds of the example. However, it should provide you a good foundation of how you make all the objects work with one another.

Summary

In this chapter, we discussed both the DataTable and the DataView objects. We discussed how to add, edit, delete, and insert new rows into each. We illustrated how to derive multiple DataViews from the same DataTable and how to modify one DataView individually and manipulate specific rows of data while not affecting the others. We then showed you how to use the SqlCommandBuilder to automatically generate SqlCommands used to save changes back to your datasource. We ended the chapter with a large code example illustrating how to use all these objects together. Specifically, the chapter explored

- An introduction to the DataTable and DataView
- Working with the DataTable
- Working with the DataView
- Using the SqlCommandBuilder to save changes
- Bringing it all together

Advanced Data Concepts

PART

IV

IN THIS PART

XML and SOAP

IN THIS CHAPTER

XML (Extensible Markup Language) and SOAP (Simple Object Access Protocol) are among the latest buzzwords in the Internet world. Unlike some buzzwords of the past, XML and SOAP actually are useful and valuable, and used heavily in the .NET Framework.

It is out of the scope of this book to explain XML and SOAP from the ground up…there are entire books on both XML and SOAP. Rather, in this chapter, you will learn how you can use XML and SOAP in your ASP.NET applications. This chapter will introduce you to the `Xml` server control, and related classes in the `System.Xml` namespace. There is much more to using XML and SOAP than what we will cover in this chapter.

In this chapter you will learn about

- `Xml` server control
- `XmlDocument` and `XmlDataDocument`
- Working with XML elements
- Reading and writing XML files with the `DataSet`
- SOAP (Simple Object Access Protocol)

What Is XML? A Quick Refresher

XML (Extensible Markup Language) is an emerging technology used to structure and describe data. It is a derivative of Standard Generalized Markup Language (SGML), much like HTML. The difference between HTML and XML is that HTML is structured and defined with common specifications. In other words, in HTML, all tags are predefined and have meaning. In XML, you define your own tags.

HTML is designed for displaying information in a browser, and that is truly its limitation. With HTML, you can define how information should look in a browser, but it is meaningless beyond that. With XML, you can define data that can be displayed in a browser, or that can be used by your application in the same manner that data from a database can be used. In other words, XML is used to describe data.

The .NET Framework and ADO.NET use XML heavily under the covers. Data that is pulled from a database into your application using one of the ADO.NET Managed Providers is persisted as XML, transmitted, and rematerialized as useful data. The real advantage in this is that XML is text based and nonproprietary. This means that any system that can read text can work with XML, whether the XML is parsed and used, or simply saved to the file system or passed on to another system. This opens the .NET Framework to being compatible with disparate systems, the true power of .NET.

The System.Xml namespace includes several classes that make working with XML, as well as XSL Transform (XSL/T) stylesheets, very easy. Creating, reading, and writing XML data becomes as simple as constructing instances of classes, altering properties, and making a few method calls. Additionally, the ASP.NET Xml server control enables the display of XML data in a browser, and the use of XSL/T stylesheets on that data, with no code other than the server control tag.

> **NOTE**
>
> To learn more about using XML in ASP.NET, read *XML for ASP.NET Developers* by Dan Wahlin, Sams Publishing, ISBN 0-672-32039-8.

Xml Server Control

The Xml server control can be used to display either raw XML output or XML data with an XSL/T stylesheet. All in all, this is a rather simple server control with only a few properties. Table 12.1 shows the properties of the Xml server control.

TABLE 12.1 Xml Server Control Properties

Property	Get or Set	Description
DocumentSource	Get/Set	Gets or sets the path to the XML file to display.
TransformSource	Get/Set	Gets or sets the path to the XSL/T stylesheet to use.
Document	Get/Set	Gets or sets the XmlDocument to display.
Transform	Get/Set	Gets or sets the XslTransform to display.

To display an XML file in the browser using the Xml server control, you obviously need an XML file. Listing 12.1 shows the products.xml file, which is made up of 10 products from the Northwind database.

> **NOTE**
>
> The products.xml file can be downloaded from the companion Web site (www.samspublishing.com).

LISTING 12.1   Products.xml

```
01: <?xml version="1.0"?>
02: <NorthwindInfo>
03:  <Products>
04:   <ProductID>1</ProductID>
05:   <ProductName>Chai</ProductName>
06:   <SupplierID>1</SupplierID>
07:   <CategoryID>1</CategoryID>
08:   <QuantityPerUnit>10 boxes x 20 bags</QuantityPerUnit>
09:   <UnitPrice>18</UnitPrice>
10:   <UnitsInStock>39</UnitsInStock>
11:   <UnitsOnOrder>0</UnitsOnOrder>
12:   <ReorderLevel>10</ReorderLevel>
13:   <Discontinued>false</Discontinued>
14:  </Products>
15:  <Products>
16:   <ProductID>2</ProductID>
17:   <ProductName>Chang</ProductName>
18:   <SupplierID>1</SupplierID>
19:   <CategoryID>1</CategoryID>
20:   <QuantityPerUnit>24 - 12 oz bottles</QuantityPerUnit>
21:   <UnitPrice>19</UnitPrice>
22:   <UnitsInStock>17</UnitsInStock>
23:   <UnitsOnOrder>40</UnitsOnOrder>
24:   <ReorderLevel>25</ReorderLevel>
25:   <Discontinued>false</Discontinued>
26:  </Products>
27:  <Products>
28:   <ProductID>3</ProductID>
29:   <ProductName>Aniseed Syrup</ProductName>
30:   <SupplierID>1</SupplierID>
31:   <CategoryID>2</CategoryID>
32:   <QuantityPerUnit>12 - 550 ml bottles</QuantityPerUnit>
33:   <UnitPrice>10</UnitPrice>
34:   <UnitsInStock>13</UnitsInStock>
35:   <UnitsOnOrder>70</UnitsOnOrder>
36:   <ReorderLevel>25</ReorderLevel>
37:   <Discontinued>false</Discontinued>
38:  </Products>
39:  <Products>
40:   <ProductID>4</ProductID>
41:   <ProductName>Chef Anton's Cajun Seasoning</ProductName>
42:   <SupplierID>2</SupplierID>
43:   <CategoryID>2</CategoryID>
44:   <QuantityPerUnit>48 - 6 oz jars</QuantityPerUnit>
```

LISTING 12.1   Continued

```
45:     <UnitPrice>22</UnitPrice>
46:     <UnitsInStock>53</UnitsInStock>
47:     <UnitsOnOrder>0</UnitsOnOrder>
48:     <ReorderLevel>0</ReorderLevel>
49:     <Discontinued>false</Discontinued>
50:   </Products>
51:   <Products>
52:     <ProductID>5</ProductID>
53:     <ProductName>Chef Anton's Gumbo Mix</ProductName>
54:     <SupplierID>2</SupplierID>
55:     <CategoryID>2</CategoryID>
56:     <QuantityPerUnit>36 boxes</QuantityPerUnit>
57:     <UnitPrice>21.35</UnitPrice>
58:     <UnitsInStock>0</UnitsInStock>
59:     <UnitsOnOrder>0</UnitsOnOrder>
60:     <ReorderLevel>0</ReorderLevel>
61:     <Discontinued>true</Discontinued>
62:   </Products>
63:   <Products>
64:     <ProductID>6</ProductID>
65:     <ProductName>Grandma's Boysenberry Spread</ProductName>
66:     <SupplierID>3</SupplierID>
67:     <CategoryID>2</CategoryID>
68:     <QuantityPerUnit>12 - 8 oz jars</QuantityPerUnit>
69:     <UnitPrice>25</UnitPrice>
70:     <UnitsInStock>120</UnitsInStock>
71:     <UnitsOnOrder>0</UnitsOnOrder>
72:     <ReorderLevel>25</ReorderLevel>
73:     <Discontinued>false</Discontinued>
74:   </Products>
75:   <Products>
76:     <ProductID>7</ProductID>
77:     <ProductName>Uncle Bob's Organic Dried Pears</ProductName>
78:     <SupplierID>3</SupplierID>
79:     <CategoryID>7</CategoryID>
80:     <QuantityPerUnit>12 - 1 lb pkgs.</QuantityPerUnit>
81:     <UnitPrice>30</UnitPrice>
82:     <UnitsInStock>15</UnitsInStock>
83:     <UnitsOnOrder>0</UnitsOnOrder>
84:     <ReorderLevel>10</ReorderLevel>
85:     <Discontinued>false</Discontinued>
86:   </Products>
87:   <Products>
88:     <ProductID>8</ProductID>
```

LISTING 12.1 Continued

```
89:     <ProductName>Northwoods Cranberry Sauce</ProductName>
90:     <SupplierID>3</SupplierID>
91:     <CategoryID>2</CategoryID>
92:     <QuantityPerUnit>12 - 12 oz jars</QuantityPerUnit>
93:     <UnitPrice>40</UnitPrice>
94:     <UnitsInStock>6</UnitsInStock>
95:     <UnitsOnOrder>0</UnitsOnOrder>
96:     <ReorderLevel>0</ReorderLevel>
97:     <Discontinued>false</Discontinued>
98:   </Products>
99:   <Products>
100:    <ProductID>9</ProductID>
101:    <ProductName>Mishi Kobe Niku</ProductName>
102:    <SupplierID>4</SupplierID>
103:    <CategoryID>6</CategoryID>
104:    <QuantityPerUnit>18 - 500 g pkgs.</QuantityPerUnit>
105:    <UnitPrice>97</UnitPrice>
106:    <UnitsInStock>29</UnitsInStock>
107:    <UnitsOnOrder>0</UnitsOnOrder>
108:    <ReorderLevel>0</ReorderLevel>
109:    <Discontinued>true</Discontinued>
110:   </Products>
111:   <Products>
112:    <ProductID>10</ProductID>
113:    <ProductName>Ikura</ProductName>
114:    <SupplierID>4</SupplierID>
115:    <CategoryID>8</CategoryID>
116:    <QuantityPerUnit>12 - 200 ml jars</QuantityPerUnit>
117:    <UnitPrice>31</UnitPrice>
118:    <UnitsInStock>31</UnitsInStock>
119:    <UnitsOnOrder>0</UnitsOnOrder>
120:    <ReorderLevel>0</ReorderLevel>
121:    <Discontinued>false</Discontinued>
122:   </Products>
123: </NorthwindInfo>
```

The Xml server control can be used to display raw XML data very easily. Simply placing the Xml server control in a Web Form, and setting a value for the DocumentSource property will suffice. This is seen in Listing 12.2.

12

> **WARNING**
>
> Netscape Navigator 4.x and prior do not have the ability to render raw XML files. The example in Listing 12.2 will not work in older Netscape browsers.

LISTING 12.2   Using the Xml Server Control to Display an XML File

[VB & C#]

```
01: <%@ Page ContentType="text/xml" %>
02: <asp:xml id="myxml" runat="server" DocumentSource="products.xml" />
```

Notice in Listing 12.2 that you set the @ Page directive's ContentType attribute to text/xml. This ensures the browser will read and display the XML data correctly. On line 2 of Listing 12.2, you use the Xml server control, and set the DocumentSource property to the products.xml file from Listing 12.1. (This example assumes both this Web Form and the products.xml file are in the same directory.) The browser display is seen in Figure 12.1.

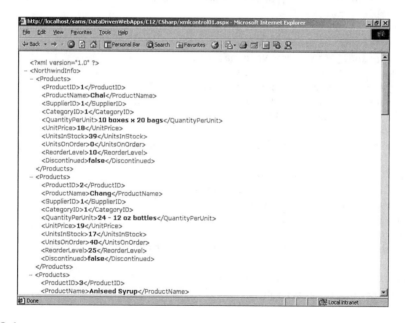

FIGURE 12.1

The Xml *server control can be used to display raw XML data in the browser.*

Although interesting, the capability to render XML data in the browser is not new. After all, pointing a browser to the actual XML file would achieve the same result. What would be more interesting and useful would be to easily apply an XSL/T transform on the XML data, and render the data in a viewer-friendly format.

The Xml server control makes this simple. The TransformSource property allows you to specify the path to an .xsl stylesheet that will be applied to the XML data. Listing 12.3 shows the NorthwindInfo.xsl stylesheet.

> **NOTE**
>
> The NorthwindInfo.xsl file can be downloaded from the companion Web site (www.samspublishing.com).

LISTING 12.3   NorthwindInfo.xsl

```
01: <xsl:stylesheet version='1.0'
02: xmlns:xsl='http://www.w3.org/1999/XSL/Transform'>
03: <xsl:template match="/">
04:   <style>
05:   .title { font: bold 10pt Verdana, Arial; color: black;}
06:   .description { font: 8pt Verdana, Arial;}
07:   .header { font: bold 9pt Verdana, Arial;
      background-color:tan; color: black;}
08:   .subheader { font: bold 8pt Arial; color: black;}
09:   .value { font: 8pt Arial;}
10:   </style>
11:   <table border="0" cellspacing="0" cellpadding="4">
12:   <tr>
13:    <th class="header">ID</th>
14:    <th class="header">Product Name</th>
15:    <th class="header">Qty/Unit</th>
16:    <th class="header">Unit Price</th>
17:   </tr>
18:   <xsl:for-each select='NorthwindInfo/Products'>
19:    <tr>
20:    <td class="value" nowrap="true" align="center">
21:     <xsl:value-of select='ProductID'/></td>
```

LISTING 12.3   Continued

```
22:    <td class="value" nowrap="true">
23:     <xsl:value-of select='ProductName'/></td>
24:    <td class="value" nowrap="true">
25:     <xsl:value-of select='QuantityPerUnit'/></td>
26:    <td class="value" nowrap="true" align="right">
27:     $<xsl:value-of select='UnitPrice'/></td>
28:    </tr>
29:   </xsl:for-each>
30:   </table>
31:  </xsl:template>
32:  </xsl:stylesheet>
```

The XSL stylesheet shown in Listing 12.3 uses the `xsl:for-each` function to loop through the XML data and apply the defined HTML styles to the output. Listing 12.4 shows the revised Web Form from Listing 12.2. Listing 12.4 uses the `Xml` server control with the `TransformSource` property to apply the XSL/T stylesheet to the `products.xml` data.

LISTING 12.4   Using the `Xml` Server Control with an XSL/T File

```
[VB & C#]

01: <html>
02: <body>
03: <asp:xml id="myxml" runat="server" DocumentSource="products.xml"
04:    TransformSource="NorthwindInfo.xsl" />
05: </body>
06: </html>
```

In Listing 12.4, you add the `TransformSource` property to the `Xml` server control, and specify the XSL/T stylesheet to apply to the XML data. This example assumes that the XSL/T stylesheet, the XML file, and the Web Form are all in the same directory. Figure 12.2 shows the rendered output from Listing 12.4.

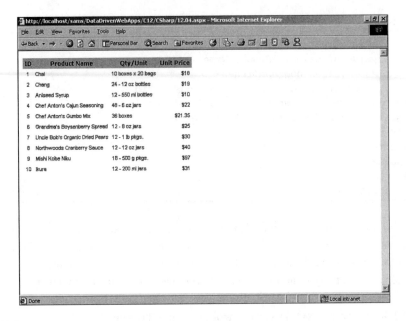

The Xml *server control can be used to easily apply an XSL/T stylesheet to XML data.*

XmlDocument and XslTransform

In the same manner that you can point the DocumentSource and TransformSource properties of the Xml server control to XML and XSL/T files on your file system and render them in the browser, you can use the Document and Transform properties of the Xml server control to render XmlDocument and XslTransform classes in the browser. There are many reasons why you might need to do this, such as rendering dynamically generated, nonpersistent XML data (that is, XML data not persisted to the file system), or even rendering the results of a call to a Web service (see Chapter 14, "Exposing Data Through a Web Service," for more information on building and consuming Web services).

As I take you through the following examples, you will learn how to use the XmlDocument and XslTransform classes with the Xml server control. For simplicity in showing how this works, I will be using XML and XSL/T files persisted on the file system. You certainly are not limited to this use, but it will demonstrate how these properties work.

Listing 12.5 shows the users.xml file. This is a simple XML file representing usernames and passwords for an application.

NOTE

The users.xml file can be downloaded from the companion Web site (www.samspublishing.com).

LISTING 12.5   The users.xml File

```
01: <?xml version="1.0" standalone="yes"?>
02: <Users>
03: <User>
04:  <Name>Doug Seven</Name>
05:  <Email>doug.seven@dotnetjunkies.com</Email>
06:  <Password>thisisafakepassword</Password>
07: </User>
08: <User>
09:  <Name>Donny Mack</Name>
10:  <Email>donny.mack@dotnetjunkies.com</Email>
11:  <Password>soisthis</Password>
12: </User>
13: <User>
14:  <Name>Eric Neff</Name>
15:  <Email>eric.neff@codejunkies.net</Email>
16:  <Password>thisonetoo</Password>
17: </User>
18: <User>
19:  <Name>Lance Hayes</Name>
20:  <Email>lance.hayes@codejunkies.net</Email>
21:  <Password>thisoneisreal</Password>
22: </User>
23: </Users>
```

Along with the users.xml file, I have a users.xsl stylesheet, as seen in Listing 12.6.

NOTE

The users.xsl file can be downloaded from the companion Web site (www.samspublishing.com).

LISTING 12.6   The users.xsl Stylesheet

```
01: <xsl:stylesheet version='1.0'
02: xmlns:xsl='http://www.w3.org/1999/XSL/Transform'>
03: <xsl:template match="/">
04:  <table border="0" cellspacing="0" cellpadding="4">
05:  <tr>
06:   <th class="header">Name</th>
07:   <th class="header">E-Mail</th>
08:   <th class="header">Password</th>
09:  </tr>
10:  <xsl:for-each select='Users/User'>
11:   <tr>
12:   <td class="value" nowrap="true"><xsl:value-of select='Name'/></td>
13:   <td class="value" nowrap="true"><xsl:value-of select='Email'/></td>
14:   <td class="value" nowrap="true"><xsl:value-of select='Password'/></td>
15:   </tr>
16:  </xsl:for-each>
17:  </table>
18: </xsl:template>
19: </xsl:stylesheet>
```

The XmlDocument and XslTransform classes represent XML and XSL data. Among their properties and methods, each of these classes exposes a Load() method, which can be used to load an XML or an XSL/T file, respectively, persisted on the file system, or persisted on another system. This can occur, provided that the XML or XSL/T file is accessible via a URL. To load the XML and XSL/T files into instances of the XmlDocument and XslTransform classes, you can use the Server.MapPath() method. Listing 12.7 shows a Web Form that uses the XmlDocument and XslTransform classes to load the users.xml and users.xsl files, and render the XML data using the Xml server control.

NOTE

> The XmlDocument class is part of the System.Xml namespace, whereas the XslTransform class is part of the System.Xml.Xsl namespace.

LISTING 12.7   Using the XmlDocument and XslTransform Classes to Load Data into the Xml
                Server Control

```
[VB]

01: <%@ Import Namespace="System.Xml" %>
02: <%@ Import Namespace="System.Xml.Xsl" %>
03: <script language="VB" runat=server>
```

LISTING 12.7 Continued

```
04: Protected Sub Page_Load(Sender As Object, E As EventArgs)
05:  Dim xmlDoc As XmlDocument = New XmlDocument()
06:  xmlDoc.Load(Server.MapPath("users.xml"))
07:  myXml.Document = xmlDoc
08:
09:  Dim xslTrans As XslTransform = New XslTransform()
10:  xslTrans.Load(Server.MapPath("users.xsl"))
11:  myXml.Transform = xxslTrans
12: End Sub
13: </script>

[C#]

01: <%@ Import Namespace="System.Xml" %>
02: <%@ Import Namespace="System.Xml.Xsl" %>
03: <script language="C#" runat=server>
04: protected void Page_Load(Object sender, EventArgs e){
05:  XmlDocument xmlDoc = new XmlDocument();
06:  xmlDoc.Load(Server.MapPath("users.xml"));
07:  myXml.Document = xmlDoc;
08:
09:  XslTransform xslTrans = new XslTransform();
10:  xslTrans.Load(Server.MapPath("users.xsl"));
11:  myXml.Transform = xslTrans;
12: }
13: </script>

[VB & C#]

14: <html>
15: <head>
16: <title>Programming Datadriven Web Apps - Chapter 12</title>
17: <style rel="stylesheet" type="text/css">
18:  H3 { font: bold 11pt Verdana, Arial, sans-serif;}
19:  .label { font: bold 9pt Verdana, Arial, sans-serif;}
20:  .header { font: bold 9pt Verdana, Arial, sans-serif;
➥   background-color:tan; color: black;}
21:  .value { font: 8pt Verdana, Arial, sans-serif;}
22: </style>
23: </head>
24: <body>
25: <form runat="server">
26: <H3>Current Users</H3>
27: <asp:xml id="myXml" runat="server" />
28: </form>
29: </body>
30: </html>
```

In Listing 12.7, you create a Web Form that uses the XmlDocument and XslTransform classes to load the users.xml and users.xsl files and render the XML data using the Xml server control. On lines 1 and 2, you import the necessary namespaces to use the XmlDocument and XslTransform classes. You load the XML and XSL/T files the same way for each class. On line 5, you create a new instance of the XmlDocument class, and on line 6 you use the Load() method with Server.MapPath() to load the users.xml file into the class. On line 7, you set the Xml server control's Document property to the instance of the XmlDocument class into which you loaded the XML data (xmlDoc).

The same process is used for the XslTransform class, but you load the users.xsl file, and set it to the Xml server control's Transform property. Figure 12.3 shows the rendered page from Listing 12.7.

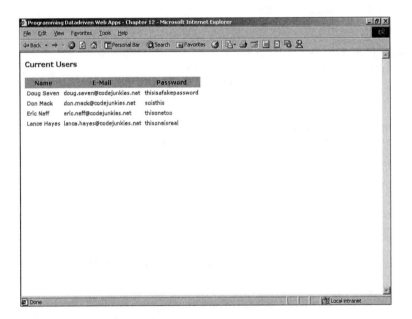

FIGURE 12.3

The Xml *server control exposes* Document *and* Transform *properties for use with the* XmlDocument *and* XslTransform *classes.*

XmlDataDocument

The XmlDataDocument class can be used to convert data in a DataSet to XML for display using the Xml server control. The XmlDataDocument class derives from the XmlDocument class, and is synchronized with the DataSet class. The XmlDataDocument constructor has an overloaded option that accepts a DataSet as a single argument. When the XmlDataDocument class is constructed with a populated `DataSet`, each row in each `DataTable` in the `DataSet` becomes an element in the `XmlDocument`, and the fields of each row become child elements. Listing 12.8 shows how to fill a `DataSet` with products from the Northwind database, and display the results using the `Xml` server control.

> **WARNING**
>
> Netscape Navigator 4.x and prior do not have the ability to render raw XML files. The example in Listing 12.8 will not work in older Netscape browsers.

LISTING 12.8 Displaying Database Query Results with the `Xml` Server Control and the `XmlDataDocument` Class

`[VB]`

```
01: <%@ Page ContentType="text/xml" %>
02: <%@ Import Namespace="System.Data" %>
03: <%@ Import Namespace="System.Data.SqlClient" %>
04: <%@ Import Namespace="System.Xml" %>
05: <script language="VB" runat=server>
06: Sub Page_Load(Sender as Object, E as EventArgs)
07:   Dim myDataSet As New DataSet()
08:   Dim myDataAdapter as New
➥ SqlDataAdapter("SELECT TOP 10 * FROM Products",
➥ "server=localhost;database=Northwind;uid=sa;pwd=;")
09:   myDataAdapter.Fill(myDataSet, "Products")
10:   myDataSet.DataSetName = "ProductList"
11:   Dim xmlDoc as XmlDataDocument = New XmlDataDocument(myDataSet)
12:   myXml.Document = xmlDoc
13: End Sub
14: </script>
```

`[C#]`

```
01: <%@ Page ContentType="text/xml" %>
02: <%@ Import Namespace="System.Data" %>
03: <%@ Import Namespace="System.Data.SqlClient" %>
04: <%@ Import Namespace="System.Xml" %>
05: <script language="C#" runat=server>
06: protected void Page_Load(Object sender, EventArgs e){
07:   DataSet myDataSet = new DataSet();
08:   myDataSet.DataSetName = "NorthwindInfo";
09:   SqlDataAdapter myDataAdapter = new
➥ SqlDataAdapter("SELECT TOP 10 * FROM Products",
➥ "server=localhost;database=Northwind;uid=sa;pwd=;");
```

12

XML AND SOAP

LISTING 12.8   Continued

```
10:  myDataAdapter.Fill(myDataSet, "Products");
11:  XmlDataDocument xmlDoc = new XmlDataDocument(myDataSet);
12:  myXml.Document = xmlDoc;
13: }
14: </script>

[VB & C#]

15: <asp:xml id="myXml" runat="server" />
```

In Listing 12.8, you query the Northwind database for the first 10 products in the Products table using the Sql Managed Provider. After filling the DataSet, you create a new XmlData Document. On line 11, you use the overloaded constructor to create the XmlDataDocument based on the DataSet. This creates an XML document similar (if not identical) to the XML document in Listing 12.1. On line 12, you use the Xml server control's Document property to apply the XmlDataDocument to the Xml server control. The rendered output from Listing 12.8 is shown in Figure 12.4.

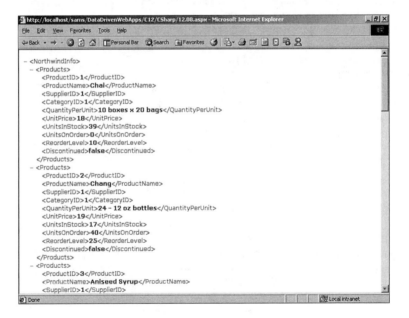

FIGURE 12.4

The XmlDataDocument *class has an overloaded constructor to create an instance of the class based on a populated* DataSet.

Because a DataSet can hold multiple DataTables, the XmlDataDocument can be created with multiple element types. For example, if you were to fill the DataSet with the Products data in Listing 12.8, and then fill a new DataTable in the same DataSet with data from the Customers table, you could create an XmlDataDocument that had both Products and Customers elements. If you tie that together with an XSL/T stylesheet, you can do some interesting things. Listing 12.9 shows a revised version of the NorthwindInfo.xsl stylesheet, named NorthwindInfo2.xsl.

> **NOTE**
>
> The NorthwindInfo2.xsl file can be downloaded from the companion Web site (www.samspublishing.com).

LISTING 12.9   The Revised NorthwindInfo.xsl Stylesheet

```
01: <xsl:stylesheet version='1.0'
02: xmlns:xsl='http://www.w3.org/1999/XSL/Transform'>
03: <xsl:template match="/">
04:  <style>
05:  .title { font: bold 10pt Verdana, Arial; color: black;}
06:  .description { font: 8pt Verdana, Arial;}
07:  .header { font: bold 9pt Verdana, Arial;
     background-color:tan; color: black;}
08:  .subheader { font: bold 8pt Arial; color: black;}
09:  .value { font: 8pt Arial;}
10:  </style>
11:  <table border="0" cellspacing="0" cellpadding="4">
12:  <tr>
13:   <th class="header">ID</th>
14:   <th class="header">Product Name</th>
15:   <th class="header">Qty/Unit</th>
16:   <th class="header">Unit Price</th>
17:  </tr>
18:  <xsl:for-each select='NorthwindInfo/Products'>
19:   <tr>
20:   <td class="value" nowrap="true" align="center">
21:    <xsl:value-of select='ProductID'/></td>
22:   <td class="value" nowrap="true">
23:    <xsl:value-of select='ProductName'/></td>
24:   <td class="value" nowrap="true">
25:    <xsl:value-of select='QuantityPerUnit'/></td>
26:   <td class="value" nowrap="true" align="right">
27:    $<xsl:value-of select='UnitPrice'/></td>
28:   </tr>
```

LISTING 12.9   Continued

```
29:  </xsl:for-each>
30:  </table>
31:  <table border="0" cellspacing="0" cellpadding="4">
32:  <tr>
33:   <th class="header">Customer ID</th>
34:   <th class="header">Company Name</th>
35:   <th class="header">Contact Name</th>
36:   <th class="header">Phone</th>
37:   <th class="header">Fax</th>
38:  </tr>
39:  <xsl:for-each select='NorthwindInfo/Customers'>
40:   <tr>
41:   <td class="value" nowrap="true" align="center">
42:    <xsl:value-of select='CustomerID'/></td>
43:   <td class="value" nowrap="true">
44:    <xsl:value-of select='CompanyName'/></td>
45:   <td class="value" nowrap="true">
46:    <xsl:value-of select='ContactName'/></td>
47:   <td class="value" nowrap="true">
48:    <xsl:value-of select='Phone'/></td>
49:   <td class="value" nowrap="true">
50:    <xsl:value-of select='Fax'/></td>
51:   </tr>
52:  </xsl:for-each>
53:  </table>
54: </xsl:template>
55: </xsl:stylesheet>
```

The `NorthwindInfo2.xsl` file has two `xsl:for-each` functions to control the style of two different elements, `Products` and `Customers`. Listing 12.10 shows the code for a Web Form that queries the Northwind database and fills a `DataSet` with two `DataTables`, `Products` and `Customers`. The `DataSet` then is passed into the overloaded `XmlDataDocument` constructor, before being assigned to the `Xml` server control. The `NorthwindInfo2.xsl` stylesheet is loaded into the `XslTransform` class and applied to the same `Xml` server control.

LISTING 12.10   Creating an `XmlDataDocument` with a `DataSet` That Has More Than One `DataTable`

```
[VB]

01: <%@ Import Namespace="System.Data" %>
02: <%@ Import Namespace="System.Data.SqlClient" %>
03: <%@ Import Namespace="System.Xml" %>
04: <%@ Import Namespace="System.Xml.Xsl" %>
```

LISTING 12.10   Continued

```
05: <script language="VB" runat="server">
06: Sub Page_Load(Sender as Object, E as EventArgs)
07:   Dim myDataSet As New DataSet()
08:   myDataSet.DataSetName = "NorthwindInfo"
09:   Dim myDataAdapter as New
➥   SqlDataAdapter("SELECT TOP 10 * FROM Products",
➥   "server=localhost;database=Northwind;uid=sa;pwd=;")
10:   myDataAdapter.Fill(myDataSet, "Products")
11:   myDataAdapter.SelectCommand.CommandText =
➥   "SELECT TOP 10 * FROM Customers"
12:   myDataAdapter.Fill(myDataSet, "Customers")
13:   Dim XmlDoc as XmlDataDocument = New XmlDataDocument(myDataSet)
14:   Dim xslTrans As XslTransform = New XslTransform()
15:   xslTrans.Load(Server.MapPath("NorthwindInfo2.xsl"))
16:   myXml.Document = xmlDoc
17:   myXml.Transform = xslTrans
18: End Sub
19: </script>

[C#]

01: <%@ Import Namespace="System.Data" %>
02: <%@ Import Namespace="System.Data.SqlClient" %>
03: <%@ Import Namespace="System.Xml" %>
04: <%@ Import Namespace="System.Xml.Xsl" %>
05: <script language="C#" runat=server>
06: protected void Page_Load(Object sender, EventArgs e){
07:   DataSet myDataSet = new DataSet();
08:   myDataSet.DataSetName = "NorthwindInfo";
09:   SqlDataAdapter myDataAdapter = new
➥   SqlDataAdapter("SELECT TOP 10 * FROM Products",
➥   "server=localhost;database=Northwind;uid=sa;pwd=;");
10:   myDataAdapter.Fill(myDataSet, "Products");
11:   myDataAdapter.SelectCommand.CommandText =
➥   "SELECT TOP 10 * FROM Customers";
12:   myDataAdapter.Fill(myDataSet, "Customers");
13:   XmlDataDocument xmlDoc = new XmlDataDocument(myDataSet);
14:   XslTransform xslTrans = new XslTransform();
15:   xslTrans.Load(Server.MapPath("NorthwindInfo2.xsl"));
16:   myXml.Document = xmlDoc;
17:   myXml.Transform = xslTrans;
18: }
19: </script>

[VB & C#]

20: <html>
21: <body>
```

LISTING 12.10 Continued

```
22: <form runat="server">
23: <asp:xml id="myXml" runat="server" />
24: </form>
25: </body>
26: </html>
```

In Listing 12.10, you create a Web Form that uses the Sql Managed Provider to run two queries on the Northwind database and fill the data into two DataTables in a DataSet. On line 13 you create a new XmlDataDocument by passing the DataSet into the constructor. This creates an XML document with an element for each row in each DataTable. On lines 14 and 15, you create a new XslTransform object and load it with the NorthwindInfo2.xsl stylesheet. On lines 16 and 17, you set the Xml server control's Document and Transform properties to the XmlDataDocument and the XslTransform objects, respectively.

The XslTransform will apply the XSL/T stylesheet to the XML data. Because the XSL/T stylesheet has xsl:for-each loops for both the Products and Customers elements, two tables will be rendered to the page, one table of products, and one of customers. The rendered output from Listing 12.10 is seen in Figure 12.5.

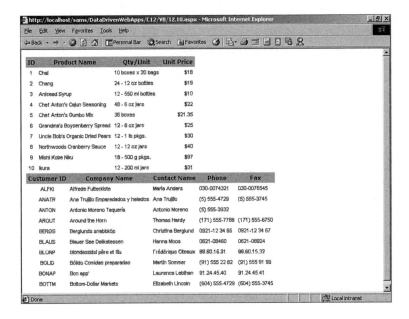

FIGURE 12.5

The XmlDataDocument class can be constructed from a DataSet with multiple DataTables. Using an XSL/T stylesheet, you can control the look of the output.

Working with XML Elements

Often it is necessary to do more than simply read and/or display XML data; often you want to add data to an XML document. The XmlElement class is used to create new elements that can be appended to an existing XmlDocument object. Much like creating new DataRows in a DataTable, XmlElements are created by setting an instance of the XmlElement class to the result of calling XmlDocument.CreateElement(*[element name]*). For example, it would be very useful to add new users to the users.xml document in the previous examples. Effectively, you could create a Web Form for adding new users to your application by accepting the user information in a form and creating a new <User> element in the users.xml document.

Creating an instance of the XmlNode class that represents the root element of the XML document is the first step in adding new elements to an XmlDocument. You then create a new XmlElement for each element that you are adding by calling XmlDocument.CreateElement(). After the XmlElements have been created, and their values set, you append the elements to the XmlDocument by calling XmlNode.AppendChild(XmlElement), where XmlNode is an instance of the XmlDocument's root element. Listing 12.11 shows how to do this.

LISTING 12.11   Adding Elements to the XmlDocument Class

```VB
[VB]
01: <%@ Import Namespace="System.Xml" %>
02: <script language="VB" runat=server>
03: Protected Sub Page_Load(Sender As Object, E As EventArgs)
04:   If Not IsPostBack Then
05:     Dim xmlDoc As XmlDocument = New XmlDocument()
06:     xmlDoc.Load(Server.MapPath("users.xml"))
07:     myXml.Document = xmlDoc
08:   End If
09: End Sub
10:
11: Protected Sub Submit_Click(Sender As Object, E As EventArgs)
12:   Dim xmlDoc As XmlDocument = New XmlDocument()
13:   xmlDoc.Load(Server.MapPath("users.xml"))
14:
15:   Dim xmlRoot As XmlNode = xmlDoc.DocumentElement
16:
17:   Dim xmlUser As XmlElement = xmlDoc.CreateElement("User")
18:   Dim xmlName As XmlElement = xmlDoc.CreateElement("Name")
19:   Dim xmlEmail As XmlElement = xmlDoc.CreateElement("Email")
20:   Dim xmlPassword As XmlElement = xmlDoc.CreateElement("Password")
21:
22:   xmlName.InnerXml = Name.Text
23:   xmlEmail.InnerXml = Email.Text
```

12

XML AND SOAP

LISTING 12.11   Continued

```
24:   xmlPassword.InnerXml = Password.Text
25:
26:   xmlUser.AppendChild(xmlName)
27:   xmlUser.AppendChild(xmlEmail)
28:   xmlUser.AppendChild(xmlPassword)
29:   xmlRoot.AppendChild(xmlUser)
30:
31:   xmlDoc.Save(Server.MapPath("users.xml"))
32:   xmlDoc.Load(Server.MapPath("users.xml"))
33:   myXml.Document = xmlDoc
34: End Sub
35: </script>
```

[C#]

```
01: <%@ Import Namespace="System.Xml" %>
02: <script language="C#" runat=server>
03: protected void Page_Load(Object sender, EventArgs e){
04:   if(!IsPostBack){
05:   XmlDocument xmlDoc = new XmlDocument();
06:   xmlDoc.Load(Server.MapPath("users.xml"));
07:   myXml.Document = xmlDoc;
08:   }
09: }
10:
11: protected void Submit_Click(Object sender, EventArgs e){
12:   XmlDocument xmlDoc = new XmlDocument();
13:   xmlDoc.Load(Server.MapPath("users.xml"));
14:
15:   XmlNode xmlRoot = xmlDoc.DocumentElement;
16:
17:   XmlElement xmlUser = xmlDoc.CreateElement("User");
18:   XmlElement xmlName = xmlDoc.CreateElement("Name");
19:   XmlElement xmlEmail = xmlDoc.CreateElement("Email");
20:   XmlElement xmlPassword = xmlDoc.CreateElement("Password");
21:
22:   xmlName.InnerXml = Name.Text;
23:   xmlEmail.InnerXml = Email.Text;
24:   xmlPassword.InnerXml = Password.Text;
25:
26:   xmlUser.AppendChild(xmlName);
27:   xmlUser.AppendChild(xmlEmail);
28:   xmlUser.AppendChild(xmlPassword);
29:   xmlRoot.AppendChild(xmlUser);
30:
```

LISTING 12.11 Continued

```
31: xmlDoc.Save(Server.MapPath("users.xml"));
32: xmlDoc.Load(Server.MapPath("users.xml"));
33: myXml.Document = xmlDoc;
34: }
35: </script>

[VB & C#]

36: <html>
37: <head>
38: <title>Programming Datadriven Web Apps - Chapter 12</title>
39: <style rel="stylesheet" type="text/css">
40: H3 { font: bold 11pt Verdana, Arial, sans-serif;}
41: .label { font: bold 9pt Verdana, Arial, sans-serif;}
42: .header { font: bold 9pt Verdana, Arial, sans-serif;
➡       background-color:tan; color: black;}
43: .value { font: 8pt Verdana, Arial, sans-serif;}
44: </style>
45: </head>
46: <body>
47: <form runat="server">
48: <H3>Add a New User</H3>
49: <table border="0" cellpadding="2" cellspacing="0">
50: <tr>
51:  <td class="label">Name:</td>
52:  <td>
53:  <asp:TextBox runat="server" id="Name" Width="200"
54:   BorderStyle="Solid" BorderWidth="1"
55:   Font-Size="8pt" Font-Name="Verdana" />
56:  </td>
57: </tr>
58: <tr>
59:  <td class="label">E-Mail:</td>
60:  <td>
61:  <asp:TextBox runat="server" id="Email" Width="200"
62:   BorderStyle="Solid" BorderWidth="1"
63:   Font-Size="8pt" Font-Name="Verdana" />
64:  </td>
65: </tr>
66: <tr>
67:  <td class="label">Password:</td>
68:  <td>
69:  <asp:TextBox runat="server" id="Password" Width="200"
70:   BorderStyle="Solid" BorderWidth="1"
71:   Font-Size="8pt" Font-Name="Verdana" />
```

LISTING 12.11   Continued

```
72:   </td>
73:  </tr>
74:  <tr>
75:   <td></td>
76:   <td>
77:   <asp:Button runat="server" id="Submit" Text="Submit New User"
78:    OnClick="Submit_Click" Width="200"
79:    BorderStyle="Solid" BorderWidth="1"
80:    Font-Size="8pt" Font-Name="Verdana" />
81:   </td>
82:  </tr>
83:  </table>
84:  <H3>Current Users</H3>
85:  <asp:xml id="myXml" runat="server" TransformSource="Users.xsl" />
86:  </form>
87:  </body>
88:  </html>
```

In Listing 12.11, you create a Web Form that has TextBoxes for inputting the user name, e-mail, and password (for sample purposes, the password TextBox does not mask the password when it is entered). Clicking on the Submit New User button fires the Submit_Click() event handler. In the Submit_Click() event handler, you reload the XML document and add the new elements to it.

On line 15, you create an instance of the XmlNode class and set it to the xmlDoc.DocumentElement property. This is the parent, or root element, of the XmlDocument. On lines 17 through 20, you create a new instance of the XmlElement class for each element you are adding. On lines 22 through 24, you set the InnerXml property of each XmlElement to the appropriate values from the TextBoxes. On lines 26 through 28, you append the child elements—<Name>, <Email>, and <Password> to the <User> element. On line 29, you append the <User> element to the XmlNode object, which represents the XmlDocument root element. Basically what you have done is add the following XML element to the XmlDocument object:

```
<User>
 <Name>Willy Wonka</Name>
 <Email>willy.wonka@chocolatefactory.com</Email>
 <Password>goldenticket</Password>
</User>
```

Of course, the primary goal here is to persist the revised XmlDocument to disk. This is done by calling XmlDocument.Save() to write the XmlDocument to the file system. You pass in the path to save to as the only argument. This is done on line 31. Before exiting the Submit_Click()

event handler, you reload the XmlDocument and set it to the Xml server control's Document property. The reloading is only to show you that the XML data was written to the users.xml file. Figure 12.6 shows the rendered Web Form after the Submit New User button has been clicked.

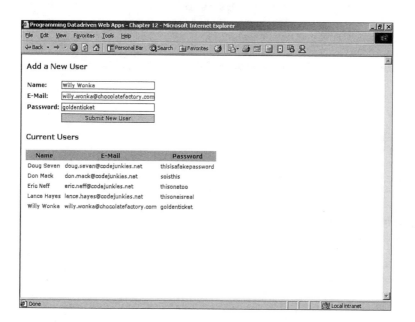

FIGURE 12.6
New elements can be added to an XML document by creating instances of the XmlElement class and appending them to the XmlDocument's root element.

Reading and Writing XML Files with the DataSet

The Xml server control is not your only option for rendering XML data in a browser. You also can read XML documents into a DataSet and bind the DataSet to any available server control, such as the DataGrid. Using the System.IO.StreamReader class, you can stream in XML data and use the DataSet.ReadXml() method to dynamically create a DataTable based on the XML data. Listing 12.12 shows how to do this in a Web Form.

LISTING 12.12 Reading XML Data into a DataSet and Binding It to a DataGrid

```
[VB]

01: <%@ Import Namespace="System.Data" %>
02: <%@ Import Namespace="System.Xml" %>
```

LISTING 12.12 Continued

```
03: <script language="VB" runat=server>
04: Protected Sub Page_Load(Sender As Object, E As EventArgs)
05:  Dim myDataSet As New DataSet
06:  Dim myStreamReader As System.IO.StreamReader =
➥  New System.IO.StreamReader(Server.MapPath("users.xml"))
07:  myDataSet.ReadXml( myStreamReader )
08:  myStreamReader.Close()
09:  myDataGrid.DataSource = myDataSet.Tables(0).DefaultView
10:  Page.DataBind()
11: End Sub
12: </script>

[C#]
01: <%@ Import Namespace="System.Data" %>
02: <%@ Import Namespace="System.Xml" %>
03: <script language="C#" runat=server>
04: protected void Page_Load(Object sender, EventArgs e){
05:  DataSet myDataSet = new DataSet();
06:  System.IO.StreamReader myStreamReader =
➥  new System.IO.StreamReader(Server.MapPath("users.xml"));
07:  myDataSet.ReadXml( myStreamReader );
08:  myStreamReader.Close();
09:  myDataGrid.DataSource = myDataSet.Tables[0].DefaultView;
10:  Page.DataBind();
11: }
12: </script>

[VB & C#]

13: <html>
14: <head>
15: <title>Programming Datadriven Web Apps - Chapter 12</title>
16: <style rel="stylesheet" type="text/css">
17:  H3 { font: bold 11pt Verdana, Arial, sans-serif;}
18:  .label { font: bold 9pt Verdana, Arial, sans-serif;}
19:  .header { font: bold 9pt Verdana, Arial, sans-serif;
➥  background-color:tan; color: black;}
20:  .value { font: 8pt Verdana, Arial, sans-serif;}
21: </style>
22: </head>
23: <body>
24: <form runat="server">
25: <H3>Current Users</H3>
26: <asp:DataGrid id="myDataGrid" runat="server"
27: BorderWidth="0" Cellpadding="2" Cellspacing="0"
28: HeaderStyle-CssClass="header" ItemStyle-CssClass="value" />
```

LISTING 12.12 Continued

```
29: </form>
30: </body>
31: </html>
```

In Listing 12.12, you create a Web Form that streams in XML data from the `users.xml` file. On line 6, you create a `System.IO.StreamReader` using the path to the `users.xml` file. On line 7, you use the `DataSet.ReadXml()` method to read the `StreamReader` into the `DataSet`. This creates a new `DataTable` representing the `users.xml` file. You then simply bind the `DataTable` to a `DataGrid`. Figure 12.7 shows the rendered output from Listing 12.12.

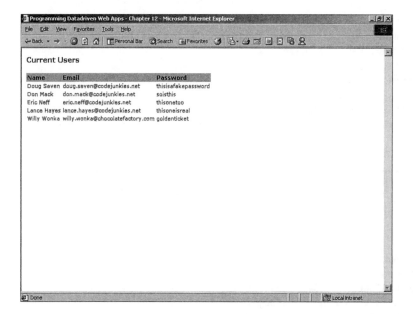

FIGURE 12.7
You can read XML data into a `DataSet` *using a* `StreamReader` *and the* `DataSet.ReadXml()` *method.*

As much as you read and wrote XML data using the `XmlDocument` and `XmlElement` classes in the previous listings, you can use the `DataSet` to read and write XML data. In Listing 12.12, you used the `StreamReader` class to stream in XML data, and the `DataSet.ReadXml()` method to create a `DataTable` from the XML data. In Listing 12.13 you extend this to have a form identical to that in Listing 12.11. In the `Submit_Click()` event handler, you create a new `DataRow` in the `DataTable`, and then use the `DataSet.WriteXml()` method to write the `DataTable` to the file system as an XML document.

LISTING 12.13   Reading and Writing XML Data with the `DataSet`

[VB]

```
01: <%@ Import Namespace="System.Data" %>
02: <%@ Import Namespace="System.Xml" %>
03: <script language="VB" runat=server>
04: Protected Sub Page_Load(Sender As Object, E As EventArgs)
05:   Dim myDataSet As New DataSet
06:   Dim myStreamReader As System.IO.StreamReader =
➥   New System.IO.StreamReader(Server.MapPath("users.xml"))
07:   myDataSet.ReadXml( myStreamReader )
08:   myStreamReader.Close()
09:
10:   If IsPostBack Then
11:   Dim myNewRow As DataRow = myDataSet.Tables(0).NewRow()
12:   myNewRow("Name") = Name.Text
13:   myNewRow("Email") = Email.Text
14:   myNewRow("Password") = Password.Text
15:   myDataSet.Tables(0).Rows.Add(myNewRow)
16:   myDataSet.AcceptChanges()
17:   myDataSet.WriteXml(Server.MapPath("users.xml"), XmlWriteMode.IgnoreSchema)
18:   End If
19:
20:   myDataGrid.DataSource = myDataSet.Tables(0).DefaultView
21:   Page.DataBind()
22: End Sub
23: </script>
```

[C#]

```
01: <%@ Import Namespace="System.Data" %>
02: <%@ Import Namespace="System.Xml" %>
03: <script language="C#" runat=server>
04: protected void Page_Load(Object sender, EventArgs e){
05:   DataSet myDataSet = new DataSet();
06:   System.IO.StreamReader myStreamReader =
➥   new System.IO.StreamReader(Server.MapPath("users.xml"));
07:   myDataSet.ReadXml( myStreamReader );
08:   myStreamReader.Close();
09:
10:   if(IsPostBack){
11:   DataRow myNewRow = myDataSet.Tables[0].NewRow();
12:   myNewRow["Name"] = Name.Text;
13:   myNewRow["Email"] = Email.Text;
14:   myNewRow["Password"] = Password.Text;
15:   myDataSet.Tables[0].Rows.Add(myNewRow);
```

LISTING 12.13   Continued

```
16:   myDataSet.AcceptChanges();
17:   myDataSet.WriteXml(Server.MapPath("users.xml"),
➥     XmlWriteMode.IgnoreSchema);
18:   }
19:
20:   myDataGrid.DataSource = myDataSet.Tables[0].DefaultView;
21:   Page.DataBind();
22:   }
23:   </script>

[VB & C#]

24:   <html>
25:   <head>
26:   <title>Programming Datadriven Web Apps - Chapter 12</title>
27:   <style rel="stylesheet" type="text/css">
28:   H3 { font: bold 11pt Verdana, Arial, sans-serif;}
29:   .label { font: bold 9pt Verdana, Arial, sans-serif;}
30:   .header { font: bold 9pt Verdana, Arial, sans-serif;
➥     background-color:tan; color: black;}
31:   .value { font: 8pt Verdana, Arial, sans-serif;}
32:   </style>
33:   </head>
34:   <body>
35:   <form runat="server">
36:   <H3>Add a New User</H3>
37:   <table border="0" cellpadding="2" cellspacing="0">
38:   <tr>
39:   <td class="label">Name:</td>
40:   <td>
41:   <asp:TextBox runat="server" id="Name" Width="200"
42:    BorderStyle="Solid" BorderWidth="1"
43:    Font-Size="8pt" Font-Name="Verdana" />
44:   </td>
45:   </tr>
46:   <tr>
47:   <td class="label">E-Mail:</td>
48:   <td>
49:   <asp:TextBox runat="server" id="Email" Width="200"
50:    BorderStyle="Solid" BorderWidth="1"
51:    Font-Size="8pt" Font-Name="Verdana" />
52:   </td>
53:   </tr>
54:   <tr>
55:   <td class="label">Password:</td>
```

LISTING 12.13 Continued

```
56:    <td>
57:    <asp:TextBox runat="server" id="Password" Width="200"
58:     BorderStyle="Solid" BorderWidth="1"
59:     Font-Size="8pt" Font-Name="Verdana" />
60:    </td>
61:   </tr>
62:   <tr>
63:    <td></td>
64:    <td>
65:    <asp:Button runat="server" id="Submit" Text="Submit New User"
66:     Width="200" BorderStyle="Solid" BorderWidth="1"
67:     Font-Size="8pt" Font-Name="Verdana" />
68:    </td>
69:   </tr>
70:   </table>
71:   <H3>Current Users</H3>
72:   <asp:DataGrid id="myDataGrid" runat="server"
73:   BorderWidth="0" Cellpadding="2" Cellspacing="0"
74:   HeaderStyle-CssClass="header" ItemStyle-CssClass="value" />
75:   </form>
76:   </body>
77:  </html>
```

In Listing 12.13, you create a Web Form like that in Listing 12.11. The Web Form has TextBoxes for Name, Email, and Password. When the Submit New User button is clicked, the Page.IsPostBack property is set to True, and the If IsPostBack Then... code on line 10 is executed.

On line 11, you create a new DataRow from the DataTable that holds the XML data. On lines 12 through 14, you set the values of the three columns in the DataRow, Name, Email, and Password. On line 15, you add the DataRow to the DataTable by calling DataTable.Rows.Add(DataRow). On line 16, you call DataTable.AcceptChanges() to commit the new DataRow to the DataTable (effectively saying, "Yes, I want this row"). On line 17, you call DataSet.WriteXml() and pass in the path to write the XML as the first parameter, and XmlWriteMode.IgnoreSchema as the second parameter. The XmlWriteMode.IgnoreSchema enumerator tells the .NET Framework not to write the XML schema information to the file. You do this because the XML document did not have the schema information to begin with. If the schema were part of the original XML file, you could write the schema by using the XmlWriteMode.IgnoreSchema enumerator (the default value). Figure 12.8 shows the rendered output from Listing 12.13 after adding a new user. Table 12.2 shows the XmlWriteMode enumerators.

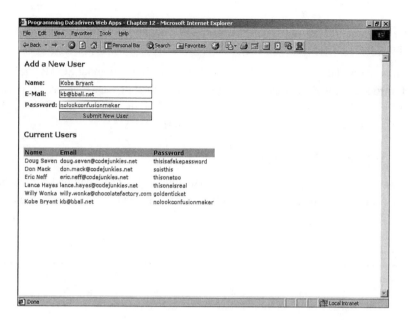

FIGURE 12.8

You can use the DataSet.WriteXml() *method to write a* DataTable *to the file system as an XML document.*

TABLE 12.2   XmlWriteMode Enumerators

Value	*Description*
DiffGram	Writes the entire DataSet as a DiffGram, including current and original values.
IgnoreSchema	Writes the current contents of the DataSet as XML data without an XSD schema. The XSD can be written separately using DataSet.WriteXmlSchema().
WriteSchema	Writes the current contents of the DataSet as XML data with the relational structure as inline XSD schema. This is the default value.

SOAP (Simple Object Access Protocol)

SOAP (Simple Object Access Protocol) was introduced to the world in late 1999. Its purpose was to provide an RPC-like structure for managing distributed objects over the Internet. The original standard called for the use of HTTP as the transport protocol, and XML as the data structure. SOAP is the carrier...the pickup truck for moving objects serialized as XML across the Internet. SOAP is a lightweight, message-based protocol that is built on XML and Internet standards. Every SOAP message is a one-way transmission, but SOAP messages can be combined to implement patterns such as request/response.

Although it is out of the scope of this book to go into much detail about SOAP, I felt that a very brief introduction was in order. I am not spending much of your time on this because you do not need to know how to construct and work with SOAP messages when building ASP.NET applications. However, a slight familiarity couldn't hurt.

The Structure of SOAP

A SOAP message is basically a chunk of data that contains an XML payload, which can be simple XML data, or a complex, serialized object. The basic SOAP structure is seen in Listing 12.14.

LISTING 12.14   Basic SOAP Structure

```
01: <soap:Envelope
02: xmlns:xsi="http://www.w3.org/2000/10/XMLSchema-instance"
03: xmlns:xsd="http://www.w3.org/2000/10/XMLSchema"
04: xmlns:soap="http://schemas.xmlsoap.org/soap/envelope">
05:   <soap:Body>
06:   <User xmlns:m="User-Uri/">
07:     <Name>Willy Wonka</Name>
08:     <Email>willy.wonka@chocolatefactory.com</Email>
09:   </User>
10:   </soap:Body>
11: </soap:Envelope>
```

Every SOAP message is an Envelope, containing an optional Header (SOAP-ENV:Header) and a required Body (SOAP-ENV:Body). The Header can carry specific data, such as a username and password for authentication when making a SOAP method call.

When looking at the SOAP structure in Listing 12.14, you can see why SOAP can be useful in Internet-based, distributed applications. The SOAP message is XML-based text, which can be read by any system that can parse XML. The payload, the XML data in the Body, can be raw data, or a representation of an object, such as a representation of a User object that exposes Name and Email properties.

SOAP Abstraction in .NET

The .NET Framework does a great job of abstracting SOAP functionality. In Chapter 14, you will learn about Web services, and how to consume Web services using SOAP messages in a request/response format. You will see how to transfer raw data and serialized objects from a provider to a consumer via SOAP. Because of the .NET Framework's abstraction of SOAP functionality, you will never need to build your own SOAP message; the .NET Framework will assemble the SOAP messages for distributing the data and objects between the provider and consumer.

> **NOTE**
>
> For a great book on SOAP, read *Understanding SOAP* by Kennard Scribner and Mark C. Stiver, Sams Publishing, ISBN 0-672-31922-5.

Summary

XML has emerged as a technology to be reckoned with. Its wide acceptance has proven that XML is here to stay…at least for a while. ASP.NET and ADO.NET rely heavily on XML under the covers. Data that is moved around with the ADO.NET Managed Providers is persisted and transmitted as XML. Although all of this happens without any interaction by you, the System.Xml namespace provides a set of classes that enables easy integration of XML into your ASP.NET applications.

The `XmlDocument` and `XmlDataDocument` classes make reading and working with XML data simple. You easily can read and write XML data to the file system, or use the Xml server control to display the XML data in the browser. Add the `XslTransform` class into the mix, and you easily can format the data into a user-friendly display.

In this chapter, you learned how to use the Xml server control to display XML data in the browser. As you progressed through the chapter, you learned how to use the `XmlDocument` class and the `XmlElement` class to manipulate XML data. You also learned how to use the `XmlData Document` to pull XML data into a `DataSet` and bind it to a data server control, like the `DataGrid`.

In addition, you also read a brief introduction to SOAP. This was more for conceptual purposes as the .NET Framework abstracts the use of SOAP away from you. In Chapter 14, you will learn how to use SOAP and XML to exchange data between systems with Web services.

In this chapter you learned about:

- `Xml` server control
- `XmlDocument` and `XmlDataDocument`
- Working with XML elements
- Reading and writing XML files with the `DataSet`
- SOAP (Simple Object Access Protocol)

BLOB Uploading and Displaying

IN THIS CHAPTER

This chapter is dedicated to the saving and displaying of database-stored binary files known as BLOBs (Binary Large Objects) in your ASP.NET Web applications. I will be discussing how to easily enable file uploading using ASP.NET and how to manipulate the file attributes after it has been uploaded to the server. Then I will discuss how to save an uploaded image directly into your database without ever saving the image to hard disk. Finally, I will demonstrate an easy way to display images derived from a database in your Web application. I will be going over the following in this chapter:

- Using the `HtmlInputFile` class to upload files to gain programmatic access to the uploaded file
- Using the `HttpPostedFile` class to manipulate and extract information from the uploaded file
- Saving uploaded images to your database
- Displaying images derived from a database

Saving BLOBS in a database has advantages and disadvantages and you have to weigh both when designing your web application. The following two lists contains some pros and cons of saving Binary Large Object Bitmaps in your database:

PROS:

- All information is stored in one place. For example, if you have a member table which contains a memberid, membername, address, and a picture of the member. If the user cancelled their membership it would be easier to delete one row from the table than to delete the row and then an image file(s) that could be on an entirely different server.
- Updating information can be made in one centralized location.
- Retrieving information can be done in one centralized location.
- Accidental changes to the file system on your servers where images are located won't break links. For instance, a system administrator inadvertently changes the name of an image directory.

CONS:

- In most cases files will load more quickly from the hard drive.
- Higher memory requirement.
- All pages that contain these images need to be server pages and dynamically generated. Note: Once created they can be cached.
- Bloats database—BLOB fields such as an `Image` is very large.

Just because there are more pros than cons in the preceding lists doesn't mean you should automatically store images in your database. Quite the contrary; it always falls back on the question, "What type of application am I building?" Sometimes using BLOBS makes sense with the architecture of the application you're building and other times it makes no sense at all. The preceding lists are just some things to think about.

Uploading Files Using `HtmlInputFile`

ASP.NET provides an easy way to enable users to upload files to a server using the `HtmlInputFile` class. The `HtmlInputFile` class enables you to have programmatic access to the `INPUT` control of the `FILE` type. For those of you not familiar with what the `File INPUT` control is, see the following example:

```
<input type="file" id="UploadFile">
```

When this control is inserted into your page, you'll receive the following when the page is rendered: a textbox with a button directly to the right of it with the text `Browse` on it.

FIGURE 13.1

Rendered page with `File INPUT` *control inserted.*

Notice in Figure 13.1 that a `Browse` button is rendered along with a `textbox`. This enables the user to browse his local hard drive for a file to upload. Users using older browsers might not receive a button and would have to manually enter the path to the file. Notice I use the `ID` attribute of the Input control. This becomes important when we want programmatic access to the control. In this example I used `UploadFile`.

When using the `HtmlInputFile` control, you must do three things for object posting to work properly. The first is to remember to put the `Runat="server"` attribute within the `Input` controls starting and ending tags. The second is to assign an `ID` attribute to the `HtmlInputFile` control so you can access it programmatically. Finally, you have to set the `enctype` attribute of the `FORM` to `multipart/form-data`.

The `HtmlInputFile` HTML server control supports all the same style attributes as its HTML equivilant element does, but there are some additional attributes worth noting that the `HtmlInputFile` control supports. The following list contains the name and a short description of each:

- `Accept`—The accept attribute enables you to get or set a comma separated list of MIME encodings that the user can upload. The following example allows all Images and Microsoft Windows Video files to be uploaded:

```
<input type="file" runat="server"
Accept="image/*,videa/x-msvideo"
Id="UploadFile" />
```

*This property is browser dependent.

- `MaxLength`—The maximimum file length the user can enter in the textbox.

```
<input type="file" runat="server"
MaxLength="50"
Id="UploadFile" />
```

*This property is browser dependent.

- `Size`—The width of the textbox that is rendered. The value is rendered as a percent, but is entered as an integer.

```
<input type="file" runat="server"
MaxLength="50"
Id="UploadFile" />
```

Contained in Listing 13.1 is a basic code example illustrating the process of uploading an image to your web server using the `HtmlInputFile` control. I will be using images for all sample code in this chapter, although you can apply the same code towards other file types. In this example the image is not saved to a database; rather, it is saved directly to the server's hard drive.

LISTING 13.1 Simple Image Uploading Example

```
[VisualBasic.NET]

01: <%@ Import Namespace="System.IO" %>
02: <script language="vb" runat="server">
```

LISTING 13.1 Continued

```
03:
04:  public sub SubmitImage(sender as Object, e as EventArgs)
05:
06:   dim UpFile as HttpPostedFile = UP_FILE.PostedFile
07:
08:   if UpFile.ContentLength = nothing then
09:
10:    message.Text = "<b>* You must pick a file to upload</b>"
11:
12:   else
13:
14:    UpFile.SaveAs(Server.MapPath("images") & "/" &
➥ Path.GetFileName(UpFile.FileName))
15:    message.Text = "<b>* Your image has been uploaded</b>"
16:
17:   end if
18:
19:  end sub
20:
21: </script>
```

[C#.NET]

```
01: <%@ Import Namespace="System.IO" %>
02: <script language="c#" runat="server">
03:
04:  void SubmitImage(Object sender, EventArgs e) {
05:
06:   HttpPostedFile UpFile = UP_FILE.PostedFile;
07:
08:   if (UpFile.ContentLength == 0) {
09:
10:    message.Text = "<b>* You must pick a file to upload</b>";
11:
12:   } else {
13:
14:    UpFile.SaveAs(Server.MapPath("images") + "/" +
➥ Path.GetFileName(UpFile.FileName));
15:    message.Text = "<b>* Your image has been uploaded</b>";
16:
17:   }
18:
19:  }
20:
21: </script>
```

13

BLOB
UPLOADING AND
DISPLAYING

LISTING 13.1   Continued

```
[VisualBasic.NET & C#.NET]
23: <html>
24: <body>
25: <form enctype="multipart/form-data" runat="server">
26: <h1>Simple Upload to Hard Drive</h1>
27: <asp:Table runat="server" width="700" align="left" >
28:  <asp:TableRow>
29:   <asp:TableCell>
30:    <b>Upload New Image</b>
31:   </asp:TableCell>
32:   <asp:TableCell>
33:    <input type="file" id="UP_FILE" runat="server"
34:     Size="34" accept="image/*" />
35:   </asp:TableCell>
36:  </asp:TableRow>
37:  <asp:TableRow>
38:   <asp:TableCell>
39:      
40:   </asp:TableCell>
41:   <asp:TableCell>
42:    <asp:Button runat="server" width="239"
43:     OnClick="SubmitImage" text="Upload Image"/>
44:   </asp:TableCell>
45:  </asp:TableRow>
46:  <asp:TableRow>
47:   <asp:TableCell>
48:      
49:   </asp:TableCell>
50:   <asp:TableCell>
51:    <asp:Label runat="server" id="message"
52:     forecolor="red" maintainstate="false" />
53:   </asp:TableCell>
54:  </asp:TableRow>
55: </asp:Table>
56:
57: </form>
58: </body>
59: </html>
```

For Listing 13.1 to work properly I created a sub-directory in the same folder that this web form exists. In this example I use a sub-directory named images, but you can name it anything you like. If you name the folder something other than `images` change the name used as a parameter in the `Server.MapPath` method on line 14 to reflect the change.

In lines 33 and 34 of Listing 13.1, you will see the `HtmlInputFile` control with an ID of `UP_FILE`. The `Button` control is used to submit the form (lines 42 and 43) and, when clicked, the `SubmitImage` method is executed on the server (lines 4 through 19). On line 6 I create a local `HttpPostedFile` object so it isn't necessary to drill down through the `HtmlInputFile` class to expose it—I will dive deeper into the `HttpPostedFile` class in the next section. An `if...then` statement on line 8 makes sure an image/file was uploaded to the server by checking the `UpFile` (`HttpInputFile`) `ContentLength` (the size of the file in bytes). If it is found to be null, then a file wasn't uploaded to the server. If the `ContentLength` is not found to be null then a file with the size of at least 1 byte was uploaded. I then use the `HttpPostedFile` classes `SaveAs` method to save the file in the `Images` folder. An illustration of this page after an image was uploaded can be found in Figure 13.2.

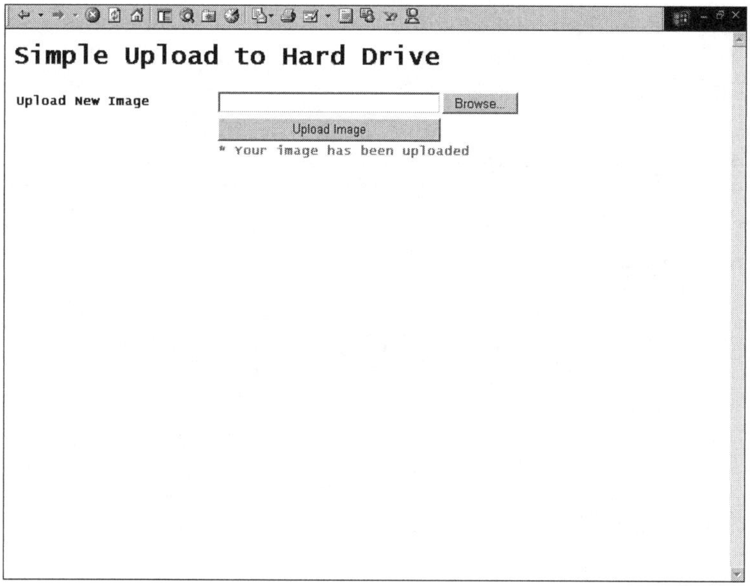

FIGURE 13.2
After an image is uploaded, a message is printed out to the page, "Your image has been uploaded."

Using the `HttpPostedFile`

As stated in the previous section, the `HttpPostedFile` class enables programmatic access to the uploaded file on the server. This class exposes a number of valuable attributes that you can use to work with the uploaded file and is accessed through the `HtmlInputFile`'s `PostedFile` property. These attributes include:

- `ContentLength`—This property `Gets` the size of the uploaded object in bytes. You can use this property to verify that an object was indeed uploaded, and that it doesn't exceed any size restrictions you might have for uploaded files.

- `ContentType`—This property `Gets` the MIME content type of the object uploaded. You can use this attribute to properly display an image after it is inserted into the database.

- `FileName`—This property `Gets` the full page of the uploaded file—this path is the path from the client's machine. You can use this attribute to retrieve the file name and extension of the uploaded object

- `InputStream`—This property `Gets` a Stream object, which points to the uploaded file. You can use this to put the binary data from the image file into a byte array so that you can insert it into a database.

Listing 13.2 illustrates working with the file after it is uploaded. I will be illustrating how to use all the above attributes except for the `InputStream` attribute, which will be covered, in the section following this one.

LISTING 13.2   Working with the Uploaded File

```
[VisualBasic.NET]
01: <%@ Import Namespace="System.IO" %>
02: <script language="vb" runat="server">
03:
04:  public sub SubmitImage(sender as Object, e as EventArgs)
05:   dim UpFile as HttpPostedFile = UP_FILE.PostedFile
06:   dim sMessage as new StringBuilder()
07:
08:   if UpFile.ContentLength = nothing then
09:
10:    sMessage.Append("You must pick a file to upload")
11:
12:   else
13:    '//File Path
14:    dim FilePath as string = UpFile.FileName
15:     sMessage.Append("<b>File Path:</b> ")
16:     sMessage.Append(FilePath)
17:     sMessage.Append("<br>")
18:    '//File Name
19:    dim FileName as string = Path.GetFileName(FilePath)
20:     sMessage.Append("<b>File Name:</b> ")
21:     sMessage.Append(FileName)
```

LISTING 13.2 Continued

```
22:     sMessage.Append("<br>")
23:     '//File Extension
24:     dim FileExtension as string = Path.GetExtension(FileName)
25;     sMessage.Append("<b>File Extension:</b> ")
26:     sMessage.Append(FileExtension)
27:     sMessage.Append("<br>")
28:     '//Content Type
29:     dim ContentInfo as string = UpFile.ContentType
30:     sMessage.Append("<b>Content Type:</b> ")
31:     sMessage.Append(ContentInfo)
32:     sMessage.Append("<br>")
33:     '//File Size
34:     dim FileSize as string = UpFile.ContentLength.ToString() & " Bytes"
35:     sMessage.Append("<b>File Size (in Bytes):</b> ")
36:     sMessage.Append(FileSize)
37:     sMessage.Append("<br>")
38:     '//Save File Under New Name
39:     dim SaveAsFilePath as string
40:     '//If it is a gif save to images/jpg directory
41:     if (FileExtension = ".jpg") then
42:
43:        SaveAsFilePath = Server.MapPath("images/jpg") + "\WhateverWhenever" +
➥FileExtension
44:        UpFile.SaveAs(SaveAsFilePath)
45:
46:        '//If it is a jpg save to images/gif directory
47:     else if (FileExtension = ".gif") then
48:
49:        SaveAsFilePath = Server.MapPath("images/gif") + "\WhateverWhenever" +
➥FileExtension
50:        UpFile.SaveAs(SaveAsFilePath)
51:
52:     else
53:
54:        SaveAsFilePath = Server.MapPath("images") + "\WhateverWhenever" +
➥FileExtension
55:        UpFile.SaveAs(SaveAsFilePath)
56:
57:     end if
58:
59:     '//New File path
60:     sMessage.Append("<b>SaveAs File Path:</b> ")
61:     sMessage.Append(SaveAsFilePath)
62:     sMessage.Append("<br>")
```

Listing 13.2 Continued

```
63:    '//Show saved image in image control
64:    sMessage.Append("<b>Uploaded Image:</b> ")
65:    sMessage.Append("<br>")
66:    sMessage.Append("<img src='")
67:    sMessage.Append(SaveAsFilePath)
68:    sMessage.Append("' border='0'>")
69:
70:   end if
71:
72:   message.Text = sMessage.ToString()
73:
74:  end sub
75:
76: </script>
```

[C#.NET]

```
01: <%@ Import Namespace="System.IO" %>
02: <script language="c#" runat="server">
03:
04:  void SubmitImage(Object sender, EventArgs e) {
05:   HttpPostedFile UpFile = UP_FILE.PostedFile;
06:   StringBuilder sMessage = new StringBuilder();
07:
08:   if (UpFile.ContentLength == 0) {
09:
10:    sMessage.Append("You must pick a file to upload");
11:
12:   } else {
13:    //File Path
14:    string FilePath = UpFile.FileName;
15:    sMessage.Append("<b>File Path:</b> ");
16:    sMessage.Append(FilePath);
17:    sMessage.Append("<br>");
18:    //File Name
19:    string FileName = Path.GetFileName(FilePath);
20:    sMessage.Append("<b>File Name:</b> ");
21:    sMessage.Append(FileName);
22:    sMessage.Append("<br>");
23:    //File Extension
24:    string FileExtension = Path.GetExtension(FileName);
25:    sMessage.Append("<b>File Extension:</b> ");
26:    sMessage.Append(FileExtension);
27:    sMessage.Append("<br>");
28:    //Content Type
```

LISTING 13.2 Continued

```
29:    string ContentInfo = UpFile.ContentType;
30:     sMessage.Append("<b>Content Type:</b> ");
31:     sMessage.Append(ContentInfo);
32:     sMessage.Append("<br>");
33:     //File Size
34:     string FileSize = UpFile.ContentLength.ToString() + " Bytes";
35:     sMessage.Append("<b>File Size (in Bytes):</b> ");
36:     sMessage.Append(FileSize);
37:     sMessage.Append("<br>");
38:     //Save File Under New Name
39:     string SaveAsFilePath;
40:     //If it is a gif save to images/jpg directory
41:     if (FileExtension == ".jpg") {
42:
43:      SaveAsFilePath = Server.MapPath("images/jpg") + "\\WhateverWhenever" +
➥FileExtension;
44:      UpFile.SaveAs(SaveAsFilePath);
45:
46:     //If it is a jpg save to images/gif directory
47:     } else if (FileExtension == ".gif") {
48:
49:      SaveAsFilePath = Server.MapPath("images/gif") + "\\WhateverWhenever" +
➥FileExtension;
50:      UpFile.SaveAs(SaveAsFilePath);
51:
52:     } else {
53:
54:      SaveAsFilePath = Server.MapPath("images") + "\\WhateverWhenever" +
➥FileExtension;
55:      UpFile.SaveAs(SaveAsFilePath);
56:
57:     }
58:
59:     //New File path
60:     sMessage.Append("<b>SaveAs File Path:</b> ");
61:     sMessage.Append(SaveAsFilePath);
62:     sMessage.Append("<br>");
63:     //Show saved image in image control
64:     sMessage.Append("<b>Uploaded Image:</b> ");
65:     sMessage.Append("<br>");
66:     sMessage.Append("<img src='");
67:     sMessage.Append(SaveAsFilePath);
68:     sMessage.Append("' border='0'>");
69:
```

13

**BLOB
UPLOADING AND
DISPLAYING**

LISTING 13.2   Continued

```
70:    }
71:
72:    message.Text = sMessage.ToString();
73:
74:  }
75:
76: </script>

[VisualBasic.NET & C#.NET]

78: <html>
79: <body>
80: <form enctype="multipart/form-data" runat="server">
81:
82: <h1>Working With File Names</h1>
83:
84: <asp:Table runat="server" width="800" align="left" >
85:  <asp:TableRow>
86:   <asp:TableCell>
87:    <b>Upload New Image</b>
88:   </asp:TableCell>
89:   <asp:TableCell>
90:    <input type="file" id="UP_FILE" runat="server"
91:     Size="34" accept="image/*" />
92:   </asp:TableCell>
93:  </asp:TableRow>
94:  <asp:TableRow>
95:   <asp:TableCell>
96:      
97:   </asp:TableCell>
98:   <asp:TableCell>
99:    <asp:Button runat="server" width="239"
100:     OnClick="SubmitImage" text="Upload Image"/>
101:   </asp:TableCell>
102:  </asp:TableRow>
103:  <asp:TableRow>
104:   <asp:TableCell>
105:      
106:   </asp:TableCell>
107:   <asp:TableCell>
```

LISTING 13.2   Continued

```
108:    <asp:Label runat="server" id="message"
109:     forecolor="red" maintainstate="false" />
110:   </asp:TableCell>
111:  </asp:TableRow>
112: </asp:Table>
113:
114: </form>
115: </body>
116: </html>
```

For Listing 13.2, I created two new sub-directories in the Images directory to demonstrate how to selectively save different image types to different directories. The two new directories are named jpg and gif.

In this example we demonstrate many different ways to extract and manipulate data of the file that was uploaded. First, on line 14, I retrieve the uploaded files path by using the HttpPostedFile classes FileName property—the FileName property retrieves the full path of the file from the clients machine (C:\MyImage.Gif). On line 19, I use members of the Path class from the System.IO namespace to extract the actual file name from the path. Specifically, I use the GetFileName method and pass in the full file path I retrieved on line 14. On line 24, I retrieve the extension of the file uploaded by using the GetExtension method of the Path class passing in FileName retrieved on line 19. On line 29, I retrieve the ContentType of the uploaded file by using the HttpPostedFile classes ContentType property (ex: image/gif). This is important information when displaying the image after it is saved in the database, as you will see in a later section. Next, on line 34, I retrieve the size of the file in bytes by using the ContentLength property of the HttpPostedFile class. In lines 39–57, I create a new file name for the image and save it to hard disk. I use an if statement to determine in what directory to save the file by checking the FileExtension variable. If the value of the FileExtension is .jpg then it is saved to images/jpg. If the value is .gif then it is saved to images/gif. All other image types are saved to images. In lines 64–68 I show the newly uploaded image by creating an <img> element and setting its SRC attribute equal to the path of the image using the SaveAsFile variable. The last thing I do is set the Message Label controls Text attribute to show all the data. Figure 13.3 shows the page after an image has been uploaded.

13

FIGURE 13.3
All file information and image is displayed on the page.

Working with the In Memory File—Saving it to a Database

The HttpInputFile's InputStream property makes saving binary data to a database very simple because it exposes a stream object pointer to the uploaded file automatically. All you must do is use a Stream to read the bytes from the uploaded file, put them into a local byte array, and save it to the database. A Stream object simply provides a way to read and write bytes to and from a source object, which in this case is an image.

Even though you might have a table that already exists in the *Northwind* database with a field of the Image type, we are going to create our own table for these examples. The reason is that some older versions of *Access* and *SQL Server* don't contain this field in the Employees table. Use the following SQL code in Query Analyzer to make a new table named Images (see Listing 13.3). If you are not using SQL Server you will have to manually design this table in design mode.

LISTING 13.3 SQL Code to Create a New Images Table

```
01: CREATE TABLE Images
02: (
03: [ImageID] int IDENTITY(1,1) NOT NULL PRIMARY KEY,
04: [Image] Image,
05: [ContentType] VarChar(50),
06: [ImageDescription] VarChar(100),
07: [ByteSize] int
08: )
```

This `Images` table has 5 fields in it. The first (`ImageID`) is the Primary Key for the table. It is an Auto Number that will increment by 1 automatically when a new row is added to the table. The second field is `Image` and it will hold the image uploaded. The third field is `ContentType` and it will be populated with the value of the `HttpPostedFile`'s `ContentType` attribute. The fourth field is `ImageDescription` and it will be populated by the contents of the `ImageDescription` TextBox. This will be a short description of the image being uploaded as described by the user. The final field is `ByteSize` and it will be populated with the value of the `HttpPostedFile`'s `ContentLength` attribute. This information isn't necessary, but will help increase performance when we want to take the image out of the database and display it. This will be explained further in the section following this one. Listing 13.4 contains code to delete this table if you want after you are done with this chapter.

LISTING 13.4 SQL Code Used to Delete the Image Table

```
01: DROP TABLE Images
```

Now that you have a table that you can use to insert an image, let's make an image upload page. Listing 13.5 takes an uploaded file that is still in memory and not saved on hard disk and saves it to a database.

LISTING 13.5 Saving an Image to Your Database

```
[VisualBasic.NET]

01: <%@ Import Namespace="System.IO" %>
02: <%@ Import Namespace="System.Data" %>
03: <%@ Import Namespace="System.Data.SqlClient" %>
04:
05: <script language="vb" runat="server">
06:
07:   public sub SubmitImage(sender as Object, e as EventArgs)
08:
```

Listing 13.5   Continued

```
09:    dim UpFile as HttpPostedFile = UP_FILE.PostedFile
10:    dim sMessage as new StringBuilder()
11:
12:    if UpFile.ContentLength = nothing then
13:
14:     sMessage.Append("<b>* You must pick a file to upload</b>")
15:
16:    else
17:
18:     dim StreamObject as Stream
19:     dim FileLength as Integer = UpFile.ContentLength
20:     dim FileByteArray(FileLength) as Byte
21:     StreamObject = UpFile.InputStream
22:     StreamObject.Read(FileByteArray,0,FileLength)
23:
24:     dim sCon as new
➥SqlConnection("server=localhost;uid=sa;pwd=;database=northwind")
25:
26:     dim SqlCmd as new StringBuilder()
27:      SqlCmd.Append("INSERT INTO Images")
28:      SqlCmd.Append("(Image, ContentType, ImageDescription, ByteSize)")
29:      SqlCmd.Append("Values(@Image, @ContentType, @ImageDescription,
➥@ByteSize)")
30:
31:     dim SqlCmdObj as new SqlCommand(SqlCmd.ToString(),sCon)
32:     dim param as SqlParameter
33:      param = SqlCmdObj.Parameters.Add(new SqlParameter("@Image",
➥SqlDbType.Image))
34:      param.value = FileByteArray
35:      param = SqlCmdObj.Parameters.Add(new SqlParameter("@ContentType",
➥SqlDbType.VarChar,50))
36:      param.value = UpFile.ContentType
37:      param = SqlCmdObj.Parameters.Add(new SqlParameter("@ImageDescription",
➥SqlDbType.VarChar,100))
38:      param.value = ImageDescription.Text
39:      param = SqlCmdObj.Parameters.Add(new SqlParameter("@ByteSize",
➥SqlDbType.Int))
40:      param.value = UpFile.ContentLength
41:
42:     sCon.Open()
43:     SqlCmdObj.ExecuteNonQuery
44:     sCon.Close()
45:
46:     sMessage.Append("<p><b>* Your image has been uploaded</b>")
```

LISTING 13.5   Continued

```
47:
48:   end if
49:    message.Text = sMessage.ToString()
50:  end sub
51:
52: </script>
53:

[C#.NET]

01: <%@ Import Namespace="System.IO" %>
02: <%@ Import Namespace="System.Data" %>
03: <%@ Import Namespace="System.Data.SqlClient" %>
04:
05: <script language="c#" runat="server">
06:
07:  void SubmitImage(Object sender, EventArgs e) {
08:
09:    HttpPostedFile UpFile = UP_FILE.PostedFile;
10:    StringBuilder sMessage = new StringBuilder();
11:
12:    if (UpFile.ContentLength == 0) {
13:
14:     sMessage.Append("<b>* You must pick a file to upload</b>");
15:
16:    } else {
17:
18:     Stream StreamObject;
19:     int FileLength = UpFile.ContentLength;
20:     Byte[] FileByteArray = new Byte[FileLength];
21:     StreamObject = UpFile.InputStream;
22:     StreamObject.Read(FileByteArray,0,FileLength);
23:
24:     SqlConnection sCon = new
➥SqlConnection("server=localhost;uid=sa;pwd=;database=northwind");
25:
26:     StringBuilder SqlCmd = new StringBuilder();
27:      SqlCmd.Append("INSERT INTO Images");
28:      SqlCmd.Append("(Image, ContentType, ImageDescription, ByteSize)");
29:      SqlCmd.Append("Values(@Image, @ContentType, @ImageDescription,
➥@ByteSize)");
30:
31:     SqlCommand SqlCmdObj = new SqlCommand(SqlCmd.ToString(),sCon);
32:     SqlParameter param;
```

Listing 13.5   Continued

```
33:      param = SqlCmdObj.Parameters.Add(new SqlParameter("@Image",
➥SqlDbType.Image));
34:      param.Value = FileByteArray;
35:      param = SqlCmdObj.Parameters.Add(new SqlParameter("@ContentType",
➥SqlDbType.VarChar,50));
36:      param.Value = UpFile.ContentType;
37:      param = SqlCmdObj.Parameters.Add(new SqlParameter("@ImageDescription",
➥SqlDbType.VarChar,100));
38:      param.Value = ImageDescription.Text;
39:      param = SqlCmdObj.Parameters.Add(new SqlParameter("@ByteSize",
➥SqlDbType.VarChar,100));
40:      param.Value = UpFile.ContentLength;
41:
42:    sCon.Open();
43:    SqlCmdObj.ExecuteNonQuery();
44:    sCon.Close();
45:
46:    sMessage.Append("<p><b>* Your image has been uploaded</b>");
47:
48:    }
49:    message.Text = sMessage.ToString();
50:  }
51:
52: </script>

[VisualBasic.NET & C#.NET]

54: <html>
55: <body>
56: <form enctype="multipart/form-data" runat="server">
57: <h1>File Upload Example to a Database</h1>
58: <asp:Table runat="server" width="700" align="left" >
59:  <asp:TableRow>
60:   <asp:TableCell>
61:    <b>Upload New Image</b>
62:   </asp:TableCell>
63:   <asp:TableCell>
64:    <input type="file" id="UP_FILE" runat="server" width="200"
➥accept="image/*" />
65:   </asp:TableCell>
66:  </asp:TableRow>
67:  <asp:TableRow>
68:   <asp:TableCell>
69:    <b>Give a Description</b>
70:   </asp:TableCell>
```

Listing 13.5 Continued

```
71:    <asp:TableCell>
72:      <asp:TextBox runat="server" width="239" id="ImageDescription"
MaintainState="false" />
73:    </asp:TableCell>
74:    </asp:TableRow>
75:    <asp:TableRow>
76:      <asp:TableCell>
77:      <asp:Label runat="server" id="message" forecolor="red"
maintainstate="false" />
78:    </asp:TableCell>
79:    <asp:TableCell>
80:      <asp:Button runat="server" width="239" OnClick="SubmitImage"
text="Upload Image"/>
81:    </asp:TableCell>
82:    </asp:TableRow>
83:  </asp:Table>
84:  </form>
85:  </body>
86:  </html>
```

Let's walk through the code in Listing 13.5. When the page first loads, you will receive a page with one HtmlInputFile control, one TextBox control, and a Button control. The TextBox control enables the user to give the file they are going to upload a description. After the user selects an image and a gives it a description, the user should click the Upload Image button. The SubmitImage method is then executed on the server. For ease of programming I put the uploaded file into a local variable, UpFile (line 9). Before you do anything you should make sure that a file was indeed uploaded. On line 12, I create an If statement that checks the HttpPostedFile's (UpFile) ContentLength (the size of the file in bytes). If the file is nothing or zero bytes, then no file was uploaded, and a message is given to the user "You must pick a file to upload." If a file is found, the else block is executed.

In lines 18 through 22, I read the bytes from the uploaded file's InputStream into a local byte array (FileByteArray). This needs to be done to insert the image into the database. In lines 25 through 42, I create the database connection, construct the SQL insert statement, set the values for all parameters, and execute a non-query SQL statement against the database. That's it—the image has been inserted into your database.

Now that you know how to insert images into the database, you might be thinking, "How the heck do I show the images now?" In the next section, I'll demonstrate one way to do this.

Retrieving and Showing an Image from a Database

In this example, the image is created from the Image field in the Images table from the Northwind database on-the-fly and once again is never saved to hard disk. Then, the image is displayed using the Image server control. We will use one Web Form to create and implement an image, and another to display it. Listing 13.6 contains the image Web Form, which will retrieve the image from the database and create a Web-usable image.

LISTING 13.6 Web Form Used to Create the Image from a Database for Web Use

```vb
[VisualBasic.NET]

01: <%@ OutputCache Duration="30" VaryByParam="ImageID" %>
02: <%@ Import Namespace="System.Data" %>
03: <%@ Import Namespace="System.Data.SqlClient" %>
04:
05: <script language="vb" runat="server">
06:
07: protected sub Page_Init(sender as Object, e as EventArgs)
08:
09:  dim ImageID as string = Request.QueryString("ImageID")
10:
11:  if not ImageID = nothing then
12:
13:  dim SqlCon as new
➥SqlConnection("server=localhost;uid=sa;pwd=;database=northwind")
14:  dim SqlCmd as new StringBuilder()
15:   SqlCmd.Append("SELECT Image, ContentType, ByteSize ")
16:   SqlCmd.Append("FROM Images WHERE ImageID = @ImageID")
17:
18:  dim sqlcommand as new SqlCommand(SqlCmd.ToString(), SqlCon)
19:   sqlcommand.Parameters.Add(new SqlParameter("@ImageID", SqlDbType.Int))
20:   sqlcommand.Parameters("@ImageID").Value = ImageID
21:  SqlCon.Open()
22:  dim SqlDr as SqlDataReader =
➥sqlcommand.ExecuteReader(CommandBehavior.CloseConnection)
23:
24:  SqlDr.Read()
25:
26:  Response.ContentType = SqlDr("ContentType")
27:
28:  Response.OutputStream.Write(SqlDr("Image"), 0, SqlDr("ByteSize"))
29:
30:  Response.End()
31:
```

LISTING 13.6 Continued

```
32:   end if
33:
34: end sub
35:
36: </script>
```

[C#.NET]

```csharp
01: <%@ OutputCache Duration="30" VaryByParam="ImageID" %>
02: <%@ Import Namespace="System.Data" %>
03: <%@ Import Namespace="System.Data.SqlClient" %>
04:
05: <script language="c#" runat="server">
06:
07: protected void Page_Init(Object sender, EventArgs e) {
08:
09:   string ImageID = Request.QueryString["ImageID"];
10:
11:   if (ImageID != null) {
12:
13:   SqlConnection SqlCon = new
➡SqlConnection("server=localhost;uid=sa;pwd=;database=northwind");
14:   StringBuilder SqlCmd = new StringBuilder();
15:    SqlCmd.Append("SELECT Image, ContentType, ByteSize ");
16:    SqlCmd.Append("FROM Images WHERE ImageID = @ImageID");
17:
18:   SqlCommand sqlcommand = new SqlCommand(SqlCmd.ToString(), SqlCon);
19:    sqlcommand.Parameters.Add(new SqlParameter("@ImageID", SqlDbType.Int));
20:    sqlcommand.Parameters["@ImageID"].Value = ImageID;
21:   SqlCon.Open();
22:   SqlDataReader SqlDr =
➡sqlcommand.ExecuteReader(CommandBehavior.CloseConnection);
23:
24:   SqlDr.Read();
25:
26:   Response.ContentType = (string)SqlDr["ContentType"];
27:
28:   Response.OutputStream.Write((byte[])SqlDr["Image"], 0,
➡(int)SqlDr["ByteSize"]);
29:
30:   Response.End();
31:
32:   }
33:
34: }
35:
36: </script>
```

13

BLOB
UPLOADING AND
DISPLAYING

In Listing 13.6, you will notice I enable output caching using the `@OuputCache` directive. The `@OuputCache` directive `VaryByParam` attribute varies caching based on the value of the parameter specified (ImageID); so for every `ImageID` sent to this page as a parameter, a separate cache item will be made. Hence subsequent calls for the same image will be served from the cache rather than dynamically generating them each time. (I will dive deep into caching in Chapter 16, "Data Caching.")

On line 9 I create an `ImageID` variable, which determines which image from the database will be shown. Its value is determined by the query string `ImageID` parameters value. On line 11 I use an `if` statement to verify that there is an `ImageID` value present. If it doesn't have a value then code execution stops and no image will be shown. On a production site this would probably not be an option so in this case there should be a mechanism in place for recovery such as a default `ImageID` value.

If the `ImageID` value is present, then the code to generate the image is executed (lines 13 through 32). I create a new connection, construct the SQL statement, and execute a query to retrieve the `Image`, `ContentType`, and `ByteSize` fields for the `ImageID` specified (lines 13–22). You might be wondering why I chose to use an `SqlDataReader` rather than a `DataSet` to retrieve the data. Well, there is a good reason for this: PERFORMANCE. Remember, the `SqlDataReader` and `OleDbDataReader` objects read a data stream directly from the database connection. And since we are working with rather large objects we will use less memory and CPU time by streaming the data in.

On line 26 I set the pages `ContentType` equal to the `ContentType` field in the database. Next, on line 28, I write the images binary data to the response stream by using the `HttpResponse.OutputStream`. There are 3 paramaters passed into the `Write` method—first is the buffer (the contents of the `Image` field) which is cast into a byte array. Second is the `offset`—*where to begin copying bytes into the stream*, in this case the very beginning - `0`. Finally, `count`—the number of bytes from the buffer that should be written to the stream we use the `ByteSize` field as this value.

Even though this page will execute by itself and will show an image (if you hardcode the `ImageID` value), you couldn't write out any other HTML content because the `ContentType` of the page will be that of an image.

Let's now consume or use this "image utility" page from another page to illustrate how multiple images can be derived from a database. Listing 13.7 shows how to use the `Listing13.6.aspx` page to show images.

LISTING 13.7   Web Form Client That Uses the Images.aspx page to Show Images.

```
[VisualBasic.NET]

01: <%@ Import Namespace="System.Data" %>
02: <%@ Import Namespace="System.Data.SqlClient" %>
03:
04: <script language="vb" runat="server">
05:
06: public sub Page_Load(sender as Object, e as EventArgs)
07:
08:   dim Url as string = "Listing13.6.aspx?ImageID="
09:   dim sdr as SqlDataReader
10:   dim sCon as new SqlConnection("server=localhost;
➥ uid=sa;pwd=;database=northwind")
11:   dim SqlCmd as string = "SELECT ImageID,ImageDescription FROM Images"
12:   dim sCmd as new SqlCommand(SqlCmd,sCon)
13:   sCon.Open()
14:   sdr = sCmd.ExecuteReader()
15:
16:   dim row as TableRow
17:   dim cell as TableCell
18:   dim ICtrl as Image
19:
20:   while (sdr.Read())
21:
22:     row = new TableRow()
23:     cell = new TableCell()
24:     cell.Controls.Add(new LiteralControl("<b>" & sdr.GetString(1) & "</b>"))
25:     cell.VerticalAlign = VerticalAlign.Top
26:     cell.Width = Unit.Pixel(400)
27:     row.Cells.Add(cell)
28:
29:     cell = new TableCell()
30:     ICtrl = new Image()
31:     ICtrl.ImageUrl = Url & sdr.GetSqlInt32(0).ToString()
32:     ICtrl.Width = Unit.Pixel(200)
33:     ICtrl.AlternateText = sdr.GetString(1)
34:     cell.Controls.Add(ICtrl)
35:     row.Cells.Add(cell)
36:
37:     ImageTable.Rows.Add(row)
38:
39:   end while
40:
41: end sub
42: </script>
```

LISTING 13.7   Continued

[C#.NET]

```
01: <%@ Import Namespace="System.Data" %>
02: <%@ Import Namespace="System.Data.SqlClient" %>
03:
04: <script language="c#" runat="server" >
05:
06: void Page_Load(Object sender, EventArgs e) {
07:
08:   string Url = "Listing13.6.aspx?ImageID=";
09:   SqlDataReader sdr;
10:   SqlConnection sCon = new SqlConnection("server=localhost;
➥   uid=sa;pwd=;database=northwind");
11:   string SqlCmd = "SELECT ImageID,ImageDescription FROM Images";
12:   SqlCommand sCmd = new SqlCommand(SqlCmd,sCon);
13:   sCon.Open();
14:   sdr = sCmd.ExecuteReader();
15:
16:   Image ICtrl;
17:   TableRow row;
18:   TableCell cell;
19:
20:   while (sdr.Read()) {
21:
22:     row = new TableRow();
23:     cell = new TableCell();
24:     cell.Controls.Add(new LiteralControl("<b>" + sdr.GetString(1) +
➥"</b>"));
25:     cell.VerticalAlign = VerticalAlign.Top;
26:     cell.Width = Unit.Pixel(400);
27:     row.Cells.Add(cell);
28:
29:     cell = new TableCell();
30:     ICtrl = new Image();
31:     ICtrl.ImageUrl = Url + sdr.GetSqlInt32(0).ToString();
32:     ICtrl.Width = Unit.Pixel(200);
33:     ICtrl.AlternateText = sdr.GetString(1);
34:     cell.Controls.Add(ICtrl);
35:     row.Cells.Add(cell);
36:
```

LISTING 13.7 Continued

```
37:     ImageTable.Rows.Add(row);
38:
39:   }
40:
41: }
42: </script>

[VisualBasic.NET & C#.NET]

44: <html>
45: <body>
46:   <asp:Table id="ImageTable" runat="server" cellpadding="4"
47:     cellspacing="4" width="600" align="left" />
48: </body>
49: </html>
```

To display the image with the `Images.aspx` Web form (the image generator), use the following code

```
<img src="Listing13.6.aspx?ImageID=ImageID >
```

where `ImageID` is equal to the `ImageID` field in the `Images` table of the database. I wanted to show every image in the `Images` table in Listing 13.7, so you first retrieve all the records and use a `DataReader` to work with them (lines 8 through 14). The fields I am returning in the SQL query are `ImageDescription` and `ImageID`. In lines 16 through 18, you create the building blocks for the `Table` and `Image` controls. Then, starting on line 20, I loop through the result set dynamically constructing the `Table` that will contain the images and descriptions.

The dynamically generated table will have two columns—one for the description and the other for the image. On lines 22 and 23 I create a new `TableRow` and the first `TableCell` object. I insert a new `LiteralControl` into the cell containing the image description, and then I set some of the `TableCells` attributes and add the `TableCell` to the `TableRow`. On line 29 the second `TableCell` is created—this `TableCell` will hold the image. On line 30 I create a new `Image` control and set its `ImageUrl` attribute equal to the `Url` variable and concatenate the `ImageId` field to the end. Next I set some of its attributes and add it to the `TableCell`. Then I immediately add the `TableCell` to the `TableRow` and then the `TableRow` to the `Table`. Figure 13.4 illustrates this page.

13

BLOB UPLOADING AND DISPLAYING

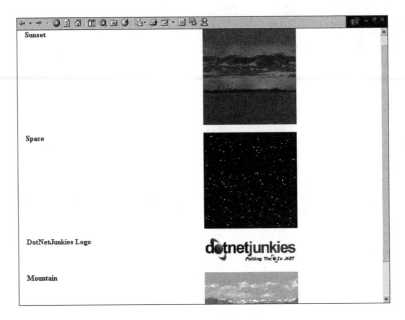

FIGURE 13.4
All images from the Images table.

Summary

In this chapter, I discussed how .NET enables us to very easily implement file uploading from the client to the server using the `HttpPostedFile` and `HtmlInputFile` classes. I demonstrated different ways you can abstract information about the uploaded file including filenames, types, and sizes using some of the `HttpPostedFile` classes' members along with members of the `System.IO` namespace. We dove headfirst into how to enable the uploading of images and how to save those images back to your database. I then showed one method you can use to display images stored in a database by using a web form to implement the image and then in turn using that as the `Image` controls `ImageUrl` or an `<img>` html elements `SRC` attribute.

Specifically I went over the following subjects in this chapter:

- Using the `HtmlInputFile` class to upload files to gain programmatic access to the uploaded file
- Using the `HttpPostedFile` class to manipulate and extract information from the uploaded file
- Saving uploaded images to your database
- Displaying images derived from a database

The examples given in this chapter focused on BLOBS of the image type, but the code here can be applied to any type of BLOB. For instance, you can use Listing 13.5 to upload a Microsoft Word document and save it in your database. Then you can use Listing 13.6 to open it by hard coding the `ImageID` to that of the saved Word Document and directly requesting that page.

Exposing Data Through Web Services

IN THIS CHAPTER

As the Internet has grown, the need to share data across Web sites, and a variety of backend applications has grown with it. With the variety of Web server platforms, database applications, programming languages, and proprietary data management applications, sharing data has become increasingly difficult. As more applications develop into Web-based solutions, and more companies rely on the Internet as a vessel for data exchange, it becomes obvious that an easy way of enabling this is needed. The solution to enabling Internet-based data exchange is .NET Web services.

Through the development of Internet standards, such as XML, you have the ability to exchange data in a common format with another application, even when the two applications run on different systems, running different applications, written in different languages, using different data storage applications. Much like HTTP provided a standard protocol by which a browser and a Web server could interact, and HTML provided a standard presentation mark-up format for documents, XML provides a standard data exchange format that can be used by a variety of disparate systems.

In this chapter, you will learn how Web services bring the programmable Web to life.

What Are Web Services?

Web services are pieces of programming logic that provide functionality to a variety of potentially disparate systems through the use of Internet standards. These pieces of logic can include such things as mathematical calculations, data look-up logic, authorization services—virtually any type of programming function you can think of. Through the use of Internet standards like XML and SOAP, your Web services can be used by any number of disparate systems, or locally by your own applications.

As you look at what Web services are, you must remember that three things are required for Web services to be successful:

- **Systems must be loosely coupled.**

  Two systems must be able to exchange data or functionality with each other, understanding no more than what inputs are required, and what outputs to expect.

- **Systems must provide ever-present communication.**

  For a Web service to be successful the provider of the service must be available at all times. As Internet technology has grown, the capability to provide a constant online presence has become easier, nearly to a point of being assumed that a constant online presence is available.

- **Web services must use a universal data format.**

  Because Web services are intended to enable disparate systems to interact and exchange data, universally understood data formats are required. The use of common standards like XML enables any system capable of understanding the standards to make use of Web services.

Common Standards

Web services are designed to work with common Internet standards. Following is a brief overview of these standards.

SOAP

SOAP, or Simple Object Access Protocol, is an XML-based data exchange protocol. SOAP uses XML's structure to represent objects and their properties and methods. Since SOAP uses existing Internet architecture, such as HTTP, the integration of SOAP into Web services is nearly seamless. SOAP is a lightweight, message-based protocol that is built on XML and Internet standards. Every SOAP message is a one-way transmission, but SOAP messages can be combined to implement patterns such as request/response.

WSDL

WSDL, or Web Service Description Language, is an XML-based document that describes the format of messages that the Web service understands. Every Web service must have a WSDL. The WSDL is basically an agreement that the provider and the consumer use to describe the behavior, inputs, outputs, and data types exchanged in the Web service. The WSDL describes, conceptually, what will happen when the consumer provides a properly formatted message to the Web service.

DISCO

DISCO, or Web service discovery, is the process of locating and interrogating Web service descriptions (WSDLs). This is a preliminary step to actually consuming a Web service. The discovery process enables consumers to find a Web service, learn its capabilities, and learn how to properly interact with the Web service. Providers of Web services can create a `*.disco` file, which is an XML document that contains links to other files that describe the Web service, such as the location of the WSDL. Providers are not required to provide a means for public discovery of their Web services. Often the provider can design the Web services for their use only. The discovery process is used only for Web services that are meant to be consumed publicly.

UDDI

UDDI, or Universal Description Discovery Integration, is analogous to the Yellow Pages of Web services. UDDI is a project put forth by technology leaders such as Microsoft, IBM, and

14

EXPOSING DATA
THROUGH WEB
SERVICES

Ariba to standardize how Web services are found on the Internet. UDDI creates a platform-independent, open framework for describing services, discovering businesses, and integrating business services using the Internet. UDDI defines how companies can expose their business applications as Web services. The UDDI project involves the shared implementation of a Web service, the UDDI Business Registry, which acts as an Internet directory of businesses and the applications they have exposed as Web services. Businesses will use the UDDI Web service to find other Web services in a manner similar to how people use Internet search engines today.

> **NOTE**
>
> You can learn more about UDDI by visiting the Microsoft UDDI Web site at `http://uddi.microsoft.com`, or the UDDI community Web site at `http://www.uddi.org`.

Usable Protocols

Web services are designed to be as accessible as possible. One of the primary goals of the Web service architecture is to exchange data in a common format that is not tied to a single operating system or language. Binary protocols like DCOM, RMI, and COBRA work by riding on top of a proprietary communication protocol. Although they can be used with Web services, because of their proprietary nature, they limit the acceptance of the Web service only to consumers who support the protocol.

Using Internet standard protocols enables Web services to be widely accepted and used. By using common protocols, businesses can exchange data, such as purchase orders and order-tracking information, without the hassles of cross-system data exchange. I once worked in a shop where we struggled with RMI calls to exchange data between a COM system and a Java class system. It was painful to say the least. We spent an excessive amount of time opening a VPN and making RMI calls—activities that could have been done easily and in much less time using Web services and standard HTTP-based protocols.

Http-Get and Http-Post

Http-Get and Http-Post are standard HTTP-based protocols that use name/value pairs to pass data to the Web service. Http-Get passes its name/value pairs as UUencoded text appended to the URL of the server handling the request. Http-Post also passes the name/value pairs as UUencoded text; however, the name/value pairs are passed in the request header, rather than in the URL.

Web services can be accessed using either Http-Get or Http-Post. For example, to implement a Web service exposed on the DotNetJunkies.com Web site, you simply type in the URL and append it with the name/value pairs expected as input by the Web service:

```
http://www.dotnetjunkies.com/services/TrivialFunTools.asmx/
➥RandomNumberGenerator?LowNumber=1&HighNumber=7
```

In this example, you use Http-Get to execute a Web service exposed by DotNetJunkies.com. The Web service, `RandomNumberGenerator`, is an exposed method of the `TrivialFunTools` Web service. The Web service expects two input parameters, `LowNumber` and `HighNumber`. These parameters are appended to the URL in the form of a `QueryString`:

```
http://server?name=value&name=value
```

The actual HTTP request header looks like this:

```
GET /services/TrivialFunTools.asmx/RandomNumberGenerator?
➥LowNumber=1&HighNumber=7 HTTP/1.1
Host: http://www.dotnetjunkies.com
```

The result of making this call is an XML document representing the results:

```
<?xml version="1.0" ?>
<int xmlns="http://tempuri.org/">5</int>
```

Using Http-Post works much in the same manner, but the name/value pairs are passed in the HTTP request header:

```
POST /services/TrivialFunTools.asmx/RandomNumberGenerator HTTP/1.1
Host: http://www.dotnetjunkies.com
Content-Type: application/x-www-form-urlencoded
Content-Length: length

LowNumber=1&HighNumber=7
```

SOAP

SOAP, like Http-Get and Http-Post, can be used to invoke a Web service and return the results. SOAP defines XML grammar for identifying the Web service method name and wrapping the method parameters. It also defines an XML grammar for returning results. SOAP is the most extensible mechanism of the three protocols (Http-Get, Http-Post, and SOAP). Although Http-Get and Http-Post enable the exchange of multiple data types and value classes, SOAP also enables the exchange of classes, structs, and `DataSets`. The offset is that the payload of a SOAP message is much larger than the Http-Get and Http-Post request headers.

A call to the `RandomNumberGenerator` Web service will look like the following as a SOAP message:

```
POST /services/TrivialFunTools.asmx HTTP/1.1
Host: http://www.dotnetjunkies.com
Content-Type: text/xml; charset="utf-8"
Content-Length: nnnn
SOAPAction: "http://www.dotnetjunkies.com/RandomNumberGenerator"
```

14

```xml
<?xml version="1.0" encoding="utf-8"?>
<soap:Envelope xmlns:xsi="http://www.w3.org/2001/XMLSchema-instance"
    xmlns:xsd="http://www.w3.org/2001/XMLSchema"
    xmlns:soap="http://schemas.xmlsoap.org/soap/envelope">
  <soap:Body>
    <RandomNumberGenerator xmlns="http://www.dotnetjunkies.com/">
      <LowNumber>1</LowNumber>
      <HighNumber>7</HighNumber>
    </RandomNumberGenerator>
  </soap:Body>
</soap:Envelope>
```

The returned result is a SOAP message that encapsulates the return value in a SOAP envelope:

```
HTTP/1.1 200 OK
Content-Type: text/xml; charset="utf-8"
Content-Length: nnnn

<?xml version="1.0" encoding="utf-8"?>
<soap:Envelope xmlns:xsi="http://www.w3.org/2001/XMLSchema-instance"
    xmlns:xsd="http://www.w3.org/2001/XMLSchema"
    xmlns:soap="http://schemas.xmlsoap.org/soap/envelope">
  <soap:Body>
    <RandomNumberGeneratorResponse xmlns="http:// www.dotnetjunkies.com/">
      <RandomNumberGeneratorResult>5</RandomNumberGeneratorResult>
    </RandomNumberGeneratorResponse>
  </soap:Body>
</soap:Envelope>
```

Figure 14.1 shows how a Web service provider and a Web service consumer interact using HTTP, DISCO, WSDL, SOAP, and XML.

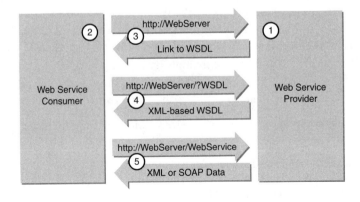

FIGURE 14.1

A provider exposes a Web service that a consumer uses.

Figure 14.1 shows how a Web service provider and consumer interact. A Web service provider (1) makes a Web service publicly available on the Internet. The consumer (2) goes through the discovery process (3) to find out what Web services are available from the provider. The discovery process returns a link to the WSDL document. When the consumer knows where to find the WSDL, she can request it by appending the URL with ?WSDL (4). The WSDL can be used to build classes for consuming the Web service. The consumer then can call the Web service with an Http-Get, Http-Post, or a SOAP message (5). The data is returned to the client as either an XML document, or XML-formatted data in a SOAP message.

Building Simple Output Web Services

Now that you are familiar with what a Web service is, and the standards and protocols that are usable by Web services, it is time to get your hands dirty by building some Web services. In the following section, I will show you how to build a simple Web service (the classic "Hello World" example. . . you didn't think you could get through a programming book without writing Hello World, did you?). You will build on the concepts learned while building a simple Web service, and build bigger, more complex Web services.

WebMethod

Building a basic Web service is really no different than creating a custom class and exposing public methods. Listing 14.1 shows the code to create a HelloWorld class (not a Web service, yet).

LISTING 14.1   Building a Custom HelloWorld Class

```
[VB]

01: Public Class HelloWorld
02:
03:  Public Function SayHello() As String
04:   Return "Hello World!"
05:  End Function
06: End Class

[C#]

01: public class HelloWorld{
02:
03:  public string SayHello(){
04:   return "Hello World!";
05:  }
06: }
```

14

EXPOSING DATA
THROUGH WEB
SERVICES

In Listing 14.1, you create a class named HelloWorld. The class has one public instance method, on lines 3 through 5, named SayHello().

To turn the SayHello() method into a Web-callable method (a Web service), you only need to change a few things.

1. Web services are saved as files with the .asmx extension. This identifies them as Web services.

2. Similar to how a Web Form uses the @ Page directive, a Web service uses the @ WebService directive. The directive specifies the class name for the Web service.

3. The methods you are exposing in the service need to be declared as WebMethods.

Listing 14.2 shows how to make the HelloWorld class into a Web service.

LISTING 14.2   Making the HelloWorld Web Service

```
[VB]

01: <%@ WebService Language="VB" Class="HelloWorld" %>
02:
03: Imports System.Web.Services
04:
05: <WebService(Namespace:="http://www.dotnetjunkies.com")> _
06: Public Class HelloWorld
07:
08:  <WebMethod(Description:="Say Hello to the world!")> _
09:  Public Function SayHello() As String
10:    Return "Hello World!"
11:  End Function
12: End Class

[C#]

01: <%@ WebService Language="C#" Class="HelloWorld" %>
02:
03: using System.Web.Services;
04:
05: [WebService(Namespace="http://www.dotnetjunkies.com")]
06: public class HelloWorld{
07:
08:  [WebMethod(Description="Say Hello to the world!")]
09:  public string SayHello(){
10:    return "Hello World!";
11:  }
12: }
```

When you create a Web service, you use the @ WebService directive (line 1) to tell the .NET Framework that this class is exposed as a Web service. The @ WebService directive specifies the language with which the class is written and the name of the class being exposed.

On line 5 you use the optional WebService attribute to provide an XML namespace for the Web service. If you do not provide a namespace for the Web service it will default to <http://tempuri.org>. By providing an XML namespace you are distinguishing the Web service from other Web services that may be using the <http://tempuri.org> namespace.

> **NOTE**
>
> The WebService attribute is optional. If you do not specify a namespace value using the WebService attribute, the Web service will use the default namespace <http://tempuri.org>. For further information regarding using namespaces with your Web services, see the Microsoft information provided at http://tempuri.org.

In a Web service, you indicate the methods you want to expose as part of the service using the WebMethod attribute. The class and any methods declared with the WebMethod attribute must be declared publicly. Looking at Listing 14.2, you can see there are some slight differences in the syntax for WebMethods in Visual Basic and C#. In Visual Basic, the WebMethod attribute is part of the method declaration. On line 8 of the Visual Basic code, the WebMethod is exposed by prefixing the function declaration with the <WebMethod()> attribute. Notice the use of the code continuation character (_) to wrap the function declaration across two lines. On line 8 of the C# code, the WebMethod is exposed by adding the [WebMethod()] attribute on the line before the function declaration.

When you navigate to HelloWorld.asmx in a browser, you see a page that is automatically rendered by the .NET Framework. The page displays the name of the Web service (the class name) and a list of any methods declared as WebMethods. Figure 14.2 shows this page.

If you click on the name of a WebMethod, a page is rendered explaining the WebMethod. The page includes a description of the WebMethod (if one was provided), a button to invoke the WebMethod (for testing), sample SOAP request and response messages, and sample Http-Get and Http-Post request and response headers. This is seen in Figure 14.3.

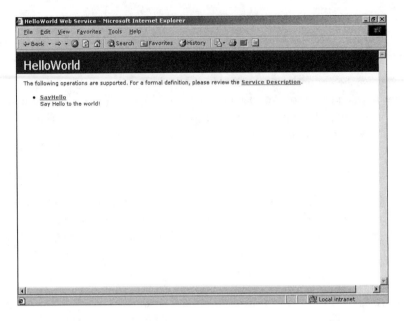

FIGURE 14.2
Web service files (.asmx) automatically render a page displaying the name of the Web service and any Web-callable methods (WebMethods) available in the service.

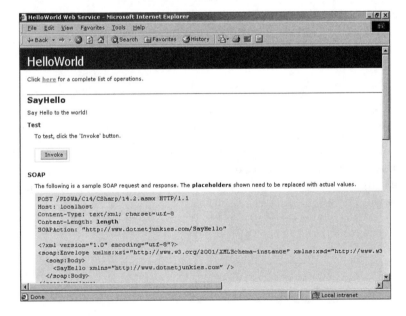

FIGURE 14.3
Clicking on a WebMethod renders a page that describes the WebMethod and the SOAP or Http-Get/Http-Post interactions.

From the `WebMethod` page, you can invoke the Web service to test the execution and see the results that are returned. These pages are provided for the developer and the consumer to test with and are not intended for normal user viewing. Figure 14.4 shows the page that is rendered when the `SayHello()` WebMethod is invoked.

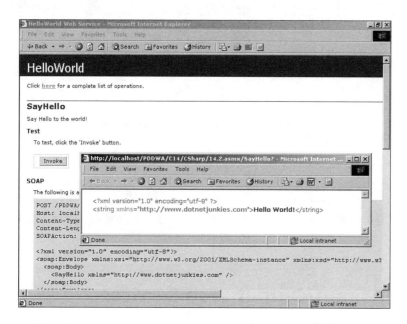

FIGURE 14.4
Invoking the `SayHello()` WebMethod *renders an XML document with the return value as an XML node.*

From the `HelloWorld.asmx` file, you also can also click a link to the Service Description, which will display the WSDL document. Figure 14.5 shows the WSDL document for the `HelloWorld` Web service.

The WSDL defines the Web service and how the client should interact with it. You will notice if you look through the WSDL that there are sections that describe how to interact using SOAP, Http-Get, and Http-Post.

14

EXPOSING DATA
THROUGH WEB
SERVICES

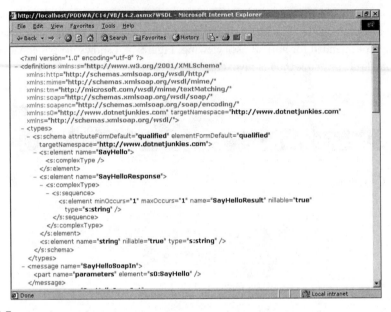

FIGURE 14.5
The WSDL for the HelloWorld *Web service is automatically created by the .NET Framework.*

Building Input/Output Web Services

In the previous example, you built a very simple Web service. No input parameters were expected, and the output was a predefined string value. Web services are capable of much more than simply providing predefined string values, of course. In this section, I will show you how to build more complex Web services that take in and return a variety of data types.

The following is a list of data types supported in Web services:

- boolean
- byte
- double
- datatype
- enumeration
- float
- int
- long
- short

- string
- unsignedByte
- unsignedInt
- unsignedLong
- unsignedShort

Like any class method, Web services can take in any number of parameters, each using different data types. The types supported by the Web service are largely dependent on the protocol used to invoke the Web service. SOAP is the most extensible protocol because it is XML message based; however, it is also the heaviest on the wire. In other words, a SOAP message uses much more bandwidth than a simple Http-Get or Http-Post. The input and output values can be serialized into XML and passed between the consumer and provider in a SOAP message. Http-Get and Http-Post are more limited, as they only work with name/value pair passed in either the URL (Http-Get) or as part of the request header (Http-Post), but are much lighter on the wire (i.e. use less bandwidth).

In the Northwind sample application, available at http://www.samspublishing.com), we have built a Web service named ProductServices. The ProductServices Web service has three Web-callable methods (WebMethods): PlaceOrder(), GetProducts(), and GetOrderDetail(). Each of these WebMethods requires input parameters provided by the consumer.

The ProductServices' Web service basic framework is shown in Listing 14.3. You will add the three WebMethods to the ProductServices class.

LISTING 14.3 The ProductServices' Web Service Framework

```
[VB]
01: <%@ WebService Language="VB" Class="Northwind.ProductServices" %>
02:
03: Imports System.Web.Services
04: Imports System
05: Imports System.Data
06: Imports System.Data.SqlClient
07:
08: Namespace Northwind
09:
10:   <WebService(Namespace:="http://www.dotnetjunkies.com/northwind/")> _
11:   Public Class ProductServices
12:
13:     Private ConString As String = _
➥        "server=localhost;database=Northwind;uid=sa;pwd=;"
14:     ' WebMethods will be inserted here
```

LISTING 14.3   Continued

```
15:   End Class
16:
17: End Namespace
```

```
[C#]
01: <%@ WebService Language="C#" Class="Northwind.ProductServices" %>
02:
03: using System.Web.Services;
04: using System;
05: using System.Data;
06: using System.Data.SqlClient;
07:
08: namespace Northwind{
09:
10:   [WebService(Namespace="http://www.dotnetjunkies.com/northwind/")]
11:   public class ProductServices{
12:
13:    private string ConString =
➡       "server=localhost;database=Northwind;uid=sa;pwd=;";
14:     // WebMethods will be inserted here
15:   }
16:
17: }
```

In Listing 14.3, you simply set up the framework in which you will build the Web service. On line 1, you identify this file as a Web service with the @ WebService directive. On lines 3 through 6, you import the required namespaces. You will be using the ADO.NET data classes and the Sql Managed Provider, so the System.Data and System.Data.SqlClient namespaces are required. The System namespace is required for some DateTime manipulation you will be doing. On line 8, you declare the classes in this Web service as part of the Northwind namespace. On line 10, you use the WebService attribute to declare the namespace of the Web service, and on line 11 you declare the public class that is your Web service, ProductServices. On line 13, you create a private string, ConString, that you will use as the ConnectionString property for any data access you do.

Building the GetProducts() WebMethod

The GetProducts() WebMethod is intended to provide a Web-callable interface for a consumer to get an XML document (a DataSet) of products and product information for a given category. The GetProducts() WebMethod takes one input parameter, the CategoryID. The category ID's are provided in the description of the Web service.

Getting products by a given category ID is a piece of application logic that you use in other parts of the Northwind Web site. You certainly do not want to duplicate the logic to do this. Rather, you want to encapsulate the logic in a class (part of the application DLL in the \bin directory), and invoke a method call on it. Web services enable this. Although the previous examples demonstrated building Web services with the application logic in the .asmx file, you are not limited to that. As with Web Forms or user controls, you can use the logic from custom classes in the Web service.

To build the GetProducts() WebMethod, first you build a Products class and then compile it into your application DLL in the bin directory. Listing 14.4 shows the code for the Products class.

LISTING 14.4   The Northwind.Products() Class

[VB]

```
01: Imports System
02: Imports System.Data
03: Imports System.Data.SqlClient
04:
05: Namespace Northwind
06:
07:   Public Class Products
08:
09:     Private ConString As String =
          "server=localhost;database=Northwind;uid=sa;pwd=;"
10:
11:     Public Function GetProductsByCategory(CategoryID As Integer)
          As SqlDataReader
12:       Dim productsReader As SqlDataReader
13:       Dim myConnection As New SqlConnection(ConString)
14:       Dim getProductsCommand As SqlCommand
15:       Dim SqlStmnt As String
16:
17:       SqlStmnt = "SELECT Products.ProductID, Products.ProductName, " & _
18:         "Suppliers.CompanyName, Categories.CategoryName, " & _
19:         "Products.QuantityPerUnit, Products.UnitPrice, " & _
20:         "Products.UnitsInStock " & _
21:         "FROM Products INNER JOIN Suppliers ON " & _
22:         "Products.SupplierID = Suppliers.SupplierID " & _
23:         "INNER JOIN Categories ON " & _
24:         "Products.CategoryID = Categories.CategoryID " & _
25:         "WHERE Categories.CategoryID = " & CategoryID
26:
27:       getProductsCommand = New SqlCommand(SqlStmnt, myConnection)
```

14

LISTING 14.4   Continued

```
28:    getProductsCommand.Connection.Open()
29:    productsReader = getProductsCommand.ExecuteReader()
30:
31:     Return productsReader
32:   End Function
33:
34:   End Class
35:
36: End Namespace
```

[C#]

```
01: using System;
02: using System.Data;
03: using System.Data.SqlClient;
04:
05: namespace Northwind{
06:
07:   public class Products{
08:
09:    private string ConString =
➡      "server=localhost;database=Northwind;uid=sa;pwd=;";
10:
11:    public SqlDataReader GetProductsByCategory(int CategoryID){
12:     SqlDataReader productsReader;
13:     SqlConnection myConnection = new SqlConnection(ConString);
14:     SqlCommand getProductsCommand;
15:     string SqlStmnt;
16:
17:     SqlStmnt = "SELECT Products.ProductID, Products.ProductName, " +
18:       "Suppliers.CompanyName, Categories.CategoryName, " +
19:       "Products.QuantityPerUnit, Products.UnitPrice, " +
20:       "Products.UnitsInStock " +
21:       "FROM Products INNER JOIN Suppliers ON " +
22:       "Products.SupplierID = Suppliers.SupplierID " +
23:       "INNER JOIN Categories ON " +
24:       "Products.CategoryID = Categories.CategoryID " +
25:       "WHERE Categories.CategoryID = " + CategoryID;
26:
27:     getProductsCommand = new SqlCommand(SqlStmnt, myConnection);
28:     getProductsCommand.Connection.Open();
29:     productsReader = getProductsCommand.ExecuteReader();
30:
31:     return productsReader;
32:    }
```

LISTING 14.4   Continued

```
33:
34:  }
35:
36: }
```

The `Products.GetProductsByCategory()` method uses the Sql Managed Provider to retrieve product information from the Northwind database and return it as a `SqlDataReader`.

> **NOTE**
>
> In Listing 14.4, you open a connection to the database (line 28) using an instance of the `SqlConnection` class. You never explicitly close and destroy the connection object. This is because the `DataReader` needs the connection to remain open while it is being used. When the calling client is done with the `DataReader` the .NET Framework will manage closing and destroying the `SqlConnection` object.

The `GetProducts()` WebMethod will create an instance of the `Products` class, and use the `GetProductsByCategory()` method to get the data that will be returned to the Web service consumer. Listing 14.5 shows the code for the `GetProducts()` WebMethod. The code in Listing 14.5 should be inserted at line 14 of Listing 14.3.

LISTING 14.5   The `ProductServices.GetProducts()` WebMethod

```
[VB]
01: <WebMethod(Description:="Return a list of products available from the " & _
02:   "Northwind Traders Company in a particular category.<br>" & _
03:   "The Categories are:" & _
04:   "<ol>" & _
05:   "<li>Beverages</li>" & _
06:   "<li>Condiments</li>" & _
07:   "<li>Confections</li>" & _
08:   "<li>Dairy Products</li>" & _
09:   "<li>Grains/Cereals</li>" & _
10:   "<li>Meat/Poultry</li>" & _
11:   "<li>Produce</li>" & _
12:   "<li>Seafood</li>" & _
13:   "</ol>")> _
14: Public Function GetProducts(CategoryID As Integer) As DataSet
15:   Dim ProductsDataSet As New DataSet()
```

LISTING 14.5   Continued

```
16:   Dim myProducts As Products = New Products()
17:   Dim productsReader As SqlDataReader
18:   Dim productsTable As DataTable = New DataTable()
19:   Dim newRow As DataRow
20:   Dim i As Integer = 0
21:
22:   productsReader = myProducts.GetProductsByCategory(CategoryID)
23:   For i = 0 to productsReader.FieldCount-1
24:    productsTable.Columns.Add(New DataColumn(productsReader.GetName(i)))
25:   Next
26:
27:   While productsReader.Read()
28:    newRow = productsTable.NewRow()
29:    For i = 0 to productsReader.FieldCount-1
30:     newRow.Item(i) = productsReader.GetValue(i)
31:    Next
32:    productsTable.Rows.Add(newRow)
33:   End While
34:
35:   ProductsDataSet.Tables.Add(productsTable)
36:   ProductsDataSet.Tables(0).TableName = "Products"
37:
38:    Return ProductsDataSet
39:   End Function
```

[C#]

```
01: [WebMethod(Description="Return a list of products available from the " +
02:   "Northwind Traders Company in a particular category.<br>" +
03:   "The Categories are:" +
04:   "<ol>" +
05:   "<li>Beverages</li>" +
06:   "<li>Condiments</li>" +
07:   "<li>Confections</li>" +
08:   "<li>Dairy Products</li>" +
09:   "<li>Grains/Cereals</li>" +
10:   "<li>Meat/Poultry</li>" +
11:   "<li>Produce</li>" +
12:   "<li>Seafood</li>" +
13:   "</ol>")]
14: public DataSet GetProducts(int CategoryID){
15:   DataSet ProductsDataSet = new DataSet();
16:   Products myProducts = new Products();
17:   SqlDataReader productsReader;
18:   DataTable productsTable = new DataTable();
```

LISTING 14.5   Continued

```
19:    DataRow newRow;
20:    int i = 0;
21:
22:    productsReader = myProducts.GetProductsByCategory(CategoryID);
23:    for(i = 0; i < productsReader.FieldCount-1; i++){
24:      productsTable.Columns.Add(new DataColumn(productsReader.GetName(i)));
25:    }
26:
27:    while(productsReader.Read()){
28:      newRow = productsTable.NewRow();
29:      for(i = 0; i < productsReader.FieldCount-1; i++){
30:        newRow[i] = productsReader.GetValue(i);
31:      }
32:      productsTable.Rows.Add(newRow);
33:    }
34:
35:    ProductsDataSet.Tables.Add(productsTable);
36:    ProductsDataSet.Tables[0].TableName = "Products";
37:
38:    return ProductsDataSet;
39:  }
```

On line 1 of Listing 14.5, you declare the method as a WebMethod, and pass into it a description for the WebMethod (lines 1 through 13). The description will be rendered on the WebMethod description page generated by the .NET Framework (see Figure 14.3). The GetProducts() WebMethod returns an XML file (a DataSet) of products for a given category. This is done by creating an instance of the Products class and calling the GetProductsBy Category() method, passing in the CategoryID passed into the WebMethod. Because the GetProductsByCategory() method returns a SqlDataReader, you have to programmatically create a DataTable, fill it with the records from the SqlDataReader, and drop the DataTable into a DataSet to be returned.

On line 18, you create an instance of the DataTable class, and an instance of the DataRow class on line 19. Although you know the names and number of columns that should be in the DataTable, based on the Products.GetProductsByCategory() method, this WebMethod should be built to allow that information to change without breaking the WebMethod. Using a For...Next loop, you loop through the first record in the SqlDataReader to create the columns in the DataTable. Using this design, the GetProductsByCategory() method can be changed to return different fields of data, and the GetProducts() WebMethod will adapt.

On line 27, you begin iterating through the data in the SqlDataReader using the Read() method. The Read() method advances the SqlDataReader one record at a time. With each

14

EXPOSING DATA
THROUGH WEB
SERVICES

record, you add a new DataRow to the DataTable. After all the rows in the SqlDataReader have been filled in the DataTable, the DataTable is added to an empty DataSet, and the DataSet is returned to the consumer.

Figure 14.6 shows the GetProducts() WebMethod description page.

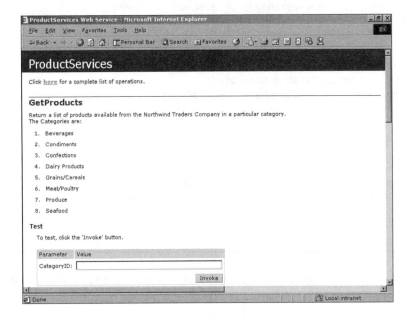

FIGURE 14.6

The GetProducts() WebMethod *page shows the* WebMethod *description, and an input box for entering a category ID for testing.*

Building the PlaceOrder() WebMethod

The PlaceOrder() WebMethod is intended to enable customers to place orders to Northwind. Because it is a WebMethod, the client can use any type of application they would like, provided it can call a Web service. For example, a customer could have a Web site that allows his product managers to place orders online. The Web application then would make a call to the Web service to send the order. The customer also could use a desktop application. The application could include an order entry screen. The application, like the Web application, would make a call to the Web service to submit the order. This type of flexibility enables you to build one Web service that can be used by many possible clients, all using different systems.

The PlaceOrder() WebMethod takes in a series of parameters that identify the customer placing the order, and an XML document, in the form of a DataSet, containing the products to order, and the quantities for each product. This WebMethod does two things. First, it adds a new entry in the Orders table in the Northwind database. Then, using the newly generated order number, the PlaceOrder() WebMethod adds a record to the Order Details table for each order entered in the DataSet. The WebMethod returns the new order number to the consumer.

For this WebMethod, you will need to add two stored procedures to the Northwind database. The first, AddNewOrder, takes in parameters for all the order information and adds a new order record. The AddNewOrder stored procedure is shown in Listing 14.6.

LISTING 14.6   The AddNewOrder SQL-Stored Procedure

```
CREATE PROCEDURE [AddNewOrder]
  @CustomerID nchar (5), @EmployeeID int, @OrderDate datetime,
  @RequiredDate datetime, @ShipVia int, @Freight money,
  @ShipName nvarchar (40), @ShipAddress varchar (60),
  @ShipCity varchar (15), @ShipRegion varchar (15),
  @ShipPostalCode varchar (10), @ShipCountry varchar (15),
  @OrderID  int output
AS
INSERT INTO Orders
(CustomerID, EmployeeID, OrderDate, RequiredDate, ShipVia,
  Freight, ShipName, ShipAddress, ShipCity, ShipRegion,
  ShipPostalCode, ShipCountry)
VALUES
(@CustomerID, @EmployeeID, @OrderDate, @RequiredDate, @ShipVia,
  @Freight, @ShipName, @ShipAddress, @ShipCity, @ShipRegion,
  @ShipPostalCode, @ShipCountry)

SELECT @OrderID = @@Identity
```

The second stored procedure, AddNewOrderDetail, takes in parameters for an order detail line, such as the order ID, product ID, and quantity ordered. The AddNewOrderDetail stored procedure is shown in Listing 14.7.

LISTING 14.7   The AddNewOrderDetail SQL-Stored Procedure

```
CREATE PROCEDURE [AddNewOrderDetail]
  @OrderID int, @ProductID int, @Quantity smallint
AS
DECLARE @UnitPrice money

SELECT @UnitPrice = UnitPrice FROM Products WHERE ProductID = @ProductID

INSERT INTO [Order Details]
```

14

LISTING 14.7   Continued

```
(OrderID, ProductID, UnitPrice, Quantity, Discount)
VALUES
(@OrderID, @ProductID, @UnitPrice, @Quantity, 0)
```

After the two stored procedures have been created, you can build the PlaceOrder()
WebMethod.

The PlaceOrder() WebMethod will take in all the necessary parameters, add a record to the
Orders table, and then insert rows into the Order Details table. Listing 14.8 shows the
PlaceOrder() WebMethod.

LISTING 14.8   The PlaceOrder() WebMethod

[VB]

```
01: <WebMethod(Description:="Submit an order for " & _
02:   "processing.  You will be given your order number as the " & _
03:   "return value.<br>" & _
04:   "The ShipVia values are:" & _
05:   "<ol>" & _
06:   "<li>Speedy Express</li>" & _
07:   "<li>United Package</li>" & _
08:   "<li>Federal Shipping</li>" & _
09:   "</ol>")> _
10  Public Function PlaceOrder(CustomerID As String, RequiredDate As DateTime, _
➡       ShipVia As Integer, ShipName As String, ShipAddress As String, _
➡       ShipCity As String, ShipRegion As String, ShipPostalCode As String, _
➡       ShipCountry As String, CustomerOrder As DataSet) As Integer
11:   Dim OrderNumber As Integer = 0
12:   Dim dt As DateTime = DateTime.Today
13:   Dim Freight As Double = 0
14:   Dim orderDetailCommand As SqlDataAdapter
15:   Dim myConnection As SqlConnection = New SqlConnection(ConString)
16:   Dim myCommand As SqlCommand
17:   Dim myParameter As SqlParameter = Nothing
18:
19:   myCommand = New SqlCommand("AddNewOrder", myConnection)
20:   myCommand.CommandType = CommandType.StoredProcedure
21:   myParameter = myCommand.Parameters.Add(new SqlParameter("@CustomerID",
➡       SqlDbType.NChar, 5))
22:   myParameter.Value = CustomerID
23:   myParameter = myCommand.Parameters.Add(new SqlParameter("@EmployeeID",
➡       SqlDbType.Int))
24:   myParameter.Value = 1
```

LISTING 14.8 Continued

```
25: myParameter = myCommand.Parameters.Add(new SqlParameter("@OrderDate",
➡    SqlDbType.DateTime))
26: myParameter.Value = dt
27: myParameter = myCommand.Parameters.Add(new SqlParameter("@RequiredDate",
➡    SqlDbType.DateTime))
28: myParameter.Value = RequiredDate
29: myParameter = myCommand.Parameters.Add(new SqlParameter("@ShipVia",
➡    SqlDbType.Int))
30: myParameter.Value = ShipVia
31: myParameter = myCommand.Parameters.Add(new SqlParameter("@Freight",
➡    SqlDbType.Money))
32: myParameter.Value = Freight
33: myParameter = myCommand.Parameters.Add(new SqlParameter("@ShipName",
➡    SqlDbType.NVarChar, 40))
34: myParameter.Value = ShipName
35: myParameter = myCommand.Parameters.Add(new SqlParameter("@ShipAddress",
➡    SqlDbType.NVarChar, 60))
36: myParameter.Value = ShipAddress
37: myParameter = myCommand.Parameters.Add(new SqlParameter("@ShipCity",
➡    SqlDbType.NVarChar, 15))
38: myParameter.Value = ShipCity
39: myParameter = myCommand.Parameters.Add(new SqlParameter("@ShipRegion",
➡    SqlDbType.NVarChar, 15))
40: myParameter.Value = ShipRegion
41: myParameter = myCommand.Parameters.Add(new SqlParameter("@ShipPostalCode",
➡    SqlDbType.NVarChar, 10))
42: myParameter.Value = ShipPostalCode
43: myParameter = myCommand.Parameters.Add(new SqlParameter("@ShipCountry",
➡    SqlDbType.NVarChar, 15))
44: myParameter.Value = ShipCountry
45: myParameter = myCommand.Parameters.Add(new SqlParameter("@OrderID",
➡    SqlDbType.Int))
46: myParameter.Direction = ParameterDirection.Output
47:
48: myConnection.Open()
49: myCommand.ExecuteNonQuery()
50: OrderNumber = CInt(myCommand.Parameters.Item("@OrderID").Value)
51:
52: orderDetailCommand = New SqlDataAdapter()
53:
54: ' Build the insert Command
55: orderDetailCommand.InsertCommand - New SqlCommand("AddNewOrderDetail",
➡    myConnection)
```

14

EXPOSING DATA
THROUGH WEB
SERVICES

LISTING 14.8 Continued

```
56: orderDetailCommand.InsertCommand.CommandType =
➥    CommandType.StoredProcedure
57:
58: myParameter = orderDetailCommand.InsertCommand.Parameters.Add(new
➥    SqlParameter("@OrderID", SqlDbType.Int))
59: myParameter.Value = OrderNumber
60:
61: myParameter = orderDetailCommand.InsertCommand.Parameters.Add(new
➥    SqlParameter("@ProductID", SqlDbType.Int))
62: myParameter.SourceVersion = DataRowVersion.Current
63: myParameter.SourceColumn = "ProductID"
64:
65: myParameter = orderDetailCommand.InsertCommand.Parameters.Add(new
➥    SqlParameter("@Quantity", SqlDbType.SmallInt))
66: myParameter.SourceVersion = DataRowVersion.Current
67: myParameter.SourceColumn = "Quantity"
68:
69: orderDetailCommand.Update(CustomerOrder, "Order")
70:
71: Return OrderNumber
72: End Function

[C#]

01: [WebMethod(Description="Submit an order for " +
02: "processing. You will be given your order number as " +
03: "the return value.<br>" +
04: "The ShipVia values are:" +
05: "<ol>" +
06: "<li>Speedy Express</li>" +
07: "<li>United Package</li>" +
08: "<li>Federal Shipping</li>" +
09: "</ol>")]
10: public int PlaceOrder(string CustomerID, DateTime RequiredDate,
➥    int ShipVia, string ShipName, string ShipAddress,
➥    string ShipCity, string ShipRegion, string ShipPostalCode,
➥    string ShipCountry, DataSet CustomerOrder){
11: int OrderNumber = 0;
12: DateTime dt = DateTime.Today;
13: Double Freight = 0;
14: SqlDataAdapter orderDetailCommand;
15: SqlConnection myConnection = new SqlConnection(ConString);
16: SqlCommand myCommand;
17: SqlParameter myParameter = null;
18:
```

LISTING 14.8 Continued

```
19:  myCommand = new SqlCommand("AddNewOrder", myConnection);
20:  myCommand.CommandType = CommandType.StoredProcedure;
21:  myParameter = myCommand.Parameters.Add(new SqlParameter("@CustomerID",
➥    SqlDbType.NChar, 5));
22:  myParameter.Value = CustomerID;
23:  myParameter = myCommand.Parameters.Add(new SqlParameter("@EmployeeID",
➥    SqlDbType.Int));
24:  myParameter.Value = 1;
25:  myParameter = myCommand.Parameters.Add(new SqlParameter("@OrderDate",
➥    SqlDbType.DateTime));
26:  myParameter.Value = dt;
27:  myParameter = myCommand.Parameters.Add(new SqlParameter("@RequiredDate",
➥    SqlDbType.DateTime));
28:  myParameter.Value = RequiredDate;
29:  myParameter = myCommand.Parameters.Add(new SqlParameter("@ShipVia",
➥    SqlDbType.Int));
30:  myParameter.Value = ShipVia;
31:  myParameter = myCommand.Parameters.Add(new SqlParameter("@Freight",
➥    SqlDbType.Money));
32:  myParameter.Value = Freight;
33:  myParameter = myCommand.Parameters.Add(new SqlParameter("@ShipName",
➥    SqlDbType.NVarChar, 40));
34:  myParameter.Value = ShipName;
35:  myParameter = myCommand.Parameters.Add(new SqlParameter("@ShipAddress",
➥    SqlDbType.NVarChar, 60));
36:  myParameter.Value = ShipAddress;
37:  myParameter = myCommand.Parameters.Add(new SqlParameter("@ShipCity",
➥    SqlDbType.NVarChar, 15));
38:  myParameter.Value = ShipCity;
39:  myParameter = myCommand.Parameters.Add(new SqlParameter("@ShipRegion",
➥    SqlDbType.NVarChar, 15));
40:  myParameter.Value = ShipRegion;
41:  myParameter = myCommand.Parameters.Add(new SqlParameter("@ShipPostalCode",
➥    SqlDbType.NVarChar, 10));
42:  myParameter.Value = ShipPostalCode;
43:  myParameter = myCommand.Parameters.Add(new SqlParameter("@ShipCountry",
➥    SqlDbType.NVarChar, 15));
44:  myParameter.Value = ShipCountry;
45:  myParameter = myCommand.Parameters.Add(new SqlParameter("@OrderID",
➥    SqlDbType.Int));
46:  myParameter.Direction = ParameterDirection.Output;
47:
48:  myConnection.Open();
49:  myCommand.ExecuteNonQuery();
```

14

EXPOSING DATA
THROUGH WEB
SERVICES

LISTING 14.8 Continued

```
50:  OrderNumber = (int)myCommand.Parameters["@OrderID"].Value;
51:
52:  orderDetailCommand = new SqlDataAdapter();
53:
54:  // Build the insert Command
55:  orderDetailCommand.InsertCommand = new SqlCommand("AddNewOrderDetail",
➥    myConnection);
56:  orderDetailCommand.InsertCommand.CommandType =
➥    CommandType.StoredProcedure;
57:
58:  myParameter = orderDetailCommand.InsertCommand.Parameters.Add(new
➥    SqlParameter("@OrderID", SqlDbType.Int));
59:  myParameter.Value = OrderNumber;
60:
61:  myParameter = orderDetailCommand.InsertCommand.Parameters.Add(new
➥    SqlParameter("@ProductID", SqlDbType.Int));
62:  myParameter.SourceVersion = DataRowVersion.Current;
63:  myParameter.SourceColumn = "ProductID";
64:
65:  myParameter = orderDetailCommand.InsertCommand.Parameters.Add(new
➥    SqlParameter("@Quantity", SqlDbType.SmallInt));
66:  myParameter.SourceVersion = DataRowVersion.Current;
67:  myParameter.SourceColumn = "Quantity";
68:
69:  orderDetailCommand.Update(CustomerOrder, "Order");
70:
71:  return OrderNumber;
72: }
```

For simplicity's sake, I have broken the PlaceOrder() WebMethod in Listing 14.8 into two parts. The first part, lines 1 through 51, adds a new order to the Orders table. The second part, lines 52 through 72, adds each order entry to the Order Details table and returns the order number to the consumer.

> **NOTE**
>
> For a real business application, this WebMethod should be built to use a transaction. You wouldn't want to commit the order entry unless the order detail entry was successful, and vice versa. Transactional processing is out of the scope of this chapter, and was omitted to simplify this example.

PlaceOrder() Part 1

Part 1 of the `PlaceOrder()` WebMethod works in the same fashion as many of the samples in previous chapters of this book. You have a series of input parameters that are passed to a stored procedure using a `SqlCommand` object. The `SqlCommand` has a parameters collection that includes a parameter for each input expected by the stored procedure. On lines 45 and 46, you define an output parameter to capture the `OrderID` that is returned from the stored procedure. The `OrderID` value is assigned to a variable that will be used in Part 2, and returned to the consumer.

You use the `ExecuteNonQuery()` method of the `SqlCommand` class to execute the stored procedure. The `OrderID` is captured by checking the `SqlCOmmand.Parameters["@OrderID"].Value` after the `ExecuteNonQuery()` method has been called.

PlaceOrder() Part 2

In Part 2 of the `PlaceOrder()` WebMethod, you use the `SqlDataAdapter.Update()` method to do a batch insert of all the order detail. In Chapter 11, "Editing and Filtering Data," you used the `Update()` method to update and insert records in an existing `DataSet`. Here you have a new `DataSet` being passed into the WebMethod. Because none of these records exist in the database (it is a new order after all), the `Update()` method will only be executing the `SqlDataAdapter.InsertCommand`.

On line 52, you instantiate a new `SqlDataAdapter`. There is no need to construct it with a SQL statement or `SqlCommand` because you will not be using the `SelectCommand`, only the `InsertCommand`. On line 54, you assign values to the `InsertCommand` property of the `SqlData Adapter`; you assign a stored procedure name, `AddNewOrderDetail`, and a `SqlConnection`. On line 58, you create one of the three `SqlParameters` that the `AddNewOrderDetail` requires, the `@OrderID` parameter. This parameter uses the order number returned from the `SqlCommand` in Part 1. The `OrderID` is used to map the record in the `Order Details` table to the order record in the `Order` table.

On lines 61 through 67, you create the other two parameters. These two parameters are a bit different from the previous one; these parameters have to dynamically grab a value from the `DataSet` and pass it to the stored procedure. Each of these parameters has a line to set the `SqlParameter.SourceVersion` property. This property is used to determine which version of the `DataTable` column to pass into the parameter. In this case, because the `DataSet/DataTable` are new, and none of the records exist in the database, you want to use the `DataRow Version.Current` property. This property specifies that the current version of the data should be used because that is the only version that exists in the `DataSet/DataTable`. You follow that by setting the `SqlParameter.SourceColumn` property, which specifies which column of the `DataTable` will be used for this parameter.

14

Finally, you call the `SqlDataAdapter.Update()` method and pass in the `DataSet` and the name of the table to update. The `Update()` method executes the `InsertCommand` for any records that are in the `DataTable`, but not in the database. It also executes the `UpdateCommand` for any records that are in the `DataTable` or the database, that have changes because the `DataTable` was created. All the records in the `DataTable` are new, and not yet in the database; only the `InsertCommand` is called.

After the `Update()` has executed, you return the `OrderID` to the calling client (line 71).

Figure 14.7 shows the `PlaceOrder()` WebMethod description page. Because one of the input parameters is an XML file (a `DataSet`), the Http-Get and Http-Post protocols cannot be used. Only the SOAP protocol information is rendered to the page.

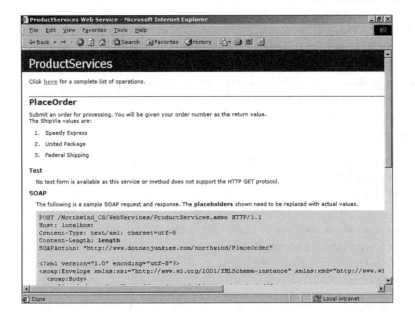

FIGURE 14.7

The `PlaceOrder()` WebMethod *page shows the* WebMethod *description.*

Building the `GetOrderDetail()` WebMethod

The last WebMethod in the Northwind `ProductServices` Web service is the `GetOrderDetail()` WebMethod. This WebMethod is used to return a `DataSet` of the order detail for a given order number. A consumer can pass in an order number and get back a `DataSet` of items ordered and their quantities.

Like the `GetProducts()` WebMethod, the `GetOrderDetail()` WebMethod uses functionality used in the rest of the Northwind application, so it will instantiate the `Products` class and invoke the `Products.GetOrderDetails()` method. The `Products.GetOrderDetails()` method returns a `SqlDataReader`, so the WebMethod will need to dynamically create a `DataTable` and a `DataSet` to return to the calling client. This WebMethod is nearly identical to the `GetProducts()` WebMethod.

The code for the `Products.GetOrderDetails()` method is shown in Listing 14.9. This code should be added to the `Products` class, and the class must be recompiled.

LISTING 14.9   The `GetOrderDetails()` Class

[VB]

```
01: Public Function GetOrderDetails(OrderID As Integer) As SqlDataReader
02:   Dim orderDetailReader As SqlDataReader
03:   Dim myConnection As SqlConnection = new SqlConnection(ConString)
04:   Dim orderDetailCommand As SqlCommand = new SqlCommand("CustOrdersDetail",
➥     myConnection)
05:   Dim myParameter As SqlParameter = Nothing
06:
07:   orderDetailCommand.CommandType = CommandType.StoredProcedure
08:   myParameter = orderDetailCommand.Parameters.Add(new
➥     SqlParameter("@OrderID", SqlDbType.Int))
09:   myParameter.Value = OrderID
10:
11:   orderDetailCommand.Connection.Open()
12:   orderDetailReader = orderDetailCommand.ExecuteReader()
13:
14:   Return orderDetailReader
15: End Function
```

[C#]

```
01: public SqlDataReader GetOrderDetails(int OrderID){
02:   SqlDataReader orderDetailReader;
03:   SqlConnection myConnection = new SqlConnection(ConString);
04:   SqlCommand orderDetailCommand = new SqlCommand("CustOrdersDetail",
➥     myConnection);
05:   SqlParameter myParameter = null;
06:
07:   orderDetailCommand.CommandType = CommandType.StoredProcedure;
08:   myParameter = orderDetailCommand.Parameters.Add(new
➥     SqlParameter("@OrderID", SqlDbType.Int));
09:   myParameter.Value = OrderID;
10:
```

14

EXPOSING DATA
THROUGH WEB
SERVICES

LISTING 14.9   Continued

```
11:  orderDetailCommand.Connection.Open();
12:  orderDetailReader = orderDetailCommand.ExecuteReader();
13:
14:  return orderDetailReader;
15: }
```

In Listing 14.9, you create a method that takes in one argument, the OrderID (line 1). You create a SqlDataReader on line 2, and execute a stored procedure, on line 12, that takes the OrderID as its only parameter. You do not need to add the CustOrderDetail-stored procedure, as it is included with the Northwind database when it is installed.

The Products.GetOrderDetails() method returns a SqlDataReader to the calling component. Listing 14.10 shows the code for the GetOrderDetail() WebMethod, which will invoke the Products.GetOrderDetails() method.

LISTING 14.10   The GetOrderDetail() WebMethod

[VB]

```
01: <WebMethod(Description:="Look up a customer order by OrderID.")> _
02: Public Function GetOrderDetail(OrderID As Integer) As DataSet
03:  Dim OrderDataSet As New DataSet()
04:  Dim myProducts As Products = New Products()
05:  Dim orderDetailReader As SqlDataReader
06:  Dim orderDetailTable As DataTable = New DataTable()
07:  Dim newRow As DataRow
08:  Dim i As Integer = 0
09:
10:  orderDetailReader = myProducts.GetOrderDetails(OrderID)
11:  For i = 0 to orderDetailReader.FieldCount-1
12:   orderDetailTable.Columns.Add(New
➥     DataColumn(orderDetailReader.GetName(i)))
13:  Next
14:
15:  While orderDetailReader.Read()
16:   newRow = orderDetailTable.NewRow()
17:   For i = 0 to orderDetailReader.FieldCount-1
18:    newRow.Item(i) = orderDetailReader.GetValue(i)
19:   Next
20:   orderDetailTable.Rows.Add(newRow)
21:  End While
22:
```

LISTING 14.10 Continued

```
23:   OrderDataSet.Tables.Add(orderDetailTable)
24:   OrderDataSet.Tables(0).TableName = "OrderDetail"
25:
26:   Return OrderDataSet
27: End Function

[C#]

01: [WebMethod(Description="Look up a customer order by OrderID.")]
02: public DataSet GetOrderDetail(int OrderID){
03:   DataSet OrderDataSet = new DataSet();
04:   Products myProducts = new Products();
05:   SqlDataReader orderDetailReader = null;
06:   DataTable orderDetailTable = new DataTable();
07:   DataRow newRow;
08:   int i = 0;
09:
10:   orderDetailReader = myProducts.GetOrderDetails(OrderID);
11:   for(i = 0; i < orderDetailReader.FieldCount-1; i++){
12:    orderDetailTable.Columns.Add(new
➥       DataColumn(orderDetailReader.GetName(i)));
13:   }
14:
15:   while(orderDetailReader.Read()){
16:    newRow = orderDetailTable.NewRow();
17:    for(i = 0; i < orderDetailReader.FieldCount-1; i++){
18     newRow[i] = orderDetailReader.GetValue(i);
19:    }
20:    orderDetailTable.Rows.Add(newRow);
21:   }
22:
23:   OrderDataSet.Tables.Add(orderDetailTable);
24:   OrderDataSet.Tables[0].TableName = "OrderDetail";
25:
26:   return OrderDataSet;
27: }
```

14

In Listing 14.10, you create the GetOrderDetail() WebMethod on lines 1–2. This WebMethod works similar to the GetProducts() WebMethod. On line 2 the OrderID is passed into the WebMethod. The WebMethod invokes the Products.GetOrderDetails() method on line 10, and returns a DataSet to the consumer.

Figure 14.8 shows the WebMethod description page for GetOrderDetail().

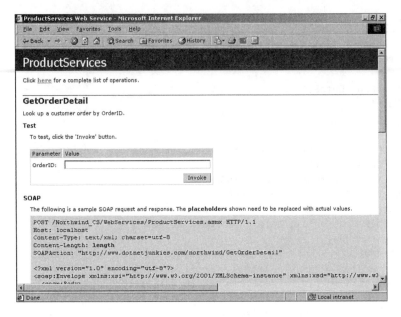

FIGURE 14.8

The GetOrderDetail() WebMethod *page shows the* WebMethod *description.*

Consuming Web Services

After a Web service is created and published on the Internet another entity, such as a business partner, client, or customer can use the Web service. This is referred to as *consuming* a Web service. The consumer can make a call to the Web service using any of the available protocols, Http-Get, Http-Post, or SOAP. The consumer of a Web service can be a Web application, a desktop application with Internet access, or another Web service.

To utilize a Web service, the consumer makes a proxy client, which provides programmatic access to all the exposed WebMethods in the Web service. The proxy client can be coded by hand, but it is much easier to use a utility to generate the proxy client. The .NET Framework SDK ships with a utility, named WSDL.exe, which is capable of generating proxy clients for Web services.

WSDL.exe

The *WSDL.exe* utility is a command-line utility used to generate proxy classes for consuming Web services. The WSDL.exe utility can generate proxy clients using any of the three protocols. The utility evaluates the WSDL provided by the Web service, and generates a proxy class in either Visual Basic, C#, or JScript. The proxy class then is compiled into a DLL and can be accessed by the consumer application. The proxy class provides methods for each of the `WebMethods` exposed by the Web service.

The WSDL.exe has a number of possible parameters, as seen in Table 14.1.

TABLE 14.1 Parameters of the WSDL.exe Utility

Parameter	Description
`/?`	Help. Entering `wsd.exe /?` at the command line will list all the parameters accepted by the WSDL utility.
`/nologo`	Suppresses the banner.
`/language:<language>`	Specifies the language used to write the proxy class. Accepted values are VB, CS, or JS. The default value is CS. `/l:` is the short form.
`/server:`	Generates an abstract class for a Web service implementation based on the contracts. The default is to create a proxy class.
`/namespace:<namespace>`	Specifies the namespace to assign to the proxy class. `/n:` is the short form.
`/out:<filename>`	Specifies the filename for the proxy class. The proxy class is created in the same directory in which the WSDL utility is run, unless a different path is defined.
`/protocol:<protocol>`	Specifies the protocol the proxy client should use to call the Web service. Possible values are SOAP, Http-Get, or Http-Post. The default is SOAP.
`/username:<username>`	Specifies the username to use when connecting to a server that requires authentication. `/u:` is the short form.
`/password:<password>`	Specifies the password to use when connecting to a server that requires authentication. `/p:` is the short form.
`/domain:<domain>`	The domain to use when connecting to a server that requires a domain name for authentication. `/d:` is the short form.

14

EXPOSING DATA
THROUGH WEB
SERVICES

To create a client proxy class, you must know the URL of the WSDL document. The WSDL.exe utility takes in the URL and any specified parameters, and generates the proxy class. An example of a command to execute the WSDL utility is

```
wsdl.exe http://localhost/myService.asmx?WSDL /l:VB
➥/out:myProxyClient.vb /n:MyApp /p:HttpPost
```

In the previous examples, you built a Web service for the Northwind application. You can create a proxy class to be used with the Northwind Web service. Included on the companion Web site for this book (`http://www.samspublishing.com`) is a sample client application, The Big Cheese, which is a customer of the Northwind Trading Company. The Big Cheese can consume the Northwind Web service and implement its own order processing by calling the Web service.

To create the structure for a new Web application for The Big Cheese, follows these steps:

1. Create a directory on your computer named `C:\Inetpub\wwwroot\TheBigCheese`.

2. Create a subdirectory named `\bin`.

3. Create another subdirectory named `\codebase`.

4. Copy the aspx, css, images, js, and usercontrols directories from the companion Web site into the `\TheBigCheese` directory on your computer.

5. In the Internet Services Manager, create a new virtual directory named `BigCheese`, and point it to the `\TheBigCheese` directory.

After the Big Cheese Web application structure is in place, you can begin creating the proxy class.

Open a command line and enter the command in Listing 14.11.

LISTING 14.11   Executing the WSDL.exe Utility

```
[VB]
wsdl http://localhost/northwind_vb/WebServices/ProductServices.asmx?WSDL
➥ /l:VB /n:Northwind.ProductServices /nologo
➥ /out:C:\Inetpub\wwwroot\TheBigCheese_VB\codebase\
➥ NorthwindProductServices_proxy.vb
[C#]
wsdl http://localhost/northwind_cs/WebServices/ProductServices.asmx?WSDL
➥ /l:CS /n:Northwind.ProductServices /nologo
➥ /out:C:\Inetpub\wwwroot\TheBigCheese_CS\codebase\
➥ NorthwindProductServices_proxy.cs
```

The WSDL.exe utility will generate a proxy class in the `\codebase` directory of the `\TheBigCheese` directory. After the proxy client has been created, compile it into a DLL using a command-line compiler, as seen in Listing 14.12.

LISTING 14.12   Compiling the Proxy Class with a Command-Line Compiler

```
[VB]

vbc /t:library /out:D:\TheBigCheese\bin\Northwind.ProductServices.dll
➥ C:\Inetput\wwwroot\TheBigCheese\codebase\
➥ NorthwindProductServices_proxy.vb
➥ /r:System.Web.Services.dll /r:System.dll /r:System.Xml.dll
➥ /r:System.Data.dll
[C#]

csc /t:library /out:D:\TheBigCheese\bin\Northwind.ProductServices.dll
➥ C:\Inetput\wwwroot\TheBigCheese\codebase\
➥ NorthwindProductServices_proxy.cs
➥/r:System.Web.Services.dll /r:System.dll /r:System.Xml.dll
➥ /r:System.Data.dll
```

Building the Consumer Web Form

A *Web service consumer* is an application that accesses a Web service. Using the WSDL.exe utility, you create a proxy client class that can be implemented to make calls to the exposed WebMethods of the Web service. The Big Cheese sample consumer application can be used to consume the Northwind ProductServices Web service. You can build a Web Form that calls the GetProducts() WebMethod. After the user has entered quantities for each product he wants to order, you can make a programmatic call to the PlaceOrder() WebMethod and the GetOrderDetail() WebMethod.

Listing 14.13 shows the code to build a consumer for the ProductServices() Web service. This code is for a Web Form (named BigCheese_Order.aspx) that provides a user interface for placing an order, and calls the Web service to process the order. The Web Form built in Listing 14.13 belongs in the BigCheese directory.

LISTING 14.13   Consuming the ProductServices_Web Service

```
[VB]

01: <%@ Page Language="VB" %>
02: <%@ Register TagPrefix="bigcheese" TagName="top"
➥   Src="user_controls/top.ascx" %>
03: <%@ Register TagPrefix="bigcheese" TagName="copyright"
➥   Src="user_controls/copyright.ascx" %>
04: <%@ Import Namespace="System.Data" %>
05: <%@ Import Namespace="Northwind.ProductServices" %>
06: <script runat="server">
07:   Protected Sub Page_Load(Sender As Object, E As EventArgs)
```

LISTING 14.13   Continued

```
08:    If Not IsPostBack Then
09:      Dim dt As DateTime = DateTime.Today
10:      dt = dt.AddDays(7)
11:      Dim NWND_Products As Northwind.ProductServices.ProductServices =
➡  New Northwind.ProductServices.ProductServices()
12:      Dim getProducts As DataSet = NWND_Products.GetProducts(1)
13:
14:      RequiredDate.SelectedDate = dt
15:      RequiredDate.VisibleDate = dt
16:
17:      PlaceOrder.Visible = True
18:      FinalOrder.Visible = False
19:      Products.DataSource = getProducts.Tables("Products").DefaultView
20:      Products.DataBind()
21:    End If
22:  End Sub
23:
24:  Protected Sub Submit_Click(Sender As Object, E As EventArgs)
25:    Dim OrderID As Integer = 0
26:
27:    ' Create the DataSet to be passed to the Web Service
28:    Dim CustomerOrder As New DataSet
29:
30:    ' Add the required Order table to the DataSet
31:    CustomerOrder.Tables.Add("Order")
32:
33:    ' Add the ProductID and Quantity column to the Order table
34:    Dim ProductID As DataColumn = New DataColumn()
35:    ProductID.DataType = System.Type.GetType("System.Int32")
36:    ProductID.ColumnName = "ProductID"
37:    CustomerOrder.Tables("Order").Columns.Add(ProductID)
38:
39:    Dim Quantity As DataColumn = New  DataColumn()
40:    Quantity.DataType = System.Type.GetType("System.Int32")
41:    Quantity.ColumnName = "Quantity"
42:    CustomerOrder.Tables("Order").Columns.Add(Quantity)
43:
44:    ' Create the objects to be used in the For() loop
45:    Dim newRow As DataRow
46:    Dim ProductQuantity As TextBox
47:    Dim i As Integer = 0
48:    Dim newQnty As Integer
49:    Dim itemCount As Integer = 0
50:
```

LISTING 14.13 Continued

```
51:    ' Any item with a quantity greater than 0 should be added to the order
52:    For i = 0 To Products.Items.Count-1
53:      ProductQuantity = Products.Items(i).FindControl("Qnty")
54:      newQnty = Integer.Parse(ProductQuantity.Text)
55:
56:      If newQnty > 0 Then
57:        newRow = CustomerOrder.Tables("Order").NewRow()
58:        newRow("ProductID") = Integer.Parse(Products.Items(i).Cells(0).Text)
59:        newRow("Quantity") = newQnty
60:        CustomerOrder.Tables("Order").Rows.Add(newRow)
61:        itemCount = itemCount + 1
62:      End If
63:    Next
64:
65:    ' Place the order by calling the Web Service if there are 1 or more items
66:    If itemCount > 0 Then
67:      Dim NWND_Products As Northwind.ProductServices.ProductServices =
➥  New Northwind.ProductServices.ProductServices()
68:
69:      ' "THEBI" is the CustomerID for The Big Cheese.
70:      ' This is the client page for Big Cheese, so the value is hard coded.
71:      OrderID = NWND_Products.PlaceOrder("THEBI", RequiredDate.SelectedDate,
➥  1, ShipName.Text, ShipAddress.Text, ShipCity.Text, ShipRegion.Text,
➥  ShipPostalCode.Text, ShipCountry.Text, CustomerOrder)
72:
73:      ErrorMsg.Text = "Order Number: " & OrderID.ToString()
74:
75:      GetNewOrder(OrderID)
76:    Else
77:      ErrorMsg.Text = "<H5>Error: No quantities over zero (0) were entered.
➥  Your order was not placed.</H5>"
78:    End If
79:  End Sub
80:
81:  Protected Sub GetNewOrder(OrderID As Integer)
82:    Dim OrderInfo As DataSet
83:    Dim NWND_Products As Northwind.ProductServices.ProductServices = New
➥Northwind.ProductServices.ProductServices()
84:    OrderInfo = NWND_Products.GetOrderDetail(OrderID)
85:
86:    Products.Visible = False
87:    Submit.Visible = False
88:    PlaceOrder.Visible = False
89:    FinalOrder.Visible = True
90:
```

14

LISTING 14.13   Continued

```
91:    FinalOrder.DataSource = OrderInfo.Tables("OrderDetail").DefaultView
92:    FinalOrder.DataBind()
93:   End Sub
94: </script>
```

[C#]

```
01: <%@ Page Language="C#" %>
02: <%@ Register TagPrefix="bigcheese" TagName="top"
➥  Src="user_controls/top.ascx" %>
03: <%@ Register TagPrefix="bigcheese" TagName="copyright"
➥  Src="user_controls/copyright.ascx" %>
04: <%@ Import Namespace="System.Data" %>
05: <%@ Import Namespace="Northwind.ProductServices" %>
06: <script runat="server">
07:  protected void Page_Load(Object sender, EventArgs e){
08:   if(!IsPostBack){
09:    DateTime dt = DateTime.Today;
10:    dt = dt.AddDays(7);
11:    Northwind.ProductServices.ProductServices NWND_Products =
➥  new Northwind.ProductServices.ProductServices();
12:    DataSet getProducts = NWND_Products.GetProducts(1);
13:
14:    RequiredDate.SelectedDate = dt;
15:    RequiredDate.VisibleDate = dt;
16:
17:    PlaceOrder.Visible = true;
18:    FinalOrder.Visible = false;
19:    Products.DataSource = getProducts.Tables["Products"].DefaultView;
20:    Products.DataBind();
21:   }
22:  }
23:
24:  protected void Submit_Click(Object sender, EventArgs e){
25:   int OrderID = 0;
26:
27:   // Create the DataSet to be passed to the Web Service
28:   DataSet CustomerOrder = new DataSet();
29:
30:   // Add the required Order table to the DataSet
31:   CustomerOrder.Tables.Add("Order");
32:
33:   // Add the ProductID and Quantity column to the Order table
34:   DataColumn ProductID = new  DataColumn();
35:   ProductID.DataType = System.Type.GetType("System.Int32");
```

LISTING 14.13 Continued

```
36:    ProductID.ColumnName = "ProductID";
37:    CustomerOrder.Tables["Order"].Columns.Add(ProductID);
38:
39:    DataColumn Quantity = new  DataColumn();
40:    Quantity.DataType = System.Type.GetType("System.Int32");
41:    Quantity.ColumnName = "Quantity";
42:    CustomerOrder.Tables["Order"].Columns.Add(Quantity);
43:
44:    // Create the objects to be used in the for() loop
45:    DataRow newRow;
46:    TextBox ProductQuantity;
47:    int i = 0;
48:    int newQnty;
49:    int itemCount = 0;
50:
51:    // Any item with a quantity greater than 0 should be added to the order
52:    for(i=0; i < Products.Items.Count-1; i++){
53:     ProductQuantity = (TextBox)Products.Items[i].FindControl("Qnty");
54:     newQnty = int.Parse(ProductQuantity.Text);
55:
56:     if(newQnty > 0){
57:      newRow = CustomerOrder.Tables["Order"].NewRow();
58:      newRow["ProductID"] = int.Parse(Products.Items[i].Cells[0].Text);
59:      newRow["Quantity"] = newQnty;
60:      CustomerOrder.Tables["Order"].Rows.Add(newRow);
61:      itemCount = itemCount + 1;
62:     }
63:    }
64:
65:    //Place the order by calling the Web Service if there are 1 or more items
66:    if(itemCount > 0){
67:     Northwind.ProductServices.ProductServices NWND_Products =
➥  new Northwind.ProductServices.ProductServices();
68:
69:     // "THEBI" is the CustomerID for The Big Cheese.
70:     // This is the client page for Big Cheese, so the value is hard coded.
71:     OrderID = NWND_Products.PlaceOrder("THEBI", RequiredDate.SelectedDate,
➥  1, ShipName.Text, ShipAddress.Text, ShipCity.Text, ShipRegion.Text,
➥  ShipPostalCode.Text, ShipCountry.Text, CustomerOrder);
72:
73:     ErrorMsg.Text = "Order Number: " + OrderID.ToString();
74:
75:     GetNewOrder(OrderID);
76:    }else{
```

LISTING 14.13   Continued

```
77:    ErrorMsg.Text = "<H5>Error: No quantities over zero (0) were entered.
➥ Your order was not placed.</H5>";
78:    }
79:  }
80:
81:  protected void GetNewOrder(int OrderID){
82:    DataSet OrderInfo;
83:    Northwind.ProductServices.ProductServices NWND_Products =
➥ new Northwind.ProductServices.ProductServices();
84:    OrderInfo = NWND_Products.GetOrderDetail(OrderID);
85:
86:    Products.Visible = false;
87:    Submit.Visible = false;
88:    PlaceOrder.Visible = false;
89:    FinalOrder.Visible = true;
90:
91:    FinalOrder.DataSource = OrderInfo.Tables["NewOrder"].DefaultView;
92:    FinalOrder.DataBind();
93:  }
94: </script>

[VB & C#]

95: <html>
96: <body style="font: 8pt Verdana, Arial, sans-serif">
97: <form runat="server" method="post">
98: <bigcheese:top runat="server" Title="Beverage Order Form" />
99: <asp:Label runat="server" ID="ErrorMsg" EnableViewState="False"
100:  ForeColor="Red" Font-Bold="True" Width="740"   />
101: <table runat="server" ID="PlaceOrder" CellPadding="0"
102:  CellSpacing="0" Width="740">
103:  <tr>
104:   <td>
105:    <table cellpadding="4" cellspacing="0">
106:     <tr>
107:      <td style="font: 9pt Verdana, Arial, sans-serif">
108:       <b>Ship To Name:</b>
109:      </td>
110:      <td>
111:       <asp:TextBox runat="server" id="ShipName"
112:        Text="The Big Cheese - Store #7"
113:        Width="300" Font-Name="Verdana" Font-Size="9pt" />
114:      </td>
115:      <td style="font: 9pt Verdana, Arial, sans-serif">
116:       <b>Date Required:</b>
```

LISTING 14.13   Continued

```
117:        </td>
118:        </tr>
119:        <tr>
120:        <td style="font: 9pt Verdana, Arial, sans-serif">
121:         <b>Ship To Address:</b>
122:        </td>
123:        <td>
124:         <asp:TextBox runat="server" id="ShipAddress" Text="123 Main Street"
125:          Width="300" Font-Name="Verdana" Font-Size="9pt" />
126:        </td>
127:        <td rowspan="5"style="font: 9pt Verdana, Arial, sans-serif">
128:         <asp:Calendar runat="server" ID="RequiredDate"
129:          TitleStyle-BackColor="Maroon" TitleStyle-ForeColor="White"
130:          TitleStyle-Font-Size="9pt" TitleStyle-Font-Bold="True"
131:          DayHeaderStyle-BackColor="Tan" DayHeaderStyle-ForeColor="Black"
132:          DayHeaderStyle-Font-Size="8pt" DayHeaderStyle-Font-Bold="True"
133:          DayStyle-BackColor="Tan" DayStyle-ForeColor="Black"
134:          DayStyle-Font-Size="8pt"
135:          SelectedDayStyle-BackColor="Maroon"
136:          SelectedDayStyle-ForeColor="White"
137:          Width="278"
138:         />
139:        </td>
140:        </tr>
141:        <tr>
142:        <td style="font: 9pt Verdana, Arial, sans-serif">
143:         <b>Ship To City:</b>
144:        </td>
145:        <td>
146:         <asp:TextBox runat="server" id="ShipCity" Text="Seattle"
147:          Width="300" Font-Name="Verdana" Font-Size="8pt" />
148:        </td>
149:        </tr>
150:        <tr>
151:        <td style="font: 9pt Verdana, Arial, sans-serif">
152:         <b>Ship To Region:</b>
153:        </td>
154:        <td>
155:         <asp:TextBox runat="server" id="ShipRegion" Text="WA"
156:          Width="300" Font-Name="Verdana" Font-Size="8pt" />
157:        </td>
158:        </tr>
159:        <tr>
160:        <td style="font: 9pt Verdana, Arial, sans-serif">
```

14

EXPOSING DATA
THROUGH WEB
SERVICES

LISTING 14.13   Continued

```
161:        <b>Ship To Postal Code:</b>
162:        </td>
163:        <td>
164:        <asp:TextBox runat="server" id="ShipPostalCode" Text="98101"
165:         Width="300" Font-Name="Verdana" Font-Size="8pt" />
166:        </td>
167:      </tr>
168:      <tr>
169:        <td style="font: 9pt Verdana, Arial, sans-serif">
170:        <b>Ship To Country:</b>
171:        </td>
172:        <td>
173:        <asp:TextBox runat="server" id="ShipCountry" Text="USA"
174:         Width="300" Font-Name="Verdana" Font-Size="8pt" />
175:        </td>
176:      </tr>
177:     </table>
178:    </td>
179:   </tr>
180:   <tr>
181:    <td>
182:     <asp:DataGrid runat="server" ID="Products" AutoGenerateColumns="False"
183:      BorderWidth="1" BorderStyle="Solid" Gridlines="Both" BorderColor="Tan"
184:      Cellpadding="2" CellSpacing="0" Width="740"
185:      HeaderStyle-BackColor="Maroon"
186:      HeaderStyle-ForeColor="White"
187:      HeaderStyle-Font-Bold="True"
188:      HeaderStyle-Font-Name="Verdana"
189:      HeaderStyle-Font-Size="9pt"
190:      ItemStyle-Font-Name="Verdana"
191:      ItemStyle-Font-Size="8pt">
192:      <Columns>
193:       <asp:BoundColumn DataField="ProductID" HeaderText="SKU" />
194:       <asp:BoundColumn DataField="ProductName" HeaderText="Product Name" />
195:       <asp:BoundColumn DataField="ProductName" HeaderText="Product Name" />
196:       <asp:BoundColumn DataField="QuantityPerUnit"
197:        HeaderText="Quantity/Unit" />
198:       <asp:BoundColumn DataField="UnitPrice" HeaderText="Unit Price"
199:        DataFormatString="{0:c}" ItemStyle-HorizontalAlign="Right" />
200:       <asp:TemplateColumn HeaderText="Quantity"
201:        ItemStyle-HorizontalAlign="Center">
202:        <ItemTemplate>
203:         <asp:TextBox runat="server" id="Qnty" Text="0" Width="50"
204:          Font-Size="8pt" Font-Name="Verdana" BorderStyle="Solid"
```

LISTING 14.13 Continued

```
205:          BorderWidth="1" />
206:        </ItemTemplate>
207:       </asp:TemplateColumn>
208:      </Columns>
209:     </asp:DataGrid>
210:    </td>
211:   </tr>
212:   <tr>
213:    <td align="right">
214:     <asp:Button runat="server" ID="Submit" OnClick="Submit_Click"
215:      Text="Place Order" BorderStyle="Solid" BackColor="Maroon"
216:      ForeColor="White" Font-Bold="True" Font-Name="Verdana"
217:      Font-Size="9pt" style="cursor: hand;" />
218:    </td>
219:   </tr>
220: </table>
221: <asp:DataGrid runat="server" ID="FinalOrder" AutoGenerateColumns="False"
222:   BorderWidth="1" BorderStyle="Solid" Gridlines="Both" BorderColor="Tan"
223:   Cellpadding="2" CellSpacing="0" Width="740"
224:   HeaderStyle-BackColor="Maroon"
225:   HeaderStyle-ForeColor="White"
226:   HeaderStyle-Font-Bold="True"
227:   HeaderStyle-Font-Name="Verdana"
228:   HeaderStyle-Font-Size="9pt"
229:   ItemStyle-Font-Name="Verdana"
230:   ItemStyle-Font-Size="8pt">
231:   <Columns>
232:    <asp:BoundColumn DataField="ProductName" HeaderText="Product Name" />
233:    <asp:BoundColumn DataField="UnitPrice" HeaderText="Unit Price"
234:     DataFormatString="{0:c}" ItemStyle-HorizontalAlign="Right" />
235:    <asp:BoundColumn DataField="Quantity" HeaderText="Quantity"
236:     ItemStyle-HorizontalAlign="Center" />
237:    <asp:BoundColumn DataField="Discount" HeaderText="Discount"
238:     ItemStyle-HorizontalAlign="Center" />
239:    <asp:BoundColumn DataField="ExtendedPrice" HeaderText="Sub Total"
240:     DataFormatString="{0:c}" ItemStyle-HorizontalAlign="Right" />
241:   </Columns>
242: </asp:DataGrid>
243: <bigcheese:copyright runat="server" />
244: </form>
245: </body>
246: </html>
```

14

EXPOSING DATA
THROUGH WEB
SERVICES

In Listing 14.13, you build a consumer Web Form for the Northwind `ProductServices` Web service. The Web Form renders a series of `TextBoxes` for inputting the shipping information (required by the `PlaceOrder()` WebMethod). Each of the `TextBoxes` has a default value. The Web Form also renders a `Calendar` control for setting the `RequiredDate` parameter required by `PlaceOrder()`. The `Calendar`'s default date is set to seven days from the current date. The Web Form also renders a `DataGrid` of products based on the `GetProducts()` WebMethod. The last column in the `DataGrid` is filled with `TextBoxes` for entering the quantity of the product that is being ordered. Figure 14.9 shows the rendered Web Form before an order is placed.

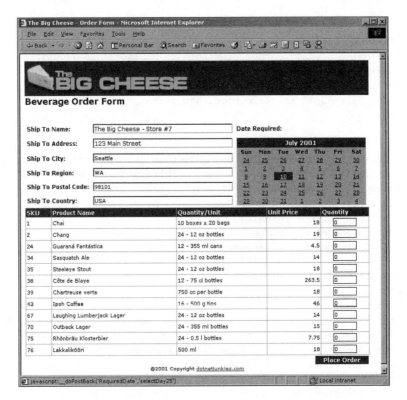

Figure 14.9

The Web Form calls to the `GetProducts()` WebMethod in the Northwind `ProductServices` Web service. Server controls are rendered to input all the ordering information.

On lines 7 through 22 of Listing 14.13, you create the `Page_Load()` event handler. In the `Page_Load()` event on line 11, you create an instance of the `Northwind.ProductServices` proxy client class. On line 12, you create an instance of the `DataSet` class with the return value of the `GetProducts()` WebMethod. You pass the number 1 into the `GetProducts()` method, which is the value for beverages. The proxy class creates a SOAP message with the number 1 in the body of the message. The SOAP message is sent to the Web service, which calls the Products.GetProductsByCategory() method. The Web service returns a DataSet in a SOAP message to the Big Cheese consumer, and the getProducts DataSet is created. All of this is done without you having to create a SOAP message, or handle the return of a SOAP message. The page is rendered, and the beverages are bound to the Products DataGrid.

When the user clicks the Place Order button, the Submit_Click() event handler is called. In the Submit_Click() event handler, you programmatically create a new DataSet (line 28) and a new DataTable in the DataSet, named Order (line 31). On lines 33 through 42, you create two DataColumns in the Order DataTable, and assign a name and a data type to them. On lines 51 through 63, you loop through the DataGrid.Items collection and create a new DataRow for any item that has a quantity greater than 0. This is done by programmatically creating a TextBox and using the FindControl() method (line 53) to locate the TextBox in the last column of the DataGrid row. You assign it to the TextBox instance. On line 54, you use the int.Parse() [Integer.Parse()] method to parse the Text property of the TextBox and set it to an integer variable. On lines 56 through 63, you add a new DataRow to the Order DataTable if the value in the TextBox is greater than 0. As you do this, you keep a running tally using the itemCount variable, on line 61, of how many products are being ordered (not their individual quantities). This tally is used to determine if the PlaceOrder() WebMethod should be called. If the Place Order button was clicked, even though no quantities were entered, the PlaceOrder() WebMethod will not be called, and an error message will be displayed to the user.

If the itemCount variable is greater than 0, then at least one product was ordered, and the PlaceOrder() WebMethod should be called. On line 67, you create a new instance of the ProductServices proxy client. You set the OrderID variable to the return value of the Place Order() WebMethod. You pass into the PlaceOrder() call the values from the TextBoxes, and the DataSet you programmatically created. Like the GetProducts() WebMethod, a SOAP message is built and sent to the Web service. The order is processed, and the order number is returned in a SOAP message, and assigned to the OrderID variable.

Using the OrderID variable, you call the GetOrderDetail() WebMethod. Again, a SOAP message is sent to the Web service. A SOAP message is returned, and a DataSet is created with the order detail. Figure 14.10 shows the Web Form after the order has been processed.

14

EXPOSING DATA
THROUGH WEB
SERVICES

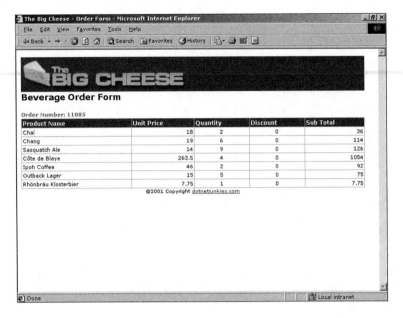

FIGURE 14.10

The user enters quantities for the order and clicks the Place Order *button. The* PlaceOrder() WebMethod *is called, and an order number is returned.*

Summary

Web services might very likely be the key to unlocking the potential of the Internet as a primary means of interbusiness communication. With Web services, disparate systems can communicate and exchange data in a useful manner. Web services leverage their power by working on a set of common Internet standards, such as HTTP, XML, and SOAP. The use of common standards enables communication and interaction between a variety of systems, regardless of their operating systems, applications, or languages.

In this chapter you learned

- What Web services are
- How to build simple Web services
- How to build complex input/output Web service
- How to consume Web services

You built both simple and complex Web services. Using the WSDL.exe utility, you built a proxy client class. The proxy client class enabled programmatic access to the Web service's exposed methods from a consumer application in the same way that you would access methods of any class local to the application.

Web services can be used for a variety of applications. You can build Web services to expose data to consumers, or to exchange data, perform critical business functions, or automate business processes. You are limited only by your imagination.

Authentication

IN THIS CHAPTER

Authentication is the process of verifying a user's identity against some authority such as an XML file or a database. Authentication is analogous to visiting an airport. Visitors are allowed in and can go into some areas. To get into other areas, such as the baggage handling area, a person must provide credentials to prove that he has the security clearance appropriate for the area. The level of clearance that a particular person has determines into which areas he is allowed. Web site authentication works in a similar fashion. With many Web sites, any visitor can view a portion of the Web site. Frequently, Web sites have "members-only" areas that require the user to be identified (authenticated).

When the user is authenticated, in other words, when the application can identify users, their requests for resources such as Web pages must be authorized. *Authorization* is the process of evaluating a user's credentials to determine if she can have access to the requested resource. In this chapter you will learn about the authentication types available to you in ASP.NET and how to authorize user requests. Specifically you will learn

- Types of authentication
- Security configuration options
- Working with forms authentication
- Enabling role-based authentication

ASP.NET provides a configuration file structure for maintaining user credentials. The default authentication format uses the configuration file, which includes usernames and passwords. The authentication classes are built with security in mind, and they provide methods for encrypting the passwords automatically.

Security Configuration

Together, the .NET Framework and IIS manage ASP.NET security. The ASP.NET configuration file, `web.config`, contains a hierarchical structure of global data, of which security information is a part (see Chapter 12, "XML and SOAP"). Listing 15.1 shows an example of the security section of the `web.config` file.

LISTING 15.1 A Sample Security Section of `web.config`

```
01: <authentication mode="[Windows/Forms/Passport/None]">
02:   <forms name="[name]" loginUrl="[url]" >
03:     <credentials passwordFormat="[Clear, SHA1, MD5]">
04:       <user name="[UserName]" password="[password]"/>
05:     </credentials>
06:   </forms>
07:   <passport redirectUrl="internal" />
08: </authentication>
09:
```

LISTING 15.1 Continued

```
10: <authorization>
11:   <allow users="[comma separated list of users]"
12:     roles="[comma separated list of roles]"/>
13:   <deny  users="[comma separated list of users]"
14:     roles="[comma separated list of roles]"/>
15: </authorization>
16:
17:   <identity impersonate ="[true/false]"/>
```

Listing 15.1 is not a usable security hierarchy, but it does demonstrate the possible values for security. Following is a description of each of the security settings.

- Line 1: `authentication mode`
  This determines the type of authentication used for the ASP.NET application. `Windows` is the default value. Other values are `Forms`, `Passport`, and `None`.

- Line 2: `forms`
  When the authentication mode is set to `Forms`, this element defines the cookie used by the client. The `name` is the identifier given to the cookie. ASP.NET will look for this cookie when authenticating a user. The `loginUrl` is the redirection path to send unauthenticated users to. This is a forms-based page where users can supply their credentials, such as their username and password.

- Line 3: `credentials passwordFormat`
  Usernames and passwords can be listed in the `<credentials>` section of the `web.config` file. The `passwordFormat` attribute is used to define the hashing algorithm used on the passwords. Three `passwordFormat` values are available:

  `MD5`   Passwords are stored using an `MD5` hash digest. When credentials are validated, the user password will be hashed using the `MD5` algorithm and compared for equality with this value. The clear text password is never stored or compared when using this value. Use this algorithm for best speed as compared to `SHA1`.

  `SHA1`   Passwords are stored using the `SHA1` hash digest. When credentials are validated, the user password will be hashed using the `SHA1` algorithm and compared for equality with this value. The clear text password is never stored or compared when using this value. Use this algorithm for best security.

  `Clear`   Passwords are stored in clear text. The user password is compared directly against this value without further transformation.

- Line 4: `username and password`
  Usernames and passwords can be defined in the `web.config` file. Each user is defined with a new `<user>` child element of the `<credentials>` element. Users can also be defined in a separate data source, such as a database table.

15

AUTHENTICATION

- Line 7: `passport redirectUrl`
  When the authentication mode is set to `Passport`, this element defines the redirect URL that an unauthenticated user is sent to when requesting a restricted resource.

- Line 10: `authorization`
  The `authorization` element contains optional values for defining which users or roles are granted access to a resource.

- Lines 11 and 12: `allow users` and `roles`
  The `<allow>` element defines which users may be granted access to a particular resource or set of resources. The default value is `"*"` (all users). You can also define a set of usernames, separated by commas, with the `users` attribute. The `roles` attribute enables you to define a set of roles, separated by commas, which may be given access to the requested resource.

- Lines 13 and 14: `deny users` and `roles`
  The `<deny>` element works the same as the `<allow>` element. To deny all users, set the `users` attribute to `"*"`. To deny only unauthenticated users, set the `users` attribute to `"?"`.

- Line 17: `identity`
  The `<identity>` element contains a boolean value for enabling impersonation. Impersonation enables the ASP.NET process to execute with the identity of a given user.

Types of Authentication

ASP.NET enables three different authentication schemes: `Windows`, `Passport`, and `Cookie` authentication.

Windows Authentication

Windows authentication works in tandem with IIS authentication. The authentication is performed by IIS in one of three ways, called Basic, Digest, and Integrated Windows Authentication. The authenticated identity is then passed to the .NET Framework and used by ASP.NET. Windows authentication is the default authentication scheme used by ASP.NET. Listing 15.2 shows the security section of the `web.config` file to enable Windows authentication.

Listing 15.2 Using Windows Authentication

```
01: <authentication mode="Windows" />
02:
03: <authorization>
04:   <deny  users="?" />
05: </authorization>
06:
07:   <identity impersonate ="true"/>
```

With Windows authentication, NTFS file permissions dictate which resources the user can access. For instance, if a subdirectory of your ASP.NET Web application is restricted to users in the Administrators role, using Windows authentication only users in that role will be granted access to files in that directory.

Windows authentication is ideal for intranets and extranets in which a network administrator controls the user base permissions. Windows authentication enables access for valid users of a network, but not any others. This is not an ideal authentication scheme for public Web sites, since not every visitor to your Web site is a valid network user. For public Web sites, you should use either Passport or Forms authentication.

Passport Authentication

Passport authentication uses the Microsoft Passport technology to authenticate users. Only users with valid Microsoft Passports will be granted access to restricted resources. The Microsoft Passport service maintains a centralized user database, including user profiles, that is available to member sites. End users are not required to have usernames and passwords for every site they visit. Instead, they can use their Microsoft Passport to gain access to any Web site that enables Passport authentication.

Passport authentication is ideal for public Web sites where you will restrict part or all of the Web site to authenticated users, but you do not want to maintain your own user data. Microsoft maintains the user data and exposes a limited amount of information to the Passport member Web sites. Each user can choose how much of his personal data you can access. There is an annual membership fee for using Passport services, and you must apply to be a Passport services member site.

> **NOTE**
>
> To learn more about enabling Passport authentication in your Web application, visit the Microsoft Passport Web site at http://www.passport.com/business.

Forms Authentication

Forms authentication is the de facto standard for Web site authentication for a public user base. *Forms authentication* uses a text file, called a cookie, stored in memory or persisted to disk on the client machine. The identity of the user is stored in the cookie upon authentication. The cookie information is sent to the Web server with each page request. If the user information is compatible with the security requirements for the requested resource, access is granted. Forms authentication uses HTML-based forms as the interface for a user to provide his credentials. The credentials are compared to the stored credentials in the Web application (either in the

15

AUTHENTICATION

web.config file, an XML file, or a database), and if valid, an AuthenticationTicket is created. The AuthenticationTicket can be encoded either as a cookie on the client or as a query string value. The following section of this chapter describes forms authentication in detail.

Using Forms Authentication

Forms authentication uses an HTML form–based login interface. The user supplies her credentials, typically a username and password, via the form. The credentials are authenticated against some authority, such as a database or XML file of users. When authenticated, a cookie is issued to the client. On each subsequent request, the cookie is appended to the request header. On each request, the user is authenticated and, if she is authorized for the requested resource, the requested resource is returned to the client. Listing 15.3 shows the security section of the web.config file to enable Forms Authentication.

LISTING 15.3 Enabling Forms Authentication

```
01: <authentication mode="Forms">
02:   <forms name="MyApp" loginUrl="PDDWA/C15/CSharp/login.aspx">
03:     <credentials passwordFormat="SHA1">
04:       <user name="WillyWonka"
➥         password="E8F97FBA9104D1EA5047948E6DFB67FACD9F5B73" />
05:     </credentials>
06:   </forms>
07: </authentication>
08:
09: <authorization>
10:   <allow users="*" />
11: </authorization>
```

In Listing 15.3, you create the <authentication> and <authorization> sections of the web.config file, enabling Forms Authentication for the Web application by setting the <authentication> element's mode attribute to Forms (line 1). On line 2, you create the <forms> element. The loginUrl value defines a Web Form named login.aspx in the top-level directory as the form where the user can provide his credentials. The name attribute assigns MyApp as the name applied to the cookie.

Using the <credentials> element on lines 3 through 5, you specify one user for this Web application, "WillyWonka", whose password is "password". On line 3 you specify SHA1 as the passwordFormat. This means that passwords are stored in the configuration file, encrypted using SHA1 encryption. When authenticating a user from the login form, the username and password will be compared against <user> elements in the <credentials> section. The user will supply his password as regular text. The password will be automatically encrypted and compared to the value in the configuration file. On line 10, you set the `allow` element of the `<authorization>` section to allow all users access to the Web application.

> **NOTE**
>
> You can encrypt passwords using the `FormsAuthentication` class' `HashPasswordForStoringInConfigFile()` method:
>
> ```
> string = FormsAuthentication.HashPasswordForStoringInConfigFile("password",
> "SHA1")
> ```

Specific resources such as `.aspx` files or subdirectories can be defined to use different authorization rules. This can be done in two ways, by using the `<location>` element in the `web.config` file, or by putting a `web.config` file in the subdirectory. Configuration files below the root directory cannot redefine the authentication scheme, but they can redefine the authorization rules for the directory that they are in and for all child directories. Listing 15.4 shows a `<location>` element that can be added to the `web.config` file to restrict access to a resource to authenticated users only.

LISTING 15.4   Restricting Access to Specific Resources

```
01: <location path="protected_page.aspx">
02:   <system.web>
03:     <authorization>
04:       <deny users="?" />
05:     </authorization>
06:   </system.web>
07: </location>
```

In Listing 15.4, you create a `<location>` element that restricts access to a Web Form (`protected_page.aspx`) to authenticated users only. The `path` attribute, on line 1, of the `<location>` element defines the relative path to the resource of which to restrict access. The `<deny>` element, on line 4, uses the `users` attribute to identify unauthenticated users.

> **WARNING**
>
> The following listings depend on a file named `protected_page.aspx`. Create a file by this name and put only the text "This is a protected page." in it. This page is only for testing the Forms Authentication.

If an unauthenticated user requests `protected_page.aspx`, he will be redirected to the login page. The `QueryString` is automatically appended with the originally requested URL, like this:

```
http://localhost/login.aspx?
➥ReturnUrl=
➥http%3a%2f%2flocalhost%2fprotected_page.aspx
```

If you need to apply access restrictions to a subdirectory of the root directory, you can do it with a `<location>` element in the root `web.config` file, or you can create a limited `web.config` file in the subdirectory. The limited `web.config` file contains only an `<authorization>` section with `<allow>` and/or `<deny>` elements to define the access available. Listing 15.5 shows the `web.config` file used in the Members subdirectory of the Northwind sample application.

LISTING 15.5   Using a Limited `Config.Web` in a Subdirectory

```
01: <?xml version="1.0" encoding="utf-8" ?>
02: <configuration>
03:   <system.web>
04:     <authorization>
05:       <deny users="?" />
06:     </authorization>
07:   </system.web>
08: </configuration>
```

Listing 15.5 is a sample of the entire `web.config` file you would use in a subdirectory of your application. The configuration file has only an `<authorization>` section. By using the `<deny>` element on line 5, you restrict access to this subdirectory, and all its child files and directories, to authenticated users only. Any unauthenticated user requesting a resource in this subdirectory or any of its child directories will be redirected to the `loginUrl` specified in the root `web.config` file.

> **NOTE**
>
> When setting allow and deny values, you can use a comma delimited list of usernames, or a * to represent all users and a ? to represent all unauthenticated users.

Creating an Authentication Ticket Cookie

When a user is authenticated, an *authentication ticket* is generated, and a text-based cookie is sent to the client. To create the authentication ticket, you must handle the submission of the login form, and call to the `Authenticate()` method of the `FormsAuthentication` class. By default the `Authenticate()` method checks the `<credentials>` element of the `web.config` file for the username and password values submitted. If the `Authenticate()` method returns `True`, the user can be redirected to the originally requested resource using the `FormsAuthentication.RedirectFromLoginPage()` method. This method takes two parameters, the username and a boolean value indicating whether or not a persistent cookie should be created. When the `RedirectFromLoginPage()` method is called, an Authentication Ticket is created, and the `SetCookie()` method is called. The cookie is sent to the client using the name in the `web.config` file, and date and expiration values based on whether the cookie was intended to be persisted or not. Listing 15.6 shows the login page (`login.aspx`).

LISTING 15.6   The Login Web Form

```
[VB]
```

```vb
01: <script runat="server" language="VB">
02:  Protected Sub Login_OnClick(Sender As Object, E As EventArgs)
03:   If FormsAuthentication.Authenticate(UserName.Text, Password.Text) Then
04:     FormsAuthentication.RedirectFromLoginPage(UserName.Text,
PersistCookie.Checked)
05:   End If
06:  End Sub
07:
08:  Protected Sub Signout_OnClick(Sender As Object, E As EventArgs)
09:   FormsAuthentication.SignOut()
10:   HttpContext.Current.Response.Redirect("login.aspx")
11:  End Sub
12: </script>
```

```
[C#]
```

```csharp
01: <script runat="server" language="C#">
02:  protected void Login_OnClick(Object sender, EventArgs e){
03:   if(FormsAuthentication.Authenticate(UserName.Text, Password.Text)){
04:     FormsAuthentication.RedirectFromLoginPage(UserName.Text,
PersistCookie.Checked);
05:   }
06:  }
07:
08:  protected void Signout_OnClick(Object sender, EventArgs e){
09:   FormsAuthentication.SignOut();
10:   HttpContext.Current.Response.Redirect("login.aspx");
11:  }
12: </script>
```

```
[VB & C#]
```

```
13: <html>
```

15

AUTHENTICATION

LISTING 15.6   Continued

```
14: <head>
15:  <title>Programming Datadriven Web Apps - Chapter 15</title>
16: </head>
17: <body>
18: <form runat="server">
19: <H4>Account Logon</H4>
20:  <b>E-Mail:</b><br/>
21:  <asp:TextBox runat="server" ID="UserName" /><br/>
22:  <b>Password:</b><br/>
23:  <asp:TextBox runat="server" ID="Password" TextMode="Password" /><br/>
24:  <b>Remember Me</b><br/>
25:  <asp:CheckBox runat="server" ID="PersistCookie" /><br/>
26:  <asp:Button runat="server" ID="Login"
27:   Text="Login"
28:   OnClick="Login_OnClick" />
29:
30:  <asp:Button runat="server" ID="Signout"
31:   Text="Sign-Out"
32:   OnClick="Signout_OnClick" />
33: </form>
34: </body>
35: </html>
```

In Listing 15.6, you create an event handler for a button click, `Login_OnClick()`. The event handler calls the `Authenticate()` method of the `FormsAuthentication` class (line 3), passing it the username and password values submitted by the user. If the `Authenticate()` method returns `True`, then the `RedirectFromLoginPage()` method is called (line 4), which issues a cookie to the client and redirects the client browser to the originally requested resource. If the `PersistCookie` CheckBox was checked, the `PersistCookie.Checked` value is `True`, and a persistent cookie is written to the client machine; otherwise a non-persistent cookie is issued.

Manually Creating a Forms Authentication Ticket

In Listing 15.6, you used the `FormsAuthentication.Authenticate()` method to validate a user's credentials against the `<credentials>` section of the `web.config` file. You can also validate users against an alternative data store, such as a database table. Since `Forms Authentication.Authenticate()` uses the `<credentials>` section to authenticate users, you must use an alternative validation method. After the credentials are validated, a call to `FormsAuthentication.RedirectFromLoginPage()` or `FormsAuthentication.SetAuthCookie()` will create an authentication ticket and pass a cookie to the client machine. The `Redirect FromLoginPage()` method will redirect the browser to the originally requested page, whereas

`SetAuthCookie()` will create an authentication ticket and issue a cookie to the client, but will not perform a redirect.

Authenticating Users From a Database Table

You can authenticate users from credentials stored in a database table. Once the user submits their credentials, you compare it to the data in the database. If the credentials are valid, you create an authentication ticket by either calling `FormsAuthentication.SetAuthCookie()` or `FormsAuthentication.RedirectFromLoginPage()`.

In Listing 15.7 you create a login Web Form that validates the user's credentials against the Users table of the Samples database.

> **WARNING**
>
> The following listings depend on a database named "samples". On the companion Web site (http://www.samspublishing.com) you can download the SQL Server script and text files to create this database, or an Access 2000 version of this database.

LISTING 15.7   Authenticating Users From a Database Table

```
[VB]
01: <%@ Import Namespace="System.Data" %>
02: <%@ Import Namespace="System.Data.SqlClient" %>
03:
04: <script runat="server" language="VB">
05:   Protected Sub Login_OnClick(Sender As Object, E As EventArgs)
06:    Dim SqlStmt As String = "SELECT COUNT(*) FROM Users WHERE Email='" & _
07:      UserName.Text.Trim() & "' " & _
08:      "AND Password = '" & _
09:      Password.Text.Trim() & "'"
10:
11:    Dim con As SqlConnection = New
➡      SqlConnection("server=localhost;database=samples;uid=sa;pwd=;")
12:    Dim cmd As SqlCommand = New SqlCommand(SqlStmt, con)
13:    Dim reader As SqlDataReader = Nothing
14:
15:    con.Open()
16:    reader = cmd.ExecuteReader()
17:    While reader.Read()
18:     If Int32.Parse(reader(0).ToString()) >= 1 Then
19:      FormsAuthentication.RedirectFromLoginPage(UserName.Text,
➡       PersistCookie.Checked)
20:     Else
```

15

LISTING 15.7   Continued

```
21:      ErrorMsg.Text = "<p><b><font color='#CC3300'>User not found,
➥      or bad credentials - try again!</font></b></p>"
22:    End If
23:  End While
24:  End Sub
25:
26:  Protected Sub Signout_OnClick(Sender As Object, E As EventArgs)
27:   FormsAuthentication.SignOut()
28:   HttpContext.Current.Response.Redirect("login_database.aspx")
29:  End Sub
30: </script>
```

```
[C#]

01: <%@ Import Namespace="System.Data" %>
02: <%@ Import Namespace="System.Data.SqlClient" %>
03:
04: <script runat="server" language="C#">
05:  protected void Login_OnClick(Object sender, EventArgs e){
06:   string SqlStmt = "SELECT COUNT(*) FROM Users WHERE Email='" +
07:     UserName.Text.Trim() + "' " +
08:     "AND Password = '" +
09:     Password.Text.Trim() + "'";
10:
11:   SqlConnection con = new
➥      SqlConnection("server=localhost;database=samples;uid=sa;pwd=;");
12:   SqlCommand cmd = new SqlCommand(SqlStmt, con);
13:   SqlDataReader reader = null;
14:
15:   con.Open();
16:   reader = cmd.ExecuteReader();
17:   while(reader.Read()){
18:    if(Int32.Parse(reader[0].ToString()) >= 1){
19:     FormsAuthentication.RedirectFromLoginPage(UserName.Text,
➥      PersistCookie.Checked);
20:    }else{
21:     ErrorMsg.Text = "<p><b><font color='#CC3300'>User not found,
➥      or bad credentials - try again!</font></b></p>";
22:    }
23:   }
24:  }
25:
26:  protected void Signout_OnClick(Object sender, EventArgs e){
27:   FormsAuthentication.SignOut();
28:   HttpContext.Current.Response.Redirect("login_database.aspx");
29:  }
```

LISTING 15.7 Continued

```
30: </script>

[VB & C#]

31: <html>
32: <head>
33:  <title>Programming Datadriven Web Apps - Chapter 15</title>
34: </head>
35: <body style="font:9pt Verdana, Arial, sans-serif;">
36: <form runat="server">
37: <H4>Account Logon Using a Database</H4>
38:  <asp:Label runat="server" id="ErrorMsg" />
39:  <b>E-Mail:</b><br/>
40:  <asp:TextBox runat="server" ID="UserName" /><br/>
41:  <b>Password:</b><br/>
42:  <asp:TextBox runat="server" ID="Password" TextMode="Password" /><br/>
43:  <b>Remember Me</b><br/>
44:  <asp:CheckBox runat="server" ID="PersistCookie" /><br/>
45:
46:  <asp:Button runat="server" ID="Login"
47:   Text="Login"
48:   OnClick="Login_OnClick" />
49:
50:  <asp:Button runat="server" ID="Signout"
51:   Text="Sign-Out"
52:   OnClick="Signout_OnClick" />
53: </form>
54: </body>
55: </html>
```

NOTE

On the companion Web site (http://www.samspublishing.com) you can download
the OleDb Managed Provider version of the code in Listing 15.7.

In Listing 15.7 you create a login Web Form that authenticates users from a database table.
Lines 5–24 are the `Login_OnClick()` event handler. In this event handler you create Managed
`Connection` (line 11) and `Command` (line 12) objects, and use a `DataReader` (line 16) to catch the
results of a `SELECT COUNT(*)` SQL statement. The SQL statement looks for e-mail and password values that match those entered by the user. If one or more matching fields are found (in

15

AUTHENTICATION

the event of duplicate user entries), the result is one or greater, and the user is authenticated. If no matching records are found, an error message (line 21) is displayed to the user.

If the user is to be authenticated, you create an authentication ticket by calling Forms Authentication.RedirectFromLoginPage() on line 19. This method creates an authentication ticket, and a cookie. If the PersistCookie.Checked value is True, then the cookie is written to the client machine, otherwise it is persisted in memory, and is lost when the browser window is closed.

On lines 26-29 you create a SignOut_OnClick() event handler for the Sign-Out button. On line 27 you call the FormsAuthentication.SignOut() method to remove the authentication ticket, effectively un-authenticating the user. To access restricted resources the user will have to login again. On line 28 you use Response.Redirect() to redirect the browser back to a refreshed version of the login Web Form. Doing this clears out any input values, and ensures the ViewState is clear.

Authenticating Users From an XML File

In the same manner that you authenticate users from a database, you can authenticate users from an XML file. You compare the users credentials to the credentials in an XML file, and if valid, you issue an authentication ticket and cookie.

Listing 15.8 shows the Users.xml file, which is simply the same user data from the Users table in the Sample database.

LISTING 15.8   The Users.xml File

```
01: <?xml version="1.0"?>
02: <Users>
03:   <User>
04:     <UserID>1</UserID>
05:     <Email>doug.seven@dotnetjunkies.com</Email>
06:     <Password>password</Password>
07:     <FName>Doug</FName>
08:     <LName>Seven</LName>
09:   </User>
10:   <User>
11:     <UserID>2</UserID>
12:     <Email>billg@microsoft.com</Email>
13:     <Password>money</Password>
14:     <FName>Bill</FName>
15:     <LName>Gates</LName>
16:   </User>
17:   <User>
18:     <UserID>3</UserID>
```

LISTING 15.8   Continued

```
19:    <Email>kobe@bball.com</Email>
20:    <Password>slamdunk</Password>
21:    <FName>Kobe</FName>
22:    <LName>Bryant</LName>
23:    </User>
24: </Users>
```

Listing 15.8 is simply an XML file of usernames, passwords, first names, and last names.

In Listing 15.9 you create a login Web Form that authenticates user credentials against the Users.xml file. Listing 15.9 uses the same HTML as Listing 15.7, so I have not duplicated it here.

LISTING 15.9   Authenticating Users From an XML File

```
[VB]

01: <%@ Import Namespace="System.Data" %>
02:
03: <script runat="server" language="VB">
04:   Protected Sub Login_OnClick(Sender As Object, E As EventArgs)
05:     Dim ds As New DataSet
06:     ds.ReadXml(Server.MapPath("Users.xml"))
07:
08:     Dim i As Integer
09:     For i = 0 to ds.Tables("User").Rows.Count - 1
10:       If (ds.Tables("User").Rows(i)("Email").ToString()
➥        = UserName.Text.Trim() AND
➥        ds.Tables("User").Rows(i)("Password").ToString()
➥        = Password.Text.Trim()) Then
11:        FormsAuthentication.RedirectFromLoginPage(UserName.Text,
➥        PersistCookie.Checked)
12:       End If
13:     Next i
14:
15:     ErrorMsg.Text = "<p><b><font color='#CC3300'>User not found,
➥        or bad credentials - try again!</font></b></p>"
16:   End Sub
17:
18:   Protected Sub Signout_OnClick(Sender As Object, E As EventArgs)
19:     FormsAuthentication.SignOut()
20:     HttpContext.Current.Response.Redirect("login_xml.aspx")
21:   End Sub
22: </script>
```

15

AUTHENTICATION

LISTING 15.9   Continued

```csharp
[C#]
01: <%@ Import Namespace="System.Data" %>
02:
03: <script runat="server" language="C#">
04:  protected void Login_OnClick(Object sender, EventArgs e){
05:    DataSet ds = new DataSet();
06:    ds.ReadXml(Server.MapPath("Users.xml"));
07:
08:    int i;
09:    for(i=0; i < ds.Tables["User"].Rows.Count; i++){
10:     if(ds.Tables["User"].Rows[i]["Email"].ToString()
➥       == UserName.Text.Trim() &&
➥       ds.Tables["User"].Rows[i]["Password"].ToString()
➥       == Password.Text.Trim()){
11:      FormsAuthentication.RedirectFromLoginPage(UserName.Text,
➥       PersistCookie.Checked);
12:     }
13:    }
14:
15:    ErrorMsg.Text = "<p><b><font color='#CC3300'>User not found,
➥       or bad credentials - try again!</font></b></p>";
16:  }
17:
18:  protected void Signout_OnClick(Object sender, EventArgs e){
19:    FormsAuthentication.SignOut();
20:    HttpContext.Current.Response.Redirect("login_xml.aspx");
21:  }
22: </script>
```

In Listing 15.9 you authenticate users against an XML file. On line 6 you read the Users.xml file into a DataSet using the DataSet.ReadXml() method. This creates a DataTable named "User", with a row for each <User> element in the XML file. On line 9 you begin to iterate through the User DataTable. On line 10 you evaluate the current record for a matching e-mail address and password. If a complete match is found, you issue an authentication ticket using the FormsAuthentication.RedirectFromLoginPage() method. If no matches are found, the code executes down to the ErrorMsg on line 15, and an error message is displayed to the user.

Role-based Forms Authentication

The .NET Framework enables role-based authentication; users can be assigned to roles and allowed access to resources based on those roles. Role access privileges are defined in the configuration file, either the root configuration file using a <location> element, or a configuration file in a subdirectory.

In Listing 15.10 you create a web.config file to be placed in a subdirectory called /adminonly.

LISTING 15.10   Restricting Access by User Roles

`[VB & C#]`

```
01: <?xml version="1.0" encoding="utf-8" ?>
02: <configuration>
03:  <system.web>
04:   <authorization>
05:    <allow roles="Administrator" />
06:    <deny users="*" />
07:   </authorization>
08:  </system.web>
09: </configuration>
```

In Listing 15.10 you create a web.config configuration file in a subdirectory of your application. On lines 4–7 you override the application authorization settings for this subdirectory, and any subdirectories under this one. On line 5 you use the <allow> element to specify that users in the role "Administrators" are allowed access, and on line 6 you deny all other users.

To enable role-based authentication you must assign the user roles to the current *principal object*. The principal object represents the security context under which the current code is being executed. To create a new principal object you must create an instance of a class that implements the IPrincipal interface and set its identity and roles arguments. The System.Security.Principal.GenericPrincipal class does just that. The GenericPrincipal class is constructed with a GenericIdentity object (which implements IIdentity), and a string array of roles. The GenericIdentity class is used to specify the username and the authentication type that is being used.

In Listing 15.11 you create a login form that retrieves user roles from the Samples database, and issues an authentication ticket and cookie to the client.

LISTING 15.11   Authenticating Users With Roles

`[VB]`

```
01: <%@ Import Namespace="System.Data" %>
02: <%@ Import Namespace="System.Data.SqlClient" %>
03: <%@ Import Namespace="System.Text" %>
04: <%@ Import Namespace="System.Security.Principal" %>
05: <script runat="server" language="VB">
06:  Protected Sub Login_OnClick(Sender as Object, E As EventArgs)
07:   Dim context As HttpContext = HttpContext.Current
08:
```

15

LISTING 15.11   Continued

```
09:   Dim SqlStmt As String = "SELECT [Roles].[RoleName]
➥      FROM [Users_to_Roles] " & _
10:    "INNER JOIN [Users] ON [Users].[UserID] =
➥      [Users_to_Roles].[UserID] " & _
11:    "INNER JOIN [Roles] ON [Users_to_Roles].[RoleID] =
➥      [Roles].[RoleID] " & _
12:    "WHERE [Users].[Email] = '" & UserName.Text & "' AND " & _
13:    "[Users].[Password] = '" & Password.Text & "'"
14:
15:   Dim reader As SqlDataReader = Nothing
16:   Dim con As SqlConnection = New
➥      SqlConnection("server=localhost;database=samples;uid=sa;pwd=;")
17:   Dim cmd As SqlCommand = New SqlCommand(SqlStmt, con)
18:
19:   Try
20:    con.Open()
21:    reader = cmd.ExecuteReader()
22:
23:    If reader.FieldCount > 0 Then
24:     Dim cookieRoles As New StringBuilder
25:     While reader.Read()
26:      cookieRoles.Append(reader("RoleName").ToString())
27:      cookieRoles.Append(".")
28:     End While
29:
30:      ' Save the Roles in a client Cookie for future requests
31:      Dim RoleCookie As HttpCookie = New HttpCookie("Roles")
32:      RoleCookie.Value = cookieRoles.ToString()
33:      Response.Cookies.Add(RoleCookie)
34:
35:      FormsAuthentication.RedirectFromLoginPage(UserName.Text,
➥       PersistCookie.Checked)
36:
37:    Else
38:     ErrorMsg.Text = "User not found, or bad credentials - try again!<br>"
39:    End If
40:
41:
42:    Catch ex As Exception
43:     ErrorMsg.Text = ex.ToString() + "<br>"
44:   End Try
45:  End Sub
46:
47:  Protected Sub Signout_OnClick(Sender as Object, E As EventArgs)
```

LISTING 15.11   Continued

```vb
48:    Dim context As HttpContext = HttpContext.Current
49:    FormsAuthentication.SignOut()
50:    context.Response.Cookies.Remove("Roles")
51:   End Sub
52: </script>
```

[C#]

```csharp
01: <%@ Import Namespace="System.Data" %>
02: <%@ Import Namespace="System.Data.SqlClient" %>
03: <%@ Import Namespace="System.Text" %>
04: <%@ Import Namespace="System.Security.Principal" %>
05: <script runat="server" language="C#">
06:  protected void Login_OnClick(Object sender, EventArgs e){
07:   HttpContext context = HttpContext.Current;
08:
09:   string SqlStmt = "SELECT [Roles].[RoleName] FROM [Users_to_Roles] " +
10:    "INNER JOIN [Users] ON [Users].[UserID] = [Users_to_Roles].[UserID] " +
11:    "INNER JOIN [Roles] ON [Users_to_Roles].[RoleID] = [Roles].[RoleID] " +
12:    "WHERE [Users].[Email] = '" + UserName.Text + "' AND " +
13:    "[Users].[Password] = '" + Password.Text + "'";
14:
15:   SqlDataReader reader = null;
16:   SqlConnection con = new
➥      SqlConnection("server=localhost;database=samples;uid=sa;pwd=;");
17:   SqlCommand cmd = new SqlCommand(SqlStmt, con);
18:
19:   try{
20:    con.Open();
21:    reader = cmd.ExecuteReader();
22:
23:    if(reader.FieldCount > 0){
24:     StringBuilder cookieRoles = new StringBuilder();
25:     while(reader.Read()){
26:      cookieRoles.Append(reader["RoleName"].ToString());
27:      cookieRoles.Append(".");
28:     }
29:
30:     //Save the Roles in a client Cookie for future requests
31:     HttpCookie RoleCookie = new HttpCookie("Roles");
32:     RoleCookie.Value = cookieRoles.ToString();
33:     Response.Cookies.Add(RoleCookie);
34:
35:     FormsAuthentication.RedirectFromLoginPage(UserName.Text,
➥     PersistCookie.Checked);
```

15

LISTING 15.11   Continued

```
36:
37:    }else{
38:     ErrorMsg.Text = "User not found, or bad credentials - try again!<br>";
39:    }
40:   }
41:
42:   catch(Exception ex){
43:    ErrorMsg.Text = ex.ToString() + "<br>";
44:   }
45:  }
46:
47:  protected void Signout_OnClick(Object sender, EventArgs e){
48:   HttpContext context = HttpContext.Current;
49:   FormsAuthentication.SignOut();
50:   context.Response.Cookies.Remove("Roles");
51:  }
52: </script>

[VB & C#]

53: <html>
54: <head>
55:  <title>Programming Datadriven Web Apps - Chapter 15</title>
56: </head>
57: <body>
58: <form runat="server">
59: <H4>Account Logon</H4>
60:  <asp:Label runat="server" id="ErrorMsg" />
61:  <b>E-Mail:</b><br/>
62:  <asp:TextBox runat="server" ID="UserName" /><br/>
63:  <b>Password:</b><br/>
64:  <asp:TextBox runat="server" ID="Password" TextMode="Password" /><br/>
65:  <b>Remember Me</b><br/>
66:  <asp:CheckBox runat="server" ID="PersistCookie" /><br/>
67:  <asp:Button runat="server" ID="Login"
68:   Text="Login"
69:   OnClick="Login_OnClick" />
70:
71:  <asp:Button runat="server" ID="Signout"
72:   Text="Sign-Out"
73:   OnClick="Signout_OnClick" />
74: </form>
75: </body>
76: </html>
```

In Listing 15.11 you create a login Web Form that authenticates a user and assigns roles to the user based on information in the Samples database.

On lines 9–13 you create a SQL statement to return all the RoleNames associated with a specific user, based on his username and password. The results are returned in a SqlDataReader. If any records are returned, the reader.FieldCount will be greater than 0, as evaluated on line 23. If records are returned, you build a string of RoleNames delimited by a period. This string (cookieRoles) will be saved to a non-persistent cookie on the client machine.

Rather than having to retrieve the RoleNames on each request, you should persist them somehow. This can be done by placing the cookieRoles object in a Session variable or a client-side cookie. Since it is likely that you have thousands of users accessing your Web site at any time, using a Session variable could be very resource intensive. By using a client-side cookie you move the resources required to the client, keeping your server resources free.

On line 31 you create a new cookie named "Roles". You assign the string representation of the cookieRoles object to the cookie, and add it to the client-side Cookies collection, on line 33. Once the cookie has been set you call FormsAuthentication.RedirectFromLoginPage() to set the authentication ticket and redirect the user to the originally requested resource.

At this point the user is authenticated, but the roles are not set to the current principal (HttpContext.User). You need to create a GenericPrincipal object with the user roles as an argument. The principal object is not persisted across requests, and must be recreated on each new request. This is why you stored the roles in a client-cookie.

To create a new GenericPrincipal object on each request, you use the global.asax Application_AuthenticateRequest() event handler. This handler is called each time a user request is authenticated. In this event handler you create a new GenericPrincipal object and assign it to the current principal instance. The roles in the current principal instance are compared against any <allow roles> or <deny roles> elements in the configuration file. You are not required to write any code to compare the roles; you only need to set the current principal instance.

In Listing 15.12 you create the Application_AuthenticateRequest() event handler in the global.asax file (in the root of your application).

LISTING 15.12 Creating a New Principal in the Global.asax

[VB]

```
01: <%@ Import Namespace="System.Security.Principal" %>
02: <script language="VB" runat="server">
03:   Public Sub Application_AuthenticateRequest()
04:     Dim context As HttpContext = HttpContext.Current
```

15

AUTHENTICATION

LISTING 15.12   Continued

```
05:   If Not context.User Is Nothing AndAlso
➡        context.User.Identity.IsAuthenticated Then
06:     ' Create a generic identity.
07:     Dim userIdentity As GenericIdentity = New
➡        GenericIdentity(context.User.Identity.Name, "Forms")
08:     ' Create a generic principal.
09:     Dim userPrincipal As GenericPrincipal = New
➡        GenericPrincipal(userIdentity,
➡        context.Request.Cookies("Roles").Value.Split("."))
10:     ' Set the new Principal to the Current User
11:     context.User = userPrincipal
12:   End If
13: End Sub
14: </script>
```

```
[C#]
01: <%@ Import Namespace="System.Security.Principal" %>
02: <script language="C#" runat="server">
03:   public void Application_AuthenticateRequest(){
04:   HttpContext context = HttpContext.Current;
05:   if(context.User != null && context.User.Identity.IsAuthenticated){
06:     //Create a generic identity.
07:     GenericIdentity userIdentity = new
➡        GenericIdentity(context.User.Identity.Name, "Forms");
08:     //Create a generic principal.
09:     GenericPrincipal userPrincipal = new
➡        GenericPrincipal(userIdentity,
➡        context.Request.Cookies["Roles"].Value.Split(new Char[] {'.'}));
10:     //Set the new Principal to the Current User
11:     context.User = userPrincipal;
12:   }
13:   }
14: </script>
```

On line 5 of Listing 15.12 you evaluate the current principal (`HttpContext.Current.User`) to see if it is not null. If it is null, then no principal exists, and you do not need to proceed setting up the roles. You also use the bitwise operator `AndAlso` (`&&` in C#) to evaluate the `IsAuthenticated` property of the principal only when the first evaluation returns `True`.

If the principal exists, and the user has been authenticated (when the authentication ticket was issued in the login Web Form), you need to create new `GenericIdentity` and `GenericPrincipal` objects.

On line 7 you create a new `GenericIdentity` object, specifying the value from the `HttpContext.Current.User.Identity.Name` property as the `name` argument, and the word "Forms" as the `type` argument. The `GenericIdentity` represents the user and authentication type being used. The `GenericIdentity` object is used as the `identity` argument when creating the new `GenericPrincipal` object, on line 9. The second argument in the `GenericPrincipal` constructor is a string array of roles. This string array is created by using the `Split()` method of the `String` class on the Roles cookie issued in the login Web Form.

On line 39 you assign the `GenericPricipal` object, which contains the user roles in an array, to the current instance of the `HttpContext.Current.User` class, which makes the `GenericPrincipal` the current principal object.

At this point, the current principal object contains the username (supplied by the user when he logged in), and an array of roles that will be compared against the configuration file.

Summary

In this chapter, you learned about ASP.NET Authentication. You learned how to set up the configuration file, `web.config`, to use one of three authentication schemes, `Windows`, `Passport`, and `Cookie`. Specifically you learned:

- Types of authentication
- Security configuration options
- Working with Forms Authentication
- Enabling Role-based authentication

You can use any of the authentication types to restrict access to resources in your Web application. Windows Authentication is ideal for intranets and extranets when all of the users have accounts in the Windows network. Passport Authentication is useful when you do not want to maintain your own user database, but it does require a fee for use and you must apply to Microsoft to be a Passport Web site.

In the bulk of this chapter you worked with Forms Authentication, which is the de facto standard for public Web site authentication. With Forms Authentication you provide an HTML forms-based login form to collect user credentials. By adding code in the `global.asax` file you can enable role-based authentication to restrict access based on user roles, such as Premier User and Standard User.

15

AUTHENTICATION

Data Caching

IN THIS CHAPTER

Here we are, at the last chapter in the book. You know what they say, "Save the best for last." Well, in my opinion, that is true for this book. In this chapter we'll put the "frosting on the cake." You'll learn how to enable and take advantage of caching in your Web applications.

ASP.NET has many different types of caching. There is page output caching, in which the responses for requested documents are cached and subsequent requests for that document are served from this cached version(s). Second on the list is fragment caching. Fragment caching enables you to cache portions of a page while other portions are dynamically generated for each response. Then there is data caching or object caching, in which you can cache objects such as a `DataSet` or `ArrayList`. You even can cache the output of Web services with one line of code. This chapter will cover it all. NOTE: Among other things, output caching is only available in *ASP.NET Premium Edition*.

In the first part of the chapter, I'll be discussing what caching is; because what one person might think of caching might be quite different from another person's perception. Within this section, I will give you a very high-level caching code example to study. Then, after you are familiar with what ASP.NET caching is, the chapter will jump head first into page output caching, which covers both the `HttpCachePolicy` class and the `@OutputCache` directive. `HttpCachePolicy` class enables you to implement output caching programmatically, and the `@OutputCache` directive is a high-level wrapper for the `HttpCachePolicy` class that enables you to enable output caching using a directive.

After the page output caching section, we'll be going over fragment or partial page caching, which is exactly what it sounds like. Fragment caching enables you to cache portions of a page using *User Controls* (`*.ascx`) while other portions are dynamically generated on each request.

The next section will cover data or object caching, which enables you to put objects such as a `DataSet` or `ArrayList` into the cache using the Cache APIs found in the `System.Web.Caching` namespace. Finally, I'll show you how to enable output caching within a Web service.

Specifically, the chapter discusses the following:

- What is caching?
- Using page output caching
- Using fragment caching
- Using the Cache API's
- Implementing caching in Web services

What Is Caching?

Caching isn't a new term to developers, but, historically, caching dynamic Web pages hasn't been a very easy or manageable task. *Caching* is the method of saving data of any kind in

memory. When the cached data is needed, instead of re-creating the data, the application provides it to the client or requestor from the in-memory version of the data. The in-memory data
is referred to as the *cached version*. The data can range from a letter in the alphabet to a complete Web page.

Implementing caching in your application increases performance because you can serve Web
pages to clients without having to re-create the pages on every request. For instance, if you
have a page that is dynamically built through a database query, but the data rarely changes,
why not cache the entire page on the first request of the day and serve every additional request
for the page to the client from the cache? Then, at midnight, take the page out of the cache and
do it again the next day.

Using this technique has many advantages. The first is that you limit the amount of database
calls each day. If that page gets requested 20,000 times per day, you will limit the number of
expensive calls to your database by that many calls. This alone should be enough to convince
you that caching is a good thing, but there is more.

Pages that implement caching are served more quickly to the client because the pages and data
used to create them are served from a memory resident version. The following list contains
some frequently asked questions regarding caching. I thought I would answer these questions
for you now, and explain their details later:

Do I have control over how long items are in the cache?

Yes, you can set varying expiration times for cache items. For instance, you can cache
one item for 10 seconds and another for 10 hours.

What happens if I change the code in a cached page?

If you change the code for an item that is in the cache, .NET will recognize the change
and remove the item from the cache. The first new request for the page will re-cache the
page, and the user will never know that the code changed.

Can I cache based on certain criteria?

Yes, there are many techniques available to cache pages based on any number of criteria.
For example, you can vary the cache based on query string values or by browser types or
combinations.

Can I cache pages only?

No, data caching using the Cache APIs enables you to cache objects such as a `DataSet`,
an `Array`, or user controls.

After I put an item into the cache, can I take it out?

Yes, just as you have complete control over how and when an item is cached, you also
have the ability to take items out of the cache whenever you want.

I can talk about caching until my head explodes, but I bet you want to see some source code. Listing 16.1 contains a very basic example of how to implement caching within a Web Form. This example demonstrates the bare minimum that you have to do to enable output caching.

LISTING 16.1 Using the `@OutputCache` Directive to Enable Page Output Caching

```
[VisualBasic.NET & C#.NET]
01: <%@ OutputCache Duration="60" VaryByParam="none"%>
02: <html>
03: <body>
04: This page was cached at:
05: <b>
06:   <%=DateTime.Now.ToString("G")%>
07: </b>
08: </body>
09: </html>
```

Caching in Listing 16.1 is enabled through the use of the `@OutputCache` directive on line 1. This line accomplishes three things necessary to enable output caching on your server using the `@OutputCache` directive. First, it supplies a valid expiration policy through the use of the `Duration` attribute, which is a required attribute. Second, the cache is public cache visible (see `HttpCacheability` enumeration—covered later in the chapter). This is done automatically by using the `@OutputCache` directive. Third, a value was given for the `VaryByParam` attribute (another required attribute which varies how documents are cached based on parameters)— none was supplied as a value so only one version of the page will be cached.

The rendered page will display the current server time; the time displayed will not change if the page is refreshed before the expiration policy has expired (60 seconds), or the Web application is restarted. You can test this by refreshing the page before 60 seconds have elapsed, and then again after 60 seconds have elapsed. Only after the 60 seconds have elapsed will the time printed to the page change to the current server time again.

I am sure that you have many more questions, but I am also sure that, after you are finished with this chapter, each of your questions will be answered exhaustively. Now let's begin by discussing page output caching.

Using the Page Output Cache

Page output caching is the method of caching the output of an entire page. After the page is rendered and cached, all subsequent requests for the page are served from the memory resident version until it is removed—*taken out of the cache.*

Page output caching can be done in two ways. The first uses the @OutputCache directive (seen in Listing 16.1), and the second uses the HttpCachePolicy class. Essentially, they accomplish the same thing, but by using the @OutputCache directive, you are accessing the HttpCachePolicy class through a higher-level, user-friendly wrapper.

In this section, I will discuss how to use both methods to enable page output caching. I will review their properties that enable you to vary the way in which the items are cached, based on different criteria, such as query string parameters or browser types.

Using the @OutputCache Directive to Enable Caching

Listing 16.1 illustrated how to use the @OutputChache directive to quickly enable page output caching. However, the directive's implementation is a catchall caching mechanism. The @OutputCache directive has five attributes available to control output caching in web forms. These attributes control how long an item can be cached, where an item can be cached (Server, Client Browsers), and ways to create multiple representations of one document. Before going into each attribute available, let's look at the @OutputCache directives general syntax:

```
01: <%@ OutputCache Duration="value" Location="value" VaryByCustom="value"
➥    VaryByHeader="value" VaryByParam="value" %>
```

We will be going over each of these attributes in the following sections.

The Duration Attribute

The Duration attribute appeared in Listing 16.1. The Duration attribute specifies the duration in seconds that an item should remain in a cache. Unlike other caching mechanisms, such as the cache APIs, there is no way to designate an exact time to take items out of the cache using the Duration attribute. (I will discuss absolute expiration times later in the chapter.)

Duration is one of the @OutuputCache directives required attributes and you would receive an exception if you didn't include it. Listing 16.2 contains an example using the @OutputCache's Duration attribute.

LISTING 16.2   Using the Duration Attribute

```
[VisualBasic.NET & C#.NET]

01: <%@ OutputCache Duration="60" VaryByParam="none" %>
02: <html>
03: <body>
04: This page was cached at:
05: <b>
06:   <%=DateTime.Now.ToString("G")%>
07: </b>
```

LISTING 16.2   Continued

```
08: </body>
09: </html>
```

The `Duration` attribute is set on line 1 within the `@OutputCache` directive. When this page is rendered, it will be cached for 60 seconds. After the 60 seconds has elapsed, the next request for the page will be placed in the cache.

The `Location` Attribute

The `Location` attribute enables you to control where an item can be cached. For instance, using the `Location` attribute, you can specify that you only want the cached documents to be located on the server that processed the original request. Or, you could stipulate that only clients, such as Internet browsers, can cache the page.

The following values can be used for the `Location` attribute. They can be found in the `OutputCacheLocation` enumeration within the `System.Web.UI` namespace:

- `Any`   The output cache can be located on the server that processed the request, on the client's browser, or on a downstream server. Essentially, caching will take place anywhere it can. `Any` is the default value for the `Location` attribute.
- `Client`   The output cache can be only on the client's browser.
- `Downstream`   The output cache can be only on a server downstream from the server that processed the request.
- `None`   The output cache is disabled for the requested page.
- `Server`   The output cache can be only on the server that processed the request.

Listing 16.3 contains an example of using the `Location` attribute. I recommend playing with all five possible values of this attribute so you can see how changing the value affects caching.

LISTING 16.3   Using the `Location` Attribute

```
[VisualBasic.NET & C#.NET]

01: <%@ OutputCache Duration="60" VaryByParam="none" Location="Server" %>
02: <html>
03: <body>
04: This page was cached at:
05: <b>
06:   <%=DateTime.Now.ToString("G")%>
07: </b>
08: </body>
09: </html>
```

In Listing 16.3 I used `Server` as the value for the `Location` attribute, which means that the cached document will always be supplied to the client from the server. I recommend playing with all the different attributes so you can see the differences. One example I suggest trying would be to set the value to `Client`, if the value is `Client`, the browser will maintain control of the cache until the cache duration time has elapsed (if caching is enabled on the client). Unlike when server caching is enabled, if the *Refresh* button is clicked; a request will be made to the server and the server dynamically generates a new version of the document for the client. When the *Refresh* button is clicked with server caching enabled, documents are still served by the server to the client on each request, but clients are served the cached version rather than a version that is being dynamically generated.

The `VaryByParam` Attribute

You have seen how to control where a document is cached using the `Location` attribute, and how to control the amount of time that it should remain in the cache using the `Duration` attribute, but you haven't seen how to vary the way that a document is cached. By "vary," I mean being able to have multiple representations of the same document cached. The `VaryByParam` is one of the `@OutputCache` attributes that enables you to do this by using query string parameter values and the parameters of a Form `POST`.

As you'll recall in Listing 16.3, the `VaryByParam` attribute has a value of `none`. When the value is set to `none`, only one representation of the page is cached. However, page content often varies based on parameters, so using `none` as a value would not be an option. For example, a page might have `Mode` passed as a query string parameter (Ex: `news.aspx?mode=#`)—`mode=1` renders current news and `mode=2` renders old news. Using the `VaryByParam` attribute enables you to cache two representations of `news.aspx` by using the values of `Mode`, `1` and `2`. After each version of `news.aspx` document is cached, subsequent requests would be served from either of the two cached versions. For this example, you would write your `@OutputCache` directive as follows:

```
<%@ OutputCache Duration="69" VaryByParam="Mode" %>
```

You are not limited to just one value; you can specify multiple values to vary the cache on by separating the values with semicolons:

```
<%@ OutputCache Duration="69" VaryByParam="Mode;Newstype" %>
```

You also might choose to vary the cache by every possible combination. You can use an `*` as the value to do this:

```
<%@ OutputCache Duration="69" VaryByParam="*" %>
```

Listing 16.4 and 16.5 illustrate how to cache multiple representations of the same document based on query string parameters.

LISTING 16.4   Using the `VaryByParam` Attribute to Vary How a Document Is Cached Based on Query String Parameter Values

[VisualBasic.NET]

```vb
01: <%@ OutputCache Duration="160" Location="Server" VaryByParam="num;num2" %>
02:
03: <%@ Import Namespace="System.Data" %>
04: <%@ Import Namespace="System.Data.SqlClient" %>
05:
06: <script language="vb" runat="server">
07:
08:  public sub Page_Load(sender as Object, e as EventArgs)
09:
10:   try
11:
12:    dim nvc as NameValueCollection = Request.QueryString
13:    dim sqlCmd as new StringBuilder()
14:    dim sQueryStringValues as new StringBuilder()
15:    dim i,ii as Integer
16:    dim KeyArray(),ValueArray() as String
17:
18: '*** Build string to show query string keys in Label control
19:    KeyArray = nvc.AllKeys
20:
21:    sQueryStringValues.Append("<b>Query string parameter(s):<br>")
22:
23:    for i = 0 to KeyArray.Length - 1
24:     sQueryStringValues.Append(KeyArray(i))
25:     ValueArray = nvc.GetValues(i)
26:     for ii = 0 to ValueArray.Length - 1
27:      sQueryStringValues.Append("=" & ValueArray(ii) & "<br>")
28:     next ii
29:    next i
30:
31:    sQueryStringValues.Append("</b>")
32:
33:    QueryStringValues.Text = sQueryStringValues.ToString()
34: '*** End
35:
36: '*** Get data from database based on num value
37:    if nvc.GetValues("num")(0) <> nothing then
38:
39:     dim ds as new DataSet()
40:     dim sCon as new SqlConnection("server=localhost;" & _
41:       "uid=sa;pwd=;database=northwind")
42:
```

LISTING 16.4 Continued

```
43:
44:    sqlCmd.Append("SELECT TOP ")
45:    sqlCmd.Append(nvc.GetValues("num")(0))
46:    sqlCmd.Append(" * FROM Products")
47:
48:    dim sda as new SqlDataAdapter(sqlCmd.ToString(),sCon)
49:    sda.Fill(ds,"Products")
50:
51:    dg1.DataSource = ds.Tables(0).DefaultView
52:    dg1.DataBind()
53:
54:    end if
55: '*** End
56: catch nullEx as NullReferenceException
57:  ErrorMessage.Text = nullEx.Message
58: end try
59:   end sub
60:
61: </script>
```

[C#.NET]

```
06: <script language="c#" runat="server">
07:
08:   void Page_Load(Object sender , EventArgs e){
09:
10:   try {
11:
12:    NameValueCollection nvc = Request.QueryString;
13:    StringBuilder sqlCmd = new StringBuilder();
14:    StringBuilder sQueryStringValues = new StringBuilder();
15:    int i,ii;
16:    string[] KeyArray,ValueArray;
17:
18: //'*** Build string to show query string keys in Label control
19:    KeyArray = nvc.AllKeys;
20:
21:    sQueryStringValues.Append("<b>Query string parameter(s):<br>");
22:
23:    for (i = 0; i < KeyArray.Length; i++){
24:     sQueryStringValues.Append(KeyArray[i]);
25:     ValueArray = nvc.GetValues(i);
26:     for (ii = 0; ii < ValueArray.Length; ii++) {
27:      sQueryStringValues.Append("=" + ValueArray[ii] + "<br>");
28:      }
29:     }
```

LISTING 16.4   Continued

```
30:
31:    sQueryStringValues.Append("</b>");
32:
33:    QueryStringValues.Text = sQueryStringValues.ToString();
34: //'*** End
35:
36: //'*** Get data from database based on num value
37:    if (nvc.GetValues("num")[0] != null){
38:
39:      DataSet ds = new DataSet();
40:      SqlConnection sCon = new SqlConnection("server=localhost;" +
41:        "uid=sa;pwd=;database=northwind");
42:
43:
44:      sqlCmd.Append("SELECT TOP ");
45:      sqlCmd.Append(nvc.GetValues("num")[0]);
46:      sqlCmd.Append(" * FROM Products");
47:
48:      SqlDataAdapter sda = new SqlDataAdapter(sqlCmd.ToString(),sCon);
49:      sda.Fill(ds,"Products");
50:
51:      dg1.DataSource = ds.Tables[0].DefaultView;
52:      dg1.DataBind();
53:
54:    }
55: //'*** End
56: } catch (NullReferenceException nullEx) {
57:    ErrorMessage.Text = nullEx.Message;
58:    }
59: }
60:
61: </script>

[VisualBasic.NET & C#.NET]

62: <html>
63: <body>
64:
65: This page was cached at: <b><%=DateTime.Now.ToString("G")%></b>
66: <br>
67: <asp:Label id="QueryStringValues" runat="server" />
68: <p>
69: <asp:datagrid runat="server" id="dg1" font-size="10" />
70: <p>
71: <asp:Label id="ErrorMessage" runat="server" />
```

LISTING 16.4 Continued

```
72: </body>
73: </html>
```

The @OutputCache directive is located on line 1 of Listing 16.4. Notice that the VaryByParam attribute contains two values separated by a semicolon, num and num2. This means that this document will be cached based on the values of both these names (parameters). When this page renders, you will see three things: the date and time this document was cached, a list of the query string parameters passed in the URL, and a DataGrid control with (n) number of rows. The num query string parameter determines the value of (n).

The second half of this example, found in Listing 16.5, contains the code for the start page. This page contains only a handful of links that navigate to Listing 16.4 with different query string values.

LISTING 16.5 The Start Page for Listing 16.4

```
[VisualBasic.NET & C#.NET]

01: <html>
02: <body>
03: <b><u>Pick how many rows to show</u>:</b>
04:   <p>
05: <b>Show Top 5</b>
06:   <br>
07:   <a href="Listing16.4.aspx?num=5">
08:   [Listing16.4.aspx?num=5]
09:   </a>
10:   <br>
11:   <a href="Listing16.4.aspx?num=5&num2=1">
12:   [Listing16.4.aspx?num=5&num2=1]
13:   </a>
14:   <p>
15: <b>Show Top 15</b>
16:   <br>
17:   <a href="Listing16.4.aspx?num=15">
18:   [Listing16.4.aspx?num=15]
19:   </a>
20:   <br>
21:   <a href="Listing16.4.aspx?num=15&num2=1">
22:   [Listing16.4.aspx?num=15&num2=1]
23:   </a>
```

LISTING 16.5   Continued

```
24:   <p>
25:   <b>Show Top 10</b>
26:   <br>
27:   <a href="Listing16.4.aspx?num=10">
28:   [Listing16.4.aspx?num=10]
29:   </a>
30:   <br>
31:   <a href="Listing16.4.aspx?num=10&num2=1">
32:   [Listing16.4.aspx?num=10&num2=1]
33:   </a>
34:   <p>
35:   <b>Show Top 20</b>
36:   <br>
37:   <a href="Listing16.4.aspx?num=20">
38:   [Listing16.4.aspx?num=20]
39:   </a>
40:   <br>
41:   <a href="Listing16.4.aspx?num=20&num2=1">
42:   [Listing16.4.aspx?num=20&num2=1]
43:   </a>
44:   </body>
45:   </html>
```

Listing 16.5 contains eight different links to the same page (Listing 16.4). Each link has the same set of parameters; however, the values of each are different. Using these links, I will demonstrate how to cache multiple representations of the same document. After you have the start page up, you should receive a page similar to Figure 16.1.

If you walk through the following steps, you will get a better handle on how the VaryByParam parameter affects caching:

1. Start at the Show Top 5 links. Click and navigate to the Listing 16.4 page. (Make a note of the time that the document was cached on each.)

2. Proceed down the line until you have navigated to every link and made a note of the cache time.

3. Start back at the Show Top 5 section and navigate all the hyperlinks again. While doing this, check the cache times with the cache times of your first pass through.

During your first pass through, you will find that every one of the links produces a new cache time. This is because the values of one or more of the parameters are always different, so a new cache is created. On your second pass through, you'll find that all the cache times did not change from the first pass through. This is because, on the second pass through, the documents are being served from the cached documents that have the same parameter values. You can also open two different browsers and request the same page from both. You will produce the same results as the previous walk through—both browsers will have the same cache time.

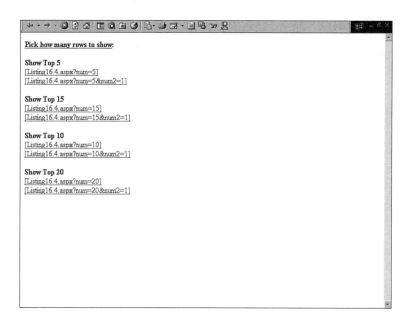

FIGURE 16.1

The start page for Listing 16.4, which contains eight different links with the same parameters, but with different values.

Try adding a third parameter on the results page, but don't change the original parameters. You'll find that the document is still served from a cached document matching the first two parameters because the third parameter is not set as a value in the VaryByParam attribute. If you were to add the newly added parameter to the VaryByParam attribute, an additional cache item would be created. Figures 16.2 and 16.3 show the results page after the first and second Show Top 5 links are selected, respectively. The cache times are different.

In Figure 16.2, the cache time is 9:13:01 p.m.

In Figure 16.3 the cache time is 9:13:12 p.m. By setting the VaryByParam attribute to both num and num2, I have created and cached two representations of the document. The next time that either of these two documents is requested before their cache duration expires, the document will be served to the client from the server cache.

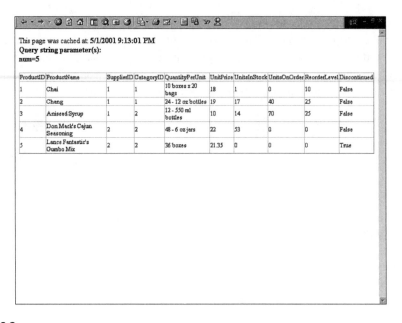

FIGURE 16.2

The results page after Show Top 5 with one parameter is selected.

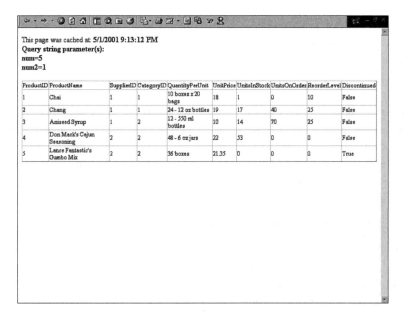

FIGURE 16.3

Results page after Show Top 5 with two parameters is selected.

You may, at this point, have concerns over all these memory resident items eating up your memory. Every item put into the cache has both a priority (its priority in the cache over other objects) and decay rate (the rate an items priority falls when its not frequently accessed— Normal to Low). As memory fills up items are taken out of the cache based on these values. The output cache by default has a very low priority rate and a very high decay rate. Therefore, if there are pages in the cache that are not frequently accessed they will be taken out of the cache to free up memory, while others that are accessed frequently are kept in the cache longer.

The VaryByCustom Attribute

You might want to vary the way that a document is cached to something other than the inherent attributes. The ASP.NET development team realized this and created a VaryByCustom attribute. VaryByCustom enables you to specify a string as a value, and caching will take place based on the value of this string. The VaryByCustom attribute does have one "Out of the box" value that you can use—Browser. When set to Browser, a new cache item is created for each type of browser that requests the document based on the *browser name* and *major version*.

You can use a custom value for the VaryByCustom attribute by overriding the HttpApplication.GetVaryByCustomString method in the Global.asax file. Listing 16.6 demonstrates implementing your own value for the VaryByCustom attribute. This example creates a new cache item based on a user. Listing 16.7 contains the code for the global.asax file. Listing 16.8 is code to put into your Web.config file to implement authentication. And, finally, Listing 16.9 contains a mock login page. For this example to work properly you must have all four examples in one Web application and a request must first be made to Listing 16.6.

LISTING 16.6 Web Form Implementing the VaryByCustom Attribute.

```
[VisualBasic.NET]

01: <%@ OutputCache Duration="160" Location="Server"
➥    VaryByCustom="UserProfile" VaryByParam="none" %>
02:
03: <%@ Import Namespace="System.Data" %>
04: <%@ Import Namespace="System.Data.SqlClient" %>
05:
06: <script language="vb" runat="server">
07:
08:   public sub Page_Load(sender as Object, e as EventArgs)
09:
10:     try
11:
12:       UserName.Text = Context.User.Identity.Name
13:
14:       dim sqlCmd as new StringBuilder()
```

LISTING 16.6   Continued

```
15:    dim ds as new DataSet()
16:    dim sCon as new SqlConnection("server=localhost;" & _
17:     "uid=sa;pwd=;database=northwind")
18:
19:    sqlCmd.Append("SELECT TOP 5")
20:    sqlCmd.Append(" * FROM Products")
21:
22:    dim sda as new SqlDataAdapter(sqlCmd.ToString(),sCon)
23:    sda.Fill(ds,"Products")
24:
25:    dg1.DataSource = ds.Tables(0).DefaultView
26:    dg1.DataBind()
27:
28:  catch Sex as SqlException
29:
30:   ErrorMessage.Text = Sex.Message
31:
32:  end try
33:
34: end sub
35:
36: public sub SignOutNow(sender as Object, e as EventArgs)
37:
38:  FormsAuthentication.SignOut()
39:
40: end sub
41:
42: </script>
```

[C#.NET]

```
01: <%@ OutputCache Duration="160" Location="Server"
➥ VaryByCustom="UserProfile" VaryByParam="none" %>
02:
03: <%@ Import Namespace="System.Data" %>
04: <%@ Import Namespace="System.Data.SqlClient" %>
05:
06: <script language="c#" runat="server">
07:
08:  void Page_Load(Object sender, EventArgs e) {
09:
10:    try {
11:
12:     UserName.Text = Context.User.Identity.Name;
13:
14:     StringBuilder sqlCmd = new StringBuilder();
```

LISTING 16.6   Continued

```
15:    DataSet ds = new DataSet();
16:    SqlConnection sCon = new SqlConnection("server=localhost;" +
17:      "uid=sa;pwd=;database=northwind");
18:
19:    sqlCmd.Append("SELECT TOP 5");
20:    sqlCmd.Append(" * FROM Products");
21:
22:    SqlDataAdapter sda = new SqlDataAdapter(sqlCmd.ToString(),sCon);
23:    sda.Fill(ds,"Products");
24:
25:    dg1.DataSource = ds.Tables[0].DefaultView;
26:    dg1.DataBind();
27:
28:  } catch (SqlException Sex) {
29:
30:    ErrorMessage.Text = Sex.Message;
31:
32:  }
33:
34: }
35:
36: public void SignOutNow(Object sender, EventArgs e) {
37:
38:   FormsAuthentication.SignOut();
39:
40: }
41:
42: </script>
```

[VisualBasic.NET & C#.NET]

```
43: <html>
44: <body>
45: <form runat="server" >
46: This page was cached at: <b><%=DateTime.Now.ToString("G")%></b>
47: <br>
48: Hello: <asp:Label id="UserName" runat="server" />
49: <p>
50: <asp:Button id="SignOut" OnClick="SignOutNow"
51:   Text="Sign Out" runat="Server" />
52: <p>
53: <asp:datagrid runat="server" id="dg1" font-size="10" />
54: <p>
55: <asp:Label id="ErrorMessage" runat="server" />
56: </form>
57: </body>
58: </html>
```

On line 1 of Listing 16.6, the @OutputCache directive's VaryByCustom attribute is set to
UserProfile. During the Page_Load event, I set the UserName Label controls Text property
to the authenticated user (line 12). On line 46, I printed out the time that this document was
cached. Listing 16.7 contains the code needed to implement the UserProfile as a valid value
for the VaryByCustom attribute within the global.asax file. Notice the "Sign Out" button in
the page; you can use this to sign out and become unauthenticated or to test how caching differs between users.

LISTING 16.7   Overriding the GetVaryByCustomString in the global.asax File

[VisualBasic.NET]

```
01: <script lanaguage="vb" runat="server">
02:
03: public overrides function GetVaryByCustomString
➡    (Context As HttpContext, CustomArgs As String) As String
04:
05:   select CustomArgs
06:   case "UserProfile"
07:     return "UserName=" & Context.User.Identity.Name
08:   case else
09:     return "Browser=" & Context.Request.Browser.Browser
10:   end select
11:
12: end function
13:
14: </script>
```

 [C#.NET]

```
01: <script language="c#" runat="server">
02:
03: public override string GetVaryByCustomString
➡    (HttpContext Context, string arg){
04:
05:   switch (arg){
06:    case "UserProfile":
07:     return "UserName=" + Context.User.Identity.Name;
08:     break;
09:    default:
10:     return "Browser=" + Context.Request.Browser.Browser;
11:     break;
12:   }
13:
14: }
15:
16: </script>
```

Start off by overriding the GetVaryByCustomString method in Listing 16.7. This method has two parameters, and the first is the HttpContext. The second is a string that will be the value of the VaryByCustom attribute. The VaryByCustom attribute within Listing 16.6 is UserProfile, so this is what will be passed in as a parameter when the page is requested. On line 5, I used a select statement (C# switch) for the CustomArgs parameter. I did this because each page can implement its own VaryByCustom attribute, so that you potentially can have multiple custom attributes being passed into this method. The GetVaryByCustomString method returns a string that determines how the cache is varied. If the method returns a string on which the cache has already been varied, then it is considered a hit, and the document isn't cached. If the method returns a string on which the cache has not already been varied, then it is considered a miss, and the document will be cached. Listing 16.8 contains the code necessary to implement authentication to test out the VaryByCustom attribute. In this example, a new cache item for this document will be created for each authenticated user.

Listing 16.8 has the code for the web.config file, used to implement forms authentication. Listing 16.9 contains the code for login.aspx, which must be saved in the application root directory. Otherwise, you must change the LoginUrl attribute to reflect any directory changes.

LISTING 16.8   Code for web.config File

```
01: <configuration>
02:   <system.web>
03:     <authentication mode="Forms">
04:       <forms name=".DOTNETJUNKIE"
➥      loginUrl="C16/listing16.6.aspx" protection="all" timeout="60" />
05:       </authentication>
06:       <authorization>
07:       <deny users="?" />
08:       </authorization>
09:   </system.web>
10: </configuration>
```

> **NOTE**
>
> You might need to change the loginUrl attribute in Listing 16.8 to reflect your Web application, like this:
>
> ```
> loginUrl="Directory/WebForm.aspx"
> ```

LISTING 16.9   Web Form for the Login Page

```
01: <script language="vb" runat="server">
02:
```

LISTING 16.9   Continued

```
03:   public sub Login_Click(sender as Object, e as EventArgs)
04:
05:    FormsAuthentication.RedirectFromLoginPage(username.Text, true)
06:
07:   end sub
08:
09: </script>
```

[C#]

```
01: <script language="c#" runat="server">
02:
03:   void Login_Click(Object sender, EventArgs e)
04:   {
05:
06:    FormsAuthentication.RedirectFromLoginPage(username.Text, true);
07:
08:   }
09: </script>
```

[VisualBasic.NET & C#.NET]

```
10: <html>
11: <body>
12: <form runat="server">
13: <h3>Login Form</h3>
14: User Name: <asp:TextBox id="username" runat="server" />
15: <br>
16: <asp:Button runat="server" onclick="Login_Click" id="Login" text="Login" />
17: </form>
18: </body>
19: </html>
```

Because the code in Listings 16.8 and 16.9 doesn't demonstrate caching and is used only to implement authentication, I haven't analyzed it.

After all code is implemented and a page request is made to Listing 16.6, your browser will be redirected to Listing16.6.aspx. After you enter a login name and click the login button, you will be redirected back to the page from Listing 16.6. You will see the cache time, your login name, and a DataGrid rendered to the page. To really see the variation in the cache, you will either have to request the page from a computer other than localhost, or log out and log back in using the Log Out button. Also, if you have two different types of browsers installed on your computer (IE and Netscape) you can open the page in each and log in under a different name since they won't share sessions. Figure 16.4 and Figure 16.5 contain screen shots of two requests from two different users.

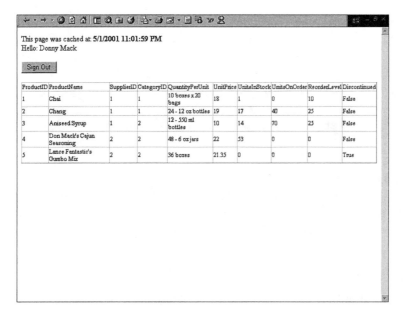

FIGURE 16.4

Listing 16.6 after logging in as Donny Mack. Note the difference in the cache time from Figure 16.5.

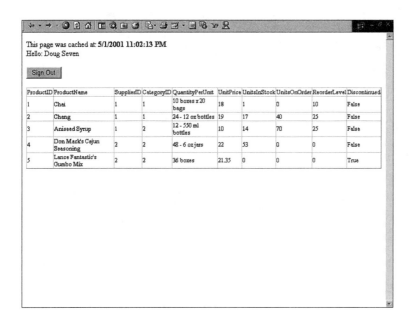

FIGURE 16.5

Listing 16.6 logging in as Doug Seven on a different computer.

As you can see, the cache time is different for both users. This trend will continue for each and every new user who logs on to your site. As users leave and new users log on, cache items automatically will be taken out of the cache based on time and importance.

> **CAUTION**
>
> The `VaryByCustom` attribute is not supported by user controls.

The `VaryByHeader` attribute

Another way you can vary how a page is cached is by `HTTP Header` information that is passed to the server by the client during a page request. The attribute that allows this type of caching is `VaryByHeader`. An example would be `User-Agent`, which is a description of the browser that made the original request:

```
"Mozilla/4.0 (compatible; MSIE 5.5; Windows NT 5.0)"
```

The following lists useful Request `HTTP Headers` you can use as a value for the `VaryByHeader` attribute:

- Accept
- Accept-Charset
- Accept-Encoding
- Accept-Language
- Authorization
- Content-Encoding
- Expect
- From
- Host
- If-Match
- If-Modified-Since
- If-None-Match
- If-Range
- If-Unmodified-Since
- Max-Forwards
- Proxy-Authorization
- Range

- Referer
- TE
- User-Agent

Using the VaryByHeader attribute is just a matter of adding one or more Header names, separated by semicolons (;) as a value for VaryByHeader:

```
<%@ OutputCache Duration="60" VaryByParam="none"
➥   VaryByHeader="User-Agent; Referer%>
```

In the preceding code, the requested document will be cached based on both the User-Agent Header (browser information) and the Referer (the location that the user navigated from to request this document).

> **CAUTION**
>
> The VaryByHeader attribute is not supported by user controls.

Using the `HttpCachePolicy` Class to Enable Output Caching

As previously mentioned, the @OutputCache directive is derived from the HttpCachePolicy class, which gives you lower-level access to the output cache. The HttpCachePolicy class is exposed through the HttpResponse.Cache property; and it is a member of the System.Web namespace. You would want to use the HttpCachePolicy rather than the @OutputCache when you need to dynamically set the output cache settings. For instance, if you want to dynamically set how long the item should remain in the cache.

The @OutputCache directive exposes nearly all the functionality available from using the HttpCachePolicy class, but the class does offer more functionality than @OutputCache. For instance, when using the @OutputCache directive, you can only set the cache expiration time in seconds. The HttpCachePolicy class enables you to set either an absolute—DateTime.Parse ("11:59:00PM") or a relative expiration time—DateTime.Now.AddMinutes(2).

Because I went over nearly all the attributes for the HttpCachePolicy class in the @OutputCache directive section, I will not go into great detail about each here. However, I will provide a code example of implementing caching using the HttpCachePolicy class in Listing 16.10.

LISTING 16.10   Implementing Output Caching Using the `HttpCachePolicy` Class

[VisualBasic.NET]

```vb
 1: <script language="vb" runat="server" >
 2:
 3:  public sub Page_Load(sender as Object, e as EventArgs)
 4:
 5:    Response.Cache.SetExpires(DateTime.Now.AddMinutes(2))
 6:    Response.Cache.SetCacheability(HttpCacheability.Public)
 7:
 8:  end sub
 9:
10: </script>
```

[C#.NET]

```csharp
01: <script language="c#" runat="server" >
02:
03:   void Page_Load(Object sender, EventArgs e) {
04:
05:    Response.Cache.SetExpires(DateTime.Now.AddMinutes(2));
06:    Response.Cache.SetCacheability(HttpCacheability.Public);
07:
08:  }
 9:
10: </script>
```

[VisualBasic.NET & C#.NET]

```html
11: <html>
12: <body>
13: <b>This page was cached at</b>: <%=DateTime.Now.ToString("G")%>
14: </body>
15: </html>
```

In Listing 16.10, caching is enabled on lines 5 and 6. On line 5, the `HttpCachePolicy.Set Expires` method sets the cache duration (`SetExpires` will be discussed in the following section). On line 6, the `SetCacheability` method sets the cache to public visibility, passing in a member of the `HttpCacheability` enumeration. (These objects are covered in the following section.)

The following list details members of the `HttpCachePolicy` class. I will not give a full code example for each member in this section because I went over the effect of using these members in the `@OutputCache` directive section, just under a different context.

- `SetExpires`—Used to set an absolute date and time that the cache shall expire. In Listing 16.8 I used `DateTime.Now.AddMinutes(2)` as the expiration time, which takes the current time and adds 2 minutes. Alternatively, you can put in a hard-coded value such as `"12:00:00AM".ToDateTime()`. This is comparable to the `@OutputCache`'s `Duration` attribute, but takes an absolute date and time rather than a value of seconds.

- `SetCacheability`—Used to control where documents are cached, whether only on the server or on both clients and the server. This is similar to the `@OuputCache`'s `Location` attribute. The value passed into this method must be a member of the `HttpCachePolicy` enumeration (a member of `System.Web`). A list and description of each value follows:

  - `HttpCachePolicy.Server` Documents are only cached on the server that processed the request

  - `HttpCachePolicy.Public` Documents can be cached on by the client, downstream server, or the original server that processed the request.

  - `HttpCachePolicy.Private` Documents can only be cached on the client.

  - `HttpCachePolicy.NoCache` Prevents caching from taking place.

- `SetMaxAge`—Used to set the maximum time span the cache item should be considered valid. The parameter for this method should be a `TimeSpan` type, such as

  `Response.Cache.SetMaxAge(TimeSpan)`

- `SetNoServerCaching`—Used to restrict any caching from taking place on the server that processed the request. This method expects no parameters:

  `Response.Cache.SetNoServerCaching()`

- `SetSlidingExpiration`—Used to turn sliding expiration on or off. This method expects a Boolean value as a parameter:

  `Response.Cache.SetSlidingExpiration(true | false)`

- `SetVaryByCustom`—Used to set the `VaryByCustom` string. This method expects a string as a parameter (for example, Platform):

  `Response.Cache.SetVaryByCustom(string)`

- `HttpCacheVaryByHeaders`—Class used to control the cache to vary by a Header(s).

- `HttpCacheVaryByParams`—Class used to control the cache to vary by a parameter(s).

Using Fragment Caching

So far, you have seen how to enable caching for entire pages. You might be thinking, "This is all well and good, but I make money off advertising. I can't have my ad banners cached because they are rotating banners and need to change on every request." Perhaps your site serves some dynamic content that must be refreshed on every request—for instance an up-to-the-minute news flash.

You are in luck because, in this section, we will be discussing *fragment caching*, the technique of caching the output of portions of pages, rather than complete documents. It might sound complicated, but it is very easy.

You can take advantage of fragment caching by including one or more cache-enabled user controls within your web form. For example, you might have a standard Web Form with three user controls included. You can set the first user control cache for 1 minute, the second for 15 minutes, and the third for 30 minutes. If you don't have caching enabled anywhere else on the page (other user controls or the web form) then all content will be dynamically created on each request except for the three user controls whose cached version will be used.

Enabling caching within a user control is done the same way as in a Web Form, so I will not explain the semantics of enabling caching in this section. As previously mentioned, there are some attributes of the @OutputCache directive that are not supported by user controls. On the flip side, there is a new attribute added to the directive specifically for user controls. Table 16.1 lists supported and non-supported attributes for the @OutputCache directive when it is used in a user control.

TABLE 16.1   Supported and Non-Supported Attributes of the @OutputCache Directive When Used in a User Control

Attribute	Supported	Description
Duration	Yes—Required	Length in seconds that the item should remain in the cache.
Location	No	N/A
VaryByCustom	Yes	Varies the document cache by a custom string. Default value "Browser".
VaryByHeader	No	N/A
VaryByParam	Yes—Required	Varies the document cache by parameters. * Varies for all parameters; none of them disables the VaryByParam attribute.
VaryByControl	Yes—Not supported by Web Forms	Varies the user control cache by property names. An example follows.

Listings 16.11, 16.12, and 16.13 contain sample code for two user controls and a Web Form to demonstrate fragment caching.

LISTING 16.11   User Control That Displays a DataGrid and Cache Time—Duration is set to 60

```
[VisualBasic.NET]

01: <%@ OutputCache Duration="60" VaryByParam="none" %>
02: <%@ Import Namespace="System.Data" %>
03: <%@ Import Namespace="System.Data.SqlClient" %>
04:
05: <script language="vb" runat="server">
06:  public sub Page_Load(sender as Object, e as EventArgs)
07:    dim sCon as new SqlConnection("server=localhost;" & _
08:     "uid=sa;pwd=;database=northwind")
09:    dim SqlCmd as String = "SELECT TOP 10 * FROM Products"
10:    dim sda as new SqlDataAdapter(SqlCmd,sCon)
11:    dim ds as new DataSet()
12:    sda.Fill(ds,"Products")
13:
14:    dgUC1.DataSource = ds.Tables(0).DefaultView
15:    dgUC1.DataBind()
16:
17:  end sub
18: </script>
19: <b>This user control was cached at:</b><%=DateTime.Now.ToString("G")%>
20: <p>
21: <asp:DataGrid runat="server" id="dgUC1" font-size="10" />

[C#.NET]

01: <%@ OutputCache Duration="60" VaryByParam="none"  %>
02: <%@ Import Namespace="System.Data" %>
03: <%@ Import Namespace="System.Data.SqlClient" %>
04:
05: <script language="c#" runat="server">
06:  void Page_Load(Object sender, EventArgs e) {
07:    SqlConnection sCon = new SqlConnection("server=localhost;" +
08:     "uid=sa;pwd=;database=northwind");
09:    string SqlCmd = "SELECT TOP 10 * FROM Products";
10:    SqlDataAdapter sda = new SqlDataAdapter(SqlCmd,sCon);
11:    DataSet ds = new DataSet();
12:    sda.Fill(ds,"Products");
13:
14:    dgUC1.DataSource = ds.Tables[0].DefaultView;
```

LISTING 16.11 Continued

```
15:   dgUC1.DataBind() ;
16:
17:   }
18: </script>
19: <b>This user control was cached at:</b><%=DateTime.Now.ToString("G")%>
20: <p>
21: <asp:DataGrid runat="server" id="dgUC1" font-size="10" />
```

Listing 16.11 renders a DataGrid control with the top 10 rows from the Products table and the time that the user control is cached—in this example, 60 seconds. In Listing 16.12, you add a new attribute, VaryByControl. Its value is one of this user control's public properties.

LISTING 16.12 User Control That Displays a DataGrid and Cache Time—Duration is set to 30

```
[VisualBasic.NET]

01: <%@ OutputCache  Duration="30" VaryByParam="none"
➡   VaryByControl="PageSize" %>
02: <%@ Import Namespace="System.Data" %>
03: <%@ Import Namespace="System.Data.SqlClient" %>
04:
05: <script language="vb" runat="server">
06:
07:   public PageSize as integer
08:
09:   public sub Page_Load(sender as Object, e as EventArgs)
10:     dim sCon as new SqlConnection("server=localhost;" & _
11:      "uid=sa;pwd=;database=northwind")
12:     dim SqlCmd as String = "SELECT TOP " & PageSize & " * FROM Suppliers"
13:     dim sda as new SqlDataAdapter(SqlCmd,sCon)
14:     dim ds as new DataSet()
15:     sda.Fill(ds,"Products")
16:
17:     dgUC1.DataSource = ds.Tables(0).DefaultView
18:     dgUC1.DataBind()
19:
20:   end sub
21: </script>
```

LISTING 16.12   Continued

```
22: <b>This user control was cached at:</b><%=DateTime.Now.ToString("G")%>
23: <p>
24: <asp:DataGrid runat="server" id="dgUC1" font-size="10" />
```

```
[C#.NET]
```

```
01: <%@ OutputCache  Duration="30" VaryByParam="none"
➥    VaryByControl="PageSize" %>
02: <%@ Import Namespace="System.Data" %>
03: <%@ Import Namespace="System.Data.SqlClient" %>
04:
05: <script language="c#" runat="server">
06:
07:   public int PageSize;
08:
09:   void Page_Load(Object sender, EventArgs e) {
10:     SqlConnection sCon = new SqlConnection("server=localhost;" +
11:       "uid=sa;pwd=;database=northwind");
12:     string SqlCmd = "SELECT TOP " + PageSize + " * FROM Suppliers";
13:     SqlDataAdapter sda = new SqlDataAdapter(SqlCmd,sCon);
14:     DataSet ds = new DataSet();
15:     sda.Fill(ds,"Products");
16:
17:     dgUC1.DataSource = ds.Tables[0].DefaultView;
18:     dgUC1.DataBind() ;
19:
20:   }
21: </script>
22: <b>This user control was cached at:</b><%=DateTime.Now.ToString("G")%>
23: <p>
24: <asp:DataGrid runat="server" id="dgUC1" font-size="10" />
```

Listing 16.12 renders a DataGrid control with the top (n) rows from the Products table and the time the user control is cached. This example takes advantage of the VaryByControl attribute to vary the cache of the control based on the PageSize variable, which sets the number of rows returned from the SQL query. This user control is set to cache for 30 seconds. The code in Listing 16.13 will work for both the C#.NET and VisualBasic.NET files.

LISTING 16.13   Web Form with Two User Controls Included, Each with Different Cache Durations

```
[VisualBasic.NET & C#.NET]

01: <%@ Register TagPrefix="DotNetJunkies"
➥    TagName="UserControl1" Src="Listing16.11.ascx" %>
02: <%@ Register TagPrefix="DotNetJunkies"
➥    TagName="UserControl2" Src="Listing16.12.ascx" %>
04:   <body>
05:    <asp:Table>
06:     <asp:TableRow>
07:      <asp:TableCell>
08:   <p>
09:   <DotNetJunkies:UserControl1 runat="server"/>
10:      </asp:TableCell>
11:     </asp:TableRow>
12:     <asp:TableRow>
13:      <asp:TableCell>
14:   <p>
15:   <DotNetJunkies:UserControl2 PageSize="2" runat="server"/>
16:   <br>
17:   <DotNetJunkies:UserControl2 PageSize="4" runat="server"/>
18:      </asp:TableCell>
19:     </asp:TableRow>
20:    </asp:Table>
21:   </body>
22:  </html>
```

The Web Form in Listing 16.13 demonstrates fragment caching. You will notice that I have registered the two different user controls from Listing 16.11 and Listing 16.12. Within the code, I put each control in its own row in a Table control. Located on lines 15 and 17 is the user control that has the VaryByControl attribute set to vary the cache based on the PageSize variable. The first has a PageSize value of 2, and the second, a PageSize value of 4. When this page is executed, you will receive a page similar to Figure 16.6. There will be three DataGrid controls and three cache times rendered. After 30 seconds has elapsed, try refreshing the page. Only the bottom two DataGrids displaying the Suppliers table will refresh.

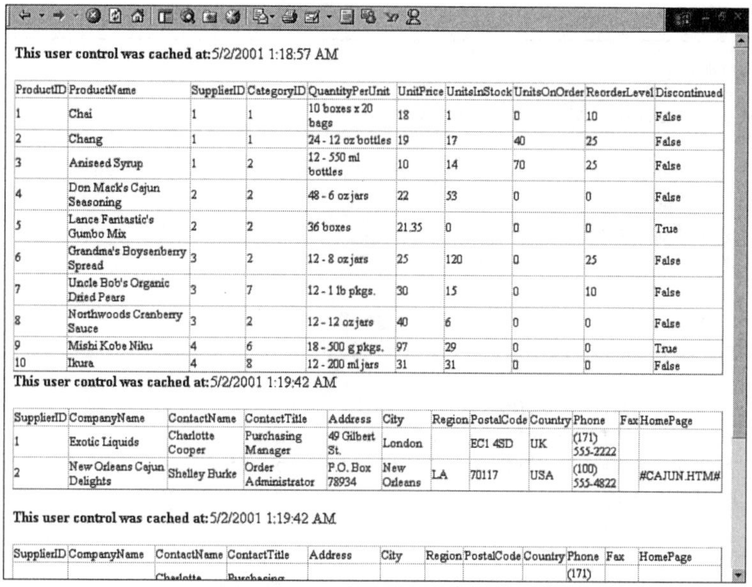

This user control was cached at:5/2/2001 1:18:57 AM

ProductID	ProductName	SupplierID	CategoryID	QuantityPerUnit	UnitPrice	UnitsInStock	UnitsOnOrder	ReorderLevel	Discontinued
1	Chai	1	1	10 boxes x 20 bags	18	1	0	10	False
2	Chang	1	1	24 - 12 oz bottles	19	17	40	25	False
3	Aniseed Syrup	1	2	12 - 550 ml bottles	10	14	70	25	False
4	Don Mack's Cajun Seasoning	2	2	48 - 6 oz jars	22	53	0	0	False
5	Lance Fantastic's Gumbo Mix	2	2	36 boxes	21.35	0	0	0	True
6	Grandma's Boysenberry Spread	3	2	12 - 8 oz jars	25	120	0	25	False
7	Uncle Bob's Organic Dried Pears	3	7	12 - 1 lb pkgs.	30	15	0	10	False
8	Northwoods Cranberry Sauce	3	2	12 - 12 oz jars	40	6	0	0	False
9	Mishi Kobe Niku	4	6	18 - 500 g pkgs.	97	29	0	0	True
10	Ikura	4	8	12 - 200 ml jars	31	31	0	0	False

This user control was cached at:5/2/2001 1:19:42 AM

SupplierID	CompanyName	ContactName	ContactTitle	Address	City	Region	PostalCode	Country	Phone	Fax	HomePage
1	Exotic Liquids	Charlotte Cooper	Purchasing Manager	49 Gilbert St.	London		EC1 4SD	UK	(171) 555-2222		
2	New Orleans Cajun Delights	Shelley Burke	Order Administrator	P.O. Box 78934	New Orleans	LA	70117	USA	(100) 555-4822		#CAJUN.HTM#

This user control was cached at:5/2/2001 1:19:42 AM

SupplierID	CompanyName	ContactName	ContactTitle	Address	City	Region	PostalCode	Country	Phone	Fax	HomePage
		Charlotte	Purchasing						(171)		

FIGURE 16.6

Web Form with two user controls included. If you refresh the page after 30 seconds, only the `Suppliers` *user control will refresh.*

Using the Cache APIs

Up to this point, you have only seen how to enable output caching. There is another side to caching, named *data caching*. This enables you to cache objects such as a `DataSet` or an `ArrayList` and share these objects application wide. For instance, say you have a `DataSet` that is created and used in more than one place in your application, yet it is always the same data. You can use data caching to place that `DataSet` into the cache the first time it is created and then access the `DataSet` from the cache when and where it's needed within your application. You can take it a step further by using page output caching on top of that.

In this section, I will give you samples of how to put data into the cache and how to access it. I'll also be discussing how to set expiration times, remove items from the cache, and how to work with file dependent data (ex: An XML file from which a `DataSet` is populated). First, let's look at a simple example of inserting objects into the cache using the `Cache.Insert` method. Listing 16.14 contains an example that puts an `ArrayList` object and a `DateTime` object into the cache.

Listing 16.14   Putting an ArrayList and a DateTime Object into the Cache

[VisualBasic.NET]

```
01: <script language="vb" runat="server">
02:
03:  public sub Page_Load(sender as Object, e as EventArgs)
04:
05:    dim LocalTime as DateTime
06:    dim LocalArrayList as ArrayList
07:
08:    '***Check if LocalTime is nothing***
09:    if Cache.Get("TimeCache") is nothing then
10:
11:      LocalTime = DateTime.Now
12:      Cache.Insert("TimeCache",LocalTime)
13:      lblCacheTime.Text = "<b>DateTime object put in the cache:</b> " &
➥  LocalTime.ToString("G")
14:
15:    else
16:
17:      LocalTime = CType(Cache.Get("TimeCache"), DateTime)
18:      lblCacheTime.Text = "<b>DateTime object from the cache:</b> " &
➥   LocalTime.ToString("G")
19:
20:    end if
21:    '***End***
22:
23:    '***Check if LocalArrayList is nothing***
24:    if Cache.Get("ArrayListCache") is nothing then
25:
26:      dim i as integer
27:      LocalArrayList= new ArrayList()
28:      for i = 0 to 10
29:       LocalArrayList.Add("Item - " & i)
30:      next i
31:
32:      Cache.Insert("ArrayListCache", LocalArrayList)
33:      ArrayListContents.DataSource = LocalArrayList
34:      ArrayListContents.DataBind()
35:      lblArrayListMessage.Text = "<b>ArrayList object put in the cache:
➥  </b> "
36:
37:    else
38:
39:      LocalArrayList = CType(Cache.Get("ArrayListCache"),ArrayList)
40:      ArrayListContents.DataSource = LocalArrayList
```

LISTING 16.14 Continued

```
41:    ArrayListContents.DataBind()
42:    lblArrayListMessage.Text = "<b>ArrayList object from the cache:
➡  </b> "
43:
44:  end if
45:  '***End***
46:
47:  end sub
48: </script>
49:

[C#.NET - Replace server code]

01: <script language="c#" runat="server">
02:
03:  void Page_Load(Object sender, EventArgs e) {
04:
05:    DateTime LocalTime;
06:    ArrayList LocalArrayList;
07:
08:    //'***Check if LocalTime is nothing***
09:    if (Cache.Get("TimeCache") == null) {
10:
11:     LocalTime = DateTime.Now;
12:     Cache.Insert("TimeCache",LocalTime);
13:     lblCacheTime.Text = "<b>DateTime object put in the cache:</b> " +
➡  LocalTime.ToString("G");
14:
15:    } else {
16:
17:     LocalTime = (DateTime) Cache.Get("TimeCache");
18:     lblCacheTime.Text = "<b>DateTime object from the cache:</b> " +
➡  LocalTime.ToString("G");
19:
20:    }
21:    //'***End***
22:
23:    //'***Check if LocalArrayList is nothing***
24:    if (Cache.Get("ArrayListCache") == null) {
25:
26:     int i;
27:     LocalArrayList= new ArrayList();
28:     for (i = 0; i < 11; i++) {
29:      LocalArrayList.Add("Item - " + i);
30:     }
```

LISTING 16.14 Continued

```
31:
32:     Cache.Insert("ArrayListCache", LocalArrayList);
33:     ArrayListContents.DataSource = LocalArrayList;
34:     ArrayListContents.DataBind();
35:     lblArrayListMessage.Text = "<b>ArrayList object put in the cache:
➥   </b> ";
36:
37:   } else {
38:
39:     LocalArrayList = (ArrayList) Cache.Get("ArrayListCache");
40:     ArrayListContents.DataSource = LocalArrayList;
41:     ArrayListContents.DataBind();
42:     lblArrayListMessage.Text = "<b>ArrayList object from the cache:
➥   </b> ";
43:
44:   }
45:   //'***End***
46:
47:  }
48: </script>
50:

[VisualBasic.NET & C#.NET]

50: <html>
51: <body>
52:   <asp:Label runat="server" id="lblCacheTime" />
53:   <p>
54:   <asp:Label runat="server" id="lblArrayListMessage" />
55:   <asp:DropDownList id="ArrayListContents" runat="server" />
56:   <p>
57: </body>
58: </html>
```

In Listing 16.14, you are putting two objects into the cache, an ArrayList and a DateTime object. The first thing you want to do whenever you are getting and working with an object from the cache is check if they exist; if the item doesn't exist in the cache and you try to work with the returned object, you will receive a NullReferenceException. I check if these objects are in the cache on lines 9 (the DateTime object) and 24 (the ArrayList object). I use the Get method to retrieve the object and check whether it is null (C#.NET syntax) or nothing (VB.NET syntax). If either of the objects is found to be null, then you know that you have to re-create them and insert them back into the cache. If this is the first request to the page, then both the `ArrayList` and `DateTime` objects should be null. Because they both are null, the `If` statement is executed, and new `DateTime` and `ArrayList` objects are created (`DateTime`, on line 11) and (`ArrayList`, on lines 26–30). After the item is created, you call the `Cache.Insert` method to insert each object into the cache (lines 12 and 32). This particular overload of `Cache.Insert` expects only two parameters:

- `string`   This string will be the `Key` for the cached item. The Key is used to access the object after it is in the cache.
- `Object`   The object you want to cache.

> **NOTE**
>
> This is the first overload for the `Insert` statement (the additional overloads are described in the following section). Using this overload of the `Insert` statement, cached items will remain in the cache for the lifetime of the application or until the runtime automatically takes it out due to lack of use or memory constraints.

You can see a screen shot of this page the first time it is requested in Figure 16.7. Notice that the `Label` control has the information from the `If` block—"Object put into cache".

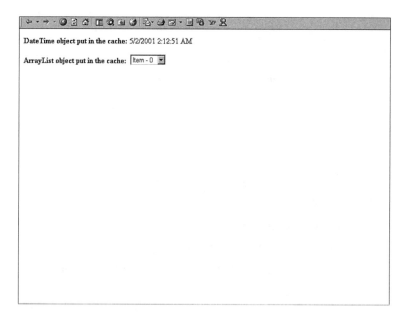

FIGURE 16.7

First request: Controls bound to dynamic data.

Now refresh the page. You will notice that the Label controls text now reads something like, "From the cache" (see Figure 16.8) On the page refresh, instead of dynamically creating each object, both objects were found in the cache. Hence, the else statement was executed, and the server controls were bound to the object obtained from the cache.

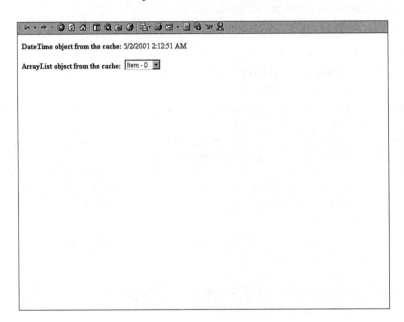

FIGURE 16.8
Second request: Controls bound to cached objects.

Now that you have a basic understanding of how to insert an item into the cache, let's go through the Insert method in detail.

The Insert Method

There are three other overloads to the Cache.Insert method available for your use. The following list contains all four:

- Cache.Insert(String, Object)
- Cache.Insert(String, Object, CacheDependency)
- Cache.Insert(String, Object, CacheDependency, DateTime, TimeSpan)
- Cache.Insert(String, Object, CacheDependency, DateTime, TimeSpan, CacheItemPriority, CacheItemPriorityDecay, CacheItemRemovedCallback)

The `Cache.Insert` method has the following parameters:

- `String`—The name of the key for the cache item.
- `Object`—The object you want to put into the cache.
- `CacheDependency`—A file or additional key of a cache item on which this cache item depends. If a change is made to a `CacheDependency` object (an XML Document), then this cache item becomes invalid and is taken out of the cache.
- `DateTime`—Sets the absolute expiration time for the cache item.
- `TimeSpan`—Sets the sliding expiration time for the cache item.
- `CacheItemPriority`—Sets the priority of the cache item relative to other cache items. The value of this parameter must be a member of the `CacheItemPriority` enumeration. A cache item with a lower priority will be taken out of the cache before one with a higher priority, in the event the server is under load.
- `CacheItemPriorityDecay`—Sets the rate at which an item declines in priority within the cache. The value of this parameter must be a member of the CacheItemPriorityDecay enumeration. With every thing else equal, a cache item that decays slowly will stay in the cache longer than one with a fast decay.
- `CacheItemRemovedCallback`—A delegate that will be called when the item is removed from the cache. One possible use could be to re-create an item when the item is taken out of the cache.

Using these parameters, you have incredible control over how an item is cached, and when the item is taken out of the cache. You now have all the possible overloads available to you using the `Cache.Insert` statement, so let's walk through inserting different types objects into the cache using a couple of them.

In Listing 16.15, I'll demonstrate how to insert an item into the cache that has a `CacheDependency`. This example uses the XML file `Authors.xml`, which is installed with the .NET SDK. `Authors.xml` can also be found in this book's source file.

LISTING 16.15   Inserting an Item into the Cache That Has a `CacheDependency`

```
[VisualBasic.NET]
01: <%@ Import Namespace="System.IO" %>
02: <%@ Import Namespace="System.Data" %>
03:
04: <script langauge="vb" runat="server">
05:
06:   public sub Page_Load(sender as Object, e as EventArgs)
07:
```

LISTING 16.15 Continued

```
08:   dim XmlDataSet as DataSet = CType(Cache.Get("XmlDataSetCache"),DataSet)
09:
10:   if XmlDataSet is nothing then
11:
12:     Response.Write("<b>Dynamically Created</b><p>")
13:
14:     dim ds as new DataSet()
15:     dim FStream as new FileStream(Server.MapPath("authors.xml"), _
16:      FileMode.Open, FileAccess.Read)
17:     dim SReader as new StreamReader(FStream)
18:     ds.ReadXml(SReader)
19:     FStream.Close()
20:
21:     dg1.DataSource = ds
22:     dg1.DataBind()
23:
24:     Cache.Insert("XmlDataSetCache", ds, _
25:      new CacheDependency(Server.MapPath("authors.xml")), _
26:      DateTime.Now.AddSeconds(10), TimeSpan.Zero)
27:
28:   else
29:
30:     Response.Write("<b>From Cache</b><p>")
31:
32:     dg1.DataSource = XmlDataSet
33:     dg1.DataBind()
34:
35:   end if
36:
37: end sub
38:
39: </script>

[C#.NET]
04: <script language="C#" runat="server">
05:
06:   void Page_Load(Object sender, EventArgs e){
07:
08:     DataSet XmlDataSet = (DataSet) Cache.Get("XmlDataSetCache");
09:
10:     if (XmlDataSet == null) {
11:
12:       Response.Write("<b>Dynamically Created</b><p>");
13:
```

LISTING 16.15 Continued

```
14:    DataSet ds = new DataSet();
15:    FileStream FStream = new FileStream(Server.MapPath("authors.xml"),
16:     FileMode.Open, FileAccess.Read);
17:    StreamReader SReader = new StreamReader(FStream);
18:    ds.ReadXml(SReader);
19:    FStream.Close();
20:
21:    dg1.DataSource = ds;
22:    dg1.DataBind();
23:
24:    Cache.Insert("XmlDataSetCache", ds,
25:      new CacheDependency(Server.MapPath("authors.xml")),
26:      DateTime.Now.AddSeconds(10), TimeSpan.Zero);
27:
28:    } else {
29:
30:    Response.Write("<b>From Cache</b><p>");
31:
32:    dg1.DataSource = XmlDataSet;
33:    dg1.DataBind();
34:
35:    }
36:
37: }
38:
39: </script>

[VisualBasic.NET & C#.NET]

41: <html>
42: <body>
43:
44:    <asp:DataGrid id="dg1" runat="server" font-size="10" />
45:
46: </body>
47: </html>
```

When the code from Listing 16.15 executes, the first thing you should do is check if the cache item exists already (lines 8 and 10). If the item is not found in the cache, then you create the DataSet object and bind the DataGrid by using the FileStream and StreamReader objects to retrieve the XML document and filling the DataSet by calling the DataSet.ReadXML method (lines 14–22). Next, insert the file dependent DataSet into the cache (lines 24–26). I used the third overload for the Insert method in this example. The first parameter is the name (Key) I want to use when referencing this cache item. The second parameter is the object I wanted to insert into the cache (the `DataSet` named ds). The third parameter is a `CacheDependency` object. The `CacheDependency` object is created by passing in the path to the file on which you want this cache item to be dependent. The fourth parameter is the absolute expiration for the cache item and in this example it is set for 10 seconds. The fifth parameter is the cache items sliding expiration and in this example I used the `Zero` field that effectively set no sliding expiration. If the cache item does exist, then the `DataGrid` is bound directly to the `XmlDataSet` (lines 32 and 33). Figure 16.9 contains a screen shot of this page on the second request. Notice that "From Cache" is printed on the page.

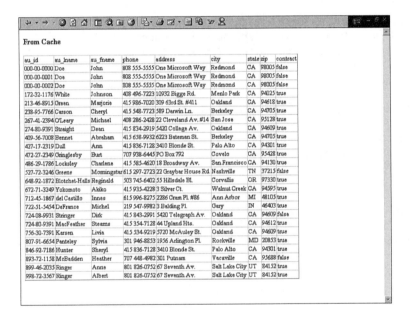

FIGURE 16.9

The `DataGrid` is bound directly to the file-dependent `DataSet` retrieved from the cache.

We briefly went over the `CacheDependency` object in the proceeding paragraph. In Listing 16.15 we used a single file as the `CacheDependency`. There are two other overloads when constructing a `CacheDependency` object:

- `CacheDependency(string)`—Monitors a single file or directory for changes. The parameter is a file and/or directory path.

- `CacheDependency(string[])`—Monitors an array of files or directories for changes. The parameter is a string array of file and/or directory paths.

- CacheDependency(string[], string[])—The first parameter monitors an array of files or directories for changes. The second monitors an array of cache keys (other items in the cache). You can use one or the other or both at the same time. If you choose to just monitor by an array of cache keys specify null as the first parameter. The first parameter is a string array of file and/or directory paths. The second parameter is a string array of cache keys.

The Get Method

Getting an item from the cache is very easy. It is just a matter of calling the Cache.Get method and passing in the Key value of the object you want to retrieve. Because this method retrieves an object you can use it as though it were a local object by casting it. However, if you need to manipulate the data, it is a good idea to put it into a local variable.

Listing 16.16 illustrates a couple different methods you can use to work with data from the cache. This example inserts a new ArrayList into the cache and then retrieves it.

LISTING 16.16   Using the Get Method to Retrieve Cached Items

```
[VisualBasic.NET]
01: <script language="vb" runat="server">
02:
03:  public sub Page_Load(sender as Object, e as EventArgs)
04:
05:  if CType(Cache.Get("ArrayListCache"),ArrayList) is nothing then
06:
07:    dim LocalArrayList as new ArrayList()
08:    dim i as integer
09:    for i = 0 to 10
10:     LocalArrayList.Add("Item - " & i)
11:    next i
12:
13:    Cache.Insert("ArrayListCache", LocalArrayList)
14:    ArrayListContents.DataSource = LocalArrayList
15:    ArrayListContents.DataBind()
16:    lblArrayListMessage.Text = "<b>ArrayList object put in the cache:
➥   </b> "
17:
18:   else
19:
20:    ArrayListContents.DataSource = CType(Cache.Get("ArrayListCache"),
➥  ArrayList)
21:    ArrayListContents.DataBind()
```

LISTING 16.16 Continued

```
22:    lblArrayListMessage.Text = "<b>ArrayList object from the cache:
➡ </b> "
23:
24:  end if
25:
26:  end sub
27:
28: </script>
```

[C#.NET]

```
01: <script language="c#" runat="server">
02:
03:  void Page_Load(Object sender, EventArgs e){
04:
05:  if (Cache.Get("ArrayListCache") == null){
06:
07:   ArrayList LocalArrayList = new ArrayList();
08:   int i;
09:   for(i = 0; i < 11; i++){
10:    LocalArrayList.Add("Item - " + i);
11:   }
12:
13:   Cache.Insert("ArrayListCache", LocalArrayList);
14:   ArrayListContents.DataSource = LocalArrayList;
15:   ArrayListContents.DataBind();
16:   lblArrayListMessage.Text = "<b>ArrayList object put in the cache:
➡ </b> ";
17:
18:  } else {
19:
20:   ArrayListContents.DataSource = (ArrayList) Cache.Get("ArrayListCache");
21:   ArrayListContents.DataBind();
22:   lblArrayListMessage.Text = "<b>ArrayList object from the cache:
➡ </b> ";
23:
24:  }
25:
26: }
27:
28: </script>
```

[VisualBasic.NET & C#.NET]

```
30: <html>
31: <body>
32: <asp:Label runat="server" id="lblArrayListMessage" />
```

LISTING 16.16   Continued

```
33: <asp:DropDownList id="ArrayListContents" runat="server" />
34: <p>
35: </body>
36: </html>
```

The `Cache.Get` method is first called on line 5 to check if the cache item exists. The `Cache.Get` method only requires one parameter and that is the cache `Key` or the name of the cache item you want to get. As in the previous example, check to see if the object is actually valid by using an `if...then` statement. If the object is not in the cache, re-create it and put it into the cache (lines 7–16) and bind the `DropDownList` control. If it is in the cache, bind the `DropDownList` directly to the object (lines 20–22).

The `GetEnumerator` Method

At some point, you might need to iterate through all the cache items. The `Cache.Get Enumerator` method can be used to return a `IDictionaryEnumerator` object you can use to do just that. The `IDictionaryEnumerator` object returned contains the Keys and their values. Listing 16.17 contains an example using the `Cache.GetEnumerator` method to print out all cache items to the page.

LISTING 16.17   Retrieving a `Dictionary` Object of All Cached Items with the `GetEnumerator` Method

```
[VisualBasic.NET]

01: <script language="vb" runat="server">
02: public sub Page_Load(sender as Object, e as EventArgs)
03:
04:  dim myEnumerater As IDictionaryEnumerator
05:  myEnumerater = Cache.GetEnumerator()
06:  while(myEnumerater.MoveNext)
07:   Response.Write(myEnumerater.Key.ToString() & "<BR>")
08:  end while
09:
10: end sub
11:
12: </script>

[C#.NET]

01:  <script language="c#" runat="server">
02: void Page_Load(Object sender, EventArgs e){
03:
```

LISTING 16.17   Continued

```
04:  IdictionaryEnumerator myEnumerater;
05:  myEnumerater = Cache.GetEnumerator();
06:  while(myEnumerater.MoveNext()) {
07:   Response.Write(myEnumerater.Key.ToString() + "<BR>");
08:  }
09:
10: }
11:
12: </script>

[VisualBasic.NET & C#.NET]

13: <html>
14: <body>
15:
16: </body>
17: </html>
```

When the code in Listing 16.17 executes, you will receive a list of all items currently in the cache similar to Figure 16.10. Notice in that screen shot that the XmlDataSetCache cache item from the previous example is still in the cache.

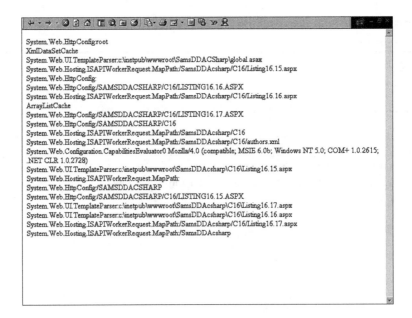

FIGURE 16.10

The contents of this application's current cache. Notice that the XmlDataSetCache and ArrayListCache cache items are still present from the previous code examples.

> Because the contents of the cache might be changing constantly, some items returned by the Cache.GetEnumerator method might or might not still be in the cache.

The Remove Method

You might run into the need to remove items from the cache before they expire, either to refresh the data or because it is no longer needed and is just taking up memory. You can use the Cache.Remove method to removeq items from the cache. The Remove method takes only one parameter and that is the Key for the cached item and its return value is the object that was taken out of the cache. Listing 16.18 contains an example using the Cache.Remove method. In this example, you will remove the DataSet you inserted in Listing 16.15 (XmlDataSetCache). If it has been a while since you ran that example, you might want to extend the expiration time and run the page again to put the DataSet back into the cache.

LISTING 16.18 Using the Remove Method to Remove a Cached Item

```
[VisualBasic.NET]

01: <script language="vb" runat="server">
02:
03:  public sub Page_Load(sender as Object, e as EventArgs)
04:
05:   Cache.Remove("XmlDataSetCache")
06:
07:  end sub
08:
09: </script>

[C#.NET]

01: <script language="c#" runat="server">
02:
03:  void Page_Load(Object sender, EventArgs e) {
04:
05:   Cache.Remove("XmlDataSetCache");
06:
07: }
08: </script>

[VisualBasic.NET & C#.NET]

11: <html>
```

LISTING **16.18**   Continued

```
12: <body>
13: </body>
14: </html>
```

In Listing 16.18, the Cache.Remove method is called on line 5. The Remove method only expects one parameter, the Key for the cache item. If the cache item is found, it will be returned by the method and removed from the cache; if it doesn't exist, it will return a null reference. After running this page, go back and execute Listing 16.17 and you can verify that the item was indeed taken out of the cache.

Caching in Web Services

Inherently, Web services support output caching by use of the CacheDuration property of the WebMethodAttribute class. The CacheDuration WebMethodAttribute is similar to the @OuputCache Duration attribute in that you set its value equal to the number of seconds that a response should remain in the cache. In Listing 16.9 I'll demonstrate how to enable output caching for a WebMethod that returns a DataSet.

Listing 16.19 illustrates how to cache the output of a Web service which returns a DataSet object.

LISTING **16.19**   Implementing Output Caching in the GetProducts Method

```
[VisualBasic.NET]

01: <%@ WebService Language="vb" Class="ProductServices" %>
02:
03: imports System.Data
04: imports System.Data.SqlClient
05: imports System.Web.Services
06:
07:  public class ProductServices : inherits WebService
08:
09:    <WebMethod(CacheDuration := 60)> _
10:    Public Function GetProducts(RecordCount As Integer) As DataSet
11:    _
12:        dim ProductsDataSet ad new DataSet()
13:        dim sCon as new SqlConnection("server=localhost;" & _
14:        "uid=sa;pwd=;database=northwind")
15:        dim SqlCmd as string = "SELECT TOP " & RecordCount &
➥ " * FROM Suppliers"
16:        dim sda as new SqlDataAdapter(SqlCmd,sCon)
17:
```

LISTING 16.19 Continued

```
18:          sda.Fill(ProductsDataSet,"Products")
19:
20:
21:          return ProductsDataSet
22:    end function
23: end class
```

```
[C#.NET]
01: <%@ WebService Language="c#" Class="ProductServices" %>
02:
03: using System.Data;
04: using System.Data.SqlClient;
05: using System.Web.Services;
06:
07: public class ProductServices : WebService {
08:
09:   [ WebMethod(CacheDuration=10) ]
10:       public DataSet GetProducts(int RecordCount) {
11:
12:          DataSet ProductsDataSet = new DataSet();
13:          SqlConnection sCon = new SqlConnection("server=localhost;" +
14:          "uid=sa;pwd=;database=northwind");
15:          string SqlCmd = "SELECT TOP " + RecordCount + " * FROM Suppliers";
16:          SqlDataAdapter sda = new SqlDataAdapter(SqlCmd,sCon);
17:
18:          sda.Fill(ProductsDataSet,"Products");
19:
20:
21:          return ProductsDataSet;
22:       }
23: }
```

Listing 16.19 illustrates a very simple example of how to implement output caching within a Web service. It is actually a very complex process, but, with my superb programming skills, I was able to simplify it. . . okay, it is this easy. Simply use the CacheDuration WebMethod Attribute, and assign an amount in seconds. In this example, I cached the output for 10 seconds.

Before you invoke the GetProducts Web method, you must enter an integer value equal to the number of rows you want returned in the DataSet from the Products table. This integer value will be the value by which the cache varies. Go through and invoke the method using 2 for the value, and then 4. Make a mental note of the approximate length of time the response takes.

Now go through and do it again. You will notice that the response is quicker. This is because the response is now being served from the output cache.

In addition to output caching, you also can take advantage of data caching in Web services. However, you need to access it a little differently than in output caching. First, you have to include the System.Web namespace within your Web service. The System.Web namespace contains all the classes and interfaces that enable browser and server communication. Specifically, it contains information about the current HTTP request object. This is what you use to access the Web applications' cache. Listing 16.20 presents a simple example of using data caching within a Web service. The example has one GetString Web method that puts a string into the cache and then returns the string from the cache.

LISTING 16.20   Using Data Caching Within a Web Service

```
[VisualBasic.NET]
01: <%@ WebService Language="vb" Class="StringService" %>
02:
03: imports System.Web.Services
04: imports System.Web
05:
06: public class StringService : inherits WebService
07:
08:     <WebMethod()> _
09:     Public Function _GetString() As string
10:
11:       dim MyString as string ="The Mack is back!"
12:       HttpContext.Current.Cache.Insert("MyStringCache", MyString)
13:
14:       return CType(HttpContext.Current.Cache.Get("MyStringCache"), string)
15:
16:    end function
17: end class

[C#.NET]
01: <%@ WebService Language="c#" Class="StringService" %>
02:
03: using System.Data;
04: using System.Data.SqlClient;
05: using System.Web.Services;
06: using System.Web;
07:
08: public class StringService : WebService {
09:
10:   [ WebMethod() ]
```

LISTING 16.20 Continued

```
11:     public string GetString() {
12:
13:       string MyString ="The Mack is back!";
14:       HttpContext.Current.Cache.Insert("MyStringCache", MyString);
15:
16:       return (string) HttpContext.Current.Cache.Get("MyStringCache");
17:
18:     }
19: }
```

In Listing 16.20, the applications cache is accessed through HttpContext.Current (the HttpContext object for the current HTTP Request) Cache property (lines 14 and 16). After you have a handle on the Cache object for the current Web application, you just need to call its respective methods (Insert and Get) to work with it. Figure 16.11 contains an image of this Web service after the GetString Web method has been invoked.

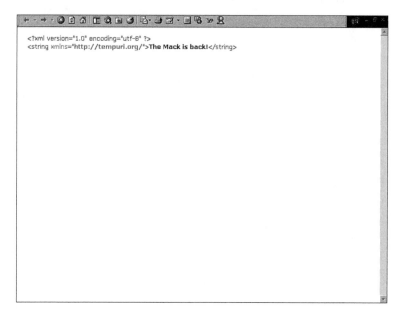

FIGURE 16.11
"The Mack is Back!" is returned by the Web method. This string was returned by the Web method directly from the cache.

Summary

In this final chapter, you learned a variety of caching techniques available to you when developing ASP.NET solutions. First, we briefly explored what caching is. We followed that by introducing page output caching, using both the `HttpCachePolicy` class and its high-level wrapper, the `@OutputCache` directive to cache entire pages. Next, we presented you with fragment caching, which enables you to cache parts of pages by using user controls. We then introduced data caching, which you can use to cache objects for application-wide object sharing using the `Cache` class. Finally, we covered caching in Web services by implementing output caching in the `GetProducts` Web method and data caching using the `GetString` Web method. Specifically, the chapter presented the following:

- What is caching?
- Using page output caching
- Using fragment caching
- Using the Cache APIs
- Implementing caching in Web services

Appendixes

IN THIS PART

ASP.NET Server Controls Reference

IN THIS APPENDIX

ASP.NET Intrinsic Server Controls

Button

TABLE A.1   Button Properties

Property	Get/Set	Description
AccessKey	Get and Set	Gets or sets the keyboard shortcut key (AccessKey) for setting focus to the Web control.
Attributes	Get	Gets the collection of arbitrary attributes (for rendering only) that do not correspond to properties on the control.
BackColor	Get and Set	Gets or sets the background color of the Web control.
BorderColor	Get and Set	Gets or sets the border color of the Web control.
BorderStyle	Get and Set	Gets or sets the border style of the Web control.
BorderWidth	Get and Set	Gets or sets the border width of the Web control.
CausesValidation	Get and Set	Gets or sets a value indicating whether validation is performed when the Button control is clicked.
ClientID	Get	Gets the server control identifier generated by ASP.NET.
CommandArgument	Get and Set	Gets or sets an optional parameter passed to the Command event along with the associated CommandName.
CommandName	Get and Set	Gets or sets the command name associated with the Button control that is passed to the Command event.
Controls	Get	Gets a ControlCollection object that represents the child controls for a specified server control in the UI hierarchy.
ControlStyle	Get	Gets the style of the Web control. This property is primarily used by control developers.

TABLE A.1   Continued

Property	Get/Set	Description
CssClass	Get and Set	Gets or sets the CSS class rendered by the Web control.
Enabled	Get and Set	Gets or sets a value indicating whether the Web control is enabled.
EnableViewState	Get and Set	Gets or sets a value indicating whether the server control maintains its view state, and the view state of any child controls it contains, when the current page request ends.
Font	Get	Gets font information of the Web control.
ForeColor	Get and Set	Gets or sets the foreground color (typically the color of the text) of the Web control.
Height	Get and Set	Gets or sets the height of the Web control.
ID	Get and Set	Gets or sets the programmatic identifier assigned to the server control.
NamingContainer	Get and Set	Gets a reference to the server control's naming container, which creates a unique namespace for differentiating between server controls with the same Control.ID property value.
Page	Get	Gets a reference to the Page instance that contains the server control.
Parent	Get	Gets a reference to the server control's parent control in the page UI hierarchy.
Site	Get	Gets information about the Web site to which the server control belongs.
Style	Get	Gets a collection of text attributes that will be rendered as a style attribute on the outer tag of the Web control.
TabIndex	Get and Set	Gets or sets the tab index of the Web control.
TemplateSourceDirectory	Get	Gets the virtual directory of the Page or UserControl that contains the current server control.

A

ASP.NET SERVER CONTROLS REFERENCE

Table A.1   Continued

Property	Get/Set	Description
Text	Get and Set	Gets or sets the text caption displayed in the `Button` control.
ToolTip	Get and Set	Gets or sets the tool tip for the Web control to be displayed when the mouse cursor is over the control.
UniqueID	Get	Gets the unique, hierarchically-qualified identifier for the server control.
Visible	Get and Set	Gets or sets a value that indicates whether a server control is rendered as UI on the page.
Width	Get and Set	Gets or sets the width of the Web control.

Table A.2   Button Public Instance Methods

Method	Description
ApplyStyle	Copies any non-blank elements of the specified style to the Web control, overwriting any existing style elements of the control. This method is primarily used by control developers.
CopyBaseAttributes	Copies the `AccessKey`, `Enabled`, `ToolTip`, `TabIndex`, and `Attributes` properties onto the Web control from the specified source control. This method is primarily used by control developers.
DataBind	Binds a data source to the invoked server control and all of its child controls.
Dispose	Enables a server control to perform final clean up before it is released from memory.
Equals	Overloaded. Determines whether two `Object` instances are equal.
FindControl	Overloaded. Searches the current naming container for the specified server control.
GetHashCode	Serves as a hash function for a particular type, suitable for use in hashing algorithms and data structures like a hash table.
GetType	Gets the `Type` of the current instance.

TABLE A.2   Continued

Method	Description
HasControls	Determines if the server control contains any child controls.
MergeStyle	Copies any non-blank elements of the specified style to the Web control, but will not overwrite any existing style elements of the control. This method is primarily used by control developers.
RenderBeginTag	Renders the HTML begin tag of the control into the specified writer. This method is primarily used by control developers.
RenderControl	Outputs server control content to a provided HtmlTextWriter object, then checks if tracing is enabled for the containing page and retrieves trace information about the server control.
RenderEndTag	Renders the HTML end tag of the control into the specified writer. This method is primarily used by control developers.
ResolveUrl	Resolves a relative URL to the absolute URL where the page or user control associated with this request resides.
SetRenderMethodDelegate	Assigns an event handler delegate to render the server control and its content into its parent control.
ToString	Returns a String that represents the current Object.

A

ASP.NET SERVER
CONTROLS
REFERENCE

TABLE A.3   Button Public Instance Events

Event	Description
Click	Occurs when the Button is clicked.
Command	Occurs when the Button is clicked.
DataBinding	Occurs when the server control binds to a data source.
Disposed	Occurs when a server control is released from memory, which is the last stage of the server control lifecycle when an ASP.NET page is requested.
Init	Occurs when the server control is initialized, which is the first step in the lifecycle.
Load	Occurs when the server control is loaded into the Page object.
PreRender	Occurs when the server control is about to render to its containing Page object.
Unload	Occurs when the server control is unloaded from memory.

CheckBox

TABLE A.4 CheckBox Properties

Property	Get/Set	Description
AccessKey	Get and Set	Gets or sets the keyboard shortcut key (AccessKey) for setting focus to the Web control.
Attributes	Get	Gets the collection of arbitrary attributes (for rendering only) that do not correspond to properties on the control.
AutoPostBack	Get and Set	Gets or sets a value indicating whether the CheckBox state automatically posts back to the server when clicked.
BackColor	Get and Set	Gets or sets the background color of the Web control.
BorderColor	Get and Set	Gets or sets the border color of the Web control.
BorderStyle	Get and Set	Gets or sets the border style of the Web control.
BorderWidth	Get and Set	Gets or sets the border width of the Web control.
Checked	Get and Set	Gets or sets a value indicating whether the CheckBox control is checked.
ClientID	Get	Gets the server control identifier generated by ASP.NET.
Controls	Get	Gets a ControlCollection object that represents the child controls for a specified server control in the UI hierarchy.
ControlStyle	Get	Gets the style of the Web control. This property is primarily used by control developers.
CssClass	Get and Set	Gets or sets the CSS class rendered by the Web control.
Enabled	Get and Set	Gets or sets a value indicating whether the Web control is enabled.

TABLE A.4 Continued

Property	Get/Set	Description
EnableViewState	Get and Set	Gets or sets a value indicating whether the control should maintain its view state, and the view state of any child control it contains, when the current page request ends.
Font	Get	Gets font information of the Web control.
ForeColor	Get and Set	Gets or sets the foreground color (typically the color of the text) of the Web control.
Height	Get and Set	Gets or sets the height of the Web control.
ID	Get and Set	Gets or sets the programmatic identifier assigned to the server control.
NamingContainer	Get and Set	Gets a reference to the server control's naming container, which creates a unique namespace for differentiating between server controls with the same Control.ID property value.
Page	Get	Gets a reference to the Page instance that contains the server control.
Parent	Get	Gets a reference to the server control's parent control in the page UI hierarchy.
Site	Get	Gets information about the Web site to which the server control belongs.
Style	Get	Gets a collection of text attributes that will be rendered as a style attribute on the outer tag of the Web control.
TabIndex	Get and Set	Gets or sets the tab index of the Web control.
TemplateSourceDirectory	Get	Gets the virtual directory of the Page or UserControl that contains the current server control.
Text	Get and Set	Gets or sets the text label associated with the CheckBox.

A

**ASP.NET SERVER
CONTROLS
REFERENCE**

TABLE A.4   Continued

Property	Get/Set	Description
TextAlign	Get and Set	Gets or sets the alignment of the text label associated with the CheckBox control.
ToolTip	Get and Set	Gets or sets the tool tip for the Web control to be displayed when the mouse cursor is over the control.
UniqueID	Get	Gets the unique, hierarchically-qualified identifier for the server control.
Visible	Get and Set	Gets or sets a value that indicates whether a server control is rendered as UI on the page.
Width	Get and Set	Gets or sets the width of the Web control.

TABLE A.5   CheckBox Public Instance Methods

Method	Description
ApplyStyle	Copies any non-blank elements of the specified style to the Web control, overwriting any existing style elements of the control. This method is primarily used by control developers.
CopyBaseAttributes	Copies the AccessKey, Enabled, ToolTip, TabIndex, and Attributes properties onto the Web control from the specified source control. This method is primarily used by control developers.
DataBind	Binds a data source to the invoked server control and all of its child controls.
Dispose	Enables a server control to perform final clean up before it is released from memory.
Equals	Overloaded. Determines whether two Object instances are equal.
FindControl	Overloaded. Searches the current naming container for the specified server control.
GetHashCode	Serves as a hash function for a particular type, suitable for use in hashing algorithms and data structures like a hash table.

TABLE A.5   Continued

Method	Description
GetType	Gets the Type of the current instance.
HasControls	Determines if the server control contains any child controls.
MergeStyle	Copies any non-blank elements of the specified style to the Web control, but will not overwrite any existing style elements of the control. This method is primarily used by control developers.
RenderBeginTag	Renders the HTML begin tag of the control into the specified writer. This method is primarily used by control developers.
RenderControl	Outputs server control content to a provided HtmlTextWriter object, then checks if tracing is enabled for the containing page and retrieves trace information about the server control.
RenderEndTag	Renders the HTML end tag of the control into the specified writer. This method is primarily used by control developers.
ResolveUrl	Resolves a relative URL to the absolute URL where the page or user control associated with this request resides.
SetRenderMethodDelegate	Assigns an event handler delegate to render the server control and its content into its parent control.
ToString	Returns a String that represents the current Object.

TABLE A.6   CheckBox Public Instance Events

Event	Description
CheckedChanged	Occurs when the Checked property is changed.
DataBinding	Occurs when the server control binds to a data source.
Disposed	Occurs when a server control is released from memory, which is the last stage of the server control lifecycle when an ASP.NET page is requested.
Init	Occurs when the server control is initialized, which is the first step in its lifecycle.
Load	Occurs when the control is loaded into the Page object.
PreRender	Occurs when the server control is about to render to its containing Page object.
Unload	Occurs when the control is unloaded from memory.

DropDownList

TABLE A.7 DropDownList Properties

Property	Get/Set	Description
AccessKeys	Get and Set	Gets or sets the keyboard shortcut key (AccessKey) for setting focus to the Web control.
Attributes	Get	Gets the collection of arbitrary attributes (for rendering only) that do not correspond to properties on the control.
AutoPostBack	Get and Set	Gets or sets a value indicating whether a postback to the server automatically occurs when the user changes the list selection.
BackColor	Get and Set	Gets or sets the background color of the Web control.
BorderColor	Get and Set	Overridden. Gets or sets the border color of the control.
BorderStyle	Get and Set	Overridden. Gets or sets the border style of the control.
BorderWidth	Get and Set	Overridden. Gets or sets the border width for the control.
ClientID	Get	Gets the server control identifier generated by ASP.NET.
Controls	Get	Gets a ControlCollection object that represents the child controls for a specified server control in the UI hierarchy.
ControlStyle	Get	Gets the style of the Web control. This property is primarily used by control developers.
CssClass	Get and Set	Gets or sets the CSS class rendered by the Web control.
DataMember	Get and Set	Gets or sets the specific table in the DataSource to bind to the control.
DataSource	Get and Set	Gets or sets the data source that populates the items of the list control.

TABLE A.7   Continued

Property	Get/Set	Description
DataTextField	Get and Set	Gets or sets the field of the data source that provides the text content of the list items.
DataTextFormatString	Get and Set	Gets or sets the formatting string used to control how data bound to the list control is displayed.
DataValueField	Get and Set	Gets or sets the field of the data source that provides the value of each list item.
Enabled	Get and Set	Gets or sets a value indicating whether the Web control is enabled.
EnableViewState	Get and Set	Gets or sets a value indicating whether the server control maintains its view state, and the view state of any child controls it contains, when the current page request ends.
Font	Get	Gets font information of the Web control.
ForeColor	Get and Set	Gets or sets the foreground color (typically the color of the text) of the Web control.
Height	Get and Set	Gets or sets the height of the Web control.
ID	Get and Set	Gets or sets the programmatic identifier assigned to the server control.
Items	Get	Gets the collection of items in the list control.
NamingContainer	Get and Set	Gets a reference to the server control's naming container, which creates a unique namespace for differentiating between server controls with the same Control.ID property value.
Page	Get	Gets a reference to the Page instance that contains the server control.
Parent	Get	Gets a reference to the server control's parent control in the page UI hierarchy.

TABLE A.7   Continued

Property	Get/Set	Description
SelectedIndex	Get and Set	Overridden. Gets or sets the index of the selected item in the DropDownList control.
SelectedItem	Get	Gets the selected item with the lowest index in the list control.
Site	Get	Gets information about the Web site to which the server control belongs.
Style	Get	Gets a collection of text attributes that will be rendered as a style attribute on the outer tag of the Web control.
TabIndex	Get and Set	Gets or sets the tab index of the Web control.
TemplateSourceDirectory	Get	Gets the virtual directory of the Page or UserControl that contains the current server control.
ToolTip	Get and Set	Overridden. Gets or sets the ToolTip text displayed when the mouse pointer rests over the control.
UniqueID	Get	Gets the unique, hierarchically-qualified identifier for the server control.
Visible	Get and Set	Gets or sets a value that indicates whether a server control is rendered as UI on the page.
Width	Get and Set	Gets or sets the width of the Web control.

TABLE A.8   DropDownList Public Instance Methods

Method	Description
ApplyStyle	Copies any non-blank elements of the specified style to the Web control, overwriting any existing style elements of the control. This method is primarily used by control developers.
CopyBaseAttributes	Copies the AccessKey, Enabled, ToolTip, TabIndex, and Attributes properties onto the Web control from the specified source control. This method is primarily used by control developers.

TABLE A.8 Continued

Method	Description
DataBind	Binds a data source to the invoked server control and all of its child controls.
Dispose	Enables a server control to perform final clean up before it is released from memory.
Equals	Overloaded. Determines whether two Object instances are equal.
FindControl	Overloaded. Searches the current naming container for the specified server control.
GetHashCode	Serves as a hash function for a particular type, suitable for use in hashing algorithms and data structures like a hash table.
GetType	Gets the Type of the current instance.
HasControls	Determines if the server control contains any child controls.
MergeStyle	Copies any non-blank elements of the specified style to the Web control, but will not overwrite any existing style elements of the control. This method is primarily used by control developers.
RenderBeginTag	Renders the HTML begin tag of the control into the specified writer. This method is primarily used by control developers.
RenderControl	Outputs server control content to a provided HtmlTextWriter object, then checks if tracing is enabled for the containing page and retrieves trace information about the server control.
RenderEndTag	Renders the HTML end tag of the control into the specified writer. This method is primarily used by control developers.
ResolveUrl	Resolves a relative URL to the absolute URL where the page or user control associated with this request resides.
SetRenderMethodDelegate	Assigns an event handler delegate to render the server control and its content into its parent control.
ToString	Returns a String that represents the current Object.

TABLE A.9   DropDownList Public Instance Events

Event	Description
DataBinding	Occurs when the server control binds to a data source.
Disposed	Occurs when a server control is released from memory, which is the last stage of the server control lifecycle when an ASP.NET page is requested.
Init	Occurs when the server control is initialized, which is the first step in its lifecycle.
Load	Occurs when the server control is loaded into the Page object.
PreRender	Occurs when the server control is about to render to its containing Page object.
SelectedIndexChanged	Occurs when the selection on the list changes and is posted back to the server.
Unload	Occurs when the server control is unloaded from memory.

HyperLink

TABLE A.10   HyperLink Properties

Property	Get/Set	Description
AccessKeys	Get and Set	Gets or sets the keyboard shortcut key (AccessKey) for setting focus to the Web control.
Attributes	Get	Gets the collection of arbitrary attributes (for rendering only) that does not correspond to properties on the control.
BackColor	Get and Set	Gets or sets the background color of the Web control.
BorderColor	Get and Set	Gets or sets the border color of the Web control.
BorderStyle	Get and Set	Gets or sets the border style of the Web control.
BorderWidth	Get and Set	Gets or sets the border width of the Web control.
ClientID	Get	Gets the server control identifier generated by ASP.NET.

TABLE A.10 Continued

Property	Get/Set	Description
Controls	Get	Gets a `ControlCollection` object that represents the child controls for a specified server control in the UI hierarchy.
ControlStyle	Get	Gets the style of the Web control. This property is primarily used by control developers.
CssClass	Get and Set	Gets or sets the CSS class rendered by the Web control.
Enabled	Get and Set	Gets or sets a value indicating whether the Web control is enabled.
EnableViewState	Get and Set	Gets or sets a value indicating whether the server control maintains its view state, and the view state of any child controls it contains, when the current page request ends.
Font	Get	Gets font information of the Web control.
ForeColor	Get and Set	Gets or sets the foreground color (typically the color of the text) of the Web control.
Height	Get and Set	Gets or sets the height of the Web control.
ID	Get and Set	Gets or sets the programmatic identifier assigned to the server control.
ImageUrl	Get and Set	Gets or sets the path to an image to display for the `HyperLink` control.
NamingContainer	Get and Set	Gets a reference to the server control's naming container, which creates a unique namespace for differentiating between server controls with the same `Control.ID` property value.
NavigateUrl	Get and Set	Gets or sets the URL to link to when the `HyperLink` control is clicked.
Page	Get	Gets a reference to the `Page` instance that contains the server control.

A

ASP.NET SERVER
CONTROLS
REFERENCE

TABLE A.10 Continued

Property	Get/Set	Description
Parent	Get	Gets a reference to the server control's parent control in the page UI hierarchy.
Site	Get	Gets information about the Web site to which the server control belongs.
Style	Get	Gets a collection of text attributes that will be rendered as a style attribute on the outer tag of the Web control.
TabIndex	Get and Set	Gets or sets the tab index of the Web control.
Target	Get and Set	Gets or sets the target window or frame to display the Web page content linked to when the HyperLink control is clicked.
TemplateSourceDirectory	Get	Gets the virtual directory of the Page or UserControl that contains the current server control.
Text	Get and Set	Gets or sets the text caption for the HyperLink control.
ToolTip	Get and Set	Gets or sets the tool tip for the Web control to be displayed when the mouse cursor is over the control.
UniqueID	Get	Gets the unique, hierarchically-qualified identifier for the server control.
Visible	Get and Set	Gets or sets a value that indicates whether a server control is rendered as UI on the page.
Width	Get and Set	Gets or sets the width of the Web control.

TABLE A.11 HyperLink Public Instance Methods

Method	Description
ApplyStyle	Copies any non-blank elements of the specified style to the Web control, overwriting any existing style elements of the control. This method is primarily used by control developers.

TABLE A.11   Continued

Method	Description
CopyBaseAttributes	Copies the `AccessKey`, `Enabled`, `ToolTip`, `TabIndex`, and `Attributes` properties onto the Web control from the specified source control. This method is primarily used by control developers.
DataBind	Binds a data source to the invoked server control and all of its child controls.
Dispose	Enables a server control to perform final clean up before it is released from memory.
Equals	Overloaded. Determines whether two `Object` instances are equal.
FindControl	Overloaded. Searches the current naming container for the specified server control.
GetHashCode	Serves as a hash function for a particular type, suitable for use in hashing algorithms and data structures like a hash table.
GetType	Gets the `Type` of the current instance.
HasControls	Determines if the server control contains any child controls.
MergeStyle	Copies any non-blank elements of the specified style to the Web control, but will not overwrite any existing style elements of the control. This method is primarily used by control developers.
RenderBeginTag	Renders the HTML begin tag of the control into the specified writer. This method is primarily used by control developers.
RenderControl	Outputs server control content to a provided `HtmlTextWriter` object, then checks if tracing is enabled for the containing page and retrieves trace information about the server control.
RenderEndTag	Renders the HTML end tag of the control into the specified writer. This method is primarily used by control developers.
ResolveUrl	Resolves a relative URL to the absolute URL where the page or user control associated with this request resides.
SetRenderMethodDelegate	Assigns an event handler delegate to render the server control and its content into its parent control.
ToString	Returns a `String` that represents the current `Object`.

A

**ASP.NET SERVER
CONTROLS
REFERENCE**

TABLE A.12   HyperLink Public Instance Events

Events	Description
DataBinding	Occurs when the server control binds to a data source.
Disposed	Occurs when a server control is released from memory, which is the last stage of the server control lifecycle when an ASP.NET page is requested.
Init	Occurs when the server control is initialized, which is the first step in the its lifecycle.
Load	Occurs when the server control is loaded into the Page object.
PreRender	Occurs when the server control is about to render to its containing Page object.
Unload	Occurs when the server control is unloaded from memory.

Image

TABLE A.13   Image Properties

Property	Get/Set	Description
AccessKey	Get and Set	Gets or sets the keyboard shortcut key (AccessKey) for setting focus to the Web control.
AlternateText	Get and Set	Gets or sets the alternate text displayed in the **Image** control when the image is unavailable. Browsers that support the ToolTips feature display this text as a ToolTip.
Attributes	Get	Gets the collection of arbitrary attributes (for rendering only) that do not correspond to properties on the control.
BackColor	Get and Set	Gets or sets the background color of the Web control.
BorderColor	Get and Set	Gets or sets the border color of the Web control.
BorderStyle	Get and Set	Gets or sets the border style of the Web control.

TABLE A.13 Continued

Property	Get/Set	Description
BorderWidth	Get and Set	Gets or sets the border width of the Web control.
ClientID	Get	Gets or sets the background color of the Web control.
Controls	Get	Gets a ControlCollection object that represents the child controls for a specified server control in the UI hierarchy.
ControlStyle	Get	Gets the style of the Web control. This property is primarily used by control developers.
CssClass	Get and Set	Gets or sets the CSS class rendered by the Web control.
Enabled	Get and Set	Gets or sets a value indicating whether the Web control is enabled.
EnableViewState	Get and Set	Gets or sets a value indicating whether the server control maintains its view state, and the view state of any child controls it contains, when the current page request ends.
Font	Get	Overridden. Gets the font properties for the alternate text.
ForeColor	Get and Set	Gets or sets the foreground color (typically the color of the text) of the Web control.
Height	Get and Set	Gets or sets the height of the Web control.
ID	Get and Set	Gets or sets the programmatic identifier assigned to the server control.
ImageAlign	Get and Set	Gets or sets the alignment of the Image control in relation to other elements on the Web page.
ImageUrl	Get and Set	Gets or sets the location of an image to display in the Image control.

A

ASP.NET SERVER
CONTROLS
REFERENCE

TABLE A.13   Continued

Property	Get/Set	Description
NamingContainer	Get and Set	Gets a reference to the server control's naming container, which creates a unique namespace for differentiating between server controls with the same Control.ID property value.
Page	Get	Gets a reference to the Page instance that contains the server control.
Parent	Get	Gets a reference to the server control's parent control in the page UI hierarchy.
Site	Get	Gets information about the Web site to which the server control belongs.
Style	Get	Gets a collection of text attributes that will be rendered as a style attribute on the outer tag of the Web control.
TabIndex	Get and Set	Gets or sets the tab index of the Web control.
TemplateSourceDirectory	Get	Gets the virtual directory of the Page or UserControl that contains the current server control.
ToolTip	Get and Set	Gets or sets the tool tip for the Web control to be displayed when the mouse cursor is over the control.
UniqueID	Get	Gets the unique, hierarchically-qualified identifier for the server control.
Visible	Get and Set	Gets or sets a value that indicates whether a server control is rendered as UI on the page.
Width	Get and Set	Gets or sets the width of the Web control.

TABLE A.14   Image Public Instance Methods

Method	Description
ApplyStyle	Copies any non-blank elements of the specified style to the Web control, overwriting any existing style elements of the control. This method is primarily used by control developers.

TABLE A.14   Continued

Method	Description
CopyBaseAttributes	Copies the AccessKey, Enabled, ToolTip, TabIndex, and Attributes properties onto the Web control from the specified source control. This method is primarily used by control developers.
DataBind	Binds a data source to the invoked server control and all of its child controls.
Dispose	Enables a server control to perform final clean up before it is released from memory.
Equals	Overloaded. Determines whether two Object instances are equal.
FindControl	Overloaded. Searches the current naming container for the specified server control.
GetHashCode	Serves as a hash function for a particular type, suitable for use in hashing algorithms and data structures like a hash table.
GetType	Gets the Type of the current instance.
HasControls	Determines if the server control contains any child controls.
MergeStyle	Copies any non-blank elements of the specified style to the Web control, but will not overwrite any existing style elements of the control. This method is primarily used by control developers.
RenderBeginTag	Renders the HTML begin tag of the control into the specified writer. This method is primarily used by control developers.
RenderControl	Outputs server control content to a provided HtmlTextWriter object, then checks if tracing is enabled for the containing page and retrieves trace information about the server control.
RenderEndTag	Renders the HTML end tag of the control into the specified writer. This method is primarily used by control developers.
ResolveUrl	Resolves a relative URL to the absolute URL where the page or user control associated with this request resides.
SetRenderMethodDelegate	Assigns an event handler delegate to render the server control and its content into its parent control.
ToString	Returns a String that represents the current Object.

A

ASP.NET SERVER
CONTROLS
REFERENCE

TABLE A.15 Image Public Instance Events

Event	Description
DataBinding	Occurs when the server control binds to a data source.
Disposed	Occurs when a server control is released from memory, which is the last stage of the server control lifecycle when an ASP.NET page is requested.
Init	Occurs when the server control is initialized, which is the first step in its lifecycle.
Load	Occurs when the server control is loaded into the Page object.
PreRender	Occurs when the server control is about to render to its containing Page object.
Unload	Occurs when the server control is unloaded from memory.

ImageButton

TABLE A.16 ImageButton Properties

Property	Get/Set	Description
AccessKey	Get and Set	Gets or sets the keyboard shortcut key (AccessKey) for setting focus to the Web control.
AlternateText	Get and Set	Gets or sets the alternate text displayed in the Image control when the image is unavailable. Browsers that support the ToolTips feature display this text as a ToolTip.
Attributes	Get	Gets the collection of arbitrary attributes (for rendering only) that do not correspond to properties on the control.
BackColor	Get and Set	Gets or sets the background color of the Web control.
BorderColor	Get and Set	Gets or sets the border color of the Web control.
BorderStyle	Get and Set	Gets or sets the border style of the Web control.
BorderWidth	Get and Set	Gets or sets the border width of the Web control.

TABLE A.16 Continued

Property	Get/Set	Description
CausesValidation	Get and Set	Gets or sets a value indicating whether validation is performed when the ImageButton control is clicked.
ClientID	Get	Gets the server control identifier generated by ASP.NET.
CommandArgument	Get and Set	Gets or sets an optional argument that provides additional information about the CommandName property.
CommandName	Get and Set	Gets or sets the command name associated with the ImageButton control.
Controls	Get	Gets a ControlsCollection object that represents the child controls for a specified server control in the UI hierarchy.
ControlStyle	Get	Gets the style of the Web control. This property is primarily used by control developers.
CssClass	Get and Set	Gets or sets the CSS class rendered by the Web control.
Enabled	Get and Set	Gets or sets a value indicating whether the Web control is enabled.
EnableViewState	Get and Set	Gets or sets a value indicating whether the server control maintains its view state, and the view state of any child controls it contains, when the current page request ends.
Font	Get	Overridden. Gets the font properties for the alternate text.
ForeColor	Get and Set	Gets or sets the foreground color (typically the color of the text) of the Web control.
Height	Get and Set	Gets or sets the height of the Web control.
ID	Get and Set	Gets or sets the programmatic identifier assigned to the server control.

Table A.16 Continued

Property	Get/Set	Description
ImageAlign	Get and Set	Gets or sets the alignment of the Image control in relation to other elements on the Web page.
ImageUrl	Get and Set	Gets or sets the location of an image to display in the Image control.
NamingContainer	Get and Set	Gets a reference to the server control's naming container, which creates a unique namespace for differentiating between server controls with the same Control.ID property value.
Page	Get	Gets a reference to the Page instance that contains the server control.
Parent	Get	Gets a reference to the server control's parent control in the page UI hierarchy.
Site	Get	Gets information about the Web site to which the server control belongs.
Style	Get	Gets a collection of text attributes that will be rendered as a style attribute on the outer tag of the Web control.
TabIndex	Get and Set	Gets or sets the tab index of the Web control.
TemplateSourceDirectory	Get	Gets the virtual directory of the Page or UserControl that contains the current server control.
ToolTip	Get and Set	Gets or sets the tool tip for the Web control to be displayed when the mouse cursor is over the control.
UniqueID	Get	Gets the unique, hierarchically-qualified identifier for the server control.
Visible	Get and Set	Gets or sets a value that indicates whether a server control is rendered as UI on the page.
Width	Get and Set	Gets or sets the width of the Web control.

TABLE A.17 `ImageButton` Public Instance Methods

Method	Description
ApplyStyle	Copies any non-blank elements of the specified style to the Web control, overwriting any existing style elements of the control. This method is primarily used by control developers.
CopyBaseAttributes	Copies the `AccessKey`, `Enabled`, `ToolTip`, `TabIndex`, and `Attributes` properties onto the Web control from the specified source control. This method is primarily used by control developers.
DataBind	Binds a data source to the invoked server control and all of its child controls.
Dispose	Enables a server control to perform final clean up before it is released from memory.
Equals	Overloaded. Determines whether two `Object` instances are equal.
FindControl	Overloaded. Searches the current naming container for the specified server control.
GetHashCode	Serves as a hash function for a particular type, suitable for use in hashing algorithms and data structures like a hash table.
GetType	Gets the `Type` of the current instance.
HasControls	Determines if the server control contains any child controls.
MergeStyle	Copies any non-blank elements of the specified style to the Web control, but will not overwrite any existing style elements of the control. This method is primarily used by control developers.
RenderBeginTag	Renders the HTML begin tag of the control into the specified writer. This method is primarily used by control developers.
RenderControl	Outputs server control content to a provided `HtmlTextWriter` object, then checks if tracing is enabled for the containing page and retrieves trace information about the server control.
RenderEndTag	Renders the HTML end tag of the control into the specified writer. This method is primarily used by control developers.
ResolveUrl	Resolves a relative URL to the absolute URL where the page or user control associated with this request resides.
SetRenderMethodDelegate	Assigns an event handler delegate to render the server control and its content into its parent control.
ToString	Returns a `String` that represents the current `Object`.

A

ASP.NET SERVER CONTROLS REFERENCE

TABLE A.18 ImageButton Public Instance Events

Event	Description
Click	Occurs when the ImageButton is clicked.
Command	Occurs when the ImageButton is clicked.
DataBinding	Occurs when the server control binds to a data source.
Dispose	Occurs when a server control is released from memory, which is the last stage of the server control lifecycle when an ASP.NET page is requested.
Init	Occurs when the server control is initialized, which is the first step in its lifecycle.
Load	Occurs when the server control is loaded into the Page object.
PreRender	Occurs when the server control is about to render to its containing Page object.
Unload	Occurs when the server control is unloaded from memory.

Label

TABLE A.19 Label Properties

Property	Get/Set	Description
AccessKey	Get and Set	Gets or sets the keyboard shortcut key (AccessKey) for setting focus to the Web control.
Attributes	Get	Gets the collection of arbitrary attributes (for rendering only) that do not correspond to properties on the control.
BackColor	Get and Set	Gets or sets the background color of the Web control.
BorderColor	Get and Set	Gets or sets the border color of the Web control.
BorderStyle	Get and Set	Gets or sets the border style of the Web control.
BorderWidth	Get and Set	Gets or sets the border width of the Web control.
ClientID	Get	Gets the server control identifier generated by ASP.NET.

TABLE A.19 Continued

Property	Get/Set	Description
Controls	Get	Gets a `ControlCollection` object that represents the child controls for a specified server control in the UI hierarchy.
ControlStyle	Get	Gets the style of the Web control. This property is primarily used by control developers.
CssClass	Get and Set	Gets or sets the CSS class rendered by the Web control.
Enabled	Get and Set	Gets or sets a value indicating whether the Web control is enabled.
EnableViewState	Get and Set	Gets or sets a value indicating whether the server control maintains its view state, and the view state of any child controls it contains, when the current page request ends.
Font	Get	Gets font information of the Web control.
ForeColor	Get and Set	Gets or sets the foreground color (typically the color of the text) of the Web control.
Height	Get and Set	Gets or sets the height of the Web control.
ID	Get and Set	Gets or sets the programmatic identifier assigned to the server control.
NamingContainer	Get and Set	Gets a reference to the server control's naming container, which creates a unique namespace for differentiating between server controls with the same `Control.ID` property value.
Page	Get	Gets a reference to the `Page` instance that contains the server control.
Parent	Get	Gets a reference to the server control's parent control in the page UI hierarchy.
Site	Get	Gets information about the Web site to which the server control belongs.

TABLE A.19 Continued

Property	Get/Set	Description
Style	Get	Gets a collection of text attributes that will be rendered as a style attribute on the outer tag of the Web control.
TabIndex	Get and Set	Gets or sets the tab index of the Web control.
TemplateSourceDirectory	Get	Gets the virtual directory of the Page or UserControl that contains the current server control.
Text	Get and Set	Gets or sets the text content of the Label control.
ToolTip	Get and Set	Gets or sets the tool tip for the Web control to be displayed when the mouse cursor is over the control.
UniqueID	Get	Gets the unique, hierarchically-qualified identifier for the server control.
Visible	Get and Set	Gets or sets a value that indicates whether a server control is rendered as UI on the page.
Width	Get and Set	Gets or sets the width of the Web control.

TABLE A.20 Label Public Instance Methods

Method	Description
ApplyStyle	Copies any non-blank elements of the specified style to the Web control, overwriting any existing style elements of the control. This method is primarily used by control developers.
CopyBaseAttributes	Copies the AccessKey, Enabled, ToolTip, TabIndex, and Attributes properties onto the Web control from the specified source control. This method is primarily used by control developers.
DataBind	Binds a data source to the invoked server control and all of its child controls.
Dispose	Enables a server control to perform final clean up before it is released from memory.

TABLE A.20   Continued

Method	Description
Equals	Overloaded. Determines whether two Object instances are equal.
FindControl	Overloaded. Searches the current naming container for the specified server control.
GetHashCode	Serves as a hash function for a particular type, suitable for use in hashing algorithms and data structures like a hash table.
GetType	Gets the Type of the current instance.
HasControls	Determines if the server control contains any child controls.
MergeStyle	Copies any non-blank elements of the specified style to the Web control, but will not overwrite any existing style elements of the control. This method is primarily used by control developers.
RenderBeginTag	Renders the HTML begin tag of the control into the specified writer. This method is primarily used by control developers.
RenderControl	Outputs server control content to a provided HtmlTextWriter object, then checks if tracing is enabled for the containing page and retrieves trace information about the server control.
RenderEndTag	Renders the HTML end tag of the control into the specified writer. This method is primarily used by control developers.
ResolveUrl	Resolves a relative URL to the absolute URL where the page or user control associated with this request resides.
SetRenderMethodDelegate	Assigns an event handler delegate to render the server control and its content into its parent control.
ToString	Returns a String that represents the current Object.

TABLE A.21   Label Public Instance Events

Event	Description
DataBinding	Occurs when the server control binds to a data source.
Disposed	Occurs when a server control is released from memory, which is the last stage of the server control lifecycle when an ASP.NET page is requested.

A

ASP.NET SERVER CONTROLS REFERENCE

TABLE A.21 Continued

Event	Description
Init	Occurs when the server control is initialized, which is the first step in its lifecycle.
Load	Occurs when the server control is loaded into the Page object.
PreRender	Occurs when the server control is about to render to its containing Page object.
Unload	Occurs when the server control is unloaded from memory.

LinkButton

TABLE A.22 LinkButton Properties

Property	Get/Set	Description
AccessKey	Get and Set	Gets or sets the keyboard shortcut key (AccessKey) for setting focus to the Web control.
Attributes	Get	Gets the collection of arbitrary attributes (for rendering only) that do not correspond to properties on the control.
BackColor	Get and Set	Gets or sets the background color of the Web control.
BorderColor	Get and Set	Gets or sets the border color of the Web control.
BorderStyle	Get and Set	Gets or sets the border style of the Web control.
BorderWidth	Get and Set	Gets or sets the border width of the Web control.
CausesValidation	Get and Set	Gets or sets a value indicating whether validation is performed when the LinkButton control is clicked.
ClientID	Get	Gets the server control identifier generated by ASP.NET.
CommandArgument	Get and Set	Gets or sets an optional argument passed to the Command event handler along with the associated CommandName property.

TABLE A.22 Continued

Property	Get/Set	Description
CommandName	Get and Set	Gets or sets the command name associated with the LinkButton control. This value is passed to the Command event handler along with the CommandArgument property.
Controls	Get	Gets a ControlCollection object that represents the child controls for a specified server control in the UI hierarchy.
ControlStyle	Get	Gets the style of the Web control. This property is primarily used by control developers.
CssClass	Get and Set	Gets or sets the CSS class rendered by the Web control.
Enabled	Get and Set	Gets or sets a value indicating whether the Web control is enabled.
EnableViewState	Get and Set	Gets or sets a value indicating whether the server control maintains its view state, and the view state of any child controls it contains, when the current page request ends.
Font	Get	Gets font information of the Web control.
ForeColor	Get and Set	Gets or sets the foreground color (typically the color of the text) of the Web control.
Height	Get and Set	Gets or sets the height of the Web control.
ID	Get and Set	Gets or sets the programmatic identifier assigned to the server control.
NamingContainer	Get and Set	Gets a reference to the server control's naming container, which creates a unique namespace for differentiating between server controls with the same Control.ID property value.
Page	Get	Gets a reference to the Page instance that contains the server control.

A

ASP.NET SERVER
CONTROLS
REFERENCE

TABLE A.22   Continued

Property	Get/Set	Description
Parent	Get	Gets a reference to the server control's parent control in the page UI hierarchy.
Site	Get	Gets information about the Web site to which the server control belongs.
Style	Get	Gets a collection of text attributes that will be rendered as a style attribute on the outer tag of the Web control.
TabIndex	Get and Set	Gets or sets the tab index of the Web control.
TemplateSourceDirectory	Get	Gets the virtual directory of the Page or UserControl that contains the current server control.
Text	Get and Set	Gets or sets the text caption displayed on the LinkButton control.
ToolTip	Get and Set	Gets or sets the tool tip for the Web control to be displayed when the mouse cursor is over the control.
UniqueID	Get	Gets the unique, hierarchically-qualified identifier for the server control.
Visible	Get and Set	Gets or sets a value that indicates whether a server control is rendered as UI on the page.
Width	Get and Set	Gets or sets the width of the Web control.

TABLE A.23   LinkButton Public Instance Methods

Method	Description
ApplyStyle	Copies any non-blank elements of the specified style to the Web control, overwriting any existing style elements of the control. This method is primarily used by control developers.
CopyBaseAttributes	Copies the AccessKey, Enabled, ToolTip, TabIndex, and Attributes properties onto the Web control from the specified source control. This method is primarily used by control developers.

TABLE A.23 Continued

Method	Description
DataBind	Binds a data source to the invoked server control and all of its child controls.
Dispose	Enables a server control to perform final clean up before it is released from memory.
Equals	Overloaded. Determines whether two Object instances are equal.
FindControl	Overloaded. Searches the current naming container for the specified server control.
GetHashCode	Serves as a hash function for a particular type, suitable for use in hashing algorithms and data structures like a hash table.
GetType	Gets the Type of the current instance.
HasControls	Determines if the server control contains any child controls.
MergeStyle	Copies any non-blank elements of the specified style to the Web control, but will not overwrite any existing style elements of the control. This method is primarily used by control developers.
RenderBeginTag	Renders the HTML begin tag of the control into the specified writer. This method is primarily used by control developers.
RenderControl	Outputs server control content to a provided HtmlTextWriter object, then checks if tracing is enabled for the containing page and retrieves trace information about the server control.
RenderEndTag	Renders the HTML end tag of the control into the specified writer. This method is primarily used by control developers.
ResolveUrl	Resolves a relative URL to the absolute URL where the page or user control associated with this request resides.
SetRenderMethodDelegate	Assigns an event handler delegate to render the server control and its content into its parent control.
ToString	Returns a String that represents the current Object.

TABLE A.24   LinkButton Public Instance Events

Event	Description
Click	Occurs when the LinkButton control is clicked.
Command	Occurs when the Button control is clicked.
DataBinding	Occurs when the server control binds to a data source.
Disposed	Occurs when a server control is released from memory, which is the last stage of the server control lifecycle when an ASP.NET page is requested.
Init	Occurs when the server control is initialized, which is the first step in its lifecycle.
Load	Occurs when the server control is loaded into the Page object.
PreRender	Occurs when the server control is about to render to its containing Page object.
Unload	Occurs when the server control is unloaded from memory.

ListBox

TABLE A.25   ListBox Properties

Property	Get/Set	Description
AccessKey	Get and Set	Gets or sets the keyboard shortcut key (AccessKey) for setting focus to the Web control.
Attributes	Get	Gets the collection of arbitrary attributes (for rendering only) that do not correspond to properties on the control.
AutoPostBack	Get and Set	Gets or sets a value indicating whether a postback to the server automatically occurs when the user changes the list selection.
BackColor	Get and Set	Gets or sets the background color of the Web control.
BorderColor	Get and Set	Overridden. Gets or sets the border color of the control.
BorderStyle	Get and Set	Overridden. Gets or sets the border style of the control.

TABLE A.25 Continued

Property	Get/Set	Description
BorderWidth	Get and Set	Overridden. Gets or sets the border width for the control.
ClientID	Get	Gets the server control identifier generated by ASP.NET.
Controls	Get	Gets a ControlCollection object that represents the child controls for a specified server control in the UI hierarchy.
ControlStyle	Get	Gets the style of the Web control. This property is primarily used by control developers.
CssClass	Get and Set	Gets or sets the CSS class rendered by the Web control.
DataMember	Get and Set	Gets or sets the specific table in the DataSource to bind to the control.
DataSource	Get and Set	Gets or sets the data source that populates the items of the list control.
DataTextField	Get and Set	Gets or sets the field of the data source that provides the text content of the list items.
DataTextFormatString	Get and Set	Gets or sets the formatting string used to control how data bound to the list control is displayed.
DataValueField	Get and Set	Gets or sets the field of the data source that provides the value of each list item.
Enabled	Get and Set	Gets or sets a value indicating whether the Web control is enabled.
EnableViewState	Get and Set	Gets or sets a value indicating whether the server control maintains its view state, and the view state of any child controls it contains, when the current page request ends.
Font	Get	Gets font information of the Web control.
ForeColor	Get and Set	Gets or sets the foreground color (typically the color of the text) of the Web control.

TABLE A.25   Continued

Property	Get/Set	Description
Height	Get and Set	Gets or sets the height of the Web control.
ID	Get and Set	Gets or sets the programmatic identifier assigned to the server control.
Items	Get	Gets the collection of items in the list control.
NamingContainer	Get and Set	Gets a reference to the server control's naming container, which creates a unique namespace for differentiating between server controls with the same Control.ID property value.
Page	Get	Gets a reference to the Page instance that contains the server control.
Parent	Get	Gets a reference to the server control's parent control in the page UI hierarchy.
Rows	Get and Set	Gets or sets the number of rows displayed in the ListBox control.
SelectedIndex	Get and Set	Gets or sets the lowest ordinal index of the selected items in the list.
SelectedItem	Get and Set	Gets the selected item with the lowest index in the list control.
SelectionMode	Get and Set	Gets or sets the selection mode of the ListBox control.
Site	Get	Gets information about the Web site to which the server control belongs.
Style	Get	Gets a collection of text attributes that will be rendered as a style attribute on the outer tag of the Web control.
TabIndex	Get and Set	Gets or sets the tab index of the Web control.
TemplateSourceDirectory	Get	Gets the virtual directory of the Page or UserControl that contains the current server control.
ToolTip	Get and Set	Overridden. Gets or sets the ToolTip text displayed when the mouse pointer rests over the control.

TABLE A.25   Continued

Property	Get/Set	Description
UniqueID	Get	Gets the unique, hierarchically-qualified identifier for the server control.
Visible	Get and Set	Gets or sets a value that indicates whether a server control is rendered as UI on the page.
Width	Get and Set	Gets or sets the width of the Web control.

TABLE A.26   ListBox Public Instance Methods

Method	Description
ApplyStyle	Copies any non-blank elements of the specified style to the Web control, overwriting any existing style elements of the control. This method is primarily used by control developers.
CopyBaseAttributes	Copies the AccessKey, Enabled, ToolTip, TabIndex, and Attributes properties onto the Web control from the specified source control. This method is primarily used by control developers.
DataBind	Binds a data source to the invoked server control and all of its child controls.
Dispose	Enables a server control to perform final clean up before it is released from memory.
Equals	Overloaded. Determines whether two Object instances are equal.
FindControl	Overloaded. Searches the current naming container for the specified server control.
GetHashCode	Serves as a hash function for a particular type, suitable for use in hashing algorithms and data structures like a hash table.
GetType	Gets the Type of the current instance.
HasControls	Determines if the server control contains any child controls.
MergeStyle	Copies any non-blank elements of the specified style to the Web control, but will not overwrite any existing style elements of the control. This method is primarily used by control developers.

TABLE A.26 Continued

Method	Description
RenderBeginTag	Renders the HTML begin tag of the control into the specified writer. This method is primarily used by control developers.
RenderControl	Outputs server control content to a provided HtmlTextWriter object, then checks if tracing is enabled for the containing page and retrieves trace information about the server control.
RenderEndTag	Renders the HTML end tag of the control into the specified writer. This method is primarily used by control developers.
ResolveUrl	Resolves a relative URL to the absolute URL where the page or user control associated with this request resides.
SetRenderMethodDelegate	Assigns an event handler delegate to render the server control and its content into its parent control.
ToString	Returns a String that represents the current Object.

TABLE A.27 ListBox Public Instance Events

Events	Description
DataBinding	Occurs when the server control binds to a data source.
Disposed	Occurs when a server control is released from memory, which is the last stage of the server control lifecycle when an ASP.NET page is requested.
Init	Occurs when the server control is initialized, which is the first step in its lifecycle.
Load	Occurs when the server control is loaded into the Page object.
PreRender	Occurs when the server control is about to render to its containing Page object.
SelectedIndexChanged	Occurs when the selection on the list changes and is posted back to the server.
Unload	Occurs when the server control is unloaded from memory.

Panel

TABLE A.28 Panel Properties

Property	Get/Set	Description
AccessKey	Get and Set	Gets or sets the keyboard shortcut key (AccessKey) for setting focus to the Web control.
Attributes	Get	Gets the collection of arbitrary attributes (for rendering only) that does not correspond to properties on the control.
BackColor	Get and Set	Gets or sets the background color of the Web control.
BackImageUrl	Get and Set	Gets or sets the URL of the background image for the panel control.
BorderColor	Get and Set	Gets or sets the border color of the Web control.
BorderStyle	Get and Set	Gets or sets the border style of the Web control.
BorderWidth	Get and Set	Gets or sets the border width of the Web control.
ClientID	Get	Gets the server control identifier generated by ASP.NET.
Controls	Get	Gets a `ControlCollection` object that represents the child controls for a specified server control in the UI hierarchy.
ControlStyle	Get	Gets the style of the Web control. This property is primarily used by control developers.
CssClass	Get and Set	Gets or sets the CSS class rendered by the Web control.
Enabled	Get and Set	Gets or sets a value indicating whether the Web control is enabled.
EnableViewState	Get and Set	Gets or sets a value indicating whether the server control maintains its view state, and the view state of any child controls it contains, when the current page request ends.

A

ASP.NET SERVER CONTROLS REFERENCE

TABLE A.28   Continued

Property	Get/Set	Description
Font	Get	Gets font information of the Web control.
ForeColor	Get and Set	Gets or sets the foreground color (typically the color of the text) of the Web control.
Height	Get and Set	Gets or sets the height of the Web control.
HorizontAlign	Get and Set	Gets or sets the horizontal alignment of the contents within the panel.
ID	Get and Set	Gets or sets the programmatic identifier assigned to the server control.
NamingContainer	Get and Set	Gets a reference to the server control's naming container, which creates a unique namespace for differentiating between server controls with the same Control.ID property value.
Page	Get	Gets a reference to the server control's naming container, which creates a unique namespace for differentiating between server controls with the same Control.ID property value.
Parent	Get	Gets a reference to the server control's parent control in the page UI hierarchy.
Site	Get	Gets information about the Web site to which the server control belongs.
Style	Get	Gets a collection of text attributes that will be rendered as a style attribute on the outer tag of the Web control.
TabIndex	Get and Set	Gets or sets the tab index of the Web control.
TemplateSourceDirectory	Get	Gets the virtual directory of the Page or UserControl that contains the current server control.
ToolTip	Get and Set	Gets or sets the tool tip for the Web control to be displayed when the mouse cursor is over the control.

TABLE A.28 Continued

Property	Get/Set	Description
UniqueID	Get	Gets the unique, hierarchically-qualified identifier for the server control.
Visible	Get and Set	Gets or sets a value that indicates whether a server control is rendered as UI on the page.
Width	Get and Set	Gets or sets the width of the Web control.
Wrap	Get and Set	Gets or sets a value indicating whether the content wraps within the panel.

TABLE A.29 Panel Public Instance Methods

Method	Description
ApplyStyle	Copies any non-blank elements of the specified style to the Web control, overwriting any existing style elements of the control. This method is primarily used by control developers.
CopyBaseAttributes	Copies the AccessKey, Enabled, ToolTip, TabIndex, and Attributes properties onto the Web control from the specified source control. This method is primarily used by control developers.
DataBind	Binds a data source to the invoked server control and all of its child controls.
Dispose	Enables a server control to perform final clean up before it is released from memory.
Equals	Overloaded. Determines whether two Object instances are equal.
FindControl	Overloaded. Searches the current naming container for the specified server control.
GetHashCode	Serves as a hash function for a particular type, suitable for use in hashing algorithms and data structures like a hash table.
GetType	Gets the Type of the current instance.
HasControls	Determines if the server control contains any child controls.

TABLE A.29   Continued

Method	Description
MergeStyle	Copies any non-blank elements of the specified style to the Web control, but will not overwrite any existing style elements of the control. This method is primarily used by control developers.
RenderBeginTag	Renders the HTML begin tag of the control into the specified writer. This method is primarily used by control developers.
RenderControl	Outputs server control content to a provided HtmlTextWriter object, then checks if tracing is enabled for the containing page and retrieves trace information about the server control.
RenderEndTag	Renders the HTML end tag of the control into the specified writer. This method is primarily used by control developers.
ResolveUrl	Resolves a relative URL to the absolute URL where the page or user control associated with this request resides.
SetRenderMethodDelegate	Assigns an event handler delegate to render the server control and its content into its parent control.
ToString	Returns a String that represents the current Object.

TABLE A.30   Panel Public Instance Events

Event	Description
DataBinding	Occurs when the control binds to a data source. Notifies the control to perform any data binding during this event.
Disposed	Occurs when a control is released from memory, the last stage of the control life cycle.
Init	Occurs when the control is initialized, the first step in the page life cycle.
Load	Occurs when the control is loaded to the Page object. Notifies the control to perform any steps that need to occur on each page request.
PreRender	Occurs when the control is about to render.
Unload	Occurs when the control is unloaded from memory.

PlaceHolder

TABLE A.31 PlaceHolder Properties

Property	Get/Set	Description
ClientID	Get	Gets the server control identifier generated by ASP.NET.
Controls	Get	Gets a ControlCollection object that represents the child controls for a specified server control in the UI hierarchy.
EnableViewState	Get and Set	Gets or sets a value indicating whether the server control maintains its view state, and the view state of any child controls it contains, when the current page request ends.
ID	Get and Set	Gets or sets the programmatic identifier assigned to the server control.
NamingContainer	Get and Set	Gets a reference to the server control's naming container, which creates a unique namespace for differentiating between server controls with the same Control.ID property value.
Page	Get	Gets a reference to the Page instance that contains the server control.
Parent	Get	Gets a reference to the server control's parent control in the page UI hierarchy.
Site	Get	Gets information about the Web site to which the server control belongs.
TemplateSourceDirectory	Get	Gets the virtual directory of the Page or UserControl that contains the current server control.
UniqueID	Get	Gets the unique, hierarchically-qualified identifier for the server control.
Visible	Get and Set	Gets or sets a value that indicates whether a server control is rendered as UI on the page.

TABLE A.32 PlaceHolder Public Instance Methods

Method	Description
DataBind	Binds a data source to the invoked server control and all of its child controls.
Dispose	Enables a server control to perform final clean up before it is released from memory.
Equals	Overloaded. Determines whether two Object instances are equal.
FindControl	Overloaded. Searches the current naming container for the specified server control.
GetHashCode	Serves as a hash function for a particular type, suitable for use in hashing algorithms and data structures like a hash table.
GetType	Gets the Type of the current instance.
HasControls	Determines if the server control contains any child controls.
RenderControl	Outputs server control content to a provided HtmlTextWriter object, then checks if tracing is enabled for the containing page and retrieves trace information about the server control.
ResolveUrl	Resolves a relative URL to the absolute URL where the page or user control associated with this request resides.
SetRenderMethodDelegate	Assigns an event handler delegate to render the server control and its content into its parent control.
ToString	Returns a String that represents the current Object.

TABLE A.33 PlaceHolder Public Instance Events

Event	Description
DataBinding	Occurs when the server control binds to a data source.
Disposed	Occurs when a server control is released from memory, which is the last stage of the server control lifecycle when an ASP.NET page is requested.
Init	Occurs when the server control is initialized, which is the first step in its lifecycle.
Load	Occurs when the server control is loaded into the Page object.

TABLE A.33   Continued

Event	Description
PreRender	Occurs when the server control is about to render to its containing `Page` object.
Unload	Occurs when the server control is unloaded from memory.

RadioButton

TABLE A.34   RadioButton Properties

Property	Get/Set	Description
AccessKeys	Get and Set	Gets or sets the keyboard shortcut key (AccessKey) for setting focus to the Web control.
Attributes	Get	Gets the collection of arbitrary attributes (for rendering only) that does not correspond to properties on the control.
AutoPostBack	Get and Set	Gets or sets a value indicating whether the `CheckBox` state automatically posts back to the server when clicked.
BackColor	Get and Set	Gets or sets the background color of the Web control.
BorderColor	Get and Set	Gets or sets the border color of the Web control.
BorderStyle	Get and Set	Gets or sets the border style of the Web control.
BorderWidth	Get and Set	Gets or sets the border width of the Web control.
Checked	Get and Set	Gets or sets a value indicating whether the `CheckBox` control is checked.
ClientID	Get	Gets the server control identifier generated by ASP.NET.
Controls	Get	Gets a `ControlCollection` object that represents the child controls for a specified server control in the UI hierarchy.

TABLE A.34 Continued

Property	Get/Set	Description
ControlStyle	Get	Gets the style of the Web control. This property is primarily used by control developers.
CssClass	Get and Set	Gets or sets the CSS class rendered by the Web control.
Enabled	Get and Set	Gets or sets a value indicating whether the Web control is enabled.
EnableViewState	Get and Set	Gets or sets a value indicating whether the server control maintains its view state, and the view state of any child controls it contains, when the current page request ends.
Font	Get	Gets font information of the Web control.
ForeColor	Get and Set	Gets or sets the foreground color (typically the color of the text) of the Web control.
GroupName	Get and Set	Gets or sets the name of the group that the radio button belongs to.
Height	Get and Set	Gets or sets the height of the Web control.
ID	Get and Set	Gets or sets the programmatic identifier assigned to the server control.
NamingContainer	Get and Set	Gets a reference to the server control's naming container, which creates a unique namespace for differentiating between server controls with the same Control.ID property value.
Page	Get	Gets a reference to the Page instance that contains the server control.
Parent	Get	Gets a reference to the server control's parent control in the page UI hierarchy.
Site	Get	Gets information about the Web site to which the server control belongs.

TABLE A.34   Continued

Property	Get/Set	Description
Style	Get	Gets a collection of text attributes that will be rendered as a style attribute on the outer tag of the Web control.
TabIndex	Get and Set	Gets or sets the tab index of the Web control.
TemplateSourceDirectory	Get	Gets the virtual directory of the Page or UserControl that contains the current server control.
Text	Get and Set	Gets or sets the text label associated with the CheckBox.
TextAlign	Get and Set	Gets or sets the alignment of the text label associated with the CheckBox control.
ToolTip	Get and Set	Gets or sets the tool tip for the Web control to be displayed when the mouse cursor is over the control.
UniqueID	Get	Gets the unique, hierarchically-qualified identifier for the server control.
Visible	Get and Set	Gets or sets a value that indicates whether a server control is rendered as UI on the page.
Width	Get and Set	Gets or sets the width of the Web control.

A

ASP.NET SERVER CONTROLS REFERENCE

TABLE A.35   RadioButton Public Instance Methods

Method	Description
ApplyStyle	Copies any non-blank elements of the specified style to the Web control, overwriting any existing style elements of the control. This method is primarily used by control developers.
CopyBaseAttributes	Copies the AccessKey, Enabled, ToolTip, TabIndex, and Attributes properties onto the Web control from the specified source control. This method is primarily used by control developers.
DataBind	Binds a data source to the invoked server control and all of its child controls.

TABLE A.35 Continued

Method	Description
Dispose	Enables a server control to perform final clean up before it is released from memory.
Equals	Overloaded. Determines whether two Object instances are equal.
FindControl	Overloaded. Searches the current naming container for the specified server control.
GetHashCode	Serves as a hash function for a particular type, suitable for use in hashing algorithms and data structures like a hash table.
GetType	Gets the Type of the current instance.
HasControls	Determines if the server control contains any child controls.
MergeStyle	Copies any non-blank elements of the specified style to the Web control, but will not overwrite any existing style elements of the control. This method is primarily used by control developers.
RenderBeginTag	Renders the HTML begin tag of the control into the specified writer. This method is primarily used by control developers.
RenderControl	Outputs server control content to a provided HtmlTextWriter object, then checks if tracing is enabled for the containing page and retrieves trace information about the server control.
RenderEndTag	Renders the HTML end tag of the control into the specified writer. This method is primarily used by control developers.
ResolveUrl	Resolves a relative URL to the absolute URL where the page or user control associated with this request resides.
SetRenderMethodDelegate	Assigns an event handler delegate to render the server control and its content into its parent control.
ToString	Returns a String that represents the current Object.

TABLE A.36 RadioButton Public Instance Events

Event	Description
CheckedChanged	Occurs when the Checked property is changed.
DataBinding	Occurs when the server control binds to a data source.

TABLE A.36 Continued

Event	Description
Disposed	Occurs when a server control is released from memory, which is the last stage of the server control lifecycle when an ASP.NET page is requested.
Init	Occurs when the server control is initialized, which is the first step in its lifecycle.
Load	Occurs when the server control is loaded into the Page object.
PreRender	Occurs when the server control is about to render to its containing Page object.
Unload	Occurs when the server control is unloaded from memory.

RadioButtonList

TABLE A.37 RadioButtonList Properties

Property	Get/Set	Description
AccessKey	Get and Set	Gets or sets the keyboard shortcut key (AccessKey) for setting focus to the Web control.
Attributes	Get	Gets the collection of arbitrary attributes (for rendering only) that does not correspond to properties on the control.
AutoPostBack	Get and Set	Gets or sets a value indicating whether a postback to the server automatically occurs when the user changes the list selection.
BackColor	Get and Set	Gets or sets the background color of the Web control.
BorderColor	Get and Set	Gets or sets the border color of the Web control.
BorderStyle	Get and Set	Gets or sets the border style of the Web control.
BorderWidth	Get and Set	Gets or sets the border width of the Web control.

Table A.37   Continued

Property	Get/Set	Description
CellPadding	Get and Set	Gets or sets the distance (in pixels) between the border and the contents of the table cell.
CellSpacing	Get and Set	Gets or sets the distance (in pixels) between adjacent table cells.
ClientID	Get	Gets the server control identifier generated by ASP.NET.
Controls	Get	Gets a ControlCollection object that represents the child controls for a specified server control in the UI hierarchy.
ControlStyle	Get	Gets the style of the Web control. This property is primarily used by control developers.
CssClass	Get and Set	Gets or sets the CSS class rendered by the Web control.
DataMember	Get and Set	Gets or sets the specific table in the DataSource to bind to the control.
DataSource	Get and Set	Gets or sets the data source that populates the items of the list control.
DataTextField	Get and Set	Gets or sets the field of the data source that provides the text content of the list items.
DataTextFormatString	Get and Set	Gets or sets the formatting string used to control how data bound to the list control is displayed.
DataValueField	Get and Set	Gets or sets the field of the data source that provides the value of each list item.
Enabled	Get and Set	Gets or sets a value indicating whether the Web control is enabled.
EnableViewState	Get and Set	Gets or sets a value indicating whether the server control maintains its view state, and the view state of any child controls it contains, when the current page request ends.
Font	Get	Gets font information of the Web control.

TABLE A.37   Continued

Property	Get/Set	Description
ForeColor	Get and Set	Gets or sets the foreground color (typically the color of the text) of the Web control.
Height	Get and Set	Gets or sets the height of the Web control.
ID	Get and Set	Gets or sets the programmatic identifier assigned to the server control.
Items	Get	Gets the collection of items in the list control.
NamingContainer	Get and Set	Gets a reference to the server control's naming container, which creates a unique namespace for differentiating between server controls with the same Control.ID property value.
Page	Get	Gets a reference to the Page instance that contains the server control.
Parent	Get	Gets a reference to the server control's parent control in the page UI hierarchy.
RepeatColumns	Get and Set	Gets or sets the number of columns to display in the RadioButtonList control.
RepeatDirection	Get and Set	Gets or sets the direction that the radio buttons within the group are displayed.
RepeatLayout	Get and Set	Gets or sets the layout of radio buttons within the group.
SelectedIndex	Get and Set	Gets or sets the lowest ordinal index of the selected items in the list.
SelectedItem	Get	Gets the selected item with the lowest index in the list control.
Site	Get	Gets information about the Web site to which the server control belongs.
Style	Get	Gets a collection of text attributes that will be rendered as a style attribute on the outer tag of the Web control.
TabIndex	Get and Set	Gets or sets the tab index of the Web control.

TABLE A.37   Continued

Property	Get/Set	Description
TemplateSourceDirectory	Get	Gets the virtual directory of the Page or UserControl that contains the current server control.
TextAlign	Get and Set	Gets or sets the text alignment for the radio buttons within the group.
ToolTip	Get and Set	Gets or sets the tool tip for the Web control to be displayed when the mouse cursor is over the control.
UniqueID	Get	Gets the unique, hierarchically-qualified identifier for the server control.
Visible	Get and Set	Gets or sets a value that indicates whether a server control is rendered as UI on the page.
Width	Get and Set	Gets or sets the width of the Web control.

TABLE A.38   RadioButtonList Public Instance Methods

Method	Description
ApplyStyle	Copies any non-blank elements of the specified style to the Web control, overwriting any existing style elements of the control. This method is primarily used by control developers.
CopyBaseAttributes	Copies the AccessKey, Enabled, ToolTip, TabIndex, and Attributes properties onto the Web control from the specified source control. This method is primarily used by control developers.
DataBind	Binds a data source to the invoked server control and all of its child controls.
Dispose	Enables a server control to perform final clean up before it is released from memory.
Equals	Overloaded. Determines whether two Object instances are equal.
FindControl	Overloaded. Searches the current naming container for the specified server control.

TABLE A.38 Continued

Method	Description
GetHashCode	Serves as a hash function for a particular type, suitable for use in hashing algorithms and data structures like a hash table.
GetType	Gets the Type of the current instance.
HasControls	Determines if the server control contains any child controls.
MergeStyle	Copies any non-blank elements of the specified style to the Web control, but will not overwrite any existing style elements of the control. This method is primarily used by control developers.
RenderBeginTag	Renders the HTML begin tag of the control into the specified writer. This method is primarily used by control developers.
RenderControl	Outputs server control content to a provided HtmlTextWriter object, then checks if tracing is enabled for the containing page and retrieves trace information about the server control.
RenderEndTag	Renders the HTML end tag of the control into the specified writer. This method is primarily used by control developers.
ResolveUrl	Renders the HTML end tag of the control into the specified writer. This method is primarily used by control developers.
SetRenderMethodDelegate	Assigns an event handler delegate to render the server control and its content into its parent control.
ToString	Returns a String that represents the current Object.

TABLE A.39 RadioButtonList Public Instance Events

Events	Description
DataBinding	Occurs when the server control binds to a data source.
Disposed	Occurs when a server control is released from memory, which is the last stage of the server control lifecycle when an ASP.NET page is requested.
Init	Occurs when the server control is initialized, which is the first step in its lifecycle.
Load	Occurs when the server control is loaded into the Page object.

TABLE A.39   Continued

Events	Description
PreRender	Occurs when the server control is about to render to its containing Page object.
SelectedIndexChanged	Occurs when the selection on the list changes and is posted back to the server.
Unload	Occurs when the server control is unloaded from memory.

Table

TABLE A.40   Table Properties

Property	Get/Set	Description
AccessKey	Get and Set	Gets or sets the keyboard shortcut key (AccessKey) for setting focus to the Web control.
Attributes	Get	Gets the collection of arbitrary attributes (for rendering only) that does not correspond to properties on the control.
BackColor	Get and Set	Gets or sets the background color of the Web control.
BackImageUrl	Get and Set	Indicates the URL of the background image to display behind the table. The image will be tiled if it is smaller than the table.
BorderColor	Get and Set	Gets or sets the border color of the Web control.
BorderStyle	Get and Set	Gets or sets the border style of the Web control.
BorderWidth	Get and Set	Gets or sets the border width of the Web control.
CellPadding	Get and Set	Gets or sets the distance (in pixels) between the border and the contents of the table cell.
CellSpacing	Get and Set	Gets or sets the distance (in pixels) between table cells.

TABLE A.40 Continued

Property	Get/Set	Description
ClientID	Get	Gets the server control identifier generated by ASP.NET.
Controls	Get	Gets a `ControlCollection` object that represents the child controls for a specified server control in the UI hierarchy.
ControlStyle	Get	Gets the style of the Web control. This property is primarily used by control developers.
CssClass	Get and Set	Gets or sets the CSS class rendered by the Web control.
Enabled	Get and Set	Gets or sets a value indicating whether the Web control is enabled.
EnableViewState	Get and Set	Gets or sets a value indicating whether the server control maintains its view state, and the view state of any child controls it contains, when the current page request ends.
Font	Get	Gets font information of the Web control.
ForeColor	Get and Set	Gets or sets the foreground color (typically the color of the text) of the Web control.
Gridlines	Get and Set	Gets or sets the gridlines property of the `Table` class.
Height	Get and Set	Gets or sets the height of the Web control.
HorizontalAlign	Get and Set	Gets or sets the horizontal alignment of the table within the page.
ID	Get and Set	Gets or sets the programmatic identifier assigned to the server control.
NamingContainer	Get and Set	Gets a reference to the server control's naming container, which creates a unique namespace for differentiating between server controls with the same `Control.ID` property value.

A

ASP.NET SERVER CONTROLS REFERENCE

Table A.40   Continued

Property	Get/Set	Description
Page	Get	Gets a reference to the Page instance that contains the server control.
Parent	Get	Gets a reference to the server control's parent control in the page UI hierarchy.
Rows	Get	Gets the collection of rows within the table.
Site	Get	Gets information about the Web site to which the server control belongs.
Style	Get	Gets a collection of text attributes that will be rendered as a style attribute on the outer tag of the Web control.
TabIndex	Get and Set	Gets or sets the tab index of the Web control.
TemplateSourceDirectory	Get	Gets the virtual directory of the Page or UserControl that contains the current server control.
ToolTip	Get and Set	Gets or sets the tool tip for the Web control to be displayed when the mouse cursor is over the control.
UniqueID	Get	Gets the unique, hierarchically-qualified identifier for the server control.
Visible	Get and Set	Gets or sets a value that indicates whether a server control is rendered as UI on the page.
Width	Get and Set	Gets or sets the width of the Web control.

Table A.41   Table Public Instance Methods

Method	Description
ApplyStyle	Copies any non-blank elements of the specified style to the Web control, overwriting any existing style elements of the control. This method is primarily used by control developers.
CopyBaseAttributes	Copies the AccessKey, Enabled, ToolTip, TabIndex, and Attributes properties onto the Web control from the specified source control. This method is primarily used by control developers.

TABLE A.41 Continued

Method	Description
DataBind	Binds a data source to the invoked server control and all of its child controls.
Dispose	Enables a server control to perform final clean up before it is released from memory.
Equals	Overloaded. Determines whether two Object instances are equal.
FindControl	Overloaded. Searches the current naming container for the specified server control.
GetHashCode	Serves as a hash function for a particular type, suitable for use in hashing algorithms and data structures like a hash table.
GetType	Gets the Type of the current instance.
HasControls	Determines if the server control contains any child controls.
MergeStyle	Copies any non-blank elements of the specified style to the Web control, but will not overwrite any existing style elements of the control. This method is primarily used by control developers.
RenderBeginTag	Renders the HTML begin tag of the control into the specified writer. This method is primarily used by control developers.
RenderControl	Outputs server control content to a provided HtmlTextWriter object, then checks if tracing is enabled for the containing page and retrieves trace information about the server control.
RenderEndTag	Renders the HTML end tag of the control into the specified writer. This method is primarily used by control developers.
ResolveUrl	Resolves a relative URL to the absolute URL where the page or user control associated with this request resides.
SetRenderMethodDelegate	Assigns an event handler delegate to render the server control and its content into its parent control.
ToString	Returns a String that represents the current Object.

A

TABLE A.42   Table Public Instance Events

Event	Description
DataBinding	Occurs when the server control binds to a data source.
Disposed	Occurs when a server control is released from memory, which is the last stage of the server control lifecycle when an ASP.NET page is requested.
Init	Occurs when the server control is initialized, which is the first step in its lifecycle.
Load	Occurs when the server control is loaded into the Page object.
PreRender	Occurs when the server control is about to render to its containing Page object.
Unload	Occurs when the server control is unloaded from memory.

TableCell

TABLE A.43   TableCell Properties

Property	Get/Set	Description
AccessKey	Get and Set	Gets or sets the keyboard shortcut key (AccessKey) for setting focus to the Web control.
Attributes	Get	Gets the collection of arbitrary attributes (for rendering only) that does not correspond to properties on the control.
BackColor	Get and Set	Gets or sets the background color of the Web control.
BorderColor	Get and Set	Gets or sets the border color of the Web control.
BorderStyle	Get and Set	Gets or sets the border style of the Web control.
BorderWidth	Get and Set	Gets or sets the border width of the Web control.
ClientID	Get	Gets the server control identifier generated by ASP.NET.
ColumnSpan	Get and Set	Gets or sets the number of columns in the Table control that the cell spans.

TABLE A.43 Continued

Property	Get/Set	Description
Controls	Get	Gets a `ControlCollection` object that represents the child controls for a specified server control in the UI hierarchy.
ControlStyle	Get	Gets the style of the Web control. This property is primarily used by control developers.
CssClass	Get and Set	Gets or sets the CSS class rendered by the Web control.
Enabled	Get and Set	Gets or sets a value indicating whether the Web control is enabled.
EnableViewState	Get and Set	Gets or sets a value indicating whether the server control maintains its view state, and the view state of any child controls it contains, when the current page request ends.
Font	Get	Gets font information of the Web control.
ForeColor	Get and Set	Gets or sets the foreground color (typically the color of the text) of the Web control.
Height	Get and Set	Gets or sets the height of the Web control.
HorizontalAlign	Get and Set	Gets or sets the horizontal alignment of the contents in the cell.
ID	Get and Set	Gets or sets the programmatic identifier assigned to the server control.
NamingContainer	Get and Set	Gets a reference to the server control's naming container, which creates a unique namespace for differentiating between server controls with the same `Control.ID` property value.
Page	Get	Gets a reference to the `Page` instance that contains the server control.
Parent	Get	Gets a reference to the server control's parent control in the page UI hierarchy.

TABLE A.43   Continued

Property	Get/Set	Description
RowSpan	Get and Set	Gets or sets the number of rows in the Table control that the cell spans.
Site	Get	Gets information about the Web site to which the server control belongs.
Style	Get	Gets a collection of text attributes that will be rendered as a style attribute on the outer tag of the Web control.
TabIndex	Get and Set	Gets or sets the tab index of the Web control.
TemplateSourceDirectory	Get	Gets the virtual directory of the Page or UserControl that contains the current server control.
Text	Get and Set	Gets or sets the text contents of the cell.
ToolTip	Get and Set	Gets or sets the tool tip for the Web control to be displayed when the mouse cursor is over the control.
UniqueID	Get	Gets the unique, hierarchically-qualified identifier for the server control.
VerticalAlign	Get and Set	Gets or sets the vertical alignment of the contents in the cell.
Visible	Get and Set	Gets or sets a value that indicates whether a server control is rendered as UI on the page.
Width	Get and Set	Gets or sets the width of the Web control.
Wrap	Get and Set	Gets or sets a value that indicates whether the content of the cell wrap in the cell.

TABLE A.44   TableCell Public Instance Methods

Method	Description
ApplyStyle	Copies any non-blank elements of the specified style to the Web control, overwriting any existing style elements of the control. This method is primarily used by control developers.

TABLE A.44 Continued

Method	Description
CopyBaseAttributes	Copies the AccessKey, Enabled, ToolTip, TabIndex, and Attributes properties onto the Web control from the specified source control. This method is primarily used by control developers.
DataBind	Binds a data source to the invoked server control and all of its child controls.
Dispose	Enables a server control to perform final clean up before it is released from memory.
Equals	Overloaded. Determines whether two Object instances are equal.
FindControl	Overloaded. Searches the current naming container for the specified server control.
GetHashCode	Serves as a hash function for a particular type, suitable for use in hashing algorithms and data structures like a hash table.
GetType	Gets the Type of the current instance.
HasControls	Determines if the server control contains any child controls.
MergeStyle	Copies any non-blank elements of the specified style to the Web control, but will not overwrite any existing style elements of the control. This method is primarily used by control developers.
RenderBeginTag	Renders the HTML begin tag of the control into the specified writer. This method is primarily used by control developers.
RenderControl	Outputs server control content to a provided HtmlTextWriter object, then checks if tracing is enabled for the containing page and retrieves trace information about the server control.
RenderEndTag	Renders the HTML end tag of the control into the specified writer. This method is primarily used by control developers.
ResolveUrl	Resolves a relative URL to the absolute URL where the page or user control associated with this request resides.
SetRenderMethodDelegate	Assigns an event handler delegate to render the server control and its content into its parent control.
ToString	Returns a String that represents the current Object.

A

ASP.NET SERVER
CONTROLS
REFERENCE

TABLE A.45 TableCell Public Instance Events

Events	Description
DataBinding	Occurs when the server control binds to a data source.
Disposed	Occurs when a server control is released from memory, which is the last stage of the server control lifecycle when an ASP.NET page is requested.
Init	Occurs when the server control is initialized, which is the first step in its lifecycle.
Load	Occurs when the server control is loaded into the Page object.
PreRender	Occurs when the server control is about to render to its containing Page object.
Unload	Occurs when the server control is unloaded from memory.

TableRow

TABLE A.46 TableRow Properties

Property	Get/Set	Description
AccessKey	Get and Set	Gets or sets the keyboard shortcut key (AccessKey) for setting focus to the Web control.
Attributes	Get	Gets the collection of arbitrary attributes (for rendering only) that does not correspond to properties on the control.
BackColor	Get and Set	Gets or sets the background color of the Web control.
BorderColor	Get and Set	Gets or sets the border color of the Web control.
BorderStyle	Get and Set	Gets or sets the border style of the Web control.
BorderWidth	Get and Set	Gets or sets the border width of the Web control.
Cells	Get	Gets a collection of TableCell objects that represent the cells of a row in a Table control.

TABLE A.46 Continued

Property	Get/Set	Description
ClientID	Get	Gets the server control identifier generated by ASP.NET.
Controls	Get	Gets a `ControlCollection` object that represents the child controls for a specified server control in the UI hierarchy.
ControlStyle	Get	Gets the style of the Web control. This property is primarily used by control developers.
CssClass	Get and Set	Gets or sets the CSS class rendered by the Web control.
Enabled	Get and Set	Gets or sets a value indicating whether the Web control is enabled.
EnableViewState	Get and Set	Gets or sets a value indicating whether the server control maintains its view state, and the view state of any child controls it contains, when the current page request ends.
Font	Get	Gets font information of the Web control.
ForeColor	Get and Set	Gets or sets the foreground color (typically the color of the text) of the Web control.
Height	Get and Set	Gets or sets the height of the Web control.
HorizontalAlign	Get and Set	Gets or sets the horizontal alignment of the contents in the row.
ID	Get and Set	Gets or sets the programmatic identifier assigned to the server control.
NamingContainer	Get and Set	Gets a reference to the server control's naming container, which creates a unique namespace for differentiating between server controls with the same `Control.ID` property value.
Page	Get	Gets a reference to the `Page` instance that contains the server control.

A

ASP.NET SERVER CONTROLS REFERENCE

Table A.46   Continued

Property	Get/Set	Description
Parent	Get	Gets a reference to the server control's parent control in the page UI hierarchy.
Site	Get	Gets information about the Web site to which the server control belongs.
Style	Get	Gets a collection of text attributes that will be rendered as a style attribute on the outer tag of the Web control.
TabIndex	Get and Set	Gets or sets the tab index of the Web control.
TemplateSourceDirectory	Get	Gets the virtual directory of the Page or UserControl that contains the current server control.
ToolTip	Get and Set	Gets or sets the tool tip for the Web control to be displayed when the mouse cursor is over the control.
UniqueID	Get	Gets the unique, hierarchically-qualified identifier for the server control.
VerticalAlign	Get and Set	Gets or sets the vertical alignment of the contents in the row.
Visible	Get and Set	Gets or sets a value that indicates whether a server control is rendered as UI on the page.
Width	Get and Set	Gets or sets the width of the Web control.

Table A.47   TableRow Public Instance Methods

Method	Description
ApplyStyle	Copies any non-blank elements of the specified style to the Web control, overwriting any existing style elements of the control. This method is primarily used by control developers.
CopyBaseAttributes	Copies the AccessKey, Enabled, ToolTip, TabIndex, and Attributes properties onto the Web control from the specified source control. This method is primarily used by control developers.

TABLE A.47 Continued

Method	Description
DataBind	Binds a data source to the invoked server control and all of its child controls.
Dispose	Enables a server control to perform final clean up before it is released from memory.
Equals	Overloaded. Determines whether two Object instances are equal.
FindControl	Overloaded. Searches the current naming container for the specified server control.
GetHashCode	Serves as a hash function for a particular type, suitable for use in hashing algorithms and data structures like a hash table.
GetType	Gets the Type of the current instance.
HasControls	Determines if the server control contains any child controls.
MergeStyle	Copies any non-blank elements of the specified style to the Web control, but will not overwrite any existing style elements of the control. This method is primarily used by control developers.
RenderBeginTag	Renders the HTML begin tag of the control into the specified writer. This method is primarily used by control developers.
RenderControl	Outputs server control content to a provided HtmlTextWriter object, then checks if tracing is enabled for the containing page and retrieves trace information about the server control.
RenderEndTag	Renders the HTML end tag of the control into the specified writer. This method is primarily used by control developers.
ResolveUrl	Resolves a relative URL to the absolute URL where the page or user control associated with this request resides.
SetRenderMethodDelegate	Assigns an event handler delegate to render the server control and its content into its parent control.
ToString	Returns a String that represents the current Object.

TABLE A.48 TableRow Public Instance Events

Events	Description
DataBinding	Occurs when the server control binds to a data source.
Disposed	Occurs when a server control is released from memory, which is the last stage of the server control lifecycle when an ASP.NET page is requested.
Init	Occurs when the server control is initialized, which is the first step in its lifecycle.
Load	Occurs when the server control is loaded into the Page object.
PreRender	Occurs when the server control is about to render to its containing Page object.
Unload	Occurs when the server control is unloaded from memory.

TextBox

TABLE A.49 TextBox Properties

Property	Get/Set	Description
AccessKey	Get and Set	Gets or sets the keyboard shortcut key (AccessKey) for setting focus to the Web control.
Attributes	Get	Gets the collection of arbitrary attributes (for rendering only) that does not correspond to properties on the control.
AutoPostback	Get and Set	Gets or sets a value indicating whether an automatic postback to the server will occur whenever the user changes the content of the text box.
BackColor	Get and Set	Gets or sets the background color of the Web control.
BorderColor	Get and Set	Gets or sets the border color of the Web control.
BorderStyle	Get and Set	Gets or sets the border style of the Web control.
BorderWidth	Get and Set	Gets or sets the border width of the Web control.

TABLE A.49 Continued

Property	Get/Set	Description
ClientID	Get	Gets the server control identifier generated by ASP.NET.
Columns	Get and Set	Gets or sets the display width of the text box in characters.
Controls	Get	Gets a `ControlCollection` object that represents the child controls for a specified server control in the UI hierarchy.
ControlStyle	Get	Gets the style of the Web control. This property is primarily used by control developers.
CssClass	Get and Set	Gets or sets the CSS class rendered by the Web control.
Enabled	Get and Set	Gets or sets a value indicating whether the Web control is enabled.
EnableViewState	Get and Set	Gets or sets a value indicating whether the server control maintains its view state, and the view state of any child controls it contains, when the current page request ends.
Font	Get	Gets font information of the Web control.
ForeColor	Get and Set	Gets or sets the foreground color (typically the color of the text) of the Web control.
Height	Get and Set	Gets or sets the height of the Web control.
ID	Get and Set	Gets or sets the programmatic identifier assigned to the server control.
MaxLength	Get and Set	Gets or sets the maximum number of characters allowed in the text box.
NamingContainer	Get and Set	Gets a reference to the server control's naming container, which creates a unique namespace for differentiating between server controls with the same `Control.ID` property value.

TABLE A.49   Continued

Property	Get/Set	Description
Page	Get	Gets a reference to the Page instance that contains the server control.
Parent	Get	Gets a reference to the server control's parent control in the page UI hierarchy.
ReadOnly	Get and Set	Gets or sets a value indicating if the text box is locked from user input.
Rows	Get and Set	Gets or sets the display height of a multiline text box.
Site	Get	Gets information about the Web site to which the server control belongs.
Style	Get	Gets a collection of text attributes that will be rendered as a style attribute on the outer tag of the Web control.
TabIndex	Get and Set	Gets or sets the tab index of the Web control.
TemplateSourceDirectory	Get	Gets the virtual directory of the Page or UserControl that contains the current server control.
Text	Get and Set	Gets or sets the text content of the text box.
TextMode	Get and Set	Gets or sets the behavior mode of the text box.
ToolTip	Get and Set	Gets or sets the tool tip for the Web control to be displayed when the mouse cursor is over the control.
UniqueID	Get	Gets the unique, hierarchically-qualified identifier for the server control.
Visible	Get and Set	Gets or sets a value that indicates whether a server control is rendered as UI on the page.
Width	Get and Set	Gets or sets the width of the Web control.
Wrap	Get and Set	Gets or sets a value indicating whether the text content wraps within the text box.

TABLE A.50   TextBox Public Instance Methods

Method	Description
ApplyStyle	Copies any non-blank elements of the specified style to the Web control, overwriting any existing style elements of the control. This method is primarily used by control developers.
CopyBaseAttributes	Copies the AccessKey, Enabled, ToolTip, TabIndex and Attributes properties onto the Web control from the specified source control. This method is primarily used by control developers.
DataBind	Binds a data source to the invoked server control and all of its child controls.
Dispose	Enables a server control to perform final clean up before it is released from memory.
Equals	Overloaded. Determines whether two Object instances are equal.
FindControl	Overloaded. Searches the current naming container for the specified server control.
GetHashCode	Serves as a hash function for a particular type, suitable for use in hashing algorithms and data structures like a hash table.
GetType	Gets the Type of the current instance.
HasControls	Determines if the server control contains any child controls.
MergeStyle	Copies any non-blank elements of the specified style to the Web control, but will not overwrite any existing style elements of the control. This method is primarily used by control developers.
RenderBeginTag	Renders the HTML begin tag of the control into the specified writer. This method is primarily used by control developers.
RenderControl	Outputs server control content to a provided HtmlTextWriter object, then checks if tracing is enabled for the containing page and retrieves trace information about the server control.
RenderEndTag	Renders the HTML end tag of the control into the specified writer. This method is primarily used by control developers.
ResolveUrl	Resolves a relative URL to the absolute URL where the page or user control associated with this request resides.

A

ASP.NET SERVER CONTROLS REFERENCE

TABLE A.50 Continued

Method	Description
SetRenderMethodDelegate	Assigns an event handler delegate to render the server control and its content into its parent control.
ToString	Returns a String that represents the current Object.

TABLE A.51 TextBox Public Instance Events

Event	Description
DataBinding	Occurs when the server control binds to a data source.
Disposed	Occurs when a server control is released from memory, which is the last stage of the server control lifecycle when an ASP.NET page is requested.
Init	Occurs when the server control is initialized, which is the first step in its lifecycle.
Load	Occurs when the server control is loaded into the Page object.
PreRender	Occurs when the server control is about to render to its containing Page object.
TextChanged	Occurs when the content of the text box is changed upon server postback.
Unload	Occurs when the server control is unloaded from memory.

ASP.NET Rich Server Controls

AdRotator

TABLE A.52 AdRotator Properties

Property	Get/Set	Description
AccessKey	Get and Set	Gets or sets the keyboard shortcut key (AccessKey) for setting focus to the Web control.
AdvertisementFile	Get and Set	Gets or sets the path to an XML file that contains advertisement information.

Table A.52 Continued

Property	Get/Set	Description
Attributes	Get	Gets the collection of arbitrary attributes (for rendering only) that does not correspond to properties on the control.
BackColor	Get and Set	Gets or sets the background color of the Web control.
BorderColor	Get and Set	Gets or sets the border color of the Web control.
BorderStyle	Get and Set	Gets or sets the border style of the Web control.
BorderWidth	Get and Set	Gets or sets the border width of the Web control.
ClientID	Get	Gets the server control identifier generated by ASP.NET.
Controls	Get	Gets a `ControlCollection` object that represents the child controls for a specified server control in the UI hierarchy.
ControlStyle	Get	Gets the style of the Web control. This property is primarily used by control developers.
CssClass	Get and Set	Gets or sets the CSS class rendered by the Web control.
Enabled	Get and Set	Gets or sets a value indicating whether the Web control is enabled.
EnableViewState	Get and Set	Gets or sets a value indicating whether the server control maintains its view state, and the view state of any child controls it contains, when the current page request ends.
Font	Get	Gets font information of the Web control.
ForeColor	Get and Set	Gets or sets the foreground color (typically the color of the text) of the Web control.
Height	Get and Sct	Gets or sets the height of the Web control.

A

ASP.NET Server Controls Reference

Table A.52   Continued

Property	Get/Set	Description
ID	Get and Set	Gets or sets the programmatic identifier assigned to the server control.
KeywordFilter	Get and Set	Gets or sets a category keyword to filter for specific types of advertisements in the XML advertisement file.
NamingContainer	Get and Set	Gets a reference to the server control's naming container, which creates a unique namespace for differentiating between server controls with the same Control.ID property value.
Page	Get	Gets a reference to the Page instance that contains the server control.
Parent	Get	Gets a reference to the server control's parent control in the page UI hierarchy.
Site	Get	Gets information about the Web site to which the server control belongs.
Style	Get	Gets a collection of text attributes that will be rendered as a style attribute on the outer tag of the Web control.
TabIndex	Get and Set	Gets or sets the tab index of the Web control.
Target	Get and Set	Gets or sets the name of the browser window or frame that displays the contents of the Web page linked to when the AdRotator control is clicked.
TemplateSourceDirectory	Get	Gets the virtual directory of the Page or UserControl that contains the current server control.
ToolTip	Get and Set	Gets or sets the tool tip for the Web control to be displayed when the mouse cursor is over the control.
UniqueID	Get	Gets the unique, hierarchically-qualified identifier for the server control.
Visible	Get and Set	Gets or sets a value that indicates whether a server control is rendered as UI on the page.
Width	Get and Set	Gets or sets the width of the Web control.

TABLE A.53 AdRotator Public Instance Methods

Method	Description
ApplyStyle	Copies any non-blank elements of the specified style to the Web control, overwriting any existing style elements of the control. This method is primarily used by control developers.
CopyBaseAttributes	Copies the AccessKey, Enabled, ToolTip, TabIndex and Attributes properties onto the Web control from the specified source control. This method is primarily used by control developers.
DataBind	Binds a data source to the invoked server control and all of its child controls.
Dispose	Enables a server control to perform final clean up before it is released from memory.
Equals	Overloaded. Determines whether two Object instances are equal.
FindControl	Overloaded. Searches the current naming container for the specified server control.
GetHashCode	Serves as a hash function for a particular type, suitable for use in hashing algorithms and data structures like a hash table.
GetType	Gets the Type of the current instance.
HasControls	Determines if the server control contains any child controls.
MergeStyle	Copies any non-blank elements of the specified style to the Web control, but will not overwrite any existing style elements of the control. This method is primarily used by control developers.
RenderBeginTag	Renders the HTML begin tag of the control into the specified writer. This method is primarily used by control developers.
RenderControl	Outputs server control content to a provided HtmlTextWriter object, then checks if tracing is enabled for the containing page and retrieves trace information about the server control.
RenderEndTag	Renders the HTML end tag of the control into the specified writer. This method is primarily used by control developers.
ResolveUrl	Resolves a relative URL to the absolute URL where the page or user control associated with this request resides.

A

ASP.NET SERVER CONTROLS REFERENCE

TABLE A.53 Continued

Method	Description
SetRenderMethodDelegate	Assigns an event handler delegate to render the server control and its content into its parent control.
ToString	Returns a String that represents the current Object.

TABLE A.54 AdRotator Public Instance Events

Event	Description
AdCreated	Occurs once per round trip to the server after the creation of the control, but before the page is rendered.
DataBinding	Occurs when the server control binds to a data source.
Disposed	Occurs when a server control is released from memory, which is the last stage of the server control lifecycle when an ASP.NET page is requested.
Init	Occurs when the server control is initialized, which is the first step in its lifecycle.
Load	Occurs when the server control is loaded into the Page object.
PreRender	Occurs when the server control is about to render to its containing Page object.
Unload	Occurs when the server control is unloaded from memory.

Calendar

TABLE A.55 Calendar Properties

Property	Get/Set	Description
AccessKey	Get and Set	Gets or sets the keyboard shortcut key (AccessKey) for setting focus to the Web control.
Attributes	Get	Gets the collection of arbitrary attributes (for rendering only) that does not correspond to properties on the control.
BackColor	Get and Set	Gets or sets the background color of the Web control.

TABLE A.55 Continued

Property	Get/Set	Description
BorderColor	Get and Set	Gets or sets the border color of the Web control.
BorderStyle	Get and Set	Gets or sets the border style of the Web control.
BorderWidth	Get and Set	Gets or sets the border width of the Web control.
CellPadding	Get and Set	Gets or sets the amount of space between the contents of a cell and the cell's border.
CellSpacing	Get and Set	Gets or sets the amount of space between cells.
ClientID	Get	Gets the server control identifier generated by ASP.NET.
Controls	Get	Gets a ControlCollection object that represents the child controls for a specified server control in the UI hierarchy.
ControlStyle	Get	Gets the style of the Web control. This property is primarily used by control developers.
CssClass	Get and Set	Gets or sets the CSS class rendered by the Web control.
DayHeaderStyle	Get and Set	Gets the style properties for the section that displays the day of the week.
DayNameFormat	Get and Set	Gets or sets the name format of days of the week.
DayStyle	Get and Set	Gets the style properties for the days in the displayed month.
Enabled	Get and Set	Gets or sets a value indicating whether the Web control is enabled.
EnableViewState	Get and Set	Gets or sets a value indicating whether the server control maintains its view state, and the view state of any child controls it contains, when the current page request ends.

TABLE A.55 Continued

Property	Get/Set	Description
FirstDayOfWeek	Get and Set	Gets or sets the day of the week to display in the first day column of the Calendar control.
Font	Get	Gets font information of the Web control.
ForeColor	Get and Set	Gets or sets the foreground color (typically the color of the text) of the Web control.
Height	Get and Set	Gets or sets the height of the Web control.
ID	Get and Set	Gets or sets the programmatic identifier assigned to the server control.
NamingContainer	Get and Set	Gets a reference to the server control's naming container, which creates a unique namespace for differentiating between server controls with the same Control.ID property value.
NextMonthText	Get and Set	Gets or sets the text displayed for the next month navigation control.
NextPrevFormat	Get and Set	Gets or sets the format of the next and previous month navigation elements in the title section of the Calendar control.
NextPrevStyle	Get and Set	Gets the style properties for the next and previous month navigation elements.
OtherMonthDayStyle	Get and Set	Gets the style properties for the days on the Calendar control that are not in the displayed month.
Page	Get	Gets a reference to the Page instance that contains the server control.
Parent	Get	Gets a reference to the server control's parent control in the page UI hierarchy.
PrevMonthText	Get and Set	Gets or sets the text displayed for the previous month navigation control.
SelectedDate	Get and Set	Gets or sets the selected date.

TABLE A.55 Continued

Property	Get/Set	Description
SelectedDates	Get	Gets a collection of System.DateTime objects that represent the selected dates on the Calendar control.
SelectedDayStyle	Get	Gets the style properties for the selected dates.
SelectionMode	Get and Set	Gets or sets the date selection mode on the Calendar control that specifies whether the user can select a single day, a week, or an entire month.
SelectMonthText	Get and Set	Gets or sets the text displayed for the month selection element in the selector column.
SelectorStyle	Get	Gets the style properties for the week and month selector column.
SelectWeekText	Get and Set	Gets or sets the text displayed for the week selection element in the selector column.
ShowDayHeader	Get and Set	Gets or sets a value indicating whether the heading for the days of the week is displayed.
ShowGridLines	Get and Set	Gets or sets a value indicating whether the days on the Calendar control are separated with grid lines.
ShowNextPrevMonth	Get and Set	Gets or sets a value indicating whether the Calendar control displays the next and previous month navigation elements in the title section.
ShowTitle	Get and Set	Gets or sets a value indicating whether the title section is displayed.
Site	Get	Gets information about the Web site to which the server control belongs.
Style	Get	Gets a collection of text attributes that will be rendered as a style attribute on the outer tag of the Web control.
TabIndex	Get and Set	Gets or sets the tab index of the Web control.

TABLE A.55 Continued

Property	Get/Set	Description
TemplateSourceDirectory	Get	Gets the virtual directory of the Page or UserControl that contains the current server control.
TitleFormat	Get and Set	Gets or sets the title format for the title section.
TitleStyle	Get	Gets the style properties of the title heading for the `Calendar` control.
TodayDayStyle	Get	Gets the style properties for today's date on the `Calendar` control.
TodaysDate	Get and Set	Gets or sets the value for today's date.
ToolTip	Get and Set	Gets or sets the tool tip for the Web control to be displayed when the mouse cursor is over the control.
UniqueID	Get	Gets the unique, hierarchically-qualified identifier for the server control.
Visible	Get and Set	Gets or sets a value that indicates whether a server control is rendered as UI on the page.
VisibleDate	Get and Set	Gets or sets the date that specifies the month to display on the `Calendar` control.
WeekendDayStyle	Get and Set	Gets the style properties for the weekend dates on the `Calendar` control.
Width	Get and Set	Gets or sets the width of the Web control.

TABLE A.56 Calendar Public Instance Methods

Method	Description
ApplyStyle	Copies any non-blank elements of the specified style to the Web control, overwriting any existing style elements of the control. This method is primarily used by control developers.
CopyBaseAttributes	Copies the `AccessKey`, `Enabled`, `ToolTip`, `TabIndex` and `Attributes` properties onto the Web control from the specified source control. This method is primarily used by control developers.

TABLE A.56   Continued

Method	Description
DataBind	Binds a data source to the invoked server control and all of its child controls.
Dispose	Enables a server control to perform final clean up before it is released from memory.
Equals	Overloaded. Determines whether two `Object` instances are equal.
FindControl	Overloaded. Searches the current naming container for the specified server control.
GetHashCode	Serves as a hash function for a particular type, suitable for use in hashing algorithms and data structures like a hash table.
GetType	Gets the `Type` of the current instance.
HasControls	Determines if the server control contains any child controls.
MergeStyle	Copies any non-blank elements of the specified style to the Web control, but will not overwrite any existing style elements of the control. This method is primarily used by control developers.
RenderBeginTag	Renders the HTML begin tag of the control into the specified writer. This method is primarily used by control developers.
RenderControl	Outputs server control content to a provided `HtmlTextWriter` object, then checks if tracing is enabled for the containing page and retrieves trace information about the server control.
RenderEndTag	Renders the HTML end tag of the control into the specified writer. This method is primarily used by control developers.
ResolveUrl	Resolves a relative URL to the absolute URL where the page or user control associated with this request resides.
SetRenderMethodDelegate	Assigns an event handler delegate to render the server control and its content into its parent control.
ToString	Returns a `String` that represents the current `Object`.

TABLE A.57 Calendar Public Instance Events

Events	Description
DataBinding	Occurs when the server control binds to a data source.
DayRender	Occurs when each day is created in the control hierarchy for the Calendar control.
Disposed	Occurs when a server control is released from memory, which is the last stage of the server control lifecycle when an ASP.NET page is requested.
Init	Occurs when the server control is initialized, which is the first step in its lifecycle.
Load	Occurs when the server control is loaded into the Page object.
PreRender	Occurs when the server control is about to render to its containing Page object.
SelectionChanged	Occurs when the user selects a day, a week, or an entire month by clicking the date selector controls.
Unload	Occurs when the server control is unloaded from memory.
VisibleMonthChanged	Occurs when the user clicks on the next or previous month navigation controls on the title heading.

ASP.NET Style Objects

TableItemStyle

TABLE A.58 TableItemStyle Properties

Property	Get/Set	Description
BackColor	Get and Set	Gets or sets the background color property of the Style class.
BorderColor	Get and Set	Gets or sets the border color property of the Style class.
BorderStyle	Get and Set	Gets or sets the border style property of the Style class.
BorderWidth	Get and Set	Gets or sets the border width property of the Style class.
Container	Get	Returns the IContainer that contains the Component.

TABLE A.58 `TableItemStyle` Properties

Property	Get/Set	Description
CssClass	Get and Set	Gets or sets the CSS class property of the `Style` class.
Font	Get	Gets a `FontInfo` object that contains the font properties for the `Style` class.
ForeColor	Get and Set	Gets or sets the foreground color (typically the color of the text) property of the `Style` class.
Height	Get and Set	Gets or sets the height property of the `Style` class.
HorizontalAlign	Get and Set	Gets or sets the horizontal alignment of the cell content.
Site	Get and Set	Gets or sets the site of the `Component`.
VerticalAlign	Get and Set	Gets or sets the vertical alignment of the cell content.
Width	Get and Set	Gets or sets the width property of the `Style` class.
Wrap	Get and Set	Gets or sets a value indicating whether the cell content wraps within the cell.

TABLE A.59 `TableItemStyle` Public Instance Methods

Method	Description
CopyFrom	Overridden. Copies non-blank elements from the specified style, overwriting existing style elements if necessary.
Dispose	Overloaded. Releases the resources used by the `Component`.
Equals	Overloaded. Determines whether two `Object` instances are equal.
GetHashCode	Serves as a hash function for a particular type, suitable for use in hashing algorithms and data structures like a hash table.
GetLifetimeService	Retrieves a lifetime service object that controls the lifetime policy for this instance. For the default Lifetime service this will be an object of type `ILease`.
GetType	Gets the `Type` of the current instance.

TABLE A.59 Continued

Method	Description
InitializeLifetimeService	Objects can provide their own lease and so control their own lifetime. They do this by overriding the InitializeLifetimeService method provided on MarshalByRefObject.
MergeWidth	Overridden. Copies non-blank elements from the specified style, but will not overwrite any existing style elements.
Reset	Overridden. Clears out any defined style elements from the state bag.
ToString	Returns a String that represents the current Object.

TABLE A.60 TableItemStyle Public Instance Events

Events	Description
Disposed	Represents the method which will handle the Disposed event of a Component.

ADO.NET Object Model

IN THIS APPENDIX

The Major Components of an ADO.NET Solution

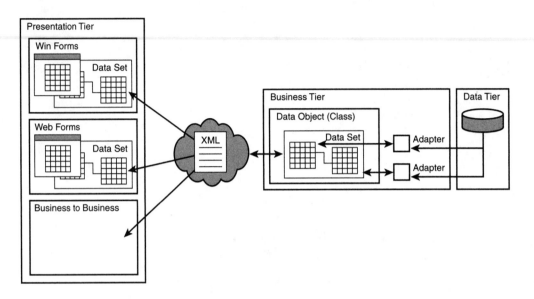

FIGURE B.1

The major components of an ADO.NET solution.

ADO.NET Object Model

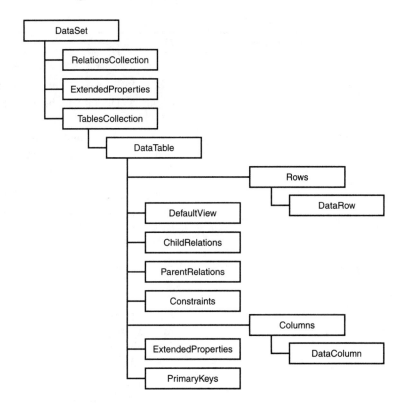

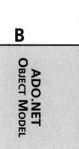

FIGURE B.2

The ADO.NET Document Object Model.

ADO.NET DbTypes

TABLE B.1   SqlDbType Compared to OleDbType

SqlDbType	OleDbType	*Description*
BigInt	BigInt	Int64—A 64-bit signed integer.
Binary	Binary	Array of type Byte—A fixed-length stream of binary data ranging between 1 and 8,000 bytes.
Bit	-	Boolean—An unsigned numeric value that can be 0, 1, or a null reference (Nothing in Visual Basic).
-	Boolean	Boolean—A boolean value (DBTYPE_BOOL).
-	BSTR	String—A null-terminated character string of Unicode characters (DBTYPE_BSTR).
Char	Char	String—A fixed-length stream of non-Unicode characters ranging between 1 and 8,000 characters.
DateTime	Date	DateTime—Date and time data ranging in value from January 1, 1753 to December 31, 9999 to an accuracy of 3.33 milliseconds.
-	DBDate	DateTime—Date data in the format yyyymmdd (DBTYPE_DBDATE).
	DBTime	TimeSpan—Time data in the format *hhmmss* (DBTYPE_DBTIME).
Decimal	Decimal	Decimal—A fixed precision and scale numeric value between −10E38 −1 and 10E38 −1.
-	Empty	Empty—No value (DBTYPE_EMPTY).
-	Error	Exception—A 32-bit error code (DBTYPE_ERROR).
-	Filetime	DateTime—A 64-bit unsigned integer representing the number of 100-nanosecond intervals since January 1, 1601 (DBTYPE_FILETIME).
Float	Double	Double—A floating point number within the range of −1.79E +308 through 1.79E +308.

TABLE B.1 Continued

SqlDbType	OleDbType	Description
Image	-	Array of type `Byte`—A variable-length stream of binary data ranging from 0 to 2E31 –1(or 2,147,483,647) bytes.
Int	Integer	Int32—A 32-bit signed integer.
-	LongVarBinary	Array of type `Byte`—A long binary value (`OleDbParameter` only).
-	LongVarWChar	`String`—A long string value (`OleDbParameter` only).
-	Numeric	`Decimal`—An exact numeric value with a fixed precision and scale (`DBTYPE_NUMERIC`).
Money	Currency	`Decimal`—Currency value ranging from –2E63 (or –922,337,203,685,477.5808) to 2E63 –1(or +922,337,203,685,477.5807) with an accuracy to a ten-thousandth of a currency unit.
NChar	-	`String`—A fixed-length stream of Unicode characters ranging between 1 and 4,000 characters.
NText	-	`String`—A variable-length stream of Unicode data with a maximum length of 2E30 –1 (or 1,073,741,823) characters.
NVarChar	-	`String`—A variable-length stream of Unicode characters ranging between 1 and 4,000 characters. Note: Implicit conversion fails if the string is greater than 4,000 characters. Explicitly set the object when working with strings longer than 4,000 characters.
-	PropVariant	`Object`—An automation `PROPVARIANT` (`DBTYPE_PROP_VARIANT`).
Real	Single	`Single`—A floating point number within the range of –3.40E +38 through 3.40E +38.
SmallDateTime	-	`DateTime`—Date and time data ranging in value from January 1, 1900 to June 6, 2079 to an accuracy of one minute.

B

TABLE B.1 Continued

SqlDbType	OleDbType	Description
SmallInt	SmallInt	Int16—A 16-bit signed integer.
SmallMoney	-	Decimal—A currency value ranging from –214,748.3648 to +214,748.3647 with an accuracy to a ten-thousandth of a currency unit.
Text	LongVarChar	String—A variable-length stream of non-Unicode data with a maximum length of 2E31 –1(or 2,147,483,647) characters.
Timestamp	DBTimestamp	DateTime—Date and time data in the format *yyyymmddhhmmss*.
TinyInt	TinyInt	Byte—An 8-bit unsigned integer.
UniqueIdentifier	Guid	Guid—A globally unique identifier (or GUID).
-	UnsignedBigInt	UInt64—A 64-bit unsigned integer (DBTYPE_UI8).
-	UnsignedInt	UInt32—A 32-bit unsigned integer (DBTYPE_UI4).
-	UnsignedSmallInt	UInt16—A 16-bit unsigned integer (DBTYPE_UI2).
-	UnsignedTinyInt	UInt8—An 8-bit unsigned integer (DBTYPE_UI1).
VarBinary	VarBinary	Array of type Byte—A variable-length stream of binary data ranging between 1 and 8,000 bytes. Note: Implicit conversion fails if the byte array is greater than 8,000 bytes. Explicitly set the object when working with byte arrays larger than 8,000 bytes.
VarChar	VarChar	String—A variable-length stream of non-Unicode characters ranging between 1 and 8,000 characters.
Variant	Variant	Object—A special data type that can contain numeric, string, binary, or date data as well as the SQL Server values Empty and Null, which is assumed if no other type is declared.

TABLE B.1 Continued

SqlDbType	OleDbType	Description
-	VarNumeric	Decimal—A variable-length numeric value (OleDbParameter only).
-	VarWChar	String—A variable-length, null-terminated stream of Unicode characters (OleDbParameter only).
-	WChar	String—A null-terminated stream of Unicode characters (DBTYPE_WSTR).

ASP.NET DataSet

TABLE B.2 DataSet Properties

Property	Get/Set	Description
CaseSensitive	Get and Set	Gets or sets a value indicating whether string comparisons within DataTable objects are case-sensitive.
Container	Get	Gets the container for the component.
DataSetName	Get and Set	Gets or sets the name of the current DataSet.
DefaultViewManager	Get	Gets a custom view of the data contained by the DataSet that allows filtering, searching, and navigating using a custom DataViewManager.
DesignMode	Get	Gets a value indicating whether the component is currently in design mode.
EnforceConstraints	Get and set	Gets or sets a value indicating whether constraint rules are followed when attempting any update operation.
ExtendedProperties	Get	Gets the collection of custom user information.
HasErrors	Get	Gets a value indicating whether there are errors in any of the rows in any of the tables of this DataSet.
Locale	Get and Set	Gets or sets the locale information used to compare strings within the table.

TABLE B.2 Continued

Property	Get/Set	Description
Namespace	Get and Set	Gets or sets the namespace of the DataSet.
Prefix	Get and Set	Gets or sets an XML prefix that aliases the namespace of the DataSet.
Relations	Get	Gets the collection of relations that link tables and allow navigation from parent tables.
Site	Get and Set	Overridden. Gets or sets an System.ComponentModel.ISite for the DataSet.
Tables	Get	Gets the collection of tables contained in the DataSet.

TABLE B.3 DataSet Public Instance Methods

Method	Description
AcceptChanges	Commits all of the changes made to this DataSet since it was loaded or the last time AcceptChanges was called.
BeginInit	Begins the initialization of a DataSet that is used on a form or by another component. The initialization occurs at runtime.
Clear	Clears the DataSet of any data by removing all rows in all tables.
Clone	Clones the structure of the DataSet, including all DataTable schemas, relations, and constraints.
Copy	Copies both the structure and data for this DataSet.
Dispose	Overloaded. Releases the resources used by the MarshalByValueComponent.
EndInit	Ends the initialization of a DataSet that is used on a form or by another component. The initialization occurs at runtime.
Equals	Overloaded. Determines whether two Object instances are equal.
GetChanges	Overloaded. Gets a copy of the DataSet containing all changes made to it since it was last loaded, or since AcceptChanges was called.

TABLE B.3 Continued

Method	Description
GetHashCode	Serves as a hash function for a particular type, suitable for use in hashing algorithms and data structures like a hash table.
GetService	Gets the implementer of the IServiceProvider.
GetType	Gets the Type of the current instance.
GetXml	Returns the XML representation of the data stored in the DataSet.
GetXmlSchema	Returns the XSD schema for the XML representation of the data stored in the DataSet.
HasChanges	Overloaded. Gets a value indicating whether the DataSet has changes, including new, deleted, or modified rows.
InferXmlSchema	Overloaded. Infers the XML schema from the specified TextReader or file into the DataSet.
Merge	Overloaded. Merges this DataSet with a specified DataSet.
ReadXml	Overloaded. Reads XML schema and data into the DataSet.
ReadXmlSchema	Overloaded. Reads an XML schema into the DataSet.
RejectChanges	Rolls back all the changes made to the DataSet since it was created, or since the last time DataSet.AcceptChanges was called.
Reset	Resets the DataSet to its original state. Subclasses should override Reset to restore a DataSet to its original state.
ToString	Returns a String that represents the current Object.
WriteXml	Overloaded. Writes XML schema and data from the DataSet.
WriteXmlSchema	Overloaded. Writes the DataSet structure as an XML schema.

B

ADO.NET
OBJECT MODEL

ASP.NET DataTable

TABLE B.4 DataTable Properties

Property	Get/Set	Description
CaseSensitive	Get and Set	Indicates whether string comparisons within the table are case-sensitive.

TABLE B.4   Continued

Property	Get/Set	Description
ChildRelations	Get	Gets the collection of child relations for this DataTable.
Columns	Get	Gets the collection of columns that belong to this table.
Constraints	Get	Gets the collection of constraints maintained by this table.
Container	Get	Gets the container for the component.
DataSet	Get	Gets the DataSet to which this table belongs.
DefaultView	Get	Gets a customized view of the table, which can include a filtered view or a cursor position.
DesignMode	Get	Gets a value indicating whether the component is currently in design mode.
DisplayExpression	Get and Set	Gets or sets the expression that will return a value used to represent this table in UI.
ExtendedProperties	Get	Gets the collection of custom user information.
HasErrors	Get	Gets a value indicating whether there are errors in any of the rows in any of the tables of the DataSet to which the table belongs.
Locale	Get and Set	Gets or sets the locale information used to compare strings within the table.
MinimumCapacity	Get and Set	Gets or sets the initial starting size for this table.
Namespace	Get and Set	Gets or sets the namespace for the DataTable.
ParentRelations	Get	Gets the collection of parent relations for this DataTable.
Prefix	Get and Set	Gets or sets the namespace for the XML representation of the data stored in the DataTable.
PrimaryKey	Get and Set	Gets or sets an array of columns that function as primary keys for the data table.

TABLE B.4   Continued

Property	Get/Set	Description
Rows	Get	Gets the collection of rows that belong to this table.
Site	Get and Set	Overridden. Gets or sets an `System.ComponentModel.Site` for the `DataTable`.
TableName	Get and Set	Gets or sets the name of the `DataTable`.

TABLE B.5   `DataTable` Public Instance Methods

Method	Description
AcceptChanges	Commits all the changes made to this table since the last time `AcceptChanges` was called.
BeginInit	Begins the initialization of a `DataTable` that is used on a form or used by another component. The initialization occurs at runtime.
BeginLoadData	Turns off notifications, index maintenance, and constraints while loading data.
Clear	Clears the `DataTable` of all data.
Clone	Clones the structure of the `DataTable`, including all `DataTable` schemas, relations, and constraints.
Compute	Computes the given expression on the current rows that pass the filter criteria.
Copy	Copies both the structure and the data for this `DataTable`.
Dispose	Overloaded. Releases the resources used by the `MarshalByValueComponent`.
EndInit	Ends the initialization of a `DataTable` that is used on a form or used by another component. The initialization occurs at runtime.
EndLoadData	Turns off notifications, index maintenance, and constraints while loading data.
Equals	Overloaded. Determines whether two `Object` instances are equal.
GetChanges	Overloaded. Gets a copy of the `DataTable` containing all changes made to it since it was last loaded, or since `AcceptChanges` was called.

B

ADO.NET OBJECT MODEL

TABLE B.5   Continued

Method	Description
GetErrors	Gets an array of DataRow objects that contain errors.
GetHashCode	Serves as a hash function for a particular type, suitable for use in hashing algorithms and data structures like a hash table.
GetService	Gets the implementer of the IServiceProvider.
GetType	Gets the Type of the current instance.
ImportRow	Copies a DataRow, including original and current values, DataRowState values, and errors, into a DataTable.
LoadDataRow	Finds and updates a specific row. If no matching row is found, a new row is created using the given values.
NewRow	Creates a new DataRow with the same schema as the table.
RejectChanges	Rolls back all changes that have been made to the table since it was loaded, or the last time AcceptChanges was called.
Select	Overloaded. Gets an array of DataRow objects.
ToString	Overridden. Gets the TableName and DisplayExpression, if there is one as a concatenated string.

RowStates of a DataRow

TABLE B.6   DataRow.RowState (uses DataRowState enumeration)

RowState	Description
Added	The row has been added to a DataRowCollection, and AcceptChanges has not been called.
Deleted	The row was deleted using the Delete method of the DataRow.
Detached	The row has been created but is not part of any DataRowCollection. A DataRow is in this state immediately after it has been created and before it is added to a collection, or if it has been removed from a collection.
Modified	The row has been modified and AcceptChanges has not been called.
Unchanged	The row has not changed since AcceptChanges was last called.

DataColumn ForeignKeyContraint

TABLE B.7 ForeignKeyConstraint (uses Rule enumeration)

Action	Description
Cascade	Delete or update related rows. This is the default.
None	No action taken on related rows.
SetDefault	Set values in related rows to the value contained in the DefaultValue property.
SetNull	Set values in related rows to DBNull.

ASP.NET Managed Providers

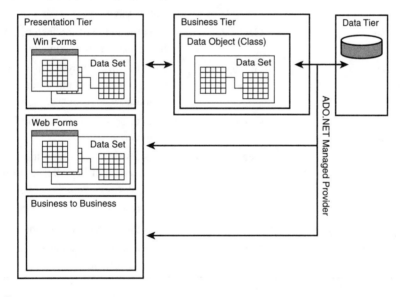

FIGURE B.3
Managed Providers are the bridge from a data store to a .NET application.

ASP.NET Managed Connection

TABLE B.8 Managed Connection Properties

Property	Get/Set	Description
ConnectionString	Get and Set	Gets or sets the string used to open a SQL Server database.
ConnectionTimeout	Get and Set	Gets the time to wait while trying to establish a connection before terminating the attempt and generating an error.
Container	Get	Returns the IContainer that contains the Component.
Database	Get	Gets the name of the current database or the database to be used once a connection is open.
DataSource	Get	Gets the name of the instance of SQL Server to which to connect.
PacketSize (SQL Managed Provider)	Get and Set	Gets the size (in bytes) of network packets used to communicate with an instance of SQL Server.
Provider (OleDB Managed Provider)	Get and Set	Gets or sets the name of the OLE DB provider.
ServerVersion	Get	Gets a string containing the version of the instance of SQL Server to which the client is connected.
Site	Get and Set	Gets or sets the site of the Component.
State	Get	Gets the current state of the connection.
WorkstationId (SQL Managed Provider)	Get	Gets a string that identifies the database client.

The Managed Command Object Model

The Managed Command (SqlCommand and OleDbCommand)

TABLE B.9 Managed Command Properties

Property	Get/Set	Description
CommandText	Get and Set	Gets or sets the Transact-SQL statement or stored procedure to execute at the data source.

TABLE B.9 Continued

Property	Get/Set	Description
CommandTimeout	Get and Set	Gets or sets the wait time before terminating the attempt to execute a command and generating an error.
CommandType	Get and Set	Gets or sets a value indicating how the CommandText property is interpreted.
Connection	Get and Set	Gets or sets the SqlConnection or OleDbConnection used by this instance of the command.
Container	Get	Returns the IContainer that contains the component.
DesignTimeVisible	Get and Set	Gets or sets a value indicating whether the command object should be visible in a Windows Forms Designer control.
Parameters	Get	Gets the SqlParametersCollection or OleDbParametersCollection.
Site	Get and Set	Gets or sets the site of the Component.
Transaction	Get and Set	Gets or sets the transaction in which the SqlCommand or OleDbCommand executes.
UpdatedRowSource	Get and Set	Gets or sets how command results are applied to the DataRow when used by the Update method of the DbDataAdapter.

B

ADO.NET OBJECT MODEL

TABLE B.10 Managed Command Public Instance Methods

Method	Description
Cancel	Cancels the execution of a command.
CreateParameter	Creates a new instance of a SqlParameter or OleDbParameter object.
Dispose	Overloaded. Releases the resources used by the Component.
Equals	Overloaded. Determines whether two Object instances are equal.
ExequteNonQuery	Executes a Transact-SQL statement against the Connection and returns the number of rows affected.
ExecuteReader	Overloaded. Sends the CommandText to the Connection and builds a DataReader.

TABLE B.10   Continued

Method	Description
ExecuteScalar	Executes the query, and returns the first column of the first row in the result set returned by the query. Extra columns or rows are ignored.
ExecuteXmlReader (SqlCommand only)	Sends the CommandText to the Connection and builds an XmlReader object.
GetHashCode	Serves as a hash function for a particular type, suitable for use in hashing algorithms and data structures like a hash table.
GetLifetimeService	Returns a lifetime service object that is used to control the lifetime policy to the object.
GetType	Gets the Type of the current instance.
InitializeLifetimeService	Objects can provide their own lease and so control their own lifetime. They do this by overriding the InitializeLifetimeService method provided on MarshalByRefObject.
Prepare	Creates a prepared (or compiled) version of the command on the data source.
ResetCommandTimeout	Resets the CommandTimeout property to the default value.
ToString	Returns a String that represents the current Object.

The DataAdapter Object Model

The DataAdapter (SqlDataAdapter and OleDbDataAdapter)

TABLE B.11   DataAdapter Properties

Property	Get/Set	Description
AcceptChangesDuringFill	Get and Set	Gets or sets a value indicating whether AcceptChanges is called on the DataRow after it is added to the DataTable.
Container	Get	Returns the IContainer that contains the Component.
DeleteCommand	Get and Set	Gets or sets a Transact-SQL statement to delete records from the data set.
InsertCommand	Get and Set	Gets or sets a Transact-SQL statement to insert new records into the data source.

TABLE B.11 Continued

Property	Get/Set	Description
MissingMappingAction	Get and Set	Determines the action to take when incoming data does not have a matching table or column.
MissingSchemaAction	Get and Set	Determines the action to take when existing DataSet schema does not match incoming data.
SelectCommand	Get and Set	Gets or sets a Transact-SQL statement used to select records in the data source.
Site	Get and Set	Gets or sets the site of the Component.
TableMappings	Get	Gets a collection that provides the master mapping between a source table and a DataTable.
UpdateCommand	Get and Set	Gets or sets a Transact-SQL statement used to update records in the data source.

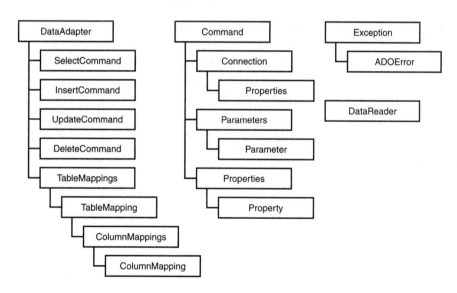

FIGURE B.4

The DataAdapter Object Model.

TABLE B.12   DataAdapter Public Instance Methods

Method	Description
Dispose	Overloaded. Releases the resources used by the Component.
Equals	Overloaded. Determines whether two Object instances are equal.
Fill	Overloaded. Overridden. Adds or refreshes rows in the DataSet to match those in the data source.
FillSchema	Overloaded. Overridden. Adds a DataTable to a DataSet and configures the schema to match that in the data source.
GetFillParameters	Overridden. Gets the parameters set by the user when executing an SQL SELECT statement.
GetHashCode	Serves as a hash function for a particular type, suitable for use in hashing algorithms and data structures like a hash table.
GetLifetimeService	Retrieves a lifetime service object that controls the lifetime policy for this instance. For the default Lifetime service this will be an object of type ILease.
GetType	Gets the Type of current instance.
InitializeLifetimeService	Objects can provide their own lease and so control their own lifetime. They do this by overriding the InitializeLifetimeService method provided on MarshalByRefObject.
ToString	Returns a String that represents the current Object
Update	Overloaded. Calls the respective INSERT, UPDATE, or DELETE statements for each inserted, updated, or deleted row in the DataSet from a DataTable named "Table".

INDEX

X-Y-Z